MW00812147

AN
ATHEIST'S
DELUSION

A Latter-Day Saint's Perspective on Richard Dawkins's Anti-Theist/Anti-Christ Book 'The God Delusion

— BY MARTIN L. BRADEN —

MLB Publications

First MLB Publication Edition 2022

First published in the United States by MLB Publications.
For information about permission to reproduce selections from this book,
write to marty.braden@gmail.com.

Scripture quotations taken from the Holy Bible KJV & JST,
Book of Mormon, Doctrine & Covenants, and the Pearl of Great Price.
KJV version Trademark is registered in the United States Patent
and Trademark Office by International Bible Society.

The Church of Jesus Christ of Latter-Day Saints Church Leadership quotes from
www.churchofjesuschrist.org website, are used by permission. All rights reserved.

ISBN: 979-8-218-12163-1
Imprint: Independently published

PRINTTED IN THE UNTIED STATES OF AMERICA

KJV version Trademark is registered in:
The United States Patent and Trademark Office by International Bible Society.

I dedicate this work to my wife Kathleen, and to my children –
Chrystal, Rachelle, Martin Jr., Garrett, Zedic, Rebecca, Adam, and Tanner,
each of whom are my most prized treasures.

The author asserts the moral right to be
identified as the author of this book.

Self-Published
An imprint of
Martin L. Braden Publications

Copyright © 2022 MLB Publications

This is not an official publication of The Church of Jesus Christ of Latter-Day Saints.

The opinions and perspectives expressed herein belong solely to the author and do not necessarily
represent the opinions or views of the leadership of The Church of Jesus Christ of Latter-Day Saints.
Permission for the use of quotes, sources, graphics, and photos
is also solely the responsibility of the author.

Acknowledgments

I give my wife, who is more precious than rubies, my most sincere appreciation for her unconditional love and unfailing encouragement that she extended to me throughout this laborious project. Her inexhaustible devotion and constructive advice have been a godsend for which I cannot repay or thank her enough.

4

TABLE OF CONTENTS

My Perspective on "The God Delusion" Chapters & Topics

Preface

Living in our ever-darkening world, with its multiplicity of complexities and competing voices, it's hard to discern which of all the voices speaks the truth, and which ones are deceptions. Learning how to discern one voice from the other is vital to one's survival, happiness, and joy. After reading Richard Dawkins book *The God Delusion*, it became clear to me that Richard's voice is one of the louder voices of deception. He may seem to be right, at first, but once you've taken his quasi-gospel of atheism 'pill', it soon takes you down the destructive road of blinded hopelessness, leaving you void of any eternal purpose. So, I decided to write *An Atheist's Delusion* in the hope that its pages will bring you, my readers, a greater understanding of why I believe my Latter-Day Saint's perspective is a voice of truth and hope crying out from the wilderness. It's the voice I have followed the entirety of my life. It's been a voice of peace and guidance, and a source of comfort throughout my life. As a member of the Church of Jesus Christ of Latter-Day Saints I have a unique perspective on all the 'Big' questions of life. Once I learned how to discern this voice from the deafening voices clamoring for our attention, I made it the guiding light in my life. As a result, I now enjoy its delicious fruits of happiness, joy, and total peace of mind.

My goal in writing my book was to give you, my readers, well-informed and highly endorsed reference legs of evidence for building out a solid circular table stand that will steadfastly support your table of belief, so you can firmly place your faith upon it. Wherever your belief cursor currently sits on Dawkins' *percentage of probability spectrum*, it will begin to move closer and closer towards the 100% marker that says *God Exists,* as I provide you with reference leg after reference leg of evidence, all the while I'm dissecting each of Dawkins' ten chapters of anti-Theist, anti-Christ dogma. By the end of my book your belief cursor will have landed solidly on the 100% *God Exists* marker, or very close to it, because your circular table stand will have been filled out with hundreds of reference legs, each stabilizing your tables' stand to the point where you will enjoy absolute confidence that your 'table of belief' is now unshakable. In other words, your table of belief will no longer wobble, nor will it be prone to collapse under the weight of doubt. Any sense of uncertainty or cognitive dissonance you may be suffering before reading my book, with its accompanying doubts, will have simply faded away like hoar frost, and your faith in God's existence will have grown ever so closer to *perfect faith* in God's existence.

In contrast to Dawkins' objective for writing his book, it being to promote his quasi-religion of atheism, my objective is to make popular the opposite perspective to the anti-Theist/anti-Christ perspective that Dawkins puts forth. Dawkins's perspective, in part, comes from the teachings of his quasi-prophet, Charles Darwin. Darwin's quasi-gospel is the anti-Theist/anti-Christ doctrine of Evolution, its chief tenant being Natural Selection. My perspective on Dawkins' book will provide you, my readers, with reasonable, well-informed, and highly endorsed reference legs that you can add to your own circular table stand of evidence to help support the belief that 'God Exists'. My Latter-Day Saint perspective will show you exactly why Evolution is a false, pernicious, anti-Theist, anti-Christ doctrine. It will also show you why I say that some of Evolutions' adherents have deliberately put forth false, deceptive interpretations of the data collected regarding man's origin, all in the hope that you and I will dismiss the living God's pure gospel and accept their false god of global, secular-humanism.

It is my hope that you, my readers, will weigh my perspective with real intent, against the unproven interpretations offered up by Richard in his faulty attempt to disprove the God Hypothesis. I ask that you honestly consider whether or not my perspective has the "ring, feeling, and spirit of truth" that usually stirs one's heart when it's presented to us. It's also my hope that you'll recognize this feeling, this *'ring of truth'* for what it is – *'the Spirit of Truth'*; delivered by the spirit and authority of the Holy Ghost, whose role it is, to manifest and testify to one's heart the truthfulness of all things. This *"voice"* of which I speak, is the still, small voice, even the voice of God spoken of in the scriptures. On the other hand, if my perspective leaves you feeling a stupor of thought in your heart and mind, then set it aside and let it go. Only you can decide if it 'feels right' to you, or not. I like what mathematician John Lennox said about his readers in the Preface to his book *'God and Stephen Hawking'*, where he said, and I quote:

"I have confidence in my readers ability to follow an argument to its conclusion. I submit what I have written here … to your judgment." (See page 9 of John's wonderful little book)

End of Quote

It is my hope that by the time you finish reading my book, and you finish writing down each and every one of the reference legs of diverse evidence I'll provide you throughout my book, each pointing to the existence of God, you will have come to the realization that it is Mr. Dawkins, and not I, who is suffering from a delusion, even *'An Atheist's Delusion'*.

AN ATHEIST'S DELUSION

A Latter-Day Saint's Perspective on Richard Dawkins's Anti-Theist/Anti-Christ Book "The God Delusion"

INTRODUCTION

Colossians 2:8-10 (KJV)

(An epistle written by the Apostle Paul while serving with his young companion Timothy)

8 Beware lest any man spoil you through *philosophy and vain deceit*, after the tradition of men, and after the *rudiments of the world*, and not after Christ.

9 For in him dwelleth all the *fulness* of the Godhead bodily.

10 And ye are *complete* in him, which is the head of all principality and power.

After reading Mr. Dawkins's book *The God Delusion*, even though Richard himself admits in his book that "*he did not and cannot prove that God doesn't exist*" [1] (Nor can I prove that God does exist with absolute, irrefutable, incontrovertible evidence), I still decided to share my Latter-Day Saint perspective on Richard's atheistic, anti-Theist/anti-Christ arguments that he put forth in his book, to show there's more than enough evidence to move one's belief cursor (wherever it currently sits on Dawkins' *'The Percentage of Probability Spectrum' relating to the "Does God exist?" question),* several percentage points beyond the 50/50 stalemate marker, and nearly to 100% 'God Exists'.

At the heart of the contemporary debate between God and Science, which has been raging on for a very, very, long time, there are still several important unanswered questions; 'Big' questions. But, before we even consider those questions, let me give my perspectives' conclusion as you, my readers, begin reading my book.

To me, this debate boils down to the fact that every individual I've ever known, appears to have chosen what they *want to believe* concerning the "Does God Exist?" question. In other words, they *choose* to believe the evidence provided by one of two worldviews, Atheism or Theism, because they *want to believe* the evidence presented by the side they want to believe in and the side that *feels* the most comfortable to them, and not because the evidence itself is incontrovertible, for, as I have already stated, "There is *no* incontrovertible evidence on either side of this debate, for or against His existence!"

I decided to put my conclusion right at the beginning of my book because the reality is, that both sides have a great deal of well-informed, highly endorsed evidence supporting their worldview, and anything Richard or I put forth as evidence, is not incontrovertible, and so it leaves all of us having to *choose to believe* or *not believe* in God's existence. The rest of my book covers my arguments in response to Richard's arguments and interpretations, from my Latter-Day Saint perspective. I am a member of the Church of Jesus Christ of Latter-Day Saints, and I sincerely hope, as you come along this deeply thought-provoking journey with me, you will enjoy the ride and even feel that it was well worth the price of admission – your precious time you'll invest in yourself by reading it. I'm confident you'll find it to not only be interesting and informative, but you'll find it to be a *transformational experience*.

Richard Dawkins has chosen to believe the evidence offered up by like-minded proponents of the worldview of Atheism; the belief that God does not exist. That, however, is just his opinion of course. Richard says, "*the evidence for God's non-existence reaches a probability percentage of more than 50%*". [2] However, I believe that you, my readers, will come to realize, as I did, that Richard simply wants to believe his delusion – *An Atheist's Delusion*. My perspective of *The God Delusion* will clearly explain why I believe this to be a true observation of Richard and almost every atheist I know.

It is also true that I have chosen to believe the evidence that my worldview, Theism, offers up, as well as my experiential and epistemic evidence I have collected from a multiplicity of sources, including from the three divine Beings we'll be discussing throughout my book. I believe it substantiates God's existence. For me, the entirety of this evidence gives me license to declare that God's existence has a *percentage of probability* that's much more than just 51%. In fact, I believe the spectrums' *percentage of probability that says God exists,* is as high as 100%, but you, my readers, will determine where your own belief cursor sits on this *percentage of probability spectrum* once you've finished reading my book.

Just like Richard's worldview, my worldview boils down to the fact that I *want to believe* and *do believe* my well-informed and highly endorsed evidence that I have collected over my lifetime of 68 years. I just cannot deny Him, nor would I. Richard, of course, disagrees, and says, "The God Hypothesis is very close to being ruled out by the laws of probability". [3] Well, we shall see.

The bottom line, for me, and it's a fact, is that neither the atheist scientists, nor the theist scientists, or anyone else for that matter, have come forth with any kind of absolute, irrefutable, incontrovertible, scientific '*proof*' to support their claim of God's existence or His non-existence – and that's what makes this debate so emotionally conflicting, as well as intellectually challenging for those of us who have joined in the debate.

After reviewing all the evidence, each of you, my readers, will be given the opportunity to make this very important choice for yourselves. I suggest that you do not make it lightly. What makes you choose one view or stack of evidence over the other sides view and stack of evidence, or what makes you *want to believe* one view is truer than the opposite side's view, I believe, will be your worldview and how serious and honest you are as you search for acceptable answers to all of the 'Big' questions of life.

That said, the purpose of my rebuttals' perspective to Richard's book, is to put forth a unique alternative, a Latter-Day Saint's perspective to Richard's atheistic views. As I said, I will show that there's far more evidence for *the probability of God's existence* than just the 50/50 draw. In fact, my well-informed, highly endorsed evidence that I have compiled for you, my readers, will show that the percentage of probability *for* God's existence is actually growing every single day, and much of this evidence for God's existence is coming from the atheist scientists' camp, and their more recent discoveries.

Today's new atheist scientists claim "to have the upper hand on the issue of God's existence" [4], but as a Latter-Day Saint, and someone who believes in a living, personal, corporeal God, I must protest that claim. I'm doing what I feel I can and should do to help all believers in God's existence to understand that they need not concede to these clever antagonists and their unproven claims that they're constantly barking out at believers in God. In some cases, they are barking outright lies, or at least designed manipulations. These anti-Christs work so very hard to distort the so-called '*facts of science*' in order to tilt them in their favor, and even worse, some scientists even keep some legitimate findings from being published. I'll cover why I feel I can say this with absolute confidence a little later in my book.

If I'm honest about my study of this debate, I have to say that it's left me feeling an obligation, even a moral duty to remind you, my readers, that not all statements *by* scientists are statements *of* science. In other words, science itself DOES NOT SAY ANYTHING, only scientists do. As John Lennox said, it is scientists themselves that make all statements or interpretations 'about the data', and therefore their statements and interpretations do not carry the authority of "authentic science" *just because they're scientists expressing their personal interpretations and opinions.*

Many scientists tout the *authority* of science in their effort to make their '*interpretations*' appear as though they are superior to their opponents' interpretations. I'm speaking of opponents like myself, who's just one of billions who believe in God. Most of their claims are just hyperbolic interpretations.

Here are more comments made by mathematician John Lennox from his book "*God and Stephen Hawking*" [5] that I have intermixed with my thoughts as part of my Introduction. I would encourage you, my readers, to go to YouTube and type *John Lennox* into the search bar and check out his many debates with Richard Dawkins and other atheists like him. He has a fun personality and I think you will enjoy watching him debate these so-called atheist intellectuals. I promise that you'll find your view of this topic expanded because of what you learn from John's many experiences and his lengthy, intensive studies that has brought him to his current beliefs and perspective of God. Anyway, here is John's quote:

"God is very much on the agenda these days. Scientists have made sure of it by publishing book after book with titles like Francis Collins' "*The Language of God*", Richard Dawkins' "*The God Delusion*", Victor Stenger's "*God: The Failed Hypothesis*", and Robert Winston's "*The Story of God*", and so on. The fact remains that people want to hear what these scientists have to say. Most of the above-mentioned books have been runaway best sellers, and now, in 2023, science has accumulated an immense cultural and intellectual authority within our sophisticated, modern psyche. One of the reasons for this societal phenomena, is the fact that the purveyors of science have been phenomenally successful in developing technologies that have benefited humanity throughout the world." [6]

End Quote

Just as Mr. Lennox suggested, today's scientists are giving us continually increasing insight into the wonders of the universe and our reality, as far as we understand it, both at the macro-world level and the micro-world level. Since its' launch into space back in December of 2021, the James Webb Telescope is expanding our cosmological understanding even further than it was at the time of its launch. In fact, it's already making some physicists question whether the Big Bang even happened. [7]

And so, people have many reasons for turning to the scientists of today, in particular, to hear what they have to say about the 'Big' questions of our existence. Those questions being:

- Why are we here?
- What is the purpose of life if there is any?
- Where are we going after we die, or do we just stop existing after death?
- Is this universe all that exists, or is there more? And on and on the list goes.

These 'Big' questions, and others like them, make us think about God, religion, our existence, and purpose, and so we ask if there's any purpose to the universe and to our lives lived out here on planet earth. We want to know what scientists have to say about God, whether or not there is any evidence for His existence, and why there is any existence after death or maybe there's nothing after it at all?

Many of the best-sellers just mentioned are written by atheist scientists, but here's the important fact to remember: ... *not all scientists are atheists*. Most atheists are saying that the number of theist scientists is declining, but even if this were true, and I'm not saying that it is, it does not negate the fact that there are still a great many of today's leading scientists who are believing, award-winning theists.

The question "Are God and science at war?" is a popular question asked by today's culture, but it would have been strongly opposed by the father of modern science, Sir Isaac Newton, a colossus without parallel in the history of science. Isaac's discoveries were at the very heart of the scientific revolution of the 17th century.

Newton's landmark work *Principia Mathematica* laid out a new understanding of the heavens and the earth. Newton saw science and faith as being one great whole. Amongst other things, Newton discovered the laws of gravitation during the philosophical revolution of the Enlightenment. This discovery transformed the way we see the world. It is also important to note that Newton, besides being the brilliant scientist that he was, was also a devout Christian with a deep interest in theology and the Holy Bible.

In his *Principia Mathematica* work, Newton said, "Science cannot explain who set the planets in motion, for God governs all things." Newton saw science as a 'garden' that God wanted him to cultivate and saw many of his pioneering discoveries as coming from the 'inspiration of the Holy Spirit'. He saw an intelligent designer behind the order of the universe, sustaining creation, and he described atheism as 'senseless'.

"This most beautiful system of the sun, planets, and comets", Newton said, "could only proceed from the counsel and dominion of an intelligent and powerful Being ... This Being governs all things, not as the soul of the world, but as LORD over all; and on account of His dominion, He is wont to be called LORD God."

Another theist I want to mention is Nikola Tesla, a Serbian American inventor who lived from 1856 to 1945. Tesla was a pioneer in the fields of electricity, radio, and x-rays. Nikola's inventions varied from the AC electricity supply system to the first remote-controlled boat that the military wanted to use as a weapon of war. Tesla invented more than one-hundred and twenty-six inventions, and he said of those inventions that *"they came onto the screen of his mind as thoughts*, each one being images with great detail". He said he would work to develop and improve them while they were still in his mind. On January 30th of 1926, Tesla even spoke about the concept of wireless communications during an interview for Collier's Magazine:

Tesla said, *"When wireless is perfectly applied the whole earth will be converted into a huge brain, which in fact it is, all things being particles of a real and rhythmic whole. We shall be able to communicate with one another instantly, irrespective of distance."* Isn't that incredible? Tesla also described cell phone technology back in 1926, saying, "Through television and telephony we shall see and hear one another as perfectly as though we were face to face, despite intervening distances of thousands of miles, and the instruments through which we shall be able to do this *will fit into our vest pockets."* What an incredible futurist mind Tesla had. This was ninety-six years ago!

Tesla said that he saw these thought-visions of inventions in such detail that he often didn't need to draw them out or write them down. Tesla's vision and prediction of data transmission without wires came true nearly a century later when the Internet and cell phones became a reality. They've blessed the entire population of the world. Tesla was also an Arch priest of the Greek Orthodox Church, but when asked if he believed in God he said, "In my heart I am deeply religious, though not in the orthodox sense of that word."

To expand on this, Tesla went on to say, *"The gift of mental energy comes from God, the supreme being, and if we concentrate our thoughts on this truth we get into harmony (Attunement) with this great power."* (Collier's Magazine, January 30th, 1926).

These examples alone tell me that we shouldn't write off the debate as being resolved by so-called 'settled science' like atheist scientists would have us do. Most atheist scientists today say that the debate in question, is a clash between science and religion, and it's true that the conflicting interpretations and opinions offered up by both sides regarding God's existence, have heightened of late, but, let me give an example of why I say the debate is *not* between science and religion. It's between ATHEISM and THEISM.

The first author on the short book list I listed earlier, is Francis Collins, the retired Director of the National Institute of Health in the USA as of December 2021, and the former Head of the Human Genome Project. His predecessor, as head of that project, was Jim Watson, winner (with Francis Crick) of the Nobel Prize for discovering the double-helix structure of DNA. Collins is a Christian. Watson an atheist. They are both top-level scientists, which shows us that what divides them is *not* their science but their 'WORLDVIEW'. There is a real conflict for sure, but it is *not* science versus religion. It is ATHEISM versus THEISM." [8]

My point here is the fact that there are scientists of high reputation on both sides of this worldview debate, and it is the fact that many atheist scientists are not being forthright with the truth about many of their findings [9] that motivated me to join in the debate, especially because there weren't any Latter-Day Saints, that I'm aware of, taking on Richard's book *The God Delusion,* directly. So, after reading Dawkins' book, I decided to join in the debate and write about my personal perspective as a Latter-Day Saint regarding Richard's anti-Theist/anti-Christ book *The God Delusion.* My perspective focuses on the real question at stake here, and that real question, for me, is *not* whether or not God exists, it's:

"Is science pointing away from God's existence, or is it pointing ever more towards His existence?" In other words, "What is the reality about God and our relationship to Him if He exists?" And "Is science's data itself ... neutral on these ideas?"

The so-called 'Secularization-Hypothesis', rashly assumed in the wake of 'The Enlightenment', or the 'Century of the Enlightened', which was a European intellectual movement of the 17th and 18th centuries in which ideas concerning God, reason, nature, and humanity were synthesized into a worldview that gained wide assent in the West and that instigated revolutionary developments in art, philosophy, and politics. Central to 'enlightenment thought' were the use and celebration of reason, the power by which humans understand the universe and improve their condition. The goals of rational humanity were considered to be knowledge, freedom, and happiness. The enlightened asserted that religion would eventually decline and even die out. But the opposite has happened. [10]

The topic of "Science and the Death of God" is still raging on. I compare the debate about God's existence to a caravan of camels, and I'm calling it "The Caravan of Truth". The caravan's camels are driven by Theists, believers in a Living God. These believers patiently and courageously cross the arid desert of doubt, looking for additional evidence to put on their dromedaries' backs, evidence that will help prove God's existence, yet all the while paying no mind to the pack of scrappy dogs that are continually yapping at their heels (the scrappy dogs being the atheists like Richard Dawkins, and other nonbelievers). The theist believers are pressing onward to the Golden City where Jesus Christ, as the resurrected Lord, will reveal all truth to the world at His 2nd coming, and begin His millennial reign.

This quip's anti-atheist attitude is reflected in this ancient descript, *"The dogs bark but the caravan moves on"*, which was stated in our day by Paul John Keating, a former Australian politician who served as the 24th Prime Minister of Australia from 1991 to 1996 and was the leader of the Labor Party. There are a variety of dogs joining in the chorus every day, with several renown hounds barking the loudest, such as the likes of Richard Dawkins and his atheist friend, who recently passed away, Christopher Hitchens. As a believer in a Living God, I simply choose to pay them no mind, except for my taking the time to write this book.

The god called 'Secularization' or 'Humanism', whose goal is to kill the idea of the Living God's existence, is driving the 'Big' question of God's existence ever higher on the agenda. Atheist scientists seem, to me, to be manifesting a fear that highly recognized scientists will soon discover that damaging evidence that says, 'Supernatural', 'Divine Intelligence', even the powerful 'beginning causal cause' in the causal chain, does in fact exist (Watch the YouTube video where Hugh Ross, an astrophysicist, Christian apologist, and author, refers to the atheist physicist Dr. Phillip Ball, the former Senior Editor for

Nature Magazine. Dr. Ball quotes what three non-believing scientists said about Dark Matter. The video's called '*Dr. Hugh Ross Conference Weekend-Session 3-Cosmic Reasons to Believe in Christ*' [11]).

Here's a few excerpts from an article written by Dr. Ross on this very topic, and I quote:

"Dark energy refers to the self-stretching property of the 'space – time' fabric of the universe. Space, because of dark energy and independent of matter, or light, stretches itself. Moreover, the larger the space-time envelope of the universe grows, the more stretching energy it gains. This gaining of stretching energy causes some science writers to refer to dark energy as an anti-gravity factor. The effect of dark energy on the space-time envelope of the universe is to make two massive bodies appear to repel one another. Moreover, the farther apart two bodies are from one another, the more strongly they will appear to repel one another. In contrast, gravity acts as a brake on cosmic expansion. In junior high physics classes, we all learned that, according to the law of gravity, two massive bodies attract one another and that the closer two massive bodies are to one another the more strongly they will attract. Since the universe contains a lot of mass, gravity works to pull the massive bodies together and thereby slows down cosmic expansion. When the universe is young and more compact, gravity's effect on cosmic dynamics would be powerful while dark energy would be weak.

However, when the universe is old and more spread out, dark energy's effect would be strong while 'gravities' would be weak. Thus, if gravity alone influences cosmic dynamics, astronomers will observe that throughout cosmic history, the expansion of the universe slows down. The slowing down effect will be seen to get progressively weaker as the universe ages. However, if both gravity and dark energy are operable, astronomers will see cosmic expansion transition from slowing down to speeding up.

"For more than two decades, many atheists and virtually all young-earth creationists have been adamant in denying the existence of dark energy. Atheists reject dark energy because it implies a relatively recent cosmic beginning. It implies a beginning so recent as to defy a naturalistic explanation for the origin of life and history of life that makes possible the origin and existence of human beings who attain a global high-technology civilization. Another reason they do not like dark energy is because of the fine-tuning design it implies.

"In 2002, Philip Ball (an atheist physicist and former senior editor for *Nature Magazine)* interviewed theoretical physicists *Lisa Dyson, Matthew Kleban, and Leonard Susskind* about a paper they had just published and quoted them as saying, "Arranging the cosmos as we think it is arranged … would have required a miracle." [12]

"In the same interview, the three physicists said, "the existence of dark energy would imply that an unknown agent intervened in the evolution [of the universe] for reasons of its own." The three physicists, all of whom are nontheists, concluded their paper with these words: "Perhaps the only reasonable conclusion is that we do not live in a world with a true cosmological constant." [13]

"The cosmological constant is another term for dark energy. They felt compelled to deny the existence of dark energy because the alternative was '*an Agent beyond space and time performing miracles for reasons of his own*'. Young-earth creationists, too, wish that dark energy would go away. They wish it, however, for a reason opposite to nontheistic scientists. If dark energy is real, it makes the universe too old for their interpretation of the Genesis 1 creation days and the Genesis 5 and 11 genealogies. Like it or not, dark energy is real. With a measure as accurate as dark energy comprising 70.8±1.2% [14] of all the stuff of the universe there isn't any rational basis for doubting its existence. It makes up more than two-thirds of the universe. Those who believe in the God of the Bible should like it. It implies that the universe had a beginning in finite time as the Bible repeatedly declares. Furthermore, '*the fine-tuning design*' implies that a known agent who can operate from beyond space and time has miraculously intervened in the history of the universe for reasons of his own." [15] This sounds a lot like what Isaac Newton said about the universe and its creator, doesn't it?

End of excerpts from an article by Dr. Ross

To be fair and balanced with this, let me share with you, my readers, what a cosmologist atheist scientist had to say about this same topic, and more particular about what he called "*starting a universe from nothing, without any supernatural shenanigans*". I'm speaking of retired professor Lawrence Maxwell Krauss who is an American Canadian, theoretical physicist, and cosmologist who previously taught at Arizona State University, Yale University, and Case Western Reserve University. Dr. Kraus did a lecture at Radcliff Institute for Advanced Study at Harvard University, titled "*A Universe from Nothing*", which is now a video on YouTube under this same title.

You, my readers, should check out the full video lecture for the complete explanation of Dr. Kraus's *belief* that the universe created itself from nothing, but I am only going to state a couple of quotes from that video lecture by Dr. Kraus on what nothing means to him.

Dr. Kraus took about 30 minutes to describe where the universe came from, as well as what the 'total gravitational energy' in the universe is, and why B/A is the quantity 'Omega' (Ω), which = 1, and the total gravitational energy = 0. And then Dr. Kraus says: "This begins to suggest that we can create a universe from 'nothing'. Everything in the Universe has a total gravitational energy of zero, and so without any '*supernatural shenanigans*', in principle, we can create a universe from 'nothing'."

Find 48:18 on the Video and then watch it going forward. Dr. Kraus goes on to discuss *three* different 'versions' of his concept of 'nothing' while giving a little jab at all philosophers and theologians, saying "they're experts at making much to do about nothing" (Watch the video to learn why he says there are three (3) versions of nothing).

Richard Dawkins, the self-appointed leader of the more popular pack of new atheists (The "Unholy Trinity" [16] as they have been tagged, or the "Four Horsemen" [17], another name given to these new atheists, with Daniel Dennett being the fourth horseman), has been frantically turning up the volume of his yapping and barking, from loud to shrill, all-the-while the logic of his arguments, in particular over the last five years or so, has started to fracture – at least in my view it has.

Many of Richard's fellow atheists are now coming to a similar conclusion as Dr. Ball has, who I just mentioned. Yet, Richard is determined to 'raise the consciousness' [18] of the public to his belief that: "God does not exist", which is his stated purpose for writing his book. He's working hard to spread his 'quasi-gospel' of atheism, preaching that it's "the only *intellectually respectable* viewpoint on today's sophisticated, scientific landscape". [19]

This kind of dogmatism reminds me of Niels Bohr and his dogged belief that Newtonian principles were incontrovertible and Einstein, with his General Law of Relativity, was demonstrably wrong. [20] But Einstein's General Law of Relativity, over time, proved to be correct, and Newton and Niels were surprisingly wrong. It took hundreds of years for this to be realized in the scientific 'world' however, and so, I say, it might take many, many years for Darwin's Theory of Organic Evolution to be fully and completely dismantled and falsified, but I believe that that is what's going to happen.

In my view, even though Dawkins' quasi-religion and anti-Christ gospel is meant to disprove God's existence and thus destroy faith in any religion, I'm confident that it will ultimately be proven a deception. More and more of its tenets are now being questioned by some of today's brightest scientific minds. Before his death, Stephen Hawking's barking was added to the Atheist Scientists yapping chorus, with Stephen giving a splendid 'howling solo performance' just before his death. Mr. Hawking wrote, "The Universe was not created by God!" And "Physics leaves no room for God!" [21] Both claims are philosophical, non-scientific statements made by Stephen in his book, "The Grand Design: Has the Grand Master of Physics checkmated the Grand Designer of the Universe?" [22]

The fact is, Hawking did NOT produce one iota of evidence in his book to establish such anti-God claims, scientifically or otherwise, in my view. His unsupported *philosophical claims* do not stand up to any 'close' scrutiny either, which you would think a scientist of his renown would have required of himself. (See John Lennox's book, "God and Stephen Hawking" for the scrutiny that should have been done by Hawking himself. I've woven many of the arguments listed in John's book, here in my Introduction). [23]

Now you might be asking yourself, "What was the epistemological path that I took to come to the conclusions of my wanting and choosing to be a theist, a true believer in God, who lives in the sidereal heavens, or what Richard calls the Sky-God?" A good part of it comes from my personal study of a variety of sources such as the following list of scientists and religious scholars, and their works:

- Dr. John Lennox – Mathematician and Dr. of the Philosophy of Science. Dr. Lennox debates with Atheist Scientists. Here are a few of the books he's written, or videos he has done:
  - Why I am Not an Atheist – YouTube Video
  - God's Undertaker: Has Science Buried God?
  - Gunning for God: Why the New Atheists are Missing the Target
  - God & Stephen Hawking
- Dr. Stephen Meyer – Geologist and Ph.D. in Philosophy of Science
  - Signature in the Cell (DNA & the Evidence for Intelligent Design)

- - The Return of the God Hypothesis – DNA and the Evidence for Intelligent Design
  - Darwin's Doubt - The Explosive Origin of Animal Life and the Case for Intelligent Design
  - In the Begging there Was Information –
- Dr. John D. Lamb – Chemist & Professor at BYU (retired) – 'Joseph Smith's 21st Century View of the World: (Scientific) Truths He Knew Before the World Accepted Them'
- Dr. Marcus Ross – Paleontologist – The Study of Rock Formation and Fossils as they relate to The Global Flood & Intelligent Design
- Dr. Andrew Snelling – 'Earth's Catastrophic Past' (Especially the footnotes)
- Dr. Kevin Anderson – Archeologist – Study of the Tower of Babel
- Dr. Kevin Anderson – Microbiologist – Mutations & Evolution Biology
- Dr. Kurt Wise – Paleontologist – Rock & Fossil Formation
- Dr. Robert Carter – Marine Biologist – Ocean Life & Intelligent Design
- Dr. Todd Wood – Biologist – Human and Ape Fossils and what he sees the differences are (They're not from the same KIND)
- Dr. Steven Boyd – Hebraic Scholar – Genesis Studies & Earth History
- Dr. Andrew Snelling – Geologist – Carbon-14 and Radiocarbon Dating
- Dr. Danny Faulkner – Astronomer – The Big Bang Theory and Creation
- Dr. Art Chadwick – Taphonomy (The branch of paleontology that deals with the processes of fossilization) – Study of Events and Systems as they relate to Fossils.
- Dr. Paul Nelson – Philosopher of Science – Evolution & Intelligent Design.
- Dr. Joe DeWeese – Biochemist – Enzymology of Proteins that regulate DNA topology, and how it relates to Intelligent Design questions.
- Dr. Stuart Burgess – Mechanical Engineer – Systems Designs
- Dr. Richard Dawkins – Biologist – Author of "The God Delusion" (An Atheist treatise on The God Hypothesis)
- Dr. Nathaniel Jeanson – Cell & Developmental Biologist – Author of "Replacing Darwin".
- Christopher Hitchens – Journalist, Philosopher, and Social Commentator (An Atheist) – One of the Four Horsemen (Hitchens; Dawkins; Harris; Bennet)
- Gregg Braden – Bachelor of Science; Computer Geologist; Structural Geologist; Marine Biologist; Computer Systems Designer – The Ancient Text from the Book of Creation (Author of many books – See https://www.greggbraden.com/about-gregg-braden/; See Wikipedia)
- Ken Ham – Christian Apologist – Founded Answers in Genesis, a Video Series about Science and The Bible (Also see "Replacing Darwin: The New Origin of Species)
- Frank Turek – Christian Apologist – Founder of Cross Examined (A Master's degree in 'Public Administration', and a Doctor of Ministry in Christian Apologetics.
- Dr. Lawrence Krause – Theoretical Physicist – Origins Project, now called ASU Interplanetary Initiative (Dr. Krause is an Atheist who does debates with well-known Theists about God and the Universe from nothing)
- Joseph Fielding Smith – LDS prophet and Apologist/Historian & 10th President of the Church of Jesus Christ of Latter-Day Saints – Wrote "Man His Origin & Destiny" in 1954 (See also Mormonism and Evolution for multiple statements from Presidencies, Prophets, and Apostles, conflicting and multiple official statements).
- Bruce R. McConkie – Apostle of the Church of Jesus Christ of Latter-Day Saints. Wrote 'Mormon Doctrine'; 'The Premortal Messiah'; 'The Mortal Messiah, and 'The Millennial Messiah' and others.
- Wayne May – Author & Researcher of American Hopewell Mound- Builders – Published 'Ancient American Magazine' for over 20 years.
- Dr. Hugh Ross – Astrophysicist, Christian apologist, and old-Earth creationist. Dr. Ross has a Ph.D. in Astronomy and a B.Sc. degree in physics. Some of his books are "Why the Universe is the Way it is", "Improbable Planet", "The Creator of the Cosmos", and many, many more books.
- Dr. James Tour – An American Chemist and Nanotechnologist. He is a Professor of Chemistry, Professor of Materials Science and Nano-Engineering, a Professor of Computer Science at Rice University, and a Christian.

It's just a beginning list from which I drew a lot of insights that now support my beliefs. There are many additional processes of learning and study that I've followed as well. I've chosen not to include all the teachings of the many prophets of God, whose teachings I have studied, both ancient and modern.

I also did not choose to include most of the scriptures from which my belief in God was formed. I've listed a sampling of source materials and resources offered by these individuals who've spoken on the varied topics Richard Dawkins has argued about in his book, each of them drawing from their own 'lane of study'. These individuals' experiences and learning have helped me grow in my knowledge and understanding of God and His nature. I only included two leaders of the Church of Jesus Christ of Latter-Day Saints on the above list, but I'll refer to many more throughout my book as I share my perspective on Richard's varied chapters.

From these individuals' research and writings, as well as from the many years of personal study and prayer, including my having repeated moments of personal inspiration (personal revelation), I acquired my own epistemic philosophy, it now spanning the entirety of my 68 years of life (As of this writing). This epistemic philosophy has gone through several iterations, just like most folks' belief systems do.

My belief in God, as a child, was mostly due to the fact that I was raised in a home where both parents were members of the Church of Jesus Christ of Latter-Day Saints, both believing in the same God and the same gospel – the gospel of Jesus Christ. Being united in their beliefs, they taught me the gospel of Jesus Christ from a very early age, along with each of my six living siblings (One sister died of spina bifida shortly after her birth due to my mother having had German measles during her pregnancy).

As a result of my upbringing, I had the seeds of the gospel of Jesus Christ planted in my heart and mind. Richard, of course, would say, "I am an example of child abuse because my parents taught me about God as a child when I didn't have the mental capacity to understand what they were teaching me." [24] I will come back to this false claim later when I review Chapter 9. My parents also taught me the Golden Rule, my place in God's Church and kingdom here on earth, as well as the Plan of Redemption and Happiness that Heavenly Father offers all of His children, as a gift, even the gift of eternal life in His presence, in the world to come.

This mindset of Richard reminds me of a garden patch my wife and I had at the side of a home we owned several years ago. We decided to roto-till that piece of dirt and then, I am sad to say, I failed to follow through with our goal to plant the variety of flower seeds that we wanted to grow in that strip of dirt, hoping that it would become a beautiful flower garden that we could enjoy by the end of that summer and for many years thereafter. Over the summer months that unattended dirt patch automatically grew a wide variety of weeds. Some weeds grew more than five feet tall if you can believe it. Some became large prickly bushes that birds could hide in. Like this weed patch, children's minds seem to automatically grow the weeds of the world's ideologies. Their ideologies come from the swirling thought-seeds that automatically land in their minds if it's not protected and left unattended.

As a result of these attitudes of mind and beliefs of the world one learns from daily associations, our minds will automatically produce a patch of 'worldly-thought-weeds'. But, if we deliberately plant beautiful, wonderful 'thought-seeds', our minds grow a beautiful garden of magnificent thought-flowers and thought-trees of intended knowledge; thought-trees that produce the good fruit of a healthy, happy ideology and lifestyle. When my parents purposefully chose to plant a garden of mental beauty in my mind, these powerful thought-seeds produced a worldview that they knew would bring me joy, peace, and happiness throughout the entirety of my life here on earth, in spite of all of the challenges they knew I would face as I grew older and lived out my life.

Throughout my childhood, thought-seeds were planted continuously; thought-seeds about God, prayer, and the story of the prophet Joseph Smith and his first vision as examples. These thought-seeds, and others, made up the topics we as a family discussed during our weekly Family Home Evenings, which we enjoyed together every Monday night. My mind's thought-garden grew positive, faith-filled mental trees, and in time those mental trees produced the fruit of healthy, positive behaviors in me that reflected the fruit of my faith, the fruit being faith in, and a love for God, and His Son, Jesus Christ.

By eight years old, after a few years of Primary (A type of Sunday School for little children) and Family Home Evenings called Family Night, as well as having participated in daily, personal prayers each morning and evening as a family, along with individual and family scripture study (Or at least we tried to do it early each morning. Ha-ha), all these good mental plants produced a tender 'seedling testimony' of God and His Son, Jesus Christ, as well as faith in the Holy Ghost, as it manifested truth within my mind and heart.

At that time, I only had a vague understanding of who and what the spiritual personage of the Holy Ghost was. This concept was planted in my mind and heart so that by the time I reached eight years old, having loving encouragement by both of my parents, versus being forced against my will, I decided to become a member of the Church of Jesus Christ of Latter-Day Saints and was baptized and confirmed a member of the Church by my father. Dad was an ordained High Priest, an office he held in the Melchizedek priesthood, after the order of the Son of God, and as such was authorized to perform these ordinances of baptism and confirmation upon me, so I could become a member of Christs' Church, the Church of Jesus Christ of Latter-Day Saints.

Though I didn't have an apologist's knowledge of the Gospel of Jesus Christ as an eight-year-old, I had had many experiences that helped me identify with the concepts of good and evil, right and wrong, and what personal sin was. In other words, I had become familiar with what the feeling or what I came to understand was my conscience, which provided me with a *sense of guilt*, and its power to convict me when I had sinned or when I was about to make wrong choices. This conviction came by way of this sense of guilt in my very core, my center, and due to that feeling in my heart, I was often moved with a desire to repent which is simply the desire to change. When I did so it allowed me to change and be the better person Heavenly Father wanted me to become. This gift of conscience and its sense of guilt reminded me of the person I can be, even what a child of the Living God should be, Jesus being our example of what a child of Heavenly Father should be.

At times I succumbed to the spirit of Satan, which spirit uses shame to influence us to continue to sin. It is a tool that Satan uses to make us feel of little value, worthless, and even unlovable by God when we sin. It, if not resisted and rejected, brings us to a point where we find ourselves giving up and saying, "What's the use? God has rejected me. He can't love me anymore", and thus we're led down the path to even greater sin and self-loathing which binds us down like a flaxen cord, instead of repenting and changing our course when we make wrong choices. When we repent, we choose to change our course and move towards becoming the kind of people God wants us, His children, to be.

Our conscience convicts us when we break the laws of God, He having written them upon our hearts by the Light of Christ. It also speaks to our minds and hearts via this sense of guilt. In other words, I knew when I was considering doing the wrong thing. When I chose to follow this Light of Christ and did the right thing, this influence of light, this prompting from my conscience, protected me from the consequences of sin. On the other hand, I felt the convicting spirit and sense of guilt in my heart whenever I chose to go against its promptings and did the wrong thing anyway. When I chose not to follow the promptings of my conscience, even the Light of Christ, I found myself moving ever closer to outright rebellion against God and His commandments. Here's an example of what I'm talking about.

There were times when I stole a piece of candy for example, or when I was unkind to a sibling or neighborhood friend; so that I soon felt the conviction or the sense of guilt speaking to me through thoughts in my mind and feelings in my core, saying, "You know better Marty. Don't do this". I distinctly remember the pain of conscious I felt after saying a dirty word or thinking a dirty thought as I was looking at the pornography magazine a neighborhood boy showed me when I was just eleven or twelve years old. Such experiences are a part of our earthly experience here on earth as human beings. We all have sinned and come short of the glory of God.

We are all fallen and therefore are broken in that sense, and it's our sins that separates us from God, and often weigh us down if we don't repent of them. This pain of conscience isn't just mental either. It's spiritual in nature. There's a difference between mental and spiritual pain from guilt, and this feeling of sadness sank deep into my bosom. It's what's called *'having a broken heart and a contrite spirit'*. The thought of disappointing my Heavenly Father, and the Savior, Jesus Christ, due to my disobedience, as well as the thought of disappointing my parents (if and when they ever learned of my bad behavior and poor choices), was a powerful emotion that entered my heart, and it's always moved me to repent.

I knew my parents loved me and understood that I was human just like they were. I knew they wanted me to grow in my faith and my knowledge of God's truth and plan for me, and they didn't condemn or shame me when I stumbled. They just loved and encouraged me to try and do better. They didn't like the behavior, of course, they just wanted me to make better choices so that I could grow in my confidence and character and be happy as I made the effort to change my behavior to be better. They loved and encouraged me, so that my 'desire to be better' increased, as did my goal to become more like the child of God I was learning how to become.

The spirit of God does not shame. It convicts us and gives us this sense of guilt as a reminder to help us move *unto* repentance so that changes in our behavior can be made, and those changes can move us ever closer to who we truly are – children of God. Making such changes are gifts to God. Repentance is a gift. It's not a punishment, nor is it something to feel shame about. God wants us to become like His

Son, the Savior Jesus Christ. Some past prophets have even called us "Children of the King of Kings" which implies that all of us are of royal birth because we're children of a Heavenly King. [25]

By the time I turned eleven years old I had developed a pretty good habit of personal prayer, and of asking for forgiveness each night and before going to Church to partake of the emblems of the sacrament to renew the covenants I had made with God at my baptism when I was eight years old. Over the many years since my baptism, I learned to see myself, in my minds' eye, reaching out for His mercy, and asking Him to heal and forgive me of my shortcomings, and find greater strength to overcome life's temptations. This thoughtful imagery came from the story of the woman who had faith that she would be healed if she could but touch Jesus' garment as he passed by her while she sat at the side of the street. I try to remember this imagery as I wait to be offered the emblems of the sacrament.

At the age of eleven, I knew I was an agent over my own will, having the power to choose what to think, how to act, and how to deepen my redemptive relationship with God. It was my choice to love God or not. I knew that I was human and had a sinful nature like everyone else, and therefore I knew I wasn't perfect, but I also knew that I had been allowed the opportunity of becoming more like my Savior through the means of His grace and mercy and through my sincere repentance. I remember an experience that illustrates how life's experiences helped me grow in my faith in God. I had just got a tiny new puppy who I named Tojo. All the neighborhood children loved him and liked to come over and play with him (Not so much with me, ha-ha). One time while we were all playing with Tojo, we were running around the front yard with him chasing and barking at our feet, and suddenly a neighbor boy accidentally kicked Tojo in the head. Tojo fell immediately to his side and went stiff, showing no movement.

Tojo's eyes were wide open but glazed over, and a greyish foam started flowing out of his mouth. I immediately ran into the house to my parent's bedroom. I shut the door and hit my knees at the side of their bed and started pleading with Heavenly Father to help Tojo. After a while I had become oblivious to what was beginning to happen outside that bedroom window, but I soon began to hear some of the kids saying, "Is he dead? Where did Marty go? What happened? What should we do?" This made me pray even more fervently.

By pray I mean, I pleaded with Heavenly Father to help Tojo be okay. I told Him that I knew He had the power to help Tojo, and even bring him back to life if necessary. It was a simple prayer offered up by an innocent eleven-year-old's believing heart. After a few more minutes of pleading to God, I heard a neighborhood friend scream out, "Marty! Marty! Come out here! Where are you? Tojo's okay! He's not dead!" And sure enough, when I got outside, I could see Tojo coming to life. He was a bit wobbly as he stood back onto his feet, but he was alive. His eyes got the light back in them, the foaming stopped, and he was once again breathing again. He was alive! At least that's what we, as little children called it. In my mind, Tojo was no longer dead because God had answered my fervent, simple, yet hopeful prayer.

As an adult, I can certainly understand it if people would choose to describe this experience as a coincidence of timing; that it just took some time for Tojo's brain to get over the concussion it had just suffered. But my mind went into hope mode, producing thoughts and images and solutions to a horrific event I was experiencing at that moment in time, especially with me being just an eleven-year-old boy. For me, this experience took my trust in my Heavenly Father, my simple belief in God and the relationship I had with Him, up to that point, to a whole new level. It made my relationship with God a 'trusting in God' kind of relationship. Being able to see God as a personal God. A God who loved me and heard my prayers, and had the power over life and death, made all the difference to me.

My faith in God today, is the fruit of hundreds of experiences just like this one. Each experience helped to take my belief in this incredible being, to the level where I knew I could trust Him completely, and that He was my friend and was always there to help me when I found myself in desperate need of His help, especially in those difficult times where I couldn't control my circumstances. When someone else's choice made my circumstance out of my control, I leaned on Him. I especially feel I need God's help whenever I feel unworthy of His love due to my poor choices. I have grown to the point where I exercise complete faith in God because I have come to understand that faith is an action word, and my role in making sure it is working in my life, is to simply exercise my faith and stand on His promises. This action of choosing to love and exercise faith in Him, is best shown by keeping His commandments.

Let me say here that there are millions and millions of people who can and do claim these same kinds of experiences and express this same kind of trust in God. To me, this principle of faith is a repeatable, predictable kind of evidence-based principle that says there is a loving God that exists. It is a testable principle that anyone and everyone can put to the test. This test of the principle called faith, has its own distinct kind of spiritual steps, so-to-speak. Like the scientific method, this spiritual method has its own spiritual steps. May I suggest that you, my readers, check out a book titled, "Lectures on Faith," [26] which is a book that goes into wonderful, delicious detail on the principle of faith, as it was studied and taught in a school for Latter-Day Saint leaders in Joseph Smith's Day, called "The School of the Prophets". [27]

I've had hundreds of these kinds of faith promoting experiences, and they peppered my early years, up and until my mission, where I went to the *Gulf States Mission* to share the message of the Restored Gospel of Jesus Christ. During the 19 years leading up to my mission, I had come to learn how to discern the *voice of the Spirit* from other competing voices, including my own voice, which spiritual voice I've heard softly speaking in my mind my entire life, and so, I've come to know the difference between these voices. This *voice of the spirit* is distinctly different from my own knowable 'self's' voice.

Over the years the spirit of the Lord's voice has become distinct, and increasingly recognizable to me, and I'm so very grateful for this gift of discernment. The Voice of the Spirit is often described in the scriptures as a "Still Small Voice":

I Kings 19:11-13

11 And he said, Go forth, and stand upon the mount before the LORD. And, behold, the LORD passed by, and a great and strong wind rent the mountains, and brake in pieces the rocks before the LORD; *but* the LORD *was* not in the wind: and after the wind an earthquake; but the LORD *was* not in the earthquake:

12 And after the earthquake a fire; *but* the LORD *was* not in the fire: and after the fire a *still small voice.*

These verses of scripture reminds me of an incredibly beautiful song sung by the talented musical artist named Sissell Kyrkjebø, called "Slow Down". You can find it on YouTube at: "Slow Down – Sissell (2019) Pioneer Concert with The Tabernacle Choir. This beautiful song attunes one's heart to the spirit of the Lord quite beautifully, and I've found that music like Sissell's song, gets that attunement done in the most unobstructed way. It's wonderful.

By the time I was old enough to go on my mission, I had developed a deeper testimony than the one I had as a child, and that's because, besides all the experiences I had had, I had also read the Book of Mormon (For a greater understanding of the people spoken of in The Book of Mormon, go to YouTube and do a search for "Wayne May Fireside" where Wayne shares evidence of the Hopewell Mound-builder people; people whose history fall perfectly into the 600 B.C. to 400 A.D timeframe. These people represent one of two theories of where the Book of Mormon took place) at least three times by the time I went on my mission at nineteen, as well as the Doctrine & Covenants and the Pearl of Great Price a couple of times, each of which is part of our canonized books of scripture for my Church. I had also read The Old Testament in its entirety twice, and the New Testament at least three times in total. In addition, I attended four years of religious seminary classes during my high school years, eleven years of Sunday School, and six years of Priesthood Quorum lessons [28] by the time my mission came around. Most of these classes were taught by terrific, humble instructors. Surprisingly, I paid attention to them for the most part. I even took notes and listed questions that came to me during these classes, which I then took home to ask my father to see what he had to say about them. These were the confusing, hard doctrine questions I found too difficult to answer for myself and so I asked my father, who loved the gospel, to help me with them.

They were questions like, "What about dinosaurs, dad?" Or "I learned about evolution in biology today, dad. I don't believe in Darwin's theory that says Man came from monkeys, and that we descended from amoebas living in a chemical soup. It just didn't ring true to me, but a lot of people who are a lot smarter than I am, believe this stuff dad", and so I asked my dad, "What do you think about evolution?" Anyway, my epistemic philosophy developed during my youth can be summed up as a philosophy influenced by others (Parents, Church leaders, teachers, and close friends) and a lot of personal study on the questions that had come to me personally, peppered with personal experiences that I had had growing up as a child. Each of these experiences helped my understanding of the true nature of God and His Son, Jesus Christ, and what having a Savior truly meant for me and everybody else too. By my nineteenth year, I had acquired a good understanding of the need for redemption, meaning being saved from both death & hell – Death, meaning Physical death, and Hell, meaning Spiritual Death, … which is separation from God due to our own personal sins and not Adam's transgressions. [29] By the time I left home to go on my mission, which was the 20th of July 1973, a lifetime ago, I had acquired my own personally developed testimony; a belief in God's existence.

Through personal effort to know God and His Son, Jesus Christ, my testimony slowly deepened line upon line, precept by precept, here a little, and there a little, especially as I continued to keep the covenants that I had made with my Heavenly Father almost eleven years earlier.

I had multiple experiences that deepened my faith and understanding of the Godhead, and because of my searching and feeling after God, I acquired a strong experiential belief in Their involvement in the details of my life. For me there were just too many coincidences to just set them aside. I knew my beliefs were quite different from other Christians, as well as those who called themselves Deists, who believe in a God, but only through unaided reason, so that they reject any theological beliefs that can't be proven by reason. As I understand it, it is the Deist's belief that God does not step into our mortal experience to reveal or manifest Himself to His children as their Living God. But, God, our Heavenly Father, told his ancient apostles that coming to *know* Him is what He called Eternal Life. [30] Here's what one of God's apostles said about that statement of Jesus. It is a recorded by the apostle John:

John 17:3

3 And this is life eternal, that they might *know thee* the only true God, and Jesus Christ, whom thou hast sent.

Anyway, it was these kinds of experiences and my personal study regarding them, that motivated me to go on a mission. My decision was like the decision to go to school for another year. It was just automatic. It was not a command or the result of being pressured to go by my parents. There was no struggle deciding whether or not I wanted to go on a mission versus just staying home and continuing with my schooling and dating. It wasn't even about being expected to go by the Church leaders either. I was excited about going on a mission from the time I was a little boy of eight years, and so I did. I had always looked forward to going on a mission because of the relationship I had developed with God and my Savior early on. At eighteen my mission call came, and I was called to go to the Gulf States Mission, which consisted of those states that form the Bible Belt. It included Arkansas, Mississippi, Louisiana, and the western half of Tennessee. I soon learned how different the South was from Boise, Idaho.

Once I was serving on my mission (I turned nineteen one week after entering the mission field), I soon learned about critics of my Church and their Anti-Mormon literature for the very first time in my life. It was probably about the third or fourth month of my mission. I don't know why, but I hadn't come across it until my mission. It consisted of pamphlets and books, as well as books and videos like "The God-Makers." [31]

I'm sure they were available for me to read or watch in Boise, but, like I said, I never saw or read anything like it before my mission. In addition to the material just mentioned, I also came across a couple of books written by Sandra Tanner, an ex-Latter-Day Saint and anti-Mormon author. [32] I quickly found that the message given by Peter in 1 Peter 3:15 was exactly what I needed to hear. Peter gave the following counsel to the Saints of his time:

1 Peter 3:15

15 But sanctify the Lord God in your hearts: and be ready always to give an answer to every man that asketh you the reason of the hope that is in you (The hope Peter is referring to, I believe, is the hope of the resurrection and of the reality of life after death, as well as the gift of returning to live in the presence of God and His holy society forever. That's quite a hope, isn't it?).

I soon learned that this was where I needed to get to knowledge-wise, and do it as quickly as possible, if I was going to be of any help to my sweet investigators. While serving in West Memphis Arkansas early on in my mission, I met a lovely man, who was the Branch President for the West Memphis Arkansas Branch (a branch is a small congregation of around one-hundred members or less), and he made available a small library of Church books for the West Memphis Branch members to purchase for their personal study.

I knew I needed to buy a few of those books and get after studying them as soon as possible. And that is what I did. I soon filled my mind with answers to gospel questions to assist me in the work. It helped me establish a habit of study that I have kept up to this very day. It was at this particular juncture of my mission that I discovered the writings of Elder Bruce R. McConkie, mentioned earlier on my list. I bought his series of the 'The Promised Messiah: The First Coming of Christ' [33]; The Mortal Messiah (4 volumes) [34] and the Millennial Messiah' [35] (Each volume being about one and a half inches thick).

I also bought a five-volume series called 'Answers to Gospel Questions' [36] by Joseph Fielding Smith, an Apostle of the Church from 1910 to 1970, and later President of the Church, as well as a 27-volume series called 'The Journal of Discourses' [37], including an Index of the many authors and quotes.

In addition to these books, I purchased a 6-Volume series called 'A Comprehensive History of The Church of Jesus Christ of Latter-Day Saints' by B. H. Roberts; a three-volume series called 'Doctrinal New Testament Commentary', again by Bruce R. McConkie, and many, many more books that fill my bookshelves today. It was my belief that I was to get and study the scriptures as well as learn and study from the best books like I just mentioned. From this list of books, you can tell that I developed an insatiable appetite for consuming religious books. As I said, I continued this habit of gospel study after returning home from my mission and throughout my adult life, post mission. I think I've read well over a hundred books, maybe more, on the topics we'll be discussing here in my book.

I've continued my studies throughout the 49 years since my mission. Man, have those 49 years flown by! As I said, it feels like a lifetime ago. During my mission I also started collecting pamphlets, such as the ones handed out by Jehovah's Witnesses called 'The Watch Tower'. I also purchased several books written by Christian authors. One such book was a book called "Religions of the World". Another was called "Mystery Babylon Religion". I now have several new books that fall into the category I've named "Other Religions & Beliefs", and Mr. Dawkins's book, *The God Delusion,* which now holds a special place in this category on my bookshelf, because it's about his quasi-religion of 'Atheism'.

I have also bought, collected, and read many books about science. One is, "The Faith of a Scientist" by Dr. Henry B. Eyring. Another is called, "Joseph Smith's 21st Century View of the World", whose author gives a scientific take on the world, the universe, and science. It's written by John David Lamb of BYU, who holds a Ph.D. in Inorganic Physical Chemistry. When I got home from my mission, I continued searching for books that fell into the category of books written by people who believe differently than I do, especially books written by the three main religions of Judaism, Christianity, and Islam. I purchased many of them so I could have them as reference books for my library. That way I could study them as part of my spiritual development.

It's been my belief that I needed to follow the commandment that says, we should "love the Lord your God with all your heart, might, 'MIND' and strength". Not only worship the God of my youth, and the God I served as a missionary, but to study Him and His gospel as an adult so that I could give cohesive, sound, reasonable answers to anyone who asks me any of the 'Big' questions, especially when they ask me "Why do you still have the hope that you do?" It's a hope gained from believing in God, especially after learning what scientists had to say about God not existing. In other words, "Why are you so confident in your faith Marty? Why do you believe God exists when scientists say He doesn't?"

Because of the struggles that some people have with the Church of Jesus Christ of Latter-Day Saints, and due to the many callings of leadership that have been extended to me over the last 45 years of my adult life (These callings include a Gospel Doctrine Teacher, a member of the High Council in three different Stakes, and currently I'm serving as a Branch President of a small congregation of residents living in a Care Center here in Bountiful Utah), I had to educate myself so that I would be comfortable with those callings that put me in the position where I needed to be prepared to answer those questions that caused doubts about the Church, or about life itself. I also bought and read books like "Faith is Not Blind" by Bruce C. Haffen, and others like it, each of which has helped me to uplift my friends and family members who were suffering from cognitive dissonance, and some who had gone into a full-blown faith crisis. As human beings we are often faced with these kinds of spiritual challenges in our daily lives.

I could go on and on listing the hundreds of books that are on my bookshelves today, but I'll leave it there. Suffice it to say, if you consider all the hours of study I have expended in reading and studying these books, I feel I have more than a college degree *in gospel learning* (But not a diploma of course). I am learned on the subjects of faith, religion, philosophy, and 'The Gospel of Jesus Christ' specifically, each of which have contributed to the development of my epistemic philosophy to which I attribute my belief in God and His existence, as well as His plan and life's purpose He has for me. With all this learning, both scientific and spiritual, I believe I have a clear understanding of God and His nature, and so, I wanted you, my readers, to know this about me *before* you read my book in its entirety. That way you can not only know what I believe about God, but you'll know *why* I believe what I do about Him. You'll know what I believe our purpose for being sent here to earth is, from a Latter-Day Saint's point of view, and, as a result you'll be prepared to understand my personal perspective I'll give on Richard's book.

It's my hope that as we go on this journey together (The journey of reviewing Richard's book from my perspective), you'll stay with me all the way to its conclusion. If you do, I believe that by the end of our journey you'll be well equipped to honestly and fairly decide whether Richard is the one who is delusional or I am. Here's a few teachings from the life and journals of the prophet Joseph Smith on the nature of God the Eternal Father, and what He has described is His purpose for you and me, His Children.

For me, these quotes made by the prophet Joseph Smith, formed the foundation of my perspective on God and His nature. One wonderful example from the more famous of Joseph Smiths' quotes, clearly describes the truth to which I have taken ownership as my core, foundational belief. I even claimed it as my purpose and goal for my life. Here it is, and I quote:

"Happiness is the object and design of our existence and will be the end thereof if we pursue the path that leads to it; and this path is virtue, uprightness, faithfulness, holiness, and keeping all the commandments of God".

End Quote

Here are a few more quotes made by the Prophet Joseph Smith which I have found to be very helpful as I'm on this journey of finding happiness wherever I am, no matter my circumstances. Joseph's quotes can be found on the following website: www.churchofjesuschrist.org. Joseph Smith taught:

"The purposes of our God are great, His love unfathomable, His wisdom infinite, and His power unlimited; therefore, the Saints (Baptized members of The Church of Jesus Christ of Latter-Day Saints are referred to as saints) have cause to rejoice and be glad." [38]

Psalm's 48:14

14 For this God *is* our God for ever and ever: he will be our guide *even* unto death.

Among Joseph Smith's progenitors were many who sought to know the true God in their Day. Joseph's parents were deeply spiritual, and although they did not find the full truth about God in the churches around them, they honored the Bible as God's word and made prayer a part of their daily life. The Prophet's brother William recalled:

"My father's religious habits were strictly pious and moral. … I was called upon to listen to prayers both night and morning. My parents, father, and mother poured out their souls to God, the donor of all blessings, to keep and guard their children and keep them from sin and all evil works. Such was the strict piety of my parents." [39] William also said:

"We always had family prayers since I can remember. I well remember father used to carry his spectacles in his vest pocket, … and when us boys saw him feel for his specs, we knew that was a signal to get ready for prayer, and if we did not notice it mother would say, "William", or whoever was the negligent one, "get ready for prayer." After the prayer, we had a song we would sing; I remember part of it yet: 'Another day has passed and gone, we lay our garments by.'" [40]

This early spiritual training sank deep into young Joseph Smith's soul, much like my experiences did as a child. When he became concerned about his eternal welfare and sought to know which church he should join, he knew he could turn to God for answers, just as I learned I could. Here's that experience in his own words, and I quote:

"I learned in the scriptures that God was the same yesterday, today, and forever, that he was no respecter to persons, for he was God. For I looked upon the sun, the glorious luminary of the earth, and also the moon rolling in [its] majesty through the heavens and also the stars shining in their courses; and the earth also upon which I stood, and the beast of the field and the fowls of heaven and the fish of the waters; and also man walking forth upon the face of the earth in majesty and the strength of beauty, [with] power and intelligence in governing the things which are so exceedingly marvelous even in the likeness of him who created them. And when I considered upon these things my heart exclaimed, 'Well hath the wise man said it is a fool that saith in his heart there is no God (Psalms 53:1)."

"My heart exclaimed, 'All these bear testimony and bespeak an omnipotent and omnipresent power, a Being who maketh laws and decreeth and bindeth all things in their bounds, who filleth eternity, who was and is and will be from all eternity to eternity. And when I considered all these things and that that Being seeketh such to worship him as worship him in spirit and truth:

John 4:23

23 But the hour cometh, and now is, when the true worshippers shall worship the Father in spirit and in truth: for the Father seeketh such to worship him.

"Therefore, I cried unto the Lord for mercy, for there was no one else to whom I could go and obtain mercy." [41]

End Quote

Joseph's faithful prayer for mercy and wisdom was answered with his First Vision. That vision gave the young prophet far greater knowledge about God than any of the churches of his Day possessed; knowledge that had been lost to the world for centuries due to apostasy (The falling away from original, pure truth). In the First Vision, Joseph learned for himself that the Father and the Son are individual, corporeal beings; that their power is greater than the power of evil; and that man is indeed fashioned in God's divine image—truths that are essential in understanding our actual relationship to our Father in Heaven. Other revelations about the nature of God followed, including many that are now recorded in our latter-day scriptures besides the Bible (Those being The Book of Mormon, The Doctrine & Covenants, and The Pearl of Great Price). As God's chosen instrument in restoring pure gospel truth to the world, the prophet Joseph testified of God throughout his ministry. Here's just one example, and I quote:

"I am going to inquire after God," he declared, "for I want you all to know Him, and to be familiar with Him. ... You will then know that I am His servant, for I speak as one having authority." [42]

"God is the loving Father of all mankind, and the source of all that is good. While one portion of the human race is judging and condemning the other without mercy, the Great Parent of the universe looks upon the whole of the human family with fatherly care and paternal regard; He views them as His offspring, and without any of those contracted feelings that influence the children of men, causes His sun to rise on the evil and the good, and sendeth rain on the just and on the unjust." [43]

Matthew 5:45

45 That ye may be the children of your Father which is in heaven: for he maketh his sun to rise on the evil and on the good, and sendeth rain on the just and on the unjust.

"We admit that God is the great source and fountain from whence proceeds all good; that He is perfect intelligence, and that His wisdom alone is sufficient to govern and regulate the mighty creations and worlds which shine and blaze with such magnificence and splendor over our heads, as though touched with His finger and moved by His Almighty word.

Psalm 19:1

1 The heavens the glory of God; and the firmament sheweth his handywork.

"And a moment's reflection is sufficient to teach every man of common intelligence, that all these are not the mere productions of *chance*, nor could they be supported by any power less than an Almighty hand." [44] "God sees the secret springs of human action and knows the hearts of all living." [45]

"The purposes of our God are great, His love unfathomable, His wisdom infinite, and His power unlimited; therefore, the Saints have cause to rejoice and be glad, knowing that 'this God is our God forever and ever, and He will be our Guide until death": [46]

Psalm 48:14

14 For this God *is* our God for ever and ever: he will be our guide *even* unto death.

"When we comprehend the character of God, we comprehend ourselves and know how to approach Him. There are but a very few beings in the world who understand rightly the character of God. The great majority of mankind do not comprehend anything, either that which is past or that which is to come, as it respects their relationship to God. They do not know, neither do they understand the nature of that relationship; and consequently, they know but little above the brute beast, or more than to eat, drink and sleep. This is all man knows about God or His existence unless it is given by the inspiration of the Almighty:

Amos 3:7

7 Surely the Lord God will do nothing but he revealeth His secret unto His servants the prophets.

"If a man learns nothing more than to eat, drink and sleep, and does not comprehend any of the designs of God, the beast comprehends the same things. It eats, drinks, sleeps, and knows nothing more about God; yet it knows as much as we do unless we can comprehend by the inspiration of Almighty God. If men do not comprehend the character of God, they do not comprehend themselves. I want to go back to the beginning, and so lift your minds into more lofty spheres and a more exalted understanding than what the human mind generally aspires to (In other words, Joseph wanted to raise our consciousness by learning of these supernal truths). The scriptures inform us that:

John 17:3

3 And this is life eternal, that they might know thee the only true God, and Jesus Christ, whom thou hast sent.

"If any man does not know God and inquires what kind of a being He is—if he will search diligently his own heart—if the declaration of Jesus and the apostles be true, he will realize that he has not eternal life; for there can be eternal life on no other principle. My first object is to find out the character of the only wise and true God, and what kind of a being He is.

"God Himself was once as we are now, and is an exalted man, and sits enthroned in yonder heavens! That is the great secret. If the veil were rent today, and the great God who holds this world in its orbit, and who upholds all worlds and all things by His power, was to make Himself visible,—I say, if you were to see Him today, you would see Him as a man in form—like yourselves in all the person, image, and very form as a man; for Adam was created in the very fashion, image and likeness of God, and received instruction from, and walked, talked and conversed with Him, as one man talks and communes with another."

Continuing with what Joseph said:

"Having a knowledge of God, we begin to know how to approach Him, and how to ask so we can receive an answer. When we understand the character of God and know how to come to Him, He begins to unfold the heavens to us (The mysteries of Godliness) and tell us all about it. When we are ready to come to Him, He is ready to come to us." [47]

"In the Godhead there are three separate and distinct personages:

Articles of Faith 1:1

1 We believe in God, the Eternal Father, and in His Son, Jesus Christ, and in the Holy Ghost." [48]

Joseph Smith taught the following in April 1843, later recorded in *Doctrine & Covenants 130:22*:

"The Father has a body of flesh and bones as tangible as man's (This is corporeal); the Son also; but the Holy Ghost has not a body of flesh and bones but is a personage of Spirit. Were it not so, the Holy Ghost could not dwell in us." [49]

"I have always declared God to be a distinct personage, Jesus Christ a separate and distinct personage from God the Father, and that the Holy Ghost was a distinct personage and a Spirit: and these three constitute three distinct personages and three Gods." [50]

"That which is without body or parts is nothing. There is no other God in heaven but that God who has flesh and bones." [51]

"The Godhead is in perfect unity, and God the Father presides. There is much said about God and the Godhead. ... The teachers of the Day say that the Father is God, the Son is God, and the Holy Ghost is God, and they are all in one body and one God. Jesus prayed that those that the Father had given him out of the world might be made one in them, as they were one:

John 17:11–23

11 And now I am no more in the world, but these are in the world, and I come to thee. Holy Father, keep through thine own name those whom thou hast given me, that they may be one, as we *are*.

12 While I was with them in the world, I kept them in thy name: those that thou gavest me I have kept, and none of them is lost, but the son of perdition; that the scripture might be fulfilled.

13 And now come I to thee; and these things I speak in the world, that they might have my joy fulfilled in themselves.

14 I have given them thy word; and the world hath hated them, because they are not of the world, even as I am not of the world.

15 I pray not that thou shouldest take them out of the world, but that thou shouldest keep them from the evil.

16 They are not of the world, even as I am not of the world.

17 Sanctify them through thy truth: thy word is truth.

18 As thou hast sent me into the world, even so have I also sent them into the world.

19 And for their sakes I sanctify myself, that they also might be sanctified through the truth.

20 Neither pray I for these alone, but for them also which shall believe on me through their word;

21 That they all may be one; as thou, Father, *art* in me, and I in thee, that they also may be one in us: that the world may believe that thou hast sent me.

22 And the glory which thou gavest me I have given them; that they may be one, even as we are one:

23 I in them, and thou in me, that they may be made perfect in one; and that the world may know that thou hast sent me, and hast loved them, as thou hast loved me.

"Peter and Stephen testify that they saw the Son of Man standing on the right hand of God. Any person that had seen the heavens opened knows that there are three personages in the heavens; that they hold the keys of power, and that one of these three, our Heavenly Father, presides over them all." [52]

"An everlasting covenant was made between three personages before the organization of this earth and relates to their dispensation of things to men on the earth. These personages are called God the first, the Creator; God the second, the Redeemer; and God the third, the Witness or Testator." [53]

"[It is] the province of the Father to preside as the Chief or President, Jesus as the Mediator, and the Holy Ghost as the Testator or Witness. The Son [has] a tabernacle and so [does] the Father, but the Holy Ghost is a personage of spirit without tabernacle." [54] The scripture says, 'I and my Father are one':

John 10:30

30 I and *my* Father are one.

… and again, that the Father, Son, and Holy Ghost are one. In what sense are they one? John says:

1 John 5:7–8

7 For there are three that bear record in heaven, the Father, the Word, and the Holy Ghost: and these three are one.

8 And there are three that bear witness in earth, the Spirit, and the water, and the blood: and these three agree in one.

"So did the Savior pray to the Father, 'I pray not for the world, but for those whom ye gave me out of the world, that we might be 'one,' or to say, be of one mind in the unity of the faith:

John 17:9, 11

9 I pray for them: I pray not for the world, but for them which thou hast given me; for they are thine.

11 And now I am no more in the world, but these are in the world, and I come to thee. Holy Father, keep through thine own name those whom thou hast given me, that they may be one, as we *are*.

But everyone being a different or separate person, so are God and Jesus Christ and the Holy Ghost separate persons, but they all *agree in one* or the selfsame thing. In word and in deed *Jesus was trying to reveal and make personal to us the true nature of His Father, our Heavenly Father.*" [55]

End of Quotes by and about Joseph Smith

The following excerpts come from a talk given by Elder Jeffery R. Holland, a current member of the Quorum of the Twelve Apostles, in October of 2003 titled, "*The Grandeur of God*". These excerpts eloquently describe what I believe about God and His Son, Jesus Christ, and *in what sense they are one*. I hope you will invest the time to read it in its entirety so that you understand my perspective and where I'm coming from as I share what I believe about the nature of God. Here's the excerpts, and I quote:

"Of the many magnificent purposes served in the life and ministry of the Lord Jesus Christ, one great aspect of that mission often goes uncelebrated. His followers did not understand it fully at the time, and many in modern Christianity do not grasp it even now, but the Savior Himself spoke of it repeatedly and emphatically. It is *the grand truth that in all that Jesus came to say and do, including and especially in His atoning suffering and sacrifice, He was showing us who and what God our Eternal Father is like, how completely devoted He is to His children in every age and nation. In word and in deed Jesus was trying to reveal and make personal to us the true nature of His Father, our Father in Heaven.*

"He did this at least in part because then and now all of us need to know God more fully in order to love Him more deeply and obey Him more completely. As both the Old and New Testaments declare, "The first of all the commandments is ... thou shalt love the Lord thy God with all thy heart, and with all thy soul, and with all thy mind, and with all thy strength: this is the first [and great] commandment." [56]

Little wonder then that the Prophet Joseph Smith taught:

"It is the first principle of the gospel to know for a certainty the character of God. I want you all to know Him," he said, "and to be familiar with Him." [57] "We must have "a *correct* idea of his ... perfections, and attributes, and admiration for the excellency of [His] character." [58]

Elder Holland continues: "Thus, the first phrase we utter in the declaration of our faith is, "We believe in God, the Eternal Father." [59] So, emphatically, did Jesus. Even as He acknowledged His singular role in the divine plan, the Savior nevertheless insisted on this prayerful preamble:

"And this is life eternal, that they might know thee the only true God." [60]

"After generations of prophets had tried to teach the family of man the will and the way of the Father, usually with little success, God in His ultimate effort to have us know Him (Richard would criticize God for making it so difficult to do this, saying "Just show us you are real and we're good"), sent to earth His Only Begotten and Perfect Son, created in His very likeness and image, to live and serve among mortals in the everyday rigors of life (Richard is ignorant of the reasons God the Father does not simply show Himself, and so the barking out criticisms continue).

"To come to earth with such a responsibility, to stand in place of Elohim—speaking as He would speak, judging and serving, loving, and warning, forbearing and forgiving as He would do—this is a duty of such staggering proportions that you and I cannot comprehend such a thing. But in the loyalty and determination that would be characteristic of a divine child, Jesus could comprehend it and He did it. Then, when the praise and honor began to come, He humbly directed all adulation to the Father (Jesus did miracles to show the people He was God's Son, and he deflected the glory back to the Fathers').

"The Father doeth the works," he said in earnest. "The Son can do nothing of himself, but what he seeth the Father do: for what things soever [the Father] doeth, these also doeth the Son likewise." On another occasion He said: "I speak that which I have seen with my Father. ... I do nothing of myself; but, as my Father hath taught me. I came down from heaven, not to do mine own will, but the will of him that sent me." [61]

Elder Holland then bares his own witness of God, the Father saying:

"I make my own heartfelt declaration of God our Eternal Father this morning because some in the contemporary world suffer from a distressing misconception of Him. Among these there is a tendency to feel distant from the Father, even estranged from Him, if they believe in Him at all. And if they do believe, many moderns say they might feel comfortable in the arms of Jesus, but they are uneasy contemplating the stern encounter of God." [62] "Through a misreading (and surely, in some cases, a mistranslation) of the Bible, these see God the Father and Jesus Christ His Son as operating very differently, this in spite of the fact that in both the Old Testament and the New, the Son of God is one and the same, acting as He always does under the direction of the Father, who is Himself the same "yesterday, today, and forever." [63]

"In reflecting on these misconceptions, we realize that one of the remarkable contributions of the Book of Mormon is its seamless, perfectly consistent view of divinity throughout that majestic book. Here there is no Malachi-to-Matthew gap, no pause while we shift theological gears, no misreading the God who is urgently, lovingly, faithfully at work on every page of that record from its Old Testament beginning to its New Testament end. Yes, in an effort to give the world back its Bible with a correct view of Deity with it, what we have in the Book of Mormon is a uniform view of God in all His glory and goodness, all His richness and complexity—including and especially as again demonstrated through a personal appearance of His Only Begotten Son, Jesus Christ.

"How grateful we are for *all* the scriptures, especially the scriptures of the Restoration that teach us the majesty of each member of the Godhead. How we would thrill, for example, if all the world would receive and embrace the view of the Father so movingly described in the Pearl of Great Price:

Moses 7:29-33, 37

29 And Enoch said unto the Lord: How is it that thou canst weep, seeing thou art holy, and from all eternity to all eternity?

30 And were it possible that man could number the particles of the earth, yea, millions of earths like this, it would not be a beginning to the number of thy creations; and thy curtains are stretched out still; and yet thou art there, and thy bosom is there; and also thou art just; thou art merciful and kind forever;

31 And thou hast taken Zion to thine own bosom, from all thy creations, from all eternity to all eternity; and naught but peace, justice, and truth is the habitation of thy throne; and mercy shall go before thy face and have no end; how is it thou canst weep?

32 The Lord said unto Enoch: Behold these thy brethren; they are the workmanship of mine own hands, and I gave unto them their knowledge, in the day I created them; and in the Garden of Eden, gave I unto man his agency;

33 And unto thy brethren have I said, and also given commandment, that they should love one another, and that they should choose me, their Father; but behold, they are without affection, and they hate their own blood;

37 But behold, their sins shall be upon the heads of their fathers; Satan shall be their father, and misery shall be their doom; and the whole heavens shall weep over them, even all the workmanship of mine hands; wherefore should not the heavens weep, seeing these shall suffer?

"There, amid a grand vision of humankind which heaven opened to his view, Enoch, observing both the blessings and challenges of mortality, turns his gaze toward the Father and is stunned to see Him weeping. He says in wonder and amazement to this most powerful Being in the universe: "How is it that thou canst weep? Thou art just [and] merciful and kind forever; ... Peace ... is the habitation of thy throne; and ... Mercy ... shall go before thy face and have no end; how is it thou canst weep?"

"Looking out on the events of almost any day, God replies:

"Behold these thy brethren; they are the workmanship of mine own hands. ... I gave unto them [a] commandment, that they should love one another, and that they should choose me, their Father; but behold, they are without affection, and they hate their own blood. Wherefore should not the heavens weep, seeing these shall suffer?" [64]

"That single, riveting scene does more to teach the true nature of God than any theological treatise could ever convey. It also helps us understand much more emphatically that vivid moment in the Book of Mormon allegory of the olive tree, when after digging and dunging, watering, and weeding, trimming, pruning, transplanting, and grafting, the great Lord of the vineyard throws down his spade and his pruning shears and weeps, crying out to any who would listen, 'What could I have done more for my vineyard?'[65]

Elder Holland continues, "What an indelible image of God's engagement in our lives! What anguish in a parent when His children do not choose Him nor the gospel of God He sent! How easy to love someone who so singularly loves us!" [66]

"Of course, the centuries-long drift away from belief in such a perfect and caring Father hasn't been helped any by the man-made creeds of erring generations which describe God variously as unknowable, formless, passionless, elusive, ethereal, simultaneously everywhere and nowhere at all. Certainly, that does not describe the Being we behold through the eyes of these prophets. Nor does it match the living, breathing, embodied Jesus of Nazareth who was and is in "the brightness of his glory, and the express image of his [Father]." [67]

"In that sense, Jesus did not come to improve God's view of man nearly so much, as He came to improve man's view of God and to plead with them to love their Heavenly Father as He has always and will always love them. The plan of God, the power of God, the holiness of God, yes, even the anger and the judgment of God, they had occasion to understand. But the love of God, the profound depth of His devotion to His children, they still did not fully know—until Christ came.

"So, feeding the hungry, healing the sick, rebuking hypocrisy, pleading for faith—this was Christ showing us the way of the Father, He who is merciful and gracious, slow to anger, long-suffering and full of goodness." [68] In His life and especially in His death, Christ was declaring, "This is God's compassion I am showing you, as well as that of my own."

"In the perfect Son's manifestation of the perfect Father's care, in Their mutual suffering and shared sorrow for the sins and heartaches of the rest of us, we see ultimate meaning in the declaration:

"For God so loved the world, that he gave his only begotten Son, that whosoever believeth in him should not perish, but have everlasting life. For God sent not his Son into the world to condemn the world; but that the world through him might be saved." [69]

"I bear personal witness this day of a personal, Living God, who knows our names, hears, and answers prayers, and cherishes us eternally as children of His spirit. I testify that amidst the wondrously complex tasks inherent in the universe, He seeks our individual happiness and safety above all other godly concerns. We are created in His very image and likeness, [70] and Jesus of Nazareth, His Only Begotten Son in the flesh, came to earth as the perfect mortal manifestation of His grandeur.

"In addition to the witness of the ancients, we also have the modern miracle of Palmyra, the appearance of God the Father and His Beloved Son, the Savior of the world, to the boy prophet Joseph Smith. I testify of that appearance, and in the words of that prophet I, too, declare:

"Our Heavenly Father is more liberal in His views, and boundless in His mercies and blessings, than we are ready to believe or receive. God does not look on sin with [the least degree of] allowance, but the nearer we get to our Heavenly Father, the more we are disposed to look with compassion on perishing souls; we feel that we want to take them upon our shoulders and cast their sins behind our backs." [71]

"I bear witness of a God who has such shoulders. And in the spirit of the holy apostleship, I say as did one who held this office anciently: "Herein [then] is love, not that we loved God, but that he loved us, and sent his Son to be the propitiation for our sins. Beloved, if God so loved us, we ought also to love one another"—and to love Him forever, I pray. In the sacred name of Jesus Christ, amen." [72]

End of excerpts from Elder Holland's Talk

My understanding and belief system today, my belief in The Church of Jesus Christ of Latter-Day Saints as Gods' true Church and Kingdom on the earth today, directs me in how I live my life and the choices I make each-and-every day of my life. I too testify of the love God has for us, His children, as well as the love His Beloved Son, Jesus Christ, has for us. It is because of this love that He made the choice to come to earth to reveal our Father in heaven to us, that way we can exercise faith in Him. As I said, I want my readers to know what my belief system is as I begin to share my comments and personal perspective on Richard Dawkins' book *The God Delusion*. Religious study alone is *not* the only type of knowledge I have sought, for I love both the scientific and spiritual knowledge that God has made available to anyone who desires to know Him. This knowledge is revealed line upon line, and precept by precept, here a little, and there a little by the Holy Ghost who reveals all knowledge to us.

All the learning I've acquired over the many years of my life, has enhanced my love for the gospel of Jesus Christ. I love studying it more than any other subject. In addition to my religious study and the little scientific study I've done here and there, I'm continually adding new knowledge that expands my epistemological philosophy which defines my worldview. This worldview's foundation is the word of God. It is not the word of man. As I have new and unexpected experiences throughout my daily life, I continue to take notes on them as well as notes on other individuals' life experiences. These experiences reveal new and informative life lessons for my list of personal experiential knowledge, each one helping me to become more enlightened. They also become new 'reference leg evidence' for my circular support stand that faithfully supports my 'Table of Belief' with absolute integrity and stability today.

Through this process I've experienced the pain of watching several people join the Church of Jesus Christ of Latter-Day Saints, only to lose their testimonies and request that their membership in God's kingdom here on earth be removed. I have seen happy couples become sad and disconnected couples, due to what they chose to make their life experiences mean to them. These life experiences and the choices these couples made as they tried to negotiate through their difficult circumstances, often resulted in them changing their entire worldview, and that change in their belief system led some of them to leave the Church and reject the faith of their youth. Such is the fruit of moral agency. I could have taken this same path many times myself, due to the hardships I've experienced during my 48 years of adult life, but I didn't, and that choice to stay on the covenant path, I believe, was due to the depth of my relationship I have with God and His Son, Jesus Christ, my Savior and Redeemer, even my Friend.

Here are just two examples of the many experiences I could share with you, where it would have been so easy to go down the same path these folks chose to take while in their time of crisis. I chose to stay on the covenant path, and I was blessed because of that choice. I believe these experiences were for a wise and glorious purpose for my life, and for my learning and experience. They truly have increased my faith in the God I love with all my heart, might, mind, and strength. That said, I also believe that many of these individuals I have known, who decided to step away from the covenant path, will have experiences that will ultimately bring them back to the covenant path.

(1ˢᵗ) As a young father of two little girls, my wife was pregnant with what we would later learn was our first son. But at the time of this experience, we didn't know our baby's sex. I think I was 26 at the time. It was about four or five days before my wife's next check-up to hear the baby's heartbeat with the sonogram and learn how the baby was doing. It was getting really close to my wife's delivery date, so we were excited. A couple of days before the appointment my wife stopped feeling the baby kick. That really scared us, and so we called and told the doctor about it, and Dr. Hulme told us to come to his office immediately so he could do a sonogram where he would move the device over Kathleen's tummy to try and find our baby's heartbeat.

After 30-minutes or more of trying to find the baby's heartbeat, Dr. Hulme could never find one. The doctor then said, "Sometimes we can't find a heartbeat, but I'm sure things are okay. Let's give it a little more time and have you come back in another week, and let's see if we can find it then, okay?" You need to remember this was more than 40 years ago when we didn't have the kind of technology we have today, such as an ultrasound etc. Anyway, you can imagine how Kathleen and I felt. What could we do? How were we to respond to such news? Just imagine what that ride back home in our little Datsun B210 two-door hatchback was like. My wife was only 22 years old, and a mother of two girls at the time. Kathleen just stared forward aimlessly, trying to hold on to hope. We both just looked out through the front windshield without looking at or speaking to each other. We just wept quietly, letting our tears stream down our cheeks all the way home.

The day before we were to return to the doctor's office with the hope that the heartbeat could be found, Kathleen said she wanted me to give her a priesthood blessing, a comfort blessing (I was an Elder in the Church of Jesus Christ of Latter-Day Saints at the time), and so I did. As a very young father, to be asked to give a priesthood blessing to my wife who had come from her doctors' appointment a week earlier where the doctor said he couldn't find her baby's heartbeat, and for over a week she still hadn't been able to feel her baby move in her womb, I'm sure you can imagine how I was feeling at that moment when I stepped up to lay my hands on my young wife's head.

I was speechless and absolutely terrified. Yet, like many times before when called upon to give blessings, I put my faith and trust (which I had developed over 18 years since my baptism and becoming a member of the Church of Jesus Christ of Latter-Day Saints) in the Lord and prayed that His spirit would guide my words. As I laid my hands on my wife's head and started to pronounce the blessing upon her, and upon our baby in her womb, it felt as though someone had suddenly stepped up next to me from behind and was steadying me because I was a bit unsteady due to the fear of not knowing what I was going to say. I almost wanted to open my eyes and turn around to see who it was, but I didn't. I just continued pronouncing the blessing. Within just a moment I found myself vocalizing the words, "Your little 'boy' has gone home to His heavenly Father."

How did I know that? I didn't. Why did I say that? It's just what came out of my mouth. I wanted to say something else. Anything else but, "Your baby is dead". Up to that moment I didn't even know that our baby was a boy, but I certainly knew it now. That is what came into my mind and out of my mouth at that very moment, and I was overcome with emotion. Right then, I felt an incredible feeling of love wash over me, and a spirit of peace and calm settled upon my heart; a kind of peace like I'd never felt before in my entire life. I since learned that it is that peace that surpasses all understanding.

There was no question in my mind after giving Kathleen that blessing, that our baby was a boy, and I knew that our baby was no longer alive in my wife's womb. His spirit had gone home to that God who had given him his heartbeat and life, as he certainly had been alive in my wife's womb. Kathleen had felt him kicking within her for more than four months, and then, out of the blue, his kicking suddenly stopped. It was now more than an eight-month pregnancy. When we went back to see Dr. Hulme the next day, Kathleen had been carrying her dead baby in her womb for more than two weeks. We didn't need to wait for its delivery to know what the sex of our baby was. We knew our son had come to get his body and had gone ahead into eternity. Yet, as I said, my heart wanted my words to give my sweetheart hope, even if it was just a little hope that would get us to the next day when we would visit the doctor, so he could say that things were going to be okay. But that was not to be. I continued the blessing, telling Kathleen that she would have many more children and that she would have the opportunity to raise this little boy during the millennium after all of us were resurrected.

After having two daughters before this still-born pregnancy, and now, after Marty Juniors' still-birth (that's what we named him), we had five more children, for a total of eight children. After going to the doctor's, Dr. Hulme confirmed our baby was dead. Upon arriving home and on through that fateful day, I felt impressed to write a song. So, later that night, in just fifteen minutes time, I wrote down the lyrics to a song, which I titled, "My Angel Child" (See the lyrics of the next page).

I then worked well into the night trying to put the appropriate music to those simple lyrics. As I was trying to write down the lyrics that I felt best expressed what I was feeling, a flow of the most incredible words came into my young mind. It was like I was reading them from off some heavenly piece of sheet music, and soon the phrase, *"You were crowned without the conflict, and became my angel child"* came into my mind. As I wrote down those words onto my paper, I just wept. What average 26-year-old young man has such beautiful words come into their mind? Certainly not me, at least not before that very moment. I then finished putting simple, but beautiful guitar chords to those lyrics. It was as though someone or something was placing all of this into my head. I now know that I was just following what the spirit of God was telling me to write. When I was done, I finally went to bed and fell asleep instantly. The next morning, when Kathleen woke up, I played the guitar as I sang the words to this song to her, and when she heard me sing the words *"You were crowned without the conflict, and became my angel child"*, she wept just like I had done. Here are the lyrics to this song that I wrote some forty plus years ago:

1st Verse

Oh, how lovely is the day, when mother and child reunite.
That day, it seems so distant, resurrections' morning bright.
I will wait my whole lifetime, and keep myself undefiled,
So, I can be found worthy, to raise you, my angel child.

(Chorus)

Angel child, my angel child, I long to be with you,
To hold you in my arms and be a mother to you.

2nd Verse

All the years they go so slowly, many times I feel like giving in,
But to lose you to someone more worthy, oh the thought stirs the will to win.
I pray each and every night, "Dear Lord help me do what is right,
So, when my life's journey ends, I'll be with you, my angel child".

(Chorus)

3rd Verse

On the day you went away, I did not re-a-lize,
What a blessing I had been given, ... Our Father in Heaven is wise.
He gave me a chance to grow, to prove my faith undefiled,
You were crowned without the conflict, ... and became my angel child.

For Kathleen and me, this song became a love letter of comfort from our Heavenly Father. In this experience, I found a peaceful sense of certainty about our baby boy and what happened to him some forty plus years ago. God's love and peace comforted both of us at this time of sadness and despair.

(2nd) A second example of the spiritual method of observing God's hand in our lives and in the lives of others, was an experience much like our Marty Jr.'s still-birth. I'm speaking of the pre-mature death of our oldest son Garrett (At 25) due to a car accident while he was parked on the side of the freeway. Candice, his bride of just seven weeks, got a migraine headache while driving to a class with our son Garrett, and said she needed to pull over and have Garrett take over driving to their class. Candice pulled over to a safe lane and right as Garrett was sitting back down into the front driver's seat, a 19-year-old young man, driving a small pickup truck at 85 to 90 miles an hour, crashed into the back left-rear of their small, parked car, killing Garrett instantly, and Candice, his young bride, was taken to the hospital to be checked and cared for (We later had to tell her that her husband was killed).

Just a few days before Garrett's car accident, he was at our home visiting us. Garrett was just 25 years old at the time and had only been married seven weeks as I said. Just before leaving, he walked into our bedroom and told both of us that he loved us, and then, mentioning his patriarchal blessing, he specifically asked if we thought his blessing might be saying that he was going to die prematurely. Of course, we said we didn't think so and reminded him that patriarchal blessings also included eternal blessings and didn't just relate to our mortal probation. That seemed to pacify him, and he hugged us and told us that he loved us, and off he went out the door. That was the last time we saw Garrett alive (Check my Church website for 'Patriarchal Blessing' to learn what they are and why they are given). Just a few days later, in the evening around 7:30 p.m., on February 23rd, 2007, I answered a phone call from a State Trooper telling us he wanted to come to our apartment, saying there was an accident.

When the officers arrived, they told us that our son Garrett had been killed in a car accident at the portion of the I-15 Freeway known as the "Spaghetti Bowl", which runs along the west side of Salt Lake City. I won't go on and on about the many *"tender mercies"* that we experienced during this difficult time, but suffice it to say, there were many. I do, however, want to mention one specific *tender mercy* that took place during the ten days of preparation and arranging for Garrett's funeral. This was a stressful time as you can imagine, where I had to spend ten days handling all the funeral arrangements so that before my head even hit the pillow each night, I fell fast asleep. But, about three days into the ten days, I had a dream come to me *three nights in a row*. It was the exact same dream night after night with no variation. It's a very sacred experience which I have held close to my heart ever since that fateful night, and so I've never shared it publicly, but for reasons unknown to me, I have felt a strong impression that I'm supposed to share it with you, my readers, and so, here goes.

All three dreams began with me sitting quietly in the Celestial Room of the Salt Lake Temple (You can search www.churchofjesuschrist.org for 'Salt Lake Temple Celestial Room' to see a picture of it. It is spectacular), where I was reflecting on our son's death, and suddenly Garrett, dressed in his temple whites, stepped through one of the doorways into the Celestial room where I was sitting. He beaconed me to come to him. He didn't say anything. I just knew it. Once he caught my eye, Garret told me in my mind to get up and follow him, and he turned to go back into the hallway. I left the Celestial Room and followed him down the hallway a little ways, into one of the sealing rooms along that hallway.

As I entered the room, I saw a figure in the room who was dressed in gloriously white robes and a sash. He had his back to me. As I said, His robes were brilliantly white, and He had shoulder-length hair that was also brilliantly white and wavy. As he turned to face me, I immediately recognized him as the Savior, Jesus Christ. He called me by my first name, saying, once again in my mind only, "Martin", as He stretched out his arms for me to come to Him. I walked into His arms, and He wrapped them around me like a warm comforter. He gave me the biggest hug while saying in my ear, "I love you, Martin." I almost collapsed to the floor.

Garret was standing just a few feet away, letting me have a private moment in the Savior's arms, and then one of Jesus's arms let go of me and He opened up our hug to allow Garrett to join us. It was the most amazing experience! I could have stayed in His arms forever, but then the dream faded, and I found myself awake in my bed, feeling a bit startled because I realized that it was just a dream. Yet, it felt so real; a real physical experience. Though a dream, it made an incredible impression on me.

This exact same dream, without any variance, came to me again the very next night, and as I said, it came to me a third time, for a total of three nights in a row. It was so incredibly glorious. I'll never forget the feeling of the Savior's divine love that He expressed for me as He took me in His arms and embraced me so lovingly. It was such an overwhelming, palpable experience. Now I'm not oblivious to the fact that most people would scoff at such a dream and my feeling that it was something more than just my brain firing off to construct spiritual comfort food for an aching heart because I had just lost my son to a fatal car accident, and that's okay for them to think that way. But, for me, I will never forget how I felt and how the Savior's eternal loving hug replaced the pain and sorrow I had been suffering with for days. It was an answer to my heartfelt prayer for comfort and assurance.

Skeptics yap and bark, "These experiences, as you've described them Marty, certainly are not proof that there's a God. It's no different than someone saying 'I dreamed a spaceship came and took me away for seven days, did tests on me, and then brought me back after erasing my memory. It felt so real'. These folks' experiences haven't provided any proof that there are real green aliens either, any more than your dream is proof of God's existence. So, don't expect us to believe your story and not theirs! Okay?" Of course, I won't. It is their personal experience, just as mine is my personal experience.

Skeptics, I've come to learn, can easily excuse away 17 million peoples' testimonies, each having the same experience of receiving a witness in their hearts and minds that the Church of Jesus Christ of Latter-Day Saints, and the Restored Gospel it proclaims, including Joseph Smiths' testimony of his First Vision of the Father and the Son appearing to Him in a grove of trees, actually happened and that all of it is true. Skeptics believe that all of us Latter-Day Saints are simply delusional and experiencing a 'group hallucination' of some kind. A hallucination that apparently has spanned over 192 years so far and continues even today. That's quite a 'red pill' if it can produce an experience that can last that long, and for that many people from all walks and backgrounds, and I'm okay with them saying that. However, saying I'm delusional doesn't change the fact of what I experienced those three nights. Anyway, from that moment on, after those three nights of dreaming the same dream, any unsettling feeling that I had about Garrett's death left me completely, and I was left feeling total and complete peace. I know even more fervently that my son lives on and that he did not simply fade into dust only to become a dirt pile.

Others can say, "You can't possibly know that it's true and that you're just believing what you want to believe", and I'm okay with folks saying that too. As I said, it doesn't change my experience one iota. With this experience, any limited knowledge that God was a real, tangible, loving being, went to a new level of certainty for me, and the peace and comfort I had been praying for throughout the experience of Garrett's death, had fully and completely enveloped me and left me with the assurance that Garrett was fine and that Jesus Christ, the Savior of the world, is as real and tangible as you and I are, and because of this *experiential knowledge*, I, of a surety, know that I too will live on after I die, just as my son has continued to live on after his car accident which took his mortal life some fifteen years ago.

These two experiences are certainly not the only reasons and evidence of why I say that "I know and believe in God's existence and that He lives", but they're two of the more tender and vivid reference legs that are at the very core and center of my 'Circular Reference Legs Stand' that continues to support my 'Table of Belief'. They're so personal and sacred and have continued to reside in my heart all these many years later. Skeptics, like Richard, would say that not one of those hundreds of reference legs are observable, tangible, testable proofs, nor do they provide factual data to support or endorse the belief that God exists. But I disagree. I believe there's a God who exists in the sidereal heavens and that His Son, Jesus Christ, is His Only Begotten Son, in the flesh, who is our Savior and Redeemer, because all of these experiential evidence, and other well endorsed evidence, tells me this is so. But the capstone evidence to my belief is the fact that all of these have been affirmed to my spirit by the spirit and power of the Holy Ghost, even the third member of the Godhead whose role is to be the Testator of all truth.

I now know that Jesus is glorious beyond all description. The love I felt while in his embrace, was and is unforgettably transformational. It was overwhelming and it made me weep because of the joy I felt while in His arms, and it helped me know that my son Garrett was okay and that he, as well as myself, are accepted by God. There's no feeling more powerful and life changing than that feeling of love, assurance, and total acceptance that the Savior expressed to me and to my son, as He called each of us by name, and held us both in the arms of His love. I pray that everyone will experience this someday. Seeing my son Garrett having a relationship with Jesus after his death, brought me to the incredible assurance that death is just a doorway to a new stage of our eternal existence. All of us will experience this doorway into eternity, where we'll continue our life as immortals. When we die, we'll await our resurrection until we receive our immortal body, which body will never be separated from our spirit personage ever again. Until the millennium, when the resurrection takes place, we'll continue to reside in the spirit world, learning more about God and His Plan of Happiness, and many of us will have the privilege of teaching His gospel to all those spirits who died without knowing anything about Jesus and His gospel, while they're in what's called 'spirit prison', while they await their resurrection.

Yes, all these examples and experiences can be tagged and rejected as just thoughts from a frenzied, unguided mind that was confronted with trauma and agonizing pain from the loss of a child, or as some other emotionally charged delusion. Yet my experience tells me otherwise. There are literally hundreds, if not thousands of experiences that I have had over my 68 years of life here on earth, as well as the numberless experiences that other people have had as I've associated with them. I continue to bind all of these experiences together, each expanding my 'Circular Stand of Reference Legs'; each of which supports my 'Table of Belief' – the belief in the reality of the Lord Jesus Christ, and of God, our Heavenly Father. Simply put, I know that my Redeemer lives and that "God, our Heavenly Father exists too".

As I said, there are many, many reference legs that have formed a solid, immovable 'circle of support'; a sturdy evidence-based stand of faith that now supports my personal 'Table of Belief'. This circular stand of reference legs evidence is made up of hundreds, maybe even thousands of reference legs as I said, that have helped remove any wobbly movement or instability that may have existed in my early years. My *table of belief* now sits atop this unshakable 'circle of support', thus allowing me to sit at it and feast upon all the delicious fruit that comes from faith and belief in the True and Living God – those fruits being happiness, joy, and peace.

Included in this stand of reference legs, are the many hundreds of YouTube videos I've watched, each of which have allowed me to discover new evidence supporting the existence of God. Besides these YouTube videos, I've read multiple new books that have confirmed for me, the same conclusion – God exists! These experiences, and so many more, have added to the development of my epistemic philosophy on God, religion, science, and all that God has said in His revelations to His living prophets, regarding the creation, life, and the spiritual journey each of us are on while living here on earth. I think it was author John Bunyan who called our lives a 'pilgrims' progress'. The books of revelation that I referred to earlier, of course, are the holy scriptures, as well as the modern-day words offered up by living prophets and apostles who serve the members of the Church of Jesus Christ of Latter-Day Saints today, as well as the entire world's population, if they're willing to come and listen to a prophet's voice.

I know that the skeptics like Richard, say that the scriptures, like the Bible for example, "are not systematically evil but just plain weird, as you would expect of a chaotically cobbled-together anthology of disjointed documents, composed, revised, translated, distorted, and 'improved' by hundreds of anonymous authors, editors, and copyists, unknown to us and mostly unknown to each other, spanning nine centuries." [73] Yet, don't scientists use extremely old, historically improved upon accounts of scientific data in an effort to try and support their theorems? We'll cover this point more thoroughly in future chapters. Most of the videos and books I'll reference throughout my book, besides the scriptures, were produced and written by scientists and philosophers who are far more intelligent than I. Some of these authors are even atheist scientists, and a few of them are theist scientists. Some of these academics are Christians, and some of them are of other faiths, with a smattering being Agnostics. I've also read several books written by members of The Church of Jesus Christ of Latter-Day Saints, with some of them being recognized scientists and scholars in their own right.

This list is not an exhaustive list of the many men and women of intelligence that I could have listed, but it is sufficient to build a case for the belief that God exists. And so, with this Introduction, I've hopefully laid the foundation upon which my perspective regarding Richard's book *The God Delusion*, an anti-Theist/anti-Christ book, rests. With all these thoughts bouncing around in my mind for many years, I thought they would make for a good Introduction to my book and what's behind my perspective on God. With that said, let's go ahead now and take on the arguments made by Richard Dawkins in his book *The God Delusion*, and show that it is he, and not I, that is suffering from an atheist's delusion.

The truth is, either I am delusional, or Richard is delusional. There is no in-between position in this debate between Richard and me. Therefore, I will list each of Richard's arguments in summary form, under each chapter's title and subtitles, referring to a few of Richard's key points he gives in each of the subtitles' topics, and then I will give my perspective on each of them, in the hope of presenting to you, my readers, the evidence as to why I honestly believe Richard is the one suffering from an atheist's delusion. Let's begin with Richards' Preface. Here's what he said:

"There are lots of people out there who have been brought up in some religion or other, that are unhappy in it, or don't believe in it anymore, or are worried about the evils that are done in the name of religion. People who feel vague yearnings to leave their parents' religion and wish they could, but just don't realize that the act of 'leaving' is an option they have … They say, 'I didn't know I could'." [74]

Richard says he wrote this book "to raise consciousness to the fact that you can be an atheist and be moral and happy, even if you leave your traditional faith. It's okay." [75]

Richard goes on to talk about the idea that says, "Imagine the world without religion. Imagine no suicide bombers; no 9/11, no 7/7, no Crusades; no witch-hunts; no Gunpowder Plot; no Indian partition; no Israeli/Palestinian wars; no Serb/Croat/Muslim massacres; no persecution of Jews as 'Christ-Killers'; no Northern Ireland 'troubles'; no honor-killings; no shiny-suited bouffant-haired televangelists fleecing gullible people of their money; no Taliban to blow up ancient statues. Imagine no public beheadings of blasphemers; no floggings of females for the crime of showing an inch of their skin; etc., etc." [76]

Richard continues his Preface by introducing the four consciousness-raisers that he feels debunks even agnosticism as a viable stance, and then declares that his later chapters will *"knock out 'Intelligent Design' and the 'God Hypothesis'*, … a pernicious delusion." [77] After reading Richard's book, his goal of disproving each of these arguments, in my opinion, fell ridiculously short. By the time you, my readers, are done reading my book and understand my perspective on Richard's claims, you will hopefully realize that there are sound, believable, alternate answers to each of the following questions Richard raises.

Here are the four consciousness-raiser statement/questions that Richard asks his readers to answer for themselves [78]:

- Why belief is so ubiquitous, but not because God exists.
- Why religion isn't needed to have objective morals.
- Why religion comes from childhood indoctrination and not God.
- Why atheism is something to be proud of and not to be embarrassed about.

In his Preface, Dawkins includes a definition of the term 'delusion' since it's a particularly descriptive word in the title of his book *The God Delusion*, as well as in my book's title, "An Atheist's Delusion". Here's the definition he gives for the word delusion:

"A delusion is a persistent, false belief, held in the face of strong contradictory evidence, especially as a symptom of psychiatric disorder." [79]

Richard then quotes Robert M. Pirsig, author of "Zen and the Art of Motorcycle Maintenance", wherein Mr. Pirsig wrote: "When one person suffers a delusion, it is called 'insanity'. When many people suffer from a delusion it's called 'Religion'." [80]

Ha-ha-ha. I thought that Mr. Pirsig's comment was quite clever and a bit comical, as it made me chuckle. According to Richard, "Any argument or explanation that believers give to the contrary of what *he* believes and writes in *his* book, are coming from a dyed-in-the-wool, faith-head position, and are delusional". [81] So, I guess by Richard's definition, I'm *a faith-head delusional*. Good honk in the morning Richard. That cracks me up! C'mon man. Richard also says, "If this book works as I intend, religious readers who open it *will be atheists when they put it down,* but if believers end up staying believers, it's because *they've been made immune to the truth of my arguments,* due to the resistance that has built up in their minds from many years of childhood indoctrination and mental and emotional child-abuse, and, from methods that took centuries to mature." [82] Again, in short, I'm a delusional 'Faith-head' who has been brainwashed as a child and hoodwinked by methods that came about throughout the entirety of my life. To this I simply say, "That, my friend, is coming from a man who believes he came from ancestral amoeba's."

Richard says, "These methods took centuries to mature *by evolution* (Did you catch that, "by evolution"?) or possibly by religious design" [83]. It is my opinion that there is a third option – God exists, and that Richard doesn't know or understand how faith is a gift from God, nor does he understand how it is developed through exercising it by doing *'experiments'* on the word of God. He is simply guessing or positing his own angst and definition of faith here, which Richard believes is simply 'blind faith'. As a member of the Church of Jesus Christ of Latter-Day Saints, which is more commonly known by its nickname 'the Mormons', although a more accurate name and fact to which I prefer to be designated, is "I'm a disciple of Jesus Christ, my Lord and King, and I love Him as my Savior". I'm an active member of His Church and Kingdom here on earth, it being the Church of Jesus Christ of Latter-Day Saints, and as such, I unequivocally believe in God's existence. Like Mr. Dawkins, I have my own opinions about many of the earth's religions, including the Catholic Church which Richard derides by blasting their doctrine of the Trinity, as well as its belief in multiple Saints, Transubstantiation, Infant Baptism, etc. [84]

I choose to fight criticism with curiosity and compassion, unlike Richard who chooses to criticize all religions. I believe that the various polytheistic and monotheistic views of God that other theists have come to believe in, are a result of what's called 'Apostasy' [85], it being the resulting state once the death of all God's living oracles take place, so that there are no longer any of His prophets, seers, and revelators who hold the keys of authority living amongst us and receiving revelation and guidance from god Himself, which His prophets can then dispense to His children. The earth's history consists of a multiplicity of dispensations that were ultimately plagued by apostasy, including the dispensation in which we're now living, the last dispensation which is called 'The Dispensation of the Fulness of Times'. Examples of apostasy are referenced in New Testament scriptures where they use the imagery of apostasy, such as a plant taking root among the rocks, but then 'withering under the hot sun of testing', etc. Here are just a few of these scriptural examples:

Mark 4:5–6, 17

5 And some fell on stony ground, where it had not much earth; and immediately it sprang up because it had no depth of earth:

6 But when the sun was up, it was scorched; and because it had no root, it withered away.

17 And have no root in themselves, and so endure but for a time: afterward, when afflictions, or persecution ariseth for the word's sake, immediately they are offended.

Or those who fall prey to the wiles of false teachers:

Matthew 24:11

11 And many false prophets shall rise and shall deceive many.

And heretical beliefs and worldliness:

1 Timothy 4:1

1 Now the Spirit speaketh expressly, that in the latter times some shall depart from the faith, giving heed to seducing spirits, and doctrines of devils;

2 Timothy 4:3–4

3 For the time will come when they will not endure sound doctrine; but after their own lusts shall they heap to themselves teachers, having itching ears;

4 And they shall turn away *their* ears from the truth, and shall be turned unto fables.

There are many more that I could give, but I will share just one more. Some of the more prominent New Testament verses describing this 'falling away' imagery, or apostasy from God's truth, are those describing the *apostasy to come*. They're found in 2 Thessalonians 2:3, wherein the apostle Paul wrote to the Thessalonians in his Day, counseling them to:

2 Thessalonians 2:3

3 Let no man deceive you by any means: for *that day shall not come (Christ's 2ⁿᵈ Coming), except there 'come' a 'falling away' first*, and that man of sin be revealed, the son of perdition;

Richard says all these faiths have "immerged over the millenniums (whether by evolution or design)." [86] I say they have all immerged out of a state of apostasy and are therefore apostate religions. The Church of Jesus Christ of Latter-Day Saints claims that the gospel of Jesus Christ was restored through the instrumentality of a chosen boy prophet whose name was Joseph Smith Jr., whom God raised up in the early 19th century after nearly two millennia of apostasy. Many events had to take place before the restoration could happen, including America being established as well as the pinnacle being both the Father and the Son appearing to the boy prophet Joseph Smith in order to restore the pure gospel, starting with the knowledge of the true nature of the Godhead. Why did God raise up another prophet like unto Moses? The answer to this question is found in Amos 3:7. The prophet Amos, from the Old Testament, confirms that God always speaks through His prophets, especially at the beginning of a new dispensation or dispensing of truth because apostasy had taken root in the minds of man such that they distorted God's pure gospel. Here's what Amos declared:

Amos 3:7

7 Surely the Lord God will do nothing except he '*revealeth*' his secret(s) (The mysteries of Godliness) to his servants the prophets.

This is exactly what God did when He opened up this, the last dispensation or dispensing of His Plan of Happiness and Redemption, even the final time before His Son, Jesus Christ's 2ⁿᵈ coming. This restoration of pure truth began in a grove of trees near Joseph Smith's home. When the Father and His Son Jesus Christ appeared to Joseph, the Father introduced Jesus, His Son, by saying, "This is my beloved Son, hear Him". On that early spring morning in 1820, Joseph said Jesus answered his question of 'which of all the churches he should join', by saying:

Joseph Smith—History 1:19

19 I was answered that I must join none of them, for they were all wrong; and the Personage who addressed me said that all their creeds were an abomination in his sight; that those professors were all corrupt; that: "they draw near to me with their lips, but their hearts are far from me; *they teach for doctrines the commandments of men (mingled with scripture)*, having a form of godliness, but they deny the power thereof."

This almost sounds like Richard said this, almost. This *restoration of all things* that closed off the two millennia of apostasy, required that the true nature of God the Father and His Son, be '*restored*' to the world. Thus, both '*The Father and The Son*' appeared to Joseph Smith, the boy prophet. "This restoration of pure truth by God Himself, and His Son Jesus Christ, established once again the *only true and living Church of God on the face of the earth today*." [87] ... 'The Church of Jesus Christ of Latter-Day Saints' is Jesus' Church, even His earthly kingdom that is now established here on earth once again. Jesus Christ is the Head of His Church and kingdom, both on earth and in heaven, and not by any man.

I want to make it clear that I do not mean to be harsh or self-righteous in any way when I say these things so candidly. I believe that most people who believe in 'their God', love their God and what they believe 'Him' to be. I do not think they are delusional for believing in the existence of their God, and not in the God of the Restoration as He's described by Joseph Smith. Of course, Richard believes any-and-all believers in God, no matter their God, are all delusional, because, for Richard, there is no such thing as "God".

I do believe that all these 'differences in beliefs' (in particular, what the true nature of God is) are born out of apostasy for the most part, as I've said, and the objects of faith in these different religions, be they Polytheistic gods or Monotheistic gods, are therefore not the True and Living God, and are not the God that the ancient patriarchs Abraham, Isaac, and Jacob knew and worshipped.

These differing beliefs are the outgrowth of apostasy, which always leads fallen men and women to fashion their own gods from the imaginations of their hearts, minds, and desires. Here are a few words of the prophet Moses, as He shares what Jehovah said to him regarding man-made gods:

Exodus 20:1-5

1 And God spake all these words, saying,

2 I *am* the Lord thy God, which have brought thee out of the land of Egypt, out of the house of bondage.

3 Thou shalt have no other gods before me.

4 Thou shalt not make unto thee any graven image, or any likeness *of anything* that *is* in heaven above, or that *is* in the earth beneath, or that *is* in the water under the earth.

The scriptures teach there is but one God, and that one God is 'God the Father':

Ephesians 4:5-6

5 One Lord, one faith, one baptism,

6 *One God and Father of all*, who *is* above all, and through all, and in you all.

All the many apostate theistic views existing out in the world have immerged out of the 'falling away' from the pure gospel that Jesus Himself taught the people in the meridian of time, and more particularly the gospel He taught to His fellow Jews during His three-year ministry, and so these modern apostate teachings beg scrutiny by any honest and sincere truth seeker.

The apostate views that have emerged from this state of apostacy have had two millennia of confusion and conflict to create the *stumbling block* that all sincere truth seekers face today. It has made it extremely difficult to know where to look for the pure gospel that Jesus taught in its fulness. Like Richard says, "all religions today, have an unshakable faith that one's religion is the only true one", [88] and that all mankind should be worshiping "their" God and worshiping Him in the way "they" worship Him, and that "their" way is the "only" true way to come unto God and live with Him forever.

The scriptures say that this is the way and nature of apostasy which takes root in the minds of both men and women who no longer enjoy the power and spirit of revelation themselves, nor do they enjoy the blessing of God giving His living servants, the prophets, revelation. It is from these prophets who God Himself reveals His secrets, that pure religion comes to the world. It is through the Gift of the Holy Ghost, even the Spirit of prophecy. It's often called the "Testimony of Jesus", which revelation He delivers to the hearts of His servants. God reveals His truth to His living prophets; even the pure gospel He wants His children to live by. He taught it to the prophet Moses, which included giving the Israelites the Ten commandments as a help to prepare them so they could live the higher law that was to come, which Law they weren't ready to live when Moses first gave it. The gospel Moses taught the Israelites placed them on the covenant path back to their Heavenly Father's presence. The bottom line with revelation is coined in this simple concept: "*God's prophets are allowed to see around the corner*".

Amos 3:7

7 Surely the Lord God will do nothing, but he revealeth his secret(s) unto his servants the prophets.

One must keep in mind that "God requires that we at least desire to believe." [89] It is this 'desire to seek out God' that helps us come to know Him. It strives in nearly all of God's children, except when it has been driven out of one's heart due to repeated sin, and or by wicked spiritual leaders. This divine gift, this spark and desire to know God, strives in all of us even before we are born into this world. God placed it in our hearts, like spiritual DNA, so that we'd seek and feel after Him, and ultimately come to know that He exists, and that He is our Father in heaven, and that He loves us divinely. He wants us to accept His *gospel invitation* when it's presented to us, because He will not force us to accept it. The power behind His *gospel invitation* to 'come unto Christ', is manifested to us by The Light of Christ. [90]

A spark of God's divinity, His light, this desire to believe, ... is in all men and women in varying degrees. This divinity in us is the desire to seek God and find out if He exists. So, I'm happy when anyone's stirred in this way and follows these promptings, that spark, that light and desire to believe, and the power one feels as this Light of Christ prompts them so that they come unto His Only Begotten Son in the flesh, the Savior of the world, who's role is to manifest the Father unto each of us, by performing the Atonement which gives each of us the opportunity to be saved *from* our sins and not saved *in* our sins. There's a big difference between these two ideas – being saved *from* our sins versus being saved *in* our sins.

The Spirit of God can and will manifest the Father to anyone who desires to know Him, by way of His Son, Jesus Christ, and His gospel. I must say that a belief in an apostate version of the True and Living God, and His pure gospel, does in fact limit a person from enjoying the *fulness of blessings* and *the deeper understanding of what Godliness and salvation really are*, and *how* they can be ours if we would only believe in the True and Living God, and in His Only Begotten Son, Jesus Christ. When we do, we're better equipped (but *not* better than others) to follow Christs' revealed truths that His Father asked Him to reveal to His living prophets, which revealed gospel they're required to share with all of us, God's children, and hopefully each of us will choose to come and listen to these prophets' voices.

But again, I'm reminded that what I just said is exactly the criticism Richard has with any religionists or religion that preaches the message of *"Here's the Truth and the only true way"*, especially a restored gospel like the restored gospel the prophet Joseph Smith taught, which is the gospel I believe in with all my heart, might, and soul. Richard has angst towards anyone who believes in any 'sky-god'. Period! [91]

Before going any further with my perspective, I also want to take a moment to address Richard's quasi-religion and what I believe is at its core. Even though Richard doesn't call it his religion, that's what it is. The religion of Atheism, which includes Humanism and Secularism, whatever you want to call it. Richards' atheist belief system is rooted in the quasi-prophet Charles Darwin's quasi-gospel of "Evolution", along with its chief tenant "Natural Selection"—the so-called 'ultimate scientific consciousness raiser'. This is a religion where god's word is rejected and is replaced by man's word.

Richard adheres to this theory of Evolution religiously. I call it a quasi-religion because it resembles a religion, but it has the spirit of anti-Christ. One definition of religion is "a particular system of faith and worship", but a second definition says "*a pursuit or interest to which someone ascribes supreme importance*" [92]. I certainly think this describes Richard's belief in atheism, don't you? Let me quote Joseph Fielding Smith, the 10th President and prophet of the Church of Jesus Christ of Latter-Day Saints who served as president of the Church from 1970 to 1972. He wrote a book titled, "Man, His Origin and Destiny", wherein he wrote the following excerpts about the anti-Christ dogma of Evolution, quote:

"Organic Evolution teaches that in some unknown way, and at some unknown time, *life* commenced in some spontaneous way within a speck of protoplasm. This postulated theory cannot explain how this speck of protoplasm, or cell, happened to be. It is merely a postulate, a guess that such a thing really happened." [93] "With this guess, mankind is beholden to no one for their existence. He is not, according to this theory, the offspring of God, for there is no God. We have no divine origin, no spirit person in our bodies that is eternal.

"Therefore, when we die, we return to the dust of this earth and our death is the end of us all. No doctrine born of this godless, anti-Christ belief, could be more destructive to one's hope than the total extinction of each of us as individuals ... at our death. '*Such a doctrine makes atheists of us all'*. [94]

"Total extinction is the reward offered up to you and I and every creature on our planet. Ridicule of religion is the natural outgrowth of such doctrines as 'Organic Evolution' and 'Natural Selection'. It places man as the natural kin of the animals, a descendant of a rat, a worm, an amoeba, as our multi-millionth great-grandparent. It, in fact, denies the Fatherhood of God and the Sonship of Jesus Christ, and brings all mankind down to the level of amoeba-hood, all with no verifiable, testable, repeatable evidence to support it." [95] (And that's because it's not observable science, it's just the historic, forensic type of science, where one gives their interpretation of the available data, it being one's best guess).

End of excerpts by President Joseph Fielding Smith

Speaking of evidence, let me share a testimony that is contrary to the non-existence of God testimony that Darwin and Dawkins have given. It's the testimony of two other men – Joseph Smith Jr., and Oliver Cowdery – born just 214 and 215 years ago respectively (As of 2022). These men testified personally of *seeing* the resurrected Jesus, which testimony and witness is recorded in a book of scripture called - "The Doctrine & Covenants". Their testimony is as follows:

Doctrine & Covenants 76:22-24

22 And now, after the many testimonies which have been given of him, this is the testimony, last of all, which we give of him: That he lives!

23 *For we saw him*, even on the right hand of God; and we heard the voice bearing record that he is the Only Begotten of the Father.

24 That by him, and through him, and of him, the worlds are and were created, and the inhabitants thereof are begotten sons and daughters unto God.

The prophet Joseph Smith Jr. was murdered by a state sanctioned mob for bearing that testimony. It is Joseph's and Oliver's eye-witness account, having the privilege of *seeing* the glorious, resurrected Christ. This visitation did not take place over 2,000 years ago. It was in our dispensation, the Dispensation of the Fullness of Times, just 190 years ago on February 16, 1832, in Hyrum, Ohio. Their testimony confirms the witness of all the prophets, past and present, each testifying that God the Son, who is Jesus Christ, lives!

In the hardness of their hearts, both men and women of the world have rejected this and all the other testimonies of prophets and believers, denying that such eyewitness testimonies are not evidence of God's existence. They are blindly pursuing their way to eternal damnation, dragging as many as they can with them, through their pernicious teachings such as Organic Evolution, and the like.

Here are just a few examples of scripture where apostles and prophets, the bearers of the keys of administering the pure gospel to God's children, have warned the people of the world about the consequences of rejecting God, His Word, and the witnesses of prophets. I would encourage you, my readers, to not take them lightly. Here's just a few sobering declarations by past prophets as they're recorded in the Bible:

1 Thessalonians 4:8

8 So, he who rejects this is not rejecting man but the God who gives His Holy Spirit to you.

1 Samuel 15:23

23 For rebellion is as the sin of divination, and insubordination is as iniquity and idolatry. Because you have rejected the word of the Lord, He has also rejected you.

Psalm 106:24

24 Then they despised the pleasant land; They did not believe in His word.

Psalm 50:17

17 For you hate discipline, and you cast My words behind you.

Isaiah 5:24

24 Therefore, as a tongue of fire consumes stubble, and dry grass collapses into the flame; So, their root will become like rot and their blossom blows away as dust; For they have rejected the law of the Lord of hosts and despised the word of the Holy One of Israel.

Isaiah 30:12

12 Therefore, thus says the Holy One of Israel, Since you have rejected this word, and have put your trust in oppression and guile, and have relied on them.

Jeremiah 6:10

10 To whom shall I speak and give warning that they may hear? Behold, their ears are closed, and they cannot listen. Behold, the word of the Lord has become a reproach to them; they have no delight in it.

Jeremiah 8:9

9 The wise men are put to shame. They are dismayed and caught; Behold, they have rejected the word of the Lord, and what kind of wisdom do they have?

Here are a few more scriptures from the Book of Mormon and the Doctrine & Covenants, where both books of scripture, of ancient and modern prophets of God, refer to those who reject God and His Word:

I Nephi 3:18

18 Jews have *rejected* the words of prophets.

I Nephi 15:17

17 The Lord will show his power unto Gentiles because Jews will *reject* him, ...

I Nephi 19:13

13 Jews shall be scourged because they *reject* signs and the power of God.

II Nephi 1:10

10 When those upon the promised land *reject* the Holy One, judgements shall rest upon them.

II Nephi 25:12

12 But, behold, they shall have wars, and rumors of wars; and when the day cometh that the Only Begotten of the Father, yea, even the Father of heaven and of earth, shall manifest himself unto them in the flesh, behold, they will reject him, because of their iniquities, and the hardness of their hearts, and the stiffness of their necks.

Here are a few scriptures talking about those Jews who *rejected* Christ because of iniquities:

II Nephi 25:18

18 Word given to Israel to convince them of the true Messiah, whom they *rejected*.

II Nephi 27:14

14 Wo unto him who *rejects* the word of God.

Jacob 4:15–17

15 And now I, Jacob, am led on by the Spirit unto prophesying; for I perceive by the workings of the Spirit which is in me, that by the stumbling of the Jews they will reject the stone upon which they might build and have safe foundation.

16 But behold, according to the scriptures, this stone shall become the great, and the last, and the only sure foundation, upon which the Jews can build.

17 And now, my beloved, how is it possible that these, after having rejected the sure foundation, can ever build upon it, that it may become the head of their corner?

By the stumbling of the Jews, they will *reject* the stone upon which they might build safe foundation.

Mosiah 14:3

3 He is despised and rejected of men; a man of sorrows, and acquainted with grief; and we hid as it were our faces from him; he was despised, and we esteemed him not.

Isaiah 53:3

3 He is despised and rejected of men; a man of sorrows, and acquainted with grief: and we hid as it were *our* faces from him; he was despised, and we esteemed him not.

Mosiah 27:30

30 I rejected my Redeemer, and denied that which had been spoken of by our fathers; but now that they may foresee that he will come, and that he remembereth every creature of his creating, he will make himself manifest unto all.

Alma *rejected* his Redeemer:

Alma 6:3

3 And it also came to pass that whosoever did belong to the church that did not repent of their wickedness and humble themselves before God—I mean those who were lifted up in the pride of their hearts—the same were rejected, and their names were blotted out, that their names were not numbered among those of the righteous.

Church members who do not repent are rejected:

Alma 13:4

4 And thus they have been called to this holy calling on account of their faith, while others would reject the Spirit of God on account of the hardness of their hearts and blindness of their minds, while, if it had not been for this they might have had as great privilege as their brethren.

Men reject the Spirit because of hard hearts and blindness of minds:

III Nephi 16:10

10 And thus commandeth the Father that I should say unto you: At that day when the Gentiles shall sin against my gospel, and shall reject the fulness of my gospel, and shall be lifted up in the pride of their hearts above all nations, and above all the people of the whole earth, and shall be filled with all manner of lying's, and of deceits, and of mischiefs, and all manner of hypocrisy, and murders, and priestcrafts, and whoredoms, and of secret abominations; and if they shall do all those things, and shall reject the fulness of my gospel, behold, saith the father, ... I will bring the fulness of my gospel from among them.

When Gentiles *reject* the fulness of the gospel, the Father will bring it from them:

Ether 11:22

22 And they did reject all the words of the prophets, because of their secret society and wicked abominations.

Jaredites *reject* the words of prophets because of a secret society, after they rejected so great knowledge Nephites must soon perish:

Doctrine & Covenants 39:9

9 Nevertheless, thou hast seen great sorrow, for thou hast rejected me many times because of pride and the cares of the world.

Thou hast rejected me many times because of pride:

Doctrine & Covenants 124:8

8 And that I may visit them in the day of visitation, when I shall unveil the face of my covering, to appoint the portion of the oppressor among hypocrites, where there is gnashing of teeth, if they reject my servants and my testimony which I have revealed unto them.

The fate of the wicked who reject the testimony of prophets:

Doctrine & Covenants 138:21, 32

21 Neither did the rebellious who rejected the testimonies and the warnings of the ancient prophets behold his presence, nor look upon his face.

32 Thus was the gospel preached to those who had died in their sins, without a knowledge of the truth, or in transgression, having rejected the prophets.

The rebellious reject prophets, past and present. These are prophets who declare that the author of all the lies about God and His existence, is Satan. He is the great deceiver, the 'father of lies', and the enemy of all righteousness. He who has eyes to see will notice that Satan has been true to his determination to destroy God's Plan of Redemption and Happiness. As the god of pleasure, Satan continually tempts mankind to worship him by seeking the pleasures of the world. He continues this objective even to this very day, leading mankind astray and away from a belief in the True and Living God. He calls us away from our eternal Parents who reside in the sidereal heavens. Satan, also called the adversary or the devil, is the enemy of all righteousness and of those who seek to follow God. Satan is a spirit son of God, our Heavenly Father, who was once an angel of light, even one who was in authority in the presence of God, he being called a 'Son of the Morning':

Doctrine & Covenants 76:25

25 And this we saw also, and bear record, that an angel of God who was in authority in the presence of God, ... who rebelled against the Only Begotten Son whom the Father loved and who was in the bosom of the Father, was thrust down from the presence of God and the Son, even a "Son of the Morning":

Doctrine & Covenants 76:26–27

26 And was called Perdition, for the heavens wept over him—he was Lucifer, a son of the morning.

27 And we beheld, and lo, he is fallen! is fallen, even a son of the morning!

Isaiah 14:12

12 How art thou fallen from heaven, O Lucifer, son of the morning! *how* art thou cut down to the ground, which didst weaken the nations!

In the Premortal Grand Council in Heaven, Lucifer, as Satan was then called, ultimately rebelled against God, our Heavenly Father, and when he did, war in heaven ensued. As a result of the war (A war of principles and ideologies), Satan and his followers were cast out of God's presence and were sent to earth in their spirit personage state, and they then, are the spirits who continually tempt each of us and work extremely hard to destroy each of us. They are the third part of the spirit children of God who were thrust down to our earth for rebellion.

Since that time, Satan has sought to destroy the children of God who have come to earth to get a body and experience mortality. It is Satan's desire to make all of mankind most miserable like he and his fallen minions are. They will never receive bodies and so they are furious with God and his children who have and will yet obtain mortal bodies. One primary principle fought about in this veritable conflict between God and Satan, in our pre-mortal estate, was the principle of *agency*. Agency is a precious gift given to us by God Himself. It's an essential law in His plan. Satan's rebellion against God and His law, especially his fight with Jehovah, was about "destroying the agency of man", even the law of choice:

Moses 4:1-32

1 And I, the Lord God, spake unto Moses, saying: That Satan, whom thou hast commanded in the name of mine Only Begotten, is the same which was from the beginning, and he came before me, saying—Behold, here am I, send me, I will be thy son, and I will redeem all mankind, that one soul shall not be lost, and surely I will do it; wherefore give me *thine* honor.

2 But, behold, my Beloved Son, which was my Beloved and Chosen from the beginning, said unto me—Father, thy will be done, and the glory be thine forever.

3 Wherefore, because that Satan rebelled against me, *and sought to destroy the agency of man*, which I, the Lord God, had given him, and also, that I should give unto him mine own power; by the power of mine Only Begotten, I caused that he should be cast down;

4 *And he became Satan, yea, even the devil, the father of all lies, to deceive and to blind men, and to lead them captive at his will, even as many as would not hearken unto my voice.*

5 And now the serpent was more subtle than any beast of the field which I, the Lord God, had made.

6 And Satan put it into the heart of the serpent, (for he had drawn away many after him,) and he sought also to beguile Eve, for he knew not the mind of God, wherefore he sought to destroy the world.

7 And he said unto the woman: Yea, hath God said—Ye shall not eat of every tree of the garden?

8 And the woman said unto the serpent: We may eat of the fruit of the trees of the garden;

9 But of the fruit of the tree which thou beholdest in the midst of the garden, God hath said—Ye shall not eat of it, neither shall ye touch it, lest ye die.

10 And the serpent said unto the woman: Ye shall not surely die;

11 For God doth know that in the day ye eat thereof, then your eyes shall be opened, and ye shall be as gods, knowing good and evil.

12 And when the woman saw that the tree was good for food, and that it became pleasant to the eyes, and a tree to be desired to make her wise, she took of the fruit thereof, and did eat, and also gave unto her husband with her, and he did eat.

13 And the eyes of them both were opened, and they knew that they had been naked. And they sewed fig leaves together and made themselves aprons.

14 And they heard the voice of the Lord God, as they were walking in the garden, in the cool of the day; and Adam and his wife went to hide themselves from the presence of the Lord God amongst the trees of the garden.

15 And I, the Lord God, called unto Adam, and said unto him: Where goest thou?

16 And he said: I heard thy voice in the garden, and I was afraid, because I beheld that I was naked, and I hid myself.

17 And I, the Lord God, said unto Adam: Who told thee thou wast naked? Hast thou eaten of the tree whereof I commanded thee that thou shouldst not eat, if so thou shouldst surely die?

18 And the man said: The woman thou gavest me, and commandest that she should remain with me, she gave me of the fruit of the tree and I did eat.

19 And I, the Lord God, said unto the woman: What is this thing which thou hast done? And the woman said: The serpent beguiled me, and I did eat.

20 And I, the Lord God, said unto the serpent: Because thou hast done this thou shalt be cursed above all cattle, and above every beast of the field; ... upon thy belly shalt thou go, and shalt thou eat all the days of thy life;

21 And I will put *enmity* between thee and the woman, between thy seed and her seed; and he shall bruise thy head, and thou shalt bruise his heel.

22 Unto the woman, I, the Lord God, said: I will greatly multiply thy sorrow and thy conception. In sorrow thou shalt bring forth children, and thy desire shall be to thy husband, and he shall rule over thee.

23 And unto Adam, I, the Lord God, said: Because thou hast hearkened unto the voice of thy wife, and hast eaten of the fruit of the tree of which I commanded thee, saying—Thou shalt not eat of it, cursed shall be the ground for thy sake; in sorrow shalt thou eat of it all the days of thy life.

24 Thorns also, and thistles shall it bring forth to thee, and thou shalt eat the herb of the field.

25 By the sweat of thy face shalt thou eat bread, until thou shalt return unto the ground—for thou shalt surely die—for out of it wast thou taken: for dust thou wast, and unto dust shalt thou return.

26 And Adam called his wife's name Eve, because she was the mother of all living; for thus have I, the Lord God, called the first of all women, which are many.

27 Unto Adam, and also unto his wife, did I, the Lord God, make coats of skins, and clothed them.

28 And I, the Lord God, said unto mine Only Begotten: Behold, the man is become as one of us to know good and evil; and now lest he put forth his hand and partake also of the tree of life, and eat and live forever,

29 Therefore I, the Lord God, will send him forth from the Garden of Eden, to till the ground from whence he was taken;

30 For as I, the Lord God, liveth, even so my words cannot return void, for as they go forth out of my mouth they must be fulfilled.

31 So I drove out the man, and I placed at the east of the Garden of Eden, cherubim and a flaming sword, which turned every way to keep the way of the tree of life.

32 And these are the words which I spake unto my servant Moses, and they are true even as I will; and I have spoken them unto you. See thou show them unto no man, until I command you, except to them that believe. Amen.

Satan said: "I will redeem *all* mankind, that one soul shall not be lost, and surely I will do it; wherefore give me thine honor." Satan was able to persuade "a third part" of the hosts of heaven to support him in his goal to become the Savior and God Himself, and because God chose Jehovah Satan and his followers rebelled against Jehovah and Heavenly Father's Plan of Happiness:

Doctrine & Covenants 29:36

36 And it came to pass that Adam, being tempted of the devil—for, behold, the devil was before Adam, for he rebelled against me, saying, Give me thine honor, which is my power; and also a third part of the hosts of heaven turned he away from me because of their agency;

Revelations 12:7-8

7 And there was war in heaven: Michael (Whose name was Adam while on the earth), and his angels (You and I), fought against the dragon (Lucifer/Satan); and the dragon fought with his angels (Those spirit children who were later cast out with Satan to the earth),

8 And prevailed not; neither was their place found any more in heaven.

As a result of this rebellion, Satan and his followers were cut off from God's presence and were denied the blessing of receiving a physical body, as well as the experience of having a mortal experience here on earth with all of its opportunities and blessings, and ultimately, after our time on earth, receiving the gift of resurrection. This conflict between *forced salvation* and *moral agency* continues even to this very day. It is a war of opposing ideologies – theism versus secular-humanism or Atheism.

Revelation 12:9

9 And the great dragon was cast out, that old serpent, called the Devil, and Satan, which deceiveth the whole world: he was cast out into the earth, and his angels were cast out with him.

Heavenly Father allows Satan and his followers (Those spirit children cast out of His presence for rebellion, referred to as Satans' angels in the scriptures), to tempt us as part of our experience here in mortality. The following verses of scripture were written by Lehi, as he taught his son Jacob:

II Nephi 2:11–14

11 For it must needs be, that there is an opposition in all things. If not so, my firstborn in the wilderness, righteousness could not be brought to pass, neither wickedness, neither holiness nor misery, neither good nor bad. Wherefore, all things must needs be a compound in one; wherefore, if it should be one body it must needs remain as dead, having no life neither death, nor corruption nor incorruption, happiness nor misery, neither sense nor insensibility.

12 Wherefore, it must needs have been created for a thing of naught; wherefore there would have been no purpose in the end of its creation. Wherefore, this thing must needs destroy the wisdom of God and his eternal purposes, and also the power, and the mercy, and the justice of God.

13 And if ye shall say there is no law, ye shall also say there is no sin. If ye shall say there is no sin, ye shall also say there is no righteousness. And if there be no righteousness there be no happiness. And if there be no righteousness nor happiness there be no punishment nor misery. And if these things are not there is no God. And if there is no God we are not, neither the earth; for there could have been no creation of things, neither to act nor to be acted upon; wherefore, all things must have vanished away.

14 And now, my sons, I speak unto you these things for your profit and learning; for there is a God, and he hath created all things, both the heavens and the earth, and all things that in them are, both things to act and things to be acted upon.

Doctrine & Covenants 29:39

39 And it must needs be that the devil should tempt the children of men, or they could not be agents unto themselves; ... for if they never should have bitter they could not know the sweet because Satan "seeketh that all men might be miserable like unto himself":

II Nephi 2:27

27 Wherefore, men are free according to the flesh; and all things are given them which are expedient unto man. And they are free to choose liberty and eternal life, through the great Mediator of all men, or to choose captivity and death, according to the captivity and power of the devil; for he seeketh that all men might be miserable like unto himself.

Satan and his minions (Fallen spirits/angels, even the third part of God's spirit children) try to lead us away from choosing righteousness. Heavenly Father, our Creator, does not force us to accept His authority or His love. *Our willingness to submit to His authority (Sustaining God as sovereign) is the first step in conversion to the Gospel of Jesus Christ and coming to know that there is a God who lives.* How do we do that you say? We *lay aside any feeling of pride* that is so common in the world today.

By this, I mean *'the attitude and mindset' that rejects the authority of God to rule in one's life*, which is exactly what Lucifer or Satan did and still does today. He rejected God's authority because he wanted it for himself. The Lord Himself made the prophet Joseph Smith aware of this *"attitude of rebellion"* by describing it to him when He said to Joseph in the First Vision: "They seek not the Lord to establish *His* righteousness, but every man walketh in his own way, and after the image of his (or her) own god." [96]

This *'attitude of rebellion'* manifests in people that Satan attacks with his most strenuous opposition. He attacks the most important aspects of Heavenly Father's Plan of Happiness and Redemption – the family and other divinely appointed institutions (And has done so throughout the earth's entire history). For example, he seeks to discredit the Savior and His priesthood (The authority to act in God's name), trying to cast doubt on the power of the Atonement (So that we don't repent and seek forgiveness). He uses counterfeit revelation to distract us from the truth and its divine source which leads us to disregard individual accountability (For example, teaching that there is no such thing as 'Free Will', or that we're an unintended accident of Evolution, and as such are not accountable for our own actions).

He attempts to undermine the family by confusing gender, promoting sexual relations outside of marriage saying it hurts no one, and so, there is no consequence in seeking that kind of pleasure. He ridicules marriage and discourages childbearing by married adults who would otherwise raise children in righteousness. Here's another set of scriptures quoted by an ancient prophet named Nephi, the son of Lehi. He lived in ancient America more than 580 years before the birth of Jesus Christ in Bethlehem, in the land of Jerusalem. He prophetically predicted the following:

II Nephi 28:19–21

19 For the kingdom of the devil must shake, and they which belong to it must needs be stirred up unto repentance, or the devil will grasp them with his everlasting chains (Like a flaxen chord), and they be stirred up to anger, and perish;

20 For behold, at that day (These Latter-Days), *shall he rage in the hearts of the children of men, and stir them up to anger against that which is good.*

21 And others will he pacify, and lull them away into carnal security, that they will say: All is well in Zion; yea, Zion prospereth, all is well—and thus the devil cheateth their souls, and leadeth them away *carefully* down to hell.

22 And behold, others he flattereth away, and telleth them there is no hell; and he saith unto them: I am no devil, for there is none—*and thus he whispereth in their ears, until he grasps them with his awful chains, from whence there is no deliverance.*

Let me ask, in the spirit of fair play, "Why are the advocates of the quasi-religion of Darwinism, whose believers are atheists, privileged to teach their soul-destroying doctrines and the unproven, quasi-gospel of Evolution and its tenant Natural Selection, in our public schools and colleges, when the doctrines of Jesus Christ – the doctrine of Divine Intelligence and Creationism – are barred?"

"Why are so many of the textbooks adopted in these schools, steeped in the theories of this quasi-religion and by these means the minds of our children are poisoned, and their faith destroyed, all the while non-religious books, such as "Signature in the Cell", are barred?" In this land of America, our fathers fought for religious and political freedom, but our nation is now confronted with a far more deadly enemy, whose objective is the destruction of our children's faith in the Living God. The perpetrators of this doctrine either know that they are deceivers, or else they have been completely blinded by the archenemy of divine truth, Satan, even the god of this age and his gospel of pleasure.

Only God himself knows what's in a person's heart, so I will not judge these people and will leave it there. But again, I ask, "Why should those who believe in the creation of man, and the Fall of man, and the atonement of Jesus Christ, have to submit to these imperious theories being promulgated and taught in the textbooks of our secular schools ... as though they are *settled* truths?" All Believers should take a stand for our religious freedom from this contaminating influence that is dominating so much of our education being taught throughout the world, including our schools here in America.

This same practice has prevailed in the schools of Great Britain, but there THE VICTORIA INSTITUTE, or PHILOSOPHICAL SOCIETY OF GREAT BRITAIN, which has in its membership many noted scientists, educators, lawyers, and statesmen, dared to enter a protest. By their 'Secretary' they appealed to the President of the Board of Education in the following communication:

"To the President of the Board of Education, Whitehall, London, S. W. I. October 6th, 1941", and I quote:

Sir,

I have the honor, by request of the Council of the Victoria Institute, or Philosophical Society of Great Britain, to bring to your notice a complaint that is being made in respect of the manner of teaching biology in schools.

Representations have been made to the Council that correct teachings of biology are prejudiced by the use, with official sanction, of textbooks in which the 'theory of organic evolution' is assumed to be a fact of science, and while facts that appear to favor the theory are stressed, others which tell heavily against it are left unmentioned: are, in effect suppressed; a method of teaching which, if employed, is unscientific and unphilosophical."

"... ill consequences are bound to result: not only from suppression of truth, but worse, from the harnessing of immature minds in advance to a theory, adoption of which in certain quarters as the basis of the philosophy of life has already (they have good reason to know) served to undermine belief in God and in man's accountability to Him, with disastrous results in the moral realm." [97]

End Quote

The secularist educators that run our public schools throughout the world, have been educating our children to believe man's word is the only truth – the word of scientists and atheists – and that God's word is full of fables. This century of this godless educating of our children has created doubt and cognitive dissonance in the minds of children today, so that they're rejecting God's word in great numbers. There are two foundations, two religions or worldviews toady: Man's Word vs God's Word.

Here's more of what President Joseph Fielding Smith wrote, and I quote: "Darwin, the quasi-prophet of the 'Hypothesis of Organic Evolution', found himself in a difficult struggle. In his book 'Descent of Man', in the third and fourth chapters, Mr. Darwin indulges in a rather difficult effort to try and close the gap between the mental powers of man and those of the lower animal. Darwin admits that there is an immense distance between the highest ape, whatever that happens to be: and the lowest savage, whatever that happens to be, yet they have certain instincts in common." [98]

End Quote

Let me share a few more thoughts related to the hypothetic gospel of Organic Evolution, and its chief tenet Natural Selection, before I further dive into responding to Richard's first chapter. Richard's fanaticism as a believer in this *delusion of evolution*, causes him to constantly refer to it as "the source of all creation of life, no matter its kind, including the evolution of religion itself." [99]

First of all, I, as a believer in prophets and revelation, not only those who lived in ancient days, but in those who lived early in this dispensation, as well as those who are currently walking amongst us today, starting with the first prophet of this dispensation, the prophet of the Restoration of the Gospel of Jesus Christ in its fulness and purity. I'm speaking of the prophet Joseph Smith Jr. As I shared earlier, as a boy in his fifteenth year, having a desire to know the truth regarding which of all the churches of his Day he should join, Joseph, after reading James 1:5, was stirred to go into the woods near his home to seek an answer from God. Here is that verse of scripture that Joseph read, causing him to reflect on it on again, and again, where it ultimately moved him to take God at His word and pray for an answer:

James 1:5

5 If any of you lack wisdom, let him ask of God, that giveth to all *men* liberally, and upbraideth not; and it shall be given him.

So, Joseph went into the woods near his home, with the intent of asking God which of all the churches operating in his Day he should join. This was the circumstance leading up to Joseph experiencing his First Vision, the appearance of God the Eternal Father and His Only Begotten Son, Jesus Christ, in a grove of trees. It was the result of Joseph's question and sincere prayer. I think you, my readers, should be aware of a few things that you may not know about the Prophet Joseph Smith's First Vision. You can read his full story at www.churchofjesuschrist.org, where you can learn about all *five* "First Vision Accounts" that were recorded during the years that followed Joseph's actual vison.

Joseph Smith may have lived during the first fifty years of the nineteenth century (He was born on December 23rd, 1805, and was murdered by a mob on June 27th, 1844, in his thirty-ninth year), but he saw the world in ways we are only now beginning to understand. Relying upon Joseph's own words and teachings, an award-winning professor of chemistry at BYU (2011-present), Dr. John David Lamb (Mentioned in my list of resources), authored the book titled, "Joseph Smith's 21st Century View of the World: Truths He Knew Before the World Accepted Them".

Dr. Lamb draws fascinating parallels between the latest scientific discoveries and the revelations received by the Prophet Joseph Smith. Dr. Lamb *unites science and faith*, ... as he paints a mesmerizing picture of the universe around us. Dr. Lamb begins his book with a statement by Joseph Smith the prophet, given on October 9, 1843, at Nauvoo Illinois, and I quote:

"Could you gaze into heaven five minutes you would know more than you would by reading all that ever was written on the subject." [100]

End Quote

The following are a few excerpts from Dr. Lamb's study of Joseph Smiths' vision of the world (Be sure to read Dr. Lamb's book in its entirety), and I quote:

"In producing revelation upon revelation, Joseph exposed uncanny insights into topics well beyond his ken. Among these were revelations that touch on what we call science today, referring specifically to natural science. Many of the ideas found among Joseph's insights involved concepts that were either unknown to science in his Day or were poorly or even wrongly understood." Dr. Lamb continues, "Looking back on Joseph's claims from the viewpoint of today's science, they were remarkably prescient, and it is clear that Joseph held a very forward-thinking, twenty-first-century vision of the world which came to be accepted and understood long after his death." [101]

"Science and Religion are often cast as antagonists on the world stage. Joseph did not share this view. He laid claim to any truth from any source, including science, and embraced it wholeheartedly. Indeed, his attitude on this matter may best be summed up in a quote by one of his most ardent followers and companions, Brigham Young", [102] who said, and I quote: "The idea that the religion of Christ is one thing, and science is another, is a mistaken idea, for there is no true religion without true science, and consequently there is no true science without true religion." [103]

End of Brigham Young's and Joseph Smith's quotes

Dr. Lamb also wrote, quote: "This book is not designed to single out and respond to any particular criticism of Joseph's teachings in any apologetic way. Rather, it is to illustrate how Joseph possessed a very modern view of the world, one that a twenty-first-century person would find fits quite comfortably with what science is now revealing about the world around us." [104]

End Quote

In his book Dr. Lamb took the approach, out of necessity, to simplify many aspects of the otherwise complex and fascinating topics that are at the heart of today's science. So, I respectfully ask that those experts in the many fields of science, hold off in taking exception to Dr. Lamb's generalizations for the present moment, and simply read his book as a follow-up to my perspective on Richard Dawkins' arguments as found in *The God Delusion*. I very much like these three statements made by Dr. Lamb, where he stated the following, and I quote:

First, "The path of scientific advancement has not been a smooth one, and our current understanding of the world, itself undoubtedly imperfect, has arisen from a series of fits and starts, successes and failures, which ideas coming in and out of vogue, sometimes lost and then rediscovered." [105]

Next, "Too often we tend to dwell on areas where science and religion appear to conflict. I say, appear to conflict because we must recognize that there can be only one truth, and where science and religion intersect and overlap in their claims, those who value both as reliable sources can rightly expect them to harmonize." [106]

Lastly, "There are several examples where, in recent times, past areas of apparent conflict have been wondrously resolved, so that where once there was disharmony, a new harmony has arisen. And thereby, we may entertain hope and faith that where apparent conflicts remain, with the gathering of *new* knowledge in both science and theology, those seeming discontinuities will be resolved like the ones that have already found resolution." [107]

End of Dr. Lamb quotes

It's been nearly 200 years since the light of the gospel was restored, and it has only been in the last two hundred years that science has taken on the connotation of what we can more strictly term *natural science*, embracing fields like chemistry, physics, biology, and so on. Joseph Smith taught, and I quote:

"*Knowledge does away with darkness, suspense, and doubt; for these cannot exist where knowledge is. In knowledge there is power. God has more power than all other beings because He has greater knowledge.*" [108] I would even dare to say, "He has all knowledge, for He is all knowing".

End Quote

There's a verse in the hymnal of my Church called, "The Spirit of God". It says, "The Veil O're the Earth is Beginning to Burst". Dr. Lamb wrote, quote:

"This is a truth the Prophet Joseph taught. Today we are blessed to live in that Day that he foresaw when knowledge is expanding, and the veil of darkness which obscured our vision of the true nature of the world and our place in it for many centuries, is certainly being lifted."

"As this process of research and study and revelation unfolds, new insights in both science and theology resolve old questions in some cases and raise new questions in others. It is my conviction that over time knowledge derived from both areas of understanding will come to be in perfect harmony under one complex framework of truth." [109]

End Quote

The diagram shown on the next page illustrates how wide the gap of knowledge was between the minds of the non-believers and the believers at the beginning of man's existence. Over the six thousand plus years that followed since Adam and Eve's fall, both the things of a scientific nature, as well as those things of a spiritual nature, have been moving ever so closer to intersecting where each of these two 'Magisterium's or authorities of truth', will one day be circumscribed into one great whole of truth and perfection.

With that thought in mind, I would like to remind you, my readers, what Dr. Lamb mentioned in his book "Joseph Smith's 21st Century View of the World", where the Lord promised the prophet Joseph Smith that He would reveal all things at His 2nd coming. This promise is found in the Doctrine & Covenant as follows:

Doctrine & Covenants 101:32-34

32 Yea, verily I say unto you, *in that day when the Lord shall come*, he shall reveal all things—

33 Things which have passed, and hidden things which no man knew, things of the earth, by which it was made, and the purpose and the end thereof—

34 Things most precious, things that are above, and things that are beneath, things that are in the earth, and upon the earth, and in heaven.

As this diagram shows, it is my belief that one day scientific knowledge and religious knowledge will intersect, and that day will be when science is perfectly pure, and religion is perfectly pure. But that day will not take place until Jesus Christ Himself returns at His 2nd coming, at which time He will reveal the truth of all things and begin His millennial reign as He has promised.

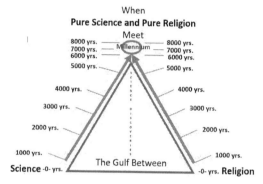

When
Pure Science and Pure Religion
Meet

Dr. Lamb continued his comments on this subject saying that as this revelation takes place, quote:

"We shall see that on several key points, Joseph Smith was remarkably prescient in his understanding of the natural world, anticipating the scientific discoveries that we have now come to understand in the twenty-first century." [110]

"Early in the nineteenth century, long after the revolutionary discoveries made by Galileo and his small telescope, most scientific observers in Joseph Smiths' Day viewed the Milky Way Galaxy as the only galaxy in the universe with its large but finite number of stars. ... Such was the status of our human understanding of the universe among scholars in Josephs' Day." [111]

"At one point in Josephs' adult life, he found himself in a dungeon-like jail in the middle of winter, jailed for a crime he did not commit. While in Liberty Jail Joseph received a revelation wherein God told Joseph that during this last dispensation of time (Our time), much would be revealed about the universe, and after nearly 200 years that promise has literally come to pass." [112]

End of quote

Consider these verses in the Doctrine & Covenants. It's the revelation Joseph received from the Lord while he was incarcerated in the Liberty jail:

Doctrine & Covenants 88:36-38, 47

36 All kingdoms have a law given;

37 And there are many kingdoms; for there is no space in the which there is no kingdom; and there is no kingdom in which there is no space, either a greater or a lesser kingdom.

38 And unto every kingdom is given a law; and unto every law there are certain bounds also and conditions (The Laws of Physics are just one example).

47 Behold, all these are kingdoms, and any man who hath seen any or the least of these hath seen God moving in his majesty and power.

Here's a brief review of what humankind has learned on this subject since the restoration of the gospel in its fulness through the instrumentality of Joseph Smith, beginning in the 1820's on through the 1840's:

"Question – How many stars do scientists say there are today? Today, we know there are literally billions, and perhaps trillions of stars in our universe. Just as the Lord promised, over the 200 years since the Lord told Joseph that He would reveal much about the universe, considerable knowledge about our universe has been revealed and accumulating at a breathtaking rate. The most recent and dramatic contributions to our knowledge and understanding of the real scope of the universe was the International Thermonuclear Experimental Reactor (ITER) in 1988, which was to replicate the fusion processes of the Sun to create energy on the Earth, somewhere between 14 and 18 billion dollars expense. Next was the launching of the Hubble Space Telescope in 1990, at a cost of one and a half-billion dollars. And then there is the James Webb telescope. It was successfully launched on Christmas Day, December 25th, 2021, after 30 years in development and at a cost of 10 billion dollars. What's next?

"Using the Hubble telescope, scientists pointed it to a small, supposedly empty black patch in the heavens, wherein they found that there were galaxies everywhere. So, the answer to our question here, is that there are about 200 billion stars in the Milky Way Galaxy alone, and there are between 100 and 1,000 billion galaxies in the universe" (As far as our best guessing goes).

Recorded in the Book of Moses is a revelation from God that says:

Moses 7:30

30 And were it possible that man could number the particles of the earth, yea, millions of earths like this, it would not be a beginning to the number of thy creations and thy curtains are stretched out still.

In the Book of Abraham 3:11-12, another revelation received by the prophet Joseph Smith, it says:

Abraham 3:11-12

11 Thus I, Abraham, talked with the Lord, face to face, as one man talkest with another; and he told me of the works which his hands had made; And he said unto me: My son, my son (and his hand was stretched out), behold I will show you all these.

12 And he put his hand upon mine eyes, and I saw those things which his hands had made, which were many; and they multiplied before mine eyes, and I could *not* see the end thereof.

And again, in the book of Moses, in the Pearl of Great Price, it says:

Moses 1:28-29

28 And he beheld also the inhabitants thereof, and there was not a soul which he beheld not; and he discerned them by the Spirit of God; and their numbers were great, ... even numberless as the sand upon the seashore.

29 And he beheld many lands; and each land was called earth, and there were inhabitants on the face thereof.

"Carl Sagan himself used the same metaphor of a sandy beach to describe the large numbers relating to the stars in our universe. He said, "Lo and behold, the number of stars in the known universe is greater than the number of grains of sand on all the beaches of planet earth." [113]

"Our understanding has come a great distance from the time of Joseph Smith and how the scientists of his Day viewed the universe, yet Joseph knew the scriptures and had received new revelations that gave him this knowledge and understanding, and he was ridiculed by the world at that Day for saying it. Just before Joseph Smith's Day, scientists like Kant and Herschel (They died in 1804 and 1822), in Europe, and Benjamin Franklin in America (Who died in 1790), had been speculating about the existence of multiple worlds. But Joseph Smith, a contemporary to Kant and Herschel, went much further, and in his 'works of revelation', referring to the writings of Moses and Abraham as I cited earlier, as well as Josephs' revelations in the Doctrine & Covenants, Joseph made claims about the number of stars and planets that were outlandish and unsubstantiated in his Day, and that held him up for possible ridicule and eventual discrediting.

"Joseph even claimed that there were countless inhabited planets, an outrageous proposition for the science of his Day, but now it's considered to be a serious possibility by respected scientists. One must ask, "Why would Joseph risk criticism like this, unnecessarily, if he were inventing these things as a ruse?" Why would he continue to do so even under the threat of death until he ultimately was killed.

"In the intervening years he has been vindicated by scientific discoveries, and this stands as a significant witness (Dare I say a reference leg of evidence) to his prophetic calling." [114]

Here are more excerpts from Dr. Lamb's book:

"Let me give just a couple more modern discoveries that Joseph spoke of and taught openly about a hundred and seventy years before such discoveries occurred in our Day. In Doctrine & Covenants 76:10 we read:

Doctrine & Covenants 76:10

10 For by my *Spirit* will I enlighten them, and by my *power* will I make known unto *them* the secrets of my will – yes, even those things which eye has not *seen*, nor ear heard, nor yet entered into the heart of man.

"Science is certainly the search for knowledge about our world and what reality is. 'What the eye can't see', for centuries, was where things were left, or should I say, remained unknown ... which drew scientists to dig deeper in their search of that unseen knowledge. Normally, you and I rely on our five senses to gather information about the world around us. And for thousands of years, humans had no way to augment these senses beyond what the unaided sensory organs could perceive."

"That is why astronomy is the 'oldest' of the sciences – because regularities in the heavens could only be observed with the naked eye. But with the invention of the telescope, and the microscope around the same time, we began to realize that there existed things in nature that we previously had no idea existed (Things or ideas that mankind had never seen, nor had they ever imagined them before)."

"In the early 1,600's, Galileo saw moons circling Jupiter using his 'primitive' telescope. At about the same time, Van Leeuwenhoek saw microorganisms in a droplet of water using his 'primitive' microscope. Today, with our current powerful telescopes and microscopes "What the eye can't see" has been changed to "What the eye can see". [115] We can only imagine what the James Webb telescope will reveal to us in the coming months and years. Since those early times where people questioned if what was being observed was real, or just a by-product of the device, today's binoculars, telescopes, and microscopes have become much more sophisticated, making such discoveries further and further removed from our natural senses." [116] End of Dr. Lamb's comments.

Modern people (Like Richard Dawkins), often express pride in not believing in God because He is not seen, nor are our 'spirits' that inhabit our bodies. Yet they simultaneously take for granted the existence of all kinds of things that *cannot be seen* by our natural eyes or even by scientific means, at least not so far, such as the Atom or Proton or Quarks or Dark Matter, etc., but they accept what they analyze – the *effects* that they can measure – and they then use these *effects* to proclaim their existence with confidence.

In other words, they say the new, unseen worlds are not made up of spirits and or made by the invisible God, but are made up of microbes, atoms, photons, and quarks that they cannot see. The fact is that it takes real faith for scientists to believe in these *unseen* things, just as I exercise faith. Right? Here's why.

The belief in the existence of the unseen world of the spirits, angels, and God Himself, as well as the sense that there is more to our world than just our existence in it, even though we cannot see such things with our natural eye or powerful devices, especially at the micro-level, is a driving force behind the universal human need to believe in such unseen things. It's what drives scientists to *do science*, right?

C. S. Lewis said, "This universal need by most of mankind throughout all of history, is one of the strongest evidences that proves God exists." [117] Didn't Richard say one of his consciousness raisers was, "Why belief is so ubiquitous, but not because God exists?"

I'm going to use the example of an unseen, yet real existence, of an atom and its parts, to make my point, because even today an atom has never been *seen*, even thru the highest-powered electron microscope. Yet, all scientists believe, to the point of saying they *know* that they do exist, due to this different kind of scientific tool that measures and records the atom's *effect* on things. Sound familiar? In an article written by Lynn Charles Rathbun, titled "World's Most Powerful Microscope" he said:

"The light from the thing that we want to see is magnified with lenses in a microscope and we see a virtual image of that tiny thing. The smallest thing that we can see with a 'light' microscope is about 500 nanometers. A nanometer is one-billionth (that's 1,000,000,000th) of a meter. So, the smallest thing that you can see with a light microscope is about 200 times smaller than the width of a hair. Bacteria are about 1,000 nanometers in size. The reason we can't see anything smaller is that these microscopes use light. We don't think about light as having a size, but visible light is about 500-800 nanometers. To see anything smaller we need a more powerful microscope."

"'Electron microscopes' see things *using electrons instead of light*. Electrons are much smaller than the wavelength of visible light and so much smaller things can be *seen* with these electron microscopes. The pictures that you get from an electron microscope are black and white because we need visible light to have colors. Sometimes we see electron microscope pictures that have colors. Scientists add those colors, like Dennis Kunkel, to help point out important things or sometimes because they just look cool.

"The world's most powerful microscopes don't see things with light or even electrons. They see things by 'feeling', *feeling with a very sharp tip on the end of something that looks like a needle*. Sometimes scientists put 'carbon nanotubes' on the end to make them even sharper. A tip so sharp is only a few atoms wide (Wow!). A tip so sharp that as it moves across something it '*feels its shape*' (Measures its effect around it as it *feels* the *effects*. See Picture here):

"These very powerful microscopes are called *atomic force microscopes* because they can see (*feel*) things by the forces between atoms."

"So, with an atomic force microscope, you can see things as small as a strand of DNA or even individual atoms (Of course the word *see* actually means *measuring or feeling the effects* of something that exists but is too small to actually see it in picture form using our natural eyes).

"These microscopes use computers to help convert the information from tapping on the sample to make a three-dimensional view of the object. So, with the world's most powerful microscope, scientists have been able to *see* DNA (To feel its effects and draw a picture of it) and report that it is a double helix just like Watson and Crick showed over 50 years ago!" [118]

End of Article

With this example of how scientists can *see* very small pieces of matter such as DNA, I think it's a great time to bring in a brief discussion on *matter* itself. Joseph Smith taught that "matter cannot be created or destroyed, and that *spirit matter* was just more fine or purer than other matter." [119] Like the atom, it cannot be seen with the natural eye, nor with the strongest, most powerful microscope in use today, but we know this matter exists. Here are a few excerpts from a message given by Parley P. Pratt, a close friend of Joseph Smith, titled "Eternal Duration of Matter" that I found quite enlightening, and I quote:

"By the end of the eighteenth century, modern scientific methods had begun to provide new insights into the fundamental nature of matter, and these negated the Greek philosophical position of form over matter. This *change* in scientific thinking was contemporary with the teachings of the Prophet Joseph Smith in the theological realm. Joseph's teachings returned theology to the intimate relationship between God and mankind of early Judeo-Christian writings.

"These concepts were in contrast to the position that deity is an embodiment of principles and philosophical ideals that transcend in importance the physical realities of matter.

"Furthermore, the view that matter was created from nothing (ex nihilo), a concept dominating theological and scientific thought for many centuries and is still widespread in nineteenth century thought, lost the support of modern science, and was opposed by the gospel restored by Joseph Smith. Modern scientific theories of matter, from Antoine Lavoisier's (1743-1794) to Erwin Schrödinger's (1887-1961), maintain the permanence of matter.

"In the twentieth century, the atomic theory has embodied several fundamental nuclear particles and powerful mathematical theories. Some falling outside human intuition, account for *properties* of matter newly discovered in this century. Concepts have led to the development of '*unified quantum mechanical*' and '*quantum dynamic*' theories for both matter and light. The conservation law of Lavoisier has been extended to include all equivalent 'forms' of matter and 'energy' and still constitutes one of the primary pillars of modern science. It is significant that the teachings of the Prophet Joseph Smith and the restored gospel on the eternal nature of physical matter, along with a parallel in the spiritual realm, embody these conservation principles. Here is a key statement by Joseph Smith himself, who wrote regarding this subject on matter, saying "The elements are eternal":

Doctrine & Covenants 93:33

33 For man is spirit. The elements are eternal, and spirit and element, inseparably connected, receive a fulness of joy; (It's talking about the spirit uniting with the body as a resurrected being)

"Anything created cannot be eternal; and earth, water, etc., had their existence *in an elementary state*, from eternity." [120]

End of excerpts and quotes by Dr, Lamb and Elder Pratt

Let me say here that this revelation by the Prophet Joseph Smith is one of, if not the main reason I say, "I too am a 'Naturalist or Materialist'. I'm a naturalist in the sense that I believe that everything begins as 'matter' in some form or another, especially 'spirit matter' which is a form of unseen matter (At least for now, but it is 'felt', and its *effects* are *felt and seen* if we look and search our feelings closely) and has always existed in some form or another. Addressing the issue of creation 'ex nihilo', ... Joseph Smith asserted the following in one of his final sermons before his martyrdom, and I quote:

"Now, the word 'create' does not mean to create out of nothing (ex nihilo); it means to *organize*; the same as a man would organize materials and build a ship. Hence, we infer that God had materials to organize the world out of 'chaos', and 'chaotic matter', which is element. Element had an existence from the time [God] had. The pure principles of element are principles which can never be destroyed. They may be organized and reorganized, but not destroyed. They had no beginning and can have no end." (See the website www.chruchofjesuschrist.org for the essay titled, "The Book of Abraham")

End Quote

Dr. Lamb continues, "Such reorganization of element may account for the age of our earth being tens of thousands or even billions of years old, and maybe it's why 'relics' of peoples living on it are tens of thousands or billions of years old. We just don't know of these things *to a certainty*, as yet. Extending the concept of the eternal nature of matter to the substance of spirit, Joseph Smith again revealed":

Doctrine & Covenants 131:7-8

7 There is no such thing as immaterial matter. All spirit is matter, but it is more fine or pure, and can only be discerned by purer eyes;

8 We cannot see it; but when our bodies are purified we shall see that it is all matter.

"Matter and spirit are the two great principles of all existence. Everything animate and inanimate is composed of one or the other, or both of these *eternal principles*. Matter and spirit are of equal duration; both are self-existent, they never began to exist, and they never can be annihilated. Matter, as well as spirit, is eternal, uncreated, and self-existing. However infinite the variety of its changes, forms, and shapes; eternity is inscribed in indelible characters on every particle." (*HC* 4:55)

"In strict analogy to principles governing physical matter, the revelations (By God) to Joseph Smith, stress that 'eternity' for spirits, also derives from the eternal existence of spiritual matter or elements. The preeminent manifestation of the eternal nature of both physical and spiritual matter is found in the eternal existence of God and ultimately His human children as discrete, indestructible entities. In the unique LDS doctrine, matter, in all its many forms, instead of occupying a subordinate role relative to philosophical paradigms, it assumes a sovereign position, along with the principles and laws governing its properties and characteristics." [121]

End of Dr. Lamb's excerpts

Maybe one day we'll have a way to *see* spirit-matter under the power of a super-mega-power-pure-spirit-matter-microscope, as well as the atom itself (and not have to rely on *feeling* around it so computers can draw a picture of it), learning more about the kind of spirit-matter that our spirit bodies are made of, even though it's in an extremely pure and unique spirit state. Until that day comes, either when scientists discover it or God Himself reveals it to the world, I will continue to support and promote the truth that says: "Just because we cannot see something with our natural eyes, or even with our most powerful of microscopes or telescopes *at the present time*, doesn't make it non-existent" (If scientists can say this, so can I, right?).

The apostle Paul, in the book of Hebrews said:

Hebrews 11:1

1 Faith is the *'substance'* of things hoped for and the *'evidence'* (And 'effects' for that matter), of things not seen.

That's exactly the principle of *faith in action* that scientists exercise when learning about atomic theory, right? We observe the evidence (In the case of the atom we observe the *effects* it has on things around it) that exist without actually *seeing* them. It's the *atomic force microscopes* that we use to see these effects, and so, I have to say this at this juncture in our discussion, "My scientists friends, you exercise the principle of faith in doing science, just as theists exercise the principle of faith in doing their religious work, for we all know that the principle of faith is *'the moving cause of all action'*, be it in spiritual matters or in matters of science."

There are many examples that I could go on and on to describe where we're called upon to believe in things yet unseen, or perceive with one or more of our natural senses, but I think what I have shared thus far, has sufficiently made my point. You, my readers, will be the judge.

I still have a question though. Believers are asked by God to believe in worlds and phenomena that the *eye can't see,* such as our Father in Heaven, Jesus Christ, angels, spirit bodies, the spirit world, etc.

So, my question is, "In what ways are the two exercises of faith (Scientific faith, and religious faith) similar? And in what ways are they different?" I won't take the time to tell you all that Dr. Lamb wrote or give all the examples he gives in answering these questions but let me just say that both science and religion require that we trust in *indirect evidence* (such as effects etc.) and in those similarities existing between how science and religion go about verifying the existence of things ... which our naked eye cannot see.

Dr. Lamb says quote:

"Our bodies are the most complex system in the whole universe. The more we learn about the cells that make up you and me, and the biochemical processes that make us function, the more awe-inspired we should become. Every cell in our body is an amazing little world of its own, with gates and walls, sophisticated chemical factories, a central government, and a complex and extraordinary communications system. If you or I could be the size of a protein molecule and we could set things up so that we could explore a single cell in our body (Like the folks in the movie 'Fantastic Voyage' did), we could spend a lifetime observing all the comings and goings and the busy activity in it, and never run out of interesting new things to see. And we have a hundred trillion such cells of hundreds of different kinds doing lots of different things. And some of them we haven't even discovered yet."

(As a member of the Church of Jesus Christ of Latter-Day Saints, I see the complexity of the biological world and the realm of the atom, unseen to our unaided eye, as providing one more witness of the greatness of our Heavenly Father and his creative genius. I ask that you add this to the stack of indirect yet well-informed, supporting evidence for the existence of God, or at least on the stack of evidence for moving your belief cursor further along the *percentage of probability spectrum towards* God exists)

"Today, we take the existence of these worlds as a given, in part due to the expansion of our senses through the use of amazing scientific tools, and in part, due to the existence of overwhelming, indirect evidence. We have come to rely on the fruits of our knowledge related to the worlds of atoms, molecules, and biological cells to keep us alive, healthy, and well-stocked with comforts, entertainment, and toys. By the same token, my religion teaches me about the existence of unseen worlds (Like the spirit world that's all around us), which those who make the effort to come to know it as a given." [122]

End quote from Dr. Lamb

The living prophets of today direct us to *experiment* for ourselves so we can come to experience these worlds by subtle interactions with the Spirit (Or what I call the *'Incomprehensible It'* that fills the immensity of space and is beyond the reach of time, even the Light of Christ), as well as by indirect evidence, as they yield the tangible evidence or fruits of love, joy, peace, and fulfillment, each being *feelings* that our spirits most definitely can and do measure. Here's a few more quotes by Dr. Lamb:

"By faith science recognizes the worlds of the atom, dark matter, and dark energy, and by *faith* religion recognizes the worlds created by God, the world of Spirits, and of light itself, etc. Neither philosophy is exempt from the need for exercising (well-informed) faith to accept the existence of the unseen. Indeed, neither could function without it." [123] Again, Dr. Lamb says, and I quote:

"Although scriptures are not scientific texts, on occasion, the scriptures refer to principles that overlap with scientific topics. These points of overlap are often the source of potential apparent conflict between science and religion and can be a *stumbling block* to those who question their authenticity as divinely inspired. Just such a passage occurs in Doctrine & Covenants, section 88. This section is especially rich with scientifically interesting allusions I referred to earlier, and want to come to it again:

Doctrine & Covenants 88:36-38, 47

36 All kingdoms have a law given.

37 And there are many kingdoms; for there is no space in the which there is no kingdom; and there is no kingdom in which there is no space, either a greater or a lesser kingdom.

38 And unto every kingdom is given a law; and unto every law there are certain bounds also and conditions. (The Laws of Physics)

47 Behold, all these are kingdoms, and any man who hath seen any or the least of these hath seen God moving in his majesty and power.

"I submit that these verses of scripture only make sense in light of scientific discoveries made long after Joseph Smith was dead and gone. In Joseph's Day, almost 200 years ago, the scientific community, along with everybody else, was quite confident that the universe described by Newton was well understood. The solar system was organized with the sun at the center; the planets circling in elliptical orbits held by universal gravity, and beyond existed a large number of stars, which were other suns, perhaps organized into one spiral galaxy.

"Between all these heavenly objects was *space*, which in turn was filled with a massless foggy material called the luminiferous 'aether' (The fifth element or quintessence, and another name for dark energy which is used to describe what fills the universe). At the other extreme, that of the very small, very little was understood at that time. They did have some idea of materials being composed of atoms, but it was being nourished in its infancy. It was assumed that the atoms filled all the spaces within the object, leaving no voids. How much of this advanced thinking had made its way into the purview of Joseph Smith, is hard to say.

"Whether Joseph was up to date with the current scientific thought of his Day remains irrelevant, because the fact is, that *scientific thinking* about space and matter has changed drastically since then, only to reveal that the passage I just quoted in the Doctrine & Covenants is amazingly in line with the science, NOT of Joseph's Day, but that of OUR Day, in the twenty-first century!"

"Speaking of space, it's estimated that our galaxy is 99.999999999999% empty space. The volume of space in the atom is 99.999999999999% empty space as well. The modern model of the structure of the atom dates to the early twentieth century, long after Josephs' Day. We've learned that atoms are not solid balls composed mostly of fluff. The vast majority of the mass of an atom is concentrated in a tiny nucleus at the center, which is surrounded by a few extremely tiny electrons that move about so fast we usually refer to them as a cloud. This tiny percentage of the universe occupied by matter itself (By atoms), is almost completely empty space.

"It turns out the universe we know is composed mostly of *nothing* (Yet it is something for sure). And that is something no one imagined in Joseph Smiths' Day. In his Day, to claim that there is no kingdom (Any physical realm of existence, be it in outer space or inner space, be it a galaxy, a planet, or an atom), in which there is no space, seemed to make no sense.

"Today, it certainly does. One could ask, "What does Joseph mean when he states that, "There is no space in which there is no kingdom?" Joseph taught that there are many things in the universe beyond what we can perceive with our natural senses. One of these things is the so-called 'Spirit of God' (My Incomprehensible IT, or the Light of Christ)." [124]

End of quotes by Dr. Lamb

Dr. Lamb goes into this topic at length in his book where he reviews what Joseph shares as his insights about the kingdoms of *spirit* and *space*. He speaks of it as spirit or *light*, and that it is a substance that proceeds forth from the presence of God to fill the immensity of space (I often wonder if it is what scientist say is Dark Matter along with its Dark Energy), as it is described in this verse of scripture:

Doctrine & Covenants 88:12

12 Which light proceedeth forth from the presence of God to fill the immensity of space.

Here's a little more of what Dr. Lamb said regarding this particular topic of light, and I quote:

"There is certainly plenty of room for *it between* the atoms and the stars, isn't there? Let me ask, "What does science now teach us about the space within and surrounding atoms and within and between galaxies? They have lots to say about it, much of it being speculative at this point. Just in the last few decades, scientists have postulated (Guessed) that a huge amount of *dark matter* and *dark energy* must exist (Dark, not black. It just means they do not know what it consists of). Scientists say that *they* are spread throughout creation at varying concentrations in various places. Whatever 'they' are, 'they' are probably around us at this very moment, even though we can't see them or feel them (Sounds like me describing spirit persons and the spirit world which are all around us, doesn't it?)."

"You see, dark matter and dark energy are *invisible* to us because they don't interact with normal matter. These things have little or no perceivable *effect* on your body (That we know of). In other words, *they would pass right through you without you even knowing it*. There is certainly plenty of empty space within your atoms to allow it, right?" [125]

End of Dr. Lamb's Quotes

Let me interject here what I would call a scientific source of evidence, Dr. Sam Parnias' work. Dr. Parnia is a Pulmonologist and Neuroscientist. I would encourage you to check out a YouTube video titled: "What is Consciousness?" by Closer to Truth and presented by Robert Kuhn, its host. Robert Kuhn, who has a doctorate in neuroscience, interviews Dr. Sam Parnia who helps patients that are close to death and some who have even died, which he then works with them by bringing them back to life, even hours after their brain has died.

I suggest that you watch the entirety of this video, but especially the last three minutes of the video, and then compare what Dr. Parnia says, to what I just quoted Dr. Lamb as saying. Dr. Parnia says that "When a patient flat-lines and the heart stops so that the brain stops as well, there's still the *conscious self* (I call it their Spirit body), that Dr. Parnias' equipment continues to show signs of its activity, sometimes for a few hours, even though the brain itself is completely shut down." [126]

End of quote by Dr. Parnia found on the YouTube Video

Let me ask you, my readers, "If the brain is what produces consciousness and not the mind, how is the patients' consciousness continuing on and being measured by Dr. Parnia, for several hours after the patient flat-lines and the brain is declared dead? Something to think about, right?" Dr. Lamb continues:

"Let me say that what we have learned about the nature of matter and space, solves a long-standing mystery about the so-called spirit world, and of spirits. Joseph Smith taught that the spirit world was not in some distant spot in the universe, but right here, around us (See also what President Brigham Young taught about the post-mortal spirit world and how it's right here on earth, all around us)." [127]

"This idea was ridiculed as completely incomprehensible with scientific knowledge. That criticism is no longer true. Not only do we know there's plenty of space for other *kingdoms* besides our own right here, but now, physicists themselves are talking about *previously unknown materials* residing right amid what is all around us (Such as Black Matter and Black or Dark Energy, etc.).

"What I'm saying is that whereas Josephs' religious claims of a spirit world being right here around and through us, previously made no sense scientifically, but now, in our Day, these claims are perfectly compatible with science, and similar claims are being made by atheist scientists themselves!" [128]

End of excerpts by Dr. Lamb

As you can see, as a member of the Church of Jesus Christ of Latter-Day Saints, I am not asked to express blind faith on such matters regarding reality and or doctrines. I am asked to exercise illuminated, well endorsed, evidence-based faith (Faith that hasn't become perfected yet), ... the same kind of well endorsed, evidenced-based faith that scientists are called to exercise when they talk about such things as atoms, electrons, quarks, dark energy, the edge of the universe, its creation, and other *unseen* things.

Scientists of today are saying that galaxies are being carried outward like passengers on the expanding space express (Describing matter and space like they're an expanding balloon. Do a search for the *Great Attractor* and check out what scientists are saying about that). Scientists are also claiming that the universe is 13.7 billion years old and that it zoomed out from a singularity the size of a pea. Georges Lemaître named this singularity explosion 'The Big Bang Theory' back in 1931." [129]

The postulation (Guess) is that if you run the expansion that we are seeing today, backward in time (a form of Reductionism), at some time in the past everything *must have* collapsed down to a point like the size of a pea with unimaginable packed energy. Scientists also are saying that space itself is imbued with a kind of 'hidden' energy that can spontaneously generate physical particles out of thin space, which then pop in and out of existence (Again, space is some kind of matter, and so this popping in and out of it is not out of non-existent thin air called *Nothing*; 'ex nihlo'; which also has matter of some kind in it). [130]

I could go on and on, but I'll just ask you, my readers, "Who are the ones that are putting forth ideas as though they were facts, yet we cannot see visible proof of them, except for the kinds of *effects* that scientists call evidence or *illuminated evidence*?" This claim about the universes birth by atheist scientists, should sound familiar because it is exactly what theists like me, have said and are mocked by atheist scientists for saying it. It's the very case we've been trying to make about faiths' *substance of things hoped for and evidence of things unseen*. C'mon man. You scientists can't have it both ways.

Before I leave my discussion on the comments made by Dr. Lamb in his book about Joseph Smith's teachings and revelations concerning scientific matters, and the many scientific concepts he taught well ahead of his time, let me just list a few of the other topics Dr. Lamb reviews in further detail in his book. I'm hopeful that this list of additional topics will motivate you to get and read his book in its entirety. If you do get his book, be sure to check out the chapter titled "Light in Science and Theology". In this chapter Dr. Lamb quotes Parley P. Pratt, the contemporary associate of Joseph Smith I quoted earlier.

Parley was one of Josephs' closest confidants. As I mentioned earlier, Parley Pratt published a book twenty years after Joseph's martyrdom, which he titled, "Key to the Science of Theology".

In this book, Elder Pratt spoke of light, spirit, and spirit matter, and even the Holy Spirit as being a substance (Kind of like spiritual *'packets'* of information being sent from a router). "This substance", Parley said, "like all others, is one of the elements of material or physical existence, and therefore subject to the necessary laws which govern all matter. Like all other elements, *'it's whole is composed of individual particles'*. Like them, each particle occupies space, possesses the power of motion, requires time to move from one part of space to another, and can in no wise occupy two spaces at once." [131]

I share this in the hope that you will read Dr. Lamb's book in its entirety, as well as Elder Pratt's book, as they both lay out a picture of how far ahead of scientific discoveries Joseph Smith's understanding and revelations were on these incredibly intriguing scientific subjects. Hopefully, you will add them as additional *illuminated, well-endorsed reference legs* to your circular stand of evidentiary reference legs that I've already given you in support of my perspective on Richard's 'God does not exist' delusion.

The following is a short list of scientific topics that Joseph Smith the Prophet taught, and that Dr. Lamb reviews in his book. I'm confident it will blow your mind in a very exciting and well-informed way. New knowledge and insights tend to do that.

Here are just some of the topics Dr. Lamb covers in his book:

- Space & Time
- Kingdoms in both Space & Time (Biological & Cosmological)
- Laws given for Space & time
- Light, Spirit & Truth
- The Laws of Nature
- Knowledge, Truth & Reason
- Cosmos & Chaos

Let me close off my discussion of Dr. Lamb's review of Joseph Smith's teachings on the scientific discoveries we have only recently come to understand, with this statement by Dr. Lamb:

"Certainly, the claim cannot be made that Joseph Smith anticipated the world of science in the recognition of this important principle [that the world is governed by natural law]. It is a source of marvel to me that Joseph should so clearly recognize and state it so clearly, especially at a time when many religious sects and philosophical creeds had chosen to assume that natural laws could be set aside easily by mystical methods that might be acquired by anyone.

"In some respects, the scientific test of the divine inspiration of Joseph Smith lies here. If ignorant and superstitious as his enemies say Joseph was, the mystical would have attracted to him greatly and he would have played for his own interest upon the superstitious fears of his followers. But, instead, he taught doctrines absolutely free from mysticism, and built a system of religion in which the invariable relation of cause and effect was and is the cornerstone." [132] End of statement by Dr. Lamb.

I would also encourage you, my readers, to check out another YouTube video that once again has Dr. Parnia sharing in greater detail, his views on this topic: "Is Life After Death Possible?", once again by Closer to Truth. In this video Dr. Sam Parnia is found discussing how *'life after the threshold of death'* has been breached by many hundreds of examples. Its host, Robert Kuhn, is once again Dr. Parnia's interviewer. After viewing this video, please consider what Dr. Lamb said in his book and compare it to what Dr. Parnia says in both videos that I've suggested you watch, and then ... I would have you consider what is said in the YouTube video titled *"LDS Perspective on Near-Death Experiences"*. I think you will find all three of these videos absolutely fascinating, as they discuss death, consciousness, spirit-matter, the spirit world, and the experiences real individuals describe from their NDE's (Near Death Experiences).

If you do read the books and watch these videos, I'm confident that you'll be able to see more clearly my Latter-Day Saint perspective on these 'Big' questions, whose answers are supposedly unknown to the world. God is truly keeping His promise to reveal such things, line upon line, precept by precept; here a little, there a little; which has always been His way as the Eternal Teacher. It's kind of the 'milk before the meat' method of teaching us, His children. In my mind, it's brilliant.

Anyway, let me get back to Richard and his delusion regarding Evolution and God's non-existence, as I compare it to what the Church of Jesus Christ of Latter-Day Saints teaches about these so-called controversial topics.

Richard Dawkins' *end-all-to-be-all* argument for each of the 'Big' questions about life and how it began, about the universe and how it began, about whether-or-not there is life after death, and if God does or does not exist, seems to be Evolution, and nothing but Evolution, and its so-called crane of Natural Selection. All that Richard has learned about Evolution combines to form his reason for disbelieving in God's existence, and so, let me share a few more points from Joseph Fielding Smith's book, "Man, His Origin and Destiny", to help me reaffirm my Introduction as the foundation for my counterarguments and very unique perspective on Richard's book, *The God Delusion*.

As I quoted earlier, President Joseph Fielding Smith mentioned that Charles Darwin, in his book "The Descent of Man", indulges in a rather difficult struggle to close the gap between the mental powers of man and those of the lower animals, by quoting Mr. Darwin who said, and I quote:

"Man bears in his bodily structure clear traces of his decent from some lower form; but it may be urged that, as man differs so greatly in his mental powers from all other animals, there must be some *error* in this conclusion."

And again, "If no organic being excepting man had possessed any mental powers, as if his powers had been of a wholly different nature from those of the lower animals, then we should never have been able to convince ourselves that our high faculties had been *gradually developed* (So I guess because we supposedly convinced ourselves of this guess, it shows that we are not as smart as we think we are?)

We must also admit that there is a much wider interval in mental power between one of the lowest fishes, as a lamprey or lancelet, and one of the higher apes, than between an ape and man; yet this interval is filled-up by numberless gradations." [133]

End of quoting Charles Darwin, and now quoting Joseph Fielding Smith once again:

"After this introduction, this honorable gentleman, who erroneously glories in the thought that he has an amoeba, or perhaps rather, the larvae of existing Ascidians, as very distant grandparents, laboriously endeavors to show that this great dividing gulf should not be considered as beyond bridging in course of time." [134]

Quoting Darwin again from his book "The Descent of Man": "These lower animals and man have certain instincts in common, even as it is". [135]

End of Darwin's quote, and continuing to quote Joseph Fielding Smith again:

"Then he discourses on these *instincts*, which are enumerated as 'sexual love', the 'love of a mother for her new-born offspring', the 'desire possessed by the latter to suck', and so forth. I ask myself, "Was this advocate of organic evolution unaware of the fact that it was written in the scriptures that the Lord created great whales, and every living creature that moveth, which the waters brought forth abundantly, after their Kind, and every winged fowl after his Kind; and God saw that it was good."

"Likewise, "He brought forth, cattle, and creeping things, and beasts of the earth after their Kind; and that all of these were commanded to multiply and fill the earth?" How could they do all of this and keep this commandment if they had *not* been endowed with these *instincts* in common with man (From their beginning)? Of course, it is natural for a mother to have love for their young, for the Lord endowed her with it; otherwise, the poor little animal would starve to death if it did not have the common instinct to seek its food. In all of this, these lower animals are faithfully performing the commandment the Lord gave them to obey.

"Then the discourse goes on to enumerate other *instincts* – and with this, I have no controversy with Darwin (or I, with Dawkins) – such as love, which the animals manifest. For all I know animals may be able to count more than four, at least they have the sense to distinguish between two, three, and a heard. I freely admit that many of them, in their wild state gather in flocks and herds, and it is possible that they have some social aim in doing so, as well as considering it a means of protection. As a member of Christ's Church on earth, I do not take the view that animals have no reason and therefore cannot think (I would have you, my readers, check out the YouTube video "Suda -The painting elephant", to consider what degree of intelligence and instinct God has given his animal creations).

"We have received divine knowledge (Revelation) that each of these possesses a spirit in the likeness of its body (Some might also say that they have consciousness, or a degree of it). Each was created spiritually before it was created naturally and given a body for living on the earth. Naturally, then, there is some measure of intelligence in members of the animal kingdom. The fact remains, however, that they received their place and their bounds by divine decree, which they cannot pass."

"I admit that many have a language, or some power of communication, whether it be the elephant, the bear, the fox, the bee, the ant, the spider, or the bat. Just remember though, that the amount or extent of their intelligence does not depend on the size of their brain. Judged by performance the lowly ant manifests greater intelligence than Mr. Darwin's highest ape. The busy bee can travel for many miles and knows where it is going and its way home. Bees are organized and live within communities and work harmoniously together, and so do ants. Some animals may have some sense of beauty, and Mr. Darwin is right in saying birds build nests without having previous instruction. The snake-like eel and the humble salmon follow the habits of their ancestors without having been taught, and this is more than man can do! The eel from the streams of England, Holland, or other places, finds its way to the deep waters of the Galapagos Sea, and back again from whence it started, if I am rightly informed. The salmon, for example, leaves the waters where it was spawned, for a life in the sea and then returns to the same stream from whence it left in its youth. It then comes home to spawn and die. Is this intelligence? Some might call it instinct. It certainly is a debatable question, isn't it? I have to give attention to the fact that all kingdoms have a law given to them:

Doctrine & Covenants 88:36-38

36 All kingdoms have a law given;

37 And there are many kingdoms; for there is no space in the which there is no kingdom; and there is no kingdom in which there is no space, either a greater or a lesser kingdom.

38 And unto every kingdom is given a law; and unto every law there are certain bounds also and conditions."

"Man, in the beginning, was given laws pertaining to his or her being temporal, as well as spiritual. So were the beasts, the fowl, the fish – all creatures were given laws and commandments, which they cannot pass. Among these laws was the measure of intelligence which each possesses, and beyond the bounds of this decree they cannot go. Therefore, the beast of the forest and the domesticated animal remains *within the bounds divinely set at the beginning*. Their measure of intelligence is fixed, and limited: *not so with man*, for he is the offspring of God and has been commanded to keep His commandments with the promise that he may become perfect (Be *perfect* means become *complete*), even as his Father in Heaven, etc.)."

Matthew 5:48

48 Be ye therefore perfect, even as your Father who is in Heaven is perfect.

"I could go on and on giving example after example of how we should marvel at the powers of the lower kingdom of animals that are greater than man's, such as the sense of smell of a bloodhound, or the radar of bats, but for me, there is nothing in these acknowledgments that in the least gives evidence of any relationship between beast and man *genealogically* speaking. The almighty has not placed the requirement or responsibility upon the animal world – beast, reptile, fowl, or fish – to bow down and worship him. He placed each in its sphere and gave it commandments commensurate with its purpose. They have been commanded to multiply, not to pray. They increase after their Kind, not pay homage, and to these commandments, they are true and faithful. These commandments, to believe in God, to obey his commandments, to pray to him in the name of Jesus Christ, have been given to men and women everywhere … throughout the world" (In every dispensation of time). When men and nations have *rebelled* against his authority and his commandments they soon perish.

"We, the human family, have been commanded to be obedient and worship him, the creator of the earth, and all things therein, and yet we find men and women, otherwise intelligent, in *open rebellion* and offering to him the greatest insult – denial of his existence (An Atheist's Delusion)."

"Men and women deny his Fatherhood, his right to command and direct his creations, and in their open *rebellion* they choose to worship an amoeba, a fish, a reptile, a cow, a baboon, even gods made of their own hands; gods of wood, stone, gold, and the arm of the flesh, and place some of them in their own personal, ancestral, or genealogical tree! Yes, I, as someone who has faith in this Supreme Being – God, the Eternal Father, whose offspring we are – am willing to concede to the animals some measure of intelligence, but it is not intelligence gained over millions of years from iterations of mutations. It is intelligence given to us from God. In fact, I am happy in my belief that they have some mental powers; that they can think, that they may even have a sense of beauty, that they may exercise the spirit of pleasure and happiness (See the recent YouTube Video called *"Two chimpanzees bath a dog| CCTV English"*, … where chimpanzees enjoy the pleasure of bathing a dog). They may become angry and remember a wrong committed against them. etc. All this, however, does not make them the offspring of God, nor does it indicate that the Almighty had nothing to do with their being in existence."

"It is too late to say anything that will do Mr. Darwin any good – he has gone where he has had the opportunity of learning of his folly (Delusion) – but to others who are inclined to follow his lead (Such as Mr. Dawkins), permit me to say that today, as just one example, we have the evidence that the Fuegians and the lower Botocudos (See YouTube Video titled "With the Indians of Tierra del Fuego") are descendants of a once white and delightsome people; an intelligent people, who had the guidance of the Lord and his holy prophets among them. But, because of their wickedness and rebellion against the Living God, they were brought to the deplorable condition we now find them in (It's called the state of Apostasy)."

"The same conditions came upon many additional peoples because Satan came among them after they had been taught faith in God and had been given his commandments. Satan and his minions told them "believe it not", and we are informed that men began from that time forth to be carnal, sensual, and devilish."

"Mr. Darwin and his disciples like Mr. Dawkins, speak glibly of the numberless gradations all ranging from amoeba, worm, or other infinitesimal forms of life, up through the apes to higher apes and then to man. They speak as though this gradation process has been proven as *settled* fact. It is not."

"These Evolutionists say that the whale, the shark, and other inhabitants of the deep, as well as all manner of life upon the land, have shown numberless gradations, to the final state in which man finds himself today. However, when challenged to show the world these gradations (intermediates), just one 'Kind' jumping over to a totally different 'Kind', they fail to do so, and so it begs the question:

"If there have been these numberless gradations, then the missing links connecting us with the amoeba or worm, all the way up to the higher apes, should be filling and walking upon the earth today with all their various stages of their new Kind. But there isn't any. There may be small mutations *within* each 'Kind' (Meaning within species of the same Kind), but never jumping over into a totally different Kind (For example, a dog over to a cat). All of them are in their finished, perfect form, just as God organized them when He said, "And it is 'good'. It's not necessary for our scientific brethren to search the deserts and the mountains and the depths of the sea, trying to find these 'links' which have *never* been produced." [136]

End of excerpts from President Joseph Fielding Smiths' book "Man, His Origin and Destiny".

Anyone who has bought into this scam of evolution and man's ascent from ape to what we are today, I would simply suggest that you invest the time it takes to watch the YouTube video called "Genesis Impact (Full Movie)". You will see why I feel comfortable in saying that most of this theory is indeed a scam, and in some cases, I am even persuaded to call it, a 'lie'. Watch the video and see if you agree or disagree with me.

In looking for the best resource to answer the question "Where does the Church of Jesus Christ of Latter-Day Saints" (and its leaders) stand on the question of 'Evolution'?", I came across an article in "The Daily Universe", an online Utah paper that took what I believe to be a very fair and balanced historical approach to answer the question "What is the Church of Jesus Christ of Latter-Day Saints official position on the subject of Evolution?"

Let me once again say, that my book is not an official book of the Church of Jesus Christ of Latter-Day Saints, nor do I represent the Church in any official way. That said, here is the article I found that offers what Rachel Keeler, it's author, felt the Church's official stance is on the theory of Evolution:

The Church and BYU: An evolution — of evolution
By Rachel Keeler - July 30, 2019

BYU and the theory of evolution haven't always coexisted peacefully. Over the course of more than a century, BYU and the teaching of evolution have developed harmony. According to the historical site 'Signature Books', in the early 1900s, President George H. Brimhall desired to transform Brigham Young Academy into a true university. Brimhall hired four intellectual and well-educated men who held either masters or doctoral degrees from the University of Chicago, Harvard, and Berkeley to bring scholarship to the new university. These intellectuals, brothers Joseph and Henry Peterson and Ralph and William Chamberlin, celebrated Darwinism, taught organic evolution, theology, and scriptural explanation.

1909 First Presidency Message

In 1909, the First Presidency of The Church of Jesus Christ of Latter-Day Saints caught wind of what these professors were teaching at BYU and released an official statement primarily on the theory of Evolution and the beliefs of the Church, called the "The Origin of Man." The statement reads, "It is held by some that Adam was not the first man upon this earth and that the original human being was a development from lower orders of the animal creation. These, however, are the theories of men. The word of the Lord declared that Adam was "the first man of all men." This message from the First Presidency was anti-evolution and anti-science. Because of this statement, many students at BYU became opposed to the teachings of organic evolution and its correlation with religion and were angry with the school.

Over the next two years, Brimhall dismissed the four professors to keep the peace at BYU. Sunstone magazine released an article "Campus in Crisis" with statements from the professors and an explanation of what occurred during that time. Intellectual Henry Peterson wrote a letter to The Provo Herald and spoke with Sunstone on how he felt hurt by the accusations that he was "destroying faith."

"Readers … don't let people tell you from the pulpit, or otherwise, that to accept evolution means to forsake your faith or deny God," said Peterson. "Evolution is the process by which God works."

1925 Scopes Trial

In 1925, science teacher John Scopes was prosecuted for teaching evolution at a public school in Tennessee, one of the many states which had recently made teaching evolution a misdemeanor. This trial, known as the Scopes Monkey Trial, sparked debate about the controversial topic of evolution and whether it should be legal to teach it.

The First Presidency again released an official statement during the time of the Scopes Trial, entitled "Mormon View of Evolution", which offered the Church's stance on evolution. This statement was a shorter, edited version of "The Origin of Man," and did not contain any anti-evolution material.

1930-31

Elder Joseph Fielding Smith, then an apostle, gave a General Conference talk in 1930 stating that there was no death before Adam and no such thing as "pre-Adamites". B.H. Roberts of the Seventy stated he believed otherwise and presented concerns. Elder Roberts was writing a book called "The Truth, The Way, The Life" that discussed religion and evolution cohesively, but the book was challenged by Joseph Fielding Smith and was not published until 1995. According to an article on the history of the Church's view on evolution, Joseph Fielding Smith and B.H. Roberts were called in to meet with the First Presidency to discuss the dispute. Joseph Fielding Smith referred back to the scriptures and the 1909 address, whereas B.H. Roberts brought scientific evidence and findings to the discussion.

The First Presidency released a statement to all General Authorities in 1931 with instruction to "leave science to the scholars'. Our mission is to bear the message of the restored Gospel to the people of the world," the statement reads. "Leave geology, biology, archaeology, and anthropology (And I will add Cosmology), none of which has to do with the salvation of the souls of mankind, to scientific research, while we magnify our calling in the realm of the Church."

Elder James E. Talmage, then an apostle, gave a speech about the progression of the earth and evolution called "The Earth and Man." This talk was not published until November 1931 because it was challenged by another member of the Quorum of the Twelve. The First Presidency decided to publish the speech in the newspaper and as a pamphlet because the Church's official stance on evolution was neutral and the only view from the quorum so far was Joseph Fielding Smith's anti-evolution talk.

The 1950s

Canadian scientist Howard Stutz was the first to teach a graduate course in 'evolutionary biology' at BYU (Richard Dawkins expertise). Stutz taught a class on cytogenetics, the study of chromosome mechanics. The topic of evolution was still controversial at the time, especially with the publishing of two heavily anti-evolution books from General Authorities; Joseph Fielding Smith's "Man, His Origin and Destiny" in 1954 and then-Seventy Elder Bruce R. McConkie's "Mormon Doctrine" in 1958. Despite this, Stutz continued to encourage those he taught that evolution and religion are intertwined.

"Not only is the concept of 'organic evolution' completely compatible with the gospel as found in the scriptures, but it is the very heart of it," said Stutz.

In 1957, President David O. McKay wrote a letter to University of Utah geology professor William Lee Stokes about evolution and said Joseph Fielding Smith's book was not authorized, nor looked over by the Church before it was published.

BYU evolutionary biology professor Duane Jeffery said, "By the end of the '50s and '60s, all of the seminary teachers and religious teachers had become very anti-science. Others who weren't had to be very quiet."

Professor Duane E. Jeffery

The 1960s

By the mid-60s things were loosening up a little bit. In 1965, the Church's magazine for Sunday School titled "The Instructor" published an article by BYU botanist Bertrand F. Harrison called "The Relatedness of Living Things" and James E. Talmage's speech "The Earth and Man."

Jeffery said, "BYU biology students were not that well regarded in the real world of science because of the lack of knowledge about evolution, which is a vital component to biology". Duane E. Jeffery was a Professor of Integrative Biology at Brigham Young University. He has published professionally in various biological journals and in matters of Mormonism and science. Duane explains in an interview his findings on the research he did about the history of the Church and evolution (Addie Blacker).

Jeffery was getting his Ph. D. in zoology under the direction of world-renowned geneticist Curt Stern when he got a call from BYU asking him to join its faculty. Jeffrey didn't want to teach at BYU because of its reputation in the science department, but he found out that BYU badly needed a geneticist. "I had no intention of coming," Jeffery said, "but the students weren't receiving a good education. BYU had graduate students teaching genetics."

Duane Jeffery holds his book "Mormonism and Evolution: the authoritative LDS statements." (Addie Blacker)

1969

When Jeffery arrived at BYU in 1969, Howard was known as an evolutionist on campus and Jeffery said it was spoken as a depreciative, "we tolerate the guy." Jeffery said he let it be known that when he came to BYU, he was going to propose a course on evolution.

"I asked, 'how would that be received?' And they said, 'like any other course. You put together the proposition, it will be considered by the committees and, if it looks well put together, it then goes to the Board of Trustees. And if they approve it, it goes,'" Jeffery said. Jeffery compiled his course and sent in the proposition, and it got approved. While still controversial, the evolutionary biology course was well-received. Jeffery said the religion faculty had a harder time with evolution being taught than the students.

Duane Jeffery began researching the Church's stance and history with evolution to better understand. In 1974, He published a paper titled "Seers, Savants, and Evolution: The Uncomfortable Interface," which reviewed and detailed articles, dates and events dealing with the Church and evolution.

1980-2014

Evolutionary biology professor William Bradshaw began teaching the reconciliation of evolution with theism in his classroom in the 1980s. Bradshaw gave the same test at the beginning and end of his course to collect data about the acceptance of this reconciliation. During this time, there would be BYU students who would go to their religion class and have their teacher strongly condemn evolution," Bradshaw said. "And then they would come to Biology 100 and be presented with the notion that evolution was true, but that it was not an enemy to their religious faith."

In 2014, evolutionary biology professor Jamie Jensen began giving a similar test to see if this acceptance to the reconciliation of religion and evolution had changed or improved over the past few decades since Bradshaw's time at BYU. Jensen found that the data has improved dramatically between the two time periods. She said students are much more accepting of evolution but that there are still a lot of students who felt as though they have to choose either science or religion. The following poster explains aspects of the controversy between religion and evolution at the July 2019 reconciling evolution conference. (Addie Blacker)

Our first and foremost goal is to keep people's testimonies," Jensen said. "I see so many students that are standing on a precipice that doesn't actually exist — where they feel like they have to ditch their faith because the science makes sense. There is no reason one would have to abandon their faith to accept the science." Jensen wanted to do something about this. Representative Sean Carroll from Howard Hughes Medical Institute talked with Jensen and said he was interested in funding the collection of data from other universities and hosting a conference to encourage discussion and collaboration between the science and religion worlds.

2016 to today

The BYU biology department invited four other religious universities to its first Reconciling Evolution Conference in October 2016 with President Kevin J. Worthen in attendance. In that same month, the Church released an article in the New Era titled "What does the Church believe about evolution?"

BYU opened an evolution exhibit in March 2019 in the Bean Life Science Museum that illustrates the process of evolution at a macro level. There is a plaque posted on the exhibit stating that it is not Church doctrine, and the Church has no (Official) stance on the issue. In July 2019, the BYU biology department hosted 18 different religious institutions from across the country to discuss the topic of evolution in relation to other religions and their institutions. This conference showed that the topic of combining evolution and religion for these other universities is also a difficult topic to discuss.

Although through the majority of the 1900's controversy existed in the Church and at BYU dealing with the subject of evolution, the Church has officially stated its neutral stance on evolution, and the BYU administration today has been supportive of the teaching of evolution.

THE EARTH & MAN by James E. Talmage

Genesis 1:1-2

12 In the beginning God created the heaven and the earth. And the earth was without form, and void; and darkness was upon the face of the deep. And the Spirit of God moved upon the face of the waters.

"Any question as to when that beginning was is largely futile because [it is] unanswerable. In the first place we have no time unit by which to measure back through the ages to the time at which, so far as the earth is concerned, time began. Years are as inadequate in any attempted survey of the stages of earth development as are miles to the astronomer who would span the distances of interstellar space. He speaks in terms of light-years, such unit being the distance traversed by a ray of light speeding on at the rate of approximately 186,000 miles per second throughout a year.

"Secondly, we are without information as to what stage of earth development is indicated by "the beginning". And what is a beginning in nature? At best it is but a new start in advance of what had passed up to that point of time; and every beginning is an ending of what went immediately before, even as every consummation is a commencement of something greater, higher, and therefore superior to the past.

The Earth Older Than Man

"To the thoughtful mind there can be no confusion of the beginning spoken of in the opening verse of genesis with the advent of man upon the changing earth; for by the scriptural record itself we learn of stage after stage, age after age of earth processes by which eventually this planet became capable of supporting life -- vegetable, animal, and human in due course. Whether or not scientists have been able to see, however dimly, the way by which the earth as an orb in space was formed, matters little except as a subject of academic interest. For many years it was very generally believed that the earth, once formless and void, passed through stages of cooling of superheated gas to liquid, thence to the solid state, as the Nebular Theory assumed; but this conception has given way to the later thought that the earth as a solid spheroid has resulted from the bringing together of particles once diffused in space this being the basis of the Planetesimal Hypothesis (A hypothesis in astronomy: the planets have evolved by aggregation from planetesimals, in terms of our Solar system. The 'BIG' BANG Hypothesis is a theory of how our Universe originated from a small singularity, and so our earth as well as ourselves are made from 'Stardust').

"But this we know, for both revealed and discovered truth, that is to say both scripture and science, so affirm -- that plant life antedated animal existence and that animals preceded man as tenets of earth (I would ask, "if the Son of God can turn water into wine in a minute or two, and, make the earth's rotation look as though it has stopped rotating for three days, and, make a mountain land on top of a valley during a three-day cataclysmic event, why not create each stage of creation in a day represented by 24 hours? I'm just asking, and not claiming. It's truly something to think about).

Life and Death Before Man's Advent

"According to the conception of geologists the earth passed through ages of preparation, to us unmeasured and immeasurable, during which countless generations of plants and animals existed in great variety and profusion (Did they ever die before the earth 'fell'?) and gave in part the very substance of their bodies to help form certain strata which are still existent as such. [This was written before the introduction of radioactive isotope dating techniques. The oldest, that is to say the earliest rocks thus far identified in land masses, reveal the fossilized remains of once living organisms, plant, and animal. The coal strata, upon which the world of industry so largely depends, are essentially but highly compressed and chemically changed vegetable substance. The whole series of chalk deposits and many of our deep-sea limestones contain the skeletal remains of animals.

These lived *and died*, age after age, while the earth was yet unfit for human habitation (But what about the Great Flood laying down all those strata as research has found the case to be today? Lived and died? Really? Also, what about the theory that this earth was once inhabited by a people and after its course of existence and resurrection the earth died, but was reorganized for us, a new group of God's children? I'm not saying this is what happened though. It's just another possibility, or dare I say guess).

From the Simple to the Complex

"From the fossil remains of plants and animals found in the rocks, the scientist points to a very definite order in the sequence of life embodiment, for the older rocks, the earlier formations, reveal to us organisms of simplest structure only, whether of plants or animals. These primitive species were aquatic; landforms were of later development. Some of these simpler forms of life have persisted until the present time, though with great variation as the result of changing environment. Geologists say that these very simple forms of plant and animal bodies were succeeded by others more complicated; and in the indestructible record of the rocks they read the story of advancing life from the simple to the more complex, from the single-celled protozoan to the highest animals, from the marine algae to the advanced types of flowering plant -- to the apple-tree, the rose, and the oak. What a fascinating story is inscribed upon the stony pages of the earth's crust!

"The geologists, who through long and patient effort has learned at least a little of the language in which these truths are written, finds the pages illustrated with pictures, which for fidelity of detail excel the best efforts of our modern engravers, lithographers, and half-tone artists. The pictures in the rocks are the originals, the rest at best but copies.

"In due course came the crowning work of this creative sequence, the advent of man! Concerning this all-important event, we are told that scientists and theologians are at hopeless and irreconcilable variance. I regard the assumption or claim, whichever it be, as an exaggeration. Discrepancies that trouble us now will diminish as our knowledge of pertinent facts is extended. The Creator has made record in the rocks for man to decipher; but He has also spoken directly regarding the main stages of progress by which the earth has been brought to be what it is. The accounts cannot be fundamentally opposed; one cannot contradict the other, though man's *interpretation* of either may be seriously at fault.

Adam a Historic Personage

"So, far as the history of man on the earth is concerned, the scriptures begin with the account of Adam. True, the geologist does not know Adam by name; but he knows and speaks of man as an early, continuing, and present form of earth-life, above and beyond all other living things past or present. We believe that Adam was a real personage, who stands at the head of his race chronologically. To my mind Adam is a historic personage, not a prehistoric being, unidentified and uncertain.

"If the Usher chronology be correct, or even approximately so, then the beginning of Adamic history as recorded in scripture dates back about 4,000 years before the birth of Christ. We as a Church believe that the current reckoning of time from the birth of Christ to the present is correct, namely 2022 years (As of the date of this statement) -- not from last New Year's-day January 1, ... but from the month that came to be known among the Hebrews as Nisan or Ahib, corresponding with our late March and early April. So, we believe that we are now living in the 2022nd year since the birth of Christ, and therefore 6022 years since the beginning of the Adamic record.

"This record of Adam and his posterity is the only scriptural account we have of the appearance of man upon the earth. But we have also a vast and ever-increasing volume of knowledge concerning man, his early habits and customs, his industries and works of art, his tools and implements, about which such scriptures as we have thus far received are entirely silent. Let us not try to wrest the scriptures in an attempt to explain away what we cannot explain.

"The opening chapters of Genesis, and scriptures related thereto, were never intended as a textbook of geology, archaeology, earth science or man science. Holy Scripture will endure, while the conceptions of men change with new discoveries. We do not show reverence for the scriptures when we misapply them through faulty interpretation.

Primary and Secondary Causes

"There has been much discussion over the alleged conflict between the teachings of science and the doctrines of the revealed word concerning the origin of man. Let it be remembered that the term origin is almost invariably used in a relative sense. The mind of man is unable to grasp the fundamental thought of an absolute or primary origin. Every occurrence man has witnessed is the result of some previously acting cause or purpose; and that cause in turn was the effect or result of causes yet more remote, thus a causal chain. Perhaps we have never been able to trace an effect to its primary or original cause. Man may say that he understands the origin of an oak in the acorn form from which it sprang; but is not the acorn the fruit of a yet earlier oak?

"So, in reality, rather a continuation than a beginning? Yet there is something fascinating in the thought of a beginning, the persistence of a process once started is far less mysterious than its inception. It is not enough to refer effects to the First Great Cause; it is unsatisfying and not always reverent to answer questions as to how things came to be what they are by the easy statement that God made them so. With such an answer the scientific man has little patience (Richard Dawkins being such a man). The fact that all created things are the works of God and that all processes of nature are due to Him as the administrator of law and order is to the scientific mind an axiom requiring neither argument nor demonstration. The botanist knows that God makes the plant grow; but he, weak mortal, is devoting time and energy of body, mind, and spirit, to a study of the way in which God works such a marvelous miracle.

"The geologist knows that God created the earth; but the best effort of his life is put forth in the hope of finding out in some degree, however small, the method by which the Creator wrought this wondrous world. The astronomer gazing into the starry depths sees in their orderly procession the Lord Eternal walking in His majesty and might; and in humility the student of the heavenly bodies spends days and nights striving to learn a little of the way in which God worked out the marvel of the universe. In proportion as any one of these may learn of the ways of God, he becomes wise. To be able to think as God thinks, to comprehend in any degree His purposes and methods, is to become in that measure like unto Him, and to that extent to be prepared for eventual companionship in His presence.

"The scientist is busily engaged in the study of secondary causes -- the ways and means by which God works and through which He accomplishes His miracle, ever beginning, never ending. In his search for the truth the student of science scarcely dares lift his eyes to look toward the First Great Cause, the Eternal Power that stands and operates behind and above all the secondary causes, or what we call the processes of Nature.

The Origin of Man

"The question involved in the origin of man, therefore, is not raised as a challenge to the belief and declaration that he came to earth through Divine direction, but it is in the nature of an inquiry as to 'the conditions under which he came. There are many who claim that man's advent upon the earth was 'effected' through processes of evolution from lower forms, processes that had been operative for ages, processes by which man is made kin to the brute and a development from the lowest type of organism. Others affirm that he differs from all mortal creatures of lower rank, not only in degree but in kind; in short, that he is not one with the animal creation and that therefore his coming was in no sense a natural and necessary result of earlier animal life.

"Discussion on this question has developed intense animus, and too often the quest for truth has been lost sight of in the strife for triumph. In speaking of the origin of man we generally have reference to the creation of man's body; and, of all the mistakes that man has made concerning himself, one of the greatest and the gravest is that of mistaking the body for the man.

"The body is no more truly the whole man than is the coat the body. The man, as an individual intelligence, existed before his earthly body was framed and shall exist after that body has suffered dissolution. Let it not be assumed that belief in the existence of man's spirit is a conception founded upon scriptural authority only; on the contrary, let it be known that it is in accordance with the best and most advanced scientific thought and philosophic belief of the day to hold that man consists of spirit and body; and Divine revelation makes plain that these together constitute the soul.

"We have difficulty in comprehending processes for which we find no analogy in things familiar. Even were it possible for us to know in detail the way in which the body of man was formed and then endowed with the power of procreation, ensuring the perpetuity of the race, it would throw but little light upon the subject of the ultimate origin of man. We know but little of things beyond the sphere upon which we live except as information has been revealed by a power superior to that of earth, and by an intelligence above that of man.

"Notwithstanding the assumption that man is the culmination of an evolutionary development from a lower order of beings, we know that the body of man today is in the very form and fashion of his spirit, except indeed for disfigurements and deformities. The perfect body is the counterpart of the perfect spirit and the two are the constituent entities of the soul.

By What Standard?

"Much depends upon the standard by which we judge as to whether any particular organism shall be pronounced of high or lower rank. By the standard of powers of flight, in which the bird excels, man is a very inferior being; if judged by fleetness of foot he is far below the deer; by gage [gauge] of strength he is inferior to the horse and the elephant; and yet man holds dominion over these and all other living things of earth. In certain important points of body-structure man stands low in the scale if he be graded strictly in accordance with the accepted standard of mammalian anatomy. In the course of creative events the earth came to a condition fitted for the abiding place of the sons and daughters of God; and then Adam came forth upon the earth. But the beginning of man's mortal existence upon the earth was not the beginning of man; he had lived before, even as he shall life after the earth has passed away and its place taken by a new earth and a new heaven.

Man, and the Ape

"It has been stated by certain extremists that evolution affirms that man is in the line of posterity from the ape. But scientists today discredit this view. The most that even radical evolutionists assert is that the similarity of structure between man and certain apes indicates the possibility of a common ancestor of the two, but between man and the ape there are more essential differences than resemblances. True, man does not excel in strength of limb, agility, or speed, but in the God-given powers of mind and in the possession of superior ambition and effort. Hear the words of one who until his death was regarded as among the foremost of American geologists, James D. Dana:

"Man's origin has thus far no sufficient explanation from science. His close relations in structure to the man-apes are unquestionable. They have the same number of bones, with two exceptions, and the bones are the same in kind and structure.

"The muscles are mostly the same. Both carry their young in their arms. The affiliations strongly suggest community of descent. But the divergencies especially the cases of degeneracy in man's structure, exhibited in his palpigrade feet and the primitive character of his teeth, allying him in these respects to the Lower Eocene forms, are admitted proof that he has not descended from any type of ape. In addition, man's erect posture makes the gap a very broad one.

"The brute, the ape included, has powerful muscles in the back of the neck to carry the head in its horizontal position, while man has no such muscles, as anyone of the species can prove by crawling for a while on 'all fours.' Beyond this, the great size of the brain, his eminent intellectual and moral qualities, his voice, and speech, give him sole title to the position at the head of the kingdoms of life. In this high position, he is able to use Nature as his workmate, his companion, and his educator, and to find perpetual delight in her harmonies and her revelations. Whatever the results of further search, we may feel assured, in accord with Wallace, who shares with Darwin in the authorship of the theory of 'Natural Selection', that the intervention of a Power above nature as at the basis of man's development.

"Believing that Nature exists through the will and ever-acting power of the Divine Being, and that all its great truths, its beauties, its harmonies, are manifestations of His wisdom and power, or, in the words nearly of Wallace, that the whole universe is not merely dependent on, but actually is, the will of one Supreme Intelligence. Nature, with man as its culminant species, is no longer a mystery" (James D. Dana, Manual of Geology, 4th edition, page 1036, around the year 1871). These lines were written before the death of the writer in 1895 -- and constitute his last testament and testimony as to the origin of the species to which he himself belonged.

Man's Place in Nature

In the work already cited, the same author wrote:

"Man stands in the successional line of the quadrumana, at the head of the animal kingdom. But he is not a primate among primates. The quadrumana are, as Cuvier called them, quadrumana from the first to the last. They are brute mammals, as is manifested in their carnivore-like canines and their powerful jaws; in their powerful muscular development; in their walking on all fours, and the adaption thereto exhibited in the vertebrae, producing the convexity of the back; and also, in other parts of the skeleton. Man, on the contrary, is not quadrumanes.

"Man was the first being, in the geological succession, capable of an intelligent survey of Nature and a comprehension of her laws; the first capable of augmenting his strength by bending nature to his service, rendering thereby a weak body stronger than all possible animal force; the first capable of deriving happiness from truth and goodness; of apprehending eternal right; of reaching toward a knowledge of self and God; the first, therefore, capable of conscious obedience or disobedience of a moral law, and the first subject to debasement of his moral nature through his appetites."

"There is in man, therefore, a spiritual element in which the brute has no share. His power of indefinite progress, his thoughts and desires that look onward even beyond time, his recognition of spiritual existence and of a Divinity above, all evince a nature that partakes of the infinite and divine. Man is linked to the past through the system of life, of which he is the last, the completing, creation. But, unlike other species of that closing system of the past, he, through his spiritual nature, is more intimately connected with the opening future." -- Dana, pages 1017-18.

A Later Authority

"Let me cite a later authority than Dana. Among the living no anthropologist has been more pronounced in upholding the theories of Darwin and Lamarck than Dr. Henry Fairfield Osborn. By the theories mentioned, man was said to have risen from tree-climbing ape-like ancestors. In his address as retiring president of the American Association for the Advancement of Science, December 1929, Dr. Osborn affirms the untenability of the views he had so long and aggressively advocated. He regards the human bones unearthed at Piltdown, Sussex, England, as typical of the "Dawn Man," who was in every distinguishing characteristic, a man, not part man and part ape, but as to brain capacity and other evidence of mentality equal to some races now living. Yet Osborn holds to a communal origin of man and anthropoids related in structure, away back in the late Tertiary age of geologic history. [In the 1965 Instructor version, a footnote points out that more recent analysis of the Piltdown Man skull has revealed that it is not an authentic specimen -- it had been "planted" evidently as a hoax.]

"Thus, theories come, endure for a season, and go, like the fungi of the night; nevertheless, they serve their purpose as temporary aids in human thought and endeavor.

The Time Element

"The outstanding point of difference between those who take the opening chapters of Genesis and cognate scriptures as the whole and only reliable record of the creation of earth and man, and the students of earth-science who fail to find an adequate record in scripture, is the point of time during which man in 'some' state has lived on the planet. Geologists and anthropologists say that if the beginning of Adamic history dates back but 6,000 years or less, there must have been races of human sort upon earth long before that time -- without denying, however, that Adamic history may be correct, if it be regarded solely as the history of the Adamic race. This view postulates by application of Dana's affirmation already quoted:

"That the intervention of a power above Nature" brought about the placing of, let me say, Adam upon earth. It is but fair to say that no reconciliation of these opposing conceptions has been 'effected' to the satisfaction of both parties. We have not yet learned how to correlate geologic time-periods with terms of years, except as estimates, for which no absolutely dependable foundation may be found."

Nobility of Adam's Race

"I do not regard Adam as related to -- certainly not as descended from -- the Neanderthal, the Cro-Magnon, the Peking, or the Piltdown man. Adam came as divinely directed, created, and empowered, and stands as the patriarchal head of his posterity -- a posterity, who, if true to the laws of God, are heirs to the Priesthood and to the glories of eternal lives. Were it true that man is a product of evolution from lower forms, it is but reasonable to believe that he will yet develop into something higher (In other words, to stay true to the principle of evolution, it is only natural for him to continue his evolution. If not this, then how does the process of evolution know when perfection has arrived so that it stops?).

"While it is a fact that eternal progression is a characteristic of man's Divine birthright, as yet we have learned nothing to indicate that man shall develop physically into any other form than that in which he now appears. Many attempts have been made by those who regard man as an animal, to frame some definition by which he may be distinctively described among his fellow animals; ... but of such attempts none have been satisfactorily successful. The difficulty lies in the fact already stated, that man differs from the animal creation not only in degree but in kind; he is the only being who has any conception of a preexistent state or an existence beyond the grave; the only being whose thoughts turn toward God and who feels in his soul the inspiring impulses of kinship to Deity. Believe not those who would make man but little above the brutes, when in truth he is but little below the angels, and if faithful shall pass by the angels and take his place among the exalted sons of God. The spirit of man is the offspring of the Eternal Father, and his body, if unmarred, is in the very form and fashion of that spirit.

The Ante-Mortal State

"We have been told that Jesus Christ is in very truth, our elder brother, and as to His preexistence in the spirit state there is little room for question. That His spirit was in the form of the earthly body which He afterward took, and which body was slain, buried, and resurrected, and with which body He ascended into heaven, is attested by scripture. Going back to the time immediately following the dispersion from Babel, we read of a prophet to whom the unembodied Lord revealed Himself, saying:

Ether 3:16

16 Behold, this body, which ye now behold, is the body of my spirit; and man have I created after the body of my spirit; … and even as I appear unto thee to be in the spirit … will I appear unto my people in the flesh.

"It is evident from this scripture that in His preexistent state, which is to say, in the state in which He existed prior to His earthly birth, Jesus Christ had the same form and stature that He afterward presented in the flesh. By natural processes (The process of pregnancy development) His spirit shaped for itself a body from the material of earth, which body underwent a course of graded development until it reached maturity, in which state that body was the counterpart to the spirit whose material tabernacle it was.

"As with Jesus, so with all the 'sons and daughters' of God; each had a spiritual existence before he entered upon this stage of mortal existence, and in each case the body is formed and fashioned by the power of the immortal spirit. In this process of body-shaping, the spirit may be hindered, hampered, and interfered with, through influences of heredity, through prenatal defects, or through accident and disease. As to how were formed the bodies of the first human beings to take tabernacles, the revealed word gives no details while science has practically nothing to offer by way of explanation. As Dana so positively declares in the work already cited "Man's origin has thus far no sufficient explanation from science."

"Man's mortal existence is but temporary to this earth; he came hither from another realm, in which he lived in an unembodied state and to which, in the natural order, he shall return in a disembodied state, following the change known as death. After the Body of the first man had been made ready through the direct operation of the creative power, the spirit of man entered that body. Note the sublimity of the scriptural declaration:

Genesis 2:7

7 And the Lord God formed man of the dust of the ground and breathed into his nostrils the breath of life; and man became a living soul.

A Power Above Nature

"In the study of all the created things over which he has dominion, man has found it possible to investigate with some degree of success the secondary causes, or natural processes through which the creative power has operated to bring about the system that we designate as nature; but in the study of his own eternal self he is brought at once to the contemplation of the First Great Cause as to his origin. The power that lies at the basis of man's development is "a Power above Nature."

"That is to say, man, as a mortal being, exists as the result of a special and particular creation. Through graded stages the earth was brought into a state suited to the support of life. In orderly sequence plants and animals appeared; and when at last the world was prepared for its royal ruler, he came, even as had been declared:

"And God said, let us make man in our image, after our likeness; and let them have dominion over the fish of the sea, and over the fowl of the air, and over the cattle, and over all the earth, and over every creeping thing that creepeth upon the earth;

Genesis 1:26-28

26 And God said, Let us make man in our image, after our likeness: and let them have dominion over the fish of the sea, and over the fowl of the air, and over the cattle, and over all the earth, and over every creeping thing that creepeth upon the earth.

27 So God created man in his own image, in the image of God created he him; male and female created he them.

28 And God blessed them, and God said unto them, Be fruitful, and multiply, and replentish the earth, and subdue it: and have dominion over the fish of the sea, and over the fowl of the air, and over every living thing that moveth upon the earth.

"Such is the declaration of scripture regarding Adam's advent upon earth; and such is a fair summary of our knowledge upon the subject.

Evolution, True and False

"Evolution is true so far as it means development, and progress, and advancement in all the works of God. But many of the vagaries that have been made to do duty under that name are so vague as to be unacceptable to the scientific mind. At best, the conception of the development of man's body from the lower forms through evolutionary processes has been but a theory, an unproved hypothesis. Theories may be regarded as the scaffolding upon which the builder stands while placing the blocks of truth in position. It is a grave error to mistake the scaffolding for the wall, the flimsy and temporary structure for the stable and permanent (We'll discuss this scaffolding later in my book). The scaffolding serves but a passing purpose, important though it be, and is removed as soon as the walls of that part of the edifice of knowledge have been constructed.

"Theories have their purpose and are indispensable, but they must never be mistaken for demonstrated facts. The Holy Scriptures should not be discredited by theories of men; they cannot be discredited by fact and truth. Within the Gospel of Jesus Christ there is room and place for every truth thus far learned by man or yet to be made known. The Gospel is not behind the times. On the contrary it is up-to-date and ever shall be. It is natural for the young and immature mind to think that what to it is new must of necessity be new to the world. Comparatively inexperienced students are discovering from time-to-time apparent discrepancies between the faith of their fathers and the development of modern thought; and these they are apt to magnify and exaggerate, when as a matter of fact, their great-grandfathers met the same seeming difficulties and yet survived. Believe not those who assert that the Gospel of Jesus Christ is in any way opposed to progress or inconsistent with advancement.

In the Lineage of Deity

"Man is the child of God, he is born heir to boundless possibilities, the inheritor of the eternities to come. Among mortal beings, the law holds true that the posterity of each shall be after his kind. The child therefore may become like unto the parent; and man may yet attain the rank of godship. He is born in the lineage of Deity, not in the posterity of the brute creation. I cite my words of an earlier day, with a quotation [neither the pamphlet nor the 'Instructor copy' give the citation].

Man's Relative Littleness

"The insignificance of man in comparison with the earth on which he dwells, and even with the limited topographical features of his world, has oft times been dwelt upon. Draw to scale a towering mountain and a man standing at its base or on its summit what does the man amount to? But then the earth as a planet is small compared with some others of its own system, to say nothing of the relative sizes of earth and sun. In turn, our entire solar system, in the measurement of which miles cease to have meaning -- so vast it is -- ranks low in dimensions as we gage [gauge] it with other families of worlds in the great galaxy of stars to which it belongs, and that immeasurable galaxy is but one among many, and not the greatest of them all.

Dream Vision of the Infinite

"This hour is not well suited to the presentation of mathematical data relating to the extent of the universe; though it may permit us to indulge the contemplation of thought-pictures, bewildering though that indulgence may be. John Paul Richter's 'Dream Vision of the Infinite' has been brought to English readers through several renditions; and I ask you to follow or accompany me through one of these, generally worded along the lines of the version given us by Thomas DeQuincey:

"God called up from dreams a man into the vestibule of heaven, saying 'Come thou hither and I will show thee the glories of my house.' And to the servants that stood around the throne he said, 'Take the man and strip from him his robes of flesh; cleanse his vision and put a new breath into his nostrils; only touch not with any change his human heart -- the heart that fears and trembles'. It was done; and, with a mighty angel for his guide, the man stood ready for his infinite voyage. Then, from the terraces of heaven, without sound or farewell, they wheeled away into endless space. Sometimes, with solemn flight of angel wing, they fled through Zaarrahs of darkness, through wildernesses of death that divided the worlds of life.

Sometimes they swept over frontiers that were quickening under prophetic motions from God. Then, from a distance that is counted only in heaven, light dawned for a time through a sleepy film. By unutterable pace, the light swept to them, they by unutterable pace to the light. In a moment, the rushing of planets was upon them; in a moment, the blazing of suns was around them.

"Then came eternities of twilight, that revealed, but were not revealed. To the right hand and the left towered mighty constellations, that by self-repetitions and answers from afar, that by counter-positions, built up triumphal gates, whose architraves, whose archways -- horizontal, upright -- rested, rose -- at altitudes, by spans -- that seemed ghostly from infinitude. Without measure were the architraves, past number were the archways, beyond memory the gates! Within were stairs that scaled the eternities above, that descended to the eternities below; above was below, below was above to the man stripped of gravitating body. Depth was swallowed up in height insurmountable; height was swallowed up in depth unfathomable. Suddenly, as thus they rode from infinite to infinite, suddenly as thus they tilted over abysmal worlds, a mighty cry arose -- that systems more mysterious, that worlds more billowy, other heights and other depths were coming, were nearing, were at hand!

"Then the man sighed and stopped, shuddered and wept. His overladen heart uttered itself in tears; and he said, 'Angel, I will go no further; for the spirit of man aches with this infinity. Insufferable is the glory of God. Let me lie down in the grave and hide myself from the persecutions of the infinite; for end, I see, there is none!' And from all the listening stars that shone around issued a choral chant, 'The man speaks truly; end is there none that ever yet we heard of.' 'End is there none?' the angel solemnly demanded. 'Is there, indeed, no end? And is this the sorrow that kills you? Then the angel threw up his glorious hands to the heaven of heavens, saying 'End is there none to the universe of God! Lo, also, there is no beginning!'"

The Spiritual Grandeur of Man

"What is man in this boundless setting of sublime splendor? I answer you: Potentially now, actually to be, he is greater and grander, more precious according to the celestial arithmetic of God, than all the planets and suns of space. For him were they created; they are the handiwork of God; man is His son! In this world man is given dominion over a few things; it is his privilege to achieve supremacy over many things. The psalmist David declared:

Psalms 19:1

1 The heavens declare the glory of God; and the firmament showeth His handiwork.

"Incomprehensibly grand as are the physical creations of the earth and space, they have been brought into existence as means to an end, necessary to the realization of the supreme purpose, which in the words of the Creator is thus declared (Pearl of Great Price, page 4):

"For behold, this is my work and my glory -- to bring to pass the immortality and eternal life of man."

"It is decreed that this earth shall become a celestialized, glorified sphere; such is the revealed word. Science has nothing to say on the matter; it can neither refute nor prove. But the Lord, even God, hath spoken — "and so shall it be! Amen". (James E. Talmage, "The Earth and Man" *The Instructor*, vol. 100, no. 12, Dec. 1965; and vol. 101, no. 1, Jan. 1966; [Address Delivered in the Tabernacle, Salt Lake City, Utah, Sunday, August 9, 1931.]

End of James Talmage Excerpts

What does the Church believe about evolution?

"The Church has no official position on the theory of evolution. Organic evolution, or 'changes to species' inherited traits over time, is a matter for scientific study (I would say 'changes over to different 'Kinds' has not happened). Nothing has been revealed concerning evolution. Though the details of what happened on earth *before* Adam and Eve, including how their bodies were created, have not been revealed, our teachings regarding man's origin are clear and come from revelation.

"Before we were born on earth, we were spirit children of heavenly parents, with bodies in their image. God directed the creation of Adam and Eve and placed their spirits in their bodies. We are all descendants of Adam and Eve, our first parents, who were created in God's image.

"There were no spirit children of Heavenly Father on the earth before Adam and Eve were created. In addition, "for *a time* they lived alone in a paradisiacal setting where there was neither human death nor future family." They fell from that state, and this Fall was an essential part of Heavenly Father's plan for us to become like Him (www.churchofjesuschrist.org – Elder Jeffrey R. Holland of the Quorum of the Twelve Apostles, "Where Justice, Love, and Mercy Meet," Apr. 2015 General Conference).

"For further reference, see "The Origin of Man," Improvement Era, Nov. 1909, 78; Ensign, Feb. 2002, 29. See also "Encyclopedia of Mormonism", 5 vols. (1992), "Evolution," 2:478.

"In the evolution debate, difficulties have arisen when readers assume that statements by certain leaders represent an official position beyond that expressed by the First Presidency as a body.

"As expressed by David H. Bailey, a researcher at Lawrence Berkeley Laboratory and author of numerous articles on the relationship between 'Mormonism and Science', *The Church of Jesus Christ of Latte5r-Day Saints has a great scientific tradition, including notable, respected researchers in virtually every field of modern science. Indeed, our motto is "The glory of God is intelligence."*

Why not just acknowledge that science and religion address two very different sets of questions, and that the methodology in one arena cannot settle controversies in the other? Harold B. Lee's plea may be the wisest stance, and I quote:

"Perhaps if we had the full story of the creation of the earth and man, told to us in great detail, it would be more of a mystery than the simple few statements that we have contained in the Bible, because of our lack of ability to comprehend. Therefore, for reasons best known to the Lord, He has kept us in darkness. Wait until the Lord speaks or wait until that day when He shall come (At the beginning of the millennium), and when we shall be among the privileged, either to come up out of our graves and be caught up into the clouds of heaven or shall be living upon the earth likewise to be so translated before Him. Then we shall know all things pertaining to this earth, how it was made, and all things that now as children we are groping for and trying to understand. Let's reserve judgment as to the facts concerning the Creation until we know these things for sure."

End Quote

The Church's response: Official statements regarding organic evolution:

- First Presidency letter, "The Origin of Man" (November 1909) This was reprinted in 2002 ("The Origin of Man," Ensign, Feb 2002, 26)
- First Presidency statement, "Words in Season" (December 1910)
- First Presidency letter, "'Mormon' View of Evolution" (September 1925)

Despite the fact that the Church has no official position on Evolution beyond those expressed by the First Presidency (See above), some general authorities and lay members still have considered evolution to be at variance with scriptural teaching. This view is well summarized by Elder Bruce R. McConkie's statement, quote:

"There is no harmony between the truths of revealed religion and the theories of organic evolution."

End Quote

"Other authors, including Joseph Fielding Smith, held similar views. Other Church authorities and members have seen much of value in evolutionary theory, even if they have not endorsed every aspect of it. Examples include James E. Talmage, John A. Widtsoe, and LDS chemist Henry Eyring. Gordon B. Hinckley (Served as President of the Church of Jesus Christ of Latter-Day Saints from March 1995 until his death in January 2008) stated, and I quote:

"What the church requires is only belief 'that Adam was the first man of what we would call the 'human race'." Scientists can speculate on the rest." [137]

End of The Church of Jesus Christ of Latter-Day Saints' official view on the Theory of Evolution

Let me add one more source regarding Evolution – Stephen Meyer, a well-known American author and former educator, an advocate of 'Intelligent Design' (Some call it a pseudoscientific creationist argument for the existence of God), which Stephen claims is an "evidence-based scientific theory". Richard Dawkins sees 'Intelligent Design' as being Quasi-Scientific. Stephen recently did a video called *"Evolution: Bacteria to Beethoven"* (You can find it on YouTube by searching for *"Evolution: Bacteria to Beethoven"*), in which Stephen posited the following question:

"Are there no scientific reasons to doubt the evolutionary account of life's origins?"

To answer this, Stephen mentions a scientific conference he attended in London in November 2016, whose purpose was to address the growing doubts about the modern version of Darwin's theory. He then focuses on *two of these specific reasons* (Keep in mind that there were more than just these two reasons for doubting this theory: (1) The Cambrian Explosion, and (2) what he calls the DNA Enigma).

Let's look at each of the pieces in the above paragraph. In context, it's useful to know a little about Dr. Meyer himself. Wikipedia describes him as an "advocate of the pseudoscientific principle of Intelligent Design (Like I said, an atheist contributed description I'm sure)." He is not an evolutionary biologist like Richard Dawkins is. Stephen received his Ph.D. from Cambridge in the History and Philosophy of Science.

Dr. Meyer's background immediately makes it clear his position is not one of pure unbiased scientific inquiry (I ask, "What theist scientist is?). In the video "*Evolution: Bacteria to Beethoven*" he is speaking from the point of view of someone who believes in Intelligent Design, which attempts to discredit current evolutionary theory to make room for the creation of life via some God-like Intelligent Designer.

The conference Dr. Meyer attended in London was called "New trends in evolutionary biology: biological, philosophical and social science perspectives", and it was put on by the Royal Society. From the name and the list of talks, it seems the purpose of the conference was to look at current work in evolutionary biology from a variety of points of view. It does suggest that the current view of evolutionary biology (Richard's expertise and lane of study), Neo-Darwinism, a blend of Darwin's original natural selection idea with Mendelian genetics, may need updating.

Moving on to the Cambrian Explosion, Stephens' first example of a reason to doubt Darwin's Evolution Theory, the two important things to know about it are that it lasted at least 10 million years, probably tens of millions of years longer, and most of the major animal phyla appeared during that time. The amount of time cited by Dr. Meyer in the video is 10 million years, and it is the amount of time one would likely select if you intended to discredit evolutionary theory because you don't want to give life any extra time to develop on its own. Is 10 million years sufficient to produce the explosion of life seen during this period? The answer is yes. Multiple references for this can easily be found.

Finally, let's look at the DNA Enigma, the second reason Dr. Meyer puts forth as a reason to doubt Darwin's Theory of Evolution. The most important thing to notice right away is that this is simply not a scientific phrase. "The DNA Enigma" is a phrase used by Dr. Meyer and the Intelligent Design community. Therefore, it seems unlikely that this idea even came up at a Royal Society conference talk.

So, what is the DNA Enigma? To put it simply, it has to do with the origin of life, how the first cell came to be, and how the functionally specified information in DNA arose. The fact is Charles Darwin's theory had nothing to do with the origin of life. It discusses only how life changed *after* life first came to be. Therefore, as best I can tell, the DNA Enigma is simply irrelevant when discussing evolution.

"In summary, even though this video is one man's attempt to discredit current evolutionary theory, it does open up the possibility of Intelligent Design being a true postulate. The idea of a DNA Enigma is introduced, although this has to do with the origin of life and not evolution. Contrary to the video, the rapid appearance of phyla that appeared during this period is perfectly consistent with current evolutionary theory. You will learn no biology from this video, but you may learn how people attempt to discredit evolution." [138]

As you can tell by the evidence and commentary I've given in my Introduction thus far, I'm a firm believer in God's existence, and as such I'm an active, confident, yet humble disciple of Jesus Christ. My perspective is supported by several kinds *of evidence*, each piece of evidence, or what I am calling reference legs, falls into one or all of the following categories:

- Direct and Indirect evidence …
- Circumstantial evidence …
- Physical evidence …
- Individual physical evidence …
- Class physical evidence …
- Forensic evidence …
- Trace evidence …
- Testimonial evidence …
- Historical and or Origin evidence …

When all these kinds of evidence are combined, they form the foundation for my personal Latter-Day Saint perspective on Dawkins' book *The God Delusion*. I believe all the evidence fits neatly together as a strong rebuttal to the arguments made by Richard and his ilk that claim God does not exist. All the evidence I *have* provided so far, and all that I will yet provide as we move forward and dissect Richard's book, will form an immoveable circular stand of reference legs upon which your 'table of belief' can comfortably rest. This stand will be made up of a multiplicity of *reference legs of evidence*. Each leg will move your *belief cursor* along the *percentage of probability spectrum* until it's well past the 51% marker and will ultimately close in on the 'God Exists' 100% marker.

Let me make one last point before we launch into Chapter 1. Astute scientists will almost never state that *science can prove anything without a doubt*, and that's because they understand the limitations of what experimental science or what's called operational science can show. This is why Richard focusses on *percentage of probability* rather than absolute proof. There's a powerful YouTube video titled, "Why Scientists Cannot Disprove the Bible". I suggest you watch it in its entirety. In this video Patricia Englar, a science graduate states: "One of the first things I learned in my science classes was never to write *prove* on a lab report, even if we read words like that in the media." Jane Reece, another science graduate quoted the following statement she found in her science textbook: "We can never prove that a hypothesis is true. Testing a hypothesis in different ways with different sorts of data can increase our confidence in it tremendously (Or strongly suggest that it is incorrect), but no amount of experimental testing can *prove a hypothesis beyond a shadow of a doubt* (Quote found in the Campbell Biology Ed. Don Mills Pearson, Education 2014 textbook)."

Besides Experimental or Operation Science, there is what's called Historical Science, which is sometimes referred to as Origin Science. It is the science of finding out about past events that can't be repeated over and over again like experimental or operational science can be. The fact is, scientists were not there when past events took place, and so they can't observe them anew. This kind of origin, or historical science, cannot recreate or repeat the actual event with 100% accuracy. An example of this kind of Historical Science is called Forensic Science. Forensic scientists cannot recreate a crime exactly like it happened, and so they have to *interpret the facts* that they do have and determine, *as best they can*, what story they tell.

In this same 'Answers to Genesis' video, Dr. Gabriel Weston, a member of the Royal College of Surgeons, described the difference between Origin and Historical science in this way: "Dr. Shepherd's crime case reminds us that there are two kinds of forensic science. Some is definitely forensic science (Soil analysis, murder scene, objects, etc.), but some, like Paul Kirk's investigation, is really about *opinion and interpretation*, and without proper safeguards it can" *barrow the authority" of science and disguise these opinions and hard scientific facts.* Machines and chemical analysis don't interpret facts; people do, and people can get it wrong."

What I'm saying is that Forensic, Historical, and Origin science cannot corroborate its interpretation with 100% accuracy. Period! These kinds of science are not the same kind of science that can conclude what temperature water boils at, i.e., 100°C; or what the chemical composition of water is, i.e., H_2O; or what the triple point temperature of water is, 0.1-degree Celsius. These scientific conclusions can be discovered with repeatable, observable, scientific experiments and their conclusions are never observed differently.

This is not the case with Historical or Origin science. They're the kinds of science that require men and women to give their *best guesses and interpretations*, which, as Dr. Shepherd said, can in fact be wrong. We've all experienced watching a crime show to its conclusion only to find out later that the forensic evidence that was first presented as proof that the accused killer was guilty, is now wrong due to a new piece of evidence that changes the interpretation of the entire body of evidence. This one piece of evidence helps prove the accused killer is now innocent. The scientists were forced to adjust their *interpretation* of the facts, and what happened.

My perspective regarding the topic of the ultimate origin of the universe and those facts we observe in our present world, is that *they can be observed and interpreted in different ways*, and that's because no person can actually observe how life itself began or how the universe came to be. There are basically two conflicting *interpretations* of the available data; two different stories as to *how* these things came to be – one being that God organized the universe out of chaotic matter, and the other being the result of naturalistic evolutionary forces operating over millions of years, *"once there was life"*.

It's called Organic Evolution. The conflict lies in the *different interpretation* of the Historic or Origin scientific data, and not the data itself. We cannot repeat what took place millions and millions of years ago, nor can we go back in time and observe our origin (Not even with the James Webb Telescope), and so that leaves us with the two differing, *conflicting interpretations* of the known data surrounding our universe's origin – the atheist interpretation of the data and the theist interpretation of the data. *The conflict lies in how each side of the debate has decided to interpret the Historic or Origin facts and data, and the story each interpretation describes.*

Let me give an example. When we observe soft tissue that exists in dinosaur bones, an undisputed fact in the scientific community, there are those who maintain that this discovery supports biblical history because it shows that these animals did not die millions of years ago, otherwise this tissue would have permineralized. Another example of conflicting facts and their interpretation is that of trees extending up through layers upon layers of sedimentary rock. It shows that the trees were buried rapidly and not over millions and millions of years. These very same facts are the facts that evolutionists put forth to prove their story of organic evolution and how things began millions of years ago. So again, the disagreement or conflict lies not in the facts and data alone, but in the *differing interpretations of the same exact facts and data*. Both sides acknowledge the data's existence, but each side *has its own interpretation of it* – The Atheist's interpretation called Organic Evolution versus the Theists' interpretation called Creationism.

I'm sharing this perspective on Historic Interpretational Science versus Experimental, Observable Science with you, my readers, before we begin to review our first chapter, because I want you to remember this fact about interpretations as we go over Richard's arguments as well as the comments made by other atheist scientists Richard quotes throughout his book. They are much like the "science says this, or science says that" example I already mentioned at the beginning of this Introduction.

It's not science saying anything. Facts and data don't say anything, only scientists do, and so when scientists give their best *personal interpretations* of the facts and data available, it doesn't mean that their interpretations should be viewed as having the absolute authority that usually comes from repeated, scientific *'testing and observation'*, and that's because they in fact cannot do that kind of scientific testing with its repeating and reviewing of these historical events that occurred so long ago. Just because such interpretations are being given by renowned scientists like Richard Dawkins, or others, doesn't make their interpretations automatically true or settled science. There have been some pasts scientists, and there still are some scientists doing science today, who have given and continue to give *disingenuous interpretations* as answers to the 'Big' questions we're discussing in my book.

To me, it seems as though they are doing this with the intent to mislead the average person into accepting that the 'Big' questions have in fact been answered by science, when in fact they have not. I will cover this fact a little later in my book. With that said, I think we're ready to begin my review and personal perspective on each of Richard's chapter titles, as well as their subtitle topics which Richard lays out in his book. The first chapter being – "A Deeply Religious Non-Believer".

CHAPTER 1

A DEEPLY RELIGIOUS NON-BELIEVER

In reviewing Richard's first chapter of *The God Delusion*, Richard gives several examples of what the words Religious, Believer, and Nonbeliever mean to him, as well as defining what he means by a true atheist. Here's a summary description of what Richard says an atheist is:

"An atheist, in the sense of a philosophical naturalist, is somebody who believes there is nothing beyond the natural, physical world; no *supernatural* creative intelligence lurking behind the observable universe; no soul that outlasts the body; and no miracles – except in the sense of *natural phenomena that we don't yet understand (This is also my definition of what a miracle is)*. Richard says, "If there is something that appears to lie beyond the natural world as it is now imperfectly understood, we hope *eventually* to understand it and embrace it *within the natural*." [139]

In my Introduction I shared a great deal about my belief in unseen things such as spirit-matter, the spirit world, etc. so that you, my readers, can know that I, in the strictest sense, am not a naturalist atheist like Richard describes, and says he is. But I am a *naturalist theist*, and that's because I believe that all things, including unseen spirit matter, are made up of different forms and particles of matter, and our spirits that reside in our bodies are made up of a very unique and eternal form of spirit matter called Intelligence(s), its principles also being eternal. It's a more-pure form of matter. It's so pure that we can't see it with our natural eyes, just like we cannot see atoms, neurons, photons, electrons, quarks, dark matter, and dark energy. So, in this sense I am in fact a naturalist but not in a supernatural sense.

Richard goes on to give examples of highly respected religious people that he knows, describing them as being religious but non-believers in the personal, supernatural God. These are people who grew up in a faith. They're people who Richard says, "are simply loyal to their upbringing and religious traditions, but deep down they are NOT believers in God. They simply believe in belief." [140]

After reading Richards' comments on religious non-believers, I would suggest that unless and until you meet any of the folks Richard says are in this group of believers-in-belief, and you get to speak to them yourself personally, so you can ask them directly what they believe in, only then can you have standing to say what they actually believe or have faith in, and why they do. Richard's definition makes me a religious non-believer and that's because I was raised in a home where faith in God was taught, but not in the Christians' definition of God, the God that Richard calls the supernatural sky-god.

Trying to repeat what someone said and making it sound as though it's a matter of fact, when it is two persons removed, or written down by someone other than the person who actually made the statement, is, in my opinion, a good way to find yourself heading down a slippery slope to hearsay and confusion. Exact quotes given out of context helps no one. I am not saying that these religious nonbelievers Richard is quoting, didn't say what Richard says they said. I'm simply saying that first-hand quotes by the person themselves, given to you, or to me in person, or in a book that they themselves wrote, are the strongest quotes one can have. Some of the quotes that both Richard and I have offered up to our readers, are second-hand quotes that were written down or repeated to someone, versus what the person said to us personally, and that's of course, because some of them are not alive. However, most of the quotes we give are first-hand so that they can be relied on as being authentic.

For example, I'll be quoting Joseph Smith throughout my book and these quotes are obviously from Joseph's personal journal or sermons. Often scribes wrote his comments down for him, recording what he said and taught to his audience while his scribe recorded his words at the very moment he spoke to them. In addition to Joseph Smith's quotes, I'll be quoting other people who are also deceased just as Joseph Smith is. Their quotes will be their personal thoughts and ideas that they themselves wrote down in a recorded talk or in a book that you and I can go and get, and read for ourselves, so we can verify what they in fact said.

The bottom line to my point, is that it's up to each of us to decide whether-or-not any of the quotes or statements I've attributed to the individuals named in my book, are credible and therefore acceptable as authentic statements. The same goes for Richard's quotes that he shares throughout his book *The God Delusion*. With that said, let's go to the first subtitle for this first chapter.

The first subtitle being – "Deserved Respect".

DESERVED RESPECT

Richard Dawkins says: "Physicists like Einstein and Hawking occasionally slipped into the language of religious metaphor (Which is what Hawking did with his last book I quoted in my Introduction) which then opened the door for theists to believe and say that they were believers in God, even a personal God, when in fact they were not believers in such a God, at least in the *personal god* sense." [141]

This is an example of how someone can use quotes by someone who is not alive, and then speak for them as though they knew exactly what these persons meant by their statements. Richard says that most of these scientists, and in particular the dead ones, were not believers in the supernatural God, especially the Christian God Jesus, and deserve respect for what they believed in.

These so-called enlightened scientists who seemed to be deeply religious in Richard's way of thinking, reflected their belief in the Einsteinian God for example [142], but were in fact, religious nonbelievers according to Richard's review of their comments. These were comments within their writings and within their interviews and were then quoted by those who knew these individuals personally and recorded the comments they made about God and what they believed about Him.

Richard goes on to say that the kind of religion Einstein himself believed in, is a religion he, himself, can believe in. He described it in this way: "Behind anything that can be experienced there is something that our mind cannot grasp and whose beauty and sublimity reaches us only indirectly and as a feeble reflection, this is religiousness."

Richard continues, "In this sense I am religious. In this sense I too am religious. In this sense I am religious, with the reservation that *'cannot grasp'* does not have to mean *'forever ungraspable'*. But I prefer not to call myself religious because it is misleading. It is destructively misleading because, for the vast majority of people, religion implies supernatural." [143]

In my opinion Richard is misinformed when he defines all theists as those who believe in a supernatural God. He is wrong. I say that because I am a theist. I believe in God, but the God I believe in does not fit Richard's definition of what the theistic God is, which for him is only supernatural; a supernatural kind of God. Richard defines supernatural as "a supernatural intelligence (without body, parts, or passions. See both the *Nicaean Creed as well as the *Athanasian Creed) who, in addition to his main work of creating the universe in the first place, is still around to oversee and influence the subsequent fate of his initial creation." [144]

*Here is what the Nicaean Creed says, quote: "We believe in one God, the Father, the Almighty, Maker of heaven and earth, of all that is seen and unseen. We believe in one Lord Jesus Christ, the only Son of God, eternally begotten of the Father; God from God, Light from Light, true God from true God; begotten not made, one in 'being' with the Father (Three persons in one being)."

End quote

*Here is what the Athanasian Creed says, quote: "For the right Faith is, that we believe and confess; that our Lord Jesus Christ, the Son of God, is God and Man; God, of the Substance [Essence] of the Father; begotten before the worlds; and Man, of the substance [Essence] of his mother, born in the world."

End quote

By Richard defining the Christian God, 'Yahweh', and 'Jesus', as being Supernatural in this way,[145] he's saying this supernatural God is not a God that all the enlightened religious non-believers can believe in. Like I said, I am a theist, which to me, is just someone who simply believes in God, be it God, Heavenly Fathers' pre-mortal Son Yahweh or Jehovah, or Jesus, who is Jehovah who became flesh.

I am also a Christian, and by Christian, I mean, someone who believes in Jesus Christ and therefore is one of His believing disciples, even though Christendom says that the Jesus I, as a Latter-Day Saint, believe in, is not the Jesus they believe in, their belief being that He is a 'three persons in one essence or being' kind of God, who for them is called Jesus, and that's why I am not a Christian.

Because I do not believe in the God as defined by the Nicaean Creed I just quoted, disqualifies me, and all Latter-Day Saints, as being a Christian as they define Him. Let me say that I certainly allow my Christian friends to differentiate my view of God's nature from their view of Him, but I think we would agree that both Christendom and members of The Church of Jesus Christ of Latter-Day Saints are theists, and so, I will leave it there.

The God I believe in has a body with parts and passions, as does His only Begotten Son, Jesus Christ, who is separate and distinct from the Father. Both have bodies of flesh and bones as tangible as mans, though they're immortal bodies. I also believe in the Holy Ghost who is a personage of Spirit, separate and distinct from God the Father and His Son. These three, separate and distinct eternal beings make up what we as Latter-Day Saints call *The Godhead*, each being one in truth, one in vision, one in love and purpose; but not three persons in one God/Energy/Essence/or Being like Christendom teaches.

Richard's opinion about the nonbelievers' definition of God, supports his argument that God, as a non-supernatural God, could possibly exist but not in the way the Christians' supernatural God of the Bible exists. Richard says:

"These religious non-believers believe in a God that's much different than the Christian God, and therefore these religious non-believers are truly religious in that sense, but not because they believe in and worship the Christian God Jesus." [146]

The religious non-believers, Richard says, who *don't* believe in the Christians' supernatural God, meaning the Jesus of the Bible, are the ones that deserve respect. But Christians do not. You may not realize it yet, but Richard is setting the table so he can lump *all* the gods of all people living around the entire world (Except for the god that the so-called *enlightened scientist* believers believe in), into a single group of gods: gods like Zeus, the Great Spirit, Rah, and last-but-not-least, the Christian God Jesus. This is his end goal – to eliminate all gods as delusions.

In Richards' mind, those gods, and all the other gods of the world's religions, form one single group, and the other group is the god of the non-believers in the Christian God, but believers in a god that consists of the set of physical laws that govern the universe (Such as Mother nature?). This god is the only god Richard says he could believe in and the only god deserving of his respect. Richard spent a lot of page space trying to define who or what fits into this 'Deserving Respect' group, and all the other believers in God are in the "Supernatural God Delusion" group.[147]

My response to this *defining of gods exercise* that Richard takes us through, is to say that Richard is simply trying to categorize any-and-all believers who believe in any kind of god, especially those who believe in the God named Jesus, the Son of The Living God, as being delusional. Period. If he can get you and I, and all his own readers, to buy into the lie that all gods, and especially the Son of God named Jesus, are a delusion, and anyone who believes in these gods are delusional, then, in his mind, he's accomplished his goal. But this logic falls far short of adding any proof for the non-existence of God.

What I find interesting, is that Richard appears, in my humble opinion, to be religiously ignorant and theologically immature, and that ignorance and lack of spiritual maturity has led him to have a real misunderstanding of pure religions' doctrines. His understanding appears to have come from a surface reading kind of study and lack of any positive religious experience. The fact is, that none of this back-and-forth about who is religious and who isn't, and what god fits where, doesn't add one whit of evidence to whether-or-not God exists. It only creates antagonism and contention between each group, and contention is not of God. Here's what the ancient American prophet Nephi said about contention:

III Nephi 11:29
29 He that hath the spirit of contention is not of me, but is of the devil, who is the father of contention.

Richard ends this subtitle having defined these two groups in the way I just described, and if I understood this *'defining of gods'* exercise, Richard was simply saying that, "the metaphorical or pantheistic god of the physicists (Apparently the group that is deserving of respect), are light years away from the interventionist, miracle-wreaking, thought-reading, sin-punishing, prayer-answering God of the Bible group", and 'those believers', as he describes them in the next subtitle, are "Underserved of Respect".[148]

In other words, in Richard's opinion, religion does not deserve the respect that everybody seems to want to give it, in particular the group that we'll be discussing in our next subtitle – "Underserved Respect".

UNDESERVED RESPECT

As we saw from our review of the first subtitle 'Deserved Respect', Richard says "he knows that what he's said will probably offend those theists who actually read his book, and that they'll feel he does not give their opposing views the respect they deserve." [149]

Richard also goes on to give an explanation as to why he chooses to hit religion so hard. Here's what he says, and I Quote:

"The respect extended to religion and conversation on religion, by all societies … is undeserved". He says, "The assumption that religious faith is especially vulnerable to offense, (The Holy dissed by the unholy), and therefore it should be protected by what he calls an abnormal *'wall of respect'* is undeserved". [150]

End Quote

In my mind, showing respect to others faith is just people being good and respectful to each other, in terms of what they hold sacred. It's the 'Live and Let Live' kind of kindness that is being extended believers. On the other hand, Richard feels that religion, like any other social experience, should absolutely be opened up to criticism because it most definitely has its faults, even if everybody thinks that faith and their particular teachings are holy topics and should be untouchable. I agree with Richard that religion should be open to criticism and debate. That's a given. But not uncivil criticism and disrespectful, contentious debate. To me, it sounds like Richard is just whining about religion as a whole. And so, I simply, and in jest, would ask Richard, "Do you serve 'whine' with your cheese?"

Challenging religious ideas and setting them up for open debate, is what Richard Dawkins has spent his entire adult life doing, and I am just fine with that. Like I said, I don't object to Richard expressing his criticism of religion and doggedly going after any specific faith for that matter. Even mine. However, I don't believe in being unkind and uncivil in expressing one's criticism, which seems to be Richard's chosen forte. Here are just a couple examples of Richard's criticism of religion, which proves my point:

Richard says: "Being a conscientious objector, for example, because of one's religious belief, as well as ethnic cleansing or religious cleansing, are both targets for criticism. Other targeted views are topics such as sexual or reproductive morals." [151]

Richard asks:

"Why does our society beat a path to those individuals who have such religious views, as though they had some expertise comparable to that of a moral philosopher, a family lawyer, or a doctor? Such seems to be the privileging of religion." [152] "Society's exaggerated respect for religion is often under the guise of Freedom of Religion. What is so special about religion that we grant it such *uniquely privileged* respect?" [152]

My answer to Richard's last question, is that all mankind is born with and has the Light of Christ within them. This *sense of right and wrong* that burns within our hearts such that we know and therefore acknowledge this source of our sense of what is good and right and wrong, is what's worthy of reverence. It is this *feeling of reverence* for this source of what's right and wrong within each of us, that's carried over to religion itself. That said, I don't have any qualms with Richard's attitude where he says, "There is no reason why these ideas shouldn't be as open to debate as any other idea, except that we have agreed, somehow between us, that they shouldn't be." [153]

Even though I agree that it should be discussed, I must say that pointing out that religion shouldn't be getting the world's respect like it seems to be getting, in Richard's mind, once again, doesn't add one iota of evidence for, or against the reality of God's existence. It just seems to be Richard ranting about anything-and-everything related to religion in general, due to his angst against religion.

I believe the debate between atheism and theism, no matter how much one believes in their sides view, should always be done with civility and without demeaning any believer or non-believer for their personal views. So, Richard, C'mon man. Keep the hits above the belt. That said, let's move on to chapter 2 – "The God Hypothesis".

CHAPTER 2

THE GOD HYPOTHESIS

At the start of Chapter 2 Richard once again reveals his bitterness, as well as his personal hatred towards any kind of religion, especially the religion that preaches the God of the Bible revealed in both the Old and New Testaments; that particular God being Jesus Christ, who was Jehovah of the Old Testament, and is the Son of God who became flesh, the mortal, yet divine Son of God, even Jesus of Nazareth. Richard goes on to give his personal, vitriolic description of Jehovah who is Jesus:

"God is the most unpleasant character in all fiction. God is jealous and proud of it; petty, unjust, unforgiving; a control freak; a vindictive, blood thirsty ethnic cleanser; a misogynistic, homophobic racist; an infanticidal, genocidal, filicidal, pestilential, megalomaniacal, sadomasochist, capriciously malevolent bully". [154]

Tell me how you really feel Richard. Ha-ha-ha. With this distain and hatred Richard has for this God (Which appears to be fueled by his uninformed understanding of God and His true nature, Richard has concocted and personalized his own false concept of God. This, to me, is making up a god after your own image, so you can reject the god that you disagree with or don't like). Richard continues:

"The God Hypothesis chapter is *not* going to be about *that* description of Yahweh, the God of Abraham, Isaac, and Jacob, or Jehovah (Jesus of the New Testament). I shall define the God Hypothesis more defensibly (I would ask you to remember this statement by Ricard where he says this chapter is NOT going to be about THAT description of Jehovah, and Jesus, when I bring it up a little later)." [155]

Next Richard gives his description of the God theists believe in. To him theists believe that "There exists a superhuman, supernatural intelligence who (Or that) deliberately designed and created the universe and everything in it, including each of us (From nothing, or 'ex nihlo')." [156]

Just like the theoretical physicist and cosmologist Lawrence Kraus has stated, Richard also says he doesn't believe in such a 'Supernatural God'. He says his book was written to advocate an alternative view for the God Hypothesis; an alternative to the Super Being of great complexity to which theists direct their belief. Richard says:

"Any creative intelligence of sufficient complexity to design anything, comes into existence only as the end-product of an extended process of gradual evolution." [157] Richard's start, middle, and ending 'Go-To Argument' for anything-and-everything created or living, is Evolution, with its tenant Natural Selection. It's the main doctrine of his quasi-religion of Atheism. Its chief prophet is Charles Darwin, who's chief doctrine was his naturalists' quasi-gospel of Natural Selection. Richard continues:

"Creative intelligences, being evolved, necessarily *arrived late in the universe* (How do we know this?), and therefore cannot be responsible for designing it. God, in the sense defined, is a pernicious delusion! The God Hypothesis comes in many versions since it was *founded on local traditions of private revelation* rather than on evidence (Richard sees science as being the *only* true source of what he calls evidence and implies that revelation provides no such evidence because it comes from the traditions of men)." [158]

I appreciate the fact that Richard makes a clear distinction as to what view his book is going to take. However, after reading his book, I must say that he failed to keep his commitment to keep his prejudice towards Jehovah/Jesus out of his arguments. Remember him saying, "I shall define the God Hypothesis more defensibly"? The fact is Richard went on a rant of vitriolic criticism of the God called Jehovah or Jesus, and in my view, he did not add one scintilla of evidence in support of his belief in God's non-existence. If you've read *The God Delusion* you know that Richard is quite critical of the God of the Old Testament, and in particular the God of the New Testament, whom we know to be Jesus, who Richard said he wouldn't focus on, unless I misunderstood him (As a Latter-Day Saint I believe Yahweh or Jehovah is the God of the Old Testament, and became God's Son in the flesh, even Jesus of Nazareth, as revealed in the New Testament). Maybe Richard doesn't understand or know that the God of the Old Testament, Jehovah, is Jesus from the New Testament, and so, in Richard's mind he's criticizing God the Father, Elohim, and not Jehovah. Maybe Richard thinks Jehovah is someone different than the Jesus of the New Testament. As Latter-Day Saints we believe that Jehovah is the pre-mortal Messiah and the God of the Old Testament, and that He was born as the Son of God in the flesh, whose name was Jesus.

Jehovah is Heavenly Father's firstborn spirit Son who, as part of His calling and role as the Savior, became flesh in order to give efficacy to His Father's Plan of Redemption and Happiness for His children (This is my Latter-Day Saint perspective on God the Father and His Son, Jesus Christ, and as I've said, it's the main reason why Christians say that Latter-Day Saints do not believe in the Christian view of God, who is Jesus, and therefore Latter-Day Saints are not Christian in the way they are).

In my view, Richard's 'Evolutionist Argument' wherein he states, "Any and all *creative intelligences* are and were derived from evolution over millions of years, and that alone," [159] paints him into a corner where he has to double down on such statements, even as they're fast becoming obsolete. I'll tell you, my readers, why I believe this a little later. What I will tell you now is that I believe his views, his mindset, comes from the spirit of anti-Christ, which is the spirit of Satan, which I'll also cover in a later chapter.

Speaking of *creative intelligence*, let me say that intelligence is always connected to information, and information is always connected to the mind or a mind, which Richard, for obvious reasons, says intelligence is just the result of electrons firing off in a wet machine called *the brain*. In other words, there is no 'separate mind' or 'consciousness' producing this information or intelligence. Richard believes and therefore says that the brain, and the brain *alone*, produces the creative intelligence or information he mentioned in his statement. It's all produced by and within the wet brain itself, which activity is mindless in terms of a separate source of Mind, or it could be described as mindlessness.

Richard knows that his atheist scientist friends have not been able to define what 'Mind' is, in terms of matter alone (Meaning atheist scientists of Neurology, Cosmology, Physics, and Biology). As a Naturalist, he does not believe in the unseen mind or in a spirit personage dwelling in one's body (Which together forms the soul), nor does he or his atheist scientist friends know what consciousness even is, except to say that it is the result of protons, neurons, and electrons firing off and bouncing around in an unguided, unintended fashion within the wet brain machine (The hardware of the mind in other words), whose firings have no *directed*, guided, or *intended* purpose. In other words, it is mindless, and this firing off of neurons called conscience, simply stops when the brain itself dies, so no more 'mind'.

As I said, Richard does not believe there is a spirit personage residing in the body, or that when the body is such that it cannot sustain life, the spirit leaves the body causing death to occur. I believe otherwise. This is why I suggested that you, my readers, watch the two YouTube videos of Robert Kuhn of the Closer to Truth series, where he interviews Dr. Sam Parnia, a Pulmonologist and Neuroscientist. On these videos Dr. Parnia discusses how his patients' brains stop for hours, and yet, the people continued to experience *existence* outside of their bodies for those hours and then came back into their bodies, all the while their hearts had stopped, and their brains were declared dead. These experiences are called Near Death Experiences or NDE's. If the brain produces our consciousness, how did these people still have awareness, and an awareness not only of themselves but of their surroundings?

Here's an example of what I believe about *the mind versus the wet hardware we call the brain*.

When you come up to a beach and you find the letters H … E … L … P … carved deep into the sand, you know instinctively that the ocean waves, or crabs from the ocean did not come onto that beach and write those four scribbles or informational symbols in the wet sand, especially in that specific order, making a clear statement with distinct meaning – a request for HELP. It's so obvious. I certainly hope that you, my readers, see it as obvious too. You know that an intelligent mind directed the writing of that message in the sand. This is information, period! It didn't just happen by some unguided series of waves crashing onto the shore over millions of years, or by a super intelligent crab. Even if you reduced it down to the biology and physics of the sand itself, and the water alone (reductionism), the message and the information symbols (Letters) that makes up the message HELP, is NOT of nature and elements alone. It is of the MIND, and nonbelievers like Richard will not allow themselves to admit this fact.

The thought, idea, or message *HELP* has nothing to do with physics or biology, except for the sand in which the letters HELP are written, and the electrical and chemical activity going on in the mind of the person who wrote the message in the sand in the first place. The information created by the mind, lives in the mind until it is expressed. The wet brain did not produce the information. It's just the hardware reacting to the mind's instructions. The *intelligence* is produced by the mind, which mind is part of the spirit body. Otherwise, "Where does information come from?" Just as the laptop can't come up with information by itself out of nothing, the wet brain cannot come up with its own information out of thin air. It must have the operating systems and software and the other informational programs before it can be activated; before it can compute and *do* functions. It also must have the electricity to power up and to operate … and then … it needs the person or persons to direct it and give it the instructions it needs. Otherwise, it is just a pile of hardware. This is also true of the spirit's mind housed in the brain.

To say that creative intelligence is derived from evolution over millions of years, does not come close to explaining the actual origin of the word HELP, or the letters themselves that were used by someone to write the informational message while walking on a sandy beach. This person clearly understood and was directed by the consciousness of their spirits' own mind to intentionally write the word HELP, for a specific reason. It's an 'on purpose' or 'intentional' action. They had a reason for doing so. Period!

To scientists this is a 'Big' unanswered question. It is the undiscovered Theory of Mind (ToM). To me, a simpleton Latter-Day Saint, it is quite easy to understand that it is the mind that's at work here. It is the mind that's part of the spirit personage being housed within a persons' physical body. Their consciousness is the spirit personage residing in the body, and the 'light of life' that's in and part of that spirit personage is what gives it life and the ability to function. Each of us is an eternal intelligence, a spirit personage dwelling in our tabernacle of flesh and bone. Each of us, with the assistance of our brains' hardware and the spiritual operating system and software called our spirits mind, have the capacity to think, to decide, to act, and to dream because our spirit bodies are agents with the power to think for ourselves, and to act and be acted upon. This is what an intelligence is and what it does.

Richard says, "Religion Historians (Atheist ones at least), say that there was a progression from primitive tribal animisms (Attributing a soul to plants and inanimate objects), on through polytheisms (The belief in multiple deities) such as those of the Greeks, Romans, and Norsemen, on to monotheisms. Judaism and its derivatives, Christianity, and Islam – the Big three Religions of our Day – are such monotheisms!" [160]

Richard summarizes his criticisms about all the religions that have, in his mind, risen-up over the millions of years past, when he says, "They're just different manifestations, or incarnations of the One God." [161]

Richard then takes his readers back through the millenniums giving a history lesson on the various religious iterations and their infighting and outfighting. He ends this history lesson by saying: "Such has ever been the way of theology!" [162]

To this I say, in some ways Richard is right. Apostate theology does have a way of manifesting all that Richard hates about religion. But as far as religion coming from evolution, it is simply Richard's unproven opinion and theory. These so-called *iterations of religion* Richard describes and says are *the* result of some type of deterministic natural selection iterations caused by active protons bouncing against the walls of our ancestors' wet brains, creating unguided, undirected, unintended, mindless, delusional concepts about a sky-god, is ridiculous. In reality, it is just Richard's overly educated imagination at work here, which I describe as delusional. *Evolutionary Religion* is Richard's personal, unproven, untested theory. It isn't a scientifically tested, irrefutable fact. It's just one man's incredibly delusional theory, and this theory doesn't add one iota of evidence in support of Richard's belief that God does not exist.

Next is the first subtitle for chapter 2 – "Polytheism".

POLYTHEISM

Dawkins, being a quasi-disciple of Charles Darwin, claims that the evolutionary process is the power behind the crane of natural selection (See p. 200 of his book *The God Delusion*) behind the arrival of all world religions and their espoused beliefs, and it is Richard's second *Consciousness Raiser*. In this Chapter's subtitle Richard begins with this statement:

"It is not clear why the change from *polytheism to monotheism* should be assumed to be a self-evident progressive improvement." (A process much like the theory of evolution being applied to biology's mutations taking animal species towards better states through the process of natural selection, etc., etc.) "But it widely is." [163]

Once again, it is merely conjecture and Richard's opinion that this is what supposedly took place. Richard gives no incontrovertible, tested evidence that can be used to predict this process going forward, or test it following today's scientific methods, and that's because it would take millions of years to prove out any such predictions by performing the necessary repeated testing in order to confirm his theory that 'religion evolved like man evolved', through millions of iterations. How convenient is that? The time needed to test it virtually eliminates our ability to prove or falsify this theory. So, again, Richard postulating this theory doesn't add one scintilla of evidence to help support Richard's argument for God's non-existence. Next Richard quotes a Mr. Ibn Warraq, who said: "Monotheism in its turn is doomed to subtract one more god and become atheism." [164]

Richard considers the attack on Polytheism (Polytheism being the belief in or worship of a plurality of Gods, particularly those faiths in the Middle East), by Christian religionists to be a snobbish discrimination against Polytheism. Richard's goal here, is to abandon religion altogether, and its charitable status, because he feels church preachers avoid paying taxes on contributions made by their congregants. Richard uses Oral Roberts as just one of many examples to describe what he says is "a charade, its proponents being obscene, well-healed, super-hair-doo televangelists." [165]

Richard says: "Polytheistic faiths are actually just different manifestations, or incarnations of the one God idea, each just having a different name such as Lord Braham the creator; and Lord Vishnu the preserver; and Lord Shiva the destroyer, etc." [166]

Richard then discusses the Arian Heresy saying: "Rivers of medieval ink, not to mention blood, have been squandered over the *mystery of the Trinity*, which shows its ridiculousness". [167] In fact, he says, "This was a splitting of hairs that split Christendom in two, and such civil war in the church has been the way of theology." [168]

Richard then goes into a critique of the confusion that thrives among Christians regarding the Trinity's many descriptions. Here's what he says:

"Do we have one God in three parts, or three Gods in one? Unlike science or most other branches of human scholarship – Christendom has not moved on in eighteen centuries." [169]

Richard then quotes Thomas Jefferson, who Richard says was a Deist:

"Thomas and other founding fathers subscribed to the liberal religious strand of Deism that values reason over revelation. It (Deism) also rejects traditional Christian doctrines, including the Virgin birth, Original Sin, and the Resurrection of Jesus". Richard then says Jefferson said:

"*Ridicule* is the only weapon which can be used against unintelligible propositions." [170]

"Ideas must be distinct ideas before reason can act upon them; and no man ever had a distinct idea of the Trinity. It is a mere Abracadabra of the mountebanks (A mountebank being a charlatan, someone who tricks people out of their money), calling themselves the priests of Jesus." [171]

These quotes are examples from people who Richard feels are respectable. He uses them as allies to support his criticism of religious faith and its doctrines all together. Of course, there are thousands of people who have Richard's same opinion of religion, but that, in and of itself, does not prove God's non-existence, any more than my putting forth the billions of people who say atheism is anti-Christ and therefore it is proof that God exists. It is an interesting sidebar for sure, but it doesn't add one iota of support to this debate regarding God's existence or non-existence. Richard goes on to say:

"The other thing I cannot help remarking upon is the over-weening confidence with which the religious assert minute details for which they neither have, nor could have any evidence." [172]

This certainly is just one more overstated, hyperbolic opinion given by Richard. Richard continues his constant attack of religion when he says: "The Catholic faith is a poly theological conundrum, with all its many Saints and the many iterations of the mother of Jesus. All of which are worshipped as mini gods". [173]

I suppose this is why he took the time to write about it so critically. He feels this all falls into the Polytheism category due to its many Saints, which are treated as Gods, the virgin Mary being another redeemer as is her son Jesus, as Catholics believe she is. Richard says: "Who cares? Life is too short to bother with the distinction between one figment of the imagination and many. I shall refer to all deities, whether poly- or mono-theistic, as simply God. It's all full of the richness of human gullibility." [174]

Richard certainly has a way with his wordsmithing, doesn't he? He makes me chuckle. Richard ends this chapter and its two subtitles by saying: "I am not attacking any particular version of god or gods (Although he does feel most strongly about the God of the three great monotheistic religions – Judaism, Islam, and Christianity – and a fourth if you count Mormonism which he comments on a little later in his book). I am attacking God, all gods, anything, and everything supernatural, whatever and whenever they have been or will be invented." [175]

In response to Richard's rejection of all religion on its face, and of its many gods, and of anyone who has a similar take on theism and religion, with their sky-god controlling them, I would simply say that Richard is fulfilling prophecy given by many of God's servants the prophets, who prophesied of our Day as having the fruit of apostasy.

Like I wrote earlier, these religious iterations are later-day evidence of the way of apostasy. In one sense I agree with Richard, when he talks about the well-healed, super-hair-doo televangelists. These are examples of wolves in sheep's clothing, preachers of priestcraft (*Priestcraft being when men preach and set themselves up for a light unto the world, that they may get gain and the praise of the world; but they seek not the welfare of the Church and Kingdom of God. You can do a search at www.churchofjesuschrist.org on *Priestcraft* for a full and more robust review of this false practice). [176]

Like Mr. Dawkins felt comfortable doing with his arguments, I will reference individuals who I consider to be voices of reason and of authority, even though these voices will be considered unqualified by Richard and other non-believing pseudo-intellectuals like him, and that's because they speak positively towards Religion, and so Richard will reject them out of hand. The chief voices of reason for me, are the voices of prophets from the Bible, prophets who lived in ancient America whom we learn about from the Book of Mormon and their ancient records translated by the prophet Joseph Smith Jr. in 1829, as well as the voices of living prophets walking amongst us today. These are the prophets, seers, and revelators that lead and serve Christ's Church, the Church of Jesus Christ of Latter-Day Saints. They live and serve amongst us, traveling throughout the world to share the gospel of Jesus Christ.

Joseph Smith, the prophet, was commanded of God to give warnings to the people of our Day, and having done so he was harassed, beaten, tared and feathered, wrongfully taken to court more than 200 times, and ultimately shot and killed by a state-sanctioned mob, along with his older brother Hyrum, just like the prophets of old were martyred for their testimonies of Jesus' divinity. Jesus Himself was killed by the wicked religionists of His Day, who feared their priestcraft would be found out. These wicked, false teachers feared to do it themselves, so they used the power of Rome and its guards to perform the cruelty of crucifixion, putting these religionists nemesis, Jesus of Nazareth, to death. Here's just a few examples of the Lord's prophets' giving warnings about atheists and their anti-Christ message:

II Timothy 4: 3-4 (Written by the Apostle Paul)

3 For the time will come when they (The peoples of the world) will not endure sound doctrine; but after their own lusts shall they heap to themselves *teachers*, having itching ears;

4 And they shall turn away their ears from the truth and shall be turned unto fables.

(*Describes individuals who seek out messages and doctrines that condone their wordly lifestyle, as opposed to seeking out the teachings of Jesus and His prophets).

The prophet Jerimiah wrote:

Jerimiah 5:21

21 Hear now this, O foolish people, and without understanding; which have eyes, and see not; which have ears, and hear not.

The prophet Nephi from the Book of Mormon declared:

II Nephi 9:29

28 O that cunning plan of the evil one! O the vainness, and the frailties, and the foolishness of men! When they are learned (so-called *eminently intelligent*) they think they are wise, and they hearken not unto the counsel of God, for they set it aside, supposing they know of themselves (In other words 'of science and reason alone'), wherefore, their wisdom is foolishness and it profiteth them not and they shall perish.

The Prophet Joseph Smith Jr. received and recorded this revelation that said:

Doctrine & Covenants 1:16

16 They seek not the Lord to establish *his* righteousness, but every man walketh in his own way, and after the image of his own god, whose image is in the likeness of the world, and whose *substance* is that of an idol (Having no real substance in other words. Just made of wood, or the arm of the flesh, etc.); which waxeth old and shall perish in Babylon, even Babylon the great (A *type and shadow* of the world), which shall fall.

Now that's what I call a straight-forward understanding of where I stand regarding this topic of religion and how Richard seems to despise any and all forms of it, and whether you agree with me or not, at least you now know what my perspective is on this topic and can compare it to Richard's. Let's go ahead and address the next subtitle – "Monotheism".

MONOTHEISM

Richard begins this subtitle by quoting Gore Vidal, an American intellectual and writer who seems to be focused on social and cultural *sexual norms* as he sees them through the eyes of a bisexual man. Here's the quote from Gore Vidal:

"The great unmentionable evil at the center of our culture is monotheism. From a barbaric Bronze Age text known as the Old Testament, three anti-human religions have evolved – Judaism, Christianity, and Islam. These are sky-god religions. They are literally patriarchal – God is the Omnipotent Father – hence the loathing of women for 2,000 years, in those countries afflicted by the sky-god and his earthly male delegates." [177]

With such a statement Mr. Vidal reveals his anti-Theist/anti-Christ leanings, as well as his loathing for religion itself, and in particular, his disgust for the Christian religion and its specific God, Jehovah, who is the God of the Old Testament, and was made flesh, whose name, while on earth was Jesus Christ.

Mr. Dawkins appears to have taken ownership of Gore's disliking of religion, and in particular his hatred of the God of Abraham, by making Vidal's disgust for him, his own. Here's what Richard said right after quoting Mr. Vidal:

"The oldest of the three Abrahamic religions, and the clear ancestor of the other two, is Judaism (The House of Israel, and in particular the Jews): originally a tribal cult of a single, fiercely unpleasant God (A God of Justice & Mercy), morbidly obsessed with sexual restrictions (The Law of Chastity), with the smell of charred flesh (The law of Sacrifices & Burnt Offerings as types and shadows of the sacrifice of the Lamb of God, His beloved Son, Jesus, who was to come), with his own superiority over rival gods (Eternal Sovereignty), and with the exclusiveness of his chosen desert tribe (Israel. Jacob's name was changed to Israel. See www.churchofjesuschrist.org "Why Did God Change Jacob's name to Israel?)." [178]

Quite opinionated, isn't he? The fact is, Richard doesn't seem to have any understanding of, or any clue as to what the true nature of the laws of God our Eternal Father are, and why He gave them to mankind, nor does he really know what Gods' Only Begotten Son, Jesus Christs' role was, and is, in His Eternal Plan of Happiness with any depth of understanding. Richard goes on to elaborate on the three largest religions, and the sin of using the sword to spread their gospels far and wide. Richard states:

"For my purposes, all three Abrahamic religions can be treated as indistinguishable, so I shall have Christianity mostly in mind, but only because it is the version with which I happen to be most familiar (Familiar is the operative word here. Richard is clearly unschooled in the true nature of God and His pure gospel known as the Gospel of Jesus Christ, and Jesus' role as Savior of mankind)." [179]

"The differences matter less than the similarities" Richard says, "and so, I shall not be concerned at all with other religions such as Buddhism or Confucianism, etc. Indeed, there is something to be said for treating these not as religions at all, but as ethical systems or philosophies of life." [180]

In my opinion, Richard's understanding of each of the three major Abrahamic religions and the belief systems they teach, and in particular what the nature of the object of their faith is (meaning the nature of Jehovah, the God of the Old Testament, who became Jesus of Nazareth, and the God of today's Christianity), reveals how little he comprehends the true nature of God the Father, and that of His Only Begotten Son, Jesus Christ. Nor does he know what the pure gospel of Jesus Christ is, which gospel He dispensed to the Jews in the meridian of time. As I said, Richard's misunderstanding of these things is the result of him taking what the religious world teaches, which teachings are strewn with the apostasy, it lasting nearly two millenniums now. Todays' religious teachings are not the pure gospel of Jesus Christ.

It is also my opinion that Richard is especially ill informed about my faith, the Church of Jesus Christ of Latter-Day Saints, which he calls Mormonism. It is not Mormonism. Mormonism is simply a disparaging nickname given to the Latter-Day Saint Church. It's the restored gospel of Jesus Christ, which Jesus Himself revealed to his young prophet Joseph Smith Jr. Christ's Church was restored through the instrumentality and power of God's revelation given to His Latter-Day prophet, a prophet who Jesus raised up for this very purpose – to restore His pure gospel and His authority to teach and administer it to the world in its fulness, which includes all of the principles, authority, and ordinances of Christ's gospel.

Richard places all of these religious claims squarely in the grouping of supernatural gods and manmade religions, or should I more accurately say … evolution-made religions. Richard's negative and extremely critical bias towards religion itself, and more specifically his bias towards the three major religions that sprang from Abrahams' descendants, reflects how blinded and skewed his scientific mind has become. It has become so blinded that he continually looks past the mark entirely and is therefore unable to see the forest from the trees, religiously speaking. Richard's deeply held vexation towards religion itself, has kept him from doing the work of communicating directly with believers on a personal, one-on-one basis, so that he's not allowed himself to get a clear understanding of what each group of believers truly believe, having set aside his atheistic bias. I prefer to get such information from the horses' mouth, so-to-speak, and not from religious critics. It's the honest thing to do.

Richards' arguments against monotheism, expressed throughout this subtitle, becomes one long diatribe against any-and-all religions, allowing very little other-side arguments to have any space for their views to be presented in a fair and balanced way. In my opinion, this is what has kept Richard from providing any real evidence to help prop up his claim that God does not exist. The only thing Richard has proven, so far, is that he hates religion. It's also the only thing, so far, that is incontrovertible. I feel sad for Richard for not having had a real, honest, religious experience with the pure and perfect gospel of Jesus Christ, because if he had, he might have experienced a full and complete paradigm shift.

Richard's distain towards even the idea of God's existence, overpowers his ability to be still and set aside his atheistic bias and hatred long enough to do an honest and fair search of these beliefs, such as the beliefs I have, using my own words to describe them and not using those words he found, that our critics have said about Latter-Day Saints and their beliefs. By doing so, he would have learned exactly what I and the so-called other side actually believe about God and His nature, and our perspective on all his criticisms. This is a big reason why I wrote this book. To give the real truth about my beliefs so that you, my readers, can hear it from the horse's mouth and not from Richard's cankered heart.

The fact that the Church of Jesus Christ of Latter-Day Saints has such uniquely different beliefs from all the other religions of the world in existence today, I would have thought that Richard, with his fact driven mind, would have done a more exact and honest dive into the LDS claim of the *restoration of the pure gospel of Jesus Christ through the ministration of heavenly messengers.* In reading Richard's book, I read nothing about these claims. Sure, they're spectacular, but by writing them off because they are every bit as spectacular as the angel appearing to Mary, or Jesus raising the dead, or His disciples being thrown into a fiery furnace like Shadrach, Meshach and Abednego were, who, after standing in those flames for several minutes, simply walked out alive and unharmed, doesn't make them false.

I share this because Richard appears to have gained only a veneer understanding of what I, as a member of the Church of Jesus Christ of Latter-Day Saints, believe, and that's because Richard views everything through the bifocal lens of science and the quasi-doctrine of evolution. His worldview has a life-long history of biased mapping against any-and-all religions and their spectacular claims, and that is sad to me. Richard has missed out on, and continues to miss out on, the rich story of the restoration of the Pure Gospel of Jesus Christ and the relationship he could have had with the Living Christ. A good example of what I am talking about here, is what Richard specifically said about my faith as a Latter-Day Saint in particular. Here's what he actually wrote in his book *The God Delusion*, and I quote:

"Joseph Smith, its enterprisingly mendacious inventor, went to the lengths of composing a complete new holy book, the Book of Mormon, inventing from scratch a whole new bogus American history, written in bogus seventeenth-century English." [181]

End quote

My response may surprise you, my readers, but let me share a quote from President Russel M. Nelson, the current President and Prophet leader of the Church of Jesus Christ of Latter-Day Saints, regarding the translation process of what Richard says is the *bogus Book of Mormon*, and in particular the method by which Joseph was able to translate it from what Joseph Smith described as gold plates, which plates Joseph said were given to him by a resurrected being, an angel named Moroni, and I quote:

"Joseph Smith would put the *seer stone* into a hat, and put his face in the hat, drawing it closely around his face to exclude the light; and in the darkness the *spiritual light* would shine. A piece of something resembling parchment would appear, and on that appeared the writing. One character at a time would appear, and under it was the interpretation in English. Brother Joseph would read off the English to Oliver Cowdery, who was his principal scribe, and when it was written down and repeated to Brother Joseph to see if it was correct, then it would disappear, and another character with the interpretation would appear. Thus, the Book of Mormon was *translated by the gift and power of God,* and not by any power of man, and certainly not from the mind of an unlearned man like Joseph.

End Quote

On its surface, after reading such a spectacular claim, it does have the appearance of being unbelievable and a supernatural invention of a frenzied mind, doesn't it? But we must remember that this translation took place in 1829, over a period of just 65 working days, and Joseph did not have a smart phone that would light up when turned on, revealing entire books that he could retrieve using one of several thousand apps. A cell phone certainly is spectacular, a supernatural invention that would have shocked the people of Joseph's Day. Just imagine what they might have said if they saw one.

I remember when Kindle and eBooks came out several years ago. As a reading device you would sometimes find yourself sitting in the passenger seat of your car trying to read the screen of your Kindle. Due to the brightness of the sunlight, its screen was often difficult to read, and so, what did you do when this happened? You would bend over into the covered space under the front dashboard where it was the darkest, and that enclosed darkness allowed you to read by the light of the screen. Right?

Like this example of reading a Kindle, Joseph simply was making the area in which he was receiving the translated characters and words by the Spirit of God, as dark as he could make it. That way he could see the messages on the small parchments that appeared, given to him by the spirit of God via the seer stone. I imagine that it was a little like the power of the internet we enjoy today, yet far more complex. Incredibly intelligent minds imagined the Internet and Googles' Search Engine, didn't they? As well as all the many thousands of apps, right? Certainly, God could make a stone become a viewing device.

Today's technology makes it possible for us to do and enjoy the unimaginable on the 5-inch piece of glass of our iPhones. God used a technology tool called a *seer stone*, to help develop Joseph's faith and revelatory gift, which revelatory gift and ability grew and matured over time to the point where in his later years this power of revelation had become second nature to Joseph, so that he didn't need the seer stone anymore. Had God just given him the words Joseph would not have grown in faith. Prophets of old used seer stones (or what they called 'the Urim and Thummim') much in this same way, but little is recorded on 'how' a seer stone or the Urim and the Thummim worked (They also covered heads and face with animal skins to see the revelations of God, just as Joseph used an animal skin hat):

Exodus 28:30

30 And thou shalt put in the breastplate of judgment the *Urim and the Thummim*; and they shall be upon Aaron's heart, when he goeth in before the LORD: and Aaron shall bear the judgment of the children of Israel upon his heart before the LORD continually.

Leviticus 8:8

8 And he put the breastplate upon him: also he put in the breastplate the *Urim and the Thummim*.

There is so much more to this so-called *bogus* story (as Richard called it) of the translation of the Book of Mormon, but I felt this one brief example would help you, my readers, to possibly see Richard's scathing and surface review of my religion, for what it is – uninformed, or, I think I have standing to even say that it is *intentional vitriolic mocking* of what millions of members, like me, believe.

Sharing this single example, I hope, will be sufficient to motivate you to do your own digging in the history of the Church of Jesus Christs' restoration story, so that you too, can find answers to any questions you might still have regarding my faith. That way you don't have to take Richard's biased, anti-Christ, anti-Mormon, deeply critical, surface understanding as 'gospel', without seeking the truth for yourself. Those seeking only that evidence that supports their biased viewpoint, seem to quickly take the word of critics, versus taking the time do their own time-consuming study and research, because it's hard, time-consuming work. To be fair and balanced, I believe one needs to hear both sides, and once the facts are in you can make your own decision on the matter. If you are someone who wants to be fair and balanced in your search for truth, I'm sure you will find the information you are seeking, and once you do you can make an informed, unbiased decision. Is not this fair and balanced?

In my opinion, Richard deliberately twists what he sees as an opponents' view and reconstructs it so that it fits the characterization and narrative he wants to promote. For me, that is intellectually lazy, and in most cases disingenuous. But, in fairness, I also want to say that all of us do the same thing to some degree. Even I have done it. We all recruit allies that support our side of things and ignore anything that might contradict it. It is human nature, isn't it? We want to be right, even if it's not on the side of truth. My goal is to be on the side of truth, no matter what. That said, I still want to give Richard a little slack here, and here's why. The fact is, Richard's dealing with impure, and incomplete doctrines due to the effects of apostasy. It has affected all religions, and therefore he is having to deal with the many limited understandings of the true nature of God and the universe He organized. The greatest period of apostasy known to man was the past 1,800 years (From the death of the apostles up to 1820 and Joseph's First Vision). History calls it 'The Great Apostasy', even *'The Dark Ages'.*

The true gospel of Jesus Christ is always dispensed in its purity by God Himself to mankind. It was first dispensed to Adam and Eve in the Garden, and then by an angel later-on, after they had been cast out of the Garden and became fallen mortals. Adam and Eve taught this pure gospel to their children. It was then taught by each patriarch who followed Adam, on down to Noah, and from Noah to Abraham, and then from Abraham to Isaac, and from Isaac to Jacob, who was Israel. It continued being taught by prophets, but there were gaps like the one the Israelite nation experienced, which lasted 400 years until Moses was taught by Jethro in the land of Midian. Moses' prophetic mantle was later placed upon Joshua. From there the pure gospel was taught by the prophets as apostasy popped up continually, until the time of the last prophet of the Old Testament, Malachi. After Malachi there was a new apostasy of 500 years, lasting all the way until John the Baptists' time. This pattern of prophets receiving revelation from God is the Lord's way of dispensing His Plan of Happiness and gospel of Redemption to His children on earth, but there's also the pattern where apostacy creeps in and the pure gospel becomes corrupted.

After Jehovah, He being commanded by His Father to give it to His prophet Jacob, who was later called Israel, his chosen people the Israelites found themselves enslaved by the Egyptian empire, and over the next 400 plus years in captivity they had fallen into a state of deep apostasy, having no living prophet-leader to provide and guide them with continuing revelation from Jehovah, at least not until Moses came on the scene. We all know the story of Moses, and how the Lord God Jehovah raised him up to free His people, the Israelites, from their enslavement by their wicked overseer Seti, (who reigned from c. 1318–c. 1304), and later Ramses II, the pharaoh during the Exodus (c. 1304–c. 1237). If not, it's a great story for you to learn how God dealt with His chosen people, the Israelites – the House of Israel.

As their prophet leader, Moses, having freed his people, led them to and through the wilderness for more than forty years. He taught the children of Israel the pure gospel of Jesus Christ, who was the Savior *to come* in the Meridian of Time. Moses gave them God's Ten Commandments. He gave them the ordinances contained in the law of Sacrifices and Offerings, they being used as types and shadows to teach them about the great and last sacrifice of the Lamb of God, the Savior to come, Jesus of Nazareth.

Jehovah, the invisible God of the Old Testament, was the great I AM, who Moses was allowed to see face to face. The Bible represented Him as a fire in the burning bush. Joseph Smith's translation of this story in the books of Moses, makes clear how this meeting between Jehovah and His soon-to-be prophet leader Moses, actually took place, and how Jehovah actually appeared to Moses and showed him unspeakable things, even His spirit body (Jehovah had not yet been born as Jesus so he didn't have a physical body. Moses was able to see Jehovah because the Holy Ghost rested upon him).

After bringing His people out of bondage, over the next forty years Jehovah continually instructed his prophet Moses, solemnly commanding him to warn the Israelites that if they rejected the gospel and did not keep His commandments, they would be destroyed, which in fact is what happened to those Israelites who rejected God's counsel and rebelled against Moses' warnings by making a golden calf to worship. This rejecting of the God of their Fathers, even the Great I AM, sealed their doom. The Israelites were given a chance to repent but many of them continued in their rebellion by breaking their covenants and God's commandments. Most of these wicked Israelites were destroyed by God at the time when Moses came down from Mt. Sinai and saw that they were worshipping the golden calf, and others died off over the next forty years while wandering in the wilderness. After the wicked, disbelieving Israelites had all died off, their remaining children and grandchildren were allowed to enter into the promised land called Canaan. It was these righteous 2nd and 3rd generations of Israelites that were allowed to go into the land of Canaan, which includes modern-day Palestine.

Next, Jehovah directs Israel's new prophet Joshua, to go and take possession of the land He promised to Abraham, even the land of their inheritance Canaan. It was this process of war, conquering, and human destruction that Richard uses as an excuse to rile against Israel's' God, Jehovah. Dawkins' vitriolic derision and mocking where he calls Him a power-hungry, murderous God, is to me unjustified, and uninformed criticism. I will address why I can say this in a later chapter.

One can't help but notice that the Bible contains a continuous history of God's chosen people falling away into a state of apostasy. From a careful reading of the Bible, as I said, one reads that there are in fact several falling aways, or what I call *times of apostasy*, which means there was often a need for a new dispensing of God's pure gospel, the gospel of Jehovah of the Old Testament, and the gospel of Jesus Christ of the New Testament. Each were a restoration of sorts; each being a dispensing of God's pure truth. There were many prophets called, such as Eli, Samuel, Elijah, and others. One of these prophets was Daniel. Daniel was a teen living in Jerusalem at that time of the siege of Jerusalem. Daniel and others were captured and taken to Babylon around 610 B.C. to 597 B.C., where they became servants to king Nebuchadnezzar.

Daniel was a faithful follower of Jehovah and was the young Israelite who was brought before King Nebuchadnezzar, king of Babylon, regarding a dream the king had been having. Nebuchadnezzar had been disturbed by this very troubling, reoccurring dream; a dream he couldn't even remember. Daniel was brought before the king, where he told the king what his dream was about, and then he told him what his dream meant. This prophetic, revelatory gift that Daniel had been given, was the gift of revelation. This revelatory gift helped save many of the Kings servants, including Daniel and his friends.

Another prophet was the prophet Samuel, the last of the judges and the first of the later prophets. Samuel was the prophet who anointed Jesses' youngest son David to be the King of all Israel, even while King Saul sat on the throne. David was the lad who killed the Philistines' champion soldier Goliath, who supposedly stood 9' 6" tall (He would've made a fantastic center in the NBA, wouldn't he have?). There was also the prophets Nehemiah, Jerimiah, and Lehi. Jehovah directed Lehi to take his family and flee out of Jerusalem before King Nebuchadnezzar's armies came and destroyed it around 600 BC. Lehi and his family ultimately were led to North America where they grew into two nations, the Nephites, and the Lamanites. It was a prophet from the soon-to-be extinct Nephite nation, the prophet Moroni, who was the last of the Nephite people who buried their golden plate records and later gave them to Joseph Smith to translate. Moroni's father was Mormon. Mormon was commanded by the Lord to gather up all the Nephite records, which covered their 1,000-year history, and abridge them onto thin gold plates.

After abridging these records, Moroni was then commanded by his father Mormon, to write a few words of instructions and add them to his abridged plates, and then to hide them up for a future time. Like I said, it was these gold plates written by these ancient prophet-leaders, that Joseph Smith received from the resurrected Moroni on September 22, 1827. Moroni told the prophet Joseph Smith that he would soon translate them into a book of scripture by the gift and power of God. That translated book became known as the Book of Mormon, named after the ancient writer and prophet Mormon.

As I said, there was a 500-year gap from the last of the Old Testament prophets, the prophet Malachi, to John the Baptist. At that time King Herod was tricked into having this prophet, John the Baptist, beheaded, and that evil act ended the line of worthy Old Testament prophets since Moses Day. It was just before this critical juncture that Jesus Himself, John the Baptists' cousin, entered the scene to restore His pure gospel of redemption to the earth, and to set up His Church with living apostles, evangelists, priests, and teachers, beginning with Peter, James, and John as its 1st presidency. Having been called by Heavenly Father to be The Savior of the World, Jesus' assignment included restoring the pure *Gospel of Redemption, even the Father's Plan of Happiness* time and time again. His Atonement was the crowning and central act that gave efficacy to His Father's Plan of Happiness. Yet even Jesus' personal earthly ministry, with all of His miracles He performed, could not keep the Ancient Day Saints from marching on into apostasy, even into the greatest 'falling away' foretold by Jesus' ordained apostles.

The religionists of that Day were the aristocracy of the Jews called the Sadducees and the religious separatists called the Pharisees. Both groups had fallen into a state of deep apostasy by the time John the Baptist came on the scene, John being the last of the prophets, even the bridge between the ancient prophets over to Jesus' earthly ministry. John was killed by a wicked king for preaching the pure Gospel of Jesus Christ, which required that John declare to everyone that Jesus, "whose shoe's latchet he was not worthy to unloose", was the literal Son of God and the Heavenly King of the Jews. John was the prophet called to 'prepare the way' for Jesus to come in the meridian of time.

As I said, the prophet John the Baptist, therefore, was the *bridge* of the old dispensation over to the new dispensation, which Jesus Himself opened. This new dispensing was the Dispensation of the Meridian of Times. The dispensing of the pure gospel by Jesus to the Jews, was another restoration of the pure gospel which Jesus taught during His three-year ministry. Its original purity had been lost due to apostasy. After Jesus' crucifixion and death, and soon after the death of all His living apostles, apostasy reigned for the next 1,800 years. The restored Church that Jesus Christ set-up during His ministry, *"fled into the wilderness"*, so to speak, ... until the *times of refreshing* would come, and new light would burst forth as the apostle John prophesied while on the isle of Patmos (See JST Rev. 12).

With each dispensation or *dispensing* of the true, pure Gospel of Jesus Christ, the doctrines of this Gospel of Jesus Christ are revealed to God's chosen prophet leaders, whom He raises up for the very purpose of declaring the gospel plan to the people living during their dispensation. The prophets' responsibility is to teach God's Plan of Redemption and Happiness in its purity to the people of the world, thus providing the way for all of God's children to *come unto Christ* and ultimately return back into the presence of God, our Heavenly Father.

This true gospel does not and did not evolve over millions of years of evolutionary iterations by hundreds of thousands of mumbo-jumbo-speaking soothsayers conjuring up ways to enslave the people with their priestcraft (Priestcraft, again, is the preaching and setting oneself up for a light to the world to get gain and the praise of the world, without truly caring for their congregants). [182]

The principle here, is when people dwindle into a state of unbelief called apostasy, even the state of rebellion, where they no longer have faith in the True and living God dwelling in their hearts, apostasy sets in. It also seems as though such people who are in apostasy always want to kill God's prophets. This is exactly what happened with the people over the centuries leading up to the time when Jesus, born in Bethlehem in the land of Jerusalem, inconspicuously came on the scene. It's exactly what was behind Jesus' death and was the reason for all the religious wars that took place over the centuries that followed Christ's death, and it is the very reason behind the prophet Joseph Smith's martyrdom.

The religionists of Jesus' Day almost instantly wanted to kill Jesus. They were in full apostasy, enjoying their priestcraft, and so they didn't want to lose that source of wealth and power they held over the people. The Jewish religionists (Using the power of the Roman state) sought to kill Jesus, and ultimately did kill Jesus with the help of Rome's' rulers and their soldiers, who crucified Him. It took place just three years after Jesus started His ministry amongst the Jews. They wanted Him out of their way because His miracles and message were threatening their religious power and authority over the Jews.

This is a good time for me to mention an incredible commentary on the life of Jesus Christ called "Jesus the Christ". It was written by an apostle of the Church of Jesus-Christ of Latter-Day Saints, James E. Talmage. Elder Talmage was commissioned by the Church to write it. This book is my favorite book on the life and teachings of the Savior. After Jesus was crucified, He returned to His Father in Heaven, and within a few short years after His ascension, his chosen apostles, having continued teaching and administering His gospel to the Jews, and after the apostle Paul had taken it to the gentiles, all of the apostles were either killed or they died off except for John the Beloved (John the Revelator), who the scriptures say, "remained on the earth even to this very day, having been translated to a *state of being* that allowed him to live on and not taste of disease or death." [183]

I won't detail how all the apostles died or how they were martyred. I'll just say that most of them were butchered. For example, the apostle Paul was beheaded, perhaps as part of the executions of Christians that were ordered by the Roman emperor Nero, following the great fire in the city in 64 CE.

If the scriptures are true, the apostle John, The Beloved, is living amongst the people of the world even now, but where he is, is unknown, and it will remain unknown until Jesus Christ returns. I guess you could call him an Immortal. Why the Lord chose to have John perform the work that he's been doing as an immortal, I do not know exactly, except that he's helping the Gospel of Jesus Christ be spread throughout the world. If you go to www.churchofjesuschrist.org you can do a search for "John, the Disciple Who Jesus Loved" by Eric D. Huntsman, professor of Ancient Scripture at Brigham Young University. This is a commentary on John the Revelator. It will help you, my readers, to understand what the Latter-Day Saints' perspective is on this beloved apostles' ministry and why he was translated, as was Enoch, Moses, Elijah and three of the ancient Nephites. For those of you who like learning about these incredible stories, I've gone ahead and included this instruction on how to access it.

Like I said earlier, even before the death of all the apostles, the seeds of the Great Apostasy had already been planted in the hearts of the people by Satan. It seems that living the Gospel of Jesus Christ is difficult, for it requires the best of us to be maintained, and for most of us that is asking a great deal, and for some it is simply asking too much. I agree that it is difficult to live the gospel of Jesus Christ without having a deep and abiding faith in Him. I would submit that we can live the Lords' gospel however, if we use the *gift of repentance* and apply Christ's atonement, with its Grace and Enabling power so that our sins don't overtake us.

The great apostasy I've been talking to you about, as I said, was a stretch of time that lasted approximately 1,800 years. It was from Christs' death until the Restoration of the Gospel of Jesus Christ in the Spring of 1820, when the boy Joseph Smith Jr. went into a grove of trees near his home to seek an answer to his question, "Which of all the Churches on the earth he should join?" Just think of the history of the world that took place during these dark ages, up until the early to mid-19th century.

Joseph Smith's search for truth resulted in his First Vision, where the Father and His Son, Jesus Christ, appeared to him. As the heavens opened, God the Father Himself, in person, introduced His Son Jesus the Christ, by saying "This is my beloved Son, hear Him". Joseph, after gaining his strength, and having faith that Jesus would answer his question, humbly asked the Lord "which of all the churches he should join?", and Jesus replied to His soon-to-be boy prophet saying, "he was to join none of them". [184]

With this singular event, the resurrected Jesus began once again to dispense His pure Gospel in its fulness; line upon line; precept by precept. A new prophet had been raised up for the purpose of revealing His Plan of Redemption and Happiness to the world again, but it was for the last time. It was the start of *The Times of Refreshing*, the *"Last Dispensation of the Fulness of Times"*, foretold by His ancient apostle Peter more than 2,000 years earlier. Here's what the apostle Peter wrote about this:

Acts 3:19-21

19 Repent ye therefore, and be converted, that your sins may be blotted out, *when the times of refreshing shall come* from the presence of the Lord;

20 And he shall send Jesus Christ, which *before* was preached unto you:

21 Whom the heaven must receive *until the times of restitution of all things*, which God hath spoken by the mouth of all his holy prophets since the world began.

The fulness of the restoration, or *restitution of all things*, is still unfolding even today, and will continue to unfold into the Millennium. Through the instrumentality of the prophet Joseph Smith Jr. the true Gospel of Jesus Christ, in its purity and fulness, was restored to the earth in our Day. This dispensing started in 1820. It is called the "Last Dispensation of the Fulness of Times", even a dispensing of God's Gospel in its purity and fulness, to the entire world for these the "Last or Latter Days".

Joseph immediately began to share his First Vision experience, but did so at great peril, and because he did, he ultimately had his life taken from him, as I said, by a state-sanctioned mob, therefore sealing his testimony with his own blood, just as many ancient Day prophets and Jesus had done before him.

Today, this restored gospel of Jesus Christ is being shared with all people throughout the world by members of the Church of Jesus Christ of Latter-Day Saints, the modern-Day Israel. A worldwide missionary force of more than 53,000 missionaries are preaching the restored gospel in every land and to every people in their own tongue, when they allow them to, just as Jesus commanded His apostles to go and do before His ascension. Here's what the Savior of the World commanded His apostles to do:

Mark 16:15-16

15 And he said unto them, Go ye into all the world, and preach the gospel to every creature.

16 He that believeth and is baptized shall be saved; but he that believeth not shall be damned.

(My perspective of what 'damned' means, is not to be 'sent to hell', as much as it is to be 'stopped', or the opposite of 'saved'. Just as a dam *stops* water from flowing forward, being damned is stopping one from progressing forward towards eternal life and exaltation. Their eternal progression is stopped.)

At the beginning of this, the last dispensing, the Lord said to the prophet Joseph Smith:

Doctrine & Covenants 112:28

28 But purify your hearts before me; and then go ye into all the world, and preach my gospel unto every creature who has not received it;

29 And he that believeth and is baptized shall be saved, and he that believeth not, and is not baptized, shall be damned.

Since receiving this charge by the Lord to go into all the world and preach His Restored Gospel for one last time before His 2nd coming, it has become a major hinge-point in history. There's a degree of apostasy already taking root in the hearts and minds of many men and women's hearts today, and it's starting within God's own Church. There are many members of the Church of Jesus Christ of Latter-Day Saints today who have faced, or are facing a faith crisis, and as such many are losing their testimonies.

In my opinion, it is due to many factors, but I believe the chief factor is because they've been deceived by the spirit of Satan. Most of these members haven't put on the whole armor of God, so that upon being confronted with complexities of faith, combined with Satan's sophistries, wiles, and lies, they made the choice to believe the lies of that great deceiver, even the father of lies. They also have chosen to listen to those who unwittingly serve him. These deceivers are people like the atheist Richard Dawkins, who uses his influence and scientific credentials to cause unsuspecting, spiritually immature souls to lose their faith in God, which is exactly what Richard states was his objective and purpose for writing his book. Most of the members who find themselves in a faith crisis, and even some who aren't there yet, have not consistently studied the Gospel on a daily basis, in order to anchor their faith in the

Savior, Jesus Christ, who is the source of all light and truth, and as a result, most of these deceived members, having failed to put on the whole armor of God as a protection and shield against such lies, are falling into cognitive dissonance and apostasy, or they're walking close to its edge. The Lord warned:

Ephesians 6:11-18

11 *Put on the whole armour of God*, that ye may be able to stand against the wiles of the devil.

12 For we wrestle not against flesh and blood, but against principalities, against powers, against the rulers of the darkness of this world, against spiritual wickedness in high *places.*

13 Wherefore take unto you the whole armour of God, that ye may be able to withstand in the evil day, and having done all, to stand.

14 Stand therefore, having your loins girt about with truth, and having on the breastplate of righteousness;

15 And your feet shod with the preparation of the gospel of peace;

16 Above all, taking the shield of faith, wherewith ye shall be able to quench all the fiery darts of the wicked.

17 And take the helmet of salvation, and the sword of the Spirit, which is the word of God:

18 Praying always with all prayer and supplication in the Spirit, and watching thereunto with all perseverance and supplication for all saints; [185]

Doctrine & Covenants 27:15-18

15 Wherefore, lift up your hearts and rejoice, and gird up your loins, and take upon you my whole armor, that ye may be able to withstand the evil day, having done all, that ye may be able to stand.

16 Stand, therefore, having your loins girt about with truth, having on the breastplate of righteousness, and your feet shod with the preparation of the gospel of peace, which I have sent mine angel's to commit unto you;

17 Taking the shield of faith wherewith ye shall be able to quench all the fiery darts of the wicked;

18 And take the helmet of salvation, and the sword of my Spirit, which I will pour out upon you, and my word which I reveal unto you, and be agreed as touching all things whatsoever ye ask of me, and be faithful until I come, and ye shall be caught up, that where I am ... ye shall be also. Amen.

With this lack of spiritual maturity and protection, along with their misunderstanding of the scriptures due to their limited scripture study and lack of faith, the scriptures have not become delicious to the taste for them. ... They have failed to take heed to the Lords' warnings, wherein He warned:

Matthew 24:23-24

23 Then if any man shall say unto you, Lo, here *is* Christ, or there; believe *it* not.

24 For there shall arise false Christs, and false prophets, and shall shew great signs and wonders; insomuch that, if *it were* possible, they shall deceive *the very elect.*

These dear members, even some of the very elect like this scripture says, are falling away, even to the point of losing their belief in God's existence all together. This is so sad to me, and this falling away will continue to increase until Jesus' 2nd coming and the millennium ushers in upon us unexpectedly.

These claims that I am making here, most certainly will be criticized and mocked by Richard and other new atheists like him, such as Lawrence Kraus, Sam Harris, Daniel Dennett, Peter Atkins, and others.

Some of those who were once members of the Church of Jesus Christ of Latter-Day Saints who have fallen or stepped away from the covenant path, have and are now joining the pack of barking and yapping dogs, each adding their critical voices to this farrago of mocking and derision towards the Church and its leaders. This is just one more sign of the times. But that's okay. I still love them and will continue to pray for them that they will one day return to the covenant path where I and others will greet them with open arms, to walk arm-and-arm with them on the path to God's presence.

The atheists, some Christians, and even the fallen elect, have entered into the Great and Spacious Building that the prophet Lehi spoke of in his *"Tree of Life Vision"*. Like barking dogs chasing the Caravan of Truth, these non-believers continually mock members of the Church of Jesus Christ of Latter-Day Saints. Our beliefs and doctrines are *peculiar* and require that we live righteous, morally pure lives, but for some reason, this offends those who choose not to live in that way. God Himself called His people to live holy lives and become a peculiar people, a chosen generation. Here's what the apostle Paul said:

Titus 2:14

14 Who gave himself for us, that he might redeem us from all iniquity, and *purify* unto himself a *peculiar people*, zealous of good works.

I Peter 2:9

9 But ye *are a chosen generation*, a royal priesthood, an holy nation, a *peculiar people*; that ye should shew forth the praises of him who hath called you out of darkness (The darkness of apostasy) into his marvelous light (The light of His life and the light of His pure gospel):

The nature of God that we, as members of Christs' Church teach, is quite different than the doctrine of the Trinity that Christendom teaches. We teach that God, His Son Jesus Christ, and the Holy Ghost, are three separate and distinct personages, though they are one in purpose and not one in essence or three persons in one *Being*, and because we teach this, we are ridiculed and mocked by those with the spirit of anti-Christ, which is the spirit of Satan who hates God the Father and His Beloved Son. Satan's only goal is to destroy God's Plan of Redemption and Happiness because he can never enjoy it himself.

As I've said, Christians don't consider members of the Church of Jesus Christ of Latter-Day Saints to be Christian in any way, shape, or form, and that's because, as I've said, our unique understanding of God and Jesus Christ's nature being so very different from theirs. We believe Jesus is just like His Father, both of them having bodies of flesh and bone as tangible as man's (Both having been resurrected). We believe we have been created in their express, divine image, having bodies like their bodies, having both parts and passions, and one day we will all become even more like them when we are *completed* on resurrections' Day, a Day where we'll receive our immortal state and degree of glory, a state of being that will allow us to enjoy eternal peace and joy in Father's and Jesus' presence and heavenly society:

Doctrine & Covenants 130:22

22 The Father has a body of flesh and bones as tangible as man's; the Son also; but the Holy Ghost has not a body of flesh and bones, but is a personage of Spirit. Were it not so, the Holy Ghost could not dwell in us. [186]

My perspective of how the Book of Mormon was translated, as well as the teachings and doctrines of the Church that I believe and espouse, seems to fit Richards' description as being truly delusional, and I, of course, completely disagree with that characterization. In due time we will all come to know the truth of all these things, and that day will be a day of pure enlightenment and joy, even a day of God's reckoning when the heavens will be rolled back like a scroll and all things will be revealed at Christ's 2nd coming. On that day all of us will see God's Son as He truly is, the True and Living God.

Either I, and every member of the Church of Jesus Christ of Latter-day Saints, as well as all believers for that matter, will be revealed as the ones suffering from the *God Delusion*, or Richard, and all his atheist friends will be revealed to be the ones suffering from *An Atheist's Delusion*. Both claims cannot be true, and so one or the other of us will be falsified, and of course, I believe Richard and his fellow atheists will be the one's proven wrong. If he's right then who cares, for when we all die, we'll be dirt!

On that day I will not be glad and say, "I told you so!" I will be sad for the nonbelievers, for I love them and hope that one day they'll come unto Christ and enjoy the peace and happiness that The Lord, Jesus Christ offers to all who will believe in and follow Him. My claim that God the Father, and His Son, Jesus Christ, appeared to the boy Joseph Smith Jr. as separate and distinct persons, even glorified, eternal, resurrected beings, causes Richard, and all non-believers like him, to feel angst and sometimes even hatred towards believers like myself. Many choose to mock and spew out vitriol against members of my Church in particular, but I choose to pay them no heed, for such is the way of the world when the influence of apostasy and the spirit of Satan are having their way with them. I choose to simply do what the Savior did, which was to pay them no mind.

Joseph's vision re-established once again the knowledge of the true nature of God. Scientific data itself comes closer to defining the truth that we, as Latter-Day Saints believe about God and His nature, than it does for any other religion being followed by the world today. I once again, refer you to Dr. John Lamb's book "Joseph Smith's 21st Century View of the World".

I've shared just the tip of the iceberg from it, regarding our understanding of the universe, of God's true nature, of light, of spirit-matter, of the spirit world, and so much more before we're done review Richard's book. My objective, however, is not to be preachy in any way here. Please understand this. I am simply wanting to enlighten your, my readers, minds with this glorious understanding of the *light of knowledge* that has been restored to the earth one last time, in our day, making it available for your honest and informed consideration.

One such doctrine or practice that stirs great angst and sometimes vitriolic ire against the Church and its members, is the Church's past practice of plural marriage. This religious practice ceased more than 190 years ago. Another practice that triggers vitriol and is deemed as being racist, was the practice of not allowing baptized and confirmed black male members of the Church, to be ordained to the priesthood, at least not until 1978 when the prophet and president of the Church at that time, President Spencer W. Kimball, received a revelation that finally allowed all worthy male members of the Church to have conferred upon them the Melchizedek priesthood and be ordained elders, thus allowing black members to participate in temple ordinances, including temple sealings and celestial marriage.

Great misunderstanding of these and other doctrines and practices of the Church of Jesus Christ of Latter-Day Saints, is usually the result of our critics not getting fully informed about the principles at the heart of our doctrines and practices. Their uninformed criticisms become a stumbling block for most non-members and even some of our less-informed members. These two issues have at times been the source of such adversarial hatred by our enemies, that it has driven them to commit acts of violence and murder against our adherents. Today's critics certainly would characterize the early saints of the Church as being delusional, but the enemies of that Day took their hatred to the extreme, believing the saints to be a threat to their political and economic lives, so that they even murdered some of our members. The chief force driving the religious leaders of that Day, just like those in Christ's Day, was the fear that their priestcraft was at risk. Many preachers lost their congregants to conversion to the LDS Church. This fear produced the mobocracy of hate and violence that our early members suffered.

Everywhere the Latter-Day Saints gathered they formed a large block of voters, which had a major impact on the politics of those states. The anti-Mormon hatred for the so-called *Mormons*, resulted in some of our women being raped, their property illegally taken, and some of our men being murdered by mobs, who, in my opinion, were inspired by the spirit of Satan, its source. Two of those murdered were the prophet Joseph Smith and his older brother Hyrum. Truly, the mobs were the delusional ones.

Such actions, I hope, would not be tolerated in today's America, but sometimes I find myself wondering if this might even happen in our Day. Ultimately, because our enemies saw our body of members as a threat to their livelihoods and political control, they formed mobs with the goal of exterminating the saints, and due to those so-called Christians having little if any conscience to inhibit their evil actions, their worse selves ruled the day, and the saints suffered a painful price. These early saints were driven from their homes and made to flee for their lives, going from state to state, even during unbearable winter months with blizzards in full swing. Men, women, and children alike, had to leave their personal property and belongings as plunder for their enemies, simply because their beliefs were so peculiarly different and contrary to the teachings of the religionists of that Day. Talk about bigotry and hate crimes! These were fellow Americans! Good honk in the morning!

I have often wondered if I and other Latter-Day Saint descendants of these Americans, Americans who were pushed off their lands, losing their property to illegal mobs with the full support of the government, should make the same kind of 'reparations demands' that our black friends and citizens are fighting for today because of how *their* ancestors were forced into slavery for more than four centuries. Their African American ancestors, most certainly, suffered immoral, evil crimes. It was an atrocity fostered upon their ancestors by fellow Americans. Let me say that my Latter-Day Saint ancestors' treatment doesn't come close to what happened to Black Americas' ancestors, but it does give me license to cry along with them, "Injustice! That was criminal!" The fact is, both groups, without question, were treated unjustly by those who should have been led by the spirit of Christianity and civility, yet these Americans were raped, murdered, and pillaged in the so-called name of Christianity.

I am sure if Richard wanted to take the time to write about the Church of Jesus Christ of Latter-Day Saints, singling it out as one of the four mainstream religions in existence today, and especially critiquing our history, our doctrines, and our persecutions, he would have a hay-day belittling it with what I know would be uninformed, false characterizations, such as "They're crazy cultists with mental illness. These are delusional nuts who believe in angels, visions, and miracles like God calling a young man of 23 years to be responsible for translating a made-up holy book from bogus gold plates!"

I'm sure the vitriol would be much like the criticisms Richard made against the God of the Old Testament, Jehovah, who was the pre-mortal Savior, even Jesus, who came to earth to live and teach His gospel. Why would Richard treat the Latter-Day Saints any differently than how he has treated any believer in God? I'm sure he wouldn't, and doesn't, and that's because he has showed his hearts' bigotry in his brief description of what he calls Mormonism, and towards our origin and peculiar beliefs.

Just the fact that Richard even mentions the Mormons in his book, shows me that my faiths' history and doctrines certainly caught his attention. I hope you, my readers, will avoid taking the surface examination route that Richard took, and do a more honest, sincere, deeper dive into what the Latter-Day Saints early history actually was and what our proclaimed doctrines actually are, and then find someone from our Church in your area that you trust will give you more than tradition-based, or a hearsay veneer kind of answer to your honest questions. Hopefully that member will be someone who can answer any question you might have, more fully and completely, and will be authentic as your guide through the maze of questions you may be asking yourself about the story of the Restoration. In other words, please go to the 'horse's mouth' to get your answers and not to our critics.

Regarding Richard's bigoted characterization of Mormonism, I simply reply, "Until it can be proven that the *perspective* I've given, and will yet give here, on the God I believe in, is in fact *bogus* and is *falsified* with evidence that is undeniable and irrefutable, hold your peace. Until the evidence put forth by our critics can show that the so-called 'God of the Mormons' does in fact NOT exist, then Richards' barking and yapping, as well as everyone else's howls, are just that … a chorus of barking critics. I apologize for the course descript here, but I sometimes find myself becoming a bit offended.

I believe the *Caravan of Truth* I'm a part of, will continue to forge ahead until the day when Jesus Christ Himself returns at His 2nd coming, a coming attended by both those still living on the earth at that time as well as those who will come with Him. I believe I'll be part of the later. All will actually see the heavens rolled back like a scroll and the Lord Himself will be revealed in all His glory, power, and magnificence, as He sets the world straight on what's real and what's not, circumscribing all truth into one great whole. Next is the sub-title – "Secularism, the Founding Fathers, and Religion of America."

SECULARISM, THE FOUNDING FATHERS, AND THE RELIGION OF AMERICA

In this subtitle Richard covers the topic of *Secularism and Secularists*. He begins with a quote by Senator Barry Goldwater, who in 1981 stated: "There is no position on which people are so immoveable as their religious beliefs. There is no more powerful ally one can claim in a debate than Jesus Christ, or God, or Allah, or whatever one calls this supreme being." [187]

After quoting this, Richard says that Barry was a staunch presidential candidate and hero of American conservatism and was someone who upheld the secular tradition of the Republic's foundation. Richard is now building his case for the U.S. being founded on *secularism* (the principle of separation of the state from religious institutions) and not on Judeo Christian principles alone. Richard says:

"The paradox has often been noted that the United States, founded in (Upon) secularism, is now the most religious country in Christendom." [188]

Richard's goal here is to postulate the idea that, "The United States was *not* founded as a Christian nation and on its Judeo-Christian values. It was founded by deists who made sure it was founded as a *secularist nation*, a nation that had the principle of the separation of the Church from the State at its core". [189] Here's an excerpt from an article I found titled, "Earthly Governments and Laws". It can be accessed on www.churchofjesuschrist.org. It begins with the following scripture:

Doctrine & Covenants 134:9 – As it relates to the Separation of Church and State

9 We do not believe it just to mingle religious influence with civil government, whereby one religious society is fostered and another proscribed in its spiritual privileges, and the individual rights of its members, as citizens, denied.

"The Church of Jesus Christ of Latter-Day Saints upholds the principle laid down by the Constitution of the United States that religion and government should be kept separate."

The Church of Jesus Christ of Latter-Day Saints' First Presidency in 1907 (Joseph F. Smith, John R. Winder, and Anthon H. Lund) stated the following:

"The Church of Jesus Christ of Latter-Day Saints holds to the doctrine of the separation of Church and State; the non-interference of church authority in political matters; and the absolute freedom and independence of the individual in the performance of his (or her) political duties. We declare that from principle and policy, we favor:

- "The absolute separation of Church and State;"
- "No domination of the State by the Church;"
- "No Church interference with the functions of the State;"
- "No State interference with the functions of the Church, or with the free exercise of religion;"
- "The absolute freedom of the individual from the domination of ecclesiastical authority in political affairs;"
- "The equality of all churches before the law." [190]

End of Excerpt

The rest of this subtitle is Richard focusing on politics and how religion drives it, and how people reject atheists who want to go into public service. Richard seems to be whining once again and saying that he and his fellow atheists are *victims* of theists. In some cases, this may be true, but not always.

Richard sees fellow atheists as victims of theists whose goal is to keep atheists from serving their fellow citizens. In today's political environment however, things have changed. In fact, one of the quotes Richard gives could be seen as describing today's political left and the '*Wokism*' they promote, such as 'Cancel Culture', 'Black Lives Matter', and the group called 'Antifa'. Here's Richard's quote:

"The factions that are growing throughout our land (religious or leftists?) are not using their 'clout' (religious or political?) with wisdom. They are trying to *force* government leaders into following their position. If you disagree with these groups on a particular moral issue, they complain, they threaten you with a loss of money, or loss of your job, or withdrawing their votes, or all the above (To me, Richard is describing what is now being called 'Cancelled' by the 'Cancel Culture')." [191]

This should sound familiar to you, my readers, when you consider what's happening in America and throughout the world today, as of 2022 (Richard's book was published back in October of 2006), especially when you consider what's been happening the past few years (2016 through 2022). In fact, it's even getting worse here in 2022. I put quotes around the words 'religion & leftists' and 'religious & Politics' so that my readers can compare today's groups that are demanding *"you must be of like mind or of the same ideology as we haves, or we'll cancel you"*, with what you've experienced with people of faith today. There are many organizations and or movements (within the two major, opposing ideologies) that are causing our country to splinter and be at odds with each other, that's for sure. There's the ideology that I just described and then there's the ideology that says, "Live and Let Live as long as you don't step across the line and break the law in order to get your way".

To help emphasize my perspective that says there are two main ideologies growing in influence and power throughout the world today, I want to bring to your attention a video I came across while I was on YouTube. It's called *"We Will Witness What Nephi Saw in Vision"* (Parts 1 & 2) [192]. It doesn't list the presenter's name other than to show what channel posted the videos. The channel is called *Light & Truth*. It's obvious to me though, that the presenter is a member of the Church of Jesus Christ of Latter-Day Saints. The presenter reviews these two growing ideologies that I just talked about, but he goes into greater detail as to what they are and how they'll affect the world in the years to come.

I want to share a few excerpts from these two videos (Part 1 and Part 2), in the hopes that this gentleman's comments will expand your understanding of what I believe is taking place today and how this *polarization* is going to affect the entire world in the next few years. Here are the excerpts:

"All of society will be *polarized into two groups* (He called these groups two 'Church's/Ideologies' and *not* specific religions or organizations). One is aligned with an emerging government, a government of tyranny, surveillance, and control, and the other group will grow in numbers to become a force that resists and stands up for liberty and trusting in God for their salvation. Satan's *collectivist ideology* will cause people to feel that they can't feel safe until every person is *compelled* to live the new world quasi-religion of *global sustainability*.

"The *polarization* of society will be brought about by an increasing display of false evidence and deception that will convince all to align themselves either for liberty or for captivity. One would naturally ask, "Do the scriptures really speak of these things?"

"Let's ponder the prophecy made by the prophet Nephi from the Book of Mormon (And other prophets too) and see what he wrote regarding this, our Day and Time." The video presenter begins by quoting President Russell M. Nelson, current president of the LDS Church as of 2022.

"The prophet and current president of the Church of Jesus Christ of Latter-Day Saints, President Russell M. Nelson has said, and I quote:

"We live in a day that our forefathers have awaited with anxious expectation. We have front-row seats to witness live what the prophet Nephi saw only in vision, that the power of the Lamb of God would descend upon the covenant people of the Lord, who were scattered upon all the face of the earth; and they were armed with righteousness and with the power of God with great glory. You, my brothers, and sisters, are among those men, women, and children whom Nephi saw. Think of that!" (This quote is from a talk titled 'Hear Him', which President Nelson gave in General Conference of 2022).

President Nelson went on to say, "Think of that. He is saying that 'We will live to see it all'." Here is what President Nelson was referring to when he spoke of Nephi and what Nephi prophesied some 2,450 years ago, concerning our Day:

I Nephi 14:7-14

7 For the time cometh, saith the Lamb of God, that I will work a great and a marvelous work among the children of men; a work which shall be everlasting, either on the one hand or on the other— either to the convincing of them unto peace and life eternal, or unto the deliverance of them to the hardness of their hearts and the blindness of their minds unto their being brought down into captivity, and also into destruction, *both temporally and spiritually*, according to the captivity of the devil, of which I have spoken.

8 And it came to pass that when the angel had spoken these words, he said unto me: Rememberest thou the covenants of the Father unto the house of Israel (This refers to the covenant God made with Abraham, called the 'Abrahamic Covenant')? I said unto him, Yea.

9 And it came to pass that he said unto me: Look, and behold that great and abominable church, which is the mother of abominations, whose founder is the devil.

10 And he said unto me: Behold there are save *two churches only*; the one is the church of the Lamb of God, and the other is the church of the devil; (Two ideologies) wherefore, whoso belongeth not to the church of the Lamb of God belongeth to that great church, which is the mother of abominations; and she is the whore of all the earth.

11 And it came to pass that I looked and beheld the whore of all the earth, and she sat upon many waters; and she had dominion over all the earth, among all nations, kindreds, tongues, and people.

12 And it came to pass that I beheld the church of the Lamb of God, and its numbers were few, because of the wickedness and abominations of the whore who sat upon many waters; nevertheless, I beheld that the church of the Lamb, *who were the saints of God*, were also upon all the face of the earth; and their dominions upon the face of the earth were small, because of the wickedness of the great whore whom I saw.

13 And it came to pass that I beheld that the great mother of abominations did gather together multitudes upon the face of all the earth, among all the nations of the Gentiles, to fight against the Lamb of God.

14 And it came to pass that I, Nephi, beheld the power of the Lamb of God, that it descended upon the saints of the church of the Lamb, *and* upon the covenant people of the Lord, who were scattered upon all the face of the earth; and they were armed with righteousness and with the power of God in great glory.

15 And it came to pass that I beheld that the wrath of God was poured out upon that great and abominable church, insomuch that there were wars and rumors of wars among all the nations and kindreds of the earth.

16 And as there began to be wars and rumors of wars among all the nations which belonged to the mother of abominations, the angel spake unto me, saying: Behold, the wrath of God is upon the mother of harlots; and behold, thou seest all these things.

17 And when the day cometh that the wrath of God is poured out upon the mother of harlots, which is the great and abominable church of all the earth, whose founder is the devil, then, at that day, the work of the Father shall commence, in preparing the way for the fulfilling of his covenants, which he hath made to his people who are of the house of Israel.

18 And it came to pass that the angel spake unto me, saying: Look!

19 And I looked and beheld a man, and he was dressed in a white robe.

20 And the angel said unto me: Behold one of the twelve apostles of the Lamb.

21 Behold, he (The apostle John) shall see and write the remainder of these things; yea, and also many things which have been.

22 And he shall also write concerning the end of the world.

23 Wherefore, the things which he shall write are just and true; and behold they are written in the book which thou beheld proceeding out of the mouth of the Jew (The Bible); and at the time they proceeded out of the mouth of the Jew, or, at the time the book proceeded out of the mouth of the Jew, the things which were written were plain and pure, and most precious and easy to the understanding of all men.

24 And behold, the things which this apostle of the Lamb shall write are many things which thou hast seen; and behold, the remainder shalt thou see.

25 But the things which thou shalt see hereafter thou shalt not write; for the Lord God hath ordained the apostle of the Lamb of God that he should write them (John the beloved, who wrote the Book of Revelation while on the isle of Patmos).

26 And also others who have been, to them hath he shown all things, and they have written them; and they are sealed up to come forth in their purity, according to the truth which is in the Lamb, in the own due time of the Lord, unto the house of Israel.

27 And I, Nephi, heard and bear record, that the name of the apostle of the Lamb was John, according to the word of the angel.

End quote of President Nelson [193]

Current apostle, Elder David A. Bednar, speaking at the Saturday morning session of General Conference back in October of 2020, quoted Elder Jeffery R. Holland who spoke at BYU Idaho in December of 1998 (That's 24 years ago!). Elder Bednar was the President of BYU Idaho in December of 1998. Elder Bednar asked Elder Holland, "If you could teach these students just one thing, what would it be?" Here's just one part of what Elder Holland gave as his answer to that searching question, and I quote:

"We are witnessing an ever-greater movement towards *polarity*. The *middle-ground options will be removed from us* as Latter-Day Saints. The middle of the road will be withdrawn." [194]

End Quote by Elder Holland

President Ezra Taft Benson, another prophet and past president of the Church of Jesus Christ of Latter-Day Saints (1985-1994) who has since passed away, stated the following in a 1988 October General Conference talk (That's 34 years ago!), titled, "I testify", and I quote:

"I testify that as the forces of evil increase under Lucifer's leadership and as the forces of good increase under the leadership of Jesus Christ (The two main forces or ideologies in the world), there will be growing battles (I.E. Abortion battles, LGBTQ battles, Woke-ism battles; Transgender battles; Free Speech battles; Climate Change battles, and others) between the two until the *final* confrontation. As the issues become clearer and more obvious, all mankind will eventually *be required* to align themselves, either for the Kingdom of God or the kingdom of the devil." [195]

End of Quote as well as the end of Excerpts from the YouTube "Light & Truth" Videos 1 & 2

I would press upon you, my readers, how important it is that you watch these two videos by "*Light & Truth*" so you can get the full and complete understanding of how these two Church's or Ideologies will play out in the years to come just prior to Christ's 2nd coming. It is important that you do so, so you can be prepared for what is coming. I'm not a doomsayer. I'm just a watchman giving a warning voice of what's to come, but you can be the judge for yourself if you choose to believe any of this, or not. I am choosing to end the excerpts there, as I think I have made my perspective clear as to what I feel about Richard's characterization of Secularism (One Ideology) being the principle or principles on which America was founded, versus the Judeo-Christian characterization (Second Ideology) and the principles which formed the foundation upon which I believe the United States was built.

Separation of Religion from State is the principle that says, "The separation of Religion and State is the foundation of secularism. It ensures religious groups don't interfere in affairs of state, and the state *doesn't* interfere in religious affairs" (You mean like how the state didn't interfere with the Mormons in 1838, where the state sanctioned the murder of Joseph Smith and his older brother Hyrum, as well as ordered the extermination of the saints, American citizens, from Illinois?).

I found an article titled "What is Secularism?" by the 'National Secular Society' that I want you, my readers, to consider as you reflect on this subtopic of *Secularism*. Here are a few excerpts from it:

"The Separation of Religion from the State is the foundation of secularism. It ensures religious groups don't interfere in affairs of state, and the state doesn't interfere in religious affairs (Is this how the State handled the "Mormons"?). In the United Kingdom there are officially two state recognized Christian denominations – the Church of England and the Presbyterian Church of Scotland. The Queen is both head of state and Supreme Governor of the Church of England. There is no established church in Northern Ireland or Wales. But the 26 unelected bishops of the Church of England who sit in the House of Lords influence laws that affect the whole of the UK. Christianity is one major influence among many that shape our current ways of life. We are a nation of many denominations and religions. Large sectors of the population do not hold, or practice religious beliefs. If Britain were truly a secular democracy, political structures would reflect the reality of changing times by separating religion from the State.

Secularism protects both believers and non-believers

"Secularism seeks to ensure and protect freedom of religious belief and practice for all citizens (Has our so-called secular government truly protected our freedoms? In my opinion it has not. One only need look at what is happening and what the so-called 'Right' is fighting for, to know this just isn't true. Consider the list of fights going on in our country as well as across the globe, starting with 'Freedom of Speech'). Secularists want freedoms of thought and conscience to apply equally to all – believers and non-believers alike. They do not wish to curtail religious freedoms (This, in my opinion, again, is also not a true statement. While ideas about religious liberty and tolerance are central to America's founding and national story, different religious groups – including Catholics, Jews, and Latter-Day Saints – have suffered discrimination in the United States at various times in our history, at the hands of the State)."

Religious Freedom

"Secularism seeks to defend the absolute freedom of religion and other beliefs and protect their right to manifest religious belief insofar as it does not impinge on the rights and freedoms of others (The key word here, is 'impinge'. The Left seems to have redefined what 'impinge' means. Just the expression of one's belief about abortion, LGBTQ & Trans issues, etc., seems to be *impinging* on their rights). Secularism ensures that the right of individuals to freedom of religion is always balanced by the right to be free *from* religion (Those who espouse freedom FROM religion, in my experience, do not express themselves in a fair and balanced way, meaning, giving the religious right the opportunity to express their views un-impinged, without being attacked if you don't have the Left's same views)."

Secularism is about democracy and fairness

"In a secular democracy all citizens are equal before the law and parliament. No religious or political affiliation gives advantages or disadvantages, and religious believers are citizens with the same rights and obligations as anyone else. Secularism champions human rights above religious demands (One such human right is a 'woman's right over her own body', yet the secularists do not protect the 'human rights' of the little unborn body in its house, the mother's womb. I could list a multiplicity of so-called rights that in fact are not championed by our secular government. These are 'the issues' that are polarizing all nations throughout the world, and the middle ground that Elder Holland said was going to disappear, so that we'd have to choose God or Satan's path). It upholds equality laws that protect women, LGBT people and minorities from religious discrimination. These equality laws ensure that non-believers have the same rights as those who identify with a religious or philosophical belief."

Access to public services

"We all share hospitals, schools, the police, and the services of local authorities. It is essential that these public services are secular at the point of use, so no-one is disadvantaged or denied access on grounds of religious belief (or non-belief). All state-funded schools should be non-religious in character, with children being educated together regardless of their parents' religion. When a public body grants a contract for the provision of services to an organization affiliated to a particular religion or belief, such services must be delivered neutrally, with no attempt to promote the ideas of that group."

Secularism is not atheism

"Atheism is a lack of belief in gods. Secularism simply provides a framework for a democratic society. Atheists have an obvious interest in supporting secularism, but secularism itself does not seek to challenge the tenets of any particular religion or belief, neither does it seek to impose atheism on anyone. Secularism is simply a framework for *ensuring equality* throughout society – in politics, education, the law, and elsewhere – for believers and non-believers alike."

Secularism protects free speech and expression

"Religious people have the right to express their beliefs publicly but so do those who oppose or question those beliefs. Religious beliefs, ideas and organizations must not enjoy privileged protection from the right to freedom of expression. In a democracy, all ideas and beliefs must be open to discussion. Individuals have rights; ideas do not. Secularism is the best chance we must create a society in which people of all religions, or none can live together fairly and peacefully." [196]

End of "What is Secularism?" article Excerpts

From my perspective, this view of secularism is a perfect description of the emerging tyranny, surveillance, and control that is taking place in our country, spoken of by President Benson 34 years ago in 1988. We are eyewitnesses of this *polarization* taking place in very obvious ways in today's societies.

In closing out this first subtopic on Secularism, Richard says, and I quote:

"The deist God, often associated with the Founding Fathers, is certainly an improvement over the monster of the Bible. Unfortunately, it is scarcely more likely that he exists, or ever did. In any of its forms, the *God Hypothesis* is unnecessary. The God Hypothesis is *very close* to being ruled out by *the law of probability* (And Richard truly believes it soon will be)." [197]

This last statement by Richard reveals the fact that he knows that he has *not* proven the hypothesis that God does *not* exist with any incontrovertible evidence. He has merely stated his opinions about the God Hypothesis, and about it being very close to being ruled out, peppering this with hyperbole in the hope that it will move the needle (Belief Cursor) of the so-called *law of probability* to the 'God Does Not Exist' end of the spectrum. He says, "It is better for our country, and for the entire world for that matter, that we accept the *idea* of God or religion as being the God Hypothesis, and that it's 'unnecessary'." [198]

Again, I wholeheartedly disagree with this view. From here, Richard spends the rest of his book trying to argue that God is unnecessary, which, again, is just Richard giving his opinion. Stating God is unnecessary doesn't make him nonexistent, nor does it offer any evidence for His non-existence.

Next is the subtitle – "The poverty of agnosticism".

THE POVERTY OF AGNOSTICISM

In this subtitle discussion, Richard turns to agnosticism, and what he defines as "the *erroneous notion* that the existence or non-existence of God is an untouchable question, forever beyond the reach of science." [199]

In this section *Richard argues that Atheism is the only intellectually respectable viewpoint on today's scientific landscape.* In addition, he says: "There is nothing wrong with being agnostic in cases where we lack evidence one way or the other. It is the reasonable position." [200]

Carl Sagan is quoted as saying, "It's okay to reserve judgment until the evidence is in," [201] which is exactly what Elder Bruce R. McConkie counseled when we're not sure of the facts. Elder McConkie counseled, "we should *withhold judgement* until we have learned more about the subject". Richard says, "We lack the evidence to do more than *shade the probabilities* one way or the other, regarding scientific questions like the Permian Extinction question, as an example. But, when it comes to the question of God's existence, should we be agnostic about Him too? Many have said definitely, 'Yes', often with an air of conviction that verges on protesting too much. Are they right?" [202]

Richard goes on to discuss two kinds of Agnosticism – "TAP (Temporary Agnosticism in Practice), and PAP (Permanent Agnosticism in Principle)". [203] Richard believes that TAP better defines the Agnostic. He says: "The view that I shall defend lies in the area of a scientific question: One day we may know the answer, and meanwhile we can say something pretty strong about the probability that God does NOT exist (Once again, Richard is just putting forth his opinion, thinking if he says it enough times you and I will start believing it to be true. [204]

Richard accepts that scientific questions, like the Permian Extinction question, fall in the TAP side of agnosticism, which basically says:

"The reasonable stance for the Permian Extinction question is that there is a truth out there and one day we hope to know it, though for the moment *we don't*." [205]

There is truth regarding God's existence *out there* indeed, and one day the entire world will come to know it, for that day will be the day when the millennium bursts upon us. But until then we all must make the choice as to what we believe, or more correctly, as to what we *want* to believe, and I choose and want to believe in God's existence. I also believe that Richard *wants* to believe God does not exist. Both Richard and I have our reasons for *wanting* to believe what we believe. For Richard, there are some scientific related questions that fit his stance. Although the scientific question of whether God exists or not has NOT yet been settled by science, and as a result Richard says: "Today's evidence against it more fully falls into the *strong probability* category of scientific study," [206] which is another way of saying "We don't know whether God exists or not, but our opinion of the data leans to 'He does not'!"

Once again, this is just Richard stating what he feels is strong evidence for the non-existence of God, having been persuaded of the *strong probability* that God doesn't exist. He states the words of atheist scientists who believe like he does, to bolster his view. But all of this is still his opinion. The fact is, there are other scientists in that same scientific study he's quoting from, who say the evidence for God's existence, or at least for an *Intelligent Designer*, more fully falls into the strong probability category for God's existence. Both sides cannot claim there's incontrovertible, settled scientific evidence regarding God's existence or His non-existence … as yet … and so the Caravan of Truth must continue on its journey in search for truth. Richard goes on to say: "The fact that we can neither prove or disprove the existence of something does *not* put existence and non-existence on an even footing." [207]

"The existence of God is a scientific hypothesis just like any other hypothesis. Even if it's hard to test it in practice, it belongs in the same TAP or temporary agnosticism box … just as the controversies over the Permian and Cretaceous extinction questions do. God's existence or non-existence is a scientific fact about the universe, discoverable in principle, if *not* in practice. If he existed and chose to reveal it, God himself could clinch the argument, noisily and unequivocally, in his favor." [208]

As I have said, Christ will certainly do this exact thing at His 2nd coming. But, to do so before that time would frustrate His and our Father's Plan of Happiness, for it requires that all His children be given the opportunity to *use their agency to choose* liberty and eternal life or *choose captivity and death*.

II Nephi 2:26-27 (In the following verses the prophet Nephi, from the Book of Mormon said):

26 And the Messiah cometh in the fulness of time, that he may redeem the children of men from the fall. And because that they are redeemed from the fall they have become free forever, *knowing good from evil*; to act for themselves and not to be acted upon, save it be by the punishment of the law at the great and last day, according to the commandments which God hath given.

27 Wherefore, men are free according to the flesh; and things are given them which are expedient unto man. And they are *free to choose liberty and eternal life, through the great Mediator of all men, or to choose captivity and death, according to the captivity and power of the devil*; for he seeketh that all men might be miserable like unto himself.

Richard continues: "And even if God's existence is never proved or disapproved with certainty one way or the other, *available evidence and reasoning <u>may</u> yield* an *estimate* or *probability* far from 50 per cent." [209]

This last statement is the whole enchilada in my mind, not only for this chapter and all its subtitles, but for Richard's entire argument against God's existence, which is the dominant goal for writing his book. For me, this last statement summarizes Richard's entire book down to one sentence. It reveals what Richard thinks and feels about today's evidence … for or against God's existence. In his view, today's evidence does not favor the hypothesis for God's existence. Richard emphatically states, "The fact that we can neither prove nor disprove the existence of something does *not* put existence and non-existence on an even footing." [210]

Really Richard? C'mon man. This may be your judgment of how this works, but it isn't mine. To Richard, it's all about the *shading of probability; a spectrum of probabilities* where you can place human judgements about the existence of God along a spectrum of probabilities, between two extremes of opposite certainty." [211] This truly is the way a scientists' brain works, isn't it? I don't fault Richard for it.

Richard simply states, "I've laid out in my book enough arguments and reasoning against the existence of God, that it (The putting forth of his books' arguments) yields a probability of more than 50% that God doesn't exist." [212] Hold this thought just a little bit longer, and I'll show you otherwise.

Richard believes anyone who reads his book and doesn't come away agreeing with it, is in fact delusional and a faith-head. The fact that Richard believes the brain, and all that it does, is the end-product of a mindless, unguided, evolutionary process ... says it all. I ask you, "Why should we trust anything that comes from an unguided, unintended process called 'luck', which Richard says is just natural selection working in our wet machine called the brain?" If this is how, in fact, things work, I must tell you that I wouldn't trust it, but I do trust the reference legs that form the stand that supports my table of belief, and that's because it's not made up of a process of luck and unintended mindlessness, which is what atheists, like Richard, believe goes on in our 'mindless' 'unguided' brains.

There are literally hundreds, and possibly thousands of books out there, written by *believing scientists*, where they outline the many religious arguments that support the God Hypothesis, and I'm confident that you, my readers, already know this, as does Richard and his readers. But there's also evidence provided by renown scientists that point to a *probability* that's far more than 51% in *favor* of the idea that there's an Intelligent Designer, a supernatural mind (I prefer to call it a *super-intelligent mind*), even the great causal cause that directed the universes' beginning where He organized everything in it with precision and perfection. But of course, my statements here, like those made by Richard, are just *informed opinions backed by reason* and supportive statements made by highly intelligent scientists, as well as by holy prophets, past and present.

Richards' opinions and my opinions are presented here for you to consider, and once you've finished reading my book it will be up to you to decide which *grouping of evidentiary opinions* and interpretations you want to believe. You will decide which pile of evidence is more convincing and resonating for you. I encourage you to look at the scientific data and each camps' *interpretation* of this data, as you reflect on the 'Big' question of whether-or-not God exists. Be sure to look at all the historical data on our origin and scriptural testimonies given about it, which includes not only my testimony, but the testimonies given by literally millions of people, including the 15 men who are living apostles, prophets, seers, and revelators walking amongst us today.

As you do so, you can determine for yourself whether-or-not such testimonies, scientific evidence, and informed arguments moves your belief cursor in the direction of the *probability* that God exists or takes it in the direction of the *probability* that God does not exist. In the end, it truly comes down to each of us having to make this choice for ourselves. I think all of us are designed with an innate desire to know the answer, and this drives us to seek the answer to this 'Biggest' of the 'Big' questions.

Don't forget, the theist or spiritual side of this debate can in fact be *tested* just as the scientific side says there's does, and millions of people have performed that spiritual test I speak of. They've acted on God's personal *invitation* to *do the experiment on His word*. He's told his prophets to invite each of us, His children, to "Prove me now herewith" by *performing this experiment on His word*, so that we can come to know for ourselves, that He in truth exists, and that He loves us and wants us to return to Him and live in His presence once again as eternal, resurrected beings.

Each-and-every one of us are given the opportunity to choose for ourselves whether-or-not we want to let Him write His law permanently upon our hearts so that we choose to obey Him, which will allow us to live with Him in His presence and experience the joy that that brings, or to choose to reject His invitation and live with Satan forever under his bondage. God allows us to make this choice for ourselves, knowing fully the consequence of our choice, which extends through all eternity. Richard, of course, chooses not to believe in God or in the idea that there's any such thing as life after death.

I'm saddened when anyone chooses to reject God. I love all of His children. I don't want any of my spirit brothers and sisters to suffer eternally or miss out on the promised blessings our Father in Heaven has in store for each of us. Jesus said He has prepared a place for those who choose to follow Him:

John 14:1-3

1 Let not your heart be troubled: ye believe in God, believe also in me.

2 In my Father's house are many mansions: if *it were* not *so,* I would have told you. I go to prepare a place for you (One can only imagine the magnificence of such a mansion and home).

3 And if I go and prepare a place for you, *I will come again*, and receive you unto myself; that where I am, *there* ye may be also.

An apostle living amongst us today, Elder D. Todd Christopherson of the Quorum of the Twelve Apostles, has explained *this invitations' experimental steps* for how we can come to know that God lives *and know that His Son, Jesus Christ, lives too.* [213] The Lord Himself said that *"there is a law, irrevocably decreed in heaven before the foundations of this world, upon which all blessings are predicated, and when we obtain any blessing from God"*, especially a knowledge of God's existence, *"it is by obedience to that law upon which it is predicated"* (Doctrine & Covenants 130:20-21), and here are the steps that this heavenly law requires of us if we are to come to know that God exists, and I quote:

"Step 1 – You must *come to understand that the gospel has been restored* (Restored because there was an apostasy from God's pure gospel which Jesus taught over 1,800 years ago), and then *willingly humble yourself* by accepting the truth that Heavenly Father, our Creator, does not force us to accept His authority. He asks us to *willingly submit our will* to *His will and authority, which requires that we humble ourselves before HIm* (Remember Jesus saying, "Thy will be done Father, not mine be done").

"As agents of our 'selves', we are to choose, and not be forced to accept His authority. This *willing submission to Him as our God*, is the *first step* in coming to know that He truly exists. But you ask, "How do we submit to Him when we don't even know that He exists?" Well, here's how:

"We lay aside any feeling of pride that is so common in the world today. We simply humble ourselves before God, whether we believe in Him or not, by getting rid of the *attitude and mindset* that *rejects and rebels* against the authority of God to rule in our lives. The Lord Himself made the prophet Joseph Smith aware of this *submission process requirement* by describing this *rebellious attitude* in these words found in the Doctrine & Covenants:

Doctrine & Covenants 1:16

16 They seek not the Lord to establish His righteousness, but every man (Or woman) walketh in his (Or her) own way, and after the image of his (Or her) own god.

This rebellious attitude that people have, that Elder Christopherson is referring to here, is manifested when people say things like, "I believe that loving who I want, and how I want, is accepted by the God I believe in. I don't believe in a controlling, Nazi Police kind of God when it comes to who I want to love or how I want to be loved."

I, of course, am referring to how people express how they want to live in terms of their sex life, so that they describe the kind of God they want their God to be. This is making a God in the image and substance of their own imaginations. It's the kind of God that allows any kind of sexual sin or perversion. This of course, is breaking the 1st Commandment of the Ten Commandments where God commands His children to have (Or make) no other Gods before Him, meaning false Gods; Gods that are simply idols with the substance of wood, stone, animals, or the arm of flesh which simply means man-made Gods with no substance, because they're made from one's own imagination.

Another example of such rebellion is when someone is asked about taking God's name in vain (Saying OMG instead of saying a cuss word like 'Oh s**t), or when asked about committing other offensive sins which people seem to commit so easily these days. I'm speaking of sins like looking at pornography, having pre-marital sex, committing adultery, and even just looking at another person with the spirit of lust in their eyes, heart, and mind. When asked if they have broken any of these laws, people quite often say things like, "Everybody does it. God isn't going to judge me for doing something that everybody else is doing, is he? I mean, we're all human, aren't we?"

Or they say things like, "I believe in a God who loves all people. The God I believe in doesn't exist to catch everybody doing something wrong, or to focus on what they do in the privacy of their own bedrooms just so He can punish them. That isn't the Good, Loving, Forgiving God I believe in." Or, they just say, "I don't believe in God at all", so that anything and everything goes for them.

At this point I would suggest that you check out a YouTube video called: "Bob Sagat Talks About Life, Death, and Jesus." [214] Make sure that you listen to what the individuals say when they're interviewed by Reverend Ray Comfort who interviews several people about God. It's very interesting and revealing.

Elder Christopherson continues:

"These expressed attitudes and mindsets are reflections of a *rebellious attitude* against God and His commandments. It's this *rebellious attitude* that Lucifer had when he rebelled against God in the premortal world before this earth was formed for us to come and live on. Lucifer rejected Heavenly Father's *sovereign authority* to declare the truth, and to establish the laws of the universe and the heaven and earth in which we were to come to earth and live by. At that time Satan wanted (and he still wants it even today) the power to declare arbitrarily what he thinks, and what he feels is right and wrong and how things should be done in this world. He has always wanted to be God and to sit in power on God's heavenly throne, as God himself."

(I think there are a ton of people who have this exact spirit of rebellion. They want the power to declare arbitrarily what they think, and what they feel is right and wrong subjectively, and how they think things should be done in this world, and that's because they believe there' is no objective moral law).

Elder Christopherson continues:

"In-order for us to grow in our understanding of the Gospel more fully and completely, we need to pray to Him like the Book of Mormon prophets Alma and Amulek taught, as it is found in the Book of Alma chapters 32, 33, and 34. The steps that Alma and Amulek speak of in these chapters, say that we need to not only read the scriptures daily, which is where the Gospel is laid out for us plainly, but we also need to study, ponder, and pray about what we read so that we understand it more completely. By study I mean reading a few verses, and then stopping to ponder upon them and to pray about them fervently, with real intent. (As we take the time to wait on the Lord, His spirit will prompt us with the answers to any questions that may have come to our mind as we ponder about what we've read. This process soon becomes a *"transformational experience"*, a *"spiritual experience"* that brings forth incredible results (fruit). This kind of *spiritual experiment or test* is described here by Alma):

Alma 32:28

28 Now, we will compare the word unto a seed. Now, if ye give place, that a seed may be planted in your heart, behold, if it be a true seed, or a good seed, if ye do not cast it out by your unbelief, behold, it will begin to swell within your breasts; and when you feel these swelling motions, ye will begin to say within yourselves—It must needs be that this is a good seed, or that the word is good, for it beginneth to enlarge my soul; yea, it beginneth to enlighten my funderstanding, yea, it beginneth to be delicious to me.

In this way we can come to know that the Gospel and its laws are being written on our heart. Jeremiah taught that we can know that God exists when the words of the Lord, taught by His prophets past and present, are beginning to feel more and more *delicious to our soul*:

Jerimiah 31: 31-34

33 But this *shall be* the covenant that I will make with the house of Israel; After those days, saith the LORD, *I will put my law in their inward parts, and write it in their hearts*; and will be their God, and they shall be my people.

34 And they shall teach no more every man his neighbour, and every man his brother, saying, Know the LORD: for they shall all know me, from the least of them unto the greatest of them, saith the LORD: for I will forgive their iniquity, and I will remember their sin no more.

Elder Christofferson continues:

"Step 2 – As we pray for this understanding, we should also pray more specifically to receive the *gift of the Love of Christ*. This love is given as a gift to those who are true followers of Jesus Christ. These followers are disciples who ask for it with all the energy of their heart. This experimental method or process, and it's resulting gifts and answers (The fruit or results of the experiment), soon becomes a provable and repeatable experimental process, and one that all of us can perform. This happened to the prophet Nephi, a prophet referred to in the Book of Mormon, when he saw in vision this pure love of Christ represented as *the fruit of the tree of life* and 'tasting' it becomes a major part of a person's conversion to the truth that God lives, and that His Son Jesus Christ lives and loves us.

"This conversion experience from following this spiritual method, happens because once any of us feels our Savior's love for us, *even the smallest part*, we begin to feel more secure in the arms of His love, and our love for the Savior and for our Heavenly Father, grows in the soul's center or in the seat of our heart and mind, so that our desire to do what these holy beings ask of us, increases within us.

"Step 3 – The next step is to *start and then continue to serve others*. Serving others is an important element of coming to know that God lives and that He has a purpose for us. It cannot be left out of the formula or equation that we are following as part of the experiment, otherwise, like Amulek taught, "Our prayers are vain, and availeth us nothing".

"In other words, we cannot be truly converted to the knowledge of God's existence and to the understanding that He wants to write His law on our heart and mind, unless *we* open our heart and let Him in (Let His Spirit and Light into our heart) to do this work of conversion. We must be the ones to open our hearts, first to a knowledge of the message of the gospel and then to the love that God has for us. Then we must put forth the effort to *put into practice* His gospel law in our daily lives by serving others. This lays out the first three steps beautifully. We cannot fully understand or appreciate this truth, His gospel law, unless we personally *apply it* in our daily lives. Jesus said he came to serve, not be served. So, it must be with each of us.

(I believe that this is why God wants to give us the gift of love for Him, His Son, and for His children, which love moves us to apply His Gospel in our daily lives as we serve others. This in fact happened to me, but that's a story I might share at another time. I'll just say that I have a personal experience that affirms this process of receiving the *Gift of love* for His children, and its fruit as I have served others).

"But 'how' you say?" By looking outward and caring about each other. By being compassionate and forgiving towards each other. By being friendly. By sharing and helping each other in small ways, and sometimes in big ways. By loving each other no matter our color, ethnicity, or faith, and by giving of ourselves in the service of others without any expectation for something coming back to us. As we do so, Heavenly Father is able to spiritually write the Law of the Gospel on our hearts (On our inner parts, our center and core, even the *seat* of our conscience), so that it becomes a part of our very being (To me this is like receiving the oil that the scriptures taught about in the 'Five Wise Virgins' story, where there were those who acquired their lamps' oil well before the day that the Wedding Feast had even begun, and the unwise virgins who hadn't acquired their oil before that day. This oil comes through the daily living of the gospel, especially through loving and serving others, thus taking on the character of Christ)."

Elder Christofferson continues:

"Step 4 – And lastly, the fourth thing we must do as we seek to become truly converted in the knowledge of God's existence, is to *offer His Son, Jesus Christ, the gift of our broken heart and contrite spirit*, which is a repentant and obedient spirit. Such should be our Christmas gift to Christ every year, as we go forward into each new year, and throughout the entire year. In reality this is the gift of yourself and what you are working to *become*. When you get rid of any impure or unworthy behavior in your life, it becomes *a gift of repentance* that you're giving to Jesus, as a show of the love you have for Him and your faith in His gift of the atonement."

"When you develop a good habit or quality that was lacking in your life, so that you adopt it and make it a part of your character, it becomes *a gift* to the Lord. These are the best gifts we can give Him, not only during this Christmas season, but for the rest of our lives!" [215]

End of excerpts from Elder Christophersons' talk on how we can come to know God exists

As we read His word, pray to Him about His word, repent (Change our behavior), and do our best to keep His commandments, *this process softens and prepares our heart in such a way that it can receive the answers we're seeking about His existence and what His nature truly* is. By following His word with real intent, we will, as He has promised, receive the Peace, Love, and Joy (The resulting proofs or fruit gained by doing the experiment) that He said would come to the honest in heart – the honest truth seeker – even the knowledge that God exists shall be given to us. The apostle James recorded:

James 1:5 – 8, 22

5 If any of you lack wisdom, let him ask of God, that giveth to all *men* liberally, and upbraideth not (won't criticize severely); and it shall be given him.

6 But let him ask in faith, nothing wavering. For he, that wavereth is like a wave of the sea driven with the wind and tossed.

7 For let not that man think that he shall receive anything of the Lord.

8 A double minded man *is* unstable in all his ways.

22 Be ye doers of the word, and not just listeners.

Another example of a prophet inviting men and women to put to the test God's gospel invitation by performing this spiritual experiment, is also found in The Book of Mormon. The prophet Moroni was the last prophet writer in the Book of Mormon. It was Moroni who buried the gold plates more than 1,600 years ago. Moroni, as a resurrected being, appeared to Joseph Smith so he could tutor and prepare him to receive and translate the plates. Moroni, before his death, gave the following invitation to all who would read the Book of Mormon. It is an invitation in the form of a *spiritual test*:

Moroni 10:3-5

3 Behold, I would exhort you that when ye shall read these things, if it be wisdom in God that ye should read them, that ye would remember how merciful the Lord hath been unto the children of men, from the creation of Adam even down until the time that ye shall receive these things, and ponder it in your hearts.

4 And when ye shall receive these things, I would exhort you that ye would ask God, the Eternal Father, in the name of Christ, if these things are not true; and if ye shall ask with a sincere heart, with real intent, having faith in Christ, he will manifest the truth of it unto you, by the power of the Holy Ghost.

5 And by the power of the Holy Ghost ye may know the truth of all things.

I could list many more examples of *God's gospel invitation to His children to test or prove His word*, as well as list for you, my readers, a plethora of people who have accepted His invitation to test His word, and after doing the experiment they received the results that God promised He would give them. These promised results come to such seekers of truth in the form of *changes in one's heart*. Upon completing the experiment, the truth seeker finds themselves enjoying a manifestation from the Holy Ghost, who writes God's law upon their hearts so that they begin to experience the gifts of Joy, Peace, and Happiness. By exercising their faith in this law upon which the *'knowledge of God is gained'*, even upon which the *"Mysteries of godliness"* are predicated, they find themselves growing in this principle of revelation until their confidence waxes strong in His presence and they trust Him completely.

The bottom line, as far as I'm concerned, is that each of us can decide for ourselves as to whether this experiment is measurable and repeatable. When we sincerely want to know if God exists, we simply accept God's invitation to test His word is a real, testable way, and its results, though spiritual, will be achieved. The fact that these results are spiritual in nature, seems to throw some people off a bit. Keep in mind that all truth comes from the *Source of all Truth*, which is God our Eternal Father, through the reception of His Spirit, and this spiritual source, for me, is the most reliable source of truth in the universe. It most certainly is not man's puny arm of the flesh (Meaning the power of mans' mind and faculty of reason alone), even though science has given us a great deal of truth about our reality. I would submit, like Newton said, all of the discoveries of science have come from the Holy Ghost. Having said this, I'm still more than willing and open to new knowledge coming from any source, and I am hopeful that I will continue to learn new truth from whatever earthly and heavenly source that may provide it, even if it comes from an atheist's scientific mind like our friend's Richard Dawkins.

Richard goes on to list seven category markers that lay along his *spectrum of probability for God's existence*, and he then shares his position on this spectrum, as follows: "I count myself in category 6 but leaning towards 7 (7 being the farthest to the left of the spectrum, which is 'God does not exist'). I am agnostic only to the extent that I am agnostic about fairies at the bottom of the garden." [216] Excuse my chuckling here. Ha-ha-ha. That was funny Richard. You crack me up.

Category 6 on Richard's *spectrum of probability* regarding God's existence or non-existence, is defined as "A very low probability, but short of zero. A De Facto atheist." He continues:

"*I cannot know for certain*, but I think God is very improvable, and I live my life on the assumption that he is *not* there. [217]

Richard lands just shy of 7 on the *probability spectrum*. My belief cursor, on the other hand, happens to land on 1 on the opposite end of the spectrum from Richards' category 6. My belief cursor lands on category 1, which is farthest to the right of center, and the very end of the *probability spectrum*, it being 100% belief that God does exist. Richard goes on to say, "The point of all these examples like the Flying Spaghetti Monster, or the Galactic Teapot, etc., (Examples of fictitious monsters) is that the burden of proof rests with believers to prove God exists. It's *not* the role of non-believers to prove God exists." [218]

"The odds in favor of these fictitious monsters existing are not good. None of us feels an obligation to disprove any of the millions of far-fetched things that a fertile or facetious imagination might dream up … We are all atheists about the gods that are worshipped by others." [219]

This last sentence that says, "we are all atheists about other gods", is certainly true. Again, the bottom line for Richard is, "What matters is not whether God is disprovable; but whether his existence is probable. … And the probability of God's existence is not even 50 percent." [220]

Again, this 'percentage' opinion is just that, Richard's opinion. To this point of view I say, "What is good for the goose ought to be good for the gander." In other words, theists or religionists should be allowed the same generous allotted place for their claims, which, granted, might seem nonsensical to Richard and other atheists like him, but they're still viable, nonetheless.

For example, in the prophet Joseph Smith's Day, it was easy for secular intellectuals (Richard would have fit perfectly in this group of *secular atheist intellectuals* of Joseph's Day), to ridicule religious belief in unseen worlds as superstitious nonsense (In other words, delusional), but it would be, and is, hypocritical for them to do so today due to all that has been revealed by God to the world regarding the unseen world, either by science or by revealed truths through the living prophets.

Richard's dogmatism regarding his opinion that it – proving God's existence – is up to the theists and believers in God *alone*, shows how little Richard understands the true nature of God and the laws by which we come to know that He exists, and then how to actually come to know Him and His Son on a personal level once we do know 'They exist', and then … how to come to know what His work and purpose for our lives is while we're living on this telestial orb called earth. By way of revelation, the answers to all these questions were given to us in the Book of Moses. Here's Jehovah speaking to Moses:

Moses 1:39

39 For behold, this is my work and my glory—to bring to pass the immortality and eternal life of man.

Father in heaven has been very clear what his work and purposes are for creating this earth and heaven and placing all of us on it (By creating I mean organizing from existing matter that was once in its state of chaos). His is a work of redemption and exaltation. He revealed this truth to His prophet named Moses who wrote it down for each of us to read and ponder.

What's His work you ask? God's *works* are endless. Here's more from the book of Moses:

Moses 1:4

4 And, behold, thou art my son; wherefore look, and I will show thee the workmanship of mine hands; but not all, *for my works are without end*, and also my words, for they never cease.

He created the universe, "worlds without number" …:

Moses 1:33

31 And behold, the glory of the Lord was upon Moses, so that Moses stood in the presence of God, and talked with him face to face. And the Lord God said unto Moses: For mine own purpose have I made these things. Here is wisdom and it remaineth in me.

… including worlds whose "inhabitants … are begotten sons and daughters unto God":

Doctrine & Covenants 76:24

24 That by him, and through him, and of him, the worlds are and were created, and the inhabitants thereof are begotten sons and daughters unto God.

And these sons and daughters of His, are the focal point of His redemptive *work*—His overriding purpose in all He does. All of His work and creations are to redeem His children and bring them home:

II Nephi 29:9

9 "My work is not yet finished; neither shall it be until the end of man, neither from that time henceforth and forever."

Just as our earthly fathers work to provide their children a comfortable home to live in and provide them with all their needs and help them learn to grow and develop until they can start a family of their own, our heavenly parent has provided everything we need to make our way until we return to Him.

You may ask, "What is His Glory? *Glory* is honor, splendor, beauty, greatness, magnificence, and *'weight of responsibility'*. God himself, finding he was in the midst of spirits and glory, because he was more intelligent, saw proper to institute laws whereby the rest could have a privilege to advance to become like himself. He has power to institute laws to instruct the weaker intelligences, that they may be exalted with himself, so that they might have one glory upon another added upon them.

"What is Immortality? Immortality is unending life; life without death; life as a resurrected being. Because of the resurrection of Jesus Christ, all people who have ever lived will be resurrected."

II Nephi 2:25.

25 Men are, that they might have joy.

Doctrine & Covenants 93:33–34

33 For man is spirit. The elements are eternal, and spirit and element, *inseparably connected*, receive a fulness of joy;

34 And when separated, man cannot receive a fulness of joy.

"What is Eternal life? Eternal life is exaltation in the highest degree of the celestial kingdom; living as God lives; living in the presence of God in a family unit – Another name for this kind of life is Eternal Life."

Articles of Faith 1:3

3 We believe that through the Atonement of Christ, all mankind may be saved, by obedience to the laws and ordinances of the Gospel.

"What is the Atonement? The Atonement of Jesus Christ makes it possible for us to inherit eternal life through obedience to the laws and ordinances of the Gospel" (Eternal Life is also another name for God's way of life, meaning the kind of life God lives, for Eternal is His name).

Doctrine & Covenants 14:7

7 And, if you keep my commandments and endure to the end you shall have eternal life, which gift is the greatest of all the gifts of God.

John 17:3

3 And this is life eternal, that they might know thee the only true God, and Jesus Christ, whom thou hast sent.

Let's not forget what The Doctrine & Covenants said about this. It said that all kingdoms have a law given to them:

Doctrine & Covenants 88:36-38, 47

36 All kingdoms have a law given;

37 And there are many kingdoms; for there is no space in the which there is no kingdom; and there is no kingdom in which there is no space, either a greater or a lesser kingdom.

38 And unto every kingdom is given a law; and unto every law there are certain bounds also and conditions.

47 Behold, all these are kingdoms, and any man who hath seen any or the least of these hath seen God moving in his majesty and power. [221]

I submit that God, the Law Giver, instituted laws whereby we, His children, were to live by in this life, including *laws for how we can come to know Him*, or, in other words, the way in which God says he will reveal Himself to us, His children. He also instituted laws for every type of 'kingdom, both the large and the small, as I mentioned in my Introduction.

Here's another excerpt from Dr. John Lamb's book "Joseph Smith's 21st Century View of the World: Truths He Knew Before the World Accepted Them":

"Having this view of the true and very nature of God, lets us see what else He has said about how we, His children, *can come to know Him*, and how we, by living these laws and principles, are able to come to that knowledge and have a personal, direct relationship with Him and His Son, Jesus Christ.

"Have you ever been to a magic show? If so, when the magician sawed someone in half or made an elephant disappear right before your very eyes, were you amazed (Think about all the America's Got Talent incredible magicians and their unbelievable magic acts)?

"Did you for a moment wonder if maybe the magic was real, or did your common sense tell you that this was just an illusion – that behind the seemingly impossible was an explanation that the magician knew, but that was kept hidden from you? Actually, … you are probably like most of us – you experienced a thrill at '*the possibility of the impossible*', while at the same time in the back of your mind (or rather in the front of your brain in the frontal lobes of logic), you knew that you were still in the world of regularity and reason. In the last few centuries, mankind has gradually been converted to the idea that the world operates on a set of rules that applies to all things at all times (The Laws of Physics). We've come to think this way about everything around us, almost without question (Except momentarily when we see a magic show perhaps).

"And therefore, it's hard for us to appreciate that for most of history people have not gone about their lives believing that nature, here on earth, is predictable because it operates on a set of fundamental rules that apply to everything." [222]

Jesus said:

John 17:3

3 And this is life eternal, that they might know thee the only true God, and Jesus Christ, whom thou hast sent.

We can receive salvation and eternal life in His presence only as we come *to know* (And believe in) the only True and Living God, and Jesus Christ, whom He did send to manifest Heavenly Father to us. Many believe that there is a God. Many say that they know there is a God, but they do not act like they *know* God. There is a great difference between *believing in* and *knowing about* God, and in *believing in* and *knowing* God personally. When we claim that we know God, it requires great responsibility from us. An ancient apostle has given us information as a way of checking our knowledge of God and our relationship with Him. The apostle John, from the New Testament, said:

1 John 2:3–6

3 And hereby we do know that we know him, *if we keep his commandments.*

4 He that saith, I know him, and keepeth not his commandments, is a liar, and the truth is not in him (This person simply knows 'of or about' Him).

5 But whoso keepeth his word, in him verily is the love of God perfected: hereby know we that we are *in* him (The apostle John just defined what being *in* the Father and in the Son means).

6 He that saith he abideth in him ought himself also so to walk, even as he walked.

And again, the ancient apostle James, from the same time period of the New Testament said:

James 2:19

19 Thou believest that there is one God; thou doest well: the devils also believe, and tremble.

Jesus was recognized by a man possessed of the devil, and the devil spoke out from him:

Mark 1:24

24 Saying, Let *us* alone; what have we to do with thee, thou Jesus of Nazareth? Art thou come to destroy us? I know thee who thou art, the Holy One of God.

The devils know the Lord God, who is Jesus, but do not respect his doctrine or keep his commandments, but they do submit to Jesus' authority. Knowing God is related to keeping his commandments. Knowledge of and knowing God comes by direct revelation from God. You cannot know God by the power of flesh and blood alone (Or logic and reason alone). Peter was taught this great lesson by Jesus Himself in the following message. Jesus asked the disciples the following question:

Matt. 16:15–18

15 He saith unto them, But whom say ye that I am?

16 And Simon Peter answered and said, Thou art the Christ, the Son of the Living God.

17 And Jesus answered and said unto him, Blessed art thou, Simon Bar-jona: for flesh and blood hath not *revealed* it unto thee (Sounds like Jesus is explaining what revelation is and how it comes, right?), but my Father which is in heaven.

18 And I say also unto thee, That thou art Peter, and upon *this rock* (The bedrock foundation of Jesus and His revelation) I will build my Church; and the gates of hell shall not prevail against '*it*'.

"From these verses we learn that the Lord said that the gates of hell cannot prevail against the rock of *revelation* that comes from Him and His Father, to any one of his children who desires to know the Living God and His Son. Here's excerpts from a talk given by Elder Bernard P. Brockbank, Assistant to the Council of the Twelve Apostles (1962-1976), titled *"Knowing God", and I quote:*

"This (Coming to know God exists) is available by divine commitment and by *divine will* to anyone desiring to know God the Eternal Father and his Son Jesus Christ. God is under commitment, for He has promised that He would reveal Himself *by revelation,* and the gates of hell cannot prevail against that commitment. God will reveal Himself through *the power and principle of revelation* directly to anyone desiring to receive that information, especially as they work to grow in the principle of revelation. *But* there are *eternal laws* as to *how* and *when* that happens. All through the life of Jesus Christ he showed his knowledge of the Living God and his loyalty and allegiance to that God, who was and is His Heavenly Father. Jesus Christ loved his Heavenly Father. He even went so far as to say:

John 10:30

30 I and *my* Father are one.

John 6:38

38 For I came down from heaven, not to do mine own will, but the will of him that sent me.

"Knowing God does not solve all life's problems, it does however, give purpose and strength to master them. Jesus, with his knowledge of his Heavenly Father, still had his problematic circumstances to face and then to work through them mentally and physically. The answers to how we come to know God the Eternal Father, and His Son, Jesus, are found in and through Jesus Christ, for He said:

John 14:6

6 Jesus saith unto him, I am the way, the truth, and the life: no man cometh unto the Father, but by me.

"In order to know God, the Eternal Father, *we must receive that knowledge through Jesus Christ,* who is our *mediator and our advocate* between us and God. Only by Him can we come *unto* the Father. Jesus also gave this information, which is often repeated and is well known by many when He said:

John 8:12

12 Then spake Jesus again unto them, saying, I am the light of the world: he that followeth me shall not walk in darkness, but shall have the light of life.

"The 'light of life' is divine light that permeates and radiates in the human soul and brings out the godlike qualities and attributes of godliness developing within us. The *light of life* is Jesus Christ and the instrumentality of His gospel, the gospel of love. The *light of life* offers us the glorious promise from God – eternal life in His heavenly kingdom. The *light of life* can bring divine truth and happiness and peace into a troubled heart. The *light of life* brings divine light into the problems and troubles of this life (Even the spirit of peace) and helps to turn life's problems into steppingstones to eternal progression, helping us develop a Christlike character called *godliness.* Jesus Himself taught:

John 3:19

19 And this is the condemnation, that *light* is come into the world, and men loved darkness rather than light, because their deeds were evil.

20 For every one that doeth evil hateth the light, neither *cometh to the light,* lest his deeds should be reproved (Or another way of saying this is "Lest his evil deeds are made manifest by the light").

21 But he that doeth truth cometh to the light, that his deeds may be made manifest, that they are wrought in God.

(No thief runs to the police right after they've committed a crime, do they? They want to avoid the punishment they know would be theirs if they were caught, or if their deeds were made known to law enforcement. The same goes for us. Deep down inside of us, we know we have broken God's laws and therefore, we hide from Him, or we even rebel openly against Him and His light).

Elder Brockbank continues:

"To know God, you must walk in the *light of life*. To know God as one of His children, we should know and understand the nature of our relationship to him, and our divine potential, and once we come to know our God, we should understand that in knowing God there is great responsibility to respect, love, and follow His counsel, His doctrines, and His commandments so we can, as His children, become more Christlike, and in doing so we can return to His presence. Jesus Christ gave this commandment and important counsel by revelation to the Prophet Joseph Smith. He told Joseph:

Doctrine & Covenants 46:7–9

7 But ye are commanded in all things to ask of God, who giveth liberally; and that which the Spirit testifies unto you even so I would that ye should do in all holiness of heart, walking uprightly before me, considering the end of your salvation, doing all things with prayer and thanksgiving, that ye may not be seduced by evil spirits, or doctrines of devils, or the commandments of men; for some are of men, and others of devils.

8 Wherefore, beware lest ye are deceived; and that ye may not be deceived seek ye earnestly the best gifts, always remembering for what they are given;

9 For verily I say unto you, they are given for the benefit of those who love me and keep all my commandments, *and him that seeketh so to do*; that all may be benefited that seek or that ask of me, that ask and not for a sign that they may consume it upon their lusts.

"We must always keep in mind that God's greatest gift is eternal life. Eternal life comes from *knowing God* and from knowing Jesus Christ, just as Jesus said:

Doctrine & Covenants 6:13

13 If thou wilt do good, yea, and hold out faithful to the end, thou shalt be saved in the kingdom of God, which is the greatest of all the gifts of God; for there is no gift greater than the gift of salvation.

"The central and basic principle of the gospel of Jesus Christ is love. He laid the basis of human brotherhood is love. It begins with God's infinite love for his children:

John 3:16

16 For God so loved the world, that he gave his only begotten Son, that whosoever believeth in him should not perish, but have everlasting life.

"As is mentioned by the Savior, 'To know God means to keep his commandments'. The Lord also expressed this in the first and great commandment relative to the importance of keeping his commandments, when we say we love God. Here is the great commandment on love:

Matthew 22:37–38

37 Jesus said unto him, Thou shalt love the Lord thy God with all thy heart, and with all thy soul, and with all thy mind.

38 This is the first and great commandment.

Jesus also said:

John 14:15

15 If ye love me, keep my commandments.

"If we love God, we should keep his commandments. We should love his plan of happiness. We should love his Only Begotten Son, whom He sent to help us meet life's challenges and to redeem us from our sins which brings upon us death and hell. Jesus did so by making the resurrection a gift to all, and eternal life possible if we choose to accept His gift of the atonement. He gives us the *light of life* that we may walk in His ways, and through His divine light learn how to become like Him – to become Christlike. Jesus said:

John 15:3

12 This is my commandment, That ye love one another, as I have loved you.

"We must keep in mind that divine programs and divine ways have been given unto us through our Lord and Savior, Jesus Christ; and the way to know God and the way to perfect the human body and mind, and to bring out its Christlike qualities so that we can be in harmony even as a little child of God lives in a way that we can know God, are all provided in the great principles of 'faith and repentance'.

"I would like to mention briefly, a few things about the principle of 'Repentance'. Jesus said:

Matthew 4:17

17 From that time Jesus began to preach, and to say, Repent: for the kingdom of heaven is at hand.

"The light is turned on in the human soul through the great principle of repentance. Jesus has asked us to repent of past sins, regrets, weaknesses, and failures, and to prepare and look ahead into the future of eternal life and salvation in the kingdom of heaven. Repentance by all who are accountable, is required for progression and preparation for entrance into the kingdom of heaven. Repentance is God's purifying program and law for cleansing the human mind and body from weakness, imperfection, and sin. Repentance through Jesus Christ's atonement makes it possible for us to progress toward God's greatest gift, the gift of salvation and eternal life.

"Repentance is a refining influence, a principle provided through the atonement and the sacrifice of Jesus Christ, which purifies our mortal minds and bodies and helps to bring out our divine nature, our Christlike qualities of character, so that we can live in the presence of God, the Eternal Father. The home where we live with our families, is the place where knowledge of God and how to come to know God should be taught, and the place where a loving God should be exemplified for our children to see (Which is the opposite of what Richard says. Richard says, "to do so is child abuse". But what would we expect from someone who has the spirit of anti-Christ?).

"It is also not possible to choose God's way of life so we can know God unless we know his Plan for us. If we only know the ways of men and the ways of the devil, then we will choose those ways automatically (Just like the weeds that automatically grew in my unmanaged plot of dirt that was at the side of my garage). Jesus Christ commanded that we search the scriptures, that we come to know the truth, and as we come to know the truth it would make us free. We find the Lord's truths in the holy scriptures, and there is no knowledge on the face of this earth greater than the knowledge we've been given by our Heavenly Father, through the teachings of Hus Son, our Savior and Redeemer Jesus Christ, and through each of His prophets, all of which is affirmed by the gift and power of the Holy Ghost. [223]

End of Elder Brockbank's excerpts

President Harold B. Lee, (1985-1984), the 11th President of the Church of Jesus Christ of Latter-Day Saints said, quote:

"The most important work you will do for the Church will be within the walls of your own home." I repeat, "The most important of the Lord's work that you will ever do will be the work you do within the walls of your own home." [224]

End quote

Let us we recall again these words of the Prophet David O. McKay (1951-1970), the 9th President of the Church of Jesus Christ of Latter-Day Saints who said the following, and I quote:

"No other success can compensate for failure in the home." [225]

End Quote

And may I add: "No other success can compensate for failing to teach one's family how to come to know the Living God and His Son, our Savior, Jesus Christ".

I would say to all parents, that your children are gifts from God. They are an inheritance from the Lord. Each one has a divine potential, and therefore, it is our sacred responsibility as their parent, to help them and guide them to in their path to learn this sacred knowledge of God, the only True and Living God, as well as the knowledge of His Only Begotten Son, Jesus Christ, and why He is our Savior and Redeemer, whom the Father sent to the world. This knowledge of what it means to come to know Him and know that He dearly loves every one of us is vital to their happiness here on earth and in the world to come.

Let us continue with the next subtitle – NOVA.

NOVA

As I consider this subtitle and what Richard says in it, I'm reminded of the English Anglican philosopher, theologian, and biblical scholar Austin Farrer. Speaking of the debate between theism and atheism, Farrer said, and I quote:

"Though argument does not create conviction, lack of it destroys belief. What seems to be proved may not be embraced; but what no one shows the ability to defend is quickly abandoned. Rational argument does not create belief, but it maintains a climate in which belief may flourish." [226]

End quote

By participating in this debate, I believe I am helping to maintain the climate in which belief in God may flourish. Both sides of this debate have conceded to the fact that neither side has incontrovertible evidence (In particular, incontrovertible *scientific* evidence) for God's existence or His non-existence. They only have the empirical, observable, experiential evidence discovered as each side has searched for the truth. The theologian Alister McGrath makes this concession by both sides of the debate the central point of his book *"Dawkins' God: Genes, Memes and the Origin of Life"*, in which he rebuts Dawkins' claim that God doesn't exist.

Here's McGrath's quote [227]:

"The undeniable but ignominiously weak point is that you cannot disprove the existence of God."

End quote

And again, invoking the famous English biologist T.H. Huxley, Alister McGrath said Huxley, due to this debates' back and forth, was fed up with both the theists and the atheists, and as a result he made this hopelessly dogmatic statement based on inadequate empirical evidence:

"The God question could not be settled on the basis of the scientific method." [228]

And quoting one more of Richard's colleagues, the American paleontologist, evolutionary biologist, and historian of science, Stephen Jay Gould, quote:

"To say it for all my colleagues and for the umpteenth millionth time (From college bull sessions to learned treaties): Science simply cannot by its legitimate methods, adjudicate the issue of God's possible superintendence of nature. We neither affirm nor deny it; we simply can't comment on it as scientists." [229]

End quote

On all these statements regarding the position scientists must take, which is to be neutral on the science of God's existence, Richard strongly disagrees with his fellow scientist's view by saying:

"A universe with a creative superintendent would be a very different kind of universe from one without one. Why then, is that not a scientific matter?" [230]

Richard continues by devoting the next several pages to this subtitle, giving reasons why *God's existence is a scientific theory* and therefore it should be addressed scientifically, meaning it should be studied using the scientific method in order to determine if this theory is valid or not. Richard shares a few thoughts about NOMA, an acronym coined by Gould that refers to a Non-Overlapping Magisterial – "The view advocated by Gould that says science and religion each represent *different* areas of inquiry: fact vs. values – so there is a difference between the "nets" over which they have "a legitimate magisterium, or *domain of teaching authority*", and the two domains do not overlap."

Richard says, "The net or magisterium of science, covers the empirical realm: (verifiable by observation or experience rather than by pure logic alone) what is the universe made of (fact) and why does it work (theory)? The magisterium of religion extends over questions of ultimate meaning and moral value." [231]

To me, Richard is saying that science is fact-based, and religion is just wishful-thinking-based, and that's pretty arrogant as far as I'm concerned. Richard is simply showing, once again, his lack of understanding of what faith is, as a principle for learning truth, and how it works in gaining truth? He thinks faith is just blind faith; having no evidence to support it, period. My retort to Richard is simply, "C'mon man! Let's be fair and balanced here."

Richard's vociferous gripe regarding this issue, is summarized by the questions he asks regarding the subject, and here they are: "But why the chaplain? Why not the gardener or the chef? Why are scientists so cravenly respectful towards the ambitions of theologians, over questions that theologians are certainly no more qualified to answer than scientists themselves?" [232]

Richard seems quite miffed at Gould for making the comments he made in his book "Rock of Ages". Richard does not accept what other people said Gould meant by his comments either. As proof of Richard's angst, let me share what Richard said about these other folks' comments:

"It is inconceivable that Gould really did intend his unequivocally strong statement that science has nothing whatever to say about the question of God's existence when he said, 'We neither affirm nor deny it; we simply can't comment on it as scientists'." [233]

"This sounds like agnosticism of the permanent and irrevocable kind, full-blown PAP. It implies that science cannot even make *probability judgements* on the question (Which is a scientific practice apparently), ... this embodies what I refer to as the *poverty of agnosticism*." [234]

Notice how Richard, in these two comments, speaks of *science making probability judgements*. I remind my readers that science does not say anything, only scientists do, and so Richard is just saying what he, as a scientist, believes the scientific data is saying about the probability of God's existence, or His non-existence. Richard is just one of many scientists who have given their opinion and interpretation of the available data regarding Gould's comments. An opinion isn't fact.

Richard finishes this subtitle's topic by saying, "There is something utterly special about the hypothesis of ultimate design, and equally special about the only known alternative – gradual evolution – in the broadest sense. They are close to being irreconcilably different. Like nothing else, evolution really does provide an explanation for the existence of entities whose improbability would otherwise, for practical purposes, rule them out. And the conclusion to the argument is close to being terminally fatal to the God Hypothesis". [235]

This is a good place in our discussion for me to bring back the visual I showed you in my Introduction, so as to help you, my readers, have a clear understanding of my perspective of the concept of NOMA versus what pure science and pure religion really are, and why I believe Pure Science and Pure Religion will one day intersect, thus showing that they are not two domains that can never overlap as Mr. Gould and Richard Dawkins seem to think. Pure Science and Pure Religion are not irreconcilably *different*.

I am not talking about the imperfect science we've dealt with up to this point and that we continue to deal with today. Nor am I speaking of the imperfect and incomplete faith and religions practiced in the world today. I am talking about what I refer to as Pure or Perfect Science and Pure or Perfect Faith.

The theories of science and religion that we've postulated throughout history, have been far from perfect and pure, and that's due to the effects that apostasy has had on our knowledge, as I have already argued. However, I believe one day we will experience the merging of these two domains as a perfect whole. And that day is when pure science and pure religion meet at their apex at Jesus Christ's 2nd coming where He'll circumscribe all truth, both of science and of religion, into one great whole.

Jesus Christs' 2nd coming will usher in the millennium where all things will be made known in their perfection, things of science with all its unanswered questions about the natural and seen worlds, and things of religion with all its unanswered questions about the unseen worlds, including all questions about the existence of God the Father and the universe He organized for all of His children to enjoy and live out both our mortal lives and then continue on to live out our immortal, eternal lives yet to come.

On the next page is the visual I designed to illustrate what I'm trying to describe here. The diagram shows how wide the gap was between science and religion at the beginning when Adam and Eve were placed on the earth before the Fall. As a result of their transgression, Adam and Eve were cast out of the garden and began to make choices between good and evil, acting as agents for themselves. They began to learn about the natural world around them. Because God gave them dominion over the earth and every creature on it, they gained even more knowledge about their physical and spiritual worlds.

As Adam and Eve began their mortal journey on this telestial globe, God presented them the pure truth of both science and religion while in the garden. After the fall, the earth became a telestial world and through the instrumentality of God's holy angels and His prophets, He continued to teach Adam and Eve. Once Adam and Eve began to have children, their children also grew up to have their own children. Adam and Eve's children, grandchildren, and beyond, had the agency to think for themselves.

This is a major reason we're all sent to live here on this earth – to exercise our agency. Many of Adam and Eve's descendants chose to step away from the covenant path their parents had started them on. These descendants chose to see the world differently than the way their parents viewed it, and so, over time, the space between science and religion became a great divide. But, after thousands of years this divide has slowly shrunk, but not completely. Both magisterium's are still moving towards perfection.

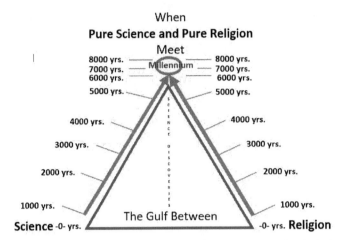

From my perspective, sometime during the next several years, starting with today's date and going forward (It probably will happen much, much sooner than later), science and religion will one day intersect as each becomes closer to perfection. When they do intersect, the truth that there wasn't a gap between them after all will be revealed. This gap only existed in the minds of people because they simply did not enjoy Pure Knowledge in its fulness, nor did they have the full and complete understanding of the answers to the so-called 'Big' questions that scientists and theologians have struggled with for millennia. Again, the gap is due to our lack of pure, complete, and perfect knowledge.

The apex cross-section event as shown at the top of my graph, as I said, will occur at the start of and then continue throughout the Millennium, which will begin at the 2nd coming of Jesus Christ. This cross-section of pure, perfect, complete truth, both in science and in religion, will be circumscribed into one great whole by Jesus Christ Himself at this great and dreadful day of His coming. This revealing of all truth by Jesus Christ is the time when every piece of incontrovertible data will be provided to both scientists and religionists so that these two magisterium's merge or intersect and become the one great whole I'm calling 'all truth' – which is things as they really were, things as they really are now, and things as they really will be – meaning, in their perfection.

Today's scientific data is not only available to both Richard and I, it's also available to anyone who wants to seek it out for themselves, but keep in mind that this data is in its current, imperfect state. We must keep in mind that these two principles or domains (Science and Religion) are incomplete and therefore imperfect, and so they must be taken with a large grain of salt and with much patience, until such time as we learn all truth regarding the 'Big' questions. That time when they will be fully and completely answered by Christ Himself, will be an incredible Day of perfect light and knowledge.

The same must be said of Faith and today's religions, as they are also in a state of apostasy, except for the gospel as taught by the Church of Jesus Christ of Latter-Day Saints. I say the gospel and _not_ its people. Though our members are imperfect, the Church's doctrines that were revealed to the prophet Joseph Smith, were and are pure. Let me also say that its members are continually falling short of the perfection these doctrines require of them, and that includes myself. We are all fallen and come short of the glory of God. As an imperfect man I ask that you don't hold me up to the mirror of perfection. Our imperfections show the need for a Savior and his gift of repentance, which gift allows us to press forward on the path towards perfection and *completeness*, which God has made possible for all of us.

I believe one day soon, when the Son of God returns at His 2nd coming, He will rule and reign on this earth, and the earth will be renewed and receive its paradisical glory once again, even as the garden of Eden was, and every question that scientists have been unable to answer, will be answered, and all the evidence that religionists have been unable to provide as irrefutable proof of God's existence, will be provided, for we all will see Jesus as He truly is, and we'll be able to feel the prints of the nails in His hands and in His feet, just as the doubting apostle Thomas did, and like Thomas, we too will hit our knees and cry, 'My Lord and my God'. This will be the *incontrovertible evidence* that answers every last one of the 'Big' questions regarding God and His Son's existence. Jesus' appearance to the entire world will be the most transcendent event since His appearance as the resurrected Christ to the people of ancient America, which appearance was recorded in the Book of Mormon. The new and additional evidence that Jesus will provide to all the world at His 2nd coming will answer every unanswered 'Big' question that the most eminent of minds, both scientific and religious, have been unable to answer ever since the dawn of mankind. Regarding this new knowledge the Lord said to His prophet Joseph:

D&C 101:32–34

32 Yea, verily I say unto you, in that day when the Lord shall come, he shall reveal all things—

33 Things which have passed, and hidden things which no man knew, things of the earth, by which it was made, and the purpose and the end thereof.

34 Things most precious, things that are above, and things that are beneath, things that are in the earth, and upon the earth, and in heaven.

I don't know about you, my readers, but these three verses are some of the grandest and most hope filled verses of scripture and prophecy I've ever read. I suggest that you go to my Church's website at www.churchofjesuschrist.org, and search for the essay titled, "The Millennium" so you can read it in its entirety. Here are just a few excerpts from this essay:

"A thousand years of peace, love, and joy will begin on the earth at the 2nd coming of Jesus Christ. This thousand-year period is called the Millennium. The scriptures and the prophets help us understand what it will be like to live on the earth during the Millennium, and there will *not* be just faithful Latter-Day Saint members. Because of the destruction of the wicked at the Savior's 2nd coming, only *righteous people of many faiths*, will live on the earth at the beginning of the Millennium. They will be those who have lived virtuous and honest lives (Thus, there will be many individuals who believe in different faiths and have different backgrounds than that of the Latter-Day Saints). These people, including the Latter-Day Saints, will inherit either the terrestrial or celestial kingdom.

"During the Millennium, mortals will still live on earth, and they will continue to have children as we do now:

Doctrine & Covenants 45:58

58 And the earth shall be given unto them for an inheritance; and they shall multiply and wax strong, and their children shall grow up without sin unto salvation.

Joseph Smith said that *"immortal beings will frequently visit the earth.* These resurrected beings will help with the government (The theocracy of the Lord Jesus Christ) and other work. People will still have their agency, and *for a time* many will be free to continue with their religions and ideas, but *eventually everyone will confess that Jesus Christ is the Savior."* [236]

Articles of Faith 1:10

10 We believe in the literal gathering of Israel and in the restoration of the Ten Tribes; that Zion (the New Jerusalem) will be built upon the American continent; that Christ will reign personally upon the earth; and, that the earth will be renewed and receive its paradisiacal glory.

"During the Millennium, Jesus will reign personally upon the earth. Joseph Smith explained: "Jesus will reign over the Saints and come down and instruct."

"What are the two great works that will be done during the Millennium? There will be two great works for members of the Church during the Millennium: temple work and missionary work. Temple work involves the ordinances that are necessary for salvation and exaltation. These include baptism, the laying on of hands for the gift of the Holy Ghost, and the temple ordinances—the endowment, temple marriage, and the sealing together of family units. Many people have died without receiving these ordinances. People on the earth must perform these ordinances for them *by proxy* (So that the dead have a choice to accept these ordinances done on their behalf or reject them, just as people must choose whether or not to accept the Savior's great act of proxy, the atonement). [237]

This work is now being done in the temples of the Lord. There is too much work to finish before the Millennium begins, so it will be completed during the millennium. Resurrected beings will help us correct the mistakes made while researching our dead ancestors' records. They'll also help us find the information we need to complete our records. The other great work that will be performed during the Millennium will be missionary work. The gospel will be taught with great power to all people on both sides of the veil. Eventually there will be no need to teach others the first principles of the gospel.

Jeremiah 31:34

34 And they shall teach no more every man his neighbour, and every man his brother, saying, Know the LORD: for they shall all know me, from the least of them unto the greatest of them, saith the LORD: for I will forgive their iniquity, and I will remember their sin no more.

"How can we prepare now for doing this work in the Millennium, with the kind of conditions we'll face during the Millennium? In what ways will life during the Millennium be different from life on the earth now? (See YouTube video – "How Bad Does It Need to Get Before the 2nd Coming? – Agency is the Key". This video adds insight to this topic; and see Joseph Fielding Smith, Doctrines of Salvation, comp. Bruce R. McConkie, 3-vol. (1954-56), 2:67, 251-52) The Prophet Joseph Smith taught:

Articles of Faith 1:10

10 We believe in the literal gathering of Israel and in the restoration of the Ten Tribes; that Zion (the New Jerusalem) will be built upon the American continent; that Christ will reign personally upon the earth; and, that the earth will be renewed and receive its paradisiacal glory.

"Satan will be Bound"

"During the Millennium, Satan will be bound. This means he will not have power to tempt those who are living at that time:

Doctrine & Covenants 45:58

58 And the earth shall be given unto them for an inheritance; and they shall multiply and wax strong, and their children shall grow up without sin unto salvation.

Doctrine & Covenants 101:28

28 And in that day Satan shall not have power to tempt any man.

"The 'children shall grow up without sin unto salvation'."

I Nephi 22:26

26 And because of the righteousness of his people, Satan has no power; wherefore, he cannot be loosed for the space of many years; for he hath no power over the hearts of the people, for they dwell in righteousness, and the Holy One of Israel reigneth.

"Peace on the Earth"

"During the Millennium, there will be no war. People will live in peace and harmony together. Things that have been used for war will be turned to useful purposes:

Isaiah 2:4

4 And he shall judge among the nations, and shall rebuke many people: and they shall beat their swords into plowshares, and their spears into pruninghooks: nation shall not lift up sword against nation, neither shall they learn war anymore.

Isaiah 11:6–7

6 The wolf also shall dwell with the lamb, and the leopard shall lie down with the kid; and the calf and the young lion and the fatling together; and a little child shall lead them.

7 And the cow and the bear shall feed; their young ones shall lie down together: and the lion shall eat straw like the ox.

Doctrine & Covenants 101:26

26 And in that day the *enmity* of man, and the enmity of beasts, yea, *the enmity of all flesh*, shall cease from before my face.

"Righteous Government" [238]

"President John Taylor taught: "The Lord will be king over all the earth, and all mankind literally under his sovereignty, and every nation under the heavens will have to acknowledge his authority and bow to his scepter. Those who serve him in righteousness will have communications with God, and with Jesus; will have the ministering of angels, and will know the past, the present, and the future; and other people, who may not yield full obedience to his laws, nor be fully instructed in his covenants, will, nevertheless, yield full obedience to his government. For it will be the reign of God upon the earth, and he will enforce his laws, and command that obedience from the nations of the world which is legitimately his right." [239]

"No Death"

"During the Millennium, there will be no death as we know it. When people have lived to an old age (Not sure what old age means), they will not die and be buried. Instead, they will be changed from their mortal condition to an immortal condition in "the twinkling of an eye."

Doctrine & Covenants 63:51

51 Wherefore, children shall grow up until they become old; old men shall die; but they shall not sleep in the dust, but they shall be changed in the twinkling of an eye.

Doctrine & Covenants 101:29–31

28 And in that day Satan shall not have power to tempt any man.

29 And there shall be no sorrow because there is no death.

30 In that day an infant shall not die until he is old; and his life shall be as the age of a tree;

31 And when he dies he shall not sleep, that is to say in the earth, but shall be changed in the twinkling of an eye, and shall be caught up, and his rest shall be glorious.

"All Things Revealed"

"Some truths have not been revealed to us. All things will be revealed during the Millennium:

Doctrine & Covenants 101:32–34

32 Yea, verily I say unto you, in that day when the Lord shall come, he shall reveal all things—

33 Things which have passed, and hidden things which no man knew, things of the earth, by which it was made, and the purpose and the end thereof—

34 Things most precious, things that are above, and things that are beneath, things that are in the earth, and upon the earth, and in heaven.

"Other Millennial Activities"

"In many ways, life will be much as it is now, except that everything will be done in righteousness. People will eat and drink and will wear clothing.

"One Final Struggle after the Millennium"

"What will be the final destiny of the earth? At the end of the 1,000 years, Satan will be set free for a short time. Some people will turn away from Heavenly Father. Satan will gather his armies, and Michael (Adam) will gather the hosts of heaven. In this great struggle, Satan and his followers will be cast out *forever*. The earth will be 'changed' into a celestial kingdom."

Here's additional Scriptures on the Millennium if you choose to search them out:

- Zechariah 14:4–9; I Nephi 22:24–25 (Jesus to reign on earth)
- Daniel 7:27 (Saints to be given the kingdom)
- D&C 88:87–110 (Conditions during the Millennium)
- Revelation 20:1–3; I Nephi 22:26 (Satan to be bound)
- D&C 101:22–31 (Enmity to cease; no death; Satan to have no power to tempt)
- Isaiah 11:1–9 (Wolf and lamb to dwell together)
- D&C 43:31; Revelation 20:7–10 (Satan loosed for a little season)

End of excerpts from the essay on the Millennium

Like I said, the most obvious, incontrovertible proof of God's existence will be Jesus' 2nd coming for all the world to see and experience first-hand, it proving that the prophets and the scriptures they taught were true regarding God's existence and that He and His Only Begotten Son, are in fact ALIVE.

The millennium will be the Day when Pure Science and Pure Faith (or Pure Religion) will intersect, each being made perfect. All truth will be revealed in its fulness for all to know and see, and it will be circumscribed into one great whole so that there no longer any confusion or conflict.

The main point that Richard tried to make in this subtitle called NOMA, was stated by Mr. Gould, which Richard will not accept as being something Gould really meant, believed, or accepted, and so let me repeat what Gould said, so that you can decide for yourselves what Gould meant:

"The net, or magisterium of science, covers the empirical realms: what is the universe made of (fact) and why does it work this way (theory).

"The net, or magisterium of religion, extends over questions of ultimate meaning and moral value. These two magisterial do not overlap, nor do they encompass all inquiry (consider for example, the magisterium of art and the meaning of beauty). To cite the old cliches, science gets the age of rocks, and religion the rock of ages; science studies how the heavens go, religion how to go to heaven." [240]

Richard finishes this sub-title by giving illustrations of what he calls 'styles' of religion, all of which he concludes to be unreasonable. Richard says, "All of these 'styles' of religion are embarrassingly popular, and unlikely to be impressed by anything as superficially reasonable as NOMA." [241]

For my concluding perspective on this subtitle and in particular my perspective on Richard's' argument about NOMA, I simply ask you, my readers, this question: "Did Richard bring to the table any new argument in his discussion of NOMA, which can be considered as additional irrefutable evidence in support of God's non-existence? In my opinion he did not. Richard, once again, simply bloviated his opinion ad nauseum without adding anything factual to the contest.

I presented a considerable amount of well-informed evidence for God's existence and what He will do when He returns to earth at His second coming (Although, this is my opinion, the fact that science and religious claims are coming closer together is obvious evidence). NOMA is "the view, advocated by Gould, that science and religion each represent *different* areas of inquiry, fact vs. values, or faith", and I disagree with this as does Richard. However, my reason for disagreeing with Gould's view is far different than Richard's disagreement.

My point of disagreement is that *ultimately science and faith will come together*, being circumscribed into one great whole by Jesus, so that *facts* and *values* will be in full harmony with each other, having no conflict or disagreement. Whether you approach a question from a scientific point of view or from a religious point of view, the pure answer will support both of these domains fully and completely, each having no conflicting laws or principles. Won't that be incredible? I certainly think it will be.

Let's move on to the next subtitle – "The Great Prayer Experiment". Richard's arguments in this subtitle cracked me up.

THE GREAT PRAYER EXPERIMENT

Richard's next Subtitle topic is a discussion about "The Great Prayer Experiment", which was a scientific study that was done to determine whether-or-not praying for hospital patients helps them recover. I would ask you, my readers, to see if Richard actually puts forth any evidence that supports the belief that God does not exist, or if Richard is just giving his opinion once again. Please read on.

Richard's reasoning is that "if prayer can be proven to be non-effective, then God doesn't exist." But you will see that Richard has a very shallow understanding of the law of prayer and those principles that make up the law of prayer. In my mind, a prayer that supposedly goes unanswered, most certainly doesn't prove God's non-existence, nor does it prove unequivocally that He does in fact exist. The principles behind people praying just prove that one prayer and answer may be different from another's prayer and answer.

Richard gives a multiplicity of examples to make the point he wanted to make regarding this topic, and that point is simply – that "Prayer, like God, isn't real". One such example Richard gives about prayer, is where he mocks those athletes who pray to win and then give thanks to God when they do. Richard retorts: "What about the other teams' players who are praying just as fervently as their opponents did? How does God decide which athlete loses and which athlete wins?" [242]

Richard, haven't you heard of 'praying amiss'?" Richard's question here, once again, shows his lack of religious literacy and understanding and his spiritual immaturity, especially about prayer. James said:

James 4:3

3 Ye ask, and receive not, because ye ask *amiss*, that ye may consume it upon your lusts.

God sees things as they really are and as they will be. We don't. In order to tap into that precious eternal perspective during our prayers, we must rely upon the promptings of the Holy Ghost. With access to this kind of pure knowledge, we would then pray for what we and or what others *should* have— (What God knows we really need—and not be motivated by pleasure). With the Spirit prompting us, we will not ask 'amiss'" (See '*Prayer*' [1977], by going to www.churchofjesuschrist.org [243]).

Another example Richard gives is a funded experiment of people who prayed for patients and others who were not being prayed for (like a placebo group), to see what the results were for them. Richard makes several sarcastic remarks about it and then states the results, which were published in the American Heart Journal of April 2006. The results were clear cut he says: "There was no difference between those patients who were prayed for and those who were not". [244]

Richard continues, "The alleged power of intercessory prayer is at least a principle within the reach of science. A double-blind experiment can be done and was in fact done. It could have yielded a positive result, and if it had, can you imagine that a single religious apologist would have dismissed it on the grounds that scientific research has no bearing on religious matters? Of course not." [245]

Richard, once again, is very critical of what any religionist or theist had to say about this so-called scientific test. Upon hearing from Oxford theologian Richard Swinburne, who after the experiment failed, wrote "I object to it on the grounds that God answers prayers only if they are offered up for good reasons", Richard said of "his reasoning about it", "This grotesque piece of reasoning, is so damningly typical of the theological mind." [246]

Again, Richard hasn't a clue regarding things spiritual, let alone the principle of prayer and the laws upon which it operates. Let me share a few thoughts regarding this so-called prayer study, and Richard's criticism of prayer itself, and the study's results, or supposed lack of results. To all the examples Richard gives in order to make his point that it is all poppycock, I simply say that I have personally experienced the power of prayer hundreds of times in my personal athletic life, much like the athletes' example Richard gave. The difference, however, is that I prayed to play my best and not to win as Richard described. I, along with millions of other believers, pray to thank God when we're given success. We pray to praise Him for being able to compete. We pray when we are successful, *and* we even give a prayer of praise when we're not successful. Prayer is about praise and expressing love to God for all that we have and experience, the good as well as the bad, for He has promised that *He will consecrate all things so that they work together for our good*, and that's because God knows all things; things as they are and things as they are to come, even those experiences like losing a football game:

Doctrine & Covenants 90:24

24 Search diligently, *pray always*, and *be believing*, and *all things shall work together for your good*, if ye walk uprightly.

This stunning promise from the Lord that "all things shall work together for our good", even when things go badly, is repeated many times in the scriptures, particularly when people and prophets find themselves suffering through difficult trials that happen in our daily lives." [247]

You might ask, "Do I go so far as to assume I will be favored over my athletic opponents?" Absolutely not, and I don't think that that was the case with the athlete Richard talked about. I do not believe that he was praying to win. At least I hope he wasn't. It's not what I pray for. I think those athletes who pray to God are simply thanking Him for the gifts He has given them, such as their bodies and the strength and skills he or she has acquired, and for a sound and healthy mind so that they can play at their best, hopefully without harm. But the fact is, football is a physically risky game so one can anticipate injury. Whether they win or lose, they're simply and humbly expressing gratitude for all their many gifts. The religious and spiritually minded give God the glory for their lives and their wondrous experiences, both the good as well as the bad. At least that's what I pray and give thanks for.

As far as the prayer experiment discussed by Richard, I have personally witnessed remarkable healings taking place after blessings I've participated in. I've also learned of many blessings that wrought positive blessings in the lives of those I've given a priesthood blessing to.

I've also heard of people who did not have a happy outcome. I want to remind my readers that as an adult male member of the Church of Jesus Christ of Latter-Day Saints, I am a priesthood holder who had the Melchizedek Priesthood conferred upon me by one having this same authority. I was first ordained to the office of an Elder, and then years later I was ordained to the office of Seventy, and then to the office of High Priest a few years later. Each priesthood ordination to these different offices within the Melchizedek Priesthood, were performed by one having the authority and power of the Melchizedek Priesthood. It once was called the Priesthood after the Order of the Son of God. [248]

All of my priesthood ordinations were performed by my father who was ordained in this same manner, after the order of the Son of God, ... and so he had the authority to ordain me in the same way he was. Both my father and I can trace our priesthood lineage back to Jesus Christ. It is back through one of the modern-day apostles down to the prophet Joseph Smith, who was ordained by resurrected Peter, James, and John, each receiving their priesthood authority directly from Jesus Christ Himself. As such, I'm an ordained minister, serving people at their homes or at hospitals or care facilities, or at church, etc. This is not unlike a protestant minister who is a pastor to his church's congregants. Although I bare the priesthood, its power and authority are not my own. It's God's authority and power that he's entrusted to me and other priesthood holders, and it is this authority that allows me to minister and serve God's children in the name of Jesus Christ and by His authority and power vested in me, not man's.

Bishops and Branch Presidents, like myself, are similar to protestant ministers or pastors. I don't, per se, preach weekly sermons like protestant pastors usually do. I give talks a couple, to three times a year to my small flock of congregates. In addition to giving talks, I also administer blessings to members of my Branch. My priesthood companion and I use consecrated oil to anoint the person wanting a blessing, and we then vocalize a blessing of healing and comfort upon them, afterwards sealing that blessing upon the head of the person who sought the blessing, closing this ordinance in the name of Jesus Christ, relying wholly upon God's power and mercy, asking God's *will* to prevail, not ours. This ordinance of administering to the sick dates back to ancient times. This priesthood power and authority was restored to Joseph Smith for the same purpose as it was used to serve the meridian-Day saints:

James 5:14-15 – (James was the oldest half-brother of Jesus)

14 Is any sick among you? let him call for the *elders* of the church; and let them pray over him, *anointing him with oil* in the name of the Lord:

15 And the *prayer of faith* shall save the sick, and the Lord shall raise him up; and if he have committed sins, they shall be forgiven him.

"There are five parts to using the priesthood authority to bless the sick: (1) the anointing of the oil, (2) the sealing of the anointing, (3) faith, (4) the words of the blessing, and (5) the will of the Lord." [249] There are literally thousands of examples of people who have given testimonies of being healed after such priesthood administrations, just as James the apostle from Jesus' Day described. This ordinance of blessing the sick and afflicted requires that both the one giving the blessing, as well as the recipient receiving the blessing, exercise their faith and trust in the Savior, the Eternal Physician, whom the Father sent to heal the world, that they might be healed both physically and spiritually, but only if it is His will. Is everyone healed immediately or miraculously? No. Are some individuals healed while others are not? From my experience, yes. Does that show favoritism by God towards one person over another? I don't think so. However, some would say "It absolutely does". But they'd be wrong. There is so much that I do not comprehend, nor do I fully understand how all this '*to be healed or not be healed*' works, though I remain hopeful that one day I will come to know everything about it. I choose to continue trusting God and exercising faith and trust in his love, as I go about doing what God has asked and called me to do, and that is to bless, administer, love, and serve others unconditionally.

It's my belief, for lack of a better analogy, that the power of prayer works much like a '*transmitting station*' does. A TV or radio station transmits radio waves for a receiver to receive its message waves, such as a song or a TV show being broadcast over the 'air waves' (The power of light, waves, protons, etc.). Such transmissions are tied to God's light and spirit, which in fact is 'matter' of a certain form and kind, which I do not fully understand, nor do I comprehend all things in this regard, but I do believe in time, that I will come to understand these things as I more fully exercise faith in this power of communication. Answers to prayers are similar to these transmissions, and the receiver that receives them is our heart and spirits' mind, much like the radio or TV receiver receives their transmissions. Prayer and faith work together in-order to have communication with God. In one of Dr. Hugh Ross's YouTube videos, he discusses how God 'could' answer four-billion prayers at the same time.

The title of his video is "Does Science Prove God's Glory? Dr. Hugh Ross, Regent University". [250]

If you go to the 6:50-minute mark on his video, Dr. Ross is answering the question that his two young boys had asked of him: "Dad, how does God answer all our prayers?" Dr. Ross answered saying, "It is one of many ways God 'could' do it." He doesn't say that it is 'the' actual way God does it. It's just one *possible* way He could do it." [251] Go watch it for his answer. Dr. Ross offers a unique possibility.

End of Dr. Ross's comments on his video

Since I'm introducing *possible* ways in which God is able to answer all our prayers simultaneously, even if there were billions of prayers ascending to Him all at once, and every minute of every day, day-in and day-out, let me share a personal 'theory' I want to postulate about how it possibly is done.

Let's say that at this very moment there are literally billions of people all across the globe who are doing searches on Google's search engine, and within a fraction of a second that incredible search engine sends back answers to every single individuals' personal inquiry. Billions of them. Pretty incredible, isn't it? You know that Google does this billions of times a day, right? Of course, it does.

Well then, let me suggest the perspective that Gods' glorious, magnificently intelligent 'Mind' has the power and capacity much like the Google search engine has to receive and answer inquiries. God's Mind receives and answers billions of prayer inquiries via His 'light of lights', His 'Incomprehensible IT', which emanates from Him continuously. It's everywhere in the immensity of space and time, being in and through all things, much like a super-transmitter that sends out its transmission waves into the air.

God's light is there to answer all these prayer requests instantly, and the recipients' heart and mind connects to this divine light to receive those divine communications. Much like router packets, back and forth they go, between the transmitter and the receiver. His 'Eternal Mind' sends His 'light of light and truth' out into the immensity of space, and each individual receives His answers as they attune their hearts and minds to His light. Another way to imagine it is it's like a receiving dial, so-to-speak, aligning itself to His 'light-of-light' transmissions. It's called our 'vibrational' mind – or what Latter-Day Saint doctrine refers to as the Light of Christ, the Spirit of the Lord that's in and through all things.

When a child of God seeks Him in prayer, even if there's five billion people praying at that same time, each expressing their own heart-felt pleadings to Him, His 'magnificent eternal receiver', His 'spiritual search engine' so-to-speak, receives prayers, and transmits answers (By His divine Mind, which I'm calling 'His Incomprehensible IT'). God receives these prayers immediately and then sends back a personalized, soul-invoking answer to each of the five billion individuals, in the way He chooses. God's answers come on His timeline and are fashioned for each individuals needs and desires. It may be immediate. It may be sent line upon line, precept by precept, here a little, and there a little. This being true, one needs to be patient. It quite often is 'No', which requires even more faith on our part as we trust in and wait on the Lord. I think most parents have said 'No' to their children a time or two, right?

Whatever answer God chooses to give us, His incredibly powerful Incomprehensible IT, His light of truth can and does answer our prayers. And yes, it is remarkable, and for some, unbelievable. One of the best methods for receiving answers to our prayers, is when we're reading and pondering our scriptures after praying, and that's because this practice of exercising our faith, helps us *attune our receiver*, our own heart and mind, to His 'light of life' transmissions He's sending out for us to attune to. That way answers can come into our heart and mind while we're studying, praying, and pondering upon Gods word. Does this seem fantastical? Yes. Is it peculiar. But it is not improbable, and here's why:

If puny human being's minds, both male and female, can come up with a nearly unlimited informational software called the 'Google Search Engine' (In my opinion it was inspired by God's spirit of inspiration, the Holy Ghost), God, with His perfectly unlimited intelligence, most certainly can have a mental 'search engine for answering prayers' kind of Mind. "The Mind of God" is, as I said, an Incomprehensible IT ("My ways are not your ways" He has said). Just think and ponder on this *possibility* for how God can answer billions of prayers all at the same time, just like Googles' search engine answers billions of searches in an instant. Ponder this for a moment. It's an interesting thought, don't you think?

I have another *possible* way in which God could answer billions of prayers simultaneously. It's called by 'Divine Investiture of Authority'. This is where God calls upon His billions of angels, who sometimes are called guardian angels, each being capable of receiving our thoughts and hearing our vocal prayers, and then by God vesting His authority in them, like He did with the angel who came to Mary, Jesus' mother, they then can answer our prayers as they stand in the stead of God, answering them as God would have answered them if He were standing right by our side. God's angels know His Mind and will.

Going back to administering blessings, as I said, it's not my authority or power that heals or doesn't heal someone. Nor was it Peters', Paul's', or any of the apostles, ... or any of the Seven Bishops that were called in Pauls' Day. It is Gods' authority and healing power, based on His will and not that of any of God's servants, nor is it the will of the person who requested the blessing. Father in Heaven either *ratifies the vocal charge of healing given to the person* who sought a blessing of healing after having done all they could do to be healed, or He chooses to let things take its course. God is all-knowing and therefore knows what's best for each persons' life-journey. He even said such experiences will be consecrated for our good. When the worthy priesthood holder, the one standing in the stead of God, attunes to God's Spirit, ... he can be directed to express the mind and will of God for that person, even at the very moment they are giving the blessing. In my Introduction I spoke of such an experience.

Having personal experience with giving a priesthood blessing many times, I will say that it is an 'experience of experiences' to have His spirit impress upon your mind the words that God wants you to pronounce. Such experiences provide you with the confidence to pronounce those words of the blessing, and do it in the name of Jesus Christ, while under the influence and power of the Holy Ghost.

There are many available options for God's plan to be fulfilled for that persons' life's journey. As I said, there are millions of individuals who have borne witness that they were in fact healed from such priesthood blessings, and I'm sure there are thousands of people who would say they were not healed. But most of them would say that they came to accept it as God's will for their lives, because they understand what 'trusting in the Lord' means. Can the non-believer say that that answer by those who did not get healed, was 'a cop-out'? I would say "Sure". But I don't believe it is a cop-out. Some may describe it as an answer of convenience. But again, I don't believe it is. No parent ever says 'yes' to every single request of their children. More often than not, as I said, their answer is "no".

There are also tens-of-thousands of people who have had a near death experience (An NDE) as well, and many of them say that after they died, they were told by beings from the other side when asked by the person if they could stay, that it wasn't their time to die, and were therefore sent back into their bodies to finish out their remaining time here on earth (I'd have you, my readers, watch a few YouTube NDE videos where individuals share such experiences. See this footnote for its title). [252]

Others were allowed to stay in the afterlife (The spirit world) and continue on with their eternal progression, while their bodies were soon to be laid down in their graves, or they were cremated and those ashes were placed in an Urn, or maybe their ashes were scattered to the wind or tossed into a watering grave to await the day of resurrection. Again, this is just one more example of how God is involved in the details of our daily lives, for death's timing is His, though personal for each of us.

After watching a few of these YouTube NDE videos I suggest that you search a specific video titled "LDS Perspective on near Death Experiences," [253] where Vincenzo gives examples of NDE's he has studied. Vincenzo discusses what these people had to say after they had their Near-Death Experience (NDE) upon returning from the spirit world. These folks referred to on this video were all members of the Church of Jesus Christ of Latter-Day Saints. Be careful not to accept as fact, everything said by everyone on these NDE videos. I just want to stimulate your mind about these kinds of after death testimonies, so that you realize there are literally tens of thousands of people that have testified that there is life after death. These are folks that have said that they literally died and came back into their bodies, after seeing the world of spirits.

After watching this video, I want you to consider what the prophet Joseph Smith taught some 200 years ago about NDE experiences. I think it will surprise you how spot on the prophet Joseph's revelatory insight was regarding the things of the spirit, the spirit world, and what the next life is like, each of these concepts being examples of what are called the 'Mysteries of Godliness'.

Remember, these particular revelations received by the prophet Joseph from the Lord, were given 200 years before science had discovered all that it has discovered since Josephs' Day. Here's one such example of what Joseph Smith taught on NDE's more than 190 years ago, and I quote:

"All men know that they must die. And it is important that we should understand the reasons and causes of our exposure to the vicissitudes of life and of death, and the designs and purposes of God in our coming into the world, our sufferings here, and our departure hence. What is the object of our coming into existence, then dying and falling away, to be here no more? It is but reasonable to suppose that God would reveal something in reference to the matter, and it is a subject we ought to study more than any other. We ought to study it day and night, for the world is ignorant in reference to their true condition and relation [to God].

If we have any claim on our Heavenly Father for anything, it is our light and knowledge on this important subject." [254]

End of Joseph Smith's Quote

Here are just a few examples of the more common repeated details of the NDE experiences given by actual Latter-Day Saint members who died and then came back to talk about their 'Near Death Experience', as related by Vincenzo Covino in the video I just mentioned and suggested that you watch it (Keep in mind I'm not listing all that I could list here. There are many, many more such examples of NDE's that I could have suggested you watch).

NDE Case Study – 1995 K.M. Dale M.D – Seeing Relatives

- 9-year-old boy w/fever
- 3 a.m. awoke and told his parents he saw relatives, including his 19-year-old sister who was away at college
- Sister had been killed just after midnight
- Parent called college only to find out she had been killed in a car accident just after midnight and we've been trying to get ahold of you

Hallucinations or Visions?

1. Netherlands, 1988 Dr. Pin van Lommel
2. Dr. Lommel did a study on 344 Cardiac Arrest Survivors
3. 18% had NDE's, 100% were on morphine meds

Light of God

George Richie 1943	Joseph Smith 1820
*A being of tremendous light and love appeared before him. Richie realizes this light is like a million welders' lamps all blazing at once."	*I saw a pillar of light exactly over my head, above the brightness of the sun … its brightness and glory defied all description.

These are just a couple of examples Vincenzo discusses on this video. I think you, my readers, will find his comments quite enlightening. I sure did. Who am I to say what God, the Father of us all, should and should not do when it comes to our lives, or what our time of death should and should not be? Only He knows the time and place we are to step through the doorway of death and walk into the light of Eternity in order to continue on our endless journey of eternal progression.

I'm absolutely sure that Richard would rail at this response to his arguments on prayer. I can hear him now. I'm sure he would say that I'm "being delusional and that my points are a cop-out, or that I am simply sidestepping the reality of things". But he cannot disregard the tens-of-thousands of personal death experiences (NDE's) shared by people, each one being different in circumstances, yet each having multiple threads of commonality in their NDE experience details, details like the bright light at the end of a tunnel, the feeling of overwhelming love, the loss of any fear of death after surviving their NDE, etc. There are thousands of NDE's stories shared by people of different faiths. Even individuals who claimed to be atheists have testified of having had similar NDE experiences with similar details.

We all are at risk of dying at any moment, due to a million possible reasons. In fact, 65 million people die every day. [255] It is my belief that God always knows when our time will be and what part our lives play in His Plan for each of us, within the grand scheme of things, even if it comes by way of what we often think is an accidental death, just like my sons' death seemed to be, when he was killed by accident some fourteen years ago, and like many of the case studies that Vincenzo shares in his video.

Many, if not most people, wrestle with and fear death. But nearly all of those who have had an NDE say that they no longer fear death, because they came away from their NDE having experienced life after they died and feeling God's overwhelming love and compassion for them. Most of these individuals say they learned their physical pain and suffering was for a great and glorious purpose.

I believe these folks who've experienced an NDE, after they realized they were dead (Meaning, their brain stopped, and their spirit left their bodies), they, (their spirit body 'selves'), entered what's described in the scriptures as the 'World of the Spirits' or the 'Spirit World'. Here's what Peter said regarding where Jesus Himself went after He died on the cross:

I Peter 3:18-20

18 For Christ also hath once suffered for sins, the just for the unjust, that he might bring us to God, being put to death in the flesh, but quickened by the Spirit:

19 By which also he went and preached unto the spirits in prison (The spirit prison is where the one malefactor went, and the other malefactor went to paradise, as Jesus said he would. Both places are in the World of Spirits);

20 Which sometime were disobedient, when once the longsuffering of God waited in the days of Noah, while the ark was a preparing, wherein few, that is, eight souls were saved by water.

The spirit world is actually all around us, here and now, but it is in a different dimension than our physical, natural world. It is a spiritual dimension (A spirit-matter dimension). It is in this world of the spirits, a world of 'pure spirit', that 'spirit beings' exist and move around, even around and through us. They can move right through us, but without seeing or bumping into us. They in fact, can and do walk right through us because they are made up of 'pure spirit matter' that is much like what *Dr. Kraus said here: "the elements that are in the unfilled space within protons are made of, which he said are "constantly popping in and out of existence". [256]

It is probably what is called a *third dimension* where the spirit persons do not see us, and we don't see them in our dimension. Just because we cannot see these spirit beings who have gone ahead, with our naked eye, doesn't mean they don't exist anymore. We just can't see them because they're made of pure spirit-matter. They can and do walk right through us as they are made up of pure light-matter, which we've learned is made up of some type of protons or particles, a type of matter that we can't see with our naked eye. The spirit world is the place where all of us living now, will go when we die. It is where we'll 'await' until the time of our resurrection, which resurrection has basically three periods: The 1st resurrection, the 2nd resurrection, and the 3rd resurrection. This state called *Resurrection* started with the 'morning of the first resurrection', Jesus being the first fruits of the resurrection. After Jesus rose from the dead, many of the saints which slept (Were in the spirit world), came forth after His resurrection:

Matthew 27:52-53

52 And the graves were opened; and many bodies of the saints which slept arose,

53 And came out of the graves after his resurrection, and went into the holy city, *and appeared unto many.*

It's hard to imagine it, isn't it? Can you imagine your 4th great grandfather walking up to you as you sat rocking in your rocking chair on your porch? Since that time there have been additional people who have been resurrected. They're examples such as John the Baptist who appeared to Joseph Smith and Oliver Cowdery to bestow the Aaronic Priesthood upon them. Next is Peter, James, and John who appeared to Oliver and Joseph to ordain them to the Melchizedek Priesthood. In addition to that prophet and those apostles, the Angel Moroni (The Moroni referred to in the Book of Mormon), returned as a resurrected being to deliver up the record of the Nephites, called the Gold Plates, to Joseph Smith when he was just 21 years old. After Joseph translated it, it became known as the Book of Mormon. Other resurrected prophets came and taught Joseph Smith throughout his ministry.

In the *Journal of Discourses*, JD 21:94, it says that "Abraham, Isaac, Jacob, Noah, Adam, Seth, Enoch, and the apostles that lived on this continent as well as those who lived on the Asiatic continent *came to Joseph Smith to teach him.* Joseph seemed to be as familiar with these people as we are with one another". Elder Orson Pratt of the Quorum of the Twelve Apostles added that Joseph Smith "often received visits from Nephi, Moroni, Peter, James, John (the beloved), John (the Baptist), Elijah, Moses, and the three Nephites", etc. etc. Moroni continued to appear to Joseph several times in an effort to tutor him until the Book of Mormons' translation was completed. These, and many more people who once lived on the earth and died, are resurrected beings now. These resurrected visitors' visits are recorded in the history of the Church as well as in the scriptures.

The 1st resurrection, which started when Jesus conquered death and was first to be resurrected, as I said, continues even today, and will continue into the millennium when the first resurrection really kicks in for the righteous, and the rest of the resurrection will take place during the millennium. You ask, "Who are to be resurrected, and when?" Those who believed in the Lord Jesus Christ (The righteous) and kept his covenants, will come forth *first*. Throughout the rest of the Millennium there will be other times of resurrection as I said, until the Millennium nears its end and the last of God's children (the wicked) are resurrected. These questions are answered in "Resurrection – A Doctrinal Study". [257]

Search for this title at www.chuchofjesuschrist.org.

Resurrection is when all of us, as spirit beings, will be reunited with our physical bodies, but this reuniting will be an inseparable connection of the physical body with its spirit body, so that each of us become immortal, eternal souls of glory, never to be separated from our bodies again.

Alma 11:42-46

42 Now, there is a death which is called a temporal death; and the death of Christ shall loose the bands of this temporal death, that all shall be raised from this temporal death.

43 The spirit and the body shall be reunited again in its perfect form; both limb and joint shall be restored to its proper frame, even as we now are at this time; and we shall be brought to stand before God, knowing even as we know now, and have a bright recollection of all our guilt.

44 Now, this restoration shall come to all, both old and young, both bond and free, both male and female, both the wicked and the righteous; and even there shall not so much as a hair of their heads be lost; but everything shall be restored to its perfect frame, as it is now, or in the body, and shall be brought and be arraigned before the bar of Christ the Son, and God the Father, and the Holy Spirit, which is one Eternal God, to be judged according to their works, whether they be good or whether they be evil.

45 Now, behold, I have spoken unto you concerning the death of the mortal body, and also concerning the resurrection of the mortal body. I say unto you that this mortal body is raised to an immortal body, that is from death, even from the first death unto life, that they can die no more; their spirits uniting with their bodies, never to be divided; thus the whole becoming spiritual and immortal, that they can no more see corruption.

46 Now, when Amulek had finished these words, the people began again to be astonished, and also Zeezrom began to tremble. And thus ended the words of Amulek, or this is all that I have written.

Each of us will receive a glorious, perfected body of flesh and bone as tangible as our temporal bodies are right now, with some measure of glory, be it telestial, terrestrial, or celestial. As such, we will have the gift of living forever and never experiencing disease and physical suffering ever again, except for the pain of seeing loved ones choosing not to follow God's Plan. Those who repent and keep the covenants of the Father, the covenants we make at baptism and all of the covenants we make with God in the temples of God, are those individuals who will be granted the opportunity to live in a state of eternal happiness, love, and peace in God's actual presence. When we live according to our covenants as members of His Church and kingdom, which is called *staying on the covenant path*, we are blessed with increased power to live righteous lives. Those spirits in the Spirit world who accept the Gospel that was taught here on earth and is now being taught to all those who have died and *didn't know of Jesus and His gospel while living on the earth* but are willing to live by God's commandments in spirit and in truth going forward, they are given the opportunity for redemption and salvation. Read what the Apostle Peter said about this doctrine of the gospel being taught to the spirits in prison (the other part of the Spirit World):

1 Peter 4:6:

6 For for this cause was the gospel preached also to them that are dead, that they might be judged according to men in the flesh, but live according to God in the spirit.

Like this scripture so plainly says, they are given the opportunity to hear the gospel and make the choice to accept it and ultimately receive a glory and place in the appropriate kingdom which the Eternal Judge will grant them as their reward for choosing to take up their cross and follow Him. Consider the Savior's promise He gave His listeners during His Sermon on the Mount. It is recorded by Matthew, where He gave a list of the "Blessed Are's", and then in verse 12 He said:

Matthew 5:12

12 Rejoice, and be exceeding glad: for great *is* your *reward* in heaven: for so persecuted they the prophets which were before you.

Let me get back on track here. To believers, prayer is the soul's sincere desire. It is man's way to communicate with their Creator, their maker, their Heavenly Father who is always ready to hear and answer our prayers with whatever means He chooses to connect and communicate with His children.

There are many ways that we can't even begin to imagine within our puny minds, with which God may choose to communicate with you or me. The power of our prayers depends on us. Attuning our mind and heart to the Great Light of the Universe (Which I'm calling the Incomprehensible IT), even His Spirit, the Spirit of the Lord, the Light of Life, or the Light of Christ, which is administered by the power and influence of the third member of the Godhead, the Holy Ghost. The influence and power of the Holy Ghost is how we can connect with the Creator of the universe. As we strive to make prayer a constant practice in our lives, we are able to grow in the principle of prayer. We should also keep in mind the counsel to keep our prayers *meaningful and specific*.

In the following verses the prophet who abridged the plates for the Book of Mormon, the prophet Mormon, gave this warning:

Moroni 7:9

9 If anyone shall pray and not with real intent of heart, it profiteth him nothing, for God receiveth none such.

To make our prayers meaningful and specific, we must pray with sincerity of heart and with all the energy of heart our faith can muster:

Moroni 7:48

48 Wherefore, my beloved brethren, pray unto the Father with all the energy of heart, that ye may be filled with this love, which he hath bestowed upon all who are true followers of his Son, Jesus Christ; that ye may become the sons of God; that when he shall appear (At His 2nd coming) we shall be like him, for we shall see him as he is; that we may have this hope; that we may be purified even as he is pure. Amen.

We must also be careful to avoid "*vain repetitions*" when we say our prayers.

Matthew 6:7

7 But when ye pray, use not vain repetitions, as the heathen *do:* for they think that they shall be heard for their much speaking.

In praying we should use language that shows love, respect, reverence, and closeness for our Lord and Heavenly King, just as we would show our earthly leaders like the Queen of England, the Crown Prince of Qatar, or the President of the United States, etc., by being respectful to their *title* when being in their presence. The application of this *principle of respect* will vary according to different languages of course, whether it is in English, Spanish, German, Mandarin, or whatever language being spoken. Reverential manner of speech is important. We should always use the pronouns of the scriptures when we address God—such as Thee, Thou, Thy, and Thine, rather than the more common, less respectful pronouns You, Your, and Yours. Certainly, new members soon learn to show such reverent language when praying to God. Regardless of the language, the principle remains the same: When we pray, we should use words that appropriately convey a loving, respectful, worshipful relationship with the objects of our worship – God, our Heavenly Father, and His Son, Jesus Christ.

Next, we should always give thanks to Heavenly Father for all that we have been given. We should "live in thanksgiving daily, for the many tender mercies and blessings with which he doth bestow upon [us]."

Alma 34:38

38 That ye contend no more against the Holy Ghost (Rebel against it), but that ye receive it, and take upon you the name of Christ; that ye humble yourselves even to the dust, and worship God, in whatsoever place ye may be in, in spirit and in truth; and that ye *live in thanksgiving daily*, for the many mercies and blessings which he doth bestow upon you.

Next, we should take time to remember our blessings, and recognize how much our Heavenly Father has done for us. We should express our thanks to Him daily and seek Heavenly Father's guidance and strength in all that we do and speak. Alma, another prophet from the Book of Mormon, counseled his son Helaman regarding this principle of prayer, in this manner:

Alma 37:36–37

36 Yea, and cry unto God for all thy support; yea, let all thy doings be unto the Lord, and whithersoever thou goest let it be in the name of the Lord; yea, let all thy thoughts be directed unto the Lord; yea, let the affections of thy heart be placed upon the Lord forever.

37 Counsel with the Lord in all thy doings, and he will direct thee for good; yea, when thou liest down at night lie down unto the Lord, that he may watch over you in your sleep; and when thou risest in the morning let thy heart be full of thanks unto God; and if ye do these things, ye shall be lifted up at the last day.

We're counseled to remember the needs of others as we pray:

Alma 34:27

27 Yea, and when you do not cry unto the Lord, let your hearts be full, drawn out in prayer unto him continually for your welfare, and also for the welfare of those who are around you.

We should ask our Heavenly Father to bless and comfort those in need. We should seek the guidance of the Holy Ghost, so we'll know what to include in our prayers. The Holy Ghost can teach us to pray and guide us in the things we should say:

Romans 8:26

26 Likewise the Spirit also helpeth our infirmities: for we know not what we should pray for as we ought: but the Spirit itself maketh intercession for us with groanings which cannot be uttered.

II Nephi 32:8

8 And now, my beloved brethren, I perceive that ye ponder still in your hearts; and it grieveth me that I must speak concerning this thing. For if ye would hearken unto the Spirit which teacheth a man to pray, ye would know that ye must pray; for the evil spirit teacheth not a man to pray, but teacheth him that he must not pray.

III Nephi 19:9, 24

9 And they did pray for that which they most desired; and they desired that the Holy Ghost should be given unto them.

24 And it came to pass that when Jesus had thus prayed unto the Father, he came unto his disciples, and behold, they did still continue, without ceasing, to pray unto him; and they did not multiply many words, for it was given unto them what they should pray, and they were filled with desire.

The Holy Ghost will help us pray "according to the will of God":

Doctrine & Covenants 46:30

30 He that asketh in the Spirit asketh according to the will of God; wherefore it is done even as he asketh.

When we make a request through prayer, we must do all we can to assist in it being granted. Heavenly Father expects us to do more than merely ask Him for blessings. When we have an important decision to make, He often will require that we "study it out in [our] mind" before He will give us an answer.

Doctrine & Covenants 9:7–8

7 Behold, you have not understood; you have supposed that I would give it unto you, when you took no thought save it was to ask me.

8 But, behold, I say unto you, that you must study it out in your mind; then you must ask me if it be right, and if it is right I will cause that your bosom shall burn within you; therefore, you shall feel that it is right.

Our prayers for guidance will be only as effective as our efforts to be receptive to the whisperings of the Holy Ghost. Our prayers for our own welfare and for the welfare of others will be in vain if we fail to care for the needy:

Alma 34:28

28 And now behold, my beloved brethren, I say unto you, do not suppose that this is all; for after ye have done all these things, if ye turn away the needy, and the naked, and visit not the sick and afflicted, and impart of your substance, if ye have, to those who stand in need—I say unto you, if ye do not any of these things, behold, your prayer is vain, and availeth you nothing, and ye are as hypocrites who do deny the faith.

If we have a difficult task before us, Heavenly Father is pleased when we get on our knees and ask for His help and then get on our feet and go to work. He will help us in all our righteous pursuits, but He seldom will do something for us that we can do for ourselves. Regarding Personal Prayer, In His Sermon on the Mount, Jesus Christ counseled:

Matthew 6:6

6 But thou, when thou prayest, enter into thy closet, and when thou hast shut thy door, pray to thy Father which is in secret; and thy Father which seeth in secret shall reward thee openly.

Personal, private prayer is an essential part of our spiritual development and connectedness with God. Every morning and every night we should find a place that is free from distractions and kneel in humility and commune with our Heavenly Father. Although sometimes we may need to pray silently, we should make an extra effort to pray vocally.

Doctrine & Covenants 19:28; 20:51

28 And again, I command thee that thou shalt pray vocally as well as in thy heart; yea, before the world as well as in secret, in public as well as in private.

51 And visit the house of each member, exhorting them to pray vocally and in secret and attend to all family duties.

Prayer is a two-way communication. As we close our prayers, we should take time to pause and reverently listen for the spirit to answer us. At times, Heavenly Father will counsel, guide, and comfort us while we are still on our knees, or, in our closets. Answers may also come later on while reading the scriptures. We should never give in to the idea that we are not worthy to pray either. This idea comes from Satan, who wants to convince us that we have no need for prayer.

II Nephi 32:8

8 And now, my beloved brethren, I perceive that ye ponder still in your hearts; and it grieveth me that I must speak concerning this thing. For if ye would hearken unto the Spirit which teacheth a man to pray, ye would know that ye must pray; for the evil spirit teacheth not a man to pray, but teacheth him that he must not pray.

We should pray especially at those times when we do not feel like praying. The solution is to pray until we finally feel like praying. The Savior has commanded:

Doctrine & Covenants 10:5

5 Pray always, that you may come off conqueror; yea, that you may conquer Satan, and that you may escape the hands of the servants of Satan that do uphold his work.

Although we cannot be continuously on our knees, always offering a personal, private prayer, we can let our hearts be full, and drawn out in prayer unto [God] continually.

Alma 34:27

27 Yea, and when you do not cry unto the Lord, let your hearts be full, drawn out in prayer unto him continually for your welfare, and also for the welfare of those who are around you.

III Nephi 20:1

1 And it came to pass that he commanded the multitude that they should cease to pray, and also his disciples. And he commanded them that they should not cease to pray in their hearts.

Throughout each day, we can maintain a constant feeling of love for our Heavenly Father and His Beloved Son. We can silently express gratitude to our Father in Heaven and ask Him to strengthen us in our responsibilities. In times of temptation or physical danger, we can silently ask for His help with the expectation that He will always help us. The Savior taught:

Matthew 7:7–8

7 Ask, and it shall be given you; seek, and ye shall find; knock, and it shall be opened unto you:

8 For every one that asketh receiveth; and he that seeketh findeth; and to him that knocketh it shall be opened.

To the Nephites (They're spoken of in the Book or Mormon) Jesus, who appeared to them after his resurrection and ascension said:

"Whatsoever ye shall ask the Father in my name, which is right, believing that ye shall receive, behold it shall be given unto you."

III Nephi 18:20

20 And whatsoever ye shall ask the Father in my name, which is right, believing that ye shall receive, behold it shall be given unto you.

Heavenly Father hears our prayers in what appears to be in a miraculous way, like I suggested earlier. He may not always answer as we expect or hope He will, but He does answer—in His own time and according to His will. Because He knows what is best for us, He may sometimes answer no, even when our petitions and pleadings are sincere and passionate. Answers to prayer also comes in many ways. They often come through the still, small voice of the Holy Ghost (See definition of "Revelation" at www.churchofjesuschrist.org), and answers may come in the circumstances of our lives or through the kindly acts of those around us. As we continue to draw near to Heavenly Father through the principle and power of prayer, we come to recognize more easily His wise answers to our pleadings. With time and experience we come to know that:

Psalm 46:1

1 God *is* our refuge and strength, a very present help in trouble.

I will end my answer to Richard's mocking of the concept of prayer, by simply saying, "I 'agree to disagree' with Richards' characterization of the power of prayer, the reality of prayer, and the fruit of prayer, and regardless of what any scientist says about the so-called data that was gathered from a so-called prayer study, proves nothing about why those prayers given in the so-called study of prayer supposedly didn't work. It is my opinion that God, in His wisdom, may have chosen not to participate in such a study, which is His prerogative, but there's no way to know if this is true, is there?

Please note that I could have listed pages and pages of examples where people have put the power of prayer to the test personally, and because of the results they experienced, meaning what their own data has told them, they've come to believe that the power of prayer is real. Others can say otherwise, for sure. But, once again, each of us are left to decide what we *want* our prayer experiences to mean to us. Regarding this question about prayer not working, I suggest you, my readers, consider the fact that millions of Latter-Day Saints and billions of other believers in God, continue to pray daily. If prayer doesn't work like Richard suggests, then why on earth do these billions of people continue to practice this principle of prayer every day of their lives without any results?

Once someone reads all the scriptural references related to prayer and exercises this principle in their personal lives over a long period of time, it is my experience that they, of course, come away with a greater understanding of why I and millions of other Latter-Day Saints, choose to believe in the power of prayer. It's why I have included my full perspective on prayer and why I have practiced daily prayer for the entirety of my life. I know for a fact that millions, if not billions of God's children offer up their prayers (At least in some form) to their God faithfully, on a daily basis, and testify they are answered.

Non-believing individuals, like Richard, are certainly free to choose not to believe in prayer or in its power to move spiritual mountains in one's life, and that's okay. Agency is a true principle, whether or not a person wants to practice it in their daily lives. But I just feel sad that they're left with having to rely *upon the arm of the flesh* alone, which is a weak and limited source of power and strength. Relying on the *arm of the flesh* only, is like placing a pavilion over oneself, thus limiting God from providing an abundance of incredible blessings in one's life. One must remember however, that exercising faith is required before God gives His promised blessings. As I said, lack of faith is like placing a pavilion over one's head, which blocks Gods' rays of truth and light from penetrating your heart.

Again, let me state that I believe that God is the Supreme Governor and Lawgiver over the universe, and that He is the Father of all mankind. I believe that coming to the knowledge that God indeed lives and is real, is key to finding happiness in this life and experiencing joy in the life to come. This is the great fruit of revelation that He's given to His prophets, and to each of us as individuals.

This knowledge is received through the instrumentality of prayer, which attunes our hearts to the manifestations of the Holy Ghost. It's through this spiritual practice of daily prayer that we can come to know God. Jesus, the Son of God, the Savior of the world, works under the direction and divine vestiture of God, our Eternal Father. Heavenly Father, and Jesus are in complete harmony with each other, and the Holy Ghost is also in complete harmony with these two members of the Godhead. These three divine beings make up the Eternal Godhead, the Heavenly Presidency, each one being one in purpose, truth, knowledge, and power, versus what the so-called Trinity that Christendom espouses as the Godhead.

All mankind are Jesus' brothers and sisters, He, being the eldest and firstborn spirit offspring of Elohim, our Heavenly Father. Most of the actions that the scriptures attribute to God the Father, were actually performed by the Lord Jehovah of the Old Testament, and by Jesus of the New Testament (And that's because Jesus is the pre-mortal Jehovah before He came to live on earth, even our advocate with the Father). Like I said, Jehovah/Jesus performed His responsibilities as the foreordained Savior of the world, under the principle of *'Divine Investiture of Authority' extended to Him by His Father, Elohim.

For example, even though Genesis says that, "God created the heavens and the earth" (Gen. 1:1), we know that it was actually the Lord Jehovah (Jesus) who was the Creator. John the apostle wrote:

John 1:1-5, 10

1 In the beginning was the Word, and the Word was with God, and the Word was God.

2 The same was in the beginning with God.

3 All things were made by him; and without him was not anything made that was made.

4 In him was life; and the life was the light of men.

5 And the light shineth in darkness; and the darkness comprehended it not.

10 He was in the world, and the world was made by him, and the world knew him not.

And, as Paul, the apostle, said, 'God created all things *by* Christ Jesus' (Another way of saying 'by divine vestiture of authority):

Ephesians 3:9

9 And to make all *men* see what *is* the fellowship of the mystery, which from the beginning of the world hath been hid in God, who created all things by Jesus Christ (His Son):

*Divine Investiture of Authority is a term sometimes used to explain when God the Father (Elohim) allows others, typically His Son Jehovah (Jesus Christ), but at other times one of His ministering angels, are commanded to speak and act "in the stead of the Father Himself". There are several scriptures that reflect this concept of 'in the stead of' God Himself. It's a lot like the General Contractor saying that he built the building, but in the physical sense it was actually the building contractor and his sub-contractors who did the actual physical labor of building the building.

The Holy Ghost is also a member of the Godhead, who is also called the Holy Spirit, the Spirit, the Spirit of God, etc., and depending on the context in which these titles are used it may be referring to the Light of Christ versus the personage of the Holy Ghost. The Holy Ghost is often confused with the Spirit of God, and so it may be difficult to know which of these titles the scriptures are referring. It takes careful, diligent reading of the scriptures to come to a greater understanding of what these titles mean and which of the members of the Godhead each scripture is referring to. God created all things and is the ruler of the universe, being omnipotent, omniscient, and omnipresent (Through the power of His Spirit, glory, and light which is everywhere and in everything), and mankind has a special relationship to Him, and that relationship differentiates man from all other creations of God: man is literally God the Father's spirit offspring, whom He made in His own divine image, whereas all other things are but the work of His hands:

Acts 17:28–29

28 For in him we live, and move, and have our being; as certain also of your own poets have said, For we are also his offspring.

29 Forasmuch then as we are the offspring of God, we ought not to think that the Godhead is like unto gold, or silver, or stone, graven by art and man's device.

The God of the scriptures is a holy, eternal being, and Man (Mankind) is commanded to become like God, our Heavenly Father, even perfect and holy as He is perfect and holy.

Leviticus 11:44–45

44 For I *am* the LORD your God: ye shall therefore sanctify yourselves, and ye shall be holy; for I *am* holy: neither shall ye defile yourselves with any manner of creeping thing that creepeth upon the earth.

45 For I *am* the LORD that bringeth you up out of the land of Egypt, to be your God: ye shall therefore be holy, for I *am* holy.

Leviticus 19:2

2 Speak unto all the congregation of the children of Israel, and say unto them, Ye shall be holy: for I the LORD your God *am* holy.

God can be known only by revelation, which principle most of us have to grow into this principle working in our lives. The Father must be revealed to man by His Son, or God will remain unknown forever to those who do not seek to know Him. I encourage you, my readers, go to my Church's website at www.churchofjesuschrist.org and do a search to read the essay titled 'God'.

Mosiah 4:9 (From the Book of Mormon)

9 Believe in God; believe that he is, and that he created all things, both in heaven and in earth; believe that he has all wisdom, and all power, both in heaven and in earth; believe that *man doth not comprehend all the things which the Lord can comprehend.*

God the Father first revealed Himself to the first man to dwell on earth, Adam (See the full chapters at Moses 5–6). God has repeatedly made Himself known by revelation to His chosen patriarchs, the prophets, from the beginning of time, on up to the present day. The present translation found in the book of John 1:18 and 1 John 4:12 is misleading. In these two separate accounts it says the following:

John 1:18

18 No man hath seen God at any time; the only begotten Son, which is in the bosom of the Father, he hath declared *him*.

I John 4:12

12 No man hath seen God at any time. If we love one another, God dwelleth in us, and his love is perfected in us.

Now let's read the Joseph Smith Translation (JST) of this verse and see if it makes more sense:

John 1:19 (JST)

19 And no man hath seen God at any time, *except He hath borne record of the Son*; for except it is through him no man can be saved.

As you can see, this is a very different translation of this verse with a very different meaning than that which the KJV relates. The KJV says no one has seen God, and the (JST) says that no man has seen God *except* he has borne record of Him by introducing His Son to that man. It's meaning is quite different, but such is the fruit of apostasy. When scripture is mistranslated it becomes corrupted. Joseph Smith's First Vision is such an example that confirms the JST of these verses. The Father, calling Joseph by name, introduced His Son to the teenager, and the Son, Jesus Christ, took it from there. Other scriptures state that there have been many who have seen God. These experiences are called 'Theophanies'. The Joseph Smith Translation (JST) of the Bible corrected these misinterpretations and mistranslations, so that it now reads that no one has seen God '*except through faith*' and '*by the power of the Holy Ghost*', and also that Jesus Christ is the only Way to God." [258]

I John 4:12 (JST)

12 No man hath seen God at any time, *except them who believe*. If we love one another, God dwelleth in us, and His love is perfected in us.

The following verses refer to the resurrected Lord appearing to followers in a closed room:

Luke 24:33-43

33 And they rose up the same hour, and returned to Jerusalem, and found the eleven gathered together, and them that were with them,

34 Saying, The Lord is risen indeed, and hath appeared to Simon.

35 And they told what things *were done* in the way (The two disciples on the road to Eumaeus), and how he was known of them in breaking of bread (As they ate with Him).

36 And as they thus spake, Jesus himself stood in the midst of them, and saith unto them, Peace be unto you (His appearance was with doors and windows closed).

37 But they were *terrified and affrighted* and supposed that they had seen a spirit.

38 And he said unto them, Why are ye troubled? and why do thoughts arise in your hearts?

39 Behold my hands and my feet, that it is I myself: handle me, and see; for a spirit hath not *flesh and bones*, as ye see me have. (Did Jesus discard His resurrected body of flesh and bones like we do a coat or jacket? I think not. This is describing the resurrected Lord, and what it means).

40 And when he had thus spoken, he shewed them *his* hands and *his* feet.

41 And while they yet believed not for joy, and wondered (They still couldn't believe what they were actually witnessing first hand), he said unto them, Have ye here any meat?

42 And they gave him a piece of a broiled fish, and of an honeycomb.

33 d he took *it* and did eat before them (Showing what a resurrected body can do).

I'm so thrilled to have these verses of holy writ. They describe what a resurrected being can do, including appearing, apparently, out of nowhere, eating food, and even disappearing or going up into the sky while others watched Him ascend, just as the apostles did later on. All of us, as resurrected beings, will have these same glorious physical attributes and capacities once we're resurrected. God the Father and His Son Jesus, have been manifested by voice, by sight, and other ways at various sundry times throughout the history of the earth, including at Jesus' own baptism:

Matthew 3:16–17

16 And Jesus, when he was baptized, went up straightway *out of the water*: and, lo, the heavens were opened unto him, and he saw the Spirit of God (The Holy Ghost) descending *like* a dove, and lighting upon him.

17 And lo a voice from heaven, saying, This is my beloved Son, in whom I am well pleased.

In these verses the three members of the Godhead are mentioned independent of each other, being identified separately – Jesus, the Holy Ghost, and God the Father who spoke by introducing His beloved Son, stating that He was well pleased with Him for obeying His commandments and fulfilling His role as the Savior of the world (My question from these verses is, "Was Jesus a ventriloquist?" I think not).

The Transfiguration:

Matthew 17:1–8

1 And after six days Jesus taketh Peter, James, and John his brother, and bringeth them up into an high mountain apart, (Mount Tabor, known as the Mount of Transfiguration)

2 And was transfigured before them: and his face did shine as the sun, and his raiment was white as the light. (This was an actual change in His body that we don't fully understand)

3 And, behold, there appeared unto them Moses and Elias talking with him.

(Moses, in company with Elijah, came to the Mount of Transfiguration and bestowed keys of the priesthood upon Peter, James, and John. From this event, which occurred before the Resurrection of Jesus, it is my understanding that Moses was a translated being, as was Elias (Elijah) and had not died a physical death as reported. It was necessary that they be *translated*, in order to have a body of flesh and bones at the time of the Transfiguration, since the Resurrection had not yet taken place. Had they been a spirit only, they could not have performed the work on that mount to *bestow the keys of the Priesthood to the mortal Peter, James, and John)*

4 Then answered Peter, and said unto Jesus, Lord, it is good for us to be here: if thou wilt, let us make here three tabernacles; one for thee, and one for Moses, and one for Elias.

5 While he yet spake, behold, a bright cloud overshadowed them: and behold a voice *out of* the cloud, which said, *This is my beloved Son, in whom I am well pleased; hear ye him.*

6 And when the disciples heard *it,* they fell on their face, and were sore afraid.

7 And Jesus came and touched them, and said, Arise, and be not afraid.

8 And when they had lifted up their eyes, they saw no man, save Jesus only.

Verse 5 says exactly, word for word, what Joseph Smith said God the Father said to him at Joseph's First Vision. Joseph testified that God the Father and Jesus appeared to him, and the Father said:

"This is my beloved Son, in whom I am well pleased; hear ye him". At Stephen's martyrdom Luke said:

Acts 7:55–56

55 But he, being full of the Holy Ghost, looked up steadfastly into heaven, and saw the glory of God, and Jesus standing on the right hand of God,

56 And said, Behold, I see the heavens opened, and the Son of man standing on the right hand of God.

And the Nephites Saw Jesus and heard the voice of the Father as well:

III Nephi 11:5-8

5 And again the third time they did hear the voice, and did open their ears to hear it; and their eyes were towards the sound thereof; and they did look steadfastly towards heaven, from whence the sound came.

6 And behold, the third time they did understand the voice which they heard; and it said unto them:

7 Behold my Beloved Son, in whom I am well pleased, in whom I have glorified my name—hear ye him.

8 And it came to pass, as they understood they cast their eyes up again towards heaven; and behold, they saw a Man descending out of heaven; and he was clothed in a white robe; and he came down and stood in the midst of them; and the eyes of the whole multitude were turned upon him, and they durst not open their mouths, even one to another, and wist not what it meant, for they thought it was an angel that had appeared unto them.

These are just four examples out of the thirty-six theophanies I have found. Joseph Smith's First Vision of the Father and the Son personally appearing to him in the Sacred Grove in the spring of 1820 near Manchester, New York, was so important because it opened the Dispensation of the Fulness of Times and launched the restoration of the pure Gospel (Read Joseph's testimony of it [259])."

Latter-Day revelation confirms the biblical account of God as the literal Father of the human family (Father of their spirit bodies), and a Being who's concerned with the welfare of mankind. He's a divine Being who hears and answers prayers. Just because we mortals may not know or understand *the exact means by which He does all of His ministering to His children,* doesn't mean he doesn't do it. These unknown ways of God, again, are called the 'Mysteries of Godliness'). [260]

I took the time to find what the scriptures said about prayer, and what prophets have taught and said regarding prayer, and how man communicates with members of the Godhead, so that you, my readers, would have my full personal perspective, in contrast to Richard's demeaning prayer argument.

Richard opened the door to my approach that I've taken here when he shared his anti-God quasi-religion in an effort to try and persuade against the validity of prayer. Let me again make it clear that I'm not trying to take advantage of you by preaching to you. That isn't what's in my heart. I'm simply stating my Latter-Day Saint perspective on these topics Richard brought up, for your consideration, as a counter to Richard's arguments against God and prayer, just like I said I would in my Introduction.

I feel comfortable sharing my pro-God and pro-Christ beliefs, and the principles Jesus taught, so that you, my readers, can get a clear idea of how powerful the principle of prayer truly is in actual practice, and hopefully you too will come to know (If you don't already) what it can do for you, just as it has for me and millions, if not billions of other people, if you'll allow yourselves to be open to it. I also wanted to share how anyone can predict, test, and even *duplicate the results* that millions of faithful believers have experienced while practicing the principle of prayer in their personal lives. As a principle it is testable, but it must be tested in the correct way as I said, for it is a *spiritual principle with a promise.*

I have clearly laid out for you the way to approach the law and principles of prayer, and if you choose to practice it in your own life, I promise you that God will answer your prayers as He has promised. Next is the subtitle "The Neville Chamberlain School of Evolution".

THE NEVILLE CHAMBERLAIN SCHOOL OF EVOLUTION

In this subtitle Richard insists "that the teaching of evolution in schools is in the front-line trench and under constant attack of a well-organized, politically well-connected, and well-financed opposition (Theists and all believers who fight against it being taught in our schools, being the opposition)." [261]

I could say the same thing about the army of atheists that oppose the God Hypothesis, and how they have been working non-stop to restrict Creationism and Intelligent Design from being taught in our schools, as well as how they're working relentlessly to destroy the promotion of Intelligent Design within the science community, saying that it doesn't *qualify* as a scientific theory. How Richard's arguments against Creationism and Intelligent Design moves the idea of God's non-existence on his scale of probability one iota towards the probability of His non-existence, isn't clear to me. In fact, I think my perspective moves the God Hypothesis several percentage points towards the probability that God in fact exists.

You, my readers, must decide for yourselves which of all the reference legs I've shared with you, so far, are moving your belief cursor along the *percentage of probability spectrum* towards your desired belief, and which ones don't? Does God exist, or does He not? I believe your heart and core, at the end, will tell you. Simply put, Richard's point that he tried to make in this subtitle is that there are evolutionists that he calls the Neville Chamberlain School of Evolution, and that they are "active fighters against creationists and creationism, yet they tend to fail in grasping the real nature of the conflict between creationists and evolutionists, *religion* being the real enemy." [262]

In short, these particular folks, in Richard's way of thinking, "give too much appeasement [NOVA acting out once again], to religion and not enough criticism of it." [263]

This is just Richard's opinion once again. I don't see how Richard's argument adds anything in the way of additional strength or evidence to Richard's overall argument against Theism or against the God Hypothesis. I've read it a few times now and feel that to belabor it or give some long list of reasons that justify why Creationism or Intelligent Design should qualify to be taught in our schools, especially if Atheism qualifies, still wouldn't get us any closer to the truth about God.

I'm just sad that the leadership of our public schools – institutions throughout the world, and in particular the hierarchy of our public school system here in the United States – don't play fair in this regard. I believe both sides of the debate – evolution versus creationism and Intelligent Design –should be presented to students, allowing them to use their own reasoning powers to come up with the decision for themselves as to what rings true for them, or not, just like Richard advocates that children should be allowed to choose what they want to believe once they are so-called *old enough* to determine for themselves what to believe or not believe. How can young adults be fully informed if they're given only one side of a topic to consider? How is that fair? C'mon man. This is not how science is done.

One of the arguments for not allowing Intelligent Design or Creationism to be taught in our schools, is the argument that this topic falls under *the separation of church and state law*. That of course is ridiculous, because the Creationism or Intelligent Design arguments are not representing any specific religion *at all*. Yet, to allow the quasi-anti-Christ-religion of atheism, which is what it is, seems to me, to be disingenuously preferential. I understand atheists say atheism is a non-religious concept, but that is disingenuous. The 3rd listed definition of religion in the Websters' Dictionary defines religion as "*a pursuit or interest to which someone ascribes supreme importance*", which defines Richard's view of atheism perfectly. Richard ascribes to and promotes atheism *religiously*. Richard uses Darwin's principle of evolution as doctrinal proof for this godless-quasi-religion. Anyway, I think I've made my point, so, let's go on to the next subtitle which is "Little Green Men". This was a fun topic and I think you'll enjoy my perspective on it. At least I hope you will.

LITTLE GREEN MEN

Earlier in his book Richard shared a little of Bertrand Russell's parable of '*The teapot in Outer Space*'. The so-called fact he stated regarding this parable and other ones like it, was that "like them, we can't prove it exists, and the only strictly rational stance to take on it … is agnosticism." [264]

Richard says, "Suppose Bertrand Russell's parable had concerned not a teapot in outer space but life in outer space – the subject of Sagan's memorable refusal to think with his gut. Once again, we cannot disprove it, and the only strictly rational stance is agnosticism." [265]

Call me a skeptic, but do you get a sense that Richard reveals a little angst in his comments regarding Carl Sagan's statement, who, by-the-way, was a fellow scientist like Richard? [266] Sagan said the following to Joel Achenbach in an interview published in The Post back in 1996:

"An atheist has to know a lot more than I know. An atheist is someone who *knows* there is no God." [267]

And again, to Robert Pope, of Windsor, Ontario, Mr. Sagan said, and I quote: "I am not an atheist. An atheist is someone who has compelling evidence that there is no Judeo-Christian-Islamic God. I am not that wise, but neither do I consider there to be anything approaching adequate evidence for such a God. Why are you in such a hurry to make up your mind? Why not *simply wait* until there is compelling evidence?" [268]

End Quote

As you, my readers know, Carl Sagan was a very renown and respected cosmologist. He was also an American astronomer, planetary scientist, astrophysicist, and astrobiologist, and as such he was known for his great understanding of cosmology, or what I call "Celestial Mathematics", in particular. The fact that Carl didn't express the same level of disbelief in God that Richard does, frustrated Richard. I believe it frustrated Richard because Carl's stance made it so Richard couldn't use Carl's world renown credibility to prop up his anti-Christ arguments against the existence of God, and that perturbed Richard. At least that's what I read between the lines in Richard's commentary on Sagan's statements.

Next, Richard gives the example of the 'Drake Equation', which says: "To estimate the number of independently evolved civilizations in the universe you must multiply seven terms together. The seven terms include the number of stars, the number of Earth-like planets per star, and the probability of this, that, and the other, which I need not list because the only point I am making is that they are all unknown or estimated with enormous margins of error. *When so many terms that are either completely or almost completely unknown are multiplied up, the product* – the estimated number of alien civilizations – *has such colossal error bars that agnosticism seems a very reasonable, if not only credible stance.*" [269]

As a follow up to this, Richard gives a lengthy review of where cosmology has been and where it is now, in terms of what has been discovered about our solar system and beyond. All the examples Richard gives is to make the point, "Science can (And is) chipping away at agnosticism in a way that Huxley bent over backwards to deny for the special case of God. I am arguing that notwithstanding the polite abstinence of Huxley, Gould, and many others, the God question is not in principle and forever outside the remit of science (Richard is circling back again to make the point that he feels the God Hypothesis is *a scientific theory* that should and must be tested)."

"As with the nature of the stars, contra Comte (Sociology must have a scientific base and be objective), and as with the likelihood of life in orbit around them, science can make at least the *probabilistic* inroads into the territory of agnosticism." [270]

Richard is saying, once again, that science (Meaning scientists) should be allowed to do something with the God question in the same way as they *do science* on other questions scientists undertake. What he's actually saying, however, is that by doing science on the God Hypothesis, he and others can make some degree of progress or inroads into the territory of eliminating agnosticism altogether, so that we're only left with the Hypothesis that God does NOT exist, or the Hypothesis that he DOES exist. I feel Richard wants to keep things in the control of science alone.

Richard, again, is making the mistake of saying that *science says this, and science says that*, when the fact is science doesn't say anything, as I've said. It's the scientists who do all the talking and guessing and interpreting what the data seems to say to them, or that it seems to have revealed and their interpretation of the data. Richard is saying what *he* believes, and what *he* hopes the scientific data is saying, so he can keep it in the realm of science alone. C'mon man. Again Richard. Let's be fair and balanced here. It is Richard's belief that science (Scientists) is working towards discovering and will one day in fact discover the *smoking gun*, the incontrovertible evidence that blows the God Hypothesis out of the water for good. That discovery being what Richard says is the Theory of Everything.

To him it is a question for science (The community working in all fields of science) and science alone to solve, but until it does, his current objective is to dismantle agnosticism, and that's because, as I said, it would remove any middle ground or fence sitting view so that we're left with only two viewpoints to choose from – theism and atheism – and not have the option of the sitting on the fence view, so-to-speak, which is agnosticism, which is where Richard says Mr. Sagan sat. Next Richard mentions Jocelyn Bell Burnell, the radio astronomer who first discovered the Pulsar in 1967 and called it LGM (Little Green Men). Of this discovery Richard says:

"Today there have been more than 1,000 pulsars found in our galaxy, and it is generally accepted that each one is a spinning neutron star emitting radio energy that sweeps around like a timescale of seconds, but just about everything we know of neutron stars is amazing. The point is that the pulsar phenomenon is now understood to be a product of simple physics, not intelligence." [271]

Simple physics Richard? Really? C'mon man. Physics is far from simple when compared to what I understand simple to be. Physics, or the laws of physics, to me, are the laws of God having been put in place to uphold the universe and keep everything within the bounds He has set. From the small to the very large. From quarks to galaxies, or even the universe in its totality. Now to the crux of "Little Green Men". Richard says:

"Whether we ever get to know about them (aliens) or not, there are very probably alien civilizations that are superhuman, to the point of being god-like in ways that exceed anything a theologian could possibly imagine. Their technical achievements would seem as supernatural to us as ours would seem to a Dark Age peasant transported to the twenty-first century." [272]

Just think of all the advances and inventions that would blow that Dark Age peasants' mind that are already in existence today. I believe the society of God, and those beings who live in it with Him, including His Son, Jesus Christ, are indeed god-like and could easily be described as super-human when compared to the Dark Age peasant. Their technological achievements; their communications; all of it is beyond our human understanding and imagination at this time. That said, I will remind you, my readers, of the testimony that Joseph Smith and Oliver Cowdery gave of seeing God, which I quoted in my Introduction. The next verse after their testimony, says:

Doctrine and Covenants 76:24

> **23** That by him, and through him, and of him, the worlds (Plural) are and were created, and the inhabitants thereof are begotten sons and daughters unto God..

Notice that this verse says worlds, in the plural, and that they are inhabited by His sons and daughters. This revelation was given more than 180 years ago, and scientists are just now alluding to the hypothesis that there might be planets that could sustain life and therefore there might be intelligent inhabitants on them, or as Richard describes them as *"aliens' who might be superhuman, to the point of being god-like"*.

The society that God and his glorified, immortal children who live in His presence, as I said, are most definitely god-like, as He is their Heavenly Father, the God of this universe. It certainly is something to think about, is it not? Richard goes on to say:

"The miracles wrought by our technology would have seemed to the ancients no less remarkable than the tales of Moses parting the waters, or Jesus, walking upon them." [273]

"Arthur C. Clarke", Richard says, "puts it this way in his Third Law: 'Any sufficiently advanced technology is indistinguishable from magic'." [274]

Near the beginning of this subtitle, Richard said, "My definition of the God Hypothesis included the words superhuman and supernatural. To clarify the difference, imagine that a SETI radio telescope did pick up a signal from outer space which showed, unequivocally, that we are not alone. In what sense, then, would the most advanced SETI aliens not be gods? In what sense would they be superhuman but not supernatural? In a very important sense, which goes to the heart of this book (This book being The God Delusion, and not mine)." [275]

"The crucial difference between gods and god-like extraterrestrials lies not in their properties but in their provenance (Beginnings). Entities that are complex enough to be intelligent are products of an evolutionary process.

(Ah-ha! We knew that evolution was going to come into this discussion, didn't we? Once again, Richard's mother-of-all-answers to everything – including god-like extraterrestrials – is evolution).

Richard continues, "No matter how god-like they may seem when we encounter them, they didn't start that way. [276]

Back in my Introduction to my book, I also mentioned a quote given by the prophet Joseph Smith, who taught:

"In knowledge there is power. ... God has more power than all other beings because he has greater knowledge; ... and hence, ... he knows how to subject all other beings to him. ... He has power over them all'." [277]

That power comes from God's Intelligence, for any knowledge is in fact intelligence, and at the risk of sounding like I'm agreeing with Richard, let me say that in a very real sense, the God I believe in, does indeed, using Richard's words, "seem as being supernatural to us just like the world in which we live would seem to be supernatural to a Dark Ages peasant when transported to the twenty-first century. Any one of our present-day advanced technologies would be indistinguishable from magic to that peasant." [278]

Almost every single theophany recorded in scripture (As I said earlier, there are multiple recorded theophanies in the Bible, in the Old and New Testaments, and other scripture) speaks of the initial fear each person felt upon seeing God, and even experienced fearful feelings when visited by one of His holy angels, so much so, that the Lord and His angels would have to say to them, "Fear not".

Many of these witnesses also testified of seeing a pillar of light, a burning bush, or a glow of light that was brighter than the noon-day sun when God was descending down with His Son Jesus, or when they showed themselves to one of God's children. Many said they were even standing above them 'in the air', or just appeared in the room with doors and windows closed. All of this seems to be supernatural, does it not? I say supernatural because we, as natural beings, certainly don't do anything close to this while in our present physical state. And so, it's hard for us to believe these kinds of visitations actually happened, especially in the way that the witnesses describe them. Just because we don't understand them or that most people don't believe they ever happened, doesn't mean they didn't happen and that those who gave such testimonies of these visitations were delusional. That said, I do understand the skepticism that most people have of such theophanies. Here's a specific example of what I'm talking about. Joseph Smith, the prophet, described the First Vision he had, which was seeing God the Father and His Son, Jesus Christ, when he was in his fifteenth year. It sounds very similar to what I just described. [279]

Joseph Smith did not say how the pillar of light worked, nor did he postulate as to where it originated from. He just said that the light came down from the sky. He didn't know, nor did any of His associates know, exactly how this worked. Heck, it could have come from an advanced transporter of some kind, like the one portrayed in the science fiction T.V. series Star Trek, where people are transported from a highly advanced spaceship up in space, far, far away (Beam me up Scotty!). We just don't know or remember that much about these mysteries of God or His realm of existence, at least not yet. I certainly don't claim to know everything, and atheists, like Richard, most certainly don't know, nor do they attempt to imagine such things regarding God and His glory, power, omniscience, and intelligence. My point is, the objects of my faith, those glorious, sentient beings called God the Father, and His Son, Jesus Christ, and the Holy Ghost, have shared very little about how they travel from where they reside, nor have they revealed how any of their advanced technologies work, such as the Urim and Thummim or the Liahona from the Book of Mormon for example. Yet, God did tell us where He and His Son reside.

The Church of Jesus Christ of Latter-Day Saints' scriptures include a record where God identifies where He lives. He said He lives near a planet called Kolob (Before you make fun of the name of this planet, think of the names that scientists have given to planets discovered in the recent past such as Pluto, a Disney character, or Celestial Dragon and Fae Fawn. Right? Good Honk in the Morning!).

This statement is recorded in the revealed scripture called *The Pearl of Great Price*, and it's specifically found in *The Book of Abraham*, starting with the 1st chapter, and continuing through the 4th chapter. The prophet Abraham is speaking about a conversation he had with the Lord God, Jehovah, regarding the Urim and Thummim. Here it is:

Abraham 3:1-4, 9

1 And I, Abraham, had the Urim and Thummim, (The Urim and Thummim is just one example of Gods' advanced technologies) which the Lord my God had given unto me, in Ur of the Chaldees; (This reminds me of the Liahona which God gave to Lehi to help navigate their travels in the wilderness and ocean. It's another advanced technology spoken of in The Book of Mormon).

2 And I saw the stars, that they were very great, *and that one of them was nearest unto the throne of God*; and there were many great ones (Stars) which were near unto it;

3 And the Lord said unto me: These are the governing ones (That governs our solar system?); and the name of the great one is Kolob, because it is near unto me, for I am the Lord thy God (Jehovah or YAH-WEH): I have set this one to govern all those which belong to the same order as that upon which thou standest.

4 And the Lord said unto me, by the Urim and Thummim, that Kolob was after the manner of the Lord, according to its times and seasons in the revolutions thereof; that one revolution was a day unto the Lord, after his manner of reckoning, it being one thousand years according to the time appointed unto that whereon thou standest. This is the reckoning of the Lord's time, according to the reckoning of Kolob."

9 And thus there shall be the reckoning of the time of one planet above another, until thou come *nigh unto Kolob*, which Kolob is after the reckoning of the Lord's time; which Kolob is set *nigh unto the throne of God*, to govern all those planets which belong to the same order as that upon which thou standest.

Abraham said that Kolob is a distant planet/star that is far, far away from earth and the *nearest* to God's throne, and that's all that God has revealed regarding that planet/star that's nearest to God's dwelling place for now, except to describe that the Celestial Kingdoms' streets (That heavenly orb's streets have the *appearance* of being paved with gold):

Doctrine & Covenants 137:1-4

1 The heavens were opened upon us, and I beheld the celestial kingdom of God, and the glory thereof, whether in the body or out I cannot tell.

2 I saw the transcendent beauty of the gate through which the heirs of that kingdom will enter, which was like unto circling flames of fire;

3 Also the blazing throne of God, whereon was seated the Father and the Son.

4 I saw the beautiful streets of that kingdom, which had *the appearance* of being paved with gold.

Does this sound outrageous? Does it sound supernatural? I suppose it would to skeptics like Richard. With CGI, movie makers can create an underworld in the deepest part of the ocean that looks supernatural and yet plausible in our minds' imaginations. Right? Much of what Joseph Smith taught 190 years ago was viewed as outrageous by the scientists of his Day, as well as today. Yet, 190 plus years later many of his concepts and beliefs have become scientifically *current* just as Dr. Lamb explained in his book "Joseph Smith's 21st Century View of the World". Other futurists, like Tesla, have told of things yet to come, and today we are living in such a prophesied world. I thought that you, my readers, might find these lyrics to a song titled "If You Could Hie to Kolob" to be interesting and informative. It was written by William W. Phelps (1792–1872), a convert to the Church of Jesus Christ of Latter-Day Saints and a close associate of Joseph Smith. Abraham 3:1–4, 9, and Moses 1:3–4, 33–39 provide the 'theme' expressed in these lyrics:

> 1.   If you could hie to Kolob
> In the twinkling of an eye,
> And then continue onward
> With that same speed to fly,
> Do you think that you could ever,
> Through all eternity,
> Find out the generation
> Where Gods began to be?

> 2.   Or see the grand beginning,
> Where space did not extend?
> Or view the last creation,
> Where Gods and matter end?
> Methinks the Spirit whispers,
> "No man has found 'pure space,'
> Nor seen the outside curtains,
> Where nothing has a place."

3.   The works of God continue,
And worlds and lives abound;
Improvement and progression
Have one eternal round.
There is no end to matter;
There is no end to space;
There is no end to spirit;
There is no end to race.

4.   There is no end to virtue;
There is no end to might;
There is no end to wisdom;
There is no end to light.
There is no end to union;
There is no end to youth;
There is no end to priesthood;
There is no end to truth.

5. There is no end to glory;
There is no end to love;
There is no end to being;
There is no death above.
There is no end to glory;
There is no end to love;
There is no end to being;
There is no death above.

Text: William W. Phelps, 1792–1872 [280]

Now I'm well aware that what I just said about God and about Kolob sounds like wacky science fiction, or as Richard would call it – delusional (But think what we're possibly going to learn from the James Webb Telescope in the years to come). Just as Richard feels distain about these and every other books of scripture, I also feel distain for what scientists often postulate. The science fiction author Daniel E. Galouye, speaks of one such theory that scientists have offered up about a possible reality:

"We live in a computer simulation" he said, "set up by some vastly superior civilization (Like the fictional city Zion, in the movie 'The Matrix', right?). But the Simulators themselves would have to come from somewhere else." Richard says, "I cannot think how to dispute it." [281]

Well, I guess neither can I, at least not with incontrovertible arguments. The theory of *computer simulations* and the *Simulators* who run them, is certainly interesting, but it's a theorem for another debate and another time. However, just as Richard asks the infinite regression question of God's beginnings, I ask the same question here, "What Simulator created this Simulator?"

All these interesting scientific and religious topics, and the questions that arise from them, are the reasons why I'm so looking forward to the Lord's 2nd coming. It will usher in the millennium, which is the hinge point I mentioned earlier. It is when all of us will have the opportunity to hear from the Lord God Himself, even Jesus Christ, as to what is real and what is not. He will answer all the 'Big' questions.

As I've said, He promised that He would reveal all things to us, even the truth of all things. But until that Day, I am content in knowing that God the Father and the Lord, Jesus Christ, His Son, exist, and in knowing that I'm the child of a Heavenly Father who loves me and all of His children, perfectly.

I might also mention that I, as a member of the Church of Jesus Christ of Latter-Day Saints, believe that when we die our spirit selves (currently housed in our physical bodies), will go to the *world of spirits*, or the *spirit world*, to await the resurrection, and I'm confident that our memory of our pre-existent life with God and Jesus, before we came to earth, will be restored in its fullness in due time, so that everything we learned up to the point at which we became mortal beings (By coming into this world as little babies), will all be restored. That's so exciting to me. I almost can't wait for the day when I remember all those things. [282] Having said that, let me say unequivocally, that God and His Son Jesus Christ, are most definitely not 'little green men' as Richard jokingly referred to them. Let's go ahead with the next chapter – "Arguments for God's Existence".

CHAPTER 3

ARGUMENTS FOR GOD'S EXISTENCE

Richard begins this next Chapter's topic by saying, "Arguments for the existence for God have been codified (Arranged for a purpose of a system) for centuries by theologians, and supplemented by others, including purveyors of misconceived common sense". [283]

I think that this statement is just a sophisticated way of saying theists and believers like myself, have, over the previous millennia, arranged the principles and laws related to God into religious systems, and they include rules (Like the Ten Commandments), which make no sense to Richard and other atheists like him. Richard's main point is that these systems and their rules didn't come from God, but were, and are, manmade, and as such, they're based on man's misconceived common sense, and are deserving of distain and disrespect.

As a counter to Richard's claim here, as well as to his arguments against God's existence that he puts forth in this chapter, let me bring in a few comments made by Stephen Meyer, a Dr. of the Philosophy of Science from the University of Cambridge. Abiogenesis is the scientific theory which states that life arose on Earth via spontaneous natural means, and so it lands in the science of Origins. Dr. Meyer works in the field of Intelligent Design, a field that atheist scientists do not consider to be a legitimate scientific theory because it opens the door to Divine Intelligence and would undermine the Theory of Evolution and Natural Selection.

Dr. Meyer, who I mentioned in my Introduction, is a well-known American author and former educator, and like I said, is an advocate of Intelligent Design, which theory has been described by its critics as being a *pseudoscientific creationist argument* for the existence of God. Pseudoscience consists of statements, beliefs, or practices that claim to be both scientific and factual but are incompatible with the scientific method (Or so say atheist scientists). Stephen presents his working theory of Intelligent Design as being *an evidence-based scientific theory*. Richard of course, rejects that claim. Critics of Stephen's work on Intelligent Design say it falls outside of *legitimate scientific norms*." [284]

In my opinion, Richard is taking this stance against Dr. Meyer's scientific research on the Theory of Intelligent Design (Which, in my opinion, lands squarely in what's called "The *Research of Life's Beginnings*" field of science. It of course is part of the study of Biology), because by saying Dr. Meyers' work is "illegitimate science", is keeping it, along with "creationism", out of our public schools' science curriculum, which keeps the debate one-sided so that there's no opposing view for students to consider.

Dr. Meyer was recently the presenter for a new PragerU video for Prager University. PragerU is an American 501-C3 nonprofit media company that creates videos on various political, economic, and sociological topics from a conservative viewpoint, using famous individuals like Dr. Meyer as their presenters. This particular video I'm referring to is found on YouTube, under the name: "5-Part Series: Science and God": [285]

Here are the titles of the five videos that Stephen reviews in this single composite of these five videos, making it a series of videos in one:

1. Are Religion and Science in Conflict?
2. How Did the Universe Begin?
3. Aliens, the Multiverse, or God?
4. What Is Intelligent Design?
5. What's Wrong with Atheism?

In reference to the 5th video titled, "What's Wrong with Atheism?", Stephen says the following, and I quote:

"Each year traditional Jews and Christians celebrate special acts of God in human history. Yet, polling data now shows that an increasing number of young people, including those from religious homes, doubt even the existence of God. Moreover, polls probing such young religiously unaffiliated agnostics and atheists, have found that science — or at least the claims of putative spokesmen for science — have played an outsized role in cementing disaffection with religious belief (In other words, they've worked to create in young people's minds *cognitive dissonance*, because it usually leads to a loss of faith and disbelief in God).

"In one, more than two-thirds of self-described atheists, and one-third of agnostics, affirm 'the findings of science make the existence of God *less probable*' (This certainly sounds like something Richard Dawkins would latch onto and promote it in support of his theory that God doesn't exist, doesn't it?). It's not hard to see how many people might have acquired this impression, as I mentioned earlier, since 2006 popular new atheist writers — Richard Dawkins, Victor Stenger, Sam Harris, Christopher Hitchens, Daniel Dennett, Stephen Hawking, Bill Nye, and Lawrence Krauss, to name just a few — have published a series of best-selling books arguing that science (Scientific Data) renders religious belief implausible.

"According to Dawkins, and the like, Darwinian evolution in particular, establishes that 'The universe we observe precisely has the properties we should expect if there is, at bottom, no design, no purpose nothing but blind, pitiless indifference'. But does science actually support this strictly materialistic vision of reality? I say that 'In fact, there were three major scientific discoveries during the last century that contradicted the expectations of scientific atheists (or materialists) and point instead in a distinctly theistic direction'.

"First, cosmologists have discovered that the physical universe likely had a beginning, contrary to the expectations of scientific materialists who had long portrayed the material universe as eternal and self-existent (And, therefore, in no need of an external Creator). The first evidence of a cosmic beginning came in the 1920s when astronomers discovered that light coming from distant galaxies was being stretched out or 'red-shifted' as if the galaxies were moving away from us (Towards some great attractor).

"Soon after, Belgian priest and physicist Georges Lemaître and Caltech astronomer Edwin Hubble independently showed that galaxies farther away from earth were receding faster than those close at hand. That suggested a spherical expansion of the universe (and space) like a balloon inflating from a singular explosive beginning — from a "big bang. Lemaître also showed that Einstein's equations describing gravity most naturally implied a dynamic, evolving universe, despite Einstein's initial attempt to gerrymander his own equations to depict the universe as eternally existing and static — i.e., neither contracting nor expanding.

"In 1931, Einstein visited Hubble at the Mt. Wilson observatory in California to view the red-shift evidence for himself. He later announced that denying the evidence of a beginning was the greatest 'blunder' of his scientific career'. This evidence of a beginning, later reinforced by other developments in observational astronomy and theoretical physics, not only contradicted the expectations of scientific materialists, it confirmed those of traditional theists.

"As physicist and Nobel Laureate Arno Penzias observed, 'The best data we have [concerning a beginning] are exactly what I would have predicted, had I nothing to go on but the first five books of Moses, the Psalms, and the Bible as a whole'.

"Second, physicists have discovered that we live in a kind of 'Goldilocks Universe'. Indeed, ever since the 1960s, physicists have determined that the fundamental physical laws and parameters of our universe have been *finely tuned*, against all odds, to make our universe capable of hosting life. Even slight alterations in the values of many independent factors — such as the strength of gravitational and electromagnetic attraction, the masses of elementary particles, and the initial arrangement of matter and energy in the universe — would have rendered life impossible. Not surprisingly many physicists have concluded that this *improbable fine-tuning* for life points to a cosmic 'fine tuner'.

"As former Cambridge astrophysicist, Sir Fred Hoyle argued: 'A common-sense interpretation of the data suggests that a super-intellect has monkeyed with physics to make life possible'. To avoid this conclusion, some physicists have postulated a vast number of other universes. This 'multiverse' idea portrays our universe as the outcome of *a grand lottery* in which some *universe-generating mechanism* spits out billions and billions of universes — so many that our universe with its 'improbable' combination of life-conducive factors would eventually *have to arise*." (This would absolutely take 'no-fact-based faith' to postulate such a theory, wouldn't it? What created the universe generating mechanism? Is this an argument Richard uses when confronted with an improbable causal cause?)

"Yet, advocates of the multiverse overlook an obvious problem. All such proposals — whether based on 'inflationary cosmology' or 'string theory' — postulate universe generating mechanisms that themselves require *prior unexplained fine-tuning* (Richard must admit that this then requires the question about the unexplained greater causal cause I just asked about, which is another infinite regress of the original cause, right?) – thus, taking us back to where we started – the need for an ultimate 'fine-tuner'.

"Finally, discoveries in molecular biology have revealed *the presence of digital code at the foundation of life*, suggesting the work of a 'master programmer'. After James Watson and Francis Crick elucidated the structure of the DNA molecule in 1953, Crick developed his famed 'sequence hypothesis'. In it, Crick proposed that the chemical constituents in DNA function like 'letters' in a 'written language' or 'digital symbols' in a 'computer code'.

"Functioning computer code depends upon a precise sequence of zeros and ones. Similarly, the DNA molecule's ability to direct the assembly of crucial protein molecules in cells depends upon specific arrangements of 'chemical constituents' called bases along the spine of its double helix structure. Thus, even Richard Dawkins has acknowledged, "the machine code of the genes is uncannily computer-like." Or as Bill Gates explains, "DNA is like a computer program, but far, far more advanced than any software we've ever created."

"No theory of undirected chemical evolution has explained the origin of the information in DNA (or RNA) needed to build the first living cell from simpler non-living chemicals. Instead, our uniform and repeated experience — the basis of all scientific reasoning — shows that systems possessing 'functional' or 'digital information' invariably arising from 'intelligent' causes. We know from experience that software comes from programmers.

"We know generally that 'information' — whether inscribed in hieroglyphics, written in a book, or encoded in radio signals (Or written in the sand on a beach) — always arises from an intelligent source. So, the discovery of information — and a complex information transmission and processing system — in every living cell, provides strong grounds for inferring that 'intelligence' played a role in life's origin. As information theorist Henry Quastler observed, 'information habitually arises from conscious activity'."

"Historian of science Fredrick Burnham notes: "The idea that God created the universe [is] a more respectable hypothesis today than at any time in the last 100 years. Recent scientific discoveries about biological and cosmological origins have decidedly theistic implications, suggesting that popular scientific reports of the death of God may have been — to adapt Mark Twain's famous quip — greatly exaggerated." [286]

This is the end of comments by Dr. Stephen Meyer during the PragerU videos

John Updike, who was an American novelist, poet, short-story writer, art critic, and literary critic, said the following:

"The most miraculous thing is happening. The physicists are getting down to the nitty-gritty ... and the last thing they ever expected to be happening is happening ... God is showing through." [287]

I just wanted you, my readers, to have these thoughts in your mind when you begin to read the perspective I'll be sharing, regarding the arguments Richard Dawkins puts forth in this 3rd chapter – "Arguments for God's Existence" – starting with the subtitle – 'Thomas Aquinas's proofs'.

THOMAS AQUINAS' PROOFS

Richard begins this subtitle by saying, "Thomas Aquinas' five proofs show a lack of thought or intelligence." [288]

In other words, they are mindless, and unguided, and do not prove anything. This of course, is just Richard expressing his opinion once again, which is also coming from an unguided, unintended, mindless wet brain, his brain, which doesn't prove anything, like he himself suggested. Next, I want to be fair and honest here. I actually agree with Richard's view on most of these so-called 'five proofs' of Aquinas, and so I guess that makes my perspective the result of my unguided, unintended, mindless wet brain too, if what Richard said is correct. Right? Ha-ha.

1. The Unmoved Mover -

Richard says, and I quote:

"Aquinas' first three arguments, the *unmoved mover*, the *uncaused cause*, and the *cosmological argument*, all involve an *infinite regress* where one answer to a question raises a prior question, and on and on into infinity." [289]

The short of it is that *something* had to *make* or *create* the first cause or mover, and theists say that God is that uncaused cause. Most Christians say God is outside of time and space and created everything from absolutely nothing (Ex Nihlo). Whereas atheists, like Richard, say "everything we see began from nothing." [290] Lawrence Kraus teaches such an unproven theorem. I will respond to Mr. Kraus's theorem that the universe came from nothing a little later.

The key argument that Richard has for giving this regress concept about an uncaused cause, is due to those theists who say, "God, as the uncaused cause, necessarily is immune to *the regress* that these arguments promote because He exists *outside* of the concept created in any way or form." Simply put, 'because he wasn't created there is no regress'.

Let me respond to Richard's angst with theists who say this. I'm going to refer to what I said earlier in my Introduction, where I quoted Dr. John Lamb. Dr. Lamb repeats what Joseph Smith taught, which was that God, His Son, and the Holy Ghost, as well as all of us for that matter, *have always existed as some* form of matter. The Godhead as well as all of us, are without beginning of days or end of life. The members of the Godhead, and each of us, existed first as intelligence(s) and eternal spirits, and so they, as well as all of us, have always existed within the universe. In other words, matter cannot be destroyed. It can be changed but not destroyed. Joseph Smith taught in the *King Follett Sermon the following*:

"The mind or the intelligence which man possesses is co-equal [co-eternal] with God himself ... The intelligence of spirits had no beginning, neither will it have an end ... There never was a time when there were not spirits; for they are co-equal [co-eternal] with our Father in heaven." [291]

Let me interject an excerpt from an essay found on my Church's website under the topic called "Intelligence, and Intelligences", to expand your, my readers, view on these two principles:

Intelligence, and Intelligences [292]
(See also Light, Light of Christ; Spirit; Truth)

"Intelligence has several meanings, three of which are: (1) It is the light of truth that gives life and light to all things in the universe. It has always existed. (2) The word *intelligences* may also refer to the spirit children of God. (3) The scriptures also may speak of intelligence as referring to the *spirit element* that existed before we were begotten as spirit children.

- Intelligence cleaveth unto intelligence:

Doctrine & Covenants 88:40

40 For intelligence cleaveth unto intelligence; wisdom recieveth wisdom; truth embraceth truth; loveth virtue; light cleaveth unto light; mercy hath compassion on mercy and claimeth her own; justice continueth its course and claimeth its own; judgment goeth before the face of him who sitteth upon the throne and governeth and executeth all things.

- Intelligence was not created or made:

Doctrine & Covenants 93:29

29 Man was also in the beginning with God; Intelligence, or the light of truth, was not created or made, neither indeed can be.

- All intelligence is independent in that sphere in which God has placed it:

Doctrine & Covenants 93:30

30 All truth is independent in that sphere in which God has placed it, to act for itself, as all intelligence also; otherwise there is no existence.

- The glory of God is intelligence:

Doctrine & Covenants 93:36–37

36 The glory of God is intelligence, or, in other words, light and truth.

37 Light and truth forsake that evil one.

- Intelligence acquired in this life rises with us in the resurrection:

Doctrine & Covenants 130:18–19

18 Whatever principle of intelligence we attain unto in this life, it will rise with us in the resurrection.

19 And if a person gains more knowledge and intelligence in this life through his diligence and obedience than another, he will have so much the advantage in the world to come.

- The Lord rules over all the intelligences:

Abraham 3:21

21 I dwell in the midst of them all; I now, therefore, have come down unto thee to declare unto thee the works which my hands have made, wherein my wisdom excelleth them all, for I rule in the heavens above, and in the earth beneath, in all wisdom and prudence, over all the intelligences thine eyes have seen from the beginning; I came down in the beginning in the midst of all the intelligences thou hast seen.

- The Lord showed Abraham the intelligences that were organized before the world was:

Abraham 3:22

22 Now the Lord had shown unto me, Abraham, the intelligences that were organized before the world was; and among all these there were many of the noble and great ones;

End of Excerpt from 'Intelligence, and Intelligences'

Let me make it very clear that I am not a spokesman for the Church of Jesus Christ of Latter-Day Saints, so I do not speak for the Church in any official capacity. My comments here are my personal views and perspective as a Latter-Day Saint. It is my belief that you, my readers, and everyone else, have always existed as a spirit child of God, our Father, or even before this, we were Intelligences, and therefore were not created in the *out of nothing* (ex nihilo) sense of the word.

It is also my belief and perspective that we existed before coming to earth as intelligent beings, even the spirit children of our eternal heavenly parents. This estate was our first estate, and because we sustained Jehovah as the Savior to be, we kept our first estate. We are now in our second estate which is mortality. After death, we'll continue to be intelligent, eternal beings, having learned from our second estates' earthly experience. At our death we will await our resurrection and begin our third estate. Each of us, when *completed*, meaning, after each of us receive our resurrected bodies which will have some degree of glory, we will continue as eternal, immortal beings, just as our heavenly parents and the Savior, Jesus Christ, who was the first fruits of the resurrection, are eternal beings.

Because Dr. Lamb's book discusses these unique elements of eternal intelligences and eternal matter, as well as the nature of the beings who make up the Godhead, and our very own nature as spirit children of the first member of the Godhead, our Eternal Father, including providing the scriptures that relate to all of this, I encourage you, my readers, to get his book and finish reading it so you can more fully understand why I say, and again, it's just my personal perspective, "the Uncaused Cause" argument that says that "God is outside of the process of *eternal, infinite regress*", is *not* an accurate understanding of God and His divine, eternal nature, and therefore this question postulated by Richard to all theists, still leaves us having to consider it more fully, and the implications it raises regarding Gods' eternality.

Richard says the question once again, becomes, "Who or what created, or organized God then?" This question makes most theists or believers a little uncomfortable as they wrestle with its implications, and for that reason many choose to side-step it by simply saying "Since God was not created, He is outside of creation." It cannot be simply answered. It is a complicated question, and this simple answer cannot be used to try and push it aside. I, as a Latter-Day Saint, do not take this position.

My perspective regarding the *infinite regression* question, is that God, as well as all of us, His children, have always existed. He, as well as all of us, was not created or organized out of nothing, nor was there a nothingness in which God existed, before He supposedly created everything out of nothing. God, Himself, did not exist in nothingness before everything else. I believe all reality and all beings, including God Himself, His Son, Jesus Christ, and the personage of the Holy Ghost, were all organized out of *something* and *not* out of nothing as Christendom would have us believe.

This creative organizing of our world and each of us, took place a very, very long time ago, the matter from which we came to be having no beginning of days, nor does any of it have an end. That *something* or *principles of eternal intelligence* and *eternal matter* cannot be seen by the natural eye in our present state, it's true, but they can be seen by those who are in an immortal, resurrected state with their purer eyes, or they can be seen when God allows it, such as in the case of the brother of Jared whose story is found in the Book of Mormon. Mahonri Moriancumer, who was the brother of Jared, saw the Lord Jehovah who was a spirit personage before He came to the earth and gained His body, as Jesus. This story can be found in the Book of Mormon in the Book of Ether, chapter 3, starting on page 492.

Our spirit bodies are formed with eternal, material element; they being *purer* than the mortal, physical matter we're able to see with our natural eyes. Our natural eyes, or any powerful microscope that's been developed so far, cannot see this pure matter, but we can and do see its *effects,* much like how we know atoms exist. The elements used in our organizing and activating, meaning the elements of intelligence and other forms of matter, are all eternal like I said, and therefore have always existed. So, *if* in fact what I am saying is true, then it dismisses the need for trying to put God outside of creation.

Joseph Smith taught that "cosmology is the description of the history and destiny of the physical and meta-physical universe, and that this cosmology is drawn out from Biblical cosmology as it's taught in the Bible, but it has many unique elements (such as those Joseph Smith taught 190 years ago) such as the pre-existence, or pre-mortal life, in which our spirits existed as the literal spirit children of heavenly parents." [293]

When our spirit bodies were *activated*, the essential *intelligence* of our spirits being eternal, and the matter making up our spirit bodies, are *without beginning or end of life* in that sense of the word (Much like our mortal bodies are activated when a sperm and egg, which contain the power of *life* in them, come together at conception, and we begin our journey of becoming a distinct, living being, an individual human person, different from all other persons. The matter forming those two beginning seeds (The sperm and the egg), is eternal. They can be changed but they cannot be destroyed. They are eternal in nature.

During our pre-mortal life our Heavenly Father (Elohim) presented a *Plan of Redemption and Happiness* to all of us, His spirit children, during a Grand Heavenly Council. Father's Plan required a Savior. Jehovah, the first born spirit child of God who became Jesus on earth, stepped forward to say, "Send Me", as did Lucifer, who was called 'a son of the morning'. Each proposed a very different way of fulfilling God's Plan of Happiness for His children. Much like politicians from opposing political parties want the same thing, but always have very different ways for going about the objective. Father chose Jehovah's offer to be our Savior, and called Him to that holy calling, even the Redeemer of the World and champion of 'moral agency', it being the central principle in Heavenly Fathers Plan. But Lucifer (Satan) insisted that he could make it so no one would be at risk from using their agency, and therefore failing to return to God. His plan would replace the principle and law of moral agency, with a different principle, a kind of forcing our actions to be in line with God, which would make it so everyone would return to live with their Heavenly Father again. Satan's approach, as I said, required that *moral agency* be replaced with some kind of, or principle of *instinct* as the heart and central principle of saving Father's children, making *choosing* right from wrong unnecessary and nonexistent.

This approach would force us to only do what he commanded us to do, resulting in all of us being unable to learn, develop, and grow. However, it would allow Satan to declare, "I, and I alone have done this, so I deserve to be called God!" When Lucifer's approach was not accepted (Due to its central principle being one of forcing all of us to unwillingly perform 'his' commandments) and Jesus' approach (Due to its central principle being *moral agency where we choose to follow God's commandments or not*) was accepted by Heavenly Father, Satan rebelled against Father and Jehovah, and instigated the *War in Heaven* that is spoken of in the book of Revelations, which war Satan ultimately lost.

As a result of Satan's rebellion and his losing this war of ideologies, Satan and his followers were cast out of heaven, and sent to earth. These followers were a third part of our spirit brothers and sisters; the third part of the hosts of heaven who fought against Gods' Plan (By fought I mean a battle between two differing ideologies, and who we wanted as our Savior). Satan and his followers were all sent down to the earth in their spirit personage state, having lost their first estate, so that they became angels of the devil and tempters to all those who have ever lived and will ever live on this earth. They make up the opposing voice to the Spirits divine voice. Here's the story found in the book of Revelations (JST):

JST, Revelation 12:1–17 (Compare KJV of Revelation 12:1–17)

6 And there was *war in heaven*; Michael (Who became Adam) and his angels fought against the dragon (Satan); and the dragon and his angels (The third part of God's spirit children) *fought against Michael;*

7 And the dragon prevailed not against Michael, neither the child, nor the woman, which was the Church of God, who had been delivered of her pains (In other words the Church having gone into the wilderness, came out from the wilderness of apostasy) and brought forth the kingdom of our God and his Christ.

8 Neither was there place found in heaven for the great dragon, who was cast out; that old serpent called the devil, and also called Satan, which deceiveth the whole world; he was cast out into the earth; and his angels were cast out with him (Cast out of Heaven down to earth to become the tempters of mankind).

According to this Plan of Happiness, under the direction of God the Father, Jehovah, His Master Builder, created (Organized) this earth as a place designed and organized for God's children to come and dwell thereon. We came here to receive our physical bodies, and to be tested, and ultimately to be redeemed so that we could return to and live with our Heavenly Father in His presence, *if* we choose Him and follow His Plan. God's work is a work of redemption. It is a work of love.

Intelligence, and Intelligences Essay excerpts continued:

"After the millennium and all of God's children are resurrected—except the third part of the spirits that chose to follow Lucifer as well as those 'sons of perdition' who fully rejected Christ and His redemptive gospel while living here on earth and as a result will be cast into outer darkness—all will face the *final* judgement and will be assigned to live in one of the three degrees of glory as they're described in the following scriptures:

John 14:2

2 In my Father's house are many mansions: if *it were* not *so,* I would have told you. I go to prepare a place for you (That place being a place of an eternal weight and glory as described in the next verses of scripture).

I Corinthians 15:40-41

40 *There are* also celestial bodies, and bodies terrestrial: but the glory of the celestial *is* one, and the *glory* of the terrestrial *is* another.

41 *There is* one glory of the sun, and another glory of the moon, and another glory of the stars: for one star differeth from *another* star in glory.

"Within the highest degree of glory, which is the celestial kingdom, there are three additional divisions within that kingdom, and those in this highest kingdom of glory, the celestial kingdom, will become gods and goddesses, and priest and priestesses *unto* God their Eternal Father, and *unto* His Son, Jesus Christ, where they enjoy the gift that is referred to as "the gift of exaltation" or "eternal progression".

(See www.thechurchofjesuschrist.org, "Our Premortal Life" for an expanded discussion of 'The *doctrine of eternal progression'* or in today's vernacular '*deification*'). "This was succinctly summarized by a past president of the Church of Jesus Christ of Latter-Day Saint, President Lorenzo Snow. President Snow described it in the following couplet:

"As man now is, God once was: As God now is, man may become."

End of the additional 'Intelligence, and Intelligences' excerpts

Here is another essay I found at www.fairlatterdaysaints.org, an LDS apologists' website, which discusses this same concept of eternal progression. It is titled "Mormonism and the Concept of Infinite Regress of Gods". Please keep in mind that this is *not* the official position of the Church. However, the quotes contained within it are historically correct and they can be easily found by going to the footnotes (Notes) at the end of each page of the essay. Here are just a few excerpts from this second essay, and I quote:

"According to Joseph Smith's 'King Follett' discourse, God the Father once passed through mortality as did Jesus, but how, when, or where that took place, (And other details we don't even know about) have not yet been revealed. The prevailing view among Latter-Day Saint faithful (I'm not convinced that it is the 'prevailing' view of most members. The language used by the author is a bit slanted) is that God once lived on a planet with his own higher God, and according to Latter-Day Saint scripture, the earth's creation was not *ex nihilo*, meaning 'out of nothing', but was 'organized' from existing, unorganized intelligence and matter in its 'chaos' state.

"This Earth is just one of many inhabited worlds Jesus organized under the direction of the Father, and there are many governing heavenly bodies, including the planet or star named Kolob, which scripture says is the nearest star to the throne of God. Having said this, let me address another question that is often asked of the Church of Jesus Christ of Latter-Day Saints regarding the concept of 'deification' (Or the issue of infinite regression).

"Is it true that LDS doctrine teaches a 'Genealogy of Gods', in which God the Father has/had a God, and this God had a God, and so forth ('Infinite regression' of Gods)? *The fact is that the doctrine of the Church of Jesus Christ of Latter-Day saints is not clearly stated on this subject and is therefore mostly speculative.*"

"Not all Latter-Day Saints accept the ideas which suggest a 'regression of divine beings', or a 'Genealogy of the Gods'. In fact, it does not play much of a role, one way or the other, in Latter-Day Saint worship or thought for it isn't a necessary knowledge for gaining salvation (Key point). It's just an interesting mystery at the present time (I call it a "Mystery of Godliness").

"Objections based on the infinite regression problem usually rely on a misunderstanding of the 'properties of infinities' and require that the critic improperly apply 'finite properties' to infinities. These problems are not unique to Latter-Day Saint theism, and so they must be confronted in some form by all believers.

"This question can only be partially answered, in part, because so very little is known about this issue in Latter-Day Saint scripture and doctrine. The basis of the question rests, in part, in the idea which the Prophet Lorenzo Snow encapsulated in his famous "couplet":

[A] As man now is, God once was, and
[B] as God now is, man may become.

"The implications of part [B] are clear, and relatively well laid out in Latter-Day Saint doctrine. This is the doctrine of *human deification*, or *theosis* (Greek: θέωσις, or deification; deification may also refer to apotheosis, lit. "making divine"). It also formed a key part of early Christian belief. However, the meaning and implication of [A] are not so clear. As President Gordon B. Hinckley, the 15th President of the Church of Jesus Christ of Latter-Day Saints indicated in a *TIME* magazine interview, wherein he stated:

"*Although we accept the first part of President Snow's couplet, we do not completely understand 'it'* ('It' implying the eternal progression of God the Father), *nor do we emphasize or teach it regularly*" (It's hard to say God is an all-knowing God, and has been eternally existing if he went through a *progression* process, doesn't it? Unless the words eternal and progression have a different meaning than what I, with my limited understanding, attributes to them).

Stance #1: God the Father had a divine Father

"This position is seemingly the dominant one in Latter-Day Saint thought. This line of thinking concludes that because God the Father had a mortal experience, He too was at one point the spirit child of another deity. This deity allowed the Father to progress through mortal life and obedience to moral law, and the Father thereby was eventually divinized – given eternal life. Implicit in this idea is the suggestion that the "Heavenly Grandfather" (So to speak) would likewise have needed to undergo a mortal experience under the patronage of yet another divine Father, and so on (Sounds like infinite regression once again, doesn't it? Much like our ancestral chain, except our mortal one stops at Adam).

"These ideas are partly based on later 19th century doctrinal extension by Joseph Smith's successors following his death. Two addresses given by Joseph Smith shortly before his death, (1) the King Follett discourse (7 April 1844) and (2) the "Sermon in the Grove" (16 June 1844). These two addresses were the key source material for these later ideas. Joseph was martyred soon after presenting these ideas publicly, and as such *did not have the opportunity to fully expand, clarify, or explain them.*

"There is some contemporary evidence from the Nauvoo Period that Joseph Smith actually taught this concept. For example, the *Anti-Mormon Nauvoo Expositor* mentioned this concept:

"Among the many items of false doctrine that are taught by the Church, is the doctrine of many Gods, one of the most direful in its effects that has characterized the world for many centuries. It is contended that there are innumerable gods as much above the God that presides over this universe, as he is above us" (Keep in mind that this is an Anti-Mormon newspaper and so its writer has a very critical view of the Latter-Day Saint Church and its teachings).

Stance #2: God the Father did NOT have a divine Father

"Joseph's remarks were not published until after his death, and no word-for-word transcription of his remarks exists. The version of these addresses with which most members of the Church are familiar, and upon which proponents of stance #1 have often mostly relied, were those that were published. Some Church members have argued, as a result, that the conclusions drawn from the commonly available versions of Joseph's talks are mistaken, and that Joseph actually, meant to teach primarily that God the Father underwent a mortal experience. Therefore, in this view, *Jesus'* mortal experience is a better model for the Father's mortality, instead of the experiences of other, fallible mortals (Meaning Jesus' life was one of perfection, and so it suggests *so was His Father's*, our Heavenly Father).

"Proponents of the second view argue that God was once as man is now, but in the sense that *Christ* was once as man is now. That is, they read Joseph Smith as asserting that the Father took on a mortal body and suffered the privations and trials of a mortal life, just as His Son, Jesus Christ did. However, as with Jesus, this does not imply that the Father was not divine prior to receiving a mortal body, nor that the Father required someone else to *atone* for or *redeem* Him" (Just as Jesus needed no redeemer to atone for Him, as he was perfect and without sin).

"It seems fairly clear to me that Joseph Smith had [the Father] being born as a mortal] in mind and not [the Father] being spiritually begotten by another Father above him]. First, immediately after discussing the fact that generation of a son necessarily requires a father, Joseph states:

"I want you to pay particular attention to what I am saying. Jesus said that the Father wrought precisely in the same way as His Father had done before Him. As the Father had done *before*? He [Jesus] laid down His life and took it up the same as His Father had done *before*."

"Thus, Joseph returns to the same explanatory principle that he had in the King Follett discourse. The Son as a mortal does "precisely" what the Father did *before* him. Many proponents of this view argue that the Father may well have played a role in providing salvation to other mortals, in the same way that Jesus did, and I quote:

"God himself, the Father of us all, dwelt on an earth, the same as Jesus Christ himself did; and I will show it from the Bible. What did Jesus say? The Scriptures inform us that Jesus said:

"As the Father hath power in Himself, even so hath the Son power—to do what? Why, what the Father did. The answer is obvious—in a manner to lay down His body and take it up again. Jesus, what are you going to do? To lay down my life as my Father did (Laid down His life) and take it up again" (Just as His Father did).

"Thus, since Jesus laid down His life as part of an atoning act, some have seen the Father in a similar role. Such ideas are perhaps plausible and consistent with the Prophet's teachings, but necessarily *remain speculative* (That's because *Joseph's teachings were incomplete on this subject*, and so I choose to leave them on my shelf of unanswered questions I have, until I learn more).

"Stance #2 has the advantage of accounting for another common theme in Joseph Smith's teaching (as well as LDS scripture) which emphasizes that there is a Most High God over all other beings called *gods*, and this is identified as the Father. For example:

Doctrine & Covenants 121:32

32 According to that which was ordained in the midst of the Council of the Eternal God *of all other gods* before this world was, that should be reserved unto the finishing and the end thereof, when every man shall enter into his eternal presence and into his immortal rest.

Abraham 3:19

9 And thus there shall be the reckoning of the time of one planet above another, until thou come nigh unto Kolob, which Kolob is after the reckoning of the Lord's time; which Kolob is set nigh unto the throne of God, to govern all those planets which belong to the same order as that upon which thou standest.

"This accords well with Joseph's remarks in the Sermon in the Grove about the Sons of God giving glory to the *Most High God*:

"I believe in these Gods that God [i.e., the Father] reveals as Gods—to be Sons of God & all can cry Abba Father–Sons of God who exalt themselves to be Gods even from before the foundation of the world & are all the only Gods I have a reverence for–John said he was a King. Jesus Christ who hath by his own blood made us Kings & Priests to God. Oh, thou God who are King of Kings & Lord of Lords..."

"Advocates of Stance #1, in reply, point out that references to a Most High God might instead apply only from our perspective, and not to the greater *multiverse* envisioned by Stance #1.

"Brigham Young seemed to believe in a backward chain (Or infinite regression) of divine beings. This teaching was linked to the so-called '*Adam-God*' theory advanced by Brigham.

"Given that the meaning of these ideas is not clear and have never been adopted into Latter-Day Saint thought or accepted as doctrine, proponents of Stance #2 have argued that Brigham's speculations on this point ought likewise to be disregarded. 'Would multiple deities threaten the sovereignty of God?' If Stance #2 is adopted, then all divine beings are subject to the Godhead of God the Father, God the Son (Jesus Christ), and God the Holy Ghost, and this is a non-issue.

"If Stance #1 is adopted, some Christians have feared that this perspective threatens the sovereignty of God, *since some other divine being could attempt to over-rule God the Father, or even seek to usurp His power (Just as Lucifer tried to usurp Father's authority and power. He was not divine as yet, and since he did not gain a body, he never can be).*

"In Latter-Day Saint thought, this possibility is of no concern, because a divine being, by definition, is engaged as a unity of love and holiness with other divine beings. The Godhead of Father, Son, and Holy Ghost retain their individuality as persons, but are '*totally united*' in love, will, and their goals.

"For one member of the Godhead to threaten this unity is unthinkable. Believers who receive divinization through divine grace are likewise invited into this same unity and love. Likewise, any other divine beings with whom the Father has a relationship, would likewise be utterly united in love, justice, mercy, and their goal to maximize the blessings and progress of God's children. In Latter-Day Saint thought, a 'conflict' between divine beings is almost a contradiction in terms, since divine beings are united by choice and nature with all other divine beings, and if they turned from it, they would cease to be a god.

"The idea of '*infinite regression*' of divine figures is not necessarily an issue for all members of the Church. However, even if one accepts Stance #1 above, this does not necessarily cause problems for Latter-Day Saint thinkers. Those who attack the Saints on these grounds often make the mistake of confusing various ideas about '*infinity*'. They may take principles that apply to finite things, and improperly extrapolate them to '*infinite things*'. Trans-finite mathematics and some aspects of the calculus deal with infinities, and show that such concepts are not irrational, nor do they share all our intuitive ideas of what infinities must involve (The issue of infinities is an ancient one in western philosophy, going at least as far back as Zeno's paradox).

"An excellent reply to those who use a variation of the '*infinite regression*' argument against Latter-Day Saint theism can be found in Blake T. Ostler, "Review of *The Mormon Concept of God: A Philosophical Analysis* by Francis J. Beckwith and Stephen E. Parrish," *FARMS Review of Books* 8/2 (1996): 99–146. off-site. [294]

End of essay's excerpts

I thought I would now share a few thoughts from *an Evangelical Christians' perspective* on this concept of deification, so that you, my readers, can compare the differences between our two perspectives of God the Father (The Latter-Day Saint perspective and the Christian perspective). Here's the article written by Christian writer Francis J. Beckwith, its title being *"The Mormon Concept of God"*, which I referenced above.

Christians of course, do not consider the Latter-Day Saint faithful to be Christians due to our concept of God, and especially our concept of Jesus Christ, the Son of God, and how different it is from their concept of these same beings (Or persons). Please keep in mind that this is by a Christian who doesn't have the best of feelings or view of the Church of Jesus Christ of Latter-Day Saints, and its doctrine. I've selected a few excerpts from his article for your consideration, and I quote:

"It is the first principle of the gospel to know for a certainty the character of God."

"Mormon leaders often like to portray their faith as merely another 'branch' of Christianity which, unlike other branches of Christianity, preaches the entirety of Christ's gospel. However, most people, even some Mormons, are unaware of how radically the Mormon view of God differs from the picture of God one finds in the Bible and traditional Christian theology.

(Keep in mind also that Mr. Beckwith's beliefs, in my view, are born out of a gospel that was born from apostasy, which apostasy is reflected in the mistranslations found in the Bible, which Mr. Beckwith believes is inerrant. In other words, his church's 'interpretation' of the Bible, and not the Bible itself, when it was in its purity when first written, has led him and the world of Christendom to believe the Bible is inerrant).

Understanding the Biblical Christian Concept of God

"In order to compare and contrast the Mormon concept of God with the biblical/Christian concept of God (Again, their interpretation of it), we must first fully understand what we mean by the 'biblical/Christian concept'. Though there are numerous aspects to God's nature that we could examine (such as that 'He' is a Trinity), for our present purposes it is sufficient to say (From our interpretation of the Bible and what we interpret it to be saying), that the God of biblical Christianity is at least (1) personal and incorporeal (*without physical parts*), (2) the Creator and sustainer of everything else that exists, (3) omnipotent (all-powerful), (4) omniscient (all-knowing), (5) omnipresent (everywhere present), (6) immutable (unchanging) and eternal, and (7) necessary and the only God that exists. Let us now briefly look at each of these attributes (He will be presenting his church's biblical interpretation for each of these attributes).

1.   God Is Personal and Incorporeal –

"According to the Bible (From his church's interpretation of the Bible, including its mistranslations), God is a personal being who has all the attributes that we may expect from a perfect Person: self-consciousness, the ability to reason, know, love, communicate, and so forth (Meaning He has a mind). This is clearly how God is described in the scriptures (The scriptures being the KJV of the Bible with its mistranslations).

"God is also incorporeal (Not composed of matter, having no material existence). Unlike humans, God is not uniquely associated with one physical entity (i.e., a body). This is why the Bible refers to God as spirit (Review the following verses and compare the mistranslated verse born from apostasy in the KJV, to the JST translation of that verse):

John 4:24 (KJV)

24 God *is* a Spirit: and they that worship him must worship *him* in spirit and in truth.

Now compare that to this Joseph Smith Translation (JST) to John 4:26 (KJV)

John 4:26 (JST)

26 *For unto such hath* God *promised his* Spirit. And they *who* worship him, must worship in spirit and in truth.

2.   God Is the Creator and Sustainer of Everything Else that Exists –

"All reality has come into existence and continues to exist because of God. Unlike a god who forms the universe out of preexistent matter (This is a dig on the Latter-Day Saint perspective of the creation/organizing of the world), the God of the Bible created the universe ex *nihilo* (out of nothing).

(As you can see, this is the opposite view or understanding to the Latter-Day Saint view regarding the nature of God. The Christian view is an interpretation of what they say the Bible is saying, thus the Bible is not the Objective Standard. The Objective Standard is actually *their interpretation of what they say the Bible says*).

"Consequently, it is on God alone that everything in the universe, indeed, the universe itself, depends for its existence.

Acts 17:25

25 Neither is worshipped with men's hands, as though he needed anything, seeing he giveth to all life, and breath, and all things;

Romans 11:36

36 For of him, and through him, and to him, *are* all things: to whom *be* glory forever. Amen.

II Corinthians 4:6

6 For God, who commanded the light to shine out of darkness, hath shined in our hearts, to give the light of the knowledge of the glory of God in the face of Jesus Christ.

Colossians 1:16-17

16 For by him were all things created, that are in heaven, and that are in earth, visible and invisible, whether *they be* thrones, or dominions, or principalities, or powers: all things were created by him, and for him:

17 And he is before all things, and by him all things exist.

Hebrews 11:3

3 Through faith we understand that the worlds were framed by the word of God, so that things which are seen were not made of things which do appear.

Revelations 4:11

11 Thou art worthy, O Lord, to receive glory and honour and power: for thou hast created all things, and for thy pleasure they are and were created.

3.   God Is Omnipotent –

"Omnipotence literally means "all-powerful." When we speak of God as omnipotent, this should be understood to mean that God can do anything that is consistent with being a personal, incorporeal, omniscient, omnipresent, immutable, wholly good, and necessary Creator. That is to say, since God is perfect, He cannot sin; because He is personal, He is incapable of making Himself impersonal; because He is omniscient; He cannot forget.

"This is supported by the Bible when its writers assert that God cannot sin:

Cannot sin for He is good:

Mark 10:18

18 And Jesus said unto him, Why callest thou me good? *there is* none good but one, *that is,* God.

Hebrews 6:18

18 That by two immutable things, in which *it was* impossible for God to lie, we might have a strong consolation, who have fled for *b*refuge to lay hold upon the hope set before us:

Cannot cease to exist:

Exodus 3:14

4 And when the LORD saw that he turned aside to see, God called unto him out of the midst of the bush, and said, Moses, Moses. And he said, here *am* I.

Malachi 3:6

6 For I *am* the LORD, I change not; therefore ye sons of Jacob are not consumed.

Cannot fail to know something:

Job 28:24

24 For he looketh to the ends of the earth, *and* seeth under the whole heaven;

Psalms 139:17-18

17 How precious also are thy thoughts unto me, O God! how great is the sum of them!

18 *If* I should count them, they are more in number than the sand: when I awake, I am still with thee.

Isaiah 46:10

10 Declaring the end from the beginning, and from ancient times *the things* that are not *yet* done, saying, My counsel shall stand, and I will do all my pleasure:

"Since God is a perfect being, He is incapable of acting in a less than perfect way - which would include sinning, ceasing to exist, and being ignorant. None of this counts against God's omnipotence (or "ability to do everything"), since, as St. Augustine points out, "[n]either do we lessen [God's] power when we say He cannot die or be deceived. This is the kind of inability which, if removed, would make God less powerful than He is. It is precisely because He is omnipotent that for Him some things are impossible.""

4.   God Is Omniscient –

"God is all-knowing and his all-knowingness encompasses the past, present, and future. He has absolute and total knowledge. Concerning God's unfathomable knowledge, the psalmist writes:

Psalms 139:17-18

17 How precious also are thy thoughts unto me, O God! how great is the sum of them!

18 *If* I should count them, they are more in number than the sand: when I awake, I am still with thee.

Psalms 147:5

5 Great is our Lord and mighty in power; his understanding has no limit.

"The author of Job writes of God: "For he views the ends of the earth and sees everything under heavens":

Job 28:24

24 For he looketh to the ends of the earth, *and* seeth under the whole heaven;

"Scripture also teaches that God has total knowledge of the past:

Isaiah 41:22

22 Let them bring *them* forth and shew us what shall happen: let them shew the former things, what they *be,* that we may consider them, and know the latter end of them; or declare us things for to come.

Isaiah 46:10

10 I make known the end from the beginning, from ancient times, what is still to come. I say: My purpose will stand and will do all that I please.

"Elsewhere, Isaiah quotes God as saying that knowledge of the future is essential for deity, something that distinguished God from the many false gods of Isaiah's day:

Isaiah 41:21-24

21 Produce your cause, saith the LORD; bring forth your strong *reasons,* saith the King of Jacob.

22 Let them bring *them* forth and shew us what shall happen: let them shew the former things, what they *be,* that we may consider them, and know the latter end of them; or declare us things for to come.

23 Shew the things that are to come hereafter, that we may know that ye *are* gods: yea, do good, or do evil, that we may be dismayed, and behold *it* together.

24 Behold, ye *are* of nothing, and your work of nought: an abomination *is he that* chooseth you.

5.   God Is Omnipresent –

"Logically following from God's omniscience, incorporeality, omnipotence, and role as Creator and sustainer of the universe is His omnipresence. Since God is not limited by a spatiotemporal body (A kind of super-essence without a body), knows everything immediately without benefit of sensory organs, and sustains the existence of all that exists, it follows that He is *in some sense* present everywhere (I have discussed what the "in some sense" is – The Incomprehensible IT; the Light of Christ – etc.). Certainly, it is the Bible's explicit teaching that God is omnipresent:

Psalms 139:7-12

7 Whither shall I go from thy spirit? or whither shall I flee from thy presence?

8 If I ascend up into heaven, thou *art* there: if I make my bed in hell, behold, thou *art there*.

9 *If* I take the wings of the morning, *and* dwell in the uttermost parts of the sea;

10 Even there shall thy hand lead me, and thy right hand shall hold me.

11 If I say, Surely the darkness shall cover me; even the night shall be light about me.

12 Yea, the darkness hideth not from thee; but the night shineth as the day: the darkness and the light *are* both alike *to thee*.

Jerimiah 23:23-24

23 *Am* I a God at hand, saith the LORD, and not a God afar off?

24 Can any hide himself in secret places that I shall not see him? saith the LORD. Do not I *fill* heaven and earth? saith the LORD.

(See this scripture as it relates to the "fill" in verse 24:)

Doctrine & Covenants 88:7-13

7 Which truth shineth. This is the Light of Christ. As also he is in the sun, and the light of the sun, and the power thereof by which it was made.

8 As also he is in the moon, and is the light of the moon, and the power thereof by which it was made;

9 As also the light of the stars, and the power thereof by which they were made;

10 And the earth also, and the power thereof, even the earth upon which you stand.

11 And the light which shineth, which giveth you light, is through him who enlighteneth your eyes, which is the same light that quickeneth your understandings;

12 Which light proceedeth forth from the presence of God *to fill* the immensity of space—

13 The light which is in all things, which giveth life to all things, which is the law by which all things are governed, even the power of God who sitteth upon his throne, who is in the bosom of eternity, who is in the midst of all things (This is the omnipresence of God as the Latter-Day Saints believe).

(We agree that God is omnipresent, we just don't agree in what *'sense'* He is present everywhere. Remember Jesus visiting His disciples in the upper room *after* his resurrection, as discussed in Luke 24? I would ask the Christians to answer these questions: "Do the Christians believe that the Resurrected Christ removes His resurrected body like one would remove their overcoat and then put it back on whenever He sees fit? Don't they believe that the resurrection is an inseparable union of the body and the Spirit?" Or is resurrection just coming back to life as Lazarus did, with a normal mortal body, but not with a glorified, eternal body, never to be separated? Something Christians should think about, right?).

6.   God Is Immutable and Eternal –

"When a Christian says that God is immutable and eternal, he or she is saying that God is unchanging (The same yesterday, today, and forever):

Isaiah 46:10

10 Declaring the ᵇend from the beginning, and from ancient times *the things* that are not *yet* done, saying, My counsel shall stand, and I will do all my pleasure:

Malachi 3:6

6 For I *am* the LORD, I change not; therefore ye sons of Jacob are not consumed.

Hebrews 6:17

17 Wherein God, willing more abundantly to shew unto the heirs of promise the immutability of his counsel, confirmed *it* by an oath:

"He has always existed as God throughout all eternity:

Psalms 90:2

2 Before the mountains were brought forth, ... or ever thou hadst formed the earth and the world even from everlasting to everlasting, thou art God.

Isaiah 40:28

28 Hast thou not known? hast thou not heard, *that* the everlasting God, the Lord, the Creator of the ends of the earth, fainteth not, neither is weary? *There is* no searching of his understanding.

Isaiah 43:12-13

12 I have declared, and have saved, and I have shewed, when *there was* no strange *god* among you: therefore ye *are* my witnesses, saith the Lord, that I *am* God.

13 Yea, before the day *was* I *am* he; and *there is* none that can deliver out of my hand: I will work, and who shall let it?

Isaiah 57:15

15 For thus saith the high and lofty One that inhabiteth eternity, whose name *is* Holy; I dwell in the high and holy *place,* with him also *that is* of a contrite and humble spirit, to revive the spirit of the humble, and to revive the heart of the contrite ones.

Rom. 1:20

20 For the invisible things of him from the creation of the world are clearly seen, being understood by the things that are made, even his eternal power and Godhead; so that they are without excuse:

1 Timothy 1:17

17 Now unto the King eternal, ¹mmortals, invisible, the only wise God, *be* honour and glory for ever and ever. Amen.

"There never was a time when God was not God. Although God certainly seems to change in response to how His creatures behave - such as in the case of the repenting Ninevites - His nature remains the same. A God who is responsive to His creatures is certainly consistent with, and seems to be entailed by, an unchanging nature that is necessarily personal. Although all biblical Christians agree that God is eternally God, they dispute whether He exists in time (i.e., the temporal eternity view) or out of time (i.e., the timeless eternity view).

7.   God is Necessary and the Only God that Exists –

"The Bible teaches that although humans at times worship some beings as if these beings were really gods:

1 Corinthians 8:4-6

4 As concerning therefore the eating of those things that are offered in sacrifice unto idols, we know that an idol *is* nothing in the world, and that *there is* none other God but one.

5 For though there be that are called gods, whether in heaven or in earth, (as there be gods many, and lords many).

6 But to us *there is but* one God, the Father, of whom *are* all things, and we in him; and one Lord Jesus Christ, by whom *are* all things, and we by him.

"There is only one True and Living God by nature:

Isaiah 43:10

10 Ye *are* my witnesses, saith the Lord, and my servant whom I have chosen: that ye may know and believe me, and understand that I *am* he: before me there was no God formed, neither shall there be after me.

Isaiah 44:6-8

6 Thus saith the Lord the King of Israel, and his redeemer the Lord of hosts; I *am* the first, and I *am* the last; and beside me *there is* no God.

7 And who, as I, shall call, and shall declare it, and set it in order for me, since I appointed the ancient people? and the things that are coming, and shall come, let them shew unto them. (This is God saying he calls and appoints His prophets to shew unto His people what is, and what is to come, etc.)

8 Fear ye not, neither be afraid: have not I told thee from that time, and have declared *it?* ye *are* even my witnesses. Is there a God beside me? yea, *there is* no God; I know not *any.*

Isaiah 45:5, 18-22

5 I *am* the LORD, and *there is* none else, *there is* no God beside me: I girded thee, though thou hast not known me:

18 For thus saith the LORD that created the heavens; God himself that formed the earth and made it; he hath established it, he created it not in vain, he formed it to be inhabited: I *am* the LORD; and *there is* none else.

19 I have not spoken in secret, in a dark place of the earth: I said not unto the seed of Jacob, Seek ye me in vain: I the LORD speak righteousness, I declare things that are right.

20 Assemble yourselves and come; draw near together, ye *that are* escaped of the nations: they have no knowledge that set up the wood of their graven image, and pray unto a god *that* cannot save.

21 Tell ye, and bring *them* near; yea, let them take counsel together: who hath declared this from ancient time? *who* hath told it from that time? *have* not I the LORD? and *there is* no God else beside me; a just God and a Saviour; *there is* none beside me.

22 Look unto me, and be ye saved, all the ends of the earth: for I *am* God, and *there is* none else.

Jerimiah 10:10

10 But the LORD *is* the true God, he *is* the Living God, and an everlasting king: at his wrath the earth shall tremble, and the nations shall not be able to abide his indignation.

John 17:3

3 And this is life *b*eternal, that they might know thee the only true God, and Jesus Christ, whom thou hast sent.

1 Corinthians 8:4-6

4 As concerning therefore the eating of those things that are offered in sacrifice Unto idols, we know that an idol is nothing in the world, and that *there is* none other God but one.

5 For though there be that are called gods, whether in heaven or in earth, (as there be gods many, and lords many,)

6 But to us *there is but* one God, the Father, of whom are all things, and we in him; and one Lord Jesus Christ, by whom *are* all things, and we by him.

Galatians 4:8

8 Howbeit then, when ye knew not God, ye did service unto them which by nature are no gods.

1 Thessalonians 1:9

9 For they themselves shew of us what manner of entering in we had unto you, and how ye turned to God from idols to serve the living and true God;

1 Timothy 2:5

5 For *there is* one God, and one mediator between God and men, the man Christ Jesus;

(How can Jesus be a mediator to Himself in this one God-Being or entity concept? He doesn't mediate to Himself. He is the Mediator '*between* us and God the Father'. Jesus is indeed the God of 'this earth'. There is no other God that we look to for salvation. Jesus is the Way, the Truth, and the Life, that's for sure. He is doing the Father's will here on the earth, having been called by God the Father to be the Savior and Redeemer for all those who will accept Him as the Savior of the world. But they are two separate beings).

"Moreover, since everything that exists depends on God, and God is unchanging and eternal, it follows that God cannot '*not*' exist. In other words, He is a necessary being, whereas everything else is contingent (or dependent on God for its existence).

"The Mormon Concept of God"

(Please keep in mind that this is Mr. Beckwith's view of what he has determined in his mind to be what the Church of Jesus Christ of Latter-Day Saints teaches, but please note that his interpretation of our doctrine is incorrect).

"Although there is certainly disagreement among Mormon scholars concerning some precise points of doctrine, it is safe to say the Church currently teaches that God is, in effect, (1) a contingent being, who was at one time not God (not necessary and not eternally God) (Not true); (2) limited in *knowledge* (not truly omniscient) (Not true), power (not omnipotent) (Not true), and being (not omnipresent or immutable) (Not true); (3) one of many gods (True, but as His children we only worship the one God called Elohim, who is God the Father. In other words, 'The' God, and His Son, 'The' Savior. We worship the Father 'in the name of His only Begotten Son Jesus Christ); (4) a corporeal (bodily) being (True), who physically dwells at a particular spatiotemporal location (This means 'belonging to both space and time or to space-time'. I would not say that God, and the other members of the Godhead, are stuck in space-time as it is presented here. God has the past, present, and future ever before Him. But that is a subject for another time) and is therefore not omnipresent like the biblical God (Not true) (Respecting His intrinsic divine nature - we are not considering the Incarnation of the Son of God here); and (5) a being who is subject to the laws and principles of a universe He did not create (Not true. God, thru His Son Jehovah, not only created the universe, God, the Father, had Jehovah be the Law Giver over His creations).

"The Mormon concept of God can best be grasped by understanding the overall Mormon worldview and how the deity fits into it. Mormonism (Again, a nickname of derision) teaches that God the Father is a resurrected, exalted human (Not true. God is immortal and eternal, and NOT human, which is a fallen man or a fallen woman) being named Elohim who was at one time not God (This is not the Church's position). Rather, he was once a mortal man on another planet who, through obedience to the precepts of his God, eventually attained exaltation, or godhood himself, through "eternal progression."

"The Mormon God, located in time and space, has a body of flesh and bone and thus is neither spirit nor omnipresent." (We as a Church, definitely have a different understanding of what Omnipresent means. The Spirit of God, not His spirit 'self' or body, is God's influence and light that emanates directly from His person. This influential 'spirit and light' is truly omnipresent. I would also say that the full understanding of this 'omnipresent' nature of God, is beyond our mortal understanding at this time, and so this perspective I've just given is my own understanding of it). Joseph Smith, founder, and prophet of Mormonism, asserts:

"God himself was once as we are now and is an exalted man (Man of Holiness) and sits enthroned in yonder heavens! . . . I am going to tell you how God came to be God. We have imagined and supposed that God was God from all eternity. I will refute this idea, and take away the veil, so that you may see. . It is the first principle of the gospel to know for a certainty the character of God, and to know that we may converse with Him, as one man converses with another, and that He was once a man like us; yea, that God himself, the Father of us all, dwelt on an earth, the same as Jesus Christ Himself did; and I will show it from the Bible . . .

"Here, then, is eternal life – to know the only wise and true God; and you have got to learn how to be gods yourselves (Become 'perfect' or 'complete' as they are perfect), and be kings and priests to God, the same as all gods have done before you, namely, by going from one small degree to another, and from a small capacity to a great one; from grace to grace, from exaltation to exaltation, until you attain to the resurrection of the dead, and are able to dwell in everlasting burnings, and to sit in glory, as do those who sit enthroned in everlasting power.

"The Father has a body of flesh and bone as tangible as man'. ..."

"*Omniscience*, according to Mormon theology, is one of the attributes one attains when reaching godhood. Here are scriptures that describes the LDS doctrine on 'Omniscience':

God, Omniscience of

- *See also* God, Foreknowledge of; God, Wisdom of; Knowledge; TG God, Omniscience of;
- All things done in wisdom of him who knoweth all things:

II Nephi 2:24

24 But behold, all things have been done in the wisdom of him who knoweth all things.

- *God* knows all things, there is not anything except he knows it:

II Nephi 9:20

20 O how great the holiness of our God! For he knoweth all things, and there is not anything save he knows it.

Mormon 8:17

17 And if there be faults they be the faults of a man. But behold, we know no fault; nevertheless God knoweth all things; therefore, he that condemneth, let him be aware lest he shall be in danger of hell fire.

- *God's* revelation reveals all things from foundation of world to end:

II Nephi 27:10

10 But the words which are sealed he shall not deliver, neither shall he deliver the book. For the book shall be sealed by the power of God, and the revelation which was sealed shall be kept in the book until the own due time of the Lord, that they may come forth; for behold, they reveal all things from the foundation of the world unto the end thereof.

- The Lord knows all works in dark:

II Nephi 27:27

27 And wo unto them that seek deep to hide their counsel from the Lord! And their works are in the dark; and they say: Who seeth us, and who knoweth us? And they also say: Surely, your turning of things upside down shall be esteemed as the potter's clay. But behold, I will show unto them, saith the Lord of Hosts, that I know all their works. For shall the work say of him that made it, he made me not? Or shall the thing framed say of him that framed it, he had no understanding?

- By help of the Creator, Jacob[2] can tell his people their thoughts:

Jacob 2:5

5 But behold, hearken ye unto me, and know that by the help of the all-powerful Creator of heaven and earth I can tell you concerning your thoughts, how that ye are beginning to labor in sin, which sin appeareth very abominable unto me, yea, and abominable unto God.

- The Spirit knoweth all things:

Alma 7:13

13 Now the Spirit knoweth all things; nevertheless the Son of God suffereth according to the flesh that he might take upon him the sins of his people, that he might blot out their transgressions according to the power of his deliverance; and now behold, this is the testimony which is in me.

- *God* knows all thoughts and intents of the heart.

Alma 18:32

32 And Ammon said: Yea, and he looketh down upon all the children of men; and he knows all the thoughts and intents of the heart; for by his hand were they all created from the beginning.

- *God* comprehends all things:

Alma 26:35

35 Now have we not reason to rejoice? Yea, I say unto you, there never were men that had so great reason to rejoice as we, since the world began; yea, and my joy is carried away, even unto boasting in my God; for he has all power, all wisdom, and all understanding; he comprehendeth all things, and he is a merciful Being, even unto salvation, to those who will repent and believe on his name.

- *God* is mindful of every people:

Alma 26:37

37 Now my brethren, we see that God is mindful of every people, whatsoever land they may be in; yea, he numbereth his people, and his bowels of mercy are over all the earth. Now this is my joy, and my great thanksgiving; yea, and I will give thanks unto my God forever. Amen.

- Ye cannot hide your crimes from *God*:

Alma 39:8

8 But behold, ye cannot hide your crimes from God; and except ye repent they will stand as a testimony against you at the last day.

- *God* knows the time when all shall come forth from dead:

Alma 40:4–5, 10, 21

4 Behold, there is a time appointed that all shall come forth from the dead. Now when this time cometh no one knows; but God knoweth the time which is appointed.

5 Now, whether there shall be one time, or a second time, or a third time, that men shall come forth from the dead, it mattereth not; for God knoweth all these things; and it sufficeth me to know that this is the case—that there is a time appointed that all shall rise from the dead.

10 And when the time cometh when all shall rise, then shall they know that God knoweth all the times which are appointed unto man.

21 But whether it be at his resurrection or after, I do not say; but this much I say, that there is a space between death and the resurrection of the body, and a state of the soul in happiness or in misery until the time which is appointed of God that the dead shall come forth, and be reunited, both soul and body, and be brought to stand before God, and be judged according to their works.

- Known unto *God* were all their cries and sufferings:

Alma 60:10

10 And now, my beloved brethren—for ye ought to be beloved; yea, and ye ought to have stirred yourselves more diligently for the welfare and the freedom of this people; but behold, ye have neglected them insomuch that the blood of thousands shall come upon your heads for vengeance; yea, for known unto God were all their cries, and all their sufferings.

- Christ knows his disciples' thoughts:

III Nephi 28:6

6 And he said unto them: Behold, I know your thoughts, and ye have desired the thing which John, my beloved, who was with me in my ministry, before that I was lifted up by the Jews, desired of me.

- The Lord shows brother of Jared[2] all inhabitants of earth who had been or would be:

Ether 3:25

25 And when the Lord had said these words, he showed unto the brother of Jared [b]all the inhabitants of the earth which had been, and also all that would be; and he [c]withheld them not from his sight, even unto the ends of the earth.

- *God* knows all things, being from everlasting to everlasting:

Moroni 7:22

22 For behold, God knowing all things, being from everlasting to everlasting, behold, he sent angels to minister unto the children of men, to make manifest concerning the coming of Christ; and in Christ there should come every good thing.

- The Lord's eyes are on all men:

Doctrine & Covenants 1:1

1 Hearken, O ye people of my church, saith the voice of him who dwells on high, and whose eyes are upon all men; yea, verily I say: Hearken ye people from afar; and ye that are upon the islands of the sea, listen together.

- *God* alone knows men's thoughts:

Doctrine & Covenants 6:16

16 Yea, I tell thee, that thou mayest know that there is none else save God that knowest thy thoughts and the intents of thy ʿheart.

Doctrine & Covenants 33:1

1 Behold, I say unto you, my servants Ezra and Northrop, open ye your ears and hearken to the voice of the Lord your God, whose word is quick and powerful, sharper than a two-edged sword, to the dividing asunder of the joints and marrow, soul and spirit; and is a discerner of the thoughts and intents of the heart.

- The Lord tells things no man knows:

Doctrine & Covenants 6:24

24 And now, behold, you have received a witness; for if I have told you things which no man knoweth have you not received a witness?

Doctrine & Covenants 15:3

3 And I will tell you that which no man knoweth save me and thee alone

- The Lord knows all things:

Doctrine & Covenants 38:2

2 The same which knoweth all things, for all things are present before mine eyes;

Doctrine & Covenants 130:7

7 But they reside in the presence of God, on a globe like a sea of glass and fire, where all things for their glory are manifest, past, present, and future, and are continually before the Lord.

- The Lord knows men's hearts:

Doctrine & Covenants 67:1

1 Behold and hearken, O ye elders of my church, who have assembled yourselves together, whose prayers I have heard, and whose hearts I know, and whose desires have come up before me.

- The Lord comprehends all things:

Doctrine & Covenants 88:6, 41

6 He that ascended up on high, as also he descended below all things, in that he comprehendeth all things, that he might be in all and through all things, the light of truth;

41 He comprehendeth all things, and all things are before him, and all things are round about him; and he is above all things, and in all things, and is through all things, and is round about all things; and all things are by him, and of him, even God, forever and ever.

- The Lord's eyes see and know all men's works:

Doctrine & Covenants 121:24

24 Behold, mine eyes see and know all their works, and I have in reserve a swift judgment in the season thereof, for them all;

- Past, present, & future are continually before the Lord:

Doctrine & Covenants 130:7

7 But they reside in the presence of God, on a globe like a sea of glass and fire, where all things for their glory are manifest, past, present, and future, and are continually before the Lord.

- All things are present with *God*:

Moses 1:6

6 And I have a work for thee, Moses, my son; and thou art in the similitude of mine Only Begotten; and mine Only Begotten is and shall be the Savior, for he is full of grace and truth; but there is no God beside me, and all things are present with me, for I know them all.

- The Lord knows all worlds that stand or have passed away:

Moses 1:35

5 Wherefore, no man can behold all my works, except he behold all my glory; and no man can behold all my glory, and afterwards remain in the flesh on the earth.

- The Lord tells Enoch all doings of men:

Moses 7:41

41 And it came to pass that the Lord spake unto Enoch, and told Enoch all the doings of the children of men; wherefore Enoch knew, and looked upon their wickedness, and their misery, and wept and stretched forth his arms, and his heart swelled wide as eternity; and his bowels yearned; and all eternity shook.

- The Lord showed Enoch[2] all things, unto end of world:

Moses 7:67

67 And the Lord showed Enoch all things, even unto the end of the world; and he saw the day of the righteous, the hour of their redemption, and received a fulness of joy;

- Jehovah knows end from beginning:

Abraham 2:8

8 My name is Jehovah, and I know the end from the beginning; therefore my hand shall be over thee.

- *God* is more intelligent than they all:

Abraham 3:19

19 And the Lord said unto me: These two facts do exist, that there are two spirits, one being more intelligent than the other; there shall be another more intelligent than they; I am the Lord thy God, I am more intelligent than they all.

"Mormons appear to be divided, however, on the meaning of omniscience. It seems that some Mormons believe omniscience to mean that God has absolute and total knowledge about the past, present, and future. This view is consistent with the biblical view. However, the *dominant* Mormon tradition teaches that God increases in knowledge and, consequently, God does not have absolute and total knowledge (This statement is absolutely untrue. It is *not* the *dominant tradition* or doctrine of our Church. God does not increase in knowledge. He is all-knowing).

"This is why Brigham Young, Smith's successor as president of the Mormon Church, and his counselors, pronounced (both in 1860 and 1865) as *false doctrine* wherein Orson Pratt claimed that "God cannot learn new truths. Ironically, Pratt's claim is consistent with the biblical view of God. Wilford Woodruff, a recognized Mormon authority (A prophet and one-time president of the Church), taught, "God Himself is increasing and progressing in knowledge, power, and dominion and will do so worlds without end. And yet another Church authority, Lorenzo Snow (Another past prophet and President of the Church), declared, "We will continue improving, advancing, and increasing in wisdom, intelligence, power, and dominion, worlds without end (We, as Latter-Day Saints, believe that God's children continue to learn and not God, for He is all knowing)."

"Once Elohim attained godhood, He then created this present world by "organizing" both eternally preexistent, inorganic matter (Not true. Intelligences and Spirit are both a form of matter of a unique kind, but they are of a much purer matter and therefore are not inorganic) and the preexistent primal intelligences from which human spirits are made.

Mormon scholar Hyrum L. Andrus explains:

"Though man's spirit is organized from a pure and fine substance which possesses certain properties of life, Joseph Smith 'seems' to have taught that within each individual spirit there is a central primal intelligence (a central directing principle of life), and that man's central primal intelligence is a personal entity possessing some degree of life and certain rudimentary cognitive powers before the time the human spirit was organized (Or 'Activated')."

"For this reason, Joseph Smith wrote that "Man was also in the beginning with God. Intelligence, or the light of truth, was not created or made, neither indeed can be." In other words, man's basic essence or primal intelligence is as eternal as God's and was not created by God (This is both interesting and thought provoking but is *not* the official position or doctrine of the Church).

"The Mormon God, by organizing this world out of preexistent matter, has granted these organized (These activated) spirits the opportunity to receive physical bodies, pass through mortality, and eventually progress to godhood - just as this opportunity was given him by his Father, God. Consequently, if human persons on earth faithfully obey the precepts of 'Mormonism' they too, ('Mormonism' and 'Mormon' once again, are slang words for the Church of Jesus Christ of Latter-Day Saints and for our beliefs. Our preferred name is the Church of Jesus Christ of Latter-Day Saints, and Latter-Day Saints, not Mormons or Mormonism) can attain godhood like Elohim before them.

"Based on the statements of Church authorities, *some* Mormon scholars contend that a premortal spirit is "organized" by God through "spirit birth." In this process, human spirits are *somehow* organized through literal sexual relations between our Heavenly Father and a mother god (A Heavenly Mother), whereby they are conceived and born as spirit children prior to entering the mortal realm (although all human persons prior to spirit birth existed as intelligences in some primal state of cognitive personal existence. Again, this is *not* the official doctrinal position of the Church, although apostles like Elder Bruce R. McConkie have stated as much — You can find elder McConkie's statement in the 1984 Melchizedek Priesthood Study Manual, where he states something similar to this).

"Since the God of Mormonism was himself organized (or spirit-birthed) by his God (I think he meant by his Heavenly Mother, as only mothers can 'birth' someone, right?), who himself is a "creation" of yet another God, and so on forever (The infinite regression issue keeps popping up again and again, doesn't it?). Mormonism teaches that the God over this world is a contingent (A being of chance? Really? I don't think so) being in an infinite lineage of gods. This is why Joseph Smith can declare, "Hence, if Jesus had a Father, can we not believe that He had a Father also? . . . I will preach the plurality of the Gods."

"Brigham Young clearly understood the logic of Smith's theology: "How many Gods there are, I do not know. But there never was a time when there were not Gods and worlds." Thus, Mormonism is a polytheistic religion which denies that God is a necessary being who has eternally existed as God (This last sentence is absolutely untrue. We do not deny any such thing. But to be fair, I do understand why Mr. Beckwith wanted to couch it in the way that he has done so here). Mormonism therefore teaches that certain basic realities have always existed and are indestructible even by God. In other words, God came from the universe; the universe did not come from God (Although he did form this planet out of preexistent matter. Again, Beckwith is conflating what we believe with his own twist on things in an effort to make things seem more extreme).

"For Mormonism, God, like man, is merely another creature in the universe (Absolutely untrue). In the Mormon universe, God is not responsible for creating or sustaining matter, energy, natural laws, human personhood, moral principles, the process of salvation (or exaltation), or much of anything (All of these things, Beckwith believes, all came out of nothing ... We believe God organized all of them from elements that always existed, but they were in a state of 'chaos' until they were organized. Yes, we see things differently). In fact, instead of the universe being subject to Him (which is the biblical view), the Mormon God is subject to the universe (If Beckwith is saying 'subject to' means 'being under one's control or jurisdiction', then what he says is absolutely *not* true. All of God's creations are subject to Him, for they are under His jurisdiction and the laws he established for them, and therefore are under His sovereignty).

"The Mormon God is far from omnipotent. He is not the God of the Bible. (The scriptures refer to the 'Most High' God. It also says 'God the Father AND His Son Jesus Christ.)

(God does not conflate Himself into One being. See the short list of scriptures on the following page which are as they're found in the Bible so that you can decide what 'Most High God'; 'Lord of Lord's', and

'King of Kings', in the plural, mean. When you combine these with the many other scriptural references and study the 'sense' in which they are used, I believe they mean just what they imply, and that is that 'God the Father', the Creator of Heaven and Earth, thru His Son Jehovah, who became Jesus in the flesh, is indeed the 'Most High' God of many gods, including God the Son, and God the Holy Ghost, and that 'god' is a 'title' for those who have been exalted and ordained unto 'godhood', just as one is ordained to the apostleship or as a Patriarch. In my *opinion* and from my perspective, the title of God is an office in the Priesthood of the Gods, it being the highest office a child of God can attain unto in the Holy priesthood after the order of the Gods. In other words, the priesthood is eternal, without beginning of days or end of life. Again, this is my perspective and opinion, and not the official stance of the Church).

Here are a few scriptures that use this title of God:

Genesis 14:18-20, 22

18 And Melchizedek king of Salem brought forth bread and wine: and he was the priest of the *Most High God.*

19 And he blessed him, and said, Blessed *be* Abram of the most high God, possessor of heaven and earth:

20 And blessed be the most high God, which hath delivered thine enemies into thy hand. And he gave him tithes of all.

22 And Abram said to the king of Sodom, I have lift up mine hand unto the LORD, the *Most High* God, the possessor of heaven and earth.

(To me, my perspective and opinion is that this is saying that of all the Gods in all the Heavenly Creations, God the Father is the "Most High God" of them all. As I said, this isn't the official doctrine of the Church of Jesus Christ of Latter-Day Saints, but I do ask, "If there's just one High God, then why not just say the "High God" here? "Most High God" implies there are lower gods, does it not?)

Daniel 3:26

26 Then Nebuchadnezzar came near to the mouth of the burning fiery furnace, *and* spake, and said, Shadrach, Meshach, and Abed-nego, ye servants of the 'Most High God', come forth, and come *hither.* Then Shadrach, Meshach, and Abed-nego, came forth out of the midst of the fire.

Daniel 5:18, 21

18 O thou king, the 'Most High God' gave Nebuchadnezzar thy father a kingdom, and majesty, and glory, and honour:

21 And he was driven from the sons of men; and his heart was made like the beasts, and his dwelling *was* with the wild asses: they fed him with grass like oxen, and his body was wet with the dew of heaven; till he knew that the 'Most High God' ruled in the kingdom of men, and *that* he appointeth over it whomsoever he will.

Hebrews 7:21

21 For those priests were made without an oath; but this with an oath by him that said unto him, The Lord sware and will not repent.

(See JST Hebrews 7:3 – "For this Melchizedek was ordained a priest after the order of the Son of God, which *order* was *without father, without mother, without descent, having neither beginning of days, nor end of life."*)

(See the next page for a special comparison chart)

Beckwith provides the following comparison:

CHRISTIAN CONCEPT OF GOD	LATTER-DAY SAINTS CONCEPT OF GOD
Personal and incorporeal (No body)	Personal and corporeal (Embodied)
Creator and sustainer of contingent existence	Organizer of the world but subject to the laws and principles of a beginningless universe (This is not what I believe)
Omnipotent	Limited in power (This is not what I believe)
Omniscient	Increasing in knowledge (This is not what I believe)
Omnipresent in being	Localized in space (This is not what I believe)
Unchanging and eternal	Changing and not eternal (as God) (This is not what I believe)
Necessary and the only God	Contingent and one of many gods (Not contingent, but yes, I believe there are many gods, and others will be ordained a god because they've become like God our Father)

End of article on the differences between the Christian God and the Mormon God [295]

After reading Mr. Beckwith's article, I decided to include it in my book in an effort to be fair and balanced as to what Christianity and Latter-Day Saints believe. I did insert several comments throughout Mr. Beckwith's excerpts, in the hopes that you, my readers, would have a clearer understanding of what Latter-Day Saints actually believe, as compared to what Mr. Beckwith says we believe. I also feel that I haven't sufficiently covered the differences between what my perspective is about God's nature, and Christendom's view of His nature, and so, I'm including the following essay titled "Becoming *Like* God" to remove any misconceptions you, my readers, might still have about my perspective .

Again, to view the footnotes listed throughout the following essay, go to my Church's website www.churchofjesuschrist.org and search for "Becoming Like God", and click on any of the footnote links to see where any of the listed statements and quotes came from. Here is the essay in its entirety:

BECOMING LIKE GOD

"One of the most common images in Western and Eastern religions alike, is of God as a parent and of human beings as God's children. Billions pray to God as their parent, invoke the brotherhood and sisterhood of all people to promote peace, and reach out to the weary and troubled out of deep conviction that each of God's children has worth.

"But people of different faiths understand the parent-child relationship between God and humans in significantly different ways. Some understand the phrase 'child of God' as an honorary title reserved only for those who believe in God and accept His guidance as they might accept a father's. Many see parent-child descriptions of God's relationship to humanity as metaphors to express His love for His creations and their dependence on His sustenance and protection.

"Latter-Say Saints see all people as children of God in a full and complete sense; they consider every person divine in origin, nature, and potential. Each has an eternal core and is 'a beloved spirit son or daughter of heavenly parents'. Each possesses seeds of divinity and must choose whether to live in harmony or tension with that divinity.

"Through the Atonement of Jesus Christ, all people may 'progress toward perfection and ultimately realize their divine destiny'. Just as a child can develop the attributes of his or her parents over time, the *divine nature* that humans inherit can be developed to become like their Heavenly Father.

"The desire to nurture the divinity in His children is one of God's attributes that most inspires, motivates, and humbles members of the Church. God's loving parentage and guidance can help each willing, obedient child of God to receive of His fulness and of His glory. This knowledge (Knowing God and His Son's nature) transforms the way Latter-Day Saints see their fellow human beings.

"The teaching that men and women have the potential to be exalted to a state of godliness (Potential deification,) clearly expands beyond what is understood by most contemporary Christian churches and expresses for the Latter-Day Saints a yearning rooted in the Bible to live as God lives, to love as He loves, and to prepare for all that our loving Father in Heaven wishes for His children.

What does the Bible say about humans' divine potential?

"Several biblical passages intimate that humans can become like God. The likeness of humans to God is emphasized in the first chapter of Genesis:

"God said, let us make man in our image, after our likeness. ... So, God created man in his own image, in the image of God created he him; male and female created he them." After Adam and Eve partook of the fruit of "the tree of the knowledge of good and evil," God said they had "become as one of us," suggesting that a process of approaching godliness was already underway. Later in the Old Testament, a passage in the book of Psalms declares, "I have said, Ye are gods; and all of you are children of the *Most High.*"

"New Testament passages also point to this doctrine. When Jesus was accused of blasphemy on the grounds that "thou, being a man, makest thyself God," He responded, echoing Psalms, "Is it not written in your law, I said, Ye are gods?" In the Sermon on the Mount, Jesus commanded His disciples to become "perfect, even as your Father which is in heaven is perfect." In turn, the Apostle Peter referred to the Savior's "exceeding great and precious promises" that we might become "partakers of the *divine nature* (The nature of God and His Son)." The Apostle Paul taught that we are "the offspring of God" and emphasized that as such "we are the children of God: and if children, then heirs; heirs of God, and joint-heirs with Christ." The book of Revelation contains a promise from Jesus Christ that "to him that overcometh will I grant to sit with me in my throne, even as I also overcame, and am set down with my Father in his throne."

"These passages can be interpreted in different ways. Yet by viewing them through the clarifying lens of revelations received by Joseph Smith, Latter-Day Saints see these scriptures as straightforward expressions of humanity's divine nature and potential. Many other Christians read the same passages far more metaphorically because they experience the Bible through the lens of *doctrinal interpretations* that developed over time after the period described in the New Testament (In other words ... the apostasy).

How have ideas about divinity shifted over Christian history?

"Latter-Day Saint beliefs would have sounded more familiar to the earliest generations of Christians than they do to many modern Christians. Many church fathers (influential theologians and teachers in early Christianity) spoke approvingly of the idea that humans can become divine. One modern scholar refers to the "ubiquity of the doctrine of deification"—the teaching that humans could become God—in the first centuries after Christ's death. The church father Irenaeus, who died about A.D. 202, asserted that Jesus Christ "did, through His transcendent love, become what we are, that He might bring us to be what He is Himself."

"Clement of Alexandria (ca. A.D. 150–215) wrote that "the Word of God became man, that thou mayest learn from man how man may become God." Basil the Great (A.D. 330–379) also celebrated this prospect—not just "being made like to God," but "highest of all, the being made God. What exactly the early church fathers meant when they spoke of becoming God is open to interpretation, but it is clear that references to *deification* became more contested in the late Roman period and were infrequent by the medieval era (The period known as the Great Apostasy). The first known objection by a church father to teaching deification came in the fifth century.

"By the sixth century, teachings on 'becoming God' appear more limited in scope, as in the definition provided by Pseudo-Dionysius the Areopagite (ca. A.D. 500):

"Deification ... is the attaining of likeness to God and union with him *so far as is possible*. Why did these beliefs fade from prominence? Changing perspectives on the creation of the world may have contributed to the gradual shift toward more limited views of human potential.

"The *earliest* Jewish and Christian commentaries on the Creation assumed that God had organized the world out of preexisting materials, emphasizing the goodness of God in shaping such a life-sustaining order. But the incursion of new philosophical ideas in the second century led to the development of a doctrine that God created the universe *ex nihilo*—'out of nothing'. This ultimately became the dominant teaching about the Creation within the Christian world. In order to emphasize God's power, many theologians reasoned that nothing could have existed for as long as He had. It became important in Christian circles to assert that God had originally been *completely alone*.

"Creation ex nihilo widened the perceived gulf between God and humans. It became less common to teach either that human souls had existed before the world or that they could inherit and develop the attributes of God in their entirety in the future. Gradually, as the depravity of humankind and the immense distance between Creator and creature were increasingly emphasized, the concept of deification faded from Western Christianity, though it remains a central tenet of Eastern Orthodoxy, one of the three major branches of Christianity.

How were ideas about deification introduced to Latter-Day Saints?

"The earliest Latter-Day Saints came from a society dominated by English-speaking Protestants, most of whom accepted both *ex nihilo creation* and the Westminster Confession's definition of God as a being without body, parts, or passion. They likely knew little or nothing about the diversity of Christian beliefs in the first centuries after Jesus Christ's ministry or about early Christian writings on deification. But revelations received by Joseph Smith diverged from the prevailing ideas of the time, and taught doctrine that, for some, reopened debates on the nature of God, creation, and humankind.

"Early revelations to Joseph Smith taught that humans are created in the image of God and that God cares intimately for His children. In the Book of Mormon, a prophet "saw the finger of the Lord" and was astonished to learn that human physical forms were truly made in the image of God. In another early revelation, Enoch (who "walked with God" in the Bible) witnessed God weeping over His creations.

When Enoch asked, "How is it thou canst weep?" he learned that God's compassion toward human suffering is integral to His love. Joseph Smith also learned that God desires that His children receive the same kind of exalted existence of which He partakes. As God declared, "This is my work and my glory—to bring to pass the immortality and eternal life of man."

"In 1832, Joseph Smith and Sidney Rigdon experienced a vision of the afterlife. In the vision, they learned that the just and unjust alike would receive immortality through a universal resurrection, but only those "who overcome by faith, and are sealed by the Holy Spirit of promise" would receive the fulness of God's glory and be "gods, even the sons of God." Another revelation soon confirmed that "the saints shall be filled with his glory and receive their inheritance and be made equal with him." Latter-Day Saints use the term *exaltation* to describe the glorious reward of *receiving one's full inheritance as a child of Heavenly Father*, which is available through the Atonement of Christ, by obedience to the laws and ordinances of the gospel.

"This striking view of each human's potential future was accompanied by revealed teachings on humanity's past. As Joseph Smith continued to receive revelations, he learned that the light or intelligence at the core of each human soul "was not created or made, neither indeed can be." God is the Father of each human spirit, and because only "spirit and element, inseparably connected, receive a fulness of joy," He presented a plan for human beings to receive physical bodies and progress through their mortal experience toward a fulness of joy. Earthly birth, then, is not the beginning of an individual's life: "Man was also in the beginning with God." Likewise, Joseph Smith taught that the material world has eternal roots, fully repudiating the concept of creation ex nihilo. "Earth, water & spirit—all these had their existence in an elementary state from Eternity," he said in an 1839 sermon. God organized the universe out of existing elements."

"Joseph Smith continued to receive revelation on the themes of divine nature and exaltation during the last two years of his life. ... In a revelation recorded in July 1843 that linked exaltation with eternal marriage, the Lord declared that those who keep covenants, including the covenant of eternal marriage, will inherit "all heights and depths." "Then," says the revelation, "shall they be gods because they have no end. They will receive "a continuation of the seeds forever and ever."

"The following April, feeling he was "never in any nearer relationship to God than at the present time," Joseph Smith spoke about the nature of God and the future of humankind to the Saints, who had gathered for a general Church conference. He used the occasion in part to reflect upon the death of a Church member named King Follett, who had died unexpectedly a month earlier. When he rose to speak, the wind was blowing, so Joseph asked his listeners to give him their "profound attention" and to "pray that the [Lord] may strengthen my lungs" and stay the winds until his message had been delivered.

"What kind of a being is God?" he asked. Human beings needed to know, he argued, because "if men do not comprehend the character of God, they do not comprehend themselves." In that phrase, the Prophet collapsed the gulf that centuries of confusion had created between God and humanity. Human nature was at its core divine. God "was once as one of us" and "all the spirits that God ever sent into the world" were likewise "susceptible of enlargement". Joseph Smith preached that long before the world was formed, God found "himself in the midst" of these beings and "saw proper to institute laws whereby the rest could have a privilege to advance like himself" and be "exalted" with Him.

"Joseph told the assembled Saints, "You have got to learn how to be a god yourself." In order to do that, the Saints needed to learn godliness, or to be more like God (Jesus and His life being the example for us to follow). The process would be ongoing and would require patience, faith, continuing repentance, obedience to the commandments of the gospel, and reliance on Christ. Like ascending a ladder, individuals needed to learn the "first [principles] of the Gospel" and continue beyond the limits of mortal knowledge until they could "learn the last [principles] of the Gospel" when the time came. "It is not all to be comprehended in this world," Joseph said. "It will take a long time after the grave to understand the whole."

"That was the last time the Prophet spoke in a general conference. Three months later, a state-sanctioned mob stormed Carthage Jail and martyred him and his brother Hyrum.

"What has been taught in the Church about *divine nature* since Joseph Smith?

"Since that sermon, known as the King Follett discourse, the doctrine that humans can progress to exaltation and godliness has been taught within the Church. Lorenzo Snow, the Church's fifth President, coined a well-known couplet: "As man now is, God once was: As God now is, man may be." Little has been revealed about the first half of this couplet, and consequently little is taught.

"When asked about this topic, Church President Gordon B. Hinckley told a reporter in 1997, "That gets into some pretty deep theology that we don't know very much about." When asked about the belief in humans' divine potential, President Hinckley responded, "Well, as God is, man may become. We believe in eternal progression. Very strongly. Eliza R. Snow, a Church leader and poet, rejoiced over the doctrine that we are, in a full and absolute sense, children of God.

"I had learned to call thee Father, / Thru thy Spirit from on high," she wrote, "But, until the key of knowledge / Was restored, I knew not why." Latter-Day Saints have also been moved by the knowledge that their divine parentage includes a Heavenly Mother as well as a Heavenly Father. Expressing that truth, Eliza R. Snow asked, "In the heav'ns are parents single?" and answered with a resounding *no:* "Truth eternal / Tells me I've a mother there." That knowledge plays an important role in Latter-Day Saint belief. As Elder Dallin H. Oaks of the Quorum of the Twelve Apostles wrote (Now a member of the First Presidency), "Our theology begins with heavenly parents. Our highest aspiration is to be like them."

"Humankind's *divine nature and potential for exaltation* have been repeatedly taught in general conference addresses, Church magazines, and in other Church materials. When Latter-Day Saint young women recite their theme, each affirms, "I am a beloved daughter of heavenly parents, with a divine nature and eternal destiny." Teaching on human beings' divine parentage, nature, and potential features prominently in *"The Family: A Proclamation to the World." Divine nature and exaltation are essential and beloved teachings in the Church (See this complete Proclamation at the end of my book).

Does belief in exaltation make Latter-Day Saints polytheists?

"For some observers, the doctrine that humans should strive for godliness may evoke images of ancient pantheons with competing deities. ... Such images are incompatible with Latter-Day Saint doctrine. Latter-Day Saints believe that God's children will always worship Him. Our progression will never change His identity as our Father and our God. Indeed, our exalted, eternal relationship with Him will be part of the "fulness of joy" He desires for us.

"Latter-Day Saints also believe strongly in the fundamental unity of the divine. They believe that God the Father, Jesus Christ the Son, and the Holy Ghost, though distinct beings, are *unified in purpose and doctrine*. It is in this light that Latter-Day Saints understand Jesus's prayer for His disciples through the ages:

"That they all may be one; as thou, Father, art in me, and I in thee, that they also may be one in us."

"If humans live out of harmony with God's goodness, they cannot grow into God's glory. Joseph Smith taught that "the powers of heaven cannot be controlled nor handled only [except] upon the principles of righteousness." When humans abandon God's selfless purposes and (Objective) standards, "the heavens withdraw themselves [and] the Spirit of the Lord is grieved." Pride is incompatible with progress; disunity is impossible between exalted beings.

How do Latter-Day Saints envision exaltation?

"Since human conceptions of reality are necessarily limited in mortality, religions struggle to adequately articulate their visions of eternal glory. As the Apostle Paul wrote, "Eye hath not seen, nor ear heard, neither have entered into the heart of man, the things which God hath prepared for them that love him." These limitations make it easy for images of salvation to become cartoonish when represented in popular culture. For example, scriptural expressions of the deep peace and overwhelming joy of salvation are often reproduced in the well-known image of humans sitting on their own clouds and playing harps after death. Latter-Day Saints' doctrine of exaltation is often similarly reduced in media to a cartoonish image of people receiving their own planets.

"A cloud and harp are hardly a satisfying image for eternal joy, although most Christians would agree that inspired music can be a tiny foretaste of the joy of eternal salvation. Likewise, while few Latter-Day Saints would identify with caricatures of having their own planet, most would agree that the awe inspired by creation hints at our creative potential in the eternities.

"Latter-Day Saints tend to imagine exaltation through the lens of the sacred in mortal experience. They see the seeds of godhood in the joy of bearing and nurturing children and the intense love they feel for those children, in the impulse to reach out in compassionate service to others, in the moments they are caught off guard by the beauty and order of the universe, in the grounding feeling of making and keeping divine covenants. Church members imagine exaltation less through images of what they will *get* and more through the relationships they have now and how those relationships might be purified and elevated. As the scriptures teach, "That same sociality which exists among us here will exist among us there, only it will be coupled with eternal glory, which glory we do not now enjoy (Or comprehend)."

How important are teachings about exaltation to Latter-Day Saint beliefs overall?

"The teaching that human beings have a divine nature and future shapes the way Latter-Day Saints view fundamental doctrine. Perhaps most significantly, belief in divine nature helps us more deeply appreciate the Atonement of Jesus Christ. While many Christian theologians have expressed the magnitude of the Savior's Atonement by emphasizing human depravity, Latter-Day Saints understand the magnitude of the Atonement of Christ in terms of the vast human potential it makes possible.

"Christ's Atonement not only provides forgiveness from sin and victory over death, but it also redeems imperfect relationships, heals the spiritual wounds that stifle growth, and strengthens and enables individuals to develop the attributes of Christ. Latter-Day Saints believe that it is only through the Atonement of Jesus Christ that we can have a sure hope of eternal glory and that the power of His Atonement is fully accessed only by faith in Jesus Christ, repentance, baptism, receiving the gift of the Holy Ghost, and enduring to the end in following the instruction and example of Christ. Thus, those who become like God and enter into a fulness of His glory are described as people who have been "made perfect through Jesus the mediator of the new covenant, who wrought out this perfect atonement through the shedding of his own blood."

"An awareness of humans' divine potential also influences Latter-Day Saints understanding of gospel principles such as the importance of divine commandments, the role of temples, and the sanctity of individual moral agency. Belief that human beings are actually God's children also changes Latter-Day Saints' behavior and attitudes. For example, even in societies where casual and premarital sex are considered acceptable, Latter-Day Saints retain a deep reverence for the God-given procreative and bonding powers of human sexual intimacy and remain committed to a higher standard in the use of those sacred powers.

Studies suggest that Latter-Day Saints place an exceptionally high priority on marriage and parenthood, a consequence in part of a strong belief in heavenly parents and a commitment to strive for that divinity.

Conclusion

"All human beings are children of loving heavenly parents and possess seeds of divinity within them. In His infinite love, God invites His children to cultivate their eternal potential by the grace of God, through the Atonement of the Lord Jesus Christ.

The doctrine of humans' eternal potential to become like their Heavenly Father is central to the gospel of Jesus Christ and inspires love, hope, and gratitude in the hearts of faithful Latter-Day Saints. [296]

End of "Becoming Like God" essay

(Footnotes for this article, as I said, are found online at www.churchofjesuschrist.org at "Becoming Like God")

The Church acknowledges the contribution of scholars to the content presented in this article; their work is used with permission'.

Having shared both sides of the Christian/Latter-Day Saint beliefs about God and man's relationship with Him, I have one last thing to share with you, my readers, before I get back to my perspective on Richard's comments regarding this subtitle about the Causal Cause of everything. I believe that to have a clear understanding of God, our Heavenly Father, and of His Son, Jesus Christ, the great and wonderous beings in the Great Causal Chain, I want to share a few comments on the concept of 'Grace' that they extend to us, God's children. I feel it fits in our debate that we're having, because like most people know, Christians believe in God's grace as being the redemptive power of God (Meaning 'forgiveness of sin'), which includes the power of Jesus' blood, to cover sins and save us from death and hell. If I understand this correctly, by vocalizing one's belief in Jesus as their Savior, it somehow activates His grace to save a believing man or women from going to hell, saving them even *in* their sins it seems. Of course, pastors will say one needs to repent as well, but it appears that giving lip service to repentance is good enough. At least it seems that way to me when I hear Christians speak about it.

In my observation of my Christian friends, they believe that just the mere expression of this kind of faith in Jesus and asking Him to save them while giving a sinners' prayer, Jesus' grace *alone* is thus sufficient for them to have the *assurance* that they are now saved and will go to heaven. The following verses are often presented as confirmation that this belief is how one is saved *without any works. To the LDS faithful, the* works are the acts of fully repenting and choosing to receive saving ordinances:

Ephesians 2:8-9

8 For by grace are ye saved *through faith; and that not of yourselves: it (Salvation) is the gift* of God:

9 *Not of works*, lest any man should boast.

Over the years, as I've studied this Christian doctrine of *'salvation by grace alone'*, and not of works, I grabbed a quote 'from here, and another one from there', not knowing I would be writing a book where I would need to remember where such quotes came from. So, please forgive me if I do not have footnotes for all of the notes I've taken from my journal, but I'm confident they'll be helpful in understanding what grace is, from my Latter-Day Saint perspective. I've titled my notes on Grace:

"Salvation by Faith Alone" (by Grace) *vs* "Salvation by Good Works Alone" (Or by both maybe?)

Here are my notes from my many years of study and research on this topic of *Saved by Grace*:

"One of the most controversial issues in Christian theology is whether salvation is the *'free gift'* of unmerited grace, meaning through faith in Jesus Christ *alone*, versus 'earning' it through doing good works, or receiving it through employing both principles. The apostle Paul's statement that "a man is justified" (Justification being a scriptural metaphor drawn from the courts of law: a judge justifies an accused person by declaring or pronouncing that person innocent or pardoned). Likewise, God may treat a person as being "not guilty", and therefore pardoned or justified of their sin.

All mortals individually need to be 'justified' because everyone of us has fallen short of perfect obedience to God's laws and commandments, resulting in our becoming "carnal, sensual, and devilish" due to our own transgressions and sins, and not just because of Adams transgressions.

Moses 5:13

13 And Satan came among them, saying: I am also a son of God; and he commanded them, Believe it not; and they believed it not, and they loved Satan more than God. And men began from that time forth to be carnal, sensual, and devilish.

Mosiah 16:3

3 For they are carnal and devilish, and the devil has power over them; yea, even that old serpent that did beguile our first parents, which was the cause of their fall; which was the cause of all mankind becoming carnal, sensual, devilish, knowing evil from good, subjecting good, subjecting themselves to the devil.

Those who transgress are "cut off" from God, and are in jeopardy of becoming "miserable forever":

II Nephi 2:5

5 And men are instructed sufficiently that they know good from evil. And the law is given unto men. And by the law no flesh is justified; or, by the law men are cut off. Yea, by the temporal law they were cut off; and also, by the spiritual law they perish from that which is good and become miserable forever.

Faith without the "deeds of the law" (The works?) is frequently cited to support the former view, while James's statement that "faith without works is dead" is often quoted in favor of the latter View:

Romans 3:28

28 Therefore we conclude that a man is justified by faith without the deeds of the law.

James 2:20

20 But wilt thou know, O vain man, that faith without works is dead?

The Latter-Day Saint doctrine on the other hand, is that salvation requires *both* grace and works (The works, as I've said, are such actions as fully repenting, being baptized, receiving the Gift of the Holy Ghost by the laying on of hands by one having the authority, each of these works forming 'the laws and ordinances of the gospel'. They are not works of 'earning' our salvation' by being better than others), and, is therefore a revealed yet commonsense reconciliation of these contradictory positions.

In his book "Mere Christianity", C. S. Lewis wrote that this dispute *"does seem to me like asking which blade in a pair of scissors is most necessary"* (p. 129). And in one way or another ... *almost all Christian denominations ultimately accept the need for both grace and works*, but the differences in *meaning* and *emphasis* among the various doctrinal traditions remain substantial (Some say grace is for Justification and works is for Sanctification. Faith in Jesus is the Tree that soon bears the Fruit of Works).

The Church of Jesus Christ of Latter-Day Saints' doctrine on grace contains an *affirmative sense of interaction* between grace and works that is unique, not only as to these concepts, but it also reflects the uniqueness of the restored gospels' view of man's nature, the Fall of Adam, the Atonement, and the process of salvation (See YouTube video titled "What the process of salvation is").

At the same time, our view as Latter-Day Saints contains features that are similar to basic elements of some other traditions as well. For example, the Latter-Day Saint insistence that such works as *ordinances* (The short list I just mentioned), be performed with proper priesthood authority, loosely resembles the Catholic teaching that its *sacraments* are the requisite channels of grace.

The Church's emphasis on the indispensability of personal faith and repentance ... in a direct relationship with God, echoes traditional Protestant teachings. The Church's position "is not a convenient eclecticism, but a repossession [through the Restoration] of a New Testament understanding that reconciles Paul and James statements on Grace (Madsen, p. 175)."

The Church's emphasis on personal responsibility and the need for self-disciplined obedience ... may seem to de-emphasize the role of Christ's grace; however, for Latter-Day Saints, *obedience is but one blade of the scissors.* All of The Church of Jesus Christ of Latter-Day Saints theology also reflects the major premise of the Book of Mormon which states that "Without grace there is no salvation":

II Nephi 25:23

23 For we know that it is by grace that we are saved, *after all we can do* (After all that's required; meaning, our part of the covenant, which we strive to do; which God says we 'can' and should do).

The source of this 'grace' and its enabling power, is the atoning sacrifice of Jesus Christ, or Atonement:

Alma 42:23

23 But God ceaseth not to be God, and mercy claimeth the penitent, and mercy cometh because of the atonement; and the atonement bringeth to pass the resurrection of the dead; and the resurrection of the dead bringeth back men into the presence of God; and thus they are restored into his presence, to be judged according to their works, according to the law and justice.

The teachings of Christian theology since the Middle Ages are rooted in the belief that, primarily because of the effects of the Fall and *original sin*, humankind has an inherently evil nature. In both the Catholic and the Protestant traditions, only the grace of God can overcome this *natural evil* (The 'natural man' as it's described in the Book of Mormon and LDS theology).

Various Christian writers have disputed the extent to which the bestowal of grace completely overcomes man's dark nature. In the fifth century, reflecting his personal struggle with what he believed to be his own inherent evil nature, Augustine saw grace as the only escape from the evil of earthly pleasures and the influence of the worldly 'city of man'. In the thirteenth century Thomas Aquinas, who I discussed earlier, was more sanguine, recognizing the serious wounding caused by what he called 'original sin', but also defending man's natural potential for good.

In the early sixteenth century, Martin Luther, through his reading of Paul and reacting against the sale of indulgences, concluded that faith, God's unilateral gift to chosen individuals, is the true source of grace and, therefore, of justification before God. Luther thus (perhaps unintentionally) broke the medieval church's control over grace, thereby unleashing the political force of the protestant reformation. For Luther, man's individual effort can in no way "earn" or otherwise be part in the righteousness infused by grace. Even the good works, demonstrated in a life of obedience to God, are but the visible *effects* of grace. This idea later influenced the development of the Puritan ethic in America.

John Calvin, Luther's contemporary, developed a complete *doctrine of predestination* based on Luther's idea that God unilaterally chooses those on whom he bestows the gifts of faith and grace. The Catholic response to Luther's challenge rejected predestination and reaffirmed both that grace is mediated by church sacraments and that grace cannot totally displace human agency. At the same time, Catholic thought underscored the primacy of God's initiative. "Prevenient grace" operates upon the 'human will' before one turns to God; yet, once touched by grace, one is still free to cooperate or not.

The interaction between divine grace and human freedom is not totally clear; however, grace is increased as one obeys God's commandments, and grace raises one's natural good works to actions of supernatural value in *a process of spiritual regeneration.*

In recent years, some Protestant theologians have questioned the way an exclusive emphasis on *unmerited grace* negates a sense of personal responsibility. Dietrich Bonhoeffer, for example, condemned the idea of "cheap grace", which falsely supposes that because "the account has been paid in advance, everything can be had for nothing" (*The Cost of Discipleship*, 1963, p. 45). [297]

John MacArthur was concerned that contemporary evangelism promises sinners that they "*can have eternal life yet continue to live in rebellion against God*" (*The Gospel According to Jesus*, 1988, pp. 15-16). And Paul Holmer wrote that stressing the dangers of works is "inappropriate if the listeners are not even trying! Most Church listeners are not in much danger of working their way into heaven" ("Law and Gospel Re-examined," *Theology Today* 10 [1953-54]:474). [298]

Some Latter-Day Saints have shared similar concerns about the limitations of a one-sided view of the grace-works controversy, just as they have shared the Catholic concern about a doctrine of grace that undercuts the fundamental nature of free will.

Elder James E. Talmage (Author of the book 'Jesus the Christ') saw Paul's writings about the inadequacy of works and 'the deeds of the law' (Rom. 3:27-28) as "referring mainly to the inadequacy of *the ritual works of the Law of Moses*, which had been superseded by the *higher requirements* of the Gospel of Jesus Christ; thus, Paul correctly regarded many of the outward forms and ceremonies of the Law of Moses as *unessential works*." [299] Here is the important distinction regarding "works".

As the prophet Abinadi declared in the Book of Mormon (c. 150 B.C.), "Salvation (And grace), doth not come by the law alone; and were it not for the Atonement, which God himself shall make for the sins and iniquities of his people, they must unavoidably perish, notwithstanding the Law of Moses."

In a broader sense, Latter-Day Saints devotion to the primary role of grace, while concurrently emphasizing self-reliance, stems from a unique doctrinal view of man's nature and destiny. As noted by Reformation scholar John Dillenberger, where he said, "In stressing human possibilities, Mormonism brought things into line, not by abandoning the centrality of grace ... but by insisting that the [real] powers of humanity reflected the actual state of humanity as such. Mormonism brought understanding to what had become an untenable problem within evangelicalism: how to reconcile the new power of humanity with the negative inherited views of humanity, without abandoning the necessity of grace."

In this way, Dillenberger concluded, "Perhaps Mormonism is the authentic American theology, for the self-reliance of revivalist fundamentalist groups stood in marked contrast to their inherited conception of the misery of humanity." [300]

In Latter-Day Saint teachings, the Fall of Adam made Christ's redemption necessary, but not because the Fall by itself made man evil. It was because of transgression that Adam and Eve were expelled from Eden into a world that was subject to death, natures evil, and evil influences such as man's individual evils. However, the Lord revealed to Adam upon his entry into mortality that "the Son of God hath atoned for original guilt"; therefore, Adam's children were not evil, but were "*whole* from the foundation of the world" (Moses 6:54). Thus, "every spirit of man was *innocent* in the beginning; and God having redeemed man from the fall, men became again, in their infant state, *innocent* before God" (Doctrine & Covenants 93:38. At least until each made choices that were transgressions and sin). As the descendants of Adam and Eve then, we become accountable for our own sins at age eight, all of us tasting sin as the result of our own free choice.

Romans 3:23

23 For all have sinned, and come short of the glory of God;

One whose cumulative experience leads her or him to love "Satan more than God":

Moses 5:28

28 And it came to pass that Cain took one of his brothers' daughters to wife, and they loved Satan more than God.

"Loving sin more than obedience to God's commandments, makes us carnal, sensual, and devilish" by nature:

Moses 5:13

13 And Satan came among them, saying: I am also a son of God; and he commanded them, saying: Believe it not; and they believed it not, and they ᶜloved Satan more than God. And men began from that time forth to be carnal, sensual, and devilish.

Moses:6:49

39 And it came to pass when they heard him, no man laid hands on him; for ᵒfear came on all them that heard him; for he walked with God.

On the other hand, one who consciously accepts Christ's grace through the Atonement by faith in Jesus as the Son of the Living God through repentance and submitting to baptism, so that we yield to "the enticing's of the Holy Spirit, we put off the natural man and become a saint through the Atonement of Christ the Lord":

Mosiah 3:19

19 For the natural man is an enemy to God, and has been from the fall of Adam, and will be, forever and ever, unless he yields to the enticings of the Holy Spirit, and putteth off the natural man and becometh a saint through the atonement of Christ the Lord, and becometh as a child, submissive, meek, humble, patient, full of love, willing to submit to all things which the Lord seeth fit to inflict upon him, even as a child doth submit to his father.

In this way, the individual takes the initiative to accept the grace made available to us by Christ's Atonement, exercising faith in Him through a willing "desire to believe":

Alma 32:27

17 Yea, there are many who do say: "If thou wilt show unto us a sign from heaven, then we shall know of a surety; then we shall believe."

That desire is often kindled by hearing others bear testimony of Christ. When this word of Christ is planted and then nourished through obedience, where it is then interacting with grace, as summarized below, the individual may "become a saint" by nature, (meaning Christlike in our very nature) thereby enjoying eternal life.

Grace is thus the source of *three* categories of blessings related to mankind's salvation:

First, many blessings of grace are *unconditional* – free and unmerited gifts – requiring no individual action. God's grace in this sense is a factor in the Creation, the Fall, the Atonement, and the Plan of Salvation. Specifically, regarding the Fall, and despite death and other conditions resulting from Adam's transgression, Christ's grace has atoned for original sin and has assured the resurrection of all humankind:

"We believe that men will be punished for their own sins, and not for Adam's transgression" (See Articles of Faith #2).

Second, the Savior has also atoned *conditionally* for *personal sins*. The application of grace to personal sins is *conditional* because it is available *only* when an individual repents, which can be a demanding form of works. Because of this condition, mercy is able to satisfy the 'demands of justice' with neither mercy nor justice robbing the other. Personal repentance is therefore a necessary *condition* of salvation, but it is *not* by itself *sufficient* to assure salvation. In addition, one must accept the ordinances of baptism and the laying-on of hands to receive the gift of the Holy Ghost, by which (By submitting oneself to this ordinance) one is 'born again' as the spirit child of Christ and may eventually become sanctified:

Doctrine & Covenants 76:51-52

51 They are they who received the testimony of Jesus, and believed on his name and were baptized after the manner of his burial, being buried in the water in his name, and this according to the commandment which he has given.

52 That by keeping the commandments they might be washed and cleansed from all their sins, and receive the Holy Spirit by the laying on of the hands of him who is ordained and sealed unto this power;

Third, after one has received Christ's gospel of faith, repentance, and baptism *unto* (Unto means 'leads to or leading to') forgiveness of sin, relying "wholly upon the merits of him who is mighty to save," one has only "entered in by the gate" to the "strait and narrow path which leads to eternal life":

II Nephi 31:17-20

17 Wherefore, do the things which I have told you I have seen that your Lord and your Redeemer should do; for, for this cause have they been shown unto me, that ye might know the gate by which ye should enter. For the gate by which ye should enter is repentance and baptism by water; and then cometh a remission of your sins by fire and by the Holy Ghost.

18 And then are ye in this strait and narrow path which leads to eternal life; yea, ye have entered in by the gate; ye have done according to the commandments of the Father and the Son; and ye have received the Holy Ghost, which witnesses of the Father and the Son, unto the fulfilling of the promise which he hath made, that if ye entered in by the way ye should receive.

19 And now, my beloved brethren, after ye have gotten into this strait and narrow path, I would ask if all is done? Behold, I say unto you, Nay; for ye have not come thus far save it were by the word of Christ with unshaken faith in him, relying wholly upon the merits of him who is mighty to save.

20 Wherefore, ye must press forward with a steadfastness in Christ, having a perfect brightness of hope, and a love of God and of all men. Wherefore, if ye shall press forward, feasting upon the word of Christ, and endure to the end, behold, thus saith the Father: Ye shall have eternal life.

In this post-baptism stage of spiritual development, one's best efforts (further spiritual works) are required to "endure to the end":

II Nephi 31:20

20 Wherefore, ye must press forward with a steadfastness in Christ, having a perfect brightness of hope, and a love of God and of all men. Wherefore, if ye shall press forward, feasting upon the word of Christ, and endure to the end, behold, thus saith the Father: Ye shall have eternal life.

These efforts include obeying the Lord's commandments and receiving the higher ordinances performed in the temples, and *continuing a repentance process* as needed to '*retain a remission of your sins*':

Mosiah 4:12

12 And behold, I say unto you that if ye do this ye shall always rejoice, and be filled with the love of God, and always retain a remission of your sins; and ye shall grow in the knowledge of the glory of him that created you, or in the knowledge of that which is just and true.

In the teachings of Martin Luther, such "works of righteousness" are not the result of personal initiative but are *the spontaneous effects of the internal grace one has received*, wholly the *fruits* of the gracious tree. In Latter-Day Saint doctrine by contrast, "men should do many things of their own free will and bring to pass much righteousness. *For the power (Of His grace) is in them*, wherein they are agents unto themselves":

Doctrine & Covenants 58:27-28

27 Verily I say, men should be anxiously engaged in a good cause, and do many things of their own free will, and bring to pass much righteousness;

28 For the power is in them, wherein they are agents unto themselves. And inasmuch as men do good they shall in nowise lose their reward.

At the same time, individuals lack the capacity to develop a Christlike nature by their own effort. The perfecting attributes such as hope, and charity, ... are ultimately *"bestowed upon all who are true followers of Jesus Christ"* by grace through his Atonement:

Moroni 7:48

48 Wherefore, my beloved brethren, pray unto the Father with all the energy of heart, that ye may be filled with this love, which he hath bestowed upon all who are true followers of his Son, Jesus Christ; that ye may become the sons of God; that when he shall appear we shall be like him, for we shall see him as he is; that we may have this hope; that we may be purified even as he is pure. Amen.

This interactive relationship between human and divine powers in Latter-Day Saint theology derives both from the significance it attaches to free will and from its optimism about the "fruits of the spirit" among the truly converted, "those who love me and keep all my commandments, *and* him that seeketh so to do".

Galatians 5:22-25

22 But the fruit of the Spirit is love, joy, peace, longsuffering, gentleness, goodness, faith,

23 Meekness, temperance: against such there is no law.

24 And they that are Christ's have crucified the flesh with the affections and lusts.

25 If we live in the Spirit, let us also walk in the Spirit.

Doctrine & Covenants 46:9

9 For verily I say unto you, they are given for the benefit of those who love me and keep all my commandments, and him that seeketh so to do; that all may be benefited that seek or that ask of me, that ask and not for a sign that they may consume it upon their lusts.

God bestows these additional, perfecting "expressions of grace" conditionally, and as he does, His grace allows forgiveness of sin. They (These expressions of Grace) are given "after all we can do"- that is, *in addition to* our best efforts. In general, this condition is related less to obeying particular commandments, than it is to one's fundamental spiritual character. For example, character traits such as "meekness and lowliness of heart":

Moroni 8:26

26 And the remission of sins bringeth meekness, and lowliness of heart; and because of meekness and lowliness of heart cometh the visitation of the Holy Ghost, which Comforter filleth with hope and perfect love, which love endureth by diligence unto prayer, until the end shall come, when all the saints shall dwell with God.

... and possessing "a broken heart and a contrite spirit":

Psalms 51:17

17 The sacrifices of God *are* a broken spirit: a broken and a contrite heart, O God, thou wilt not despise.

III Nephi 9:20

17 And as many as have received me, to them have I given to become the sons of God; and even so will I to as many as shall believe on my name, for behold, by me redemption cometh, and in me is the law of Moses fulfilled (Hafen, chap. 9).

Moroni wrote about these spiritual character traits as he was finishing writing his book that is part of the Book of Mormon, wherein he wrote:

Moroni 10:32-33

32 Yea, come unto Christ, and be perfected in him, and deny yourselves of all ungodliness; and if ye shall deny yourselves of all ungodliness, and love God with all your might, mind and strength, then is his grace sufficient for you, that by his grace ye may be perfect in Christ; and if by the grace of God ye are perfect in Christ, ye can in nowise deny the power of God.

33 And again, if ye by the grace of God are perfect in Christ, and deny not his power, then are ye sanctified in Christ by the grace of God, through the shedding of the blood of Christ, which is in the covenant of the Father unto the remission of your sins, that ye become holy, without spot.

(In other words, through *His* atoning Sacrifice we become holy without spot)

There is an additional concept if you, my readers, are to fully understand my Latter-Day Saint perspective on salvation. This concept of the Atonement of Jesus Christ not only involves Jesus' redeeming power, but it also involves His '*enabling power*'. There is a brief essay on this topic of "the enabling power we can have from the Atonement of Jesus Christ'. You can go to www.churchofjesuschrist.org and search for the title "The Enabling Power of Jesus Christ and His Atonement". Here are just a few excerpts from this essay that hopefully will inspire you, and I quote:

Philippians 4:13

13 I can do all things through Christ which strengtheneth me.

"Though we all have weaknesses, we can overcome them," says President Dieter F. Uchtdorf, a member of the Quorum of the Twelve Apostles. "Indeed, it is by the grace of God that, if we humble ourselves and have faith, weak things can become strong". Our Savior says in the Doctrine & Covenants:

Doctrine & Covenants 84:88

88 I will go before your face. I will be on your right hand and on your left, and my Spirit shall be in your hearts, and mine angels round about you, to bear you up.

"Nephi is an example of one who knew, understood, and relied upon the *enabling* power of the Savior," says Elder David A. Bednar of the Quorum of the Twelve Apostles. "Nephi's brothers bound him with cords and planned his destruction. Please note Nephi's prayer:

I Nephi 7:17 (emphasis added).

17 O Lord, according to my faith which is in thee, wilt thou deliver me from the hands of my brethren; yea, even *give me strength that I may burst these bands* with which I am bound.

"Nephi did not pray to have his circumstances changed. *Rather, he prayed for the strength to change his circumstances (To change himself so that the mountain before him was removed).* And I believe he prayed in this manner precisely because he knew, understood, and had experienced the enabling power of the Atonement to help us remove our mountains through faith on His name).

"I do not think the bands with which Nephi was bound just magically fell from his hands and wrists. Rather, I suspect he was blessed with both persistence and personal strength beyond his natural capacity, that he then 'in the strength of the Lord' worked and twisted and tugged on the cords, and ultimately and literally was enabled to break the bands. Mosiah Speaks of going forth 'in' the strength of the Lord. This is what is meant by 'enabling power':

Mosiah 9:17

17 Yea, in the strength of the Lord did we go forth to battle against the Lamanites; for I and my people did cry mightily to the Lord that he would deliver us out of the hands of our enemies, for we were awakened to a remembrance of the deliverance of our fathers.

End of Excerpts from Elder Bednar's talk titled "The Enabling Power of Jesus Christ and His Atonement" [301] as well as the end of my Journals' thoughts on the Grace Jesus' atonement offers us.

I am hopeful that you, my readers, feel confident in your understanding now, of the *difference* between my Christian friends' beliefs regarding *salvation by grace*, and my Latter-Day Saint perspective that I have of these principles of faith. Having a true knowledge of what God, the Father, and His Son, Jesus Christ's true nature is, and coming to an understanding of why we each need to develop a personal relationship with them, is so incredibly important, and that's because Christ's atonement is the one and only way in which we, as Heavenly Father's children, can return to Him, receive Eternal Life with Him, and live in His presence forever. Each of us can gain this knowledge of godliness for ourselves, individually, by exercising our faith in Jesus Christ, His Son, and receive His grace and enabling power.

It should also be noted, that like Richard has mentioned, I too want to give my perspective on the so-called problem of an *infinite past or regression*, which he says is 'the' issue or question that all Christians or believers in God must answer. Anyone who believes that God has existed forever and that He created the universe *ex nihilo* (out of nothing), must confront the difficulties this question of the infinite past and regression of God's existence poses to them. An improper or unsophisticated approach to infinities makes the idea of a God who existed 'forever' seem illogical. Critics are often quick to see their own stance on such things as 'reasonable', while believing that the Church of Jesus Christ of Latter-Day Saints' view, as well as the Christian stance on this question, are simply incoherent.

So, taking Mr. Beckwith's perspective of the nature of God in the one hand, and my Latter-Day Saint perspective in the other hand, it's very clear how different our perspectives are. Because there are these differing perspectives, you, my readers, are left to choose which perspective makes more sense to you, and which perspective you *want* to believe in, or, like many have done before you, there's a third choice where you can choose not to believe in God.

The differences in doctrine, comes down to what each believer believes the Bible is saying. On the one hand, the Christians believe only their interpretation of the Bible is the word of God, and as such it is inerrant. On the other hand, the Latter-Day Saints not only believe the Bible is the word of God, we believe our standard works are also the word of God. In addition to believing these books of scripture are the word of God, we also believe in the *continuing revelation* received and taught by the living prophets, seers, and revelators living among us today, is also the word of God, which broadens and deepens our spiritual knowledgebase even further. All these sources of scripture provide an opportunity to increase our understanding of God's true nature, which is required if we are to enjoy Eternal Life.

Because there are so many men and women who have conflicting interpretations of what the Holy Bible says and means, as I just explained, a multiplicity of religions has emerged, each of them having differing interpretations and understandings of the nature of God. Today's religious fervor, born out of all these conflicting beliefs, is due to what I have called the spirit of apostasy. It is quite similar to the religious fervor the prophet Joseph Smith experienced back in his Day, in 1820, except today there are literally hundreds, if not thousands of different churches to choose from. This being true, I certainly understand why someone like Richard feels the kind of distain he has for religion itself, and in particular his distain towards Christians and their so-called inerrant Bible.

In Ephesians we read:

Ephesians 4:4-6

4 *There is* one body, and one Spirit, even as ye are called in one hope of your calling;

5 *One Lord, one faith, one baptism,*

6 One God and Father of us all, who *is* above all, and through all, and in you all.

There should be only one true Church, yet there are at least 10 main groups, all believing different doctrines formed from the Bible. Here are seven main groups being followed today and their numbers: Catholicism: 1.2 billion; Protestantism: 600–800 million; Eastern Orthodoxy: 225–300 million; Oriental Orthodoxy: 86 million; Anglicanism: 85 million; Restorationism, Non-Trinitarianism: 41 million; and the church of Jesus Christ of Latter-Day Saints: 17 million plus.

All are worldwide groups that claim their Faith is the true and only true gospel, just as Richard has mentioned and criticized. In addition to what I just mentioned, there are at least 200 denominations in the US and a staggering 45,000 globally, each being individual churches that have 'broken off' from their 'tree of origin', with many church leaders choosing not to affiliate their church with any larger governing body (Ecclesiastical polity) that would require them to comply with only that body's prescribed doctrine and structure, though most of them have common beliefs. Even these smaller break off churches claim their doctrine to be the one true doctrine and church teaching the one true gospel of Jesus Christ.

After considering all the religions of the world, and in particular what the views of Christendom and the Church of Jesus Christ of Latter-Day Saints say regarding the true nature of God and what godliness is, you, my readers, like everyone else before you, *if* you haven't already done so, are left to decide which, out of all the religions, or as Joseph Smith said, "Which out of all the churches" is the one and only true Church on earth today? Of course, this is a question that is only asked by those who have a desire to know for themselves which of all the churches in the world is the one true and living Church. Each of us must ask ourselves, "Do I even want to know for myself? And if not, I would ask, "Why not?"

You, and only you, can do the work of deciding for yourself whether or not you want to choose to believe my perspective of God, or some other perspective of Him. You must choose and then follow those doctrines that ring true in your heart and mind. I certainly grant you that privilege of worshiping according to the dictates of your own conscious, and allow you to worship how, where, or what you may choose to worship, or not to worship at all.

It is by the revelation of God to His prophets, through the instrumentality of His spirit of truth, that I have come to know and believe in the *restored gospel* of Jesus Christ, as it was received and taught to the young prophet Joseph Smith Jr., by Jesus and His past prophets in the early nineteenth century.

Josephs' message rang true in my heart. I felt a burning in my bosom as I read and as I continue to read the Book of Mormon daily. I put forth the effort to find out for myself if it was true. I learned about Joseph's First Vision, and how he was raised up to translate the Book of Mormon, and was an instrument in God's hand in restoring the pure gospel of Jesus Christ in its fulness, including all of its laws and ordinances that bring about the salvation and exaltation of Man.

Knowing what I now know, I pray for those of you who are searching for the answer to the same question Joseph, and I had, "Which of all the churches has the fulness of God's gospel?", as well as the answers to all the rest of the 'Big' questions. I encourage you, my readers, to read the Book of Mormon in its entirety and then pray about it as Moroni counseled, because if you do, it will add a plethora of new reference legs to your circular stand upon which you can rest your table of belief confidently.

I have faith in God, and I trust that He will answer anyone's pleadings and prayers to know which of all the church's on this earth teaches His pure gospel. I know that if you, my readers, will but seek after Him with real intent, exercising faith in Jesus Christ, showing Him your willingness to humble yourself and to extend your trust in by standing on His promises, He will answer your prayers, for His promise is a 'promise of certainty'. In other words, take a leap of faith and take God at His word.

Now, let's get back to Richard's question of *Infinite Regression*. As far as my perspective on this subject goes, as a member of the Church of Jesus Christ of Latter-Day Saints, I have to tell you, my readers, that our doctrine of heavenly parents and their 'eternal ancestry', as well as our spiritual heritage and divine ancestry goes, the better question is, "Who were the *first* eternal parents in this, our universe, or even throughout all the universes, *if* there are multiple universes (and I'm not saying that there are)?" That's really what's behind Richard's '*Infinite Regression*' question, is it not?

The truth is, I'm not able to answer it, nor has any of the prophets of the Church of Jesus Christ of Latter-Day Saints been given the answer to it, or, if they have been given the answer God has not allowed them to give it to the world thus far, and so our church leaders have not given any official statement with regards to this question or doctrine, except for what I have provided thus far.

This is simply one of those subjects or questions where I have chosen to follow Elder Bruce R. McConkie's advice where he said to *withhold judgement* on the specific unanswered 'Big' questions regarding Infinite Regression, and what the eternal genealogy of our heavenly parents is, for now.

I have chosen, at the present time, to set them aside and place them on my *shelf of unknowns* until there is further light and knowledge on the subject, and I am confident it will come. I am happy to wait patiently on God to give those answers to these, and other such non-saving questions, in their fulness.

The answers, as I've said, will come in God's own due time and in His chosen way, and if it's not in my lifetime, I'm okay with that. I absolutely believe that we will come to know these long-awaited answers when Jesus Himself returns to usher in His Millennial reign at His 2nd coming, just as He has promised He would, for He has said, "He will reveal _ALL_ things, both in heaven and on earth."

Let me say here, that I believe neither Richards' arguments or my perspective on the question of _Infinite Regression_ has the power to move one's belief cursor on the Percentage of Probability Spectrum one iota, either way, and that's because there's no answer available from either side, yet. It would only be a guess. This is a perfect lead into Aquinas' next proof, "The Uncaused Cause".

2   The Uncaused Cause –

Richard says, "Nothing is caused by itself. Again, we are pushed into _infinite regress_. This must be terminated by a first cause, which theists call God". [302] The three major Abrahamic religions of our Day – Christianity, Judaism, and Islam (The Church of Jesus Christ of Latter-Day Saints is not listed here since it is supposedly so new to the world and its membership is so small when compared to the three largest religions' adherents, and because of the fact that our understanding of God's nature is so different than Christianity's understanding) – say that the God they believe in is not created; that He is uncreated, and therefore Richard Dawkins' idea of God, is a misnomer, and the question, "Who created God?", or "Where did God come from?" simply has no basis when you consider what today's theists believe about God, especially what Christians believe about Him.

As Mr. Beckwith's article said, Christians believe God is an essence that consists of three persons in one being, which being is uncreated and exists _outside_ of time-space, and therefore is from eternity to eternity, and so, the _Infinite Regression_ question does not apply and is therefore terminated. In other words, God did not have a creator, who had a creator, who had a creator, etc., and that's because He doesn't have a body of flesh and bone, and never did. The Christian God has always existed as some kind of spiritual, intangible essence; a three persons-in-one being called, _God in Trinity_.

In the Christian mind, this _Infinite Regression_ question is not only terminated because of their belief in God's special eternality, it actually can't even get started in their way of thinking, because there is no Causal Cause or Causal Chain to deal with, with their doctrine. What is interesting about Richard's _Infinite Regression_ logic is revealed in his example of "Gold and the idea of cutting a piece of Gold in half and doing it again, and again, and again until you have a single atom." [303]

This is saying that 'combined matter particles' being cut in half, over-and-over again, can no longer, at a certain point, be considered to be the material called gold. The gold, in other words, no longer exists in its _metallic state_. Only the separate atoms or even the separate quark particles remain after the atoms' nucleus is cut in half, ad Infinitum.

In the first of Aquinas' proofs, I addressed this _Infinite Regress_ conundrum by discussing eternal intelligences and forms of eternal matter, etc. I also shared several comments made by leaders of the Church of Jesus Christ of Latter-Day Saints on the subject. I mentioned that the Church of Jesus Christ of Latter-Day Saints leaders have not made any official statement regarding the principle of human deification. Human Deification is just another way of saying "becoming _like_ our Heavenly Father", which Jesus incapsulated here:

III Nephi 12:48 – "I would that ye be perfect, even as I or your Father in Heaven is perfect."

And so, other than those comments and what the 'Becoming Like God' article said about 'Deification', I've personally chosen to _reserve judgement_. I've chosen to set aside the _Infinite Regression_ question, placing it on my shelf of 'unanswered questions' until more specifics are revealed, either by the Lord to His prophets, or by scientific discovery (If and when scientists do scientific work on the subject). That said, please understand that by me not giving a full and complete answer to this 'regression' question, having set it aside for now, it doesn't in any way prove or add any evidence for God's non-existence.

In support of my taking this approach of holding off my giving an answer to the question of Infinite Regression at this time, feeling this approach is the better path to take for now, I came across an interesting article written by a past professor at BYU, who has since passed away. His name is Stephen E. Robinson. Dr. Robinson received a PhD in Biblical Studies and Classics. Dr. Robinson wrote about Anti-Mormon critics and what they have said about the Church and its official doctrinal position on subjects or questions like the Infinite Regression question Richard has posed. Here are a few excerpts from Dr. Robinson's article. I think you'll enjoy them, and I quote:

"Yet another way in which anti-Mormon critics often misrepresent LDS doctrine is in the presentation of *anomalies* as though they were the doctrine of the Church. Anomalies occur in every field of human endeavor, even in science. An anomaly is *something unexpected that cannot be explained by the existing laws or theories*, but which does not constitute evidence for changing the laws and theories. An anomaly is a *glitch*. A classic example of an anomaly in the LDS tradition is the so-called "Adam-God theory".

"During the latter half of the nineteenth century Brigham Young made some remarks about the relationship between Adam and God, that the Latter-Day Saints have never been able to understand (I include myself in this group). The reported statements conflict with LDS teachings before and after Brigham Young, as well as with statements of President Young himself during the same period of time. So, how do Latter-Day Saints deal with the phenomenon of such an anomaly? We don't; *we simply set it aside (I used conundrum in place of anomaly. Ha-ha-ha. They're similar words).*

"On occasion my colleagues and I at Brigham Young University have tried to figure out what Brigham Young might have actually said and what it might have meant, but the attempts have always failed. The reported statements simply do not compute—we cannot make sense out of them.

"This is not a matter of believing it or disbelieving it; we simply don't know what "it" is. If Brigham Young were here, we could ask him what he actually said, and what he actually meant by it, but he is not here. For the Latter-Day Saints, however, the point is moot, since whatever Brigham Young said, true or false, was never presented to the Church for a *sustaining vote*. It was not then and is not now a doctrine of the Church, and ... the Church has merely set the phenomenon aside as an anomaly." [304]

End of Excerpt from Dr. Stephen E. Robinson's essay

With this principle of *anomaly* fresh in your, my readers, mind, let me give my personal opinion and perspective on what I believe the *real issue* is with this conundrum called *Infinite Regression*. I believe this concept of *Infinite Regression* is, just as Dr. Robinson defined it, simply an anomaly. Because God, our Heavenly Father, has chosen not to reveal His personal ancestry or dare I say His heavenly ancestry in greater detail to the world, so far, or everything about *eternal intelligences* and forms of *eternal matter*, or how and in what manner eternal spirit beings exactly come to be, like you and I have come to be, or everything about what it was like when we lived in the pre-mortal world with Him, or how God Himself came to be, I've decided to set aside this *Infinite Regression* question for the time being. However, as I said, in doing so, it does not mean in any way, that I'm side-stepping Richard's question because I'm confused or want to run from it, because I'm not and I don't, and here's why:

If I tried to give this question (Or so-called argument) my best *guess*, and that's what it would be, a guess, I would be leaving myself vulnerable to the possibility of misleading you, my readers, and I don't want to do anything that would leave anyone of you feeling that I'm misrepresenting the Church of Jesus Christ of Latter-Day Saints, which I would never knowingly do, or that I was just giving some cockamamie, nonsensical argument against Richard's question just so I don't look stupid. In fact, as I said before, I do not in any way speak for the Church in any official capacity. I am simply a member of the Church of Jesus Christ of Latter-Day Saints who's chosen to jump into the debate regarding the 'Big' question of whether or not God exists. I'm simply sharing my own personal, Latter-Day Saint perspective and understanding, as well as my opinions regarding Richard's comments and arguments that he has laid out in his book *The God Delusion*. It is nothing more than that. Let's move on now, as we consider Aquinas's next argument or proof that Richard reviewed. It's called – "The Cosmological Argument".

3   The Cosmological Argument

Aquinas said, "There must have been a time when no physical things existed (An assumption that in my opinion and view of nature and reality, is most certainly a guess), and since physical things exist now, there must have been *something non-physical* to bring them into existence (From my perspective there's a few false assumptions being made by Aquinas here, not the least of which is his *something non-physical* statement, which I believe was born out of and from apostasy), and that something, again, is God." [305]

Keep in mind here that I believe Aquinas was steeped in his faith, for sure, but that faith happened to spring from the fruits of apostasy, as I've said, which was certainly in full swing in his Day (1275-1274 A.D., it being almost smack dab in the middle of the Dark Ages), and so his idea that there was a time when physical things did *not* exist (Meaning God was alone in pure nothingness), is one such false belief born out of the spirit of apostasy that leads to such false assumptions, and this false belief in ex nihlo has continued to be taught until this very Day, by Christians.

Richard opposes theist's taking the approach that says, "God Himself is immune to this question of regress because He exists outside of time and space", and "labeling Him with such characteristics as omniscience, omnipotence, goodness, creativity of design, as well as human characteristics such as the ability to listen to prayers, forgive sins and reading innermost thoughts." [306]

Richard thinks that "Omniscience and omnipotence are mutually incompatible, because God cannot change His mind, otherwise He is not omnipotent." [307]

Central to my faith as a Latter-Day Saint, a correct understanding of God the Father, and of His Son Jesus Christ, are required if one is to gain *life eternal* and receive *salvation* in the way the scriptures teach, these being the main hope-goals for any believer. As a member of the Church of Jesus Christ of Latter-Day Saints, I was taught to seek to know and to come to understand what God has revealed throughout the ages about His true nature, Jesus being the express image of His Father. Here's just a few scriptures that discuss this requirement, starting with John the apostle:

John 17:3

3 And this is life eternal, that they might know thee the only true God, and Jesus Christ, whom thou hast sent.

By learning all we can about God, the Eternal Father, we can begin to develop our relationship with Him. As we do so we come to *know* Him and His Son, Jesus Christ. This *'coming to know Them'* is described by Jesus Himself, when He spoke with His Father concerning His disciples back in the meridian of time. Here's what He said as He prayed to His Father:

John 17:21

21 That they all may be one; as thou, Father, art in me, and I in thee, that they also may be one *in* us.

I do not believe that Jesus was telling Heavenly Father that His desire for His disciples was for them to become additional persons *'in'* this One God kind of Being, or multiple persons *'in'* one Being or essence kind of Being (8 billion persons in one Being). He was praying that the Father would help them become one *in* purpose, one *in* love, one *in* unity, one *in* mind, one *in* heart, and one *in* spiritual truth with Them, which is the essence of the members of the Godhead being *one,* yet separate beings. Jesus was asking Heavenly Father to help them become *like* Him, by developing the Christlike character traits He and His Father have, so they could live in Heavenly Father's presence once again. My perspective is that the Godhead is not three persons in a *'one being essence'* called *God.* We are to become one with them by becoming *like* them via developing our character, mind, obedience, love, kindness, virtue, goodness, and completeness, and all the other godly attributes which is called *godliness.* Jesus Himself commanded us to *become perfect* even as His Father is perfect. This is, as I've laid out here, becoming <u>one with them</u> (That they might BE one with us by becoming one of us; becoming of one mind with us).

In addition to this, we must keep in mind that the scriptures don't always specify which member of the Godhead is being referred to in any given passage that includes the title of God, LORD, or Lord, so this often leads to confusion. Since the Father and the Son, and the Holy Ghost are one in all things, the scriptures often use their titles interchangeably, depending on who's speaking 'as' or 'for' God. For example, LORD (All caps) refers to God the Father. When the title Lord is used (lower caps except for the L) it's usually referring to the Son, meaning the God of the Old Testament, Jehovah, who later became Jesus incarnate (Made flesh and bone); He who condescended to become flesh like you and I.

In one sense however, it doesn't really matter which one of the members of the godhead is speaking, and that's because both the Father and the Son have the perfections, attributes, and the mind of the other members (Remember Jesus saying, "If you have seen me, you have seen the Father?", and "I only do that which I have seen my Father do? Etc.), and so they have the same thoughts of the Mind of God, the same goals, the same purpose, but different Roles, and as such, there's no conflicting comments or issues that exist between them. The following verses of scripture are just a few more examples for your consideration as you reflect on these divine attributes of God, and of His Son, Jehovah of the Old Testament and Jesus of the New Testament which are all inclusive int what is called *godliness or becoming Christlike*:

1   The existence of God is a reality:

    a.   All things denote there is a God" –

Alma 30:43-44

43 And now Korihor said unto Alma: If thou wilt show me a sign, that I may be convinced that there is a God, yea, show unto me that he hath power, and then will I be convinced of the truth of thy words (Dawkins sounds like a modern-day Korihor, doesn't he?).

44 But Alma said unto him: Thou hast had signs enough; will ye tempt your God? Will ye say, Show unto me a sign, when ye have the testimony of all these thy brethren, and also all the holy prophets? The scriptures are laid before thee, yea, and all things denote there is a God; yea, even the earth, and all things that are upon the face of it, yea, and its motion, yea, and also all the planets which move in their regular form do witness that there is a Supreme Creator.

Moses 6:63

63 And behold, all things have their likeness, and all things are created and made to bear record of me, both things which are temporal, and things which are spiritual; things which are in the heavens above, and things which are on the earth, and things which are in the earth, and things which are under the earth, both above and beneath: all things bear record of me.

Doctrine & Covenants 88:47

47 Behold, all these are kingdoms, and any man who hath seen any or the least of these hath seen God moving in his majesty and power (Sounds like Alma is describing 'Intelligent Design', right?).

   b.   God's voice has been heard from heaven:

Matthew 3:17

17 And lo a voice from heaven, saying, This is my beloved Son, in whom I am well pleased.

Matthew 17:5

5 While he yet spake, behold, a bright cloud overshadowed them: and behold a voice out of the cloud, which said, This is my beloved Son, in whom I am well pleased; hear ye him.

III Nephi 11:3–7

3 And it came to pass that while they were thus conversing one with another, they heard a voice as if it came out of heaven; and they cast their eyes round about, for they understood not the voice which they heard; and it was not a harsh voice, neither was it a loud voice; nevertheless, and notwithstanding it being a small voice it did pierce them that did hear to the center, insomuch that there was no part of their frame that it did not cause to quake; yea, it did pierce them to the very soul and did cause their hearts to burn.

4 And it came to pass that again they heard the voice, and they understood it not.

5 And again the third time they did hear the voice, and did open their ears to hear it; and their eyes were towards the sound thereof; and they did look steadfastly towards heaven, from whence the sound came.

6 And behold, the third time they did understand the voice which they heard; and it said unto them:

7 Behold my Beloved Son, in whom I am well pleased, in whom I have glorified my name—hear ye him.

Joseph Smith—History 1:17—His First Vision.

17 It no sooner appeared than I found myself delivered from the enemy which held me bound. When the light rested upon me I saw two Personages, whose brightness and glory defy all description standing above me *in the air*. One of them spake unto me, calling me by name and said, pointing to the other—*This is My Beloved Son. Hear Him!*

   c.   Prophets have testified of God's existence:

I Nephi 1:8

8 And being thus overcome with the Spirit, he was carried away in a vision, even that he saw the heavens open, and he thought he saw God sitting upon his throne, surrounded with numberless concourses of angels in the attitude of singing and praising their God.

Acts 7:55–56

55 But he, being full of the Holy Ghost, looked up steadfastly into heaven, ... and saw the glory of

God, and Jesus standing on the right hand of God,

56 And said, Behold, I see the heavens opened, and the Son of man standing on the right hand of God.

Joseph Smith—History 1:25—First Vison again

25 So it was with me. I had actually seen a light, and in the midst of that light I saw two Personages, and they did in reality speak to me; and though I was hated and persecuted for saying that I had seen a vision, yet it was true; and while they were persecuting me, reviling me, and speaking all manner of evil against me falsely for so saying, I was led to say in my heart: Why persecute me for telling the truth? I have actually seen a vision; and who am I that I can withstand God, or why does the world think to make me deny what I have actually seen? For I had seen a vision; I knew it, and I knew that God knew it, and I could not deny it, neither dared I do it; at least I knew that by so doing I would offend God, and come under condemnation.

D&C 76:19–24—Vision by Joseph & Oliver Cowdery

19 And while we meditated upon these things, the Lord touched the eyes of our understandings and they were opened, and the glory of the Lord shone round about.

20 And we beheld the glory of the Son, on the right hand of the Father, and received of his fulness;

21 And saw the holy angels, and them who are sanctified before his throne, worshiping God, and the Lamb, who worship him forever and ever.

22 And now, after the many testimonies which have been given of him, this is the testimony, last of all, which we give of him: That he lives!

23 For we saw him, even on the right hand of God; and we heard the voice bearing record that he is the Only Begotten of the Father—

24 That by him, and through him, and of him, the worlds are and were created, and the inhabitants thereof are begotten sons and daughters unto God.

2   God is the Father of all mankind:

      a.   God is literally the Father of the spirits of all mankind –

Hebrews 12:9

9 Furthermore we have had fathers of our flesh which corrected *us,* and we gave them reverence: shall we not much rather be in subjection unto *the Father of spirits*, and live?

Acts 17:28–29

28 For in him we ªlive, and move, and have our being; as certain also of your own poets have said, '*For we are also His offspring*'.

29 Forasmuch then as *we are the offspring of God*, we ought not to think that the Godhead is like unto gold, or silver, or stone, graven by art and man's device.

Numbers 16:22

22 And they fell upon their faces, and said, O God, *the God of the spirits of all flesh*, shall one man sin, and wilt thou be wroth with all the congregation?

      b.   Jesus declared that His God is our God and that His Father is our Father:

John 20:17

17 Jesus saith unto her, 'Touch me not; for I am not yet ascended to my Father: but go to my brethren, and say unto them, 'I ascend unto my Father, and your Father; and to my God, and your God.'

      c.   We are created in God's own image:

Genesis 1:26–27

26 And God said, Let us make man *in our image*, after *our likeness*: and let them have dominion over the fish of the sea, and over the fowl of the air, and over the cattle, and over all the earth, and over every creeping thing that creepeth upon the earth.

27 So God created man *in His own image*, in *the image of God created He him*; ... male and female created He them.

Alma 18:34

34 Ammon said unto him: I am a man; and man in the beginning was created *after the image of God*, and I am called by his Holy Spirit to teach these things unto this people, that they may be brought to a knowledge of that which is just and true;

Ether 3:15

15 And never have I showed myself unto man whom I have created, for never has man believed in me as thou hast. Seest thou that *ye are created after mine own image*? Yea, even all men were created in the beginning after mine own image.

Abraham 4:26–27

26 And the Gods took counsel among themselves and said: Let us go down and form man *in our image, after our likeness*; and we will give them dominion over the fish of the sea, and over the fowl of the air, and over the cattle, and over all the earth, and over every creeping thing that creepeth upon the earth.

27 So the Gods went down to *organize* man *in their own image*, in the image of the Gods to form they him, male and female to form they them.

Moses 2:26–27

26 And I, God, said unto mine Only Begotten, which was with me from the beginning: *Let us make man in our image, after our likeness*; and it was so. And I, God, said: Let them have dominion over the fishes of the sea, and over the fowl of the air, and over the cattle, and over all the earth, and over every creeping thing that creepeth upon the earth.

27 And *I, God, created man in mine own image, in the image of mine Only Begotten created I him*; male and female created I them.

Mosiah 7:27

27 And because he said unto them that Christ was the God, the Father of all things, and said that *he should take upon him the image of man*, and it should be *the image after which man was created* in the beginning; or in other words, he said that man was created after *the image of God*, and that God should come down among the children of men, and take upon him flesh and blood, and go forth upon the face of the earth.

    d.   God has love and concern for His children and all His creations:

1 John 4:7–10

7 Beloved, let us love one another: for love is of God; and every one that loveth is born of God, and knoweth God.

8 He that loveth not knoweth not God; for God is love.

9 In this was manifested the love of God toward us, because that God sent his only begotten Son into the world, that we might live through him.

10 Herein is love, not that we loved God, but that he loved us, and sent his Son *to be the propitiation* for our sins.

Matthew 10:29–31

29 Are not two sparrows sold for a farthing? and one of them shall not fall on the ground without your Father.

30 But the very hairs of your head are all numbered.

31 Fear ye not therefore, ye are of more value than many sparrows.

I Nephi 11:14–22

14 And it came to pass that I saw the heavens open; and an angel came down and stood before me; and he said unto me: Nephi, what beholdest thou?

15 And I said unto him: A virgin, most beautiful and fair above all other virgins.

16 And he said unto me: Knowest thou the condescension of God?

17 And I said unto him: I know that he loveth his children; nevertheless, I do not know the meaning of all things.

18 And he said unto me: Behold, the virgin whom thou seest is the mother of the Son of God, after the manner of the flesh.

19 And it came to pass that I beheld that she was carried away in the Spirit; and after she had been carried away in the Spirit for the space of a time the angel spake unto me, saying: Look!

20 And I looked and beheld the virgin again, bearing a child in her arms.

21 And the angel said unto me: Behold the Lamb of God, yea, even the Son of the Eternal Father! Knowest thou the meaning of the tree which thy father saw?

22 And I answered him, saying: Yea, it is the love of God, which sheddeth itself abroad in the hearts of the children of men; wherefore, it is the most desirable above all things.

John 3:16

16 For God so loved the world, that he gave his only begotten Son, that whosoever believeth in him should not perish, but have everlasting life.

  e. God's work and glory is to bring to pass the immortality and eternal life of His children.

Moses 1:39

39 For behold, this is my °work and my glory—to bring to pass the immortality and eternal life of man.

3 God is perfect in His person, character, and attributes:

  a. God is a holy, perfected personage with a body of flesh and bones –

Moses 6:57

57 Wherefore teach it unto your children, that all men, everywhere, must repent, or they can in nowise inherit the kingdom of God, for no unclean thing can dwell there, or dwell in his presence; for, in the language of Adam, Man of Holiness is his name, and the name of his Only Begotten is the Son of Man (Man of Holiness) even Jesus Christ, a righteous Judge, who shall come in the meridian of time.

Moses 7:35

35 Behold, I am God; of Holiness is my name; Man of Counsel is my name; and Endless and Eternal is my name, also.

Doctrine & Covenants 130:22

22 The Father has a body of flesh and bones as tangible as man's; the Son also; but the Holy Ghost has not a body of flesh and bones, but is a personage of Spirit. Were it not so, the Holy Ghost could not dwell in us.

Matthew 5:48

48 Be ye therefore perfect, even as your Father which is in heaven is perfect.

  b. God knows all things and has all power and might:

I Nephi 9:6

6 But the Lord knoweth all things from the beginning; wherefore, he prepareth a way to accomplish all his works among the children of men; for behold ... he hath all power unto the fulfilling of all his words. And thus it is. Amen.

Mosiah 4:9

9 Believe in God; believe that he is, and that he created all things, both in heaven and in earth; believe that he has all wisdom, and all power, both in heaven and in earth; believe that man doth not comprehend all the things which the Lord can comprehend.

II Nephi 2:24

24 But behold, all things have been done in the wisdom of him who knoweth all things.

Moroni 7:22

22 For behold, God knowing all things, being from everlasting to everlasting, behold, he sent angels to minister unto the children of men, to make manifest concerning the coming of Christ; and in Christ there should come every good thing.

    c.   God is infinite, eternal, and unchangeable:

Mormon 9:9

9 For do we not read that God is the same yesterday, today, and forever, and in him there is no variableness neither shadow of changing?

Doctrine & Covenants 20:12, 17

12 Thereby showing that he is the same God yesterday, today, and forever. Amen.

17 By these things we know that there is a God in heaven, who is infinite and eternal, from everlasting to everlasting the same unchangeable God, the framer of heaven and earth, and all things which are in them.

Doctrine & Covenants 109:77

77 O Lord God Almighty, hear us in these our petitions, and answer us from heaven, thy holy habitation, where thou sittest enthroned, with glory, honor, power, majesty, might, dominion, truth, justice, judgment, mercy, and an infinity of fulness, from everlasting to everlasting.

    d.   God is just, true, and righteous in all things:

Revelation 15:3

3 And they sing the song of Moses the servant of God, and the song of the Lamb, saying, Great and marvellous *are* thy works, Lord God Almighty; just and true *are* thy ways, thou King of saints.

Psalm 89:14

14 Justice and judgment *are* the habitation of thy throne: mercy and truth shall go before thy face.

Ether 3:12

12 And he answered: Yea, Lord, I know that thou speakest the truth, for thou art a God of truth, and canst not lie.

    e.   God is perfect in His love and mercy:

Psalm 103:17–18

17 But the mercy of the Lord *is* from everlasting to everlasting upon them that fear him, and his righteousness unto children's children;

18 To such as keep his covenant, and to those that remember his commandments to do them.

II Nephi 9:8, 53

8 O the wisdom of God, his mercy and grace! For behold, if the flesh should rise no more our spirits must become subject to that angel who fell from before the presence of the Eternal God and became the devil, to rise no more.

53 And behold how great the covenants of the Lord, and how great his condescensions unto the children of men; and because of his greatness, and his grace and mercy, he has promised unto us that our seed shall not utterly be destroyed, according to the flesh, but that he would preserve them; and in future generations they shall become a righteous branch unto the house of Israel.

Exodus 34:6–7

6 And the Lord passed by before him and proclaimed, The Lord, the Lord God, merciful and gracious, longsuffering, and abundant in goodness and truth,

7 Keeping mercy for thousands, forgiving iniquity and transgression and sin, and that will by no means clear *the guilty;* visiting the iniquity of the fathers upon the children, and upon the children's children, unto the third and to the fourth *generation.*

1 Chronicles 16:34

34   O give thanks unto the Lord; for *he is* good; for his mercy *endureth* forever.

f.   God is the source of light and life and is the law:

Doctrine & Covenants 88:12–13

12 Which light proceedeth forth from the presence of God to fill the immensity of space—

13 The light which is in all things, which giveth life to all things, which is the law by which all things are governed, even the power of God who sitteth upon his throne, who is in the bosom of eternity, who is in the midst of all things.

4   God is the Supreme Being in the universe.

a.   God the Father is greater than all:

Ephesians 4:6

6 One God and Father of all, who *is* above all, and through all, and in you all.

John 10:29

29 My Father, which gave *them* me, is greater than all; and no *man* is able to pluck *them* out of my Father's hand.

b.   As the Supreme Being, God the Father should be the object of our love and worship:

Doctrine & Covenants 18:40

40 And you shall fall down and worship the Father in my name.

Doctrine & Covenants 20:29

29 And we know that all men must repent and believe on the name of Jesus Christ, and worship the Father in his name, and endure in faith on his name to the end, or they cannot be saved in the kingdom of God.

Joshua 22:5

5   But take diligent heed to do the commandment and the law, which Moses the servant of the LORD charged you, to love the LORD your God, and to walk in all his ways, and to keep his commandments, and to cleave unto him, and to serve him with all your heart and with all your soul.

Mark 12:30

30 And thou shalt love the Lord thy God with all thy heart, and with all thy soul, and with all thy mind, and with all thy strength: this *is* the first commandment.

Doctrine & Covenants 4:2

2 Therefore, O ye that embark in the service of God, see that ye serve him with all your heart, might, mind and strength, that ye may stand blameless before God at the last day.

Luke 4:8

8 And Jesus answered and said unto him, Get thee behind me, Satan: for it is written, Thou shalt worship the Lord thy God, and him only shalt thou serve.

a.   God created all things through His Son:

Hebrews 1:1–2

1 God, who at sundry times and in divers manners spake in time past unto the fathers by the prophets,

2 Hath in these last days spoken unto us by *his* Son, whom he hath appointed heir of all things, by whom also he made the worlds;

Moses 1:32–33

32 And by the word of my power, have I created them, which is mine Only Begotten Son, who is full of grace and truth.

33 And worlds without number have I created; and I also created them for mine own purpose; and by the Son I created them, which is mine Only Begotten.

Moses 2:1

1 And it came to pass that the Lord spake unto Moses, saying: Behold, I reveal unto you concerning this heaven, and this earth; write the words which I speak. I am the Beginning and the End, the Almighty God; by mine Only Begotten I created these things; yea, in the beginning I created the heaven, and the earth upon which thou standest.

6 God the Father presides over the Godhead.

b. The Father, the Son, and the Holy Ghost are the members of the Godhead:

Articles of Faith 1:1

1 We believe in God, the Eternal Father, and in His Son, Jesus Christ, and in the Holy Ghost.

1 John 5:7

7 For there are three that bear record in heaven, the Father (God), the Word (Jesus), and the Holy Ghost (The Testator): and these three are one (One Godhead).

Alma 11:44

44 Now, this restoration shall come to all, both old and young, both bond and free, both male and female, both the wicked and the righteous; and even there shall not so much as a hair of their heads be lost; but everything shall be restored to its perfect frame (Resurrected bodies), as it is now, or in the body, and shall be brought and be arraigned before the bar of Christ the Son, and God the Father, and the Holy Spirit, which is ^cone Eternal God, to be ^djudged according to their works, whether they be good or whether they be evil.

c. Each member of the Godhead is physically separate and distinct from the others:

Doctrine & Covenants 130:22

22 The Father has a body of flesh and bones as tangible as man's; the Son also; but the Holy Ghost has not a body of flesh and bones, but is a personage of Spirit. Were it not so, the Holy Ghost could not dwell in us.

Matthew 3:16–17

16 And Jesus (One member of the Godhead), when he was baptized, went up straitway out of the water: and, lo, the heavens were opened unto him, and he saw the Spirit of God descending like a dove (Another member of the Godhead), and lighting upon him:

17 And lo a voice from heaven, saying, This is my beloved Son, in whom I am well pleased (A third member of the Godhead, God the Father. Certainly, Jesus was not a ventriloquist projecting the Father's voice).

Acts 7:55–56

55 But he, being full of the Holy Ghost, looked up steadfastly into heaven, and saw the glory of God, and Jesus standing on the right hand of God,

56 And said, Behold, I see the heavens opened, and the Son of man standing on the right hand of God.

Again, certainly God was not showing an illusion of *two* beings, that then merged into one being just to make a point. The point being made was that they are two separate and distinct personages.

d. The members of the Godhead are united in Their attributes, power, and purpose:

John 17:20–21

20 Neither pray I for these alone, but for them also which shall believe on me through their word;

21 That they all may be one; as thou, Father, *art* in me, and I in thee, that they also may be one in us: that the world may believe that thou hast sent me.

Doctrine & Covenants 20:28

28 Which Father, Son, and Holy Ghost are one God, infinite and eternal, without end. Amen.

Doctrine & Covenants 35:2

2 I am Jesus Christ, the Son of God, who was crucified for the sins of the world, even as many as will believe on my name, that they may become the sons of God, even one in me as I am one in the Father, as the Father is one in me, that we may be one (One what? One in purpose, etc.).

II Nephi 31:21

21 And now, behold, my beloved brethren, this is the way; and there is none other way nor name given under heaven whereby man can be saved in the kingdom of God. And now, behold, this is the doctrine of Christ, and the only and true doctrine of the Father, and of the Son, and of the Holy Ghost, which is one God, without end. Amen.

III Nephi 11:27

27 And after this manner shall ye baptize in my name; for behold, verily I say unto you, that the Father, and the Son, and the Holy Ghost are one; and I am in the Father, and the Father in me, and the Father and I are one (What is 'in' me mean? Again, it means one 'in' purpose, love, power, etc. For He promises that we will gain all that the Father hath).

> e. The Father is the supreme member of the Godhead:

John 14:26, 28, 31

26 But the Comforter, *which is* the Holy Ghost, whom the Father will send in my name, he shall teach you all things, and bring all things to your remembrance, whatsoever I have said unto you.

28 Ye have heard how I said unto you, I go away, and come *again* unto you. If ye loved me, ye would rejoice, because I said, I °go unto the Father: for my Father is greater than I.

31 But that the world may know that I love the Father; and as the Father gave me commandment, even so I do. Arise, let us go hence.

II Nephi 31:7, 12

7 Know ye not that he was holy? But notwithstanding he being holy, he showeth unto the children of men that, according to the flesh he humbleth himself before the Father, and witnesseth unto the Father that he would be obedient unto him in keeping his commandments.

12 And also, the voice of the Son came unto me, saying: He that is baptized in my name, to him will the Father give the Holy Ghost, like unto me; wherefore, follow me, and do the things which ye have seen me do.

III Nephi 28:11

11 And the Holy Ghost beareth record of the Father and me; and the Father giveth the Holy Ghost unto the children of men, because of me.

An additional supporting statement about God's nature by the prophet Joseph Smith (See my Footnote Pages at the end of my book):

The existence of God is a reality.

"The heavens declare the glory of God, and the firmament showeth His handiwork; and a moment's reflection is sufficient to teach every man of common intelligence, that all these are not the mere productions of *chance,* nor could they be supported by any power (The power suggested by atheists that evolution or natural selection has to evolve a cell into a man) less than an Almighty hand." [308]

Next are excerpts from speeches given by Elder John A. Widtsoe, a past apostle of the Church of Jesus Christ of Latter-Day Saints from 1921 until his death in 1952:

"The existence of God, tested by all human powers, is the most firmly established fact in man's possession. The searcher for God (You and I being the searchers) may turn for evidence to the external universe, to his own inner self, and to human history for his answer (The law written on one's heart bor inner self being just one place to look). Every process of nature is orderly. Chance, disorder, and chaos are ruled out of the physical universe. If every condition involved in a system is precisely the same, the result, anywhere, everywhere, today or at any other time, will be the same. The sun does not rise in the east today and in the west tomorrow.

"That means that the phenomena of nature are products of law. The infinitely large and the infinitely small move in obedience to law. In man's earnest search for truth, no exception to this process has been found. The universe, itself, declares that there is intelligent purpose (Intelligent intent, even intelligent design) in nature, and that there must be, therefore, a supreme intelligence directing the universe. This is God.

"The evidence for God which comes from the invisible world, the world, as yet only feebly explored by science, is equally convincing. Such, for example, is the evidence of conscience. If one seeks to do right, he is warned whenever he is tempted to stray from the proper path (For me, the conscience that tells us all what is right and what is wrong, is the greatest evidence for God's existence. The evidence for God's existence is behind our own belt-buckle so-to-speak). Similar is the evidence of prayer. The vast majority of mankind agree that prayer helps people meet or solve the problems of life. Or note the results of obedience to the laws of the Lord. They who obey His laws find a joy not otherwise to be secured. From such conformity, prayer, and heed to conscience has come to millions of people, giving them the revelation and certain conviction that God lives and guides His children on earth. The message is as real as the words issuing from the radio tuned to the broadcaster. Certain it is that man has within himself the power to find and to know God. As a supplementary evidence, is the further historical fact that a number of men have declared that they have seen God, and even spoken with Him, or that they have received messages from Him for themselves and others (These are the theophanies I spoke about earlier).

The historicity of their claims is in most cases well established. That which was done, for example, by Paul the Apostle and Joseph Smith the Prophet, after their heavenly experiences, helps confirm the truth of their claims." [309]

"God the Eternal Father, whom we designate by the exalted name-title Elohim, is the literal parent of our Lord and Savior Jesus Christ and of the spirits of the human race." [310]

"I want to tell you, each-and-every-one of you, that you are well acquainted with God our Heavenly Father, or the great Elohim. You are all well acquainted with him, for there is not a soul of you but what has lived in his house and dwelt with him year after year; and yet you are seeking to become acquainted with him, when the fact is, you have merely forgotten what you did know. There is not a person here today but what is a son or a daughter of that Being. In the spirit world your spirits were first begotten and brought forth, and you lived there with your parents for ages before you came here." [311]

"God is Father of the spirits of all flesh, not only of those that fear him, but of those who do not fear him (Fear being Reverence), and who disobey His laws. He is the Father of the spirits of all, and as is spoken of in the scriptures, 'We are His offspring and emanated from him'." [312]

"We *are* the children of God. That doctrine is not hidden away in an obscure verse. It is taught over and over again in scripture. These are clear examples from the Bible:

"All of you are children of the 'Most High':

Psalm 82:6

6 I have said, *Ye are gods*; and all of you *are* children of the most High.

"And: 'We are the offspring of God':

Acts 17:29

29 Forasmuch then as we are *the offspring of God*, we ought not to think that the Godhead is like unto gold, or silver, or stone, graven by art and man's device.

"Doctrinal truths are interrelated. There is an old saying that says, 'If you pick up one end of a stick, you automatically pick up the other end as well". So, "If you concede that we are His children, you must allow that God is our Father." [313]

"God himself was once as we are now and is an exalted man. ... If the veil were rent today, if you were to see him today, you would see him like a man in form—like yourselves in all the person, image, and very form as a man." ...

"It is the first principle of the Gospel to know for a certainty the Character of God, and to know that we may converse with him as one man converses with another, and that he was once a man like us; yea, that God himself, the Father of us all, dwelt on an earth, the same as Jesus Christ himself did; and I will show it from the Bible." [314] And, "God made man in his own image and certainly he made woman in the image of his wife-partner." [315] God is perfect in His person, character, and attributes. What did Jesus do? Why, I do the things I saw my Father do, when worlds came rolling into existence. My Father worked out His kingdom with fear and trembling, and I must do the same; and when I get my kingdom, I shall present it to my Father, so that he may obtain upon kingdom, and it will exalt Him in glory."

"He will then take a higher exaltation, and I will take his place, and thereby become exalted myself. So that Jesus treads in the tracks of his Father and inherits what God did before; and God is thus glorified and exalted in the salvation and exaltation of all his children." [316]

"God is the Supreme Being in the universe"

"By definition, God (generally meaning the Father) is the one supreme and absolute Being; the ultimate source of the universe; the all-powerful, all-knowing, all- good Creator. Ruler, and Preserver of all things." [317]

"God is the only supreme governor and independent being in whom all fullness and perfection dwell; He is omnipotent, omnipresent, and omniscient; without beginning of days or end of life; and that in him every good gift and every good principle dwell; and that he is the Father of lights; in him the principle of faith dwells independently, and he is the object in whom the faith of all other rational and accountable beings center for life and salvation." [318]

"Our relationship with the Father is supreme, paramount, and preeminent over all others. He is the God we are called to worship. It is His gospel that saves and exalts. He ordained and established the plan of salvation. He is the one who was once as we are now. The life he lives is eternal life, and if we are to gain this greatest of all the gifts of God, it will be because we become like him." [319]

"The Father presides over the Godhead."

"Three glorified, exalted, and perfected personages comprise the *Godhead* or supreme presidency of the universe. They are God the Father; God the Son; God the Holy Ghost. ... Though each God in the Godhead is a personage, separate and distinct from each of the others, yet they are one God, ... meaning that they are united as one in the attributes of perfection. For instance, each has the fulness of truth, knowledge, charity, power, justice, judgment, mercy, and faith. Accordingly, they all think, act, speak, and are alike in all things, and yet they are three separate and distinct entities. Each occupies space and is and can be in but one place at one time, but each has power and influence that is everywhere present." [320]

"Everlasting covenant was made between three personages before the organization of this earth and relates to their dispensation of things to men on the earth; these personages, according to Abraham's record, are called God the first, the Creator; God the second, the Redeemer; and God the third, the witness or Testator." [321]

And lastly by Joseph Fielding Smith, "There is a *oneness* in the Godhead as well as a distinctness of personality. This oneness is emphasized in the sayings and writings of prophets and apostles in-order-to guard against the erroneous idea that these three may be distinct and independent deities and rivals for our worship." [322]

End of Quotes

Whew! Now that that's done, I feel I have given a clear view of my perspective as a member of the Church of Jesus Christ of Latter-Day Saint, on God's nature, as well as His Son's, and therefore it should be obvious as to why I feel my perspective of God and His nature shouldn't be lumped in with Christendom's description of God, or Richard's either. I want my perspective to stand on its own. My claim is that the details I've shared about God's nature were revealed by God's Son to His prophets, both past and present, because Jesus truly wants us to know Heavenly Father more completely, so that we may return back to His presence. With that said, let's go ahead and move on to Aquinas' next argument – "The Arguments from Degree".

4   The Argument from Degree:

This is a very short argument given by Richard regarding Aquinas' fourth argument, 'The Argument from Degree', which Aquinas put forth as proof for God's existence. Here is what Aquinas said:

"Humans can be both good and bad, so the *maximum goodness* cannot rest in us. Therefore, there must be some other *maximum* to set the (Objective) *standard* for perfection, and we call that maximum God." [323]

Richard mocks this by saying, "That's an argument?" (Richard is basically saying, "C'mon man! Really?") You might as well say, people vary in smelliness but we can make the comparison only by reference to a perfect maximum of conceivable smelliness. Therefore, there must exist a pre-eminently peerless stinker, and we call him God." [324] Ha-ha-ha. That cracked me up. That's a good one Richard.

Richard's unique sense of humor shines through once again. He cracks me up. Unlike Richard, I am okay with how Aquinas worded this 'Fourth Proof' or argument. Aquinas is simply saying that "because all mankind is imperfect, _we_ cannot come up with what one would call an *Objective Standard*" for morality. I agree that only someone who is perfect and all powerful can set up the laws we, as a society, should live by, otherwise we would come up with a multiplicity of *subjective standards*, which of course would draw a multiplicity of opinions about those subjective standards. Some of us would agree with them and some of us would disagree with them, which, of course, would absolutely lead to chaos.

Only when a large majority of a society comes to an agreement as to which subjective standards will become the law, can that society keep from going into chaos. And so, to me, Aquinas is just saying that "when the vast majority of a society believes in God and in His laws, only then can they become the *standards* for all of society to follow."

That said, God is still the only source that can provide societies with that objective standard. Whether it's a standard of perfection, or a standard of morality, or a standard of objective truth, the point is, without an "objective standard" for the question "What's good and what's evil?", any act of violence becomes a matter of *subjective opinion*, and when a society is built on that kind of unstable standard, that society itself will soon becomes unstable, and in time will experience a spiral into total chaos and collapse. To illustrate my point, here's a few excerpts from an article written by Terry Lewis, an author for *Cross-Examined*, which is a Christian Apologists' non-profit organization headed up by another American apologist, Frank Turek, who is an author, a public speaker, and a successful radio host. Here are some excerpts taken from the article written by Mr. Lewis, titled: "Objective Morality: Much Ado About Nothing", and I quote:

"Imagine what would happen if our government wrote our laws like this! If tomorrow, our legislators declared that all speed limits were repealed, and law enforcement officers were empowered to arrest those who were driving "too fast". Chaos would reign! How fast is "too fast"? It's a safe bet that your idea of "too fast" is not the same as mine... and neither of us are likely to agree with the cop that has just pulled us over! Without a legal fact, a clearly written and duly established law, all legal opinions are equally valid, ... and thus are completely useless for governing anyone other than the holder of that opinion! For this reason, modern legislators and lawyers spend enormous amounts of time fretting over the exact phrasing of a document. Companies spend huge amounts of money to remove as much opinion as possible from the wording of a contract. And even after adding all the "legalese", litigants still debate the meaning of even the smallest of words.

"Our laws and regulations must be objective, based in external facts independent of any one person's opinions, in-order to be meaningful. In the same way, subjective moral opinion, in the absence of objective moral facts, is effectively no morality at all! Often at this point, the subjective moralist objects (An example of a subjective moralist would be Richard Dawkins), saying, "I can be just as moral as anyone who believes in objective morality" (This is pretty much what Richard says about himself and other Atheists). However, this objection is illogical. If moral facts do not exist, then why would it be "better" or "worse" (which are themselves, morally charged words) to be called immoral rather than moral? Why does it matter whether one breaks a non-existent standard of behavior? Can a 'subjective moralist' be a moral person? Well, yes. They can be moral and wrong about the existence of objective moral facts. Or they can be right in their belief, but neither moral nor immoral. What they cannot be though, is both right and moral. (Or to be fair, right, and immoral!)

To clarify, consider this question:

"Does a unicorn's horn glow in the dark?" The answer doesn't really matter, because the subject of the question doesn't exist, and so no answer has any meaning in the real world. In the same way, one's opinion of how we should treat others is meaningless unless there actually exists a way that we should treat others (An *objective standard* of how we should treat others)! Subjective moral opinion with no undergirding objective moral fact, is an opinion about something that does not exist. It has no more relevance to our lives than the destruction of Krypton (That's the home world of Superman and Supergirl, and the name of a material for it, as those who are under the age of 30 will attest! Ha-ha).

Subjective Moral Opinion Isn't Sufficient

"Moral opinion alone lacks the necessary scope of influence required of morality. An opinion is, by its nature, limited to one person. No two persons can share an opinion. You might describe your opinion to me, and we might hold similar opinions, but I cannot hold your opinion! Nor can you hold mine.

This means that the scope of influence of any opinion is exactly one person, but a 'standard of morality' deals largely with relationships between two or more persons. Opinions simply have insufficient scope to address relational behavior.

"For this reason, the argument that morality is a product of people in society, fails. Moral opinion can provide no binding reason that men should seek the good of others. Indeed, we instinctively resist the moral opinions of others, often with the common objection, "who are you to force YOUR morality on me!" At best, subjective morality informs a person of how they believe people should treat others, but it cannot inform a person of how they actually 'should' treat others!

Subjective Moral Opinion Cannot Explain Guilt

"How often we make excuses for our actions! The same actions that the subjective moralist claims cannot be objectively wrong, he attempts to justify to themselves and to others. This strongly indicates that at least some form of guilt is felt; one does not justify moral actions. Subjective morality cannot provide a sound explanation for guilt. Occasionally, when my oldest daughter was a toddler, she would put herself in timeout when she felt that she had done something wrong. She tearfully walked to the corner, although she had broken no rule, and neither my wife nor I had any intention of disciplining her.

"One day when this had happened, she looked over at me and asked, "May I get out of timeout now?"

I replied, "Honey... I didn't put you there! YOU put yourself there."

"In a world where morality is *not* objective, subjective moral opinion is a lot like my daughter's self-imposed timeout. With no higher authority to tell us to behave, or else "sit in the corner", and no moral facts (no objective standard on those facts) by which to judge our actions, we *'make up our own rules'* (Or we actually make up our own God and become a law unto ourselves, so-to-speak).

"Then we behave as if they were binding (Even more illogical, is we often act as if our moral opinions should be binding on others!). When we fail to live up to the rules we've created, we "put ourselves in timeout" with feelings of guilt and shame. And then we turn and ask, "Can we get out of timeout now?", ... and are answered with silence." [325]

End of Excerpts from Mr. Lewis's essay for Cross-Examined

This certainly isn't an exhaustive discussion on the topic of 'Objective and Subjective Morality' standards. I just wanted to stir the dust up a little, so that your *'consciousness is raised'* to consider where good, right, wrong, and morality come from, especially if you're an atheist and innately feel it.

Here's an example that we can apply this standard to. Let's ask ourselves, "Is a particular religions' *interpretation* of the Bible the *'objective standard'* for truth?" Christians say the authority for all truth comes from the Bible *itself*, but what they are actually saying is that the *objective standard for all truth* is *their interpretation* of the words that men said millennia ago, and that were recorded onto papyri scrolls, and later translated by religious scribes into Greek and after that into Old English. And these multiple small books (66) were then combined into one large book that is now called the Holy Bible.

The Bible, which the Christians claim is the inerrant word of God, is in fact just their interpretation of what they say the original, multiple authors said and meant. And so, this *organizational interpretation of the translated and re-transcribed words of the apostles and prophets past,* is, in fact, what they are declaring to be the inerrant, and *objective standard for all truth.* ... Their individual interpretation of the Bible, and what they say these writers meant when they spoke and wrote down their words, 'that' is what they're claiming to be inerrant, meaning without errors.

My perspective on this question is that the objective standard for all truth is found in God Himself. The question then becomes, "How do we determine what is God's untouched word, and how does it come to us, His children, perfectly? Is it from mistranslated scripture? Is it from living prophets? How does one know what is God's perfect word, and has He stopped giving it to us, or has God continued to speak to His children today through prophets? Does He need to speak to us in our Day?" I certainly believe we need Him to speak to us, especially in today's world in commotion and conflicting voices.

"Is objective morality from God?" or "Is subjective morality just something that is born out of social consensus? Does it even matter? If it does, why does it matter?" If God cannot breathe out new revelation today, as He did in times of old, as Christians claim He no longer does, then this *interpreted word of God* by multiple men, which Christians say is now complete and inerrant, for me, makes God dead to us all.

The pattern of revelation is God speaking and revealing Himself to His prophets, who then in turn teach what God revealed to them, to His children. This pattern even includes God answering our individual prayers. This is just one type of revelation that He gives to us individually. When God speaks to His living prophets it is for His children, collectively speaking. I declare that God is not dead, nor is He dead 'to' us. God, our Heavenly Father, loves us, and hears and answers our prayers, and ... He has living prophets to whom He speaks His will for us today, just as He has done throughout the whole of history.

Men's interpretation of Gods' written words alone, is most certainly a *subjective standard* that I define as the *arm of the flesh*. Such a subjective standard breeds chaos. One only needs to look at the various religions and Christian denominations we see today, each denomination having its own interpretation of the Bible to differentiate them from other denominations; each declaring their interpretation of the Bible as the inerrant word of God. Their *differing interpretation* is the reason they chose to break away from their origins. This is just one of the many fruits of apostasy that leads to this kind of religious chaos, religious chaos being another definition of apostasy. Apostasy is born out of subjective opinions, or subjective interpretations of the Bible. These subjective interpretations of God's word are the very root of the religious chaos we find in religion today. It exists throughout the entire world and will continue to grow until Christ comes and reveals pure truth once again.

Until then, God will continue to speak to His children through His living prophets (Through the principle and power of revelation, which has been God's revelatory pattern since Adam was taught by one of God's angels after leaving the garden of Eden). God has provided a plethora of witnesses who testify of His truth. As members of the Church of Jesus Christ of Latter-Day Saints, we enjoy the witness of the KJV of the Bible, including the many corrected translations that the prophet Joseph Smith received by revelation before his life was cut short by an angry mob on June 27th, 1844.

We also enjoy the witness of additional scriptures – the Book of Mormon, the Doctrine & Covenants, and the Pearl of Great Price – called the Standard Works. Each of these books of scripture are the revelatory work of prophets who testified of God's existence and the pure gospel He revealed to them. Each book of scripture is for our learning and good. Jesus said:

II Corinthians 13:1

1 This *is* the third *time* I am coming to you. In the mouth of two or three witnesses shall every word be established.

Matthew 18:15-16

15 Moreover if thy brother shall trespass against thee, go and tell him his fault between thee and him alone: if he shall hear thee, thou hast gained thy brother.

16 But if he will not hear *thee, then* take with thee one or two more, that in the mouth of two or three witnesses every word may be established.

This principle of "Out of the mouth of two or three witnesses is every word established", provides an 'objective standard' for truth because it is given directly from His own mouth to His living oracles, His prophets, which gospel is then ratified by the Holy Ghost to our hearts that it is true. God and His revelatory word become a solid, unshakeable foundation, a 'standard bulwark' upon which we're commanded to build our lives and spiritual houses, even the rock-solid foundation of Jesus and *His revelation* to His prophets. This principle of revelation was to be the foundation upon which His Church and gospel was to be built, so that we could enjoy safety and security. Here's that conversation:

Matthew 16:17-18

13 When Jesus came into the coasts of Cæsarea Philippi, he asked his disciples, saying, "Whom do men say that I, the Son of man am (The Son of the 'Man of Holiness')?"

14 And they said, Some *say that thou art* John the Baptist: some, Elias; and others, Jeremias, or one of the prophets.

15 He saith unto them, But whom say ye that I am?

16 And Simon Peter answered and said, Thou art the Christ, the Son of the Living God.

17 And Jesus answered and said unto him (Peter, His chief apostle and prophet), Blessed art thou, Simon Bar-jona: for 'flesh and blood' hath not revealed *it* unto thee, but my Father which is in heaven.

18 And I say also unto thee, That thou art Peter, and upon *this rock* (The Rock of Jesus and His Revelation by way of the Holy Ghost revealing His word to His prophets) I will build my church; and the gates of hell shall not prevail against '*it*' (Not 'prevail against *you* Peter, or against a mortal man, or 'the arm of the flesh', etc.).

Man's *interpretations* of past scripture, or the words of other men, etc. hath NOT revealed it. The objective standard is from God Himself, our Father which is in Heaven, speaking to Jesus who then speaks to His prophets by way of the Holy Ghost, even the spirit of prophesy, the testimony of Jesus. It is not mortal man's interpretations; it is not flesh and blood's interpretations. It is God's own words.

Like I made note here, Christ's church surely wasn't to be built on the man of flesh and bones named Peter, a fallible, imperfect man like the rest of us, though he was a holy man. Nor was it on the human religious leaders that followed Peter, each of whom were flawed, fallible men; especially those men who used priestcraft to gain power over their congregants. Once those who served under Peter's leadership – Paul and the rest of the apostles – were all killed off or died after Jesus' ascension (except for John the Beloved), the keys of the priesthood, Christ's authority, ceased. This resulted in the true and living Church that Jesus set up, to flee into 'the wilderness' (A metaphor for apostasy):

Revelations 12: 6, 14

6 And the woman (The true Church and Bride) fled into the wilderness, where she hath a place prepared of God, that they should feed her there a thousand two hundred *and* threescore days (JST said Years instead of Days).

14 And to the woman were given two wings of a great eagle, that she might fly into the wilderness, into her place, where she is nourished for a time, and times, and half a time, from the face of the serpent.

The woman fleeing into the wilderness is symbolic of the ancient Church being driven into the wilderness by Satan, which began the Great Apostasy, where the authority of the priesthood was taken from the earth following the deaths of Jesus Christ and His apostles. The religious leaders serving the seven churches or congregations established at the time of Paul and the early apostles, also died off and were replaced over-and-over again with flawed men, leading without a '*prophet head*' receiving revelation for the entire Church. In time the result was men, who were without direct authority, keys, or the spirit of revelation, called other men to lead the Church, so that the doctrine Jesus taught soon became diluted and corrupted as the years went by. Apostasy soon gave way to the false doctrine that there was no longer a need for revelation nor for prophets or apostles to lead the Church, which doctrine took away the Church's foundational rock upon which Christ's original Church was built. No longer was the Church firmly fixed on Jesus and His rock of revelation, as well as prophets and apostles.

The grand question for today's truth seeker is, "What or who is the objective standard for all truth today?" If we are to experience peace and happiness in this life and enjoy joy in the world to come, where do we find God's objective standard? It is my belief and perspective, as a member of the Church of Jesus Christ of Latter-Day Saints, that the objective standard for all truth is the *collective witness* of the multiple witnesses that God Himself has restored in this, the last dispensation, starting with His prophets and apostles. The following witnesses are affirmed through the great testator The Holy Ghost.

First, is the witness of God Himself, as recorded in the Standard Works. Second is the witness of the Testator, the Holy Ghost, the Spirit of the Lord, even the Light of Christ. Third is God's commandments having been written on our hearts, even our conscience convicting us of the truth. Fourth is the witness of God's prophets, past and present, each having received God's direction through the principle and spirit of prophecy and revelation, which power of revelation can be and is affirmed by the Holy Ghost to anyone wanting to know God exists. The Holy Ghost testifies to one's heart and mind that God Himself has called each of His prophets to their holy calling where they receive His secrets:

Amos 3:7

7 Surely the Lord GOD will do nothing but he revealeth his secret unto his servants the prophets. His revealed secrets.

The Mysteries of Godliness become the record of His words, written by holy men when moved upon by the power of the Holy Ghost, and then witnessed and confirmed to its readers or listeners by that same Spirit of the Holy Ghost speaking to our own spirit, even Spirit to spirit. The Holy Ghost's role is to testify of the truthfulness of Gods' word directly to our *spirit*.

There's nothing more powerful as the Holy Ghost testifying to our individual spirit selves that the word God has revealed to His prophets, who then give them to us, they being affirmed by the power of the Holy Ghost directly upon our spirit's heart. Here's what the Lord said about this affirmation:

Doctrine & Covenants 68:3-4

3 And this is the ensample unto them, that they shall speak as they are moved upon by the Holy Ghost.

4 And whatsoever they shall speak when moved upon by the Holy Ghost shall be scripture, shall be the will of the Lord, shall be the mind of the Lord, shall be the word of the Lord, shall be the voice of the Lord, and the power of God unto salvation.

The objective standard, therefore, for all truth, is God Himself revealing His words by the Holy Ghost, who is that member of the Godhead that bares record by writing them upon our hearts. God's words are given to us by way of revelation to His holy prophets whom God calls to this holy calling for our learning and correction. That is why I have referred to The Holy Ghost by the title of *The Testator*. Only when the prophets receive God's words, and then writes them down when moved upon by the Holy Ghost, do they become scripture for us living in that Day and time. Opinions do not qualify as scripture, even when the opinions are expressed by living prophets. Only when they say "Thus sayeth the Lord".

When men, having misunderstood the printed word of God, goes on to mistranslate it, or even intentionally alter the meaning of those written words from their original purity, do those words cease to be *true* scripture. The mistranslating of God's words over thousands of years by scribes, etc., is the main reason that we, as Latter-Day Saints, take the stance that "We believe the Bible to be the word of God *as far as it is translated correctly."

For me, God Himself, and His word given to His living prophets, is the objective standard and source of truth that we are to live by. Revelation from God, I believe, is the objective standard. It is not the interpretations of scripture made by a group of men or women who think they know what God's past apostles and prophets meant when they wrote their words down so long ago. It is not through man's process of intellectualizing and philosophical prowess that truth comes. It is not by the arm of the flesh.

As I have said, the Bible, in my opinion, is not the *inerrant* word of God as most Christians claim. It has multiple mistranslations, along with some intended errors that appear intermittently throughout its text. These intended errors are due to the frailties and weaknesses of men. The Bible alone, with its mistranslations and errors, therefore, cannot be inerrant and the objective standard of truth. Only God Himself and His words given to His living prophets, are the perfect, objective standard of all truth.

Please do not misunderstand what I am saying here about the Bible. I love the Bible. I truly do. It contains the gospel of Jesus Christ and is therefore a witness and testament of the central figure and corner stone in God's Plan of Happiness. The second witness or Testament of Jesus Christ is the Book of Mormon, and the third Witness and Testament of Jesus Christ is still to come. This third special record or witness of Jesus Christ is the record by the prophets who have lived amongst the Lost Ten Tribes, as foretold in latter-day scripture. Here's what the prophet Nephi said about this third witness record:

II Nephi 29:13

13 And it shall come to pass that the Jews shall have the words of the Nephites (The Book of Mormon), and the Nephites shall have the words of the Jews (The Bible); and the Nephites and the Jews shall have the words of the lost tribes of Israel (The third witness of Jesus Christ): and the lost tribes of Israel shall have the words of the Nephites and the Jews.

I will speak on this third witness a little later when Richard speaks of scripture. The day when we have this third witness of Jesus Christ will be a glorious day indeed. The next and final proof of Aquinas is – "The Theological argument".

5   The Teleological Argument (Or the Argument from Design)

The 5th and last argument put forth by Aquinas that Richard addresses in his book *The God Delusion*, is Aquinas' suggested proof that most things in the world look as though they have been *intelligently designed*, therefore there must have been an Intelligent Designer. Richard says that "a *mature* Darwin came forward" (In 1859) with what Richard calls "a devastating *rout* of popular belief by clever reasoning by Charles Darwin's destruction of the argument from design." [326]

Let me inject something here; a statement made by Darwin in a letter to John Fordyce back in May of 1879. Darwin said: *"In my most extreme fluctuations I have never been an atheist in the sense of denying the existence of a God."* It can be found in *"Darwin Correspondence Project Letter no. 12041).* Next, Richard gives his own opinion as though it is a fact, stating: "It is no longer true to say that nothing that we know looks designed unless it is designed. Evolution *by natural selection* produces an excellent simulation (or illusion) of design, mounting prodigious heights of complexity and elegance." [327]

Like the comments I shared earlier by Professor Stephen Meyers, so much has been discovered since the so-called *mature* Darwin's Day. These incredible discoveries have since brought Intelligent Design to the forefront. Two of the many discoveries are *Fine-tuning* and *DNA with Digital Code*, (Or what is referred to as *The Complexity of Life*).

These discoveries are not what anyone would expect from blind, unguided, mindless, unintended electrically charged neuronal processes, each bouncing around within the hardware called the wet brain, each having no predetermined course. It being the process that Richard refers to as "the evolutionary *natural selection* process".

I won't belabor this point by restating everything Professor Meyer said in the '5 Video Series on Science and God', as I am pretty sure that if you, my readers, took me up on my invitation to watch these videos, his statements are ringing in your ears even as you're reading this, especially when you read what Richard said about Design. Richard's arguments relating to Design are very much outdated when it comes to current scientific data. From what I have read and what I have watched, I certainly think so anyway. I will leave this subtitle for now because we will be coming back to the topics related to Intelligent Design in the up-coming chapter, chapter 4. So, let's move on to the next subtitle which covers *a Priori* and *a Posteriori* arguments – "The Ontological Argument and Other A Priori Arguments".

The ontological argument and other *a priori* arguments

Richard says, "This argument for God's existence falls into two main categories, the *a priori* and the *a posteriori* categories. Aquinas' arguments are *a priori* arguments because they rely upon inspection of the world." [328]

"The most famous of the *a priori* arguments, is the *ontological argument* proposed by St. Anselm of Canterbury in 1078 and restated in different forms by numerous philosophers ever since." [329]

Here's what my understanding of the *ontological argument* is and what it means to me in simple terms (Only because I can mentally digest *simple* far more easily than I can digest *sophisticated*). The ontological argument lies in the fact that we can imagine a perfect being, therefore there must be a God. The idea is that existing makes a good thing better than one that's only imaginary. (Or existence is more perfect than non-existence, and therefore God's existence is more perfect than His non-existence).

William Lane, one of America's renown analytic philosophers who is a Christian apologist, an author, and a Wesleyan theologian who holds the view of Molinism (Molinism is named after 16th-century Spanish Jesuit priest and Roman Catholic theologian Luis de Molina. His thesis says that God has middle knowledge. It seeks to reconcile the apparent tension of divine providence and human free will) and neo-Apollinarianism (A Christological heresy proposed by Apollinaris of Laodicea who died in 390 A.D.) which argues that Jesus had a human body and sensitive human soul, but He had a *divine mind* and not a human, rational mind.

The *Divine Logos* in other words, which takes the place of the latter (Divine Logos is defined as 'a universal divine reason', immanent in nature, yet transcending all oppositions and imperfections in the cosmos and humanity. It's an eternal and unchanging truth present from the time of creation, available to every individual who seeks it. This is very much like my version of the Incomprehensible IT that fills the immensity of space, which is in and through all things).

Speaking of Kalam Cosmology, Mr. Lane says: "The *kalam* cosmological argument is an exercise in positive apologetics aimed at proving that God exists. It may be formulated as follows:

1. Whatever *begins* to exist has a cause.
2. The universe *began* to exist.
3. Therefore, the universe has a cause.

Lane continues:

"Conceptual analysis of what it is to be the cause of the universe will recover several of the principal attributes of God, so that the cause takes on the character of a personal Creator of the universe." [330]

Thus far I've agreed with Richard's arguments against Aquinas' first three proofs. I found them to be lacking in substance. However, I agreed with Aquinas' fourth proof and this ontological argument, or the *Kalam Cosmological Argument*, which is basically the same as Aquinas' 5th proof. It too is an argument I actually agree with. Mr. Lane's attempt to explain the unexplainable, such as the perfections and greatness of God, as well as Aquinas' attempt to explain the unexplainable, come pretty close to describing what I call the Light of Christ, the Spirit of God, or the Divine Logos. The only reason I can come up as to why Richard decided to take seven pages to argue against this 5th proof and the Ontological Argument, is that Richard seems to be bent on removing any traces of any kind that might add to the proof of God's existence, even if the evidence offered by the other side is inconclusive. Either way, Richard has failed, thus far, to add any modicum of proof, of any kind, that supports his argument that God does not exist. That said, let's go on to the next subtitle which is – "The Argument from Beauty".

THE ARGUMENT FROM BEAUTY

Simply put, Richard uses the following question to describe this strand of Aquinas arguments in support of the existence of God called *beauty*. Here's Richard's question that he poses to Aquinas' second argument from his list of five proofs:

"How do you account for Shakespeare then?" [331]

Richard counters Aquinas' *a priori* argument by saying, "They (Meaning beautiful works such as music, art, architecture, etc.), are sublime if God is there and they are sublime if He isn't. They (In and of themselves) do not prove the existence of God; they prove the existence of Beethoven and of Shakespeare." [332]

Wouldn't Beethoven and Shakespeare be considered the *Intelligent Designer* of their beautiful works of music, literature, and art? I think that's something to really think about, because to my mind they are the creator-designers of their works of beauty, just as God is the creator-designer of His works of beauty, except God's works of beauty are incomprehensibly, and perfectly beautiful. Richard goes on to say, "... there is an additional point I might have made, and which needs to be made whenever religion is given credit for, let's say, the Sistine Chapel or Raphael's Annunciation. Even great artists must earn a living, and they will take commissions where they are to be had. I have no reason to doubt that Raphael and Michelangelo were Christians – It is pretty much the only option in their time – but the fact is almost incidental. If Michelangelo had been commissioned by the giant 'Museum of Science' to paint *its* ceilings, mightn't he have produced something at least as inspirational as the Sistine Chapel?" [333]

The bottom line for Richard, as he argues against the argument of beauty, is "If there's a logical argument linking the existence of great art to the existence of God it's not spelled out by its proponents. It's simply assumed to be self-evident which it most certainly is not." [334]

As I considered Richard's thoughts on this subtitle, I must say again, that it is simply his opinion. I read nothing that proves or disproves God's existence in the details of Richard's arguments he gives against beauty being proof God exists. However, that being said, I would like to give my perspective on his arguments, for what it's worth, and offer what I believe links the existence of God to such things as great art, great music, great inventions, etc. Their source is the *intelligence* and *divine character* traits of their creator-designers, and their *inherent power to create* comes from *their* Creator, even God, their Heavenly Father. It is my belief that God, and more particularly his Spirit, and the Holy Ghost using the Light of Christ, directs all men's inspiration for good, and it is Satan's spirit or lack of light and truth that directs men's inspiration for darkness and evil. One need only review, for example, what goes on in the minds of serial killers and serial rapists, as they go about their plot to murder and rape their victims, and once they do, they immediately begin to complete their plotted actions by trying to hide their crimes, which is often a herculean effort of trying to cover them up, which includes even more crimes.

These deviants think they're so smart and will get away with it. The sad fact is that many do. They have such evil, evil, evil thoughts that were repeatedly mapped onto their neuropathways, having reviewed such evil thoughts over and over again, which ultimately set in motion their horrendous action and behavior. Gods' light that permeates throughout the universe (I call it the 'Incomprehensible It'), is available to all His children to make the choice to attune to it (Using our receiver within all of us). We can turn the *mental and spiritual dials* in our own mind and heart, so-to-speak, to align our mind to be in tune with the power of the spirit, the Incomprehensible It is transmitting, and when we do, we're able to attract or receive this *light of truth and beauty* right into our heart and mind.

But alas, there is *the opposition in all things that affects everything throughout the universe.* The source of this opposition is the spirit of Satan, who is the father of lies. There is Light and Darkness; Good and Evil; and Love and Hate. We can either choose to attune our minds and hearts to light or choose to attune our minds to darkness. We can choose love or choose hate; choose good or choose evil. If we choose the influence of Satan's spirit, its evil influence will generate evil thoughts and those thoughts will be mapped onto our minds so that they ultimately manifest themselves by us choosing to create or produce works of evil such as murder, rape, pedophilia, carnal music, and pornography, sins born of these sensual thoughts.

This 'opposition in all things' is a choice between beautiful or ugly. Beautiful music, or ugly music; beautiful art or ugly art, etc. We either create works that are full of light, inspirational works, or ugly works that are full of darkness, crudeness, and carnality manifesting sensuality and devilishness. One only needs to read the lyrics of dark music to know what I am talking about. Tupac Shakur, the Notorious B.I.G., Disturbed, and Marilyn Manson are just a few examples of *Dark Music creators*. *X Rated* and *R Rated* movies visually reflect the absolute baseness of how low men and women can degrade themselves. Movies like 'Beyond the Valley of the Dolls', 'The Evil Dead', 'Female Trouble', and thousands more adult movies like them, could be added to the list of carnality, born from the god of pleasure, that god being Satan. Each of these movies provide a mirror into the minds of designing men and women who chose to produce, promote, and even act out this filth, or should I say *perform* the evil found in so-called adult entertainment.

The fact that there are some states that have legalized *whore houses*, is strong evidence that, for me, proves the spirit of Satan is alive and well. Each of us are choosing which of these two opposing forces we are going to listen to and follow every day of our lives. Are we choosing the spirit of God, and life, or are we choosing the spirit of Satan, and death.

With regards to the sins that result from people choosing to follow Satan's voice, I choose to condemn the sin or sins, and not condemn the person. Each of us are children of God who's given each of us the gift of free will, the right to choose what we desire most in our lives – either Life or Death. My point here, is that Dark is Dark, and Light is Light. There are just *two spirit-influencing voices* at play in the world; two opposing spirits that are at work, influencing all of mankind – Satan's spirit of anti-Christ and God's Spirit of Light and Truth, even the Light of Christ. We are left to choose whom we'll follow.

I heard it said that you'll know the world is ready for our Lord's 2nd coming when the *Cycle of Sin* has gone full circle. Let me explain. The cycle begins with a society being abundantly blessed because of its general obedience to God's laws. Then that society begins to become prideful due to their accomplishments that came as a result of their obedience. But soon they get prideful and begin to tout their prosperity by how they dress, where they live, so that they begin to treat people of lessor circumstances with disrespect. From there, the society starts thinking they, and they alone, achieved their prosperity, and pride begins to manifest itself and they start rebelling against God's moral law by becoming lax in keeping His Law of Chastity, which is at the very heart of all of God's laws.

Soon, the vast majority of this society has accepted fornication and adultery as no big deal. This attitude of rebellion quickly moves to a full acceptance of immorality. The society continues this downward spiral by promoting homosexuality as simply another choice of lifestyle. The next sign that's evidence that this society has become fully ripened and nearing its complete destruction, is the bottoming out of the Cycle of Sin where men and women willfully commit wanton murder and disregard the Law of Chastity entirely. The Cycle of Sin is complete when the society makes child sacrifice, such as abortion, acceptable. And then the Cycle of Sin has fully ripened when Satan has led society to openly commit the heinous act of depravity, Bestiality.

In past societies where this Cycle of Sin resulted in the society's complete destruction, as I mentioned earlier in my book, was the stage where the society's citizens openly committed human sacrifice, and more specifically child sacrifice, which was a manifestation that the society's degree of depravity and wickedness had reached its lowest state of carnality. This is called ripening for destruction. This is when God destroys them. Examples of such societies were people living before the Great Flood; the people of Sodom and Gomorrah; the people living in the land of Canaan when Joshua and the Israelites cleaned house, so-to-speak. The Lord God Jehovah told Joshua to take back the land of their inheritance, and that is what he and the Israelites did.

Another example of a people ripened for destruction was the Nephites in ancient America. God used their enemies the Lamanites, to destroy them from off the face of the land. They too had completed the Cycle of Sin and so God used the Lamanites to wipe them off the fact of the land because of their extreme wickeness.

There are many more examples throughout history that I could use to show what happens to societies who reach the end of the Cycle of Sin. I think we can agree that a large percentage of the worlds' past societies have certainly made fornication acceptable, saying "Live and let live. Who cares what someone does in the privacy of their bedrooms, as consenting adults?" According to the American Association for Marriage and Family Therapy, as of 2018, around 45% of married couples in the United States have extramarital affairs (Adultery). Data from U.S. crime reports suggest that about 1 in 5 homicide victims are killed by an intimate partner. The reports also found that over half of female homicide victims in the U.S. are killed by a current or former male intimate partner. [335]

To me, this is proof that Satan's goal is to move his victims through this *Cycle of Sin* as fast as he can, so that he can get as many of God's children to debase themselves to the point where they are motivated to commit the ultimate sin, the sin of murder, which is unforgivable. Suffice it to say, adultery and murder are major contributors to the demise that's taking place in our country today, and if we don't change things soon, which is what repentance is all about (Changing our behavior for the better), we will soon be ripened for destruction. It appears we won't stop because the scriptures say the earths' destruction *by fire* will occur at Christ's 2nd coming. The scriptures also say that there will be no fourth or fifth chance to avoid this cleansing of the earth.

An article found on *Health24* which can be found on the internet, has the title of "Bestiality is much more common than you may think". We all have heard of people taking part in the unthinkable act of bestiality (For those who've never heard of it, it is having sex with animals). One statement from the article says, and I quote:

"Few academic institutions have conducted serious studies on the matter, making it difficult to find strong estimates for the prevalence today. One recent paper (Scientific Health) which sought to find a link between sex with animals and penile cancer has offered a little insight, however. The study, which took place in Brazil and was published in the *Journal of Sexual Medicine*, found a 34% prevalence of bestiality amongst men, most of whom were from rural backgrounds, as well as determining that it was a risk factor for penile cancer." [336]

End quote

It appears that this horrendous sexual practice is becoming increasingly accepted in some societies (Even here in America), pushing societies to the point where they have come full circle in the Cycle of Sin, just as past societies that ultimately were destroyed.

You might be saying, "At least we're not performing *child sacrifice* in America." Well, I would beg to differ with that statement. More than 1-million babies are offered up as sacrifices, killed on the '*alter of convenience*' every single year in America alone. I am not sure which is worse, setting a baby on a scalding hot pair of brazen arms of the false God called Moloch, or having a doctor crush the head of a baby who is just 3 to 4 weeks in development inside its mother's womb, as well as ripping off its tiny arms and legs, and then sucking the rest of the little body out of the safety of that supposedly protective home in which it was residing, only to have all its parts laid out on a cold tray to make sure the doctor (or who I call the 'priest of abortion') got every last piece of this so-called *cluster of cells*. Certainly, child sacrifice falls into the category of outrageous evil, driven by the spirit of Satan who has been influencing women for decades to abort their babies. The following is an article I found titled, "The True History of Moloch, The Ancient God of Child Sacrifice". Here's an excerpt from this article. You, my readers, tell me which of these two crimes of child sacrifice is worse:

"Condemned by biblical prophets and Roman senators alike, few pagan deities were as reviled as Moloch, a pagan god whose bronze body was a furnace used for sacrificing children. Child sacrifice is non-existent today (Of course, we know otherwise)—but that hasn't always been the case. In ancient times, it was commonly associated with the excuse and false belief of the people who hoped for greater fertility, for either a person or the land, but one cult stands out from all the rest: the cult of Moloch, the *Canaanite* god of child sacrifice." [337]

End quote

I disagree with this claim that *child sacrifice* is non-existent today. Like I just said, millions of babies are offered upon the '*alter of the god of convenience*'. A god whose substance is that of an idol, an idol of selfishness, of shame, and of an *evil ideology*. I agree that the method for killing these sacrificial lambs (tiny pre-birth babies) may be different than the method used by the ancients, but the result, is exactly the same – a horrific and merciless death of little children!

Keep in mind that a fetus's heart *starts to beat on its own* between three to four weeks, pumping its own blood throughout the entirety of its tiny body. Some doctors even say it starts beating at three weeks and one day. To me, this is a life. What do you, my readers, think it is? With that image of this tiny humans' heart beating in your mind, imagine now today's sacrificial priest (The abortion doctor) entering into the sacrificial alter room, dressed in a white robe, with the mother ready to willingly offer up her unborn baby to him, requiring him to intrude into the sanctity of that baby's home (the mothers' womb) with his instruments of death in hand, ready to crush its tiny head, killing it instantly, and then tearing off its arms and legs, often while the mother weeps as she wonders if she's doing the right thing. It's all done in the privacy of the doctors' *chamber of horrors*.

I saw a series of short video vignettes of brand-new father's being handed their first child just after its birth. All of them cried. They were so moved by the sacredness of their having become a father, yet, young women at the tender age of 18 to 25 (some even younger), who haven't had this experience, are able to say, without blinking an eye, that if the baby is still in a mothers' womb as late as nine months, those babies, who could survive out of that mother's womb months earlier, aren't a human baby '*yet*', and therefore falls within the '*I have the right over my own body*' claim of authority. This certainly is not *scientific data* speaking. It is Satan, who's convinced these women that *life* isn't more sacred than a woman's right to control her own body. This *selfish ideology* disregards the right-to-life of these unborn babies entirely.

Imagine, once again, this *pagan practice of child sacrifice* (A quasi-sacrificial procedure) where the sacrificial priest (the paganistic abortion doctor) lays out each piece of the baby's body onto a medical tray so that he can make sure he's retrieved every single piece of the baby's body from within the mothers' womb, as a *safety precaution* for the mother! What about the baby's safety? This sacrificial slaughter is even worse than killing a live baby by placing its tiny body onto the hot, brazen arms of the pagan god-Idol Moloch, where it instantly sizzles to death, all the while the father and mother are listening to multiple drums getting louder and louder, in order to conceal the screams of their tiny sacrificial lamb – their innocent baby.

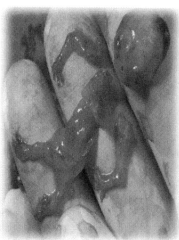

Both types of sacrifices are unimaginable and the cruelest of crimes against humanity. Let me continue sharing a few more excerpts from the "The True History of Moloch, The Ancient God of Child Sacrifice" article, and I quote: "The cult of Moloch — who is also called Molech — is said to have boiled children alive in the bowels of a big, bronze statue with the body of a man and the head of a bull. Offerings, … at least according to the Hebrew Bible, were to be reaped through either fire or war — and devotees can still be found today. The idol Moloch with seven chambers or chapels. It was believed these statues had seven chambers, one of which was reserved for child-sacrifices."

"The religion of the Canaanites was a hodgepodge of ancient Semitic faiths (Apostate ones of course), practiced by the people of the Levant region from at least the early Bronze Age. The cult of Moloch was still active into the first few centuries of the Common Era. Moloch's name was derived from the Hebrew word *mlk*, which usually stands for Melek, or "king." As this is vocalized as Molek in the Masoretic text — the authoritative text for Rabbinic Judaism — the pronunciation has become its traditional name.

"The Masoretic text dates to the Middle Ages but references to a *Molock* appear in Ancient Greek translations of old Judaic texts as well. The distinction dates back to the Second Temple period between 516 B.C. and 70 C.E. — when the Second Temple of Jerusalem stood prior to its destruction by the Romans.

"Moloch's anthropomorphized bull figure was typically pictured in Rabbinic Judaic texts as a bronze statue internally heated by a fire. It was inside this construct that priests *or parents* placed their children to be consumed by fire as a sacrificial offering (I've tried to imagine in my mind what went through the parents' mind, especially the mothers, as she came to the priests to offer her precious, innocent little newborn baby to be burned, boiled, or sizzled alive?

(What kind of grotesque human being, especially the mother, could do such a thing? Yet, the picture of millions of mother's comes to my mind today, where they actually do a similar kind of heinous offering – the sacrifice I'm calling *abortion*). Ancient Greek and Roman authors wrote tales of this sacrificial practice, with the earliest being stories of child sacrifices to Baal — or Master — Hammon in Carthage. He was their chief god, responsible for the weather and fertile agriculture. In the Bible, children were sacrificed in a *Tophet*, a shrine reserved for child sacrifice, outside of Jerusalem to Moloch's satisfaction. While certainly well-documented in religious texts, the historical and archaeological communities still debate Moloch's identity and just how active its cult was.

"Medieval French rabbi Schlomo Yitzchaki, otherwise known as Rashi, wrote an extensive commentary on the Talmud in the 12th century. His analysis of Book of Jeremiah 7:31 painted a vivid picture of the sacraments of Moloch's worship as related in the Hebrew texts:

"Topheth is Moloch, which was made of brass; and they heated him from his lower parts; and his hands being stretched out, and made hot, they put the child between his hands, and it was burnt; when it vehemently cried out; but the priests beat a drum, that the father might not hear the voice of his son, and his heart might not be moved."

"Archaeological excavations in the 1920's then discovered primary evidence of *child sacrifice* in the region and researchers also found the term *MLK* inscribed on numerous artifacts. *Child sacrifice* in Carthage, meanwhile, appears to have been common enough that it even contained a sacred grove and a temple dedicated to its cult of Baal Hammon.

"Though the Biblical account describes children being "passed through the fire" to Moloch in a Tophet, a ritual site of sacrifice in ancient Judaism, Hebrew prophets are universal in their condemnation of the practice — suggesting that such sacrifices might have been made to the Abrahamic God by some *cult* (Another manifestation of apostasy) but were condemned and cast out of the orthodox faith as anathema.

"Scholars also still debate whether or not the Carthaginian practice of *child sacrifice* differed from the cult of Moloch. It's generally understood that Carthage only sacrificed children when it was absolutely necessary — like an especially bad draught — whereas the cult of Moloch was much more regular in their sacrifices.

"Some researchers even argue that these cults didn't sacrifice children at all and that *"passing through the fire"* is a poetic term — a common feature of religious texts — that most likely referred to initiation rites that may have been painful, but not deadly. After all, the Christian term *"born again"* is not meant to be taken literally to mean passing out of your mother's womb a second time, something Jesus points out himself. Complicating matters is that there is every reason to believe these accounts were exaggerated by the Romans to make the Carthaginians appear crueler and more primitive than they were — they were the bitter enemies of Rome, after all. [338]

Here is a picture of stone slabs in the Tophet of Salammbó, which was covered by a vault built in the Roman period. It is one of the Tophets Carthaginians where children were sacrificed.

(See picture of alter on the next page)

End of excerpts from the article regarding Child Sacrifice

Let me give proof of the opposite of the spirit of Satan and it's kind of evil that is working in people's lives. That opposite being the Spirit of God, sometimes called the Spirit of Light and Truth, or The Light of Christ. Its evidence, or its fruit that becomes evidence for God's existence, can be inspected as we review the discoveries made from man's enlightenment over the centuries; discoveries I believe to be part of *Beauty*.

Such discoveries have exploded since the restoration of the fulness of the gospel of Jesus Christ and His Church, the Church of Jesus Christ of Latter-Day Saints in 1830. A plethora of magnificent scientific discoveries have exploded onto the scene, starting at 1830, and they've accelerated faster and faster Since Joseph's Day on up to our Day. When you compare the last 150 to 180 years, to the list of discoveries that were achieved during the eighteen centuries of the Dark Ages, it is mindboggling.

What took centuries and centuries for the minds of scientists living in the 16th and 17th centuries to imagine the kind of *science* that would raise the consciousness of the worlds' brightest minds, is now being imagined at a pace of more than 10 major discoveries every ten years. Over the last 180 years, scientific discoveries we're being brought forth in as little as 25 years or less, and these were major discoveries that literally changed the face of science itself. Here is a timeline of scientific discoveries that have come forth since 1735:

19th century

- 1830 – Nikolai Lobachevsky created Non-Euclidean geometry
- 1831 – Michael Faraday discovers electromagnetic induction
- 1833 – Anselme Payen isolates first enzyme, diastase
- 1837 - Charles Babbage proposes a design for the construction of a Turing complete, general purpose Computer, to be called the Analytical Engine.
- 1838 – Matthias Schleiden: all plants are made of cells
- 1838 – Friedrich Bessel: first successful measure of stellar parallax (to star 61 Cygni
- 1842 – Christian Doppler: Doppler effect
- 1843 – James Prescott Joule: Law of Conservation of energy (First law of thermodynamics), also 1847 – Helmholtz, Conservation of energy
- 1846 – Johann Gottfried Galle and Heinrich Louis d'Arrest: discovery of Neptune

- 1847 - George Boole: publishes *The Mathematical Analysis of Logic*, defining Boolean algebra; refined in his 1854 The Laws of Thought.
- 1848 – Lord Kelvin: absolute zero
- 1856 - Robert Forester Mushet develops a process for the decarbonisation, and recarbonisation of iron, thorough the addition of a calculated quantity of spiegeleisen, to produce cheap, consistently high quality steel.
- 1858 – Rudolf Virchow: cells can only arise from pre-existing cells
- 1859 – Charles Darwin and Alfred Wallace: Theory of evolution by natural selection
- 1861 – Louis Pasteur: Germ theory
- 1861 – John Tyndall: Experiments in Radiant Energy that reinforced the Greenhouse Effect
- 1864 – James Clerk Maxwell: Theory of electromagnetism
- 1865 – Gregor Mendel: Mendel's laws of inheritance, basis for genetics
- 1865 – Rudolf Clausius: Definition of entropy
- 1868 - Robert Forester Mushet discovers alloying steel with tungsten produces a harder, more durable alloy.
- 1869 – Dmitri Mendeleev: Periodic table
- 1871 – Lord Rayleigh: Diffuse sky radiation (Rayleigh scattering) explains why sky appears blue
- 1873 – Johannes Diderik van der Waals: was one of the first to postulate an intermolecular force: the van der Waals force.
- 1873 – Frederick Guthrie discovers thermionic emission.
- 1873 – Willoughby Smith discovers photoconductivity.
- 1875 – William Crookes invented the Crookes tube and studied cathode rays
- 1876 – Josiah Willard Gibbs founded chemical thermodynamics, the phase rule
- 1877 – Ludwig Boltzmann: Statistical definition of entropy
- 1880s – John Hopkinson develops Three-phase electrical supplies, mathematically proves how multiple AC dynamos can be connected in parallel, improves permanent magnets, and dynamo efficiency, by the addition of tungsten, and describes how temperature effects magnetism (Hopkinson effect).
- 1880 – Pierre Curie and Jacques Curie: Piezoelectricity
- 1884 – Jacobus Henricus van 't Hoff: discovered the laws of chemical dynamics and osmotic pressure in solutions (in his work "Etudes de dynamique chimique").
- 1887 – Albert A. Michelson and Edward W. Morley: lack of evidence for the aether
- 1888 – Friedrich Reinitzer discovers liquid crystals
- 1892 – Dmitri Ivanovsky discovers viruses
- 1895 – Wilhelm Conrad Röntgen discovers x-rays
- 1896 – Henri Becquerel discovers radioactivity
- 1896 – Svante Arrhenius derives the basic principles of the greenhouse effect
- 1897 – J.J. Thomson discovers the electron in cathode rays
  1898 – J.J. Thomson proposed the plum pudding model of an atom
- 1898 – Martinus Beijerinck: concluded a virus infectious—replicating in the host—and thus not a mere toxin and gave it the name "viru"
- 1898 - Marie Curie discovered radium and polonium

20th Century:

- 1900 – Max Planck: explains the emission spectrum of a black body

- 1905 – Albert Einstein: theory of special relativity, explanation of Brownian motion, and photoelectric effect
- 1906 – Walther Nernst: Third law of thermodynamics
- 1907 – Alfred Bertheim: Arsphenamine, the first modern chemotherapeutic agent
- 1909 – Fritz Haber: Haber Process for industrial production of ammonia
- 1909 – Robert Andrews Millikan: conducts the oil drop experiment and determines the charge on an electron
- 1910 – Williamina Fleming: the first white dwarf, 40 Eridanus B
- 1911 – Ernest Rutherford: Atomic nucleus
- 1911 – Heike Kamerlingh Onnes: Superconductivity
- 1912 – Alfred Wegener: Continental drift
- 1912 – Max von Laue : x-ray diffraction
- 1912 – Vesto Slipher : galactic redshifts
- 1912 – Henrietta Swan Leavitt: Cepheid variable period-luminosity relation
- 1913 – Henry Moseley: defined atomic number
- 1913 – Niels Bohr: Model of the atom
- 1915 – Albert Einstein: theory of general relativity – also David Hilbert
- 1915 – Karl Schwarzschild: discovery of the Schwarzschild radius leading to the identification of black holes
- 1918 – Emmy Noether: Noether's theorem – conditions under which the conservation laws are valid
- 1920 – Arthur Eddington: Stellar nucleosynthesis
- 1922 – Frederick Banting, Charles Best, James Collip, John Macleod: isolation and production of insulin to control diabetes
- 1924 – Wolfgang Pauli: quantum Pauli exclusion principle
- 1924 – Edwin Hubble: the discovery that the Milky Way is just one of many galaxies
- 1925 – Erwin Schrödinger: Schrödinger equation (Quantum mechanics)
- 1925 – Cecilia Payne-Gaposchkin: Discovery of the composition and that hydrogen is the most abundant element in the Universe
- 1927 – Werner Heisenberg: Uncertainty principle (Quantum mechanics)
- 1927 – Georges Lemaître: Theory of the Big Bang
- 1928 – Paul Dirac: Dirac equation (Quantum mechanics)
- 1929 – Edwin Hubble: Hubble's law of the expanding universe
- 1929 – Alexander Fleming: Penicillin, the first beta-lactam antibiotic
- 1929 – Lars Onsager's reciprocal relations, a potential fourth law of thermodynamics
- 1930 – Subrahmanyan Chandrasekhar discovers his eponymous limit of the maximum mass of a white dwarf star
- 1931 – Kurt Gödel: incompleteness theorems prove formal axiomatic systems are incomplete
- 1932 – James Chadwick: Discovery of the neutron
- 1932 – Karl Guthe Jansky discovers the first astronomical radio source, Sagittarius A
- 1932 – Ernest Walton and John Cockcroft: Nuclear fission by proton bombardment
- 1934 – Enrico Fermi: Nuclear fission by neutron irradiation
- 1934 – Clive McCay: Calorie restriction extends the maximum lifespan of another species
- 1938 – Otto Hahn, Lise Meitner and Fritz Strassmann: Nuclear fission of heavy nuclei

- 1938 – Isidor Rabi: Nuclear magnetic resonance
- 1943 – Oswald Avery proves that DNA is the genetic material of the chromosome
- 1945 – Howard Florey Mass production of penicillin
- 1947 – William Shockley, John Bardeen and Walter Brattain invent the first transistor
- 1948 – Claude Elwood Shannon: 'A mathematical theory of communication' a seminal paper in Information theory.
- 1948 – Richard Feynman, Julian Schwinger, Sin-Itiro Tomonaga and Freeman Dyson: Quantum electrodynamics
- 1951 – George Otto Gey propagates first cancer cell line, HeLa
- 1952 – Jonas Salk: developed and tested first polio vaccine
- 1952 – Stanley Miller: demonstrated that the building blocks of life could arise from primeval soup in the conditions present during early earth (Miller-Urey experiment)
- 1952 – Frederick Sanger: demonstrated that proteins are sequences of amino acids
- 1953 – James Watson, Francis Crick, Maurice Wilkins and Rosalind Franklin: helical structure of DNA, basis for molecular biology
- 1957 – Chien Shiung Wu: demonstrated that parity, and thus charge conjugation and time-reversals, are violated for weak interactions
- 1962 – Riccardo Giacconi and his team discover the first cosmic x-ray source, Scorpius X-1
- 1963 – Lawrence Morley, Fred Vine, and Drummond Matthews: Paleomagnetic stripes in ocean crust as evidence of plate tectonics (Vine–Matthews–Morley hypothesis).
- 1964 – Murray Gell-Mann and George Zweig: postulates quarks leading to the standard model
- 1964 – Arno Penzias and Robert Woodrow Wilson: detection of CMBR providing experimental evidence for the Big Bang
- 1965 – Leonard Hayflick: normal cells divide only a certain number of times: the Hayflick limit
- 1967 – Jocelyn Bell Burnell and Antony Hewish discover first pulsar
- 1967 – Vela nuclear test detection satellites discover the first gamma-ray burst
- 1970 - James H. Ellis proposed the possibility of "non-secret encryption", more commonly termed public-key cryptography, a concept that would be implemented by his GCHQ colleague Clifford Cocks in 1973, in what would become known as the RSA algorithm, with key exchange added by a third colleague Malcolm J. Williamson, in 1975.
- 1971 – Place cells in the brain are discovered by John O'Keefe
- 1974 – Russell Alan Hulse and Joseph Hooton Taylor, Jr. discover indirect evidence for gravitational wave radiation in the Hulse–Taylor binary

  1977 – Frederick Sanger sequences the first DNA genome of an organism using Sanger sequencing1980 – Klaus von Klitzing discovered the quantum Hall effect
- 1982 – Donald C. Backer et al. discover the first millisecond pulsar
- 1983 – Kary Mullis invents the polymerase chain reaction, a key discovery in molecular biology
- 1986 – Karl Müller and Johannes Bednorz: Discovery of High-temperature superconductivity
- 1988 – Bart van Wees [nl] and colleagues at TU Deflt and Philips Research discovered the quantized conductance in a two-dimensional electron gas.

- 1992 – Aleksander Wolszczan and Dale Frail observe the first pulsar planets (this was the first confirmed discovery of planets outside the Solar System)
- 1994 – Andrew Wiles proves Fermat's Last Theorem
- 1995 – Michel Mayor and Didier Queloz definitively observe the first extrasolar planet around a main sequence star
- 1995 – Eric Cornell, Carl Wieman and Wolfgang Ketterle attained the first Bose-Einstein Condensate with atomic gases, so called fifth state of matter at an extremely low temperature.
- 1996 – Roslin Institute: Dolly the sheep was cloned.
- 1997 – CDF and DØ experiments at Fermilab: Top quark.
- 1998 – Supernova Cosmology Project and the High-Z Supernova Search Team: discovery of the accelerated expansion of the Universe and dark energy
- 2000 – The Tau neutrino is discovered by the DONUT collaboration

21st Century: *List of years in science § 2000s, and Breakthrough of the Year*

- 2001 – The first draft of the Human Genome Project is published.
- 2003 – Grigori Perelman presents proof of the Poincaré Conjecture.
- 2004 – Andre Geim and Konstantin Novoselov isolated graphene, a monolayer of carbon atoms, and studied its quantum electrical properties.
- 2005 – Grid cells in the brain are discovered by Edvard Moser and May-Britt Moser.
- 2010 – The first self-replicating, synthetic bacterial cells are constructed.
- 2010 – The Neanderthal Genome Project presented preliminary genetic evidence that interbreeding did likely take place and that a small but significant portion of Neanderthal admixture is present in modern non-African populations.
- 2012 – Higgs boson is discovered at CERN (confirmed to 99.999% certainty)
- 2012 – Photonic molecules are discovered at MIT
- 2014 – Exotic hadrons are discovered at the LHCb
- 2016 – The LIGO team detected gravitational waves from a black hole merger
- 2017 – Gravitational wave signal GW170817 was observed by the LIGO/Virgo collaboration. This was the first instance of a gravitational wave event that was observed to have a simultaneous electromagnetic signal when space telescopes like Hubble observed lights coming from the event, thereby marking a significant breakthrough for multi-messenger astronomy.
- 2019 – The first ever image of a black hole was captured, using eight different telescopes taking simultaneous pictures, timed with extremely precise atomic clocks.
- 2020 – NASA and SOFIA (Stratospheric Observatory for Infrared Astronomy) discovered about 12oz of surface water in one of the moon's largest visible craters.
- 2021 – NASA launches the James Webb Telescope.

The significance of these modern-day discoveries, achieved over the past 180 years or so, and more particularly those from the last 25 years, reflect the *enlightenment* given to both men and women who have served, and continue to serve all of us in the natural sciences, each working in their chosen and respected fields of endeavor. These truly are individuals who have the brightest of minds.

The giver of this enlightenment, like I said, is our Heavenly Father. It is very much like the way Tesla described how his discoveries came to him by the power of the Holy Ghost. These gifts of knowledge do come through the 'power and light of God's Spirit', even His 'spirit of revelation and inspiration', which are manifestations given by the Holy Ghost's spirit. This spirit is the light of truth existing in the universe so that the minds of God's children can attune to it and receive these magnificent ideas and gifts of knowledge – even ideas of beauty – all for the betterment of mankind and societies progress. I do not believe in the idea that *the puny arm of the flesh,* with its unguided, unintended, undirected wet brain machine, blindly fires off incredible ideas out of, or from nothing at all, as the evolutionists seem to suggest. The hardware called the wet brain, is not the source of all these "brilliant ideas". I find it ironic that atheist scientists receive these discoveries by the light of light unawares.

These brilliant discoveries come from the gift and the Light of Christ, even its pure intelligence, so that *the mind can attune to this light of knowledge,* which attunement produces information just as Nicola Tesla described the way in which he received his discoveries. Science is defined as 'Knowledge', and so for me, the source of all knowledge, even the entirety of all scientific discoveries and knowledge, comes from this light of truth, and God's super-intelligent Mind is the very source of this light and truth. God's eternal light, this truth and knowledge emanating from the Creator-Designer Himself, whom the world calls God, even our Eternal Parent in Heaven, or what Richard sarcastically calls the "Sky-God". The next arguments' subtitle Richard discusses is – "The argument from personal experience."

THE ARGUMENT FROM PERSONAL EXPERIENCE

Richard is bent on destroying this next theistic argument in-order-to build his case for the probability that God does *not* exist. It is called *"the argument from (against) personal experience"*.

Richard says, "Many people believe in God because they believe they have seen a vision of him – or of an angel or a virgin in blue – with their own eyes. Or he speaks to them inside their heads."

"This argument from *personal experience* is the one that is most convincing to those who claim to have had one. But it is the least convincing to anyone else, and anyone knowledgeable about psychology.

"You say you have experienced God directly? Well, some people have experienced a pink elephant, but that probably doesn't impress you (that's a good one Richard. Ha-ha-ha!). Peter Sutcliffe, the Yorkshire Ripper, distinctly heard the voice of Jesus telling him to kill women, and he was locked up for life.

"Religious experiences are different from the psychotic stories told by the mentally ill, *only* in that the people who claim them are numerous." [339]

Richard then quotes Sam Harris, a fellow atheist, who said, quote:

"We have names for people who have many beliefs for which there is no rational justification. When their beliefs are extremely common, we call them religious; otherwise, they are likely to be called mad; psychotic or delusional.

"Clearly there is sanity in numbers. And yet, it is merely an accident of history that it is considered normal in our society to believe that the Creator of the universe can hear your thoughts, while it is demonstrative of mental illness to believe that he is communicating with you by having the rain tap in Morse Code on your bedroom window. And so, while religious people are *not* generally mad, their core beliefs absolutely are." [340]

End Quote

Richard then says, "Our brains *construct* a continuously updated model: updated by coded pulses chattering along the optic nerve, but *constructed,* nonetheless. Optical illusions are vivid reminders of this." [341]

Next Richard goes into a lengthy explanation of an illusionary mask he has of Albert Einstein. He says that it creates a visual illusion as one moves around it while staying focused on it. It appears to generate real images of Albert Einstein's face when in fact it is a hollow mask. Richard uses this as a micro lesson to demonstrate the formidable power of the brains *simulation software* to make such visuals and make them seem real. He says:

"It is well capable of *constructing* 'visions' and 'visitations' of the utmost veridical power. To *simulate* a ghost or an angel or a virgin Mary would be child's play to software of this sophistication. Constructing models is something the human brain is very good at." [342]

I certainly agree that the mind is extremely good at (producing) constructing dreams and visions. It can even imagine movies right on the spot at a moment's notice. It's incredible. I want to insert my own example of how incredible our minds are by sharing a micro lesson I have used to teach how powerful our minds truly are. If you haven't ever looked at a stereogram you've missed out on an incredible experience. A stereogram is an image that reveals a three-dimensional effect when viewed with a stereoscope or special spectacles. It can also be viewed without these visual helpers, but only if you are capable of making your eyes squint in such a way that the stereogram's 3-D image pops open on the screen of your minds. I don't know why, but I'm blessed to be able to do this. It's very cool indeed.

Quite often, people look and look and look at the stereogram picture without being able to see the 3-D image of the dragon that's hidden in the graphic. Just because someone cannot see the 3-D dragon pop out on the page in 3-D imagery, doesn't mean that it isn't there. The fact is it is there for all to see. I often use this stereogram example as my micro lesson to describe the truth that says, "Just because YOU cannot see something, does not mean OTHERS can't see it or that it is non-existent". Here's an example of what I'm talking about. It has a Dragon that is in full 3-D mode with an oval shape behind it:

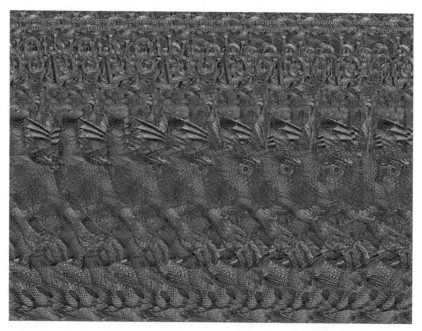

Seeing God is very much like the process of how one is able to "see" the dragon in this Stereogram picture. It takes discipline and following the rules or law of how to position your eyes of faith so that you in fact can "see' the handiwork of God, and for some they're able to see the very face of God.

Richard goes on to share several stories from his childhood such as when he heard faint voices until he saw it was the wind coming through a keyhole; or when the curtains in his home had formed a whimsical face so that his imagination took over. I agree that our minds are capable of *constructing*, or what I prefer to call *producing* incredible dream movies. In fact, I have often wondered how-on-earth my mind can produce a vivid movie on the screen of my mind, even while I am completely awake and deeply involved in something. It's especially true while I'm asleep. My mind seems to create a dream out of *nothing*. It's probably the *simulation software* at work that Richard talked about, right?

Like most people's mind, my mind has the creative capacity to construct (produce) images of people at the same time my mind's creating or projecting a dream on the movie screen of my mind, even placing people I don't even know in this movie. These are people that I have never seen or met before in my life (As far as I can remember), except at that very moment my mind is projecting them onto the screen of my mind. My mind can also place all of us in a location I've never been to before, except at the very moment it comes onto the screen of my mind. It is very surreal because it's a mixture of fact and fantasy. My mind, with its so-called *simulation software*, produces this visual story using no memory, as far as I can tell, using events that are at times spectacular and other times perfectly normal. It can even construct outrageous events such as having me fly like a fast, exotic bird over some vast ocean I've never before seen. Or, it has me flying up to the highest mountain peak that I've never imagined or seen before, all in a split second, all-the-while without having to flap non-existent wings. It's like these movies are pre-recorded 'Getty' video files that are somehow stored on my minds' visual data-storage, so that my mind can call them up in a fraction of a second, and seamlessly insert them into my ongoing *dream movie* right as it's playing on the screen of my mind. Yes, dreaming is absolutely the most surreal, incredible mental experience there is. At least I think so.

What's most interesting about this so-called *dreaming simulation software,* with its constructing (Creative producing) power to create these simulated dreams and run them on our minds' screen in a matter of moments, is the fact that they *feel so incredibly real* to us while we're experiencing them. Sometimes we can't even tell if they were real or not. Much like a Virtual Reality system can make us feel what we're watching, even though it isn't real. Sometimes our dreams warn us of impending dangers before they happen, or they provide comfort when we're in the middle of a crisis, like I received when my son died from his car accident. Some dreams are undecipherable, and many dreams aren't ever remembered once we awaken from our sleep. Here's an example of one such dreamer who had a repeating dream, but when he awoke each morning, he couldn't remember what he dreamed.

This was King Nebuchadnezzar of ancient Babylon, referred to in the Old Testament of the Bible. He had a recurring dream that caused him great concern because he couldn't even remember it as I said, but the prophet Daniel, praying to God, saw the King's dream in vision without asking the King what he remembered about it. Daniel did ask God to help him know what the king dreamed and what its interpretation was, and God answered his prayer and showed it to Daniel and then the spirit explained to Daniel what the dream meant, and because God did this for Daniel, it saved him and his fellow believers, as well as the lives of the King's counselors who were unable to help the king. I would have you, my readers, to stop and think about that one for a minute. It's quite a story, isn't it?

Joseph, a young Israelite, was another believer in God like the prophet Daniel. Joseph was sold into slavery by his brothers and ended up in Egypt. His is a similar dream-story like the story of Daniel, the prophet. Dreams are a very interesting phenomena of the mind, are they not? How does one say that the Creator of all minds doesn't know how these *principles of the mind* work, or can't use them to speak to His prophets, or to everyone else for that matter, if He wants to, be it through dreams, prayers, or otherwise?

Our minds' ability to dream is a gift, a divine trait that we inherit from our Heavenly Father. It's one of many *powers of creation* within us. It's one of our mind's divine attributes we enjoy as human beings, having inherited them, as I said, from the Father of our spirits, the Great Creator. This is just one trait we inherited from our Heavenly Parents, and it is therefore part of our divine nature. I'm pretty sure that animals' minds even experience some kind of dreaming of sorts. That's the power of a mind. This *power of the mind* is just one more evidence that Intelligence exists in our bodies, and I believe animals have some level of what I'm calling intelligence too. We, our spirit selves, enjoy this *spark of divine intelligence that we've inherited from our Creator.* This perspective on dreams has been acquired over my lifetime of study, research, and continual prayer and its reality is affirmed by the scriptures.

Richard calls this *power of the mind* our *simulation software* because it certainly acts like a computer program working in the confines of our minds' hardware, our physical wet brain. But it's really the power or programing within our *spirit selves' mind (As well as in mammals and birds' spirits' mind too),* which programming directs our physical brain to do what it does. It's simply a *function* that our spirit selves' mind engages in, as it *uses* the hardware called our physical wet brain to allow the minds' *simulation software,* so-to-speak, to do its creative work (computing). It really is quite remarkable. I'm just not sure what the minds apps are and how they work or where these spiritual apps or programs come from, but dreams do in fact happen. Maybe they are spiritual packets that contain all this creative, spiritual data, transmitting them via "light" and 'Spirit". Anyway, it's something to think about.

As I just suggested, this *simulation software* and its attributes/functions are not unique to humans alone, and that's because scientists have done tests that now show evidence that animals and birds also dream. You, my readers, should check out this footnote [343] and read up on this fact. I wonder what that says about animals' eternal future in the world to come? Interesting thought, isn't it? It is my strong belief, that we are meant to create; to imagine; to construct; and to communicate in ways we may not even understand or know we're capable of doing right now. One day we'll come to know all that we are capable of doing, but for now we can only speculate. We also don't know what we're capable of thinking or imagining by the power of our mind, if we were to use the full capacity our mind ultimately has. My guess is that it's beyond our imagination. One example of this would be the ability to 'communicate back-and-forth without having to speak out-loud'. This is called mental telepathy. This is just one of many capabilities that I believe we'll freely use one day. It's been said that our minds use a fraction of their capability or untapped cognitive potential. Scientists disagree with this statement of course, yet none have come forward with what that total capacity is or isn't. I suggest that even though today's scientists suggest that the *10% idea* that has been bandied around for years is a myth (Meaning we only use 10% of our *brains* capacity), I believe the power and cognitive capacity of our minds, not our brains alone, once it can fully function at its peak, it's capacity will be *beyond our imagination*, that's for sure.

I believe that our minds have the potential to increase in knowledge, capacity, and in light and truth continuously, even infinitely. What do you, my readers, think? God himself uses the *light of thought* to *transmit* dreams to our minds as one way He communicates with us, His children (As I said, it's much like a Radio Transmitting Station sending out its radio waves for our TV Receivers to receive them for our viewing or listening pleasure). Here are several examples of where God communicated to His prophets through transmitted dreams:

Gen. 15:12

12 And when the sun was going down, a deep sleep fell upon Abram; and, lo, an horror of great darkness fell upon him.

13 And he said unto Abram, Know of a surety that thy seed shall be a stranger in a land *that is* not theirs, and shall serve them; and they shall afflict them four hundred years (These were the Israelites who became enslaved by the Egyptians).

14 And also that nation, whom they shall serve, will I judge: and afterward shall they come out with great substance.

15 And thou shalt go to thy fathers in peace; thou shalt be buried in a good old age.

Genesis 20:3-7

3 But God came to Abimelech in a dream by night, and said to him, Behold, thou *art* a dead man, for the woman which thou hast taken; for she *is* a man's wife.

4 But Abimelech had not come near her: and he said, Lord, wilt thou slay also *a*a righteous nation?

5 Said he not unto me, She *is* my sister? and she, even she herself said, He *is* my *b*brother: in the integrity of my heart and innocency of my hands have I done this.

6 And God said unto him in a dream, Yea, I know that thou didst this in the integrity of thy heart; for I also withheld thee from sinning against me: therefore, suffered I thee not to touch her.

7 Now therefore restore the man *his* wife; for he *is* a prophet, and he shall pray for thee, and thou shalt live: and if thou restore *her* not, know thou that thou shalt surely die, thou, and all that *are* thine.

Genesis 28:12-15

12 And he dreamed, and behold a ladder set up on the earth, and the top of it reached to heaven: and behold the angels of God ascending and descending on it.

13 And, behold, the LORD stood above it, and said, I *am* the LORD God of Abraham thy father, and the God of Isaac: the land whereon thou liest, to thee will I give it, and to thy seed;

14 And thy seed shall be as the dust of the earth, and thou shalt spread abroad to the west and to the east, and to the north, and to the south: and in thee and in they seed shall all the families of the earth be blessed.

15 And, behold, I *am* with thee, and will keep thee in all *places* whither thou goest, and will bring thee again into this land; for I will not leave thee, … until I have done *that* which I have spoken to thee of.

Genesis 31:24

24 And God came to Laban the Syrian in a dream by night, and said unto him, Take heed that thou speak not to Jacob either good or bad.

Genesis 37:5-10

5 And Joseph dreamed a dream, and he told *it* his brethren: and they hated him yet the more.

6 And he said unto them, Hear, I pray you, this dream which I have dreamed:

7 For, behold, we *were* binding sheaves in the field, and, lo, my sheaf arose, and also stood upright; and, behold, your sheaves stood round about, and made obeisance to my sheaf.

8 And his brethren said to him, Shalt thou indeed reign over us? or shalt thou indeed have dominion over us? And they hated him yet the more for his dreams, and for his words.

9 And he dreamed yet another dream, and told it his brethren, and said, Behold, I have dreamed a dream more; and, behold, the sun and the moon and the eleven stars made obeisance to me.

10 And he told *it* to his father, and to his brethren: and his father rebuked him, and said unto him, What *is* this dream that thou hast dreamed? Shall I and thy mother and thy brethren indeed come to bow down ourselves to thee to the earth?

Genesis 40:5

5 And they dreamed a dream both of them, each man his dream in one night, each man according to the interpretation of his dream, the butler, and the baker of the king of Egypt, which were bound in the prison.

Genesis 41:1-28

1 And it came to pass at the end of two full years, that Pharaoh dreamed: and, behold, he stood by the river.

2 And, behold, there came up out of the river seven well favoured kind and fatfleshed; and they fed in a meadow.

3 And, behold, seven other kine came up after them out of the river, ill favoured and leanfleshed; and stood by the *other* kine upon the brink of the river.

4 And the ill favoured and leanfleshed kine did eat up the seven well favoured and fat kine. So Pharaoh awoke.

5 And he slept and dreamed the second time: and, behold, seven ears of corn came up upon one stalk, rank and good.

6 And, behold, seven thin ears and blasted with the east wind sprung up after them.

7 And the seven thin ears devoured the seven rank and full ears. And Pharaoh awoke, and behold, *it was* a dream.

8 And it came to pass in the morning that his spirit was troubled; and he sent and called for all the magicians of Egypt, and all the wise men thereof: and Pharaoh told them his dream; but *there was* none that could interpret them unto Pharaoh.

9 Then spake the chief butler unto Pharaoh, saying, I do remember my faults this day:

10 Pharaoh was wroth with his servants, and put me in ward in the captain of the guard's house, *both* me and the chief baker:

11 And we dreamed a dream in one night, I and he; we dreamed each man according to the interpretation of his dream.

12 And *there was* there with us a young man, an Hebrew, servant to the captain of the guard; and we told him, and he interpreted to us our dreams; to each man according to his dream he did interpret.

13 And it came to pass, as he interpreted to us, so it was; me he restored unto mine office, and him he hanged.

14 Then Pharaoh sent and called Joseph, and they brought him hastily out of the dungeon: and he shaved *himself,* and changed his raiment, and came in unto Pharaoh.

15 And Pharaoh said unto Joseph, I have dreamed a dream, and *there is* none that can interpret it: and I have heard say of thee, *that* thou canst understand a dream to interpret it.

16 And Joseph answered Pharaoh, saying, *It is* not in me: God shall give Pharaoh an answer of peace.

17 And Pharaoh said unto Joseph, In my dream, behold, I stood upon the bank of the river:

18 And, behold, there came up out of the river seven kine, fatfleshed and well favoured; and they fed in a meadow:

19 And, behold, seven other kine came up after them, poor and very ill favoured and leanfleshed, such as I never saw in all the land of Egypt for badness:

20 And the lean and the ill-favored kine did eat up the first seven fat kine:

21 And when they had eaten them up, it could not be known that they had eaten them; but they *were* still ill favoured, as at the beginning. So I awoke.

22 And I saw in my dream, and behold, seven ears came up in one stalk, full and good:

23 And, behold, seven ears, withered, thin, *and* blasted with the ᵉeast wind, sprung up after them:

24 And the thin ears devoured the seven good ears: and I told *this* unto the magicians; but *there was* none that could declare *it* to me.

25 And Joseph said unto Pharaoh, The dream of Pharaoh *is* one: God hath shewed Pharaoh what he is about to do.

26 The seven good kine *are* seven years; and the seven good ears *are* seven years: the dream *is* one.

27 And the seven thin and ill favoured kine that came up after them *are* seven years; and the seven empty ears blasted with the east wind shall be seven years of famine.

28 This *is* the thing which I have spoken unto Pharaoh: What God *is* about to do he sheweth unto Pharaoh.

Judges 7:13

13 And when Gideon was come, behold, *there was* a man that told a dream unto his fellow, and said, Behold, I dreamed a dream, and, lo, a cake of barley bread tumbled into the host of Midian, and came unto a tent, and smote it that it fell, and overturned it, that the tent lay along.

1 Kings 3:5

5 In Gibeon the Lord appeared to Solomon in a dream by night: and God said, Ask what I shall give thee.

Daniel 2:1, 4

1 And in the second year of the reign of Nebuchadnezzar, Nebuchadnezzar dreamed dreams, wherewith his spirit was troubled, and his sleep brake from him.

4 Then spake the Chaldeans to the king in ayrack, O king, live forever: tell thy servants the dream, and we will shew the interpretation.

Matthew 1:20

20 But while he thought on these things, behold, the angel of the Lord appeared unto him in a dream, saying, "Joseph, thou son of David, fear not to take unto thee Mary thy wife: ... for that which is conceived in her is of the Holy Ghost".

Matthew 2:12, 13, 20

12 And being warned of God in a dream that they should not return to Herod, they departed into their own country another way.

13 And when they were departed, behold, the angel of the Lord appeareth to Joseph in a dream, saying, Arise, and take the young child and his mother, and flee into Egypt, and be thou there until I bring thee word: for Herod will seek the young child to destroy him.

20 Saying, Arise, and take the young child and his mother, and go into the land of Israel: for they are dead which sought the young child's life.

Matthew 27:19

19 When he was set down on the judgment seat, his wife sent unto him, saying, Have thou nothing to do with that just man: for I have suffered many things this day in a dream because of him.

I Nephi 3:1–2

1 And it came to pass that I, Nephi, returned from speaking with the Lord, to the tent of my father.

2 And it came to pass that he spake unto me, saying: Behold I have dreamed a dream, in the which the Lord hath commanded me that thou and thy brethren shall return to Jerusalem.

I Nephi 8:2

2 And it came to pass that while my father tarried in the wilderness he spake unto us, saying: Behold, I have dreamed a dream; or, in other words, I have seen a vision.

I particularly like this verse of scripture found in Job:

Job 33:14-16

14 For God speaketh once, yea twice, *yet man* perceiveth it not.

15 In a dream, in a vision of the night, when deep sleep falleth upon men, in slumberings upon the bed;

16 Then he openeth the ears of men, and sealeth their instruction.

These few examples of God using dreams to communicate with His children, are certainly not exhaustive, for I could have listed many more examples from the scriptures where God uses dreams and visions to communicate with His children. But I think it's sufficient to show that He is no respecter of persons in this regard, for dreams (from God or otherwise) come to both the righteous and the wicked alike, just like rain falls on everyone, whether they be believers in God or nonbelievers, it matters not.

I found this essay written by a Latter-Day Saint author named Ryan C. Jenkins, titled "Quiet Slumber: Revelation through Dreams". I won't include the entirety of the essay, but I did want to share a few excerpts from it that I think will add a little insight and color to my Latter-Day Saint's view on our minds ability to imagine and to dream, and why we do. Here are some excerpts, and I quote:

"Elder Bruce R. McConkie made the distinction: "An inspired dream is a vision given to a person while he sleeps. All inspired dreams are visions, but all visions are not dreams. Visions are received in hours of wakefulness or of sleep and in some cases when the recipient has passed into a trance; it is only when the vision occurs during sleep that it is termed a dream. Sleep is something we all have in common. What satisfaction or level of enjoyment we gain from the experience varies, as does the effect it has on our mind and heart. Most of our subconscious state goes without memory. Irrational and absurd dreams are easily dismissed by an individual who has the Spirit of God. But on occasion the Lord judiciously issues dreams for his divine purposes and an individual's personal growth."

Elder Parley P. Pratt, who was himself given to prophetic dreams, said:

"In all ages and dispensations God has revealed many important instructions and warnings to men by means of dreams. When the outward organs of thought and perception are released from their activity, the nerves unstrung, and the whole of mortal humanity lies hushed in quiet slumbers, in order to renew its strength and vigor, it is then that the *spiritual organs* are at liberty, in a certain degree, to assume their wonted functions, to recall some faint outlines, some confused and half-defined recollections, of that heavenly world, and those endearing scenes of their former estate, from which they have descended in order to obtain and mature a tabernacle of flesh."

"Elder Pratt alluded to instructions and warnings as the purpose for God giving dreams to individuals at times. He also suggested that dreams are sometimes for … *recall* or *divine recollections* of our origin and purpose as we journey in the flesh and develop a 'mature tabernacle of flesh'. Mr. Jenkins continues: "Dreams may also confirm premonitions or show something that is about to happen. An inspired dream might entail a warning—a rebuke for course correction—it might convey a direct command to do something, or it might serve as spiritual assurance or bestow a promise. In every dispensation, dreams have been a prevalent spiritual gift, and the gift is validated in scripture." [344]

End of Excerpts

Merrill J. Bateman, past President of Brigham Young University, gave a talk to the university's student body titled, "Light, Visions, and Dreams". Here are a few excerpts from his talk that I think you, my readers, will find enjoyable and even insightful, and I quote some excerpts from his talk:

"Today my thoughts are centered on the dreams and visions that inspire temporal and spiritual progress and the principles that produce growth and achievement. Scientific discoveries during the last 100 years exceed the cumulative findings of all the centuries that preceded it. I do not believe that the increase in knowledge is happenstance. It is part of the Lord's plan as He bestows additional light upon the earth's inhabitants. The Lord told Joseph Smith that *the restoration of the gospel would be but a beginning to the light that He would pour out upon the earth*—not only spiritual light but also light that pertains to this temporal world":

D&C 121:26–32

26 God shall give unto you knowledge by his Holy Spirit, yea, by the unspeakable gift of the Holy Ghost, that has not been revealed since the world was until now;

27 Which our forefathers have awaited with anxious expectation to be revealed in the last times, which their minds were pointed to by the angels, as held in reserve for the fulness of their glory;

28 A time to come in the which nothing shall be withheld, *whether there be one God or many gods, they shall be manifest.*

29 All thrones and dominions, principalities and powers, shall be revealed and set forth upon all who have endured valiantly for the gospel of Jesus Christ.

30 And also, if there be bounds set to the heavens or to the seas, or to the dry land, or to the sun, moon, or stars—

31 *All the times of their revolutions, all the appointed days, months, and years, and all the days of their days, months, and years, and all their glories, laws, and set times, shall be revealed in the days of the dispensation of the fulness of times—*

32 According to that which was ordained in the midst of the Council of the Eternal God of all other gods before this world was, that should be reserved unto the finishing and the end thereof, when every man shall enter into his eternal presence and into his immortal rest.

"During the preparation of a recent talk given to the faculty and staff, I became fascinated with the *nature of light* and its characteristics. All of us are aware of the natural light that emanates from the sun, which provides the heat and light that sustains temporal life on earth. In contrast, few of the earth's inhabitants are aware of the *spiritual light* that emanates from a different Son—our "bright and morning star":

Revelation 22:16

16 I Jesus have sent mine angel to testify unto you these things in the churches (The church of the Ephesians, of the Thessalonians, etc. – 7 of them). I am the root and the offspring of David, *and* the bright and morning star.

"Even fewer people appreciate the *close relationship* between spiritual and natural light. Physicists have studied light for many years, fascinated by its dual nature. Photons of light behave like streams of particles in some circumstances and like waves in others. In a diffraction experiment, light appears to be a wave. When light is used to bombard certain materials, it appears to be composed of particles. The German physicist Max Planck developed a theory in the early 1900s that "helped explain how tiny particles, such as photons, behave like waves."

"His theory helped scientists accept the idea that light behaves like both particles and waves" (*World Book Encyclopedia*, 1974 ed., "The Nature of Light," s.v. "Light")."

"Another form of light not studied by physicists is light in the *spiritual dimension*. At Brigham Young University we are privileged to know about, access, and benefit from a more refined light that emanates from Christ. It, too, is the source of life—eternal life. This light, the Light of Christ, is the source of truth. In speaking to Joseph Smith, the Savior said:

"*For the word of the Lord is truth, and whatsoever is truth is light, and whatsoever is light is Spirit, even the Spirit of Jesus Christ.*"

Doctrine & Covenants 84:45–46

46 And the Spirit giveth light to every man that cometh into the world; and the Spirit enlighteneth every man through the world, that hearkeneth to the voice of the Spirit.

"In the study of light, physicists have discovered that light *has a spectrum*. The visible portion of that spectrum displays many colors. The light spectrum has proven useful as physicists and engineers have designed equipment that allows each color to be used as a conduit, thereby multiplying the carrying capacity of light. *The visible spectrum of light has a spiritual counterpart. The spiritual spectrum pertains to various levels of intelligence*, beginning with animal instinct and moving to more refined forms of light and truth."

"The higher gradations include man's reasoning ability and conscience, the light that comes through the Holy Ghost prior to baptism, and the light one receives through the gift of the Holy Ghost after entering the Lord's kingdom.

Finally, a fullness of light is received when one has proven worthy of the Second Comforter and receives the '*more sure word of prophecy*'."

II Peter 1:19

19 We have also a more sure word of prophecy; whereunto ye do well that ye take heed, as unto a light that shineth in a dark place, until the day dawn, and the day star arise in hearts:

Doctrine & Covenants 131:5

5 (May 17th, 1843.) The more sure word of prophecy means a man's knowing that he is sealed up unto eternal life, by revelation and the spirit of prophecy, through the power of the Holy Priesthood.

"The spiritual spectrum of light is based on statements by Parley P. Pratt in *Key to the Science of Theology*, 9th ed. [Salt Lake City: Deseret Book, 1965], 46–47; and Charles W. Penrose, JD 26:21–22. More than 100 years ago, President Charles W. Penrose, citing section 88 of the Doctrine & Covenants, stated that *the physical and spiritual spectrums of light are related and belong to one continuum.* Speaking of the Light of Christ, the Spirit of God, he said:

"*It is the light and the life of all things. It is the light and the life of man. It is the life of the animal creation. It is the life of the vegetable creation. It is in the earth; it is in the stars . . .; it is in the moon (Sagan's stardust?) ...: it is in the sun, and is the light of the sun, and the power by which it was made; and these grosser particles of light that illuminate the heavens and enable us to behold the works of nature, are from that same Spirit which enlightens our minds and unfolds the things of God. As that light comes forth from the sun, so the light of God comes to us.* [Charles W. Penrose, JD 26:21]" [345]

(This would be a good place for Richard to do his *scientific study* about the existence of God, starting with this 'spectrum of light that includes the spiritual spectrum of light').

End of quote by Charles Penrose

In closing Mr. Bateman said, and I quote:

"To acquire temporal truths, one must be diligent in pursuing an education. We encourage you to take seriously the opportunity afforded here. Do not waste time. Study daily—at least three hours for every hour in class. That still leaves more than 100 hours per week for other things. Recently I spoke to a small group of freshmen who indicated that they did not need to study in high school to obtain A's. One indicated that he was doing well here even though he had not studied thus far. There are two problems with his thinking. The first is his belief that he will do well at exam time. The second is that he could be learning so much more if he applied himself. To receive spiritual truths, one must be obedient as well as diligent.

Doctrine & Covenants 130:19

19 And if a person gains more knowledge and intelligence in this life through his diligence and obedience than another, he will have so much the advantage in the world to come.

"Spiritual light is received when one follows the doctrine of Christ—that is, the first principles and ordinances of the restored gospel. I challenge you to increase your faith by living gospel principles more precisely, by repenting when you fall short, by taking an active role in your ward, by rendering service to others, and by making prayer and scripture study a part of your everyday life. In this manner you will find true joy. In closing I turn to the words of the Prophet Joseph Smith, who wrote about *the connection between heaven and our intellect* as follows:

"*We consider that God has created man with a mind capable of instruction, and a faculty which may be enlarged in proportion to the heed and diligence given to the light communicated from heaven to the intellect; and that the nearer man approaches perfection, the clearer are his views, and the greater his enjoyments.* [TPJS, 51]" [367]

End of Excerpts by Merrill J. Bateman

Richard concludes his argument saying: "When we are asleep it is called *dreaming*; when we are awake, we call it *imagination* or, when it is exceptionally vivid, *hallucination* ... If we are gullible, we don't recognize hallucination or lucid dreaming for what it is, and we claim to have seen or heard a ghost; or an angel; or God; or – The Virgin Mary. Such visions and manifestations are certainly not good grounds for believing that ghosts or angels, gods, or virgins, are actually there. If you've had such an experience, you may well find yourself believing firmly that it was real. But don't expect the rest of us to take your word for it, especially if we have the slightest familiarity with the brain and its workings". [347]

As I've already argued in my Introduction to this book, this criticism by Richard towards the claims of visions and dreams as God's communications to His children, as well as my own personal dream experiences being from "my mind simply constructing what I wanted to see or imagined seeing", I will leave it to you, my readers, to decide if Richard's arguments are the more compelling ones, or if mine are the more convincing, even the more probable. The experiences found in scripture and the examples I've shared from my own personal experiences, as well as the tens-of-thousands of testimonies that have been given by people from all across the globe, simply cannot be written off by calling them hallucinations of a frenzied mind (Billions in fact. C'mon man. That's a lot of hallucinating minds).

I also suggest that you go to YouTube and search for the television series called "It's a Miracle", where you can check out more than three hundred stories of supposed miracles, dreams, visions, unexplainable spiritual directions, etc. Please know that I am not stating that I believe all these stories as being true miracles. I'm simply suggesting that you consider them as you reflect on this subject. I also suggest that you, my readers, think of your own experiences before making your judgement on whether-or-not dreams are real or just *constructed hallucinations* by a mis-firing wet brain.

You, my readers, should also keep in mind that there's a third option to consider besides the two I've just laid out, and that third option is, "some dreams and visions are real, and some are hallucinations". In other words, you don't necessarily have to throw the whole kit-and-caboodle out with the wash. Each of us must determine for ourselves however, which one of these three options we want to believe and hold on to as being true, and which ones we should toss out.

I want to say that if Richard is right, there are over 7.5 billion gullible, mad, psychotic, delusional people walking upon the face of this earth! These are people who are supposedly hallucinating, while experiencing their dreams or visions throughout their entire lives. 83% of South Africans believe in God or a supreme being. 78% of Mexicans and 70% of Americans do too. In Argentina it's 62%. [348] That's billions of gullible, delusional people. I say that Richard and his ilk are the ones who are under the power and influence of their delusional, mindless 'wet brains' (An Atheist's Delusion).

Literally billions of people who are walking on earth at this very moment, believe that God (Through His spirit, His light and truth) is speaking to them in their minds and hearts; that He is inspiring them with uplifting counsel, peace, and comfort, as well as prompting them as a protection for their safety. There are even highly recognized award-winning scientists who believe God is enlightening their minds with ideas and pure knowledge that ultimately have become and will yet become the next generation of beneficial technological discoveries that are and will continue to bless the lives of billions of people all across the globe, … and that alone ought to make us stop and consider the possibility of divine communications being real. The next subtitle is – 'The argument from scripture."

THE ARGUMENT FROM SCRIPTURE

Richard states, "In answer to theists putting forth the argument from scripture, one of which is C.S. Lewis who stated that, 'Since Jesus claimed to be the Son of God, he must have been either right or else insane, or a liar; Mad, Bad, or God; Lunatic, Liar, or Lord." [349]

Mr. Lewis went on to argue that Jesus in fact did make such a claim or claims and Richard, of course, disagreed (Quick note here. This statement that Richard attributes to C.S. Lewis, was actually made by P. H. Brazier in an article titled "God, or a Bad, Mad, Man". C.S. Lewis used it as part of his discourses. This was made clear by a Mr. Leslie Baynes in his article titled, "C.S. Lewis's Use of Scripture in the 'Liar, Lunatic, Lord" Argument). Richard continues, "The historical evidence that Jesus claimed any sort of divine status is minimal. In any case, as I said, there is no good historical evidence that he ever thought he was divine." [350]

I will come back to this comment by Richard a little later but let me continue with more of what Richard claims about scripture itself. Here is what Richard said about *all* scripture, but in particular, what he said about the Bible:

"Scholarly theologians have made an overwhelming case that the gospels are not reliable accounts of what happened in the history of the real world. All were written long after the death of Jesus, and also, after the epistles of Paul, which mention almost none of the alleged facts of Jesus' life. All were then copied and recopied, through many different *'Chinese Whisperers Generations'* by fallible scribes who, in any case, had their own religious agendas." [351]

Let me say with regards to this last statement by Richard, who as an atheist with bias towards religion, is actually describing the belief that the Church of Jesus Christ of Latter-Day Saint has said about the Holy Bible and its accuracy and authenticity. As I said before, "We believe the Bible to be the word of God", but only "as far as it is translated correctly".

Joseph Smith invested a considerable amount of time on his translation of the Bible (JST), but was unable to complete it before his martyrdom, and so the Church did not publish it as a fully translated Bible, nor did they canonize those portions he did translate. However, the Church leaders did include most of the JST translated verses in the footnotes of every page throughout its updated LDS version, published back in 1979. This LDS version of the Bible includes a plethora of references and footnotes that can be found at the bottom of each page of the KJV version of the Bible, and so, since they are included in this version (The JST version) it's now part of what's called the Standard Works of scripture.

Richard goes on to say, "The resulting contradictions are glaring, but consistently overlooked by the faithful … The Davinci Code, and the film made from it, are arousing huge controversy in Church circles. It is indeed fabricated from start to finish; invented, made-up fiction. In that respect, it is exactly like the gospels. The only difference between The Davinci Code and the gospels is that the gospels are ancient fiction while The Davinci Code is modern fiction." [352]

To describe the need for multiple witnesses and or testimonies of the divinity of Jesus Christ, I often give the example of someone trying to hang a large painting on a wall with just one nail. It doesn't work very well as you probably know from personal experience. You can slide the painting along the wire in either direction. By sliding I mean moving the picture from left to right, or from the right to the left, and when you do, you get a different viewpoint and angle of the painting each time. But when you add a second or third nail so that the painting is locked in at one position, these extra nails help 'fix' the painting to a single, permanent, *fixed* view. This illustrates the power that two or three witnesses have in establishing or fixing into place what is true and what's not. The apostle Paul wrote to the Corinthians about this very principle of multiple witnesses:

II Corinthians 13:1

1 This *is* the third *time* I am coming to you. In the mouth of two or three witnesses shall every word be established.

The Bible is one nations witness (The Jewish nation) of the divinity of Jesus Christ, He being the Son of the Living God (It includes the individual testimonies of witnesses who saw and knew Jesus). The Book of Mormon is another nations witness of the divinity of the Lord Jesus Christ as the Savior of the world, (The Ancient American nation). It too includes many individual testimonies of those witnesses who knew and saw the resurrected Christ. Their testimonies are recorded throughout it pages as well. The Book of Mormon is a second witness or testament of Jesus' divine Sonship as the Savior of the world. One record coming from the eastern hemisphere, and a second record or testament coming from the western hemisphere, so that we now have two distinct and separate testimonies that Jesus is the Christ.

There are additional nations who have witnesses of Jesus Christ. These witnesses have also recorded their testimonies as witnesses of the Christ, which records are yet to be revealed. In his talk, "God Will Yet Reveal", a past beloved apostle who has since passed away (July 21st, 2004), Elder Neil A. Maxwell declared the following regarding other scriptural witnesses that are yet to be revealed, and I quote:

"One of the unique features of the living Church of Jesus Christ is its ever-expanding body of fundamental spiritual knowledge about man's identity and purpose, which enlarges "the memory of this people."

Alma 37:8

8 And now, it has hitherto been wisdom in God that these things should be preserved; for behold they have *enlarged the memory of this people*, yea, and convinced many of the error of their ways, and brought them to the knowledge of their God unto the salvation of their souls.

"In fact, the Church of Jesus Christs' ninth article of faith declares that "God will *yet reveal* many great and important things pertaining to the Kingdom of God". Here' what it says:

Articles of Faith 1:9

9 We believe all that God has revealed, all that He does now reveal, and we believe that He will *yet reveal many great and important things* pertaining to the Kingdom of God.

"Thus, nourished by a menu blending antiquity and futurity, Church members need never "faint in [their] minds."

Hebrews 12:3

3 For consider him that endured such contradiction of sinners against himself, lest ye be wearied and faint in your minds.

"Instead, we can be intellectually vibrant. *Lost books are among the treasures yet to come forth.* Over twenty of these are mentioned in the existing scriptures. Perhaps most startling and voluminous will be the records of *the lost tribes of Israel*":

II Nephi 29:13

13 And it shall come to pass that the Jews shall have the words of the Nephites (The Book of Mormon), and the Nephites shall have the words of the Jews (The Bible); and the Nephites and the Jews shall have the words of *the lost tribes of Israel* (Yet to be revealed as a third witness of Jesus Christ and His divine role as the Savior of the World); and the lost tribes of Israel shall have the words of the Nephites and the Jews.

"We would not even know of the impending *third witness for Christ* except through the precious Book of Mormon, the second witness for Christ! This third set of sacred records will thus complete *a triad of truth.* Then, just as the Perfect Shepherd has said:

II Nephi 29:14

14 And it shall come to pass that my people, which are of the house of Israel, shall be gathered home unto the lands of their possessions; and my word also shall be gathered in ᶜone. And I will show unto them that fight against my word and against my people, who are of the house of Israel, that I am God, and that I covenanted with Abraham that I would remember his seed forever.

"My word also shall be gathered in one". There will be one-fold and one shepherd ...

I Nephi 22:25

25 And he gathereth his children from the four quarters of the earth; and he numbereth his sheep, and they know him; and there shall be *one-fold and one shepherd*; and he shall feed his sheep, and in him they shall find pasture.

... welding together all the Christian dispensations of human history." The Prophet Joseph Smith wrote this:

Doctrine & Covenants 128:18

18 I might have rendered a plainer translation to this, but it is sufficiently plain to suit my purpose as it stands. It is sufficient to know, in this case, that the earth will be smitten with a curse unless there is a welding ᶜlink of some kind or other between the fathers and the children, upon some subject or other—and behold what is that subject? It is the baptism for the dead. For we without them cannot be made perfect; neither can they without us be made perfect.

"Neither can they nor we be made perfect without those who have died in the gospel also; for it is necessary in the ushering in of the dispensation of the fulness of times, which dispensation is now beginning to usher in, that a whole and complete and perfect union, and *welding together of dispensations, and keys, and powers, and glories* should take place, and be revealed from the days of Adam even to the present time. And not only this, but those things which never have been revealed from the foundation of the world, but have been kept hid from the wise and prudent, shall be revealed unto babes and sucklings in this, the dispensation of the fulness of times. [353]

End of quotes by Elder Maxwell

When you combine these three records together (Like the prophet *Ezekiel describes in the verses below), they form a powerful witness for the life and reality of God and His Son Jesus Christ, and for His gospel, which is that "He came from His Father's presence to earth to redeem the world, those children of God who accept *His atoning proxy sacrifice* by believing and exercising their faith in Him, repenting, and then by making and keeping covenants with Him." Here's what Ezekiel said:

*Ezekiel 37:16 – 23

16 Moreover, thou son of man, take thee one stick, and write upon it, For Judah, and for the children of Israel his companions (The Bible): then take another stick, and write upon it (The Book of Mormon), For Joseph, the stick of Ephraim, and *for* all the house of Israel his companions:

17 And join them one to another into one stick; and they shall become one in thine hand (One complete testimony of Jesus).

18 And when the children of thy people shall speak unto thee, saying, Wilt thou not shew us what thou *meanest* by these?

19 Say unto them, Thus saith the Lord GOD; Behold, I will take the stick of Joseph, which *is* in the hand of Ephraim, and the tribes of Israel his fellows, and will put them with him, *even* with the stick of Judah, and make them one stick, and they shall be one in mine hand.

20 And the sticks whereon thou writest shall be in thine hand before their eyes.

21 And say unto them, Thus saith the Lord GOD; Behold, I will take the children of Israel from among the heathen, whether they be gone, and will gather them on every side, and bring them into their own land:

22 And I will make them one nation in the land upon the mountains of Israel; and one king shall be king to them all: and they shall be no more two nations, neither shall they be divided into two kingdoms any more at all:

23 Neither shall they defile themselves any more with their idols, nor with their detestable things, nor with any of their transgressions: but I will save them out of all their dwelling places, wherein they have sinned, and will cleanse them: so shall they be my people, and I will be their God.

The following excerpts describe the Church of Jesus Christ of Latter-Day Saints' official stance on the Bible. The full overview is found on the Church's official website at: www.churchofjesuschrist.org under the title "Doctrinal Study – Scriptures".

"The Bible is divided into two parts: The Old Testament & The New Testament. The Old Testament is a sacred record of God's dealings with His covenant people in the Holy Land. It includes the teachings of such prophets as Moses, Joshua, Isaiah, Jeremiah, and Daniel. The New Testament records the birth, mortal ministry, and Atonement of the Savior. It concludes the ministry of the Savior's disciples, including Paul who was Saul of Tarsus.

"Because the Bible has been translated many times, it is printed in different versions. In English, the King James Version of the Bible (KJV), is accepted as scripture by the Church of Jesus Christ of Latter-Day Saints. In The Church of Jesus Christ of Latter-Day Saints, we revere the Bible and its sacred teachings. We can receive strength, comfort, and guidance from the biblical accounts of God's dealings with His people. Here is The Church's view as to what scripture is (This is found in this same essay):

"When holy men of God write or speak by the power of the Holy Ghost, their words 'shall be scripture, shall be the will of the Lord, shall be the mind of the Lord, shall be the word of the Lord, shall be the voice of the Lord, and the power of God unto salvation'."

Doctrine & Covenants 68:4

4 And whatsoever they shall speak when moved upon by the Holy Ghost shall be scripture, shall be the will of the Lord, shall be the mind of the Lord, shall be the word of the Lord, shall be the voice of the Lord, and the power of God unto salvation.

"The official, canonized scriptures of the Church, often called the *Standard Works*, are the Bible, the Book of Mormon, the Doctrine & Covenants, and the Pearl of Great Price.

"The principal purpose of scriptures is to testify of Christ and to guide the children of God so they can come unto Him and receive eternal life.

John 5:39

39 Search the scriptures; for in them ye think ye have eternal life: and they are they which testify of me.

John 20:31

31 But these are written, that ye might believe that Jesus is the Christ, the Son of God; and that believing ye might have life through his name.

I Nephi 6:4

4 For the fulness of mine intent is that I may persuade men to come unto the God of Abraham, and the God of Isaac, and the God of Jacob, and be saved.

Mosiah 13:33–35

33 For behold, did not Moses prophesy unto them concerning the coming of the Messiah, and that God should redeem his people? Yea, and even all the prophets who have prophesied ever since the world began—have they not spoken more or less concerning these things?

34 Have they not said that God himself should come down among the children of men, and upon him the form of man, and go forth in mighty power upon the face of the earth?

35 Yea, and have they not said also that he should bring to pass the resurrection of the dead, and that he, himself, should be oppressed and afflicted?

The Book of Mormon prophet Mormon taught:

Helaman 3:29–30

29 Whosoever will, may lay hold upon the word of God, which is quick and powerful, which shall divide asunder all the cunning and the snares and the wiles of the devil, and lead the man of Christ in a *strait* and *narrow* course across that everlasting gulf of misery which is prepared to engulf the wicked—

30 And land their souls, yea, their immortal souls, at the right hand of God in the kingdom of heaven, to sit down with Abraham, and Isaac, and with Jacob, and with all our holy fathers, to go no more out."

"God, who is the same "yesterday, today, and forever", continues to reveal scripture in modern times as He did in ancient times.

II Nephi 29:9

9 And I do this that I may prove unto many that I am the same yesterday, today, and forever; and that I speak forth my words according to mine own pleasure. And because that I have spoken one word ye need not suppose that I cannot speak another; for my work is not yet finished; neither shall it be until the end of man, neither from that time henceforth and forever.

"Latter-Day prophets counsel people everywhere to study the scriptures daily, including the Bible, the Book of Mormon, the Doctrine & Covenants, and the Pearl of Great Price. They encourage individual and family scripture study. They encourage us, as Nephi encouraged his contemporaries, ... to *liken the scriptures to ourselves*, finding ways that the sacred accounts of old can be applied in our lives today."

I Nephi 19:23–24

23 And I did read many things unto them which were written in the books of Moses; but that I might more fully persuade them to believe in the Lord their Redeemer I did read unto them that which was written by the prophet Isaiah; for I did liken all scriptures unto us, that it might be for our profit and learning.

24 Wherefore I spake unto them, saying: Hear ye the words of the prophet, ye who are a remnant of the house of Israel, a branch who have been broken off; hear ye the words of the prophet, which were written unto all the house of Israel, and liken them unto yourselves, that ye may have hope as well as your brethren from whom ye have been broken off; for after this manner has the prophet written.

They exhort us to "search the scriptures" ...

John 5:39

39 Search the scriptures; for in them ye think ye have eternal life: and they are they which testify of me.

... and "feast upon the words of Christ."

II Nephi 32:3

3 Angels speak by the power of the Holy Ghost; wherefore, they speak the words of Christ. Wherefore, I said unto you, feast upon the words of Christ; for behold, the words of Christ will tell you all things what ye should do.

"Daily, meaningful scripture study helps individuals be *receptive* to the guidance of the Holy Ghost (It helps us to *attune* our minds to His Spirit of light and truth, the Incomprehensible IT)."

"It builds faith, fortifies against temptation, enlightens, and helps individuals draw near to our Heavenly Father and His Beloved Son." [354]

End of Excerpts regarding Scripture

I went ahead and shared all these scriptures because I felt that you, my readers, could read them more easily if I didn't make you have to take the time to go in search for them yourselves. I felt that by saving you that 'search time' it would create the best possible circumstance where you, my readers, would actually read them, and that way you would learn exactly what was said by these prophets of God, living in these ancient lands, including their testimonies concerning the man they identified as Jesus of Nazareth, and whether He was the Son of God, or not. I also felt that I had license to do it this way since Richard was so critical of the scriptures, he says he reviewed. In particular, I wanted to share with you my personal perspective about the Bible, so you, my readers, could compare it to Richard's view of the Bible, which is that it was made-up by poor peasant nobody's, and not written by holy men as they were moved upon by the power and gift of the Holy Ghost.

Anyway, I'll leave it there for now, and hope that you, my readers, will weigh both sides of this topic carefully and then decide for yourselves, what makes the most sense to you, and who provided the weightier evidence for the probability that God exists, or the probability that He doesn't. It is my hope that your personal *circular table stand,* is being built out with all the many reference legs of evidence that I've provided you so far and will yet provide you going forward. It should be feeling quite stable.

As I continue to provide you reference leg after reference leg, each one adding strength to your circular table stand, you should be seeing your *table of belief* getting increasingly stable. In fact, … by the time you've read my book, your table of belief stand should be completely immoveable. But you, of course, will be the judge of whether-or-not your *table of belief* has increased stability, like I said it would, or if it has become even less stable than before. I hope you're keeping a list of all these reference legs. Next is "The argument from admired religious scientists". This was an interesting topic for sure.

THE ARGUMENT FROM ADMIRED RELIGIOUS SCIENTISTS

Richard introduces his next argument, the argument from 'admired religious scientists', by quoting Bertrand Russell. Bertrand Arthur William Russell (1872–1970) was a British philosopher, logician, essayist, and social critic best known for his work in mathematical logic and analytic philosophy. Bertrand's most influential contributions include his championing of logicism (That's the view that mathematics is in some important sense reducible to logic), his refining of Gottlob Frege's predicate calculus (Which still forms the basis of most contemporary systems of logic), his defense of neutral monism – the view that the world consists of just one type of substance which is neither exclusively mental nor exclusively physical, and his theories of definite descriptions, logical atomism (A theoretical approach that regards something as interpretable through analysis into distinct, separable, and independent elementary components), and types. Here's his quote:

"The immense majority of *'intellectually eminent'* men disbelieve in Christian religion, but they conceal the fact in public, because they are afraid of losing their incomes." [355]

I submit that the only way one can confirm if the basis of this statement by Gottlob is true or not, is to do a controlled survey of all the so-called *'intellectually eminent'* men (And women), in the world (I would ask, "Who or what defines what the standard is for what 'intellectually eminent' means? Ha-ha-ha) and compile the data to determine if this is in fact a true statement about such intellectuals. I also believe that the controlled survey needs to be autonomous so that the participants can answer its questions without fear of judgement or risk of any kind, especially since many of these participants have a fear of losing their job if their true feelings were published.

That said, even if it were found to be a true statement, what does it say? It simply says that *supposed smart people* are ever learning and never seem to be able to come to a knowledge of the truth about the spiritual; about the reality of God's existence; what the purpose of life is; what happens after death; or even what consciousness, gravity, dark matter, and dark energy are, and I might add that this list of unanswered 'Big' questions appears to go on-and-on ad infinitum. It seems these 'Big' questions cannot be incontrovertibly proven one way or the other (Scientifically or Spiritually), and therefore the smartest person on down to the simple minded like myself, are left to weigh the data and arguments for and against the existence of God for themselves, and after they do they then must decide what, to them, is more than likely (or probably) true, and what is more than likely (or probably) false.

Again, each of us are afforded the opportunity of using our own intellect, reason, and spiritual senses to choose what we want to believe or what we want to disbelieve about the 'Big' question of whether-or-not God exists, and if He does exist, wouldn't that mean that all the other 'Big' questions, such as "Is there life after death?", or "What's the purpose of life?" are answered too? Richard says, "The nineteenth century appears to be that period of time when there was less social and judicial pressure than in earlier centuries to profess religion, and more scientific support for abandoning it. I shall concentrate mostly on scientists, because – for reasons that are perhaps not too hard to imagine – those who trot out the names of admired individuals as religious exemplars, very commonly choose scientists." [356]

I come at this 'admired individuals' topic a bit differently. I choose to trot out prophets past and present. Let me substitute a word 'here and there' to Richard's statement, so I can make a point that I think is relevant to what we're talking about here. Here's how I would restate what Richard just said:

"I shall concentrate mostly on *atheists*, because – for reasons that are perhaps not too hard to imagine – those who trot out the names of admired scientist friends as 'nonbelieving exemplars', are commonly *atheist* scientists." [357]

In other words, Richard is criticizing theists for doing what he himself has done throughout the whole of his book – trotting out individuals whom he feels are admired individuals and telling us what they said about God and things. Richard's admired allies are mostly atheists like himself. He does so, hoping that it will help his case against God's existence. If I'm honest, I too am doing the very same thing. I've been quoting admired prophets, both living ones and dead ones, in the hopes of bolstering my perspective and arguments regarding God's existence. This is just the way debates go, right?

The bottom line of Richard's argument against using admired *religious scientists*, is laid out in Richard's next statement:

"Great scientists who profess religion become harder to find through the twentieth century, but they are not particularly rare. I suspect that most of the more recent ones are religious only in the Einsteinian sense." [358]

Speaking of the three most prominent, award winning, believing theist scientists, Richard says:

"I remain baffled, not so much by their belief in *a cosmic lawgiver of some kind*, as by their belief in the *details* of the Christian religion: i.e., resurrection, forgiveness of sins and all. [359]

Richard then refers to a fellow scientist, Jim Watson, founding genius of the Human Genome Project, who is an atheist like himself. Richard asked Watson whether he knew many religious scientists, ... and Jim replied: "Virtually none. Occasionally I meet them, and I'm a bit embarrassed [laughs] because, you know, I can't believe anyone accepts truth by revelation." [360]

"There was a study done and listed in the leading journal *Nature* by Larson and Witham in 1998 which showed that American scientists considered to be eminent enough by their peers to have been elected to the National Academy of Sciences (equivalent to being a Fellow of the Royal Society in Britain), only about 7% believe in a personal God." [361]

Richard's bottom line to the *admired religious scientist's argument*, is his typical self-aggrandizing response of being more intelligent than most people he knows. Richard believes, "More highly educated people are less likely to be religious." [362]

Again, this may or may not be true, but this is just an opinion about what *the numbers* seem to be saying about scientists who are believers, versus the numbers of scientists who are not. Richard believes that *the higher the numbers are* in some way proves his opinion is true. Here's what he said:

"Meta-analysis is the technique whereby an investigator looks at all the research papers that have been published on a topic and *counts up the number of papers* that have concluded one thing, versus *the number that have concluded something else*. On the subject of religion and IQ, the only meta-analysis known to me, was published by Paul Bell in Mensa Magazine in 2002 (Mensa is the society of individuals with a high IQ, and their journal not surprisingly includes articles on the one thing that draws them together)."

"Bell concluded: "Of 43 studies carried out since 1927 on the relationship between religious belief and one's intelligence and/or educational level, all but four found an inverse connection. That is, the higher one's intelligence or education level, the less one is likely to be religious or hold religious beliefs of any kind'." [363]

My response to the logic that Mr. Bell and Richard are putting forth here, is to go back before the Middle Ages when the known population of the world, for the most part, believed the world was flat. And a little later on the supposed highly intelligent, highly educated, and influential people also imagined that the earth was at the center of the universe and that the sun revolved around it. I am sure these eminently intelligent people uses the 'greater numbers' argument to convince the majority of the people that their postulates were true. But I ask you, did the so-called *eminent intelligent minds* of that Day, along with the masses who believed in what those so-called intellectuals said was factual at that time, make their statement of belief or postulate true? It most certainly did not! They were wrong!

The so-called *meta-analysis of greater numbers* for believing the world was flat or that the sun revolved around the earth, did not make their theories true. Greater numbers supporting any idea, in-and-of themselves, do *not* make opinions or postulates true. Period! C'mon Richard, you know better. The argument that 'larger numbers of people who believe something to be true, must make it so', just doesn't fly, and implying that it does, like Richard has suggested here, makes me call into question Richard's boasting so-called *eminence of intelligence*! To me, it's just another manifestation of an atheist's delusion. The next argument is – "Pascal's Wager"

PASCAL'S WAGER

Richard's next argument is against Elaise Pascal, the great French mathematician who stated that, "However long the odds *against* God's existence might be, there is an even larger asymmetry in the penalty for guessing wrong." [364]

Put another way, Richard says to the theist, "Believing is not something you can *decide* to do as a matter of policy. At least, it is not something I can decide to do as an act of will (Interesting). I can decide to go to church, and I can decide to recite the "Nicene Creed", and I can decide to swear on a stack of Bibles that I believe every word inside them. But none of that can *make* me actually believe it ... *if I don't*. (Ah, I was asking myself, "What's the catch Richard?" and then he said it, "... *none of that can make me actually believe it if I don't*"). [365]

That's true Richard. No one can make anybody believe something if they don't believe it (Or, more especially, if they don't want to believe it, even if it is true). Richard continues:

"Pascal's Wager could only ever be an argument for feigning belief in God. And the God that you claim to believe in had better not be of the omniscient kind or he'd see through the deception. The ludicrous idea that believing is something you can *decide to do* is deliciously mocked by Douglas Adams in '*Dirk Gentley's Holistic Detective Agency*' where we meet the robotic Electric Monk, a labor-saving device that you buy 'to do your believing for you'. The *deluxe* model is advertised as 'Capable of believing things they wouldn't believe in Salt Lake City' (Ha-ha-ha. That was funny Richard. Once again you crack me up. Richard seems to be implying that folks from Salt Lake City, which includes me, believe in crazy stuff. Ha-ha-ha. That's funny)." [366]

At the risk of appearing as though I'm preaching here, I simply want to give my perspective against Richard's statement where he said: "It's ludicrous to think that *believing* is something you can *decide to do*". I want to share an example of why I believe it is absolutely true that *you can decide to believe*. In fact, it is completely normal and is what God would have us do. In the Book of Mormon, the prophet Alma was confronted by a large body of individuals who were ostracized by a community of so-called believers who viewed these poverty-stricken people as less-than-acceptable. In other words, they didn't wear the right kind of expensive clothing like these hypocrites wore, etc. What made it even worse was the fact that these impoverished believers were the ones who had done all the work of building the meeting houses where everyone came to worship. Because these poor congregants made these high-and-mighty hypocrites *feel uncomfortable* when they attended their synagogues to worship with them, they refused to let them in, and cast out anyone who had somehow made it past their guards.

Having been cast out of their place of worship they went in search for the prophet Alma to ask how they could worship when they had no church to go to anymore. As part of his answer, Alma spoke of '*faith*' and '*belief*'. His answer is a little long, but I'm confident that you, my readers, will come to feel that it was well worth the time you invest once you're done reading it, because it's such a beautiful answer; not only to their question, but to Richard's claim that "one cannot *choose to believe*". Richard said, '*none of that can make me actually believe it if I don't believe it*', and so I felt this particular discourse by the ancient prophet Alma fits beautifully as a response to Richard's comment. Alma begins his answer to these humbled members by saying:

Alma 32:26-27

26 Now, as I said concerning faith—that it was not a perfect knowledge—even so it is with my words. Ye cannot *know of their* surety *at first, unto perfection,* any more than faith is a perfect knowledge.

27 But behold, if ye will awake and arouse your faculties, even to an *experiment* (An actual scientific method kind of experiment) upon my words, and exercise a particle of faith, yea, even if ye can no more than *desire to believe, let* this desire work in you, even until ye *believe in a manner* that ye can *give place for a portion of my words."*

"Give place for a portion of my words", to me, *is deciding to believe* in a portion of the word, even if it is in a really small portion, or at least hearing and feeling it out. "Desiring to believe" so that you can give place to just a few words, such as a statement of principle, is most definitely making the *decision to believe*, even, as I said, if it is choosing to believe something as small as 'I don't know God lives, but I want to believe He does", or "because I hope that there is life after I die, I'll give place for that hope".

If God does in fact exist, then there's an afterlife in which God will judge each of us for our actions, be they good or bad, and if this is true, then it most definitely matters what you *choose to believe.* Granted, no one can force you to believe if you don't want to believe something's true. I'm okay with that. But the kind of eternity you'll experience after you die, hangs in the balance. So, *yes,* you can *choose or decide* NOT *to believe,* just as easily as you *can choose or decide* TO BELIEVE. It's our choice whether or not we want to believe in, or give place for, 'these word-seeds' to be planted in our heart in order *to see if it, the seed, will grow or take root.* These are the *seeds* which Alma is speaking of here.

Richard concludes, "Pascal (with his 'bet' argument), was probably joking when he promoted his wager, just as I am joking in my dismissal of it." [367]

Again, the penalty for guessing wrong vs guessing right, is what Pascal's wager was all about. But does proving it wrong add one iota of evidence to God's non-existence? Of course not. Again, this is just a fun point that Richard is using to toy with his readers in the hope that we will come to agree with him and therefore, move closer to his belief in God's non-existence. Richard goes on to argue *against* the idea that one can decide to believe. He says, "The ludicrous idea that believing is something you can decide to do, is an idea to be deliciously mocked." He continues, "Why do we so readily accept the idea that the one thing you must do if you want to please God is to believe in Him? Suppose we grant that there is indeed some small chance that God exists. Nevertheless, it could be said that you will lead a better, fuller life if you *bet* on his not existing, than if you *bet* on his existing and therefore squander your precious time on worshipping him, sacrificing to him, fighting, and dying for him." [368]

My perspective on the idea of *deciding to believe* as being ludicrous, is to simply say that it is obvious that Richard's conceptualization of what it means to *decide to believe* is very different from my Latter-Day Saint conceptualization of what it means to *decide to believe.* I want to expand upon the three verses I just shared with you, for just a few minutes longer, because I think it will expand your understanding of what '*belief*' really is and how a person can *decide to believe.* In fact, this decision is paramount to one being able to come to a knowledge of God's existence. The following additional verses are a continuance of the conversation Alma had begun with this humbled group of believers. Alma expands upon this concept of belief, and so I hope that his expanded answer to their question will give you, my readers, a greater understanding of my conceptualization of what *deciding to believe* really means to me as a Latter-Day Saint. My perspective is one that says *deciding to believe* in God and His word is *a gift.* It's like being given the opportunity to partake of fruit from a tree. Alma continues:

Alma 32:17-43

17 Yea, there are many who do say: If thou wilt show unto us a sign from heaven, then we shall know of a surety; then we shall believe (This perspective on what believe means, has been held from the beginning of time. Richard seems to be suffering from a very bad case of '*lack of faith*').

18 Now I ask, is this faith? Behold, I say unto you, Nay; for if a man knoweth a thing he hath no cause to *believe,* for he knoweth it.

19 And now, how much more cursed is he that knoweth the will of God and doeth it not, than he that only believeth, or only hath cause to believe, and falleth into transgression?

20 Now of this thing ye must judge. Behold, I say unto you, that it is on the one hand even as it is on the other; and it shall be unto every man according to his work (According to their personal '*effort*' to seek and then come to this kind of knowledge).

21 And now as I said concerning faith—faith is not to have a perfect knowledge of things; therefore if ye have faith ye hope for things which are not seen, which are true.

22 And now, behold, I say unto you, and I would that ye should remember, that God is merciful unto all who believe on his name; therefore he desireth, in the first place, that ye should believe, yea, even on his word.

23 And now, he imparteth his word by angels unto men, yea, not only men but women also. Now this is not all; little children do have words given unto them many times, which confound the wise and the learned.

24 And now, my beloved brethren, as ye have desired to know of me what ye shall do because ye are afflicted and cast out—now I do not desire that ye should suppose that I mean to judge you only according to that which is true—

25 For I do not mean that ye all of you have been compelled to humble yourselves; for I verily believe that there are some among you who would humble themselves, let them be in whatsoever circumstances they might.

26 Now, as I said concerning faith—that it was not a perfect knowledge—even so it is with my words. Ye cannot know of their surety at first, *unto perfection*, any more than faith is a perfect knowledge.

27 But behold, if ye will awake and arouse your faculties, even to an *experiment* upon my words, and exercise a *particle of faith*, yea, even if ye can no more than *desire to believe* (This is *'deciding to believe'*, is it not? Letting yourself consider a principle?), let this *desire* work in you, even until ye believe in a manner *that ye can give place for* (By 'give place for', I believe Alma meant 'choose' or 'desire' to believe in) a portion of my words.

28 Now, we will compare the word unto a seed. Now, if ye give place, that a seed may be planted in your heart, behold, if it be a true seed, or a good seed, if ye do not cast it out by your *unbelief, that ye will resist the Spirit of the Lord*, behold, it will begin to swell within your breasts; and when you feel these swelling motions, ye will begin to say within yourselves—It must needs be that this is a good seed, or that *the word* is good, for it beginneth to enlarge my soul; yea, it beginneth to *enlighten my understanding*, yea, it beginneth to be *delicious to me (*The fruits of experimenting on the word-seed are these very experiences).

29 Now behold, would not this increase your faith? I say unto you, Yea; nevertheless, it hath not grown up to a perfect knowledge.

30 But behold, as the seed swelleth, and sprouteth, and beginneth to grow, then you must needs say that the seed is good; for behold it swelleth, and sprouteth, and beginneth to grow (the experiments' results are positive in other words). And now, behold, will not this strengthen your faith? Yea, it will *strengthen* your faith: for ye will say I know that this is a good seed; for behold it sprouteth and beginneth to grow.

31 And now, behold, are ye sure that this is a good seed? I say unto you, Yea; for every seed bringeth forth unto its own likeness.

32 Therefore, if a seed groweth it is good, but if it groweth not, behold it is not good, therefore it is cast away (This is how the postulate or theory is falsified or not).

33 And now, behold, because ye have tried the *experiment*, and planted the seed (By choosing to give place for a portion of His words; *you chose to grow your belief* in a portion of the word *by planting that word-seed*), and it swelleth and sprouteth, and beginneth to grow, ye must needs know that *the* seed is good.

34 And now, behold, is your knowledge perfect? Yea, your knowledge is perfect *in that thing*, and your faith is dormant; and this because you know, for ye know that the word hath *swelled your souls*, and ye also know that *it hath sprouted up*, that your *'understanding'* doth begin *to be enlightened*, and your mind doth begin *to expand* (This is exactly what scientists experience from following their scientific method in order to prove out the experiment).

35 O then, is not this real? I say unto you, Yea, because it is *light*; and whatsoever is light, is good, because it is discernible, therefore ye must know that it is good; and now behold, after ye have *tasted* this light is your knowledge perfect (This is why I call it a gift from God)?

36 Behold I say unto you, Nay; neither must ye lay aside your faith, for ye have only exercised your faith *to plant the seed* (Because you chose to believe or hope to believe in a portion of the word) that ye might *try the experiment* to know if the seed was good.

37 And behold, as the tree beginneth to grow, ye will say: Let us nourish it with great care, that it may get root, that it may *grow up*, and *bring forth fruit* unto us. And now behold, if ye nourish it with much care it will get root, and grow up, and bring forth *fruit* (This is *'doing science'*, but it's applying it to a spiritual experiment and spiritual data).

38 But if ye neglect the tree, and take no thought for its nourishment, behold it will not get any root; and when the heat of the sun cometh and scorcheth it, because it hath no root it withers away, and ye pluck it up and cast it out (Deciding to believe includes continuous effort to complete the experiment or follow through with the full process).

39 Now, this is not because the seed was not good, neither is it because the fruit thereof would not be desirable; but it is because your ground is barren, and ye will not nourish the tree, therefore ye cannot have (Or enjoy) the fruit (The results) thereof.

40 And thus, if ye will not nourish the word, looking forward with an eye of faith to the fruit thereof, ye can never pluck of the fruit of the tree of life.

41 But if ye will nourish the word, yea, nourish the tree as it beginneth to grow, by your faith with great diligence, and with patience, looking forward to the fruit thereof (Don't scientists have patience, as they exercise their faith in their experimental method?), it shall take root; and behold it shall be a tree springing up unto everlasting life.

(This sounds very much like a scientific experiment that requires the faith and patience one would hopefully have in their theory; the kind of hope that produces the results you are predicting it will, as you do the work ... and in fact are hoping it will, does it not?).

42 And because of your diligence and your faith (to do the experiment; to do science so to speak) and your patience with the word in nourishing it, that it may take root in you, behold, by and by ye shall pluck the fruit thereof, which is most precious, which is sweet above all that is sweet, and which is white above all that is white, yea, and pure above all that is pure; and ye shall feast upon this fruit even until ye are filled, that ye hunger not, neither shall ye thirst (This fruit is a *gift* of knowing God lives and loves us).

Jesus Himself said He offers the kind of 'living water' where ye shall not thirst anymore, and the kind of 'bread of life' where ye would not hunger anymore. This delicious *fruit*, the delicious *results* from the *experiment*, is the fruit and life-giving bread and water Jesus promises us, they being the means for satisfying spiritual thirst and spiritual hunger. The symbolic tokens of the sacrament – the bread and water of the ordinance of the sacrament – which, if partaken of with a broken heart and a contrite spirit, and in faith – will cause a renewal in one's heart and mind, spiritually speaking. Alma continues:

43 Then, my brethren, ye shall reap the *rewards* of your faith, and your diligence, and patience, and long-suffering, waiting for *the tree* to bring forth fruit (This Spiritual fruit) unto you.

I think that makes it incredibly clear, but just to make sure there is no misunderstanding whatsoever, I want to share the following commentaries on these same verses you just read. Prophets and apostles have given these commentaries, along with other general authority leaders of the Church of Jesus Christ of Latter-Day Saints, in which they describe *'how to come to a belief in God'* (Starting with *deciding to believe*). In reading their commentaries it becomes quite evident what is meant by *'deciding to believe'*. The first of the commentaries is by the apostle, Elder Bruce R. McConkie, who died back in 1985. Here's what Elder McConkie said, who, by the way, was a hero of mine. Elder McConkie said, and I quote:

"A central point of Alma 32 (The chapter we've been discussing) is that of *having faith in* the word of God. Alma observed that when the *word of God is planted in the fertile soil of the heart* (and not on hardpan soil, which is an unbelieving heart), like a seed, it will begin to swell and grow. Through *experimenting upon the word* or *nurturing it through obedience* (It being a type of spiritual, scientific-like method for learning truth), the word of God will bring forth fruit (Results) that is most precious, and sweet above all that is sweet, white above all that is white, and pure above all that is pure" [369] (One of those experimental fruits, or gifts, is the knowledge that God exists. Isn't this planting of the seed the result of "deciding to believe just a little so that the seed you plant in your heart has a chance to grow"?).

End quote

Neglecting the word of God will result in no such fruit. As I said, this *experiment* is much like the steps of the Scientific Method, the very way we are to perform this spiritual experiment on the word-seed. It begins by starting the experiment, doing tests, and making predictions about them, and then looking for, even expecting repeatable results like the fruit mentioned by the prophet Alma to his listeners, those results or fruit being *a swelling and sprouting of the seed*, and *the seed continuing to grow*. How do we nurture our faith in the word-seed so that we may feast upon its ultimate fruit – the knowledge that God exists? President Joseph Fielding Smith (1876–1972), the 10th President and Prophet of the Church of Jesus Christ of Latter-Day Saints, taught the following regarding the 'How', quote:

"If we want to have a living, abiding faith (That God lives), we must be active in the performance of every duty as members of this Church" [370] ("Be ye doers of the word and not hearers only").

End quote

Elder Joseph B. Wirthlin (1917–2008), an apostle who served in the Quorum of the Twelve Apostles for twenty-two years (1986–2008), said the following about this "How":

"Faith exists when absolute confidence in that which we cannot see combines with action that is in absolute conformity to the will of our Heavenly Father. Without all three — **first**, absolute confidence; **second**, action; and **third**, absolute conformity—without these three, all we have is a counterfeit, a weak and watered-down faith." [371]

Elder Jeffrey R. Holland, a current member of the Quorum of the Twelve Apostles, commented on these verses from the book of Alma that we are discussing here, saying, and I quote:

"In [the] brilliant discourse [of Alma 32], Alma moves the reader from a general commentary on faith in the seedlike word of God to a focused discourse on faith in Christ as the Word of God, ... grown to *a fruit-bearing tree*, a tree whose fruit is exactly that of Lehi's earlier perception of Christ's love (Go to I Nephi 8, to read about Lehi's vision of the 'Tree of Life'). Christ is the bread of life, the living water. He is the true vine. Christ is the seed, the tree, and the fruit of eternal life. But the profound and central Tree of Life imagery in this discourse is lost, or at least greatly diminished, *if* the reader does not follow it on into the next two chapters of the Book of Mormon.

Blessed Are They Who Humble Themselves

"Alma perceived the readiness of the poor Zoramites to be taught the gospel. Their rejection by the wealthy Zoramites contributed to their state of humility." [372]

"Bishop Richard C. Edgley, past member of the Presiding Bishopric of the Church of Jesus Christ of Latter-Day Saints commented on them saying, and I quote from a talk titled "Family Pecan Tree: Planting a Legacy of Faith at Home":

"Many of us live or work in an environment where humility is often misunderstood and considered a weakness. Not many corporations or institutions include humility as a value statement or a desired characteristic of their management. Yet as we learn about the workings of God, the power of a humble and submissive spirit becomes apparent. In the kingdom of God, greatness begins with humility and submissiveness. These companion virtues are the first critical steps to opening the doors to the blessings of God and the power of the priesthood. It matters not who we are or how lofty our credentials appear. Humility and submissiveness to the Lord, coupled with a grateful heart, are our strength and our hope. Humility is important enough in the eyes of the Lord that He sometimes humbles us (Review verses 8–16 again, where it speaks of 'two ways' to become humble. Compelled being one). Verse 13 described those who are "compelled to be humble"; verses 14 and 16 speak of those who "humble themselves voluntarily because of the word." [373]

Elder Carlos E. Asay (1926–99) of the Seventy, also shared his thoughts on these two groups and what is called the *Nephite Cycle of Righteousness*:

Quote: "Most of us seem to have or are living what has been coined as the 'Nephite cycle', as part of our character (This reminds me of the Cycle of Sin). There is a point when we are teachable; our humility enables us to grow and to ride the crest of spirituality. Then there are other times when we begin to feel self-sufficient and puffed up with pride. ... How much better it would be if we kept in remembrance our God and our religion and broke *the cycle* by consistent worship and righteous living. How much better it would be if we were humbled by the word of the Lord and strong enough in spirit to remember our God ... in whatsoever circumstances we find ourselves." [374]

End quote by elder Asay

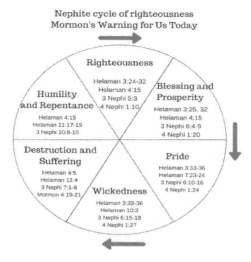

Quote: "Most of us seem to have or are living what has been coined as the 'Nephite cycle', as part of our character (This reminds me of the Cycle of Sin, right?)."

"There is a point when we are teachable; our humility enables us to grow and to ride the crest of spirituality. Then there are other times when we begin to feel self-sufficient and puffed up with pride. How much better it would be if we kept in remembrance our God and our religion and broke *the cycle* by consistent worship and righteous living. How much better it would be if we were humbled by the word of the Lord and strong enough in spirit to remember our God ... in whatsoever circumstances we find ourselves." [375]

End quote by Elder Asay

President Ezra Taft Benson (1899–1994) described ways that we could humble ourselves and avoid the trials that sometimes accompany being *compelled to be humble*. Again, this all relates to us '*deciding to believe*'. He said, quote: "We can choose to humble ourselves by conquering *enmity* toward our brothers and sisters, esteeming them as ourselves, and lifting them as high or higher ... than we are":

Doctrine & Covenants 38:24

24 And let every man esteem his brother as himself, and practice virtue and holiness before me.

Doctrine & Covenants 81:5

5 Wherefore, be faithful; stand in the office which I have appointed unto you; succor the weak, lift up the hands which hang down, and strengthen the feeble knees.

Doctrine & Covenants 84:106

106 And if any man among you be strong in the Spirit, let him take with him, him that is weak, that he may be edified in all meekness, that he may become strong also.

We can choose to humble ourselves by receiving counsel and chastisement":

Jacob 4:10

10 Wherefore, brethren, seek not to counsel the Lord, but to take counsel from his hand. For behold, ye yourselves know that he counseleth in wisdom, and in justice, and in great mercy, over all his works.

Helaman 15:3

15 Yea, wo unto this people who are called the people of Nephi except they shall repent, when they shall see all these signs and wonders which shall be showed unto them; for behold, they have been a chosen people of the Lord; yea, the people of Nephi hath he loved, and also hath he chastened them; yea, in the days of their iniquities hath he chastened them because he loveth them.

Doctrine & Covenants 63:55

55 And now behold, verily I say unto you, I, the Lord, am not pleased with my servant Sidney Rigdon; he exalted himself in his heart, and received not counsel, but grieved the Spirit;

Doctrine & Covenants 101:4 –5

4 Therefore, they must needs be chastened and tried, even as Abraham, who was commanded to offer up his only son.

5 For all those who will not endure chastening, but deny me, cannot be sanctified.

Doctrine & Covenants 108:1

1 Verily thus saith the Lord unto you, my servant Lyman: Your sins are forgiven you, because you have obeyed my voice in coming up hither this morning to receive counsel of him whom I have appointed.

Doctrine & Covenants 124:61, 84

61 That he may receive also the counsel from those whom I have set to be as plants of renown, and as watchmen upon her walls.

84 And with my servant Almon Babbitt, there are many things with which I am not pleased; behold, he aspireth to establish his counsel instead of the counsel which I have ordained, even that of the Presidency of my Church; and he setteth up a golden calf for the worship of my people.

Doctrine & Covenants 136:31

31 My people must be tried in all things, that they may be prepared to receive the glory that I have for them, even the glory of Zion; and he that will not bear chastisement is not worthy of my kingdom.

Proverbs 9:8

8 Reprove not a scorner, lest he hate thee: rebuke a wise man, and he will love thee.

"We can choose to humble ourselves by forgiving those who have offended us":

III Nephi 13:11, 14

11 And forgive us our debts, as we forgive our debtors.

14 For, if ye forgive men their trespasses your Heavenly Father will also forgive you;

Doctrine and Covenant 64:10

10 I, the Lord, will forgive whom I will forgive, but of you it is required to forgive all men.

"We can choose to humble ourselves by rendering selfless service":

Mosiah 2:16–17

16 Behold, I say unto you that because I said unto you that I had spent my days in your service, I do not desire to boast, for I have only been in the service of God.

17 And behold, I tell you these things that ye may learn wisdom; that ye may learn that when ye are in the service of your fellow beings ye are only in the service of your God.

"We can choose to humble ourselves by going on missions and preaching the word that can humble others":

Alma 4:19

19 And this he did that he himself might go forth among his people, or among the people of Nephi, that he might preach the word of God unto them, to stir them up in remembrance of their duty, and that he might pull down, by the word of God, all the pride and craftiness and all the contentions which were among his people, seeing no way that he might reclaim them save it were in bearing down in pure testimony ... against them.

Alma 31:5

5 And now, as the preaching of the word had a great tendency to lead the people to do that which was just—yea, it had had more powerful effect upon the minds of the people than the sword, or anything else, which had happened unto them—therefore Alma thought it was expedient that they should try the virtue of the word of God.

Alma 48:20

20 And thus they went forth, and the people did humble themselves because of their words, insomuch that they were highly favored of the Lord, and thus they were free from wars and contentions among themselves, yea, even for the space of four years.

"We can choose to humble ourselves by getting to the temple more frequently. And, we can choose to humble ourselves by confessing and forsaking our sins and being born of God":

Doctrine & Covenants 58:43

43 By this ye may know if a man repenteth of his sins—behold, he will confess them and forsake them.

Mosiah 27:25–26

25 And the Lord said unto me: Marvel not that all mankind, yea, men, and women, all nations, kindreds, tongues and people, must be born again; yea, born of God, changed from their carnal and fallen state, to a state of righteousness, being redeemed of God, becoming his sons and daughters;

25 And thus they become new creatures; and unless they do this, they can in nowise inherit the kingdom of God.

Alma 5:7–14, 49

7 Behold, he changed their hearts; yea, he awakened them out of a deep sleep, and they awoke unto God. Behold, they were in the midst of darkness; nevertheless, their souls were illuminated by the light of the everlasting word; yea, they were encircled about by the bands of death, and the chains of hell, and an everlasting destruction did await them.

8 And now I ask of you, my brethren, were they destroyed? Behold, I say unto you, Nay, they were not.

9 And again I ask, were the bands of death broken, and the chains of hell which encircled them about, were they loosed? I say unto you, Yea, they were loosed, and their souls did expand, and they did sing redeeming love. And I say unto you that they are saved.

10 And now I ask of you on what conditions are they saved? Yea, what grounds had they to hope for salvation? What is the cause of their being loosed from the bands of death, yea, and also the chains of hell?

11 Behold, I can tell you—did not my father Alma believe in the words which were delivered by the mouth of Abinadi? And was he not a holy prophet? Did he not speak the words of God, and my father Alma believe them?

12 And according to his faith there was a mighty change wrought in his heart. Behold I say unto you that this is all true.

13 And behold, he preached the word unto your fathers and a mighty change was also wrought in their hearts, and they humbled themselves and put their trust in the True and Living God. And behold, they were faithful until the end; therefore they were saved.

14 And now behold, I ask of you, my brethren of the church, have ye spiritually been born of God? Have ye received his image in your countenances? Have ye experienced this mighty change in your hearts?

49 And now I say unto you that this is the order after which I am called, yea, to preach unto my beloved brethren, yea, and every one that dwelleth in the land;

... yea, to preach unto all, both old and young, both bond and free; yea, I say unto you the aged, and also the middle aged, and the rising generation; yea, to cry unto them that they must repent and be born again. We can choose to humble ourselves by loving God, submitting our will to His, and putting Him first in our lives" (Just as Jesus exemplified, saying, 'Father, not my will, but thine be done"). [376]

End quote by President Ezra Taft Benson

Elder Dallin H. Oaks, first councilor in the First Presidency of the Church of Jesus Christ of Latter-Day Saints as of (June 2022), spoke of the dangers accompanying the seeking of signs for faith and belief purposes, quote:

"The showing of a sign can work to the condemnation of those who are brought to knowledge by that means. They miss the opportunity to *develop faith*, and they subject themselves to a more severe punishment for backsliding than those whose *spiritual development* is proceeding along the normal pathway of developing faith. There are other condemnations to those who seek signs *without first developing the faith God has required as a prerequisite*. One condemnation is to be misled. God warned ancient Israel against following prophets who gave signs and wonders and then sought to lead them away to the worship of strange gods (I would say Evolution and its tenant natural selection, is such a strange god):

Deuteronomy 13:1–3

1 If there arise among you a prophet, or a dreamer of dreams, and giveth thee a sign or a wonder,

2 And the sign or the wonder come to pass, whereof he spake unto thee, saying, Let us go after other gods, which thou hast not known, and let us serve them;

3 Thou shalt not hearken unto the words of that prophet, or that dreamer of dreams: for the LORD your God proveth you, to know whether ye love the LORD your God with all your heart and with all your soul.

"The Savior taught his apostles that in the last days":

JST Matt. 24:23

23 Then if any man shall say unto you, Lo, here *is* Christ, or there; believe *it* not.

Matt. 24:24

24 For there shall arise false Christs, and false prophets, and shall shew great signs and wonders; insomuch that, if *it were* possible, they shall deceive the very elect.

Mark 13:22

22 For false Christs and false prophets (Such as Charles Darwin) shall rise, and shall shew signs and wonders, to seduce, if *it were* possible, even the elect.

"There shall also arise false Christs, and false prophets, and shall show great signs and wonders, insomuch that, if possible, they shall deceive the *very elect*, who are *the elect according to the covenant*.

"In our day, God does not use miracles or signs as a way of teaching or convincing the unbeliever. As a result, we should not ask for signs for this purpose, and we should be deeply suspicious of the so-called spiritual *evidence* of those who do." [377]

End quote by Elder Oaks

President Boyd K. Packer, past President of the Quorum of the Twelve Apostles, who passed away in 2015, helps us better understand the meaning of faith when he taught, quote:

"Faith, to be faith, must center around something that is not known. Faith, to be faith, *must go beyond that for which there is confirming evidence. Faith, to be faith, must go into the unknown*. Faith, to be faith, must walk to the edge of the light, and then a few steps into the darkness."

(Much like Joshua had the Levite priests, who carried the Ark of the Covenant, take a few steps into the river Jordan *before* the river Jordan began to separate, allowing the Israelites to pass through the river on dry ground. This was the same way the Lord taught Moses and the Israelites faith, when they were facing the Red Sea on the one hand, and Pharoah's army who were at their backs on the other. Moses exercised faith and was able to, through God's power, part the Red Sea so that the Israelites were able to walk through the Red Sea on dry ground. The principle here, is that *"Faith precedes the miracle"*) Here's the Joshua and Levite Priests story in scripture:

Joshua 3:15-17

15 And as they that bare the ark were come unto Jordan, and *the feet of the priests that bare the ark were dipped in the brim of the water*, ... for Jordan over floweth all his banks all the time of harvest.

16 That the waters which came down from above *stood and rose up upon an heap* very far from the city Adam, that *is* beside Zaretan: and those that came down toward the sea of the plain, *even* the salt sea, failed, *and* were cut off: and the people passed over right against Jericho.

17 And *the priests that bare the ark of the covenant of the* LORD *stood firm on dry ground in the midst of Jordan*, and all the Israelites passed over on dry ground, until all the people were passed clean over Jordan.

"If everything has to be known, if everything has to be explained, if everything has to be certified, *then there is no need for faith*. Indeed, there is no room for it (Which is Richard's mindset).

"There are *two kinds of faith*. One of them functions ordinarily in the life of every soul. It is the kind of faith *born by experience*; it gives us certainty that a new day will dawn, that spring will come, that growth will take place. It is the kind of faith that relates us with confidence to that which is scheduled to happen. ... (An example of this kind of faith is trusting the dotted line on a two-way street. It requires the kind of faith that moves you to trust others that they too will stay on their side of the dotted line).

"There is another kind of faith, rare indeed. This is *the kind of faith that* causes *things to happen* (Joseph Smith said "This kind of Faith is the *moving cause of all action*" [378] – See "Lectures on Faith"). It is the kind of faith that is worthy and prepared and unyielding, and it calls forth things that otherwise would not be. It is the kind of faith that moves people. It is the kind of faith that sometimes moves things. It comes by gradual growth. It is a marvelous, even a transcendent power, a power as real and as invisible as electricity. Directed and channeled, it has great effect.

In a world filled with skepticism and doubt, the expression *'seeing is believing'* promotes the attitude, *'You show me, and I will believe'* (Which is what Richard lives by). We want all of the proof and all of the evidence first. It seems hard to take things on faith. When will we learn that in *spiritual things* it works the other way about—that believing is seeing – *Spiritual belief precedes spiritual knowledge*. When we believe in things that are not seen but are nevertheless true, then we have faith." [379]

End of quotes by Elder Packer

Here's a quote by Elder Neal A. Maxwell (1926–2004). As mentioned before, he was a past member of the Quorum of the Twelve Apostles. He described the relationship between hope, faith, and knowledge and explained how they exist in a profound and dynamic relationship:

"Faith and hope are constantly interactive and may not always be precisely distinguished or sequenced. Though not perfect knowledge either, ... *hope's enlivened expectations* are 'with surety' true." [380]

End quote

Let me add the following verses:

Alma 32:21–37

21 And now as I said concerning faith—faith is not to have a perfect knowledge of things; therefore if ye have faith ye hope for things which are not seen, which are true.

22 And now, behold, I say unto you, and I would that ye should remember, that God is merciful unto all who *believe* on his name; therefore he desireth, in the first place, that ye should believe, yea, even on his word.

23 And now, he imparteth his word by angels unto men, yea, not only men but women also. Now this is not all; little children do have words given unto them many times, which confound the wise and the learned.

24 And now, my beloved brethren, as ye have desired to know of me what ye shall do because ye are afflicted and cast out—now I do not desire that ye should suppose that I mean to judge you only according to that which is true—

25 For I do not mean that ye all of you have been compelled to humble yourselves; for I verily believe that there are some among you who would humble themselves, let them be in whatsoever circumstances they might.

26 Now, as I said concerning faith—that it was not a perfect knowledge—even so it is with my words. Ye cannot know of their surety at first, unto perfection, any more than faith is a perfect knowledge.

27 But behold, if ye will awake and arouse your faculties, even to an experiment upon my words, and exercise a particle of faith, yea, even if ye can no more than desire to believe, let this desire work in you, even until ye believe in a manner that ye can give place for a portion of my words.

28 Now, we will compare the word unto a seed. Now, if ye give place, that a seed may be planted in your heart, behold, if it be a true seed, or a good seed, if ye do not cast it out by your unbelief, that ye will resist the Spirit of the Lord, behold, it will begin to swell within your breasts; and when you feel these swelling motions, ye will begin to say within yourselves—It must needs be that this is a good seed, or that the word is good, for it beginneth to enlarge my soul; yea, it beginneth to enlighten my ᶠunderstanding, yea, it beginneth to be delicious to me.

29 Now behold, would not this increase your faith? I say unto you, Yea; nevertheless, it hath not grown up to a perfect knowledge.

30 But behold, as the seed swelleth, and sprouteth, and beginneth to grow, then you must needs say that the seed is good; for behold it swelleth, and sprouteth, and beginneth to grow. And now, behold, will not this strengthen your faith? Yea, it will strengthen your faith: for ye will say I know that this is a good seed; for behold it sprouteth and beginneth to grow.

31 And now, behold, are ye sure that this is a good seed? I say unto you, Yea; for every seed bringeth forth unto its own likeness.

32 Therefore, if a seed groweth it is good, but if it groweth not, behold it is not good, therefore it is cast away.

33 And now, behold, because ye have tried *the experiment*, and planted the seed, and it swelleth and sprouteth, and beginneth to grow, ye must needs know that the seed is good.

34 And now, behold, is your knowledge perfect? Yea, your knowledge is perfect in that thing, and your faith is dormant; ... and this because you know, for ye know that the word hath swelled your souls, and ye also know that it hath sprouted up, that your understanding doth begin to be enlightened, and your mind doth begin to expand.

35 O then, is not this real? I say unto you, Yea, because it is light; and whatsoever is light, is good, because it is discernible, therefore ye must know that it is good; and now behold, after ye have tasted this light is your knowledge perfect?

36 Behold I say unto you, Nay; neither must ye lay aside your faith, for ye have only exercised your faith to plant the seed that ye might try the experiment to know if the seed was good.

37 And behold, as the tree beginneth to grow, ye will say: Let us nourish it with great care, that it may get root, that it may grow up, and bring forth fruit unto us. And now behold, if ye nourish it with much care it will get root, and grow up, and bring forth fruit.

How did Alma differentiate between faith and knowledge? Go back and read Alma 32 verse 23. The faith of little children often leads to divine insights. Elder Maxwell described how their example can serve to instruct those who are older. Here's his quote:

"Children often have the 'thoughts and [the] intents of [their] hearts' focused on the Master. Though not full of years, such children are full of faith! Too young for formal Church callings, they have been 'called to serve' as exemplifiers, doing especially well when blessed with 'goodly parents':

I Nephi 1:1

1 I, Nephi, having been born of goodly parents, therefore I was taught some-what in all the learning of my father; and having seen many afflictions in the course of my days, nevertheless, having been highly favored of the Lord in all my days; yea, having had a great knowledge of the goodness and the mysteries of God, therefore I make a record of my proceedings in my days.

"Just as the scriptures assure, 'little children do have words given unto them many times":

Alma 32:23

23 And now, he imparteth his word by angels unto men, yea, not only men but women also. Now this is not all; little children do have words given unto them many times, which confound the wise and the learned.

"For example, the resurrected Jesus revealed things to the Nephite children, who then taught adults and their parents *even greater things* than Jesus had taught":

III Nephi 26:14

14 And it came to pass that he did teach and minister unto the children of the multitude of whom hath been spoken, and he did loose their tongues, and they did speak unto their fathers great and marvelous things, even greater than he had revealed unto the people; and he loosed their tongues that they could utter.

"It has been a privilege to seal several adopted children to Nan and Dan Barker, now of Arizona. Some time ago Nate, then just over three, said: 'Mommy, there is another little girl who is supposed to come to our family. She has dark hair and dark eyes and lives a long way from here". The wise mother asked, 'How do you know this?' "Jesus told me, upstairs."

"The mother noted:

'We don't have an upstairs,' but quickly sensed the significance of what had been communicated. After much travail and many prayers, the Barker family were in a sealing room in the Salt Lake Temple in the fall of 1995, where a little girl with dark hair and dark eyes, from Kazakhstan, was sealed to them for time and eternity. Inspired children still tell parents great and marvelous things." [381]

Experimenting on the Word of God Brings Conversion

Elder M. Russell Ballard, acting President of the Quorum of the Twelve Apostles, taught that a willingness to perform Alma's experiment leads to conversion:

"We know that both members and nonmembers are more likely to be thoroughly converted to the gospel of Jesus Christ when they are willing to experiment upon the word (Go back and read Alma 32:27). This is an attitude of both mind and heart that includes a *desire* to know the truth and a willingness to *act* on that desire (Leads to 'deciding to believe').

"For those investigating the Church, *the experiment* can be as simple as agreeing to read the Book of Mormon, to pray about it, and to earnestly seek to know if Joseph Smith was the Lord's prophet. True conversion comes through the power of the Spirit.

"When the Spirit touches the heart, hearts are changed. When individuals, both members and investigators, feel the Spirit working with them, or when they see the evidence of the Lord's love and mercy in their lives, they are edified and strengthened spiritually, and their faith in Him increases. These experiences with the Spirit follow naturally when a person is willing to experiment upon the word. This is how we come to *feel* the gospel is true."

"At times the swelling motions, the enlarging of souls, the enlightening of understanding, and the beginning of delicious feelings from the Spirit spoken of in Alma 32:28 are difficult to verbally express. However, being hard to express does not discount the truthfulness of these feelings.[382]

President Boyd K. Packer shared an experience that describes the difficulty of verbal expression. He bore his testimony to an atheist that "There is a God". The man said, "he could not *know* such a thing". President Packer compared his testimony and knowledge of God's existence with "knowing what salt tastes like." [Review 366 again]

In other words, it is hard to put into words of explanation. Give place, that a seed may be planted and begin to grow. Increased faith in God's word is one of the fruits that come from seeds of faith planted in the fertile ground of a soft heart. President James E. Faust (1920–2007) of the First Presidency described the necessary prerequisites for faith and knowledge to grow and mature. Here they are:

"We ... need to prepare our own seedbeds of faith. To do this we need to plow the soil through daily humble prayer, asking for strength and forgiveness. We need to harrow the soil by overcoming our feelings of pride. We need to prepare the seedbed by keeping the commandments to the best of our ability. We need to be honest with the Lord in the payment of our tithing and our other offerings."

"We need to be worthy and able to call forth the great powers of the priesthood (The authority to act in God's name) to bless ourselves, our families, and others for whom we have responsibility. There is no better place for the spiritual seeds of our faith to be nurtured than within the hallowed sanctuaries of our temples and in our homes." [383]

The planted seed of faith does not grow suddenly. President Boyd K. Packer explained the importance of patience while waiting for the seed to grow:

"My experience has been that a testimony does not burst upon us suddenly. Rather, it grows, as Alma said, from a seed of faith. ... Do not be disappointed if you have read and reread and yet have not received a powerful witness. You may be somewhat like the disciples spoken of in the Book of Mormon who were filled with the power of God in great glory 'and they knew it not':

III Nephi 9:20

20 And ye shall offer for a sacrifice unto me a broken heart and a contrite spirit. And whoso cometh unto me with a broken heart and a contrite spirit, him will I baptize with fire and with the Holy Ghost, even as the Lamanites, because of their faith in me at the time of their conversion, were baptized with fire and with the Holy Ghost, *and they knew it not.*

Do the best you can. Think of this verse:

"'See that all these things are done in wisdom and order; for it is not requisite that a man should run faster than he has strength. And again, it is expedient that he should be diligent, that thereby he might win the prize; therefore, all things must be done in order'." [384]

It Beginneth to Be Delicious to Me

Alma used the concept of taste to describe the growth of testimony. The Prophet Joseph Smith (1805–44) also used 'taste' to teach about discernment of true doctrine, here's what he said: "This is *good* doctrine. It *tastes* good. I can *taste* the principles of eternal life, and *so can you.* ... I know that when I tell you these words of eternal life as they are given to me, you *taste* them, and I know that you believe them. You say honey is sweet, and so do I. I can also *taste* the spirit of eternal life. I know that it is good; and when I tell you of these things which were given me by inspiration of the Holy Spirit, you are bound to receive them as *sweet,* and rejoice more and more." [385]

Sister Janette Hales Beckham, former General Young Women President, spoke of the feelings associated with scripture reading. Here's what she said:

"Learning to discern the teachings of the Spirit is an important part of helping faith become a reality. My daughter Karen shared her experience. She said:

"When I was just a little girl, I started reading the Book of Mormon for the first time. After many days of reading, I came one night to":

I Nephi 3:7

7 And it came to pass that I, Nephi, said unto my father: I will go and do the things which the Lord hath commanded, for I know that the Lord giveth no commandments unto the children of men, save he shall prepare a way for them that they may accomplish the thing which he commandeth them.

"I didn't know this was a famous verse, but as I read that verse, I felt strongly impressed. I was impressed that Heavenly Father would help us keep His commandments, but the deep impression was really more of a feeling.

"I had seen my parents mark verses in their scriptures with red pencils. So, I got up and searched through the house until I found a red pencil, and with a great sense of solemnity and importance, I marked that verse in my own Book of Mormon.'

Janette continued: "Over the years as I read the scriptures, that experience was repeated time and time again — reading a verse and feeling deeply impressed. In time I came to recognize that feeling as the Holy Ghost'." [386]

"O Then, Is Not This Real?"

As Alma spoke to the poor Zoramites, he asked them to discern the truth of his message for themselves. One person cannot learn a gospel principle for another. Elder Neal A. Maxwell explained that each of us can know the certainty of divine truths:

"Alma describes the growth of faith and how faith can actually become knowledge with the accompanying intellectual and emotional experiences of the believer. After the understanding of the believer has been enlarged and his mind has been expanded, Alma asks":

Alma 32:35

35 O then, is not this real? I say unto you, Yea, because it is light; and whatsoever is light, is good, because it is discernible, therefore ye must know that it is good; and now behold, after ye have tasted this light is your knowledge perfect?

"The truth of each divine doctrine is actually discernible by us in a *'system of certification and confirmation'* that justifies our saying, 'I know!'" [387]

Nourish the Word

Elder Bruce C. Hafen of the Seventy, using Alma's metaphor of cultivation, identified two aspects of nourishment that bring the blessings of the gospel into our lives:

"We grow in two ways—*removing negative weeds and cultivating positive flowers*. The Savior's grace blesses both parts—if we do our part. First and repeatedly, we must uproot the weeds of sin and bad choices. It isn't enough just to *mow* the weeds. Yank them out by the roots, repenting fully to satisfy the conditions of mercy. But being forgiven is only part of our growth. We are not just paying a debt. Our purpose is to become celestial beings. So, once we've cleared our heartland, we must continually plant, weed, and nourish the seeds of divine qualities. And then as our sweat and discipline stretch us to meet His gifts, 'the flowers of grace appear' ["There Is Sunshine in My Soul Today," *Hymns*, no. 227], like hope and meekness. Even a tree of life can take root in this heart-garden, bearing fruit so sweet that it lightens all our burdens 'through the joy of his Son'. And when the flower of charity blooms here, we will love others with the power of Christ's own love." [388]

Alma 33:23

23 And now, my brethren, I desire that ye shall plant this word in your hearts, and as it beginneth to swell even so nourish it by your faith. And behold, it will become a tree springing up in you unto everlasting life. And then may God grant unto you that your burdens may be light, through the joy of his Son. And even all this can ye do if ye will. Amen.

Moroni 7:48

48 Wherefore, my beloved brethren, pray unto the Father with all the energy of heart, that ye may be filled with this love, which he hath bestowed upon all who are true followers of his Son, Jesus Christ; that ye may become the sons of God; that when he shall appear we shall be like him, for we shall see him as he is; that we may have this hope; that we may be purified even as he is pure. Amen.

Being a Disciple of Christ

President Dieter F. Uchtdorf, a past member of the First Presidency of the Church of Jesus Christ of Latter-Day saints, and a current member of the Quorum of the Twelve Apostles, taught members of the Church how to become a disciple of Christ:

"This is the peaceable way of the follower of Jesus Christ. Nevertheless, it is not a quick fix or an overnight cure. A friend of mine recently wrote to me, confiding that he was having a difficult time keeping his testimony strong and vibrant. He ... asked for counsel.

"I wrote back to him and lovingly suggested a few specific things he could do that would align his life more closely with the teachings of the restored gospel. To my surprise, I heard back from him only a week later. The essence of his letter was:

'I tried what you suggested. It didn't work. What else have you got?'

"Brothers and sisters, we have to stay with it. We don't acquire eternal life in a sprint—this is a race of endurance. We have to apply and reapply the divine gospel principles. Day after day we need to make them part of our normal life.

"Too often we approach the gospel like a farmer who places a seed in the ground in the morning and expects corn on the cob by the afternoon. When Alma compared the word of God to a seed, he explained that the seed grows into a fruit-bearing tree gradually, as a result of our 'faith, and [our] diligence, and patience, and long-suffering'."

"It's true that some blessings come right away: soon after we plant the seed in our hearts, it begins to swell and sprout and grow, and by this we know that the seed is good. From the very moment we set foot upon the pathway of discipleship, seen and unseen blessings from God begin to attend us. But we cannot receive the fulness of those blessings if we 'neglect the tree' and take no thought for its nourishment."

"Knowing that the seed is good is not enough. We must 'nourish it with great care, that it may get root' [v. 37]. Only then can we partake of the fruit that is 'sweet above all that is sweet, and pure above all that is pure' and 'feast upon this fruit even until [we] are filled, that [we] hunger not, neither shall [we] thirst'."

"Discipleship is a journey. We need the refining lessons of the journey to craft our character and purify our hearts. By patiently walking in the path of discipleship, we demonstrate to ourselves the measure of our faith and our willingness to accept God's will rather than our own. It is not enough merely to speak of Jesus Christ or proclaim that we are His disciples. It is not enough to surround ourselves with symbols of our religion. Discipleship is not a spectator sport. We cannot expect to experience the blessings of faith by standing inactive on the sidelines any more than we can experience the benefits of health by sitting on a sofa watching sporting events on television and giving advice to the athletes."

"And yet for some, 'spectator discipleship' is a preferred if not a primary way of worshipping."

"Ours is not a secondhand religion. We cannot receive the blessings of the gospel merely by observing the good that others do. We need to get off the sidelines and practice what we preach. ... Now is the time to embrace the gospel of Jesus Christ, become His disciples, and walk in His way."

False Doctrines of the Zoramites

"Alma used the scriptures repeatedly to address the false doctrines taught by the Zoramites. He first dealt with the false notion that you can only pray while on the 'Rameumptom' (A type of ramp up to the Preaching Pulpit). Using the scriptures, he explained that they could pray and worship God anywhere; in their "wilderness;" in their "field;" in their "house;" and even in their "closet":

Alma 33:2–11

2 And Alma said unto them: Behold, ye have said that ye could not worship your God because ye are cast out of your synagogues. But behold, I say unto you, if ye suppose that ye cannot worship God, ye do greatly err, and ye ought to search the scriptures; if ye suppose that they have taught you this, ye do not understand them.

3 Do ye remember to have read what Zenos, the prophet of old, has said concerning prayer or worship?

4 For he said: Thou art merciful, O God, for thou hast heard my prayer, even when I was in the wilderness; yea, thou wast merciful when I prayed concerning those who were mine enemies, and thou didst turn them to me.

5 Yea, O God, and thou wast merciful unto me when I did cry unto thee in my field; when I did cry unto thee in my prayer, and thou didst hear me.

6 And again, O God, when I did turn to my house thou didst hear me in my prayer.

7 And when I did turn unto my closet, O Lord, and prayed unto thee, thou didst hear me.

8 Yea, thou art merciful unto thy children when they cry unto thee, to be heard of thee and not of men, and thou wilt hear them.

9 Yea, O God, thou hast been merciful unto me, and heard my cries in the midst of thy congregations.

10 Yea, and thou hast also heard me when I have been cast out and have been despised by mine enemies; yea, thou didst hear my cries, and wast angry with mine enemies, and thou didst visit them in thine anger with speedy destruction.

11 And thou didst hear me because of mine afflictions and my sincerity; and it is because of thy Son that thou hast been thus merciful unto me, therefore I will cry unto thee in all mine afflictions, for in thee is my joy; for thou hast turned thy judgments away from me, because of thy Son.

"Alma then addressed the fact that all the prophets have testified of the coming of a Christ." [389]

Hearts Drawn Out in Prayer Continually

"President Henry B. Eyring, current member and second counselor of the First Presidency explained what it means to be in a 'continuous attitude of prayer':

"When God has commanded us to pray, He has used words like 'pray unceasingly' and 'pray always' and 'mighty prayer'. Those commands do not require using many words. In fact, the Savior has told us that we need not multiply words when we pray. The diligence in prayer which God requires does not take flowery speech nor long hours of solitude. Our hearts can be drawn out to God only when they are filled with love for Him and trust in His goodness (See 'Standing on the Promises' Hymn)." [390]

A Type of Christ Was Raised in the Wilderness

"Because of the ancient Israelites' murmuring in the wilderness, the Lord sent venomous serpents to humble the spiritually poisoned. Many people died, and the repentant people turned to their prophet and pled with him to ask the Lord to remove the serpents. God told Moses to make a serpent of brass and elevate it on a pole. The Lord promised that everyone who looked upon the raised serpent would be healed:

Numbers 21:4–9

4 And they journeyed from mount Hor by the way of the Red sea, to compass the land of Edom: and the soul of the people was much discouraged because of the way.

5 And the people spake against God, and against Moses, Wherefore have ye brought us up out of Egypt to die in the wilderness? for *there is* no bread, neither *is there any* water; and our soul loatheth this light bread.

6 And the LORD sent fiery serpents among the people, and they bit the people; and much people of Israel died.

7 Therefore the people came to Moses, and said, We have sinned, for we have spoken against the LORD, and against thee; pray unto the LORD, that he take away the serpents from us. And Moses prayed for the people.

8 And the LORD said unto Moses, Make thee a fiery serpent, and set it upon a pole: and it shall come to pass, that every one that is bitten, when he looketh upon it, shall live.

9 And Moses made a serpent of brass, and put it upon a pole, and it came to pass, that if a serpent had bitten any man, when he beheld the serpent of brass, he lived.

"The brass serpent was a *type*. Elder Dallin H. Oaks explained that a *type* is "a likeness or reminder of something else." [391]

"Jesus Christ taught that the type raised up in the wilderness testified of Him:

John 3:14–15

14 And as Moses lifted up the [a] serpent in the wilderness, even so must the Son of man be lifted up:

15 That whosoever believeth in him should not perish but have eternal life.

"As Moses 'lifted up' the serpent in the wilderness, even so must the 'Son of man' be lifted up: that whosoever believeth in him should not perish but have eternal life. Because of their hard hearts and disbelief, many of the Israelites refused to take advantage of the simple manner of healing:

I Nephi 17:41

41 And he did straiten them in the wilderness with his rod; for they hardened their hearts, even as ye have; and the Lord straitened them because of their iniquity. He sent fiery flying serpents among them; and after they were bitten he prepared a way that they might be healed; and the labor which they had to perform was to look; and because of the simpleness of the way, or the easiness of it, there were many who perished.

"Alma invited everyone to "begin to believe in the Son of God":

Alma 33:22

22 If so, wo shall come upon you; but if not so, then cast about your eyes and begin to believe in the Son of God, that he will come to redeem his people, and that he shall suffer and die to atone for their sins; and that he shall ʳrise again from the dead, which shall bring to pass the resurrection, that all men shall stand before him, to be judged at the last and judgment day, according to their works.

Helaman 8:14–15

14 Yea, did he not bear record that the Son of God should come? And as he lifted up the brazen serpent in the wilderness, even so shall he be lifted up who should come.

15 And as many as should look upon that serpent should *a*live, even so as many as should look upon the Son of God with faith, having a contrite spirit, might live, even unto that life which is eternal.

"Alma promised, "nourishing this testimony lightens one's burdens and leads to everlasting life. The Atonement of Jesus Christ Is Infinite and Eternal."

"Elder Bruce R. McConkie (1915–85) of the Quorum of the Twelve Apostles defined the scope of the infinite and eternal sacrifice of the Lord with these words:

"When the prophets speak of an *infinite* atonement, they mean just that. Its effects cover all men, the earth itself and all forms of life thereon, and reaches out into the endless expanses of eternity." [392]

"Elder Russell M. Nelson, current president of the Church of Jesus Christ of Latter-Day Saints (As of 2022), when he was a member of the Quorum of the Twelve Apostles enumerated some of the ways the Atonement of Jesus Christ is infinite:

"His Atonement is infinite—without an end":

II Nephi 9:7

7 Wherefore, it must needs be an infinite atonement —save it should be an infinite atonement this corruption could not put on incorruption. Wherefore, the first judgment which came upon man must needs have remained to an endless duration. And if so, this flesh must have laid down to rot and to crumble to its mother earth, to rise no more.

II Nephi 25:16

16 And after they have been scattered, and the Lord God hath scourged them by other nations for the space of many generations, yea, even down from generation to generation until they shall be persuaded to believe in Christ, the Son of God, and the atonement, which is infinite for all mankind—and when that day shall come that they shall believe in Christ, and worship the Father in his name, with pure hearts and clean hands, and look not forward any more for another Messiah, then, at that time, the day will come that it must needs be expedient that they should believe these things.

Alma 34:10, 12, 14

10 For it is expedient that there should be a great and last sacrifice; yea, not a sacrifice of man, neither of beast, neither of any manner of fowl; for it shall not be a human sacrifice; but it must be an infinite and eternal sacrifice.

12 But the law requireth the life of him who hath murdered; therefore there can be nothing which is short of an infinite atonement which will suffice for the sins of the world.

14 And behold, this is the whole *a*meaning of the law, every whit pointing to that great and last sacrifice; and that great and last sacrifice will be the Son of God, yea, infinite and eternal.

"It was also infinite in that all humankind would be saved from never-ending death. It was infinite in terms of His immense suffering. It was infinite in time, putting an end to the preceding prototype of animal sacrifice. It was infinite in scope—it was to be done once for all [Hebrews 10:10]. And the mercy of the Atonement extends not only to an infinite number of people, but also to *an infinite number of worlds* created by Him":

Doctrine & Covenants 76:24

24 That by him, and through him, and of him, the worlds are and were created, and the inhabitants thereof are begotten sons and daughters unto God.

Moses 1:33

33 And *a*worlds without number have I created; and I also created them for mine own purpose; and by the Son I created them, which is mine Only Begotten.

"It was infinite beyond any human scale of measurement or mortal comprehension."

"Jesus was the only one who could offer such an infinite atonement, since He was born of a mortal mother and an immortal Father. Because of that unique birthright, Jesus was an infinite Being." [393]

"Every Whit Pointing to That Great and Last Sacrifice."

"Amulek declared that the whole meaning of the law of Moses was to point the people to the eventual "great and last sacrifice" of Jesus Christ in Gethsemane and Golgotha. The animal sacrifices, the feasts and festivals, and other daily rituals were full of numerous types and shadows, pointing the children of Israel to Christ. The sacrament similarly reminds us today of the atoning mission of Jesus Christ. Likewise, anciently Passover was a yearly reminder that the Lord brought Israel out of physical bondage in Egypt.

"Today Easter is a yearly reminder that through the Atonement and Resurrection of the Lord we can be redeemed out of 'spiritual bondage'.

"Faith unto Repentance."

"While serving as a member of the Seventy, Elder Robert E. Wells spoke of the faith required to bring changes in our daily lives sufficient to participate in the Atonement of Jesus Christ:

"'Just how much faith do I need for the atonement of Christ to work for me?' In other words, how much faith do I need to receive salvation? In the book of Alma … we find the answer. The prophet Amulek taught this simple but grand principle: 'The Son of God, … bringeth about *means* unto men that they may have *faith unto repentance*'.

"Please note those three words: *faith unto repentance.* That is the clue. Four times in three verses he uses that expression":

Alma 34:15–17

15 And thus he shall bring salvation to all those who shall believe on his name; this being the intent of this last sacrifice, to bring about the bowels of mercy, which overpowereth justice, and bringeth about means unto men that they may have faith unto repentance.

16 And thus mercy can satisfy the demands of justice, and encircles them in the arms of safety, while he that exercises no faith unto repentance is exposed to the whole law of the demands of justice; therefore only unto him that has faith unto repentance is brought about the great and eternal plan of redemptions.

17 Therefore may God grant unto you, my brethren, that ye may begin to exercise your faith unto repentance, that ye begin to call upon his holy name, that he would have mercy upon you;

"So, the combination of faith in Christ plus *faith unto repentance* is vitally important. That concept is one of the greatest insights we have into the importance of simple, clear faith—'faith sufficient to repent'. Apparently, faith great enough to move mountains is not required; faith enough to speak in tongues or to heal the sick is not needed; all that we need is just enough faith to recognize that we have sinned and to repent of our sins, to feel remorse for them, and to desire to sin no more but to please Christ the Lord. Then the greatest miracle of all, the Atonement, whereby Christ rescues us from our deserved punishment, is in effect in our behalf."

Mercy Can Satisfy the Demands of Justice

1. There are two aspects of justice
2. Obedience to law results in blessings that bring joy

D&C 130:20–21

20 There is a law, irrevocably decreed in heaven before the foundations of this world, upon which all blessings are predicated—

21 And when we obtain any blessing from God, it is by obedience to that law upon which it is predicated.

3. Disobedience to law results in punishments that bring sorrow:

Alma 42:22

22 But there is a law given, and a punishment affixed, and a repentance granted; which repentance mercy claimeth; otherwise, justice claimeth the creature and executeth the law, and the law inflicteth the punishment; if not so, the works of justice would be destroyed, … and God would cease to be God.

There are two ways to satisfy justice:

4   Never violate the law.

5   If you do violate the law, pay the penalty.

Problem: No flesh is *'justified'* by the law:

II Nephi 2:5

5 And men are instructed sufficiently that they know good from evil. And the law is given unto men. And by the law no flesh is justified; or, by the law men are cut off. Yea, by the temporal law they were cut off; and also, by the spiritual law they perish from that which is good and become miserable forever.

Everyone has sinned, thus a penalty must be paid:

Romans 3:23

23 For all have sinned, and come short of the glory of God;

There are two effects of sin:

6.   By temporal law we are cut off—justice is violated:

Alma 42:14

14 And thus we see that all mankind were fallen, and they were in the grasp of justice; yea, the justice of God, which consigned them forever to be cut off from his presence.

7.   By spiritual law we perish—"there cannot any unclean thing, enter into the kingdom of God":

I Nephi 15:34

34 But behold, I say unto you, the kingdom of God is not filthy, and there cannot any unclean thing enter into the kingdom of God; wherefore there must needs be a place of filthiness prepared for that which is filthy.

Jesus offereth himself a sacrifice for sin, to answer the ends of the law":

II Nephi 2:7

7 Behold, he offereth himself a sacrifice for sin, to answer the ends of the law, unto all those who have a broken heart and a contrite spirit; and unto [b]none else can the ends of the law be answered.

8.   Christ initiated the law of mercy, but how?

"He kept the law perfectly and was without sin. He was 'justified' by the law'. In the Garden of Gethsemane and on the cross, He suffered and paid the price for the penalty as though He was guilty of every sin ever committed. He is our Advocate with the Father:

Alma 33:11

11 And thou didst hear me because of mine afflictions and my sincerity; and it is because of thy Son that thou hast been thus merciful unto me, therefore I will cry unto thee in all mine afflictions, for in thee is my joy; for thou hast turned thy judgments away from me, because of thy Son.

Doctrine & Covenants 45:3–5

3 Listen to him who is the [a]advocate with the Father, who is pleading your cause before him—

4 Saying: Father, behold the sufferings and death of him who did no sin, in whom thou wast well pleased; behold the blood of thy Son which was shed, the blood of him whom thou gavest that thyself might be glorified;

5 Wherefore, Father, spare these my brethren that believe on my name, that they may come unto me and have everlasting life.

Alma 34:32–34

32 For behold, this life is the time for men to prepare to meet God; yea, behold the day of [c]this life is the day for men to perform their labors.

33 And now, as I said unto you before, as ye have had so many witnesses, therefore, I beseech of you that ye do not procrastinate the day of your repentance until the end; for after this day of life, which is given us to prepare for eternity, behold, if we do not improve our time while in this life, then cometh the night of darkness wherein there can be no labor performed.

34 Ye cannot say, when ye are brought to that awful *a*crisis, that I will repent, that I will return to my God. Nay, ye cannot say this; for that same spirit which doth possess your bodies at the time that ye go out of this life, that same spirit will have power to possess your body in that eternal world.

"Do Not Procrastinate the Day of Your Repentance."

"Procrastination and indecision can impact our efforts to return to our Heavenly Father." [394]

President Joseph Fielding Smith taught:

"Procrastination, as it may be applied to Gospel principles, is the thief of eternal life—which is life in the presence of the Father and the Son."

What circumstances did Amulek warn about that make repentance after this life, difficult?" [395]

"That Same Spirit Will Possess Us"

"Amulek made it clear that we are, by our daily choices, ultimately giving ourselves over to the control or influence of either the Spirit of the Lord or the spirit of the devil. President Harold B. Lee (1899–1973) gave the following explanation of Alma 34:35:

"To those who die in their wicked state, not having repented, the scriptures say the devil shall seal them as his own, which means that until they have paid the uttermost farthing for what they have done, they shall not be redeemed from his grasp.

"When they shall have been subjected to the buffetings of Satan sufficient to have satisfied justice, then they shall be brought forth out of the grasp of Satan and shall be assigned to that place in our Father's celestial, terrestrial, or telestial world merited by their life here upon this earth." [396]

Elder Melvin J. Ballard (1873–1939) of the Quorum of the Twelve Apostles emphasized the importance of repenting during mortality:

"This life is the time in which men are to repent. Do not let any of us imagine that we can go down to the grave not having overcome the corruptions of the flesh and then lose in the grave all our sins and evil tendencies. They will be with us. They will be with the spirit when separated from the body.

"… [Mortality] is the time when men are more pliable and susceptible." [397]

End of the commentaries by LDS Leaders on what 'Deciding to Believe' means.

So, if you made it through all these commentaries and scriptures, I hope you now can see that my conceptualization of *deciding to believe* is a full, robust, and deep understanding, and it is centered in the teachings of the prophets past and present. God Himself has revealed the principles and laws concerning desire, belief, faith, experimenting on the word, repentance, and ultimately how *knowledge of truth* is obtained, and it is not by relying on a bet, or on blind faith as Richard likes to call it.

The last of chapter 3's subtitles is – "Bayesian arguments".

BAYESIAN ARGUMENTS

The Bayesian arguments that Richard covers in this subtitle, come from a book written by Stephen Unwin, the "Probability of God". Once again, Richard brings up his belief that "the existence of God as a scientific hypothesis, is, at least in principle, investigable." [398]

"Bayes Theorem is the idea of 'coming to a conclusion' due to a mathematical engine for combining many estimated likelihoods and coming up with a verdict (Basically like one would gather circumstantial evidence for a court trial). These are usually subjectively judged with all the doubts that inevitably flow from that. It's the GIGO principle (Garbage in Garbage Out)." [399]

It comes down to 'Bayesian inference' versus 'rival statistical methods', which is what Richard is all about. Richard says, … "I have met this kind of absurdity elsewhere, when I have challenged religious but otherwise intelligent scientists to *justify their belief*, given their admission that there is no evidence. I admit that there's no evidence. There's a reason why it's called faith." [400]

No evidence? Really Richard? C'mon man! It's called "evidence-based belief", which is true faith.

Let me mention here again, that Richard's understanding of faith is rooted in his stunted belief that faith is just blind faith, meaning faith with no evidence. When in fact, faith, being an action word, is something we exercise. Faith begins with a *desire to believe*, which leads to the decision to act; to do the experiment on that word or idea expressed by God, by following multiple steps. Once those steps are completed, this 'exercised faith' brings forth *much* evidence, even the *fruit* of the experiment, which is the new knowledge and new understanding one has gained – a greater understanding of truth.

This kind of faith is not blind in any way, shape, or form. It is in fact, the kind of faith that is "the cause of all action". It is the substance of things hoped for, and the evidence of things not seen, which we've talked about already.

Richard interjects a point here that he feels shuts down Unwin's statistical theorem of God's probability. He mentions a statement from what he refers to as 'The Authoritative Oxford Companion to Philosophy'. It lists the problem of evil as "the most powerful objection to traditional theism. But it is an argument only against the existence of a good God. Goodness is no part of the definition of the God Hypothesis. It's merely a desirable add-on." [401]

I, of course, disagree with Richard's assessment of what 'Good' means as it relates to the God Hypothesis, and so, let me explain what my perspective is on what good is and means. The Lord Jesus Christ taught:

Matthew 19:17

17 And he said unto him, Why callest thou me *good*? *There is* none good but one, *that is,* God: but if thou wilt enter into life, keep the commandments.

As a Latter-Day Saint, I believe that we are commanded to become perfect "*in* Christ", and not *as* Christ is". During His Sermon on the Mount, Jesus gave His challenging command for us to '*be perfect*':

Matthew 5:48

48 Be ye therefore perfect, even as your Father which is in heaven is perfect.

But since we are all fallen human beings, and are therefore bound to make mistakes, why would God expect us to keep His commandments perfectly, knowing we would fail? Or are we misunderstanding what He means when He says *be ye therefore perfect*? Once we gain a correct understanding of God's expectations for us, we can come to know and understand what the prophet Moroni meant when he said we can become perfect '*in* Christ'. Here's what Moroni said:

Moroni 10:32–33

33 Yea, come unto Christ, and be perfected in him, and deny yourselves of all ungodliness; and if ye shall deny yourselves of all ungodliness, and love God with all your might, mind and strength, then is his grace sufficient for you, that by his grace ye may be perfect in Christ; and if by the grace of God ye are perfect in Christ, ye can in nowise deny the power of God.

34 33 And again, if ye by the grace of God are perfect in Christ, and deny not his power, then are ye sanctified in Christ by the grace of God, through the shedding of the blood of Christ, which is in the covenant of the Father unto the remission of your sins, that ye become holy, without spot.

With these verses fresh on our minds, let us look at what the phrase "*there is* none good but one, *that is,* God" and see what it means. I believe 'good' in this verse, is speaking of 'Perfect', meaning completeness or complete. But, that said, it should be asked, "What does it mean to 'Be Perfect' like our Father in Heaven is perfect?" There is a short *essay* that answers this very question. It is found on my Church's website at www.churchofjesuschrist.org. It is titled "We Believe in being Perfect – *In* Christ". Here are a few excerpts from this essay that I think is helpful to our discussion, and I quote:

"The Greek word for *perfect* can be translated as 'complete, finished, fully developed':

Again, Matthew 5:48 (footnote *b*) says:

Matthew 5:48

48 Be ye therefore perfect, even as your Father which is in heaven is perfect.

"Again, perfect in GR means complete, finished, fully developed:

Doctrine & Covenants 67:13

13 Ye are not able to abide the presence of God now, neither the ministering of angels; wherefore, continue in patience *until ye are perfected.*

"The LDS Bible Dictionary says "Perfect, or Perfection has two word-groups in the Hebrew Old Testament. They are translated "perfect" or "perfection": tamam [m'T] and calal [I;I'K]."

"The former connotes wholeness, soundness, integrity, and often takes on ethical significance; the latter connotes *completeness,* perfection, and can carry the aesthetic sense of 'comeliness or beauty'. Nearly all New Testament occurrences translate Greek words sharing the tel-stem, from which some half-dozen words are formed that bear *'the sense of completion or wholeness'.*" [402]

(See also the Latter-Day Saint Topical Guide for: the Standard of Righteousness; Godliness; Man, new, Spiritually Reborn; Man, Potential to Become like Heavenly Father; Mission of early Saints; Objection; Perfection, etc.)

"It wasn't until after Jesus' resurrection that the scriptural record of the Book of Mormon tells of Jesus' visit to the American continent where He showed Himself to those who were living there. In teaching them what they are to do and how they could become like He and His Father in Heaven are, the resurrected Jesus said something similar to what He taught the Jews. He said:

III Nephi 12:48

48 Therefore I would that ye should be perfect *even as I, or* your Father who is in heaven is perfect.

"Only after His resurrection did Jesus, having had His Father's power within Him so that He could take up His body as a resurrected being, include Himself in this command to be like 'He AND His Father' are perfect. When Jesus visited His followers in ancient America as the resurrected Christ, He had fully and completely become perfect. He had *completeness* like His Heavenly Father enjoys. Though Jesus committed no sin, He wasn't *complete* until His resurrection when He became fully like or as His Father was *Perfect* and *Complete* in every way, even bodily.

"You can read the full account from the Book of Mormon, in III Nephi, chapters 8 through 14. Because Jesus was resurrected, He was now complete and perfect, even as His Father in Heaven is perfect, and so He now included Himself in this example of *completeness.* He only included His Father as the example of perfection or completeness when He spoke to the Jews *before* His resurrection. Because He had not yet been resurrected, He only mentioned His Father in the Bible verse I just quoted earlier. Whereas now, as a resurrected being visiting the ancient day saints in ancient America, He was perfect and complete, and so He included Himself in that charge He gave the Nephites, and this same charge holds true for us even today – to be perfect and complete.

The Bible Dictionary continues:

"Our Savior asks us to become complete, finished, fully developed—to be perfected in the virtues and attributes He and our Father in Heaven exemplify" (That is why our work here on earth is to obey their commandments, and when we fail to do so we are required to repent and change our behavior so that it reflects the Christlike behavior and character we are asked to develop and exemplify as His children, which of course, is a life-long, or should I say an eternal endeavor). The perfection that the Savior envisions for us is much more than 'errorless performance'. It is the eternal expectation as expressed by the Lord in his great intercessory prayer to his Father —"that we might be made perfect and be able to dwell with them in the eternities ahead." [403]

End of Bible Dictionary Quote and the excerpts from "We Believe in being Perfect – *In* Christ".

I believe, and therefore it is my perspective, that Jesus did not intend His sermon on this subject to be a verbal hammer to batter us about, and that's because our human nature, our natural man is likely to fail continually as we make a sincere effort to keep His commandments. I believe He intended it to be a tribute to who and what God the Eternal Father is (*Good,* Complete, and Perfect), and therefore He is the example we can hold up and use as our compass while we're traveling through our wilderness of imperfection, striving all the while to live in such a way that after our resurrected we to can become complete, and return to live with our a Father in His presence for the rest of eternity, because we are like Him, even perfect "in Christ".

Elder Gerrit W. Gong of the Quorum of the Twelve Apostles, author of the message "Becoming Perfect *in* Christ", which can be found in the July 2014 Ensign magazine, found on the www.churchofjesuschrist.org website, made the following statement on this subject, and I quote:

"Understanding the Savior's freely given atoning love, can free us from self-imposed, incorrect, and *unrealistic expectations* of what perfection is." [404]

End Quote

Since all have sinned and come short of the glory of God, like the scriptures say, none of us are "Good", "Perfect", or "Complete" in the way this short essay describes. But since *perfection*, or *completeness* is an attribute of the 'Man of Holiness' (And of our Savior and Redeemer as well), it most definitely should be included in the discussion we're having about the God Hypothesis, what is meant by Good versus Evil, and what Jesus meant by saying we need to be 'perfect' as our Heavenly Father is 'perfect'.

Richard continues, "Admittedly, people of a theological bent are often chronically incapable of distinguishing what is true from what they'd like to be true. But, for a more sophisticated believer in some kind of supernatural intelligence, it is childishly easy to overcome the problem of evil."

You could turn this accusatory statement around, and simply direct it right back at Richard by saying, "As you point a finger at theists Richard, please notice that there are three fingers pointing right back at you".

Richard continues:

"Simply postulate a nasty god – such as the one who stalks every page of the Old Testament. Or, if you don't like that, invent a separate evil god, call him Satan, and blame his cosmic battle against the good god, for the evil in the world. Or – A more sophisticated solution – postulate a god with grander things to do than fuss about human distress. Or a god who is not indifferent to suffering but regards it as the price that has to be paid for *'free will'* in an orderly, lawful cosmos. Theologians can be found buying into all these ... rationalizations." [405]

Richard, as always, is overexaggerating with a bit of sarcasm once again, as he lists religionists beliefs as rationalizations. Richard finishes his point with this glib comment:

"I can't get excited about personal opinions, whether Unwin's or mine." [406]

Well Richard, neither can I. The fact is, Richard's book is filled with his personal opinions, just as mine is. The debate about God's existence, as I said, is mostly made up of people's personal opinions and perspectives, and that's because there's no incontrovertible proof that has been offered up by either side of the debate. However, I will deal with the 'problem of evil' that Richard poses here, a little later in my book, but for now, let's move on to the next chapter, chapter 4 – "Why There Almost Certainly is No God".

CHAPTER 4

WHY THERE ALMOST CERTAINLY IS NO GOD

Richard begins Chapter 4 by quoting Thomas Jefferson, who Richard claims was a Deist. Thomas said the following, and I quote:

"The priests of the different religious sects dread the advance of science as witches do the approach of daylight, … and scowl on the datal harbinger announcing the subdivision of the duperies on which they live." [407]

End quote

Richard says a little later, "The argument from probability is indeed very strong, and I suspect, unanswerable from the theist's intention. My name for the *statistical demonstration* that God almost certainly does not exist is the Ultimate Boeing 747 gambit." [408]

This analogy came from Fred Hoyle who said: "The probability of life *originating* on earth, is no greater than the chance that a hurricane, sweeping through a scrapyard, would have the luck to assemble a Boeing 747. This, in a nutshell, … is the creationist's favorite argument." [409]

Affirming Hoyle's statement, Richard follows it up by saying, "This is an argument that could be made only by somebody who doesn't understand the first thing about natural selection; somebody who thinks natural selection is a theory of chance, whereas, in the relevant sense of chance it is the opposite." [410]

Are we to accept Richard's word for it? I certainly do not. If you, my readers, were to take each of the millions of birds and animals on this planet, individually, taking them one-by-one in your hands, and consider their eyes, the color of their feathers or the uniqueness of their fur, or their internal organs, and ask, "Why are the animals or birds so perfectly complete? How come they are *finished*, and not producing any kind of offspring that has its own unique and obvious new 'Kind' mutation(s), and why aren't any of them living right here amongst us even now? Why are the offspring from the finished male and female parents of these 'Kinds' (not species) so perfect that we don't have a mutated offspring living amongst us anymore (An offspring that is 'unfinished'), where they're still evolving, so that one can 'see' them as proof of Darwin's natural selection theory?

The fact is, 'it' hasn't produced any examples of it for at least 6,000 years, maybe more. Not even one out of thousands of Kinds. Nope, not even one! I guess natural selection knows when something is finished and reached its perfection, right? But how? If evolution by natural selection was a true process for the development of all life here on earth, we absolutely would still have thousands, if not millions of examples of animals in this unique stage of 'mutating offspring' living amongst us right now. There's certainly been enough time for it, that's for sure. A bird with an evolving beak taking place within the exact same bird species, is NOT an example of this theory. I repeat, it certainly is NOT such an example.

The reason there aren't any such examples of new Kinds jumping lanes over to a totally different Kind, is because all 'Kinds' were finished and complete when the cells that made up their embryos were organized by God, which then were activated with life so that they began to grow and develop. Everything those embryos needed in order to grow to a fully developed, finished creature, was in their parents' cells – meaning, in their DNA! Period! Each are examples of *finished, perfectly created (OR organized) 'Kinds' that God said were "Good"*.

Out of the millions upon millions of species of birds, insects, and animals of every *Kind*, there's never been a single example of a *Kind* jumping over to a different lane of *Kind*, via the so-called natural selections' birth-iteration-mutation process. Period! End of story. Even with it's supposed millions of years to produce them, there's not even one, nor has there ever been one example that can be held up to support Darwin's claim that his theory is at work even today. Isn't it fantastic? Not even one! Yet, the *Complete* "It is finished and Good" Method of God's creations, offers millions of examples existing on this planet, which support His creative process! Let him who has eyes to see, see all that's available before us. I suggest that you, my readers, be honest fruit inspectors so that the truth can speak to you and set you and your mind free from this spurious, anti-Christ *Con*. I included a considerable amount of information on the subject of Evolution in my Introduction, and so I'm going to go ahead and leave it there and move on to the first subtitle of this chapter, which is – "The Ultimate Boeing 747". I'm confident that you, my readers, will find this a very interesting topic indeed. I certainly did.

THE ULTIMATE BOEING 747

Richard sets the stage for the 'Ultimate Boeing 747' argument, by saying, "Theists think improbability is evidence of design. Darwinian natural selection shows how wrong this is with respect to biological improbability."

"Darwinism teaches us to be wary of the easy assumption that design is the only alternative to chance and teaches us to seek out *graded ramps* of *slowly increasing complexity.* After Darwin, we all should feel deep in our bones, suspicious of the very idea of design. The *illusion* of design is a trap that has caught us before, and Darwin should have immunized us by raising our consciousness." [411]

As I read and reread Richard's comments in support of the idea that there almost certainly is no God, especially when he preaches his quasi-faiths' most prominent tenet – natural selection – as providing the evidence that shuts down any argument of design, I find that Richard used a slight-of-words to simply redefine what the word *chance* means. When I recognized this slight-of-words for what it was, it reminded me of a YouTube video I watched recently. It was produced by PragerU [412], where Stephen Meyer was its spokesperson. This video is titled "Evolution: Bacteria to Beethoven".

I suggest that you, my readers, take the 5-minutes that it takes to watch it.[413] It completely disassembles Richard's argument wherein he states: "After Darwin, we all should feel deep in our bones, suspicious of the very idea of design." [414] In my view, any suspicion should be directed towards evolution and all of its inherent slight-of-hand deceptions.

NATURAL SELECTION AS A CONSIOUSNESS RAISER

Richard continues, "If we were smart enough, we would see it just as Douglas Adams finally came to realize about *the truth of it,* and in having done so Adam's moved from being a believing Christian to a radical atheist (Just like Richard), with *natural selection* being the main contributing factor." [415] If you want a clearer story of Mr. Adam's conversion to atheism, do a Google search for "Douglas Adams and God – Portrait of a radical atheist". [416]

Even with Richard's constant barking out the point that natural selection answers life's 'Big' questions, the fact still remains that Darwin himself could not explain the origin and cause of variations that are generated (in species alone, and not in Kinds) during this idea or process he called evolution. Darwin emphasized the importance of the fittest organisms, and later, it has been suggested that fit *and fitter forms,* can also co-exist. The principle of inheritance was also not present during Darwin's time. It's been more than 150 years since Darwin postulated his theory of evolution, and since then not one scientist has ever been able to come up with a proven, incontrovertible explanation for *the origin and cause of variations* that are generated during this so-called *workable process* of evolution, nor have they been able to create that one *simple cell* that can duplicate itself, ... *the "itself" being the 'life' within each and every. May I suggest God placed the information in the cell so species could do this?*

Only a divine, intelligent mind can and did produce the information in each string of DNA code that exists in each and every cell of animals and every living thing that God created (Organized). Of course, since I can't prove that God created DNA, with its 4 billion letter word (Made with DNA's ACGT Code Alphabet, all of which is based on *Information* that only comes from a mind), I will say again that this is just my well-informed opinion, and I hope that you, my readers, will consider this as one more solid scientific *reference leg* of evidence that you can add to your own circular table stand supporting your personal table of belief. Keep in mind that a computer is not created in the literal sense. It is organized. Each hardware piece is organized or manufactured from material found on this planet. It's then assembled or organized anew. Then programmers place programs, such as its operating system, into it. But only when *life* is *breathed* or pumped into it can the computer *come alive* and start computing. This life energy is called *electricity,* and it too, is an unseen power just like *life* is. The fact is, all animal Kinds are complete, or what God called, "Finished and Good" (There's that word *Good* again).

There's not even one example living today, out of what many say are thousands of Kinds in existence. If you don't believe me, then go ahead and try to mate a dog with a cat for example. It doesn't work. Ask yourself, "Why can't cats and dogs mate with each other, and produce a *puppy-kitten* offspring? What keeps them from doing that successfully? Even if it looks like they're trying to do so, they will end up with no offspring, no puppy-kittens, and the reason for that is there have been boundaries placed on these Kinds. God pronounced laws that keep them within the boundaries God has set, thus keeping this *'creation of life process'* working as God intended and designed it, and not as man would have it work.

Some of those laws are their breeding behaviors, heat cycles, and especially the laws directing the DNA code within their cells, all of which combine to prevent them from being able to produce healthy, viable offspring randomly or otherwise (They cannot go beyond the bounds God has set for them. Meaning, "You shall not pass!"). Scientists have never been able to take an egg from a cat and artificially inseminate it with the sperm of a dog, in-order-to activate a new puppy-kitten Kind of offspring, meaning two different 'Kinds' becoming a totally new 'Kind' – a DogCat. Hybrid species can be created, true, but only when the animals have similar DNA to each other, such as lions and tigers, which are in the same category of species and not from different 'Kind's'. Unique and specific DNA in all animal life, including human life, exists in every cell, and when life itself is activated in those cells, it gives power and energy to that DNA which activates the DNA to start directing those cells to produce the necessary proteins needed for becoming the 'Kind' it was designed by God to become, He being the Intelligent Designer behind the DNA Information directing this 'Life' to become a complete, finished creation.

It is the DNA code, with its billions of pieces of information (The DNA's AGCT Alphabet Code), that provides the *directives* or *instructions* for all cells to manufacture and produce—like a mini-manufacturing plant—what they are meant to produce, and all this code in their respective double-helix of DNA strings, as I said, has information in it, information that has come from the gloriously intelligent, magnificently brilliant Mind of God (Which for me is the "Theory of Everything' which scientists are looking for), even the *Designer of the Universe* who organized all of the known and unknown matter. God provides the *life power* that activates the life potential that exists in every living creatures' cells.

It is a fact that mankind's parade of scientists, certainly has not been able to produce *life* itself, out of nothing. But, if-and-when they do, which I'm confident they won't, I'll happily take a second look at the *simple-to-complexity* argument of natural selection that Darwin and Dawkins claim to be the real Creator, Designer, and Director of life. *It's my belief that they're pulling the wool over many eyes, possibly even intentionally, by taking the directive process found in DNA, and renaming it *Natural Selection*. In other words, they've hijacked the directive power in DNA, and gave it to Evolution, by simply renaming DNA's directive power *Natural Selection*. I'll address this hijacking more thoroughly a little later. The next subtitle journey that Richard takes us on is called – "Irreducible Complexity."

(*Go to YouTube and watch "Have I been lied to about the Origin of Life?" - Episode 5 of Q.U.E.S.T. Questions Apologetics, to better understand why I say that some scientists have and are lying to us.)

IRREDUCCIBLE COMPLEXITY

For this sub-title Richard begins by talking about a book written by an unknown author who describes what he called a *simple-to-complexity* example called the "Venus Flowers Basket". The unknown author asks, "How can its microscopic cells *collaborate* to secrete a million glassy splinters and construct such an intricate and beautiful lattice?" [417]

Richard answers his own question by saying, "We don't know, but then religious critics pipe up to say, 'We don't know either, but one thing we do know is that *chance* is not the likely designer".[418] Then Richard continues, "The statistical improbability of phenomena such as Euplectolla's skeleton, is the central problem that any *theory of life* must solve (Scientifically not Religiously of course)." [419]

"The greater the statistical improbability, the less plausible is *Chance* as a solution: that is what improbable means. The candidate solutions to the riddle of improbability are not, as is falsely implied, Design and Chance. The problem that any theory of life must solve is the problem of 'how to escape from Chance'. The intricate elegance of flowers like the Dutchman's Pipe, moves us to ask: 'Did all of this happen by Chance?' (I'd ask, "Is it chance that everyone has their own unique fingerprints? Why?)

Richard says in response to his own question: "Of course not, but once again, Intelligent Design is not the proper alternative to Chance (This is Richard giving his opinion and not giving us facts)." [420]

"Natural Selection is not only a parsimonious (Frugal), plausible, and elegant solution, it is the *only* 'workable alternative' to chance that has ever been suggested. Once again, this is because the designer himself (herself/itself) immediately raises the bigger problem of his (Or her) own origin (This is the Infinite Regression question that Richard always asks, thinking that it is the theists greatest challenge). Any entity capable of intelligently designing something as improbable as a Dutchman's Pipe (Or fingerprints, or a universe for that matter) would have to be even *more improbable* than a Dutchman's Pipe. Far from terminating the vicious regress problem, God aggravates it with a vengeance." [421]

To begin with, let me answer the question put forth by the unknown author, which was: "How can its microscopic cells collaborate to secrete a million glassy splinters and construct such an intricate and beautiful lattice?" [422] Or, "How can a random process make individual fingerprints for billions of us?"

The answer is that "God created the DNA Code String as part of its, and our seed-cells, so that the cells *complex directives* were there from their very inception (Or fertilization, or activation, or however you want to define their beginning), directing its and our cells to develop and ultimately do the collaborative work of secreting glassy splinters, or individualizing all of our fingerprints. This is how all life was organized and designed, be it simple or complex, and it is not by chance or evolutions' natural selections' undirected process, or even by the Big Bang mindlessly, and haphazardly directing everything in our universe through a singularity explosion using the concept of evolution and natural selection.

Boiling down Richard's argument to simpler terms, he is saying that if you believe the improbability that God created or organized such incredible things like the Dutchman's Pipe, the Dragon Fly's Wing, a Bacteria Flagellar Motor, the Eagle's eye, or billions of fingerprints, you also have to believe that God has to be even more incredibly magnificent and improbable than any of these incredible creations. In short, Richards' mind (He says wet brain and not mind) just cannot comprehend that anything, a God or otherwise, can be that astonishingly intelligent and glorious. To him ... it's just too improbable.

But, on the other hand, Richard also says that if you allow billions of years for the concept of natural selection to *direct* these astonishing creations' development so that they produce enough iterations through millions of *parental mutations*, you can move the simple on to complexity quite easily, taking it up the gradual side of Mount Improbable (This is imagery that Richard uses), and 'that's the beauty of natural selection' Richard says (But, as the YouTube video on Origins said, the math doesn't add up).

Again, I ask, "Where is the proof of this *workable process* in action around us today? If it were a true theory, then shouldn't there still be millions of examples in varying stages of this kind of complex mutation going on right now, all around us, from simple offspring as well as every iteration stage in-between, on up to, and including, thousands of finished, new 'Kind' examples of full complexity? If not, then why not? Why did natural selection 'decide' to stop its process in every single 'Kind' on this planet?

The answer is "Because only finished or complete 'Kinds' existed in the first place." There are no examples from the millions of species that we can point to, as *incomplete* Kinds or Kinds still in the evolutionary process as an incomplete creation! Richard might use the flat worm, the platyhelminth and its unfinished, so-called imperfect eyes, as one such example, but this example assumes that the worms' eyes are unfinished and imperfect, which they are NOT. Their eyes work exactly as their Creator intended them to work, in the kind of environment they were created to live in.

Did this so-called *workable process* somehow *decide*, by itself, like a mind decides, to all-of-a-sudden stop directing the mutation going on within every single 'Kind' and their species, because every specie within every 'Kind' of creation had achieved perfection, so that the process said, "They are finished?" Maybe this happened, say, 6,000 years ago? Did it somehow know "They were all finished and good"?

Was its unintended, unguided, undirected, mindless, un-goal reached ... so that it no longer had to do its *survival of the fittest* decision making using its unguided, brainless, unintended process anymore? How did *it*, this mindless, unguided, unintended workable process even come to *know it* had achieved its unguided, unintended, un-goal of perfected or finished creations for every last one of the thousands of 'Kinds' on this planet? I mean, really? C'mon man! God said, "It is finished and good"! Not some false concept that somehow is able to think, evaluate, and decide something is finished or not. Good grief.

Richard went on to say:

"Natural selection is a *cumulative process* which breaks the problem of improbability up into small pieces. Each of the small pieces is slightly improbable, but not prohibitively so. When large numbers of these *slightly improbable events* are *stacked up* in a series, the end-product in the accumulation is very, very improbable indeed. [423]

Doesn't the thought process of 'breaking into pieces' take a mind? How does a mindless, undirected wet brain with no hands, get trillions of unintended neurons to continually bounce around as unguided, and undirected events and then stack them into smaller pieces? Richard calls it – a *cumulation process*?

How does an unguided, unintended, mindless process even know it's time to *choose* to break up this so-called *problem of improbability* into smaller pieces? How does it *choose* to break up these pieces into smaller, less improbable pieces, and what (in the wet brain) is making these incredible decisions, and how is *it* making them? What does *slightly improbable* even mean? What is a slightly improbable event? How does *the process even* 'know' to *stack* them up as a *series* and not stack them in some other way or order, and not create chaos? I'd like to see anything, let alone an unguided, undirected non-mind 'idea' do such a thing. If it is a so-called *workable process* like Richard's calling it, it should be able to be duplicated and tested in a lab, or however the tests would be done by today's scientists, right?

Well, scientists have never been able to test or duplicate this theory at any time, or in any way, shape, or form. And, who or what created this *workable process* called natural selection? Shouldn't Richard's Infinite Regression question be applied to natural selection like he's applied it to the God Theory? Who or what is the causal cause of natural selection and how can it be infinite and not finite?

Do you just say "Poof! It's alive?" Really Richard?

If you postulate that it is all the stuff stored in the brains of each of these participants/animals, over the many multi-millions of years and their iterations that causes each sets of their multiple parents to produce offspring with the next mutated improved cells or improved DNA code arrangements in them, you'd be wrong. It's impossible, because just one letter in the DNA code being off kilter or out of its intended sequence, keeps the cell from even getting off the ground, so-to-speak, so it can form the next *series* of proteins needed for it to grow into the new mutated iteration. It simply dies before it can · duplicate itself or themselves. IT takes too much time, and these molecules and cells die within hours.

This challenge of DNA sequencing simply means a cell would cease until the next so-called unguided, undirected, non-mind beginnings of the potential offspring cells, provided by its parents, or maybe a new set of parents that have a better chance of producing the right cells with the right kind of mutated DNA code string, generated over and over again until the right mutation just happens to survive. Really? A mutation that didn't misarrange the DNA sequence (yet was able to somehow mutate it correctly)? Talk about improbable. Sheesh! The fact is, it's impossible for this so-called workable process to produce multiple mutations of tiny, miniscule changes with its tens-of-thousands of desired protein formations accidently arranging themselves correctly, and that's because of this *busting the DNA sequence* fact.

I ask you: "Who is being improbable here?" God's DNA, or Richard's theory of natural selection? The more *probable hypothesis* is that the incredibly intelligent, brilliantly sophisticated mind, the Mind of God, is the creative genius that put the right *information* into all His creations' respective DNA Strings, all in the correct order, making every cell perfectly designed for *life* to launch! And these perfect, or complete cells grow to become beautiful, finished creations from their beginnings and those beginnings were organized before their *pre-Fall* state, and not after the Fall. After the Fall, all life of every Kind, fell into a state of mortality where the process of death came into the picture. God decreed that death would be the end of all His creations, as part of their existence here on earth goes, as a result of Adam choosing to transgress God's law. However, the earth, and all things upon it, will receive their paradisical glory once again, which God promised all His creations. So, life's cycle if life, death, and then new life.

Now, let's discuss "Irreducible complexity". Irreducible complexity (IC) is the argument that certain biological *systems* (like the Eagle's eye) cannot have evolved by successive, small modifications to pre-existing functional systems, through a natural selection process, because a less complex *system* would not be able to function without any one of its specific, individual parts being in place from the beginning.

Just like the DNA example I just ran through; every part of an irreducibly complex *system* is necessary. Take away even one part, and the entire system will no longer work, or at the least it will function poorly. Because the systems' parts are so intricate and interdependent with each of its parts, such simple and or complex systems could not possibly have been the result of little iterations of unguided, undirected, unintended, yet so-called 'workable, evolutionary processes'.

A very intelligent scientist, Michael J. Behe, is an American biochemist, author, and advocate of the pseudoscientific principle of Intelligent Design, and serves as professor of biochemistry at Lehigh University in Pennsylvania. He's also a senior fellow of the Discovery Institute's Center for Science and Culture at the time of my writing this book. Let me say up front, before I tell Behe's story, that Richard Dawkins strongly disagrees with Behe's theories, and in particular his idea about *systems* not working if one part isn't there to make the whole system work. Behe's original examples of irreducibly complex mechanisms, included the bacterial flagellum of E. coli, the blood clotting cascade, cilia, and the adaptive immune system. Behe argues that organs and biological features which are irreducibly complex cannot be wholly explained by current models of evolution. [424]

Charles Darwin himself said: "If it could be demonstrated that any complex organ existed which could not possibly have been formed by numerous, successive, slight modifications, *my theory would absolutely break down.*" [425] (Remember this quote as we work through this argument)

Bingo! With this statement, Charles Darwin provided a criterion by which his theory of evolution could be *falsified* (Meaning, 'be made to be false'). His logic was simple: "We need a 'crane', not a 'skyhook', for only a crane can do the business of working up gradually and plausibly from simplicity to otherwise improbable complexity." [426]

In other words, since evolution is a gradual process in which slight modifications produce advantages for survival, it cannot produce complex structures *in a short amount of time*. Time truly is the life-or-death enemy of evolution. Evolution requires a step-by-step *process* which may gradually build up and modify complex structures over a very long period of time (Construct over a long period of time), and so, it cannot produce or construct them suddenly.

Darwin, meet Michael Behe! Michael Behe claims to have shown exactly what Darwin claimed would destroy his theory of evolution, through a concept Behe calls *Irreducible Complexity*. In simple terms, this idea applies to any system of interacting parts in which the removal of any one part destroys the function of the entire system. An irreducibly complex system, then, requires each-and-every component to be in place *before* it will function. Behe presented one simple *irreducible complex system* – the mousetrap – as an illustration of his argument (See YouTube – "Unlocking the Mystery of Life").

It contains five interdependent parts which allow it to catch mice: the wooden platform, the spring, the hammer (the bar which crushes the mouse against the wooden base), the holding bar, and a catch. Each of these components are essential for the function of the mousetrap. For instance, if you remove the catch, you cannot set the trap and it will never catch mice, no matter how long they may dance over the contraption. Remove the spring, and the hammer will flop uselessly back and forth – certainly not much of a threat to the little rodents. Of course, removal of the holding bar will ensure that the trap never catches anything because there will again be no way to arm the system.

Now, note what this implies: an *irreducibly complex system* cannot come about in a gradual manner. One cannot begin with a wooden platform and catch a few mice, then add a spring, catching a few more mice than before, etc. No, all the components must be in place before it functions at all. A step-by-step approach to constructing such a system will result in a useless system until all the components have been added. The system requires all the components to be added at the same time, in the right configuration, before it can work at all.

How does *irreducible complexity* apply to biology? Behe notes that early this century, before biologists really understood the cell, they had a very simplistic model of its inner workings. Without the electron microscopes and other advanced techniques that now allow scientists to peer into the inner workings of the cell, it was assumed that the cell *was* a fairly simple blob of protoplasm. Behe continues:

"The living cell was a *black box* – something that could be observed to perform various functions while its inner workings were unknown and mysterious. Therefore, it was easy and justifiable to assume that the cell was a simple collection of molecules. But not anymore. Technological advances have provided detailed information about the inner workings of the cell." [427]

Michael Denton, in his book "Evolution: A Theory in Crisis", stated:

"Although the tiniest bacterial cells are incredibly small, weighing less than 10^-12 grams, each is in effect a veritable *microminiaturized factory* containing thousands of exquisitely designed pieces of intricate molecular machinery, made up altogether of one hundred thousand million atoms, far more complicated than any machine built by man and absolutely without parallel in the non-living world (Talk about a tinker-toy set! Ha, ha, ha).

"In a word, the cell is complicated; very, very complicated; and certainly not simple. In fact, Michael Behe asserts that the complicated biological structures in a cell exhibit the exact same irreducible complexity that we saw in the mousetrap example. In other words, they are all-or-nothing: either everything is there, and it works, or when something is missing, it doesn't work. Keep in mind that the twelve main parts of a single cell are made up u=of hundreds of parts themselves. Leaving just one of those hundreds of parts that make up these twelve main parts would leave the cell unable to function.

"As we saw before, such a system cannot be constructed in a gradual manner – it simply won't work until all the components are present, and Darwin's theory has no mechanism for adding all the components *at once*. Remember, Darwin's (Theoretical) mechanism (Or crane) of natural selection is one of gradual mutations and iterations leading to improved fitness for survival over millions of years.

"A less-than-complete system of this nature simply will not function, and it certainly won't help the organism to survive (A rule of natural selection). Indeed, having a half-formed, and hence, a non-functional system would actually hinder the cells survival, and would be selected against (Being broken it couldn't survive). Behe is not the only scientist to recognize *irreducible complexity* in nature." [428]

In 1986, Michael J. Katz, in his *"Templets and the explanation of complex patterns"* (Cambridge: Cambridge University Press, 1986) wrote the following:

"In the natural world, there are many *pattern-assembly systems* for which there is no simple explanation. There are useful scientific explanations for these complex systems, but the final patterns that they produce are so heterogeneous (Large and diverse) that *they cannot effectively be reduced to smaller or less intricate predecessor components*. As I will argue these patterns are, in a fundamental sense, irreducibly complex." [429]

Katz continues, stating this sort of complexity is found in biology:

"Cells and organisms are quite complex by all pattern criteria. They are built of heterogeneous elements arranged in heterogeneous configurations (Diverse in character such as solid, liquid, or gaseous as one example) and they do not self-assemble (In other words, it *can't* cause events to *stack* into a *series* as Dawkins suggested it could, nor direct, or self-assemble itself). One cannot stir together the parts of a cell or of an organism and spontaneously assemble a neuron or a walrus: to create a cell or an organism, one needs a preexisting cell or a preexisting organism, with its *attendant complex templates* (As well as the 'life' energy it needs). A fundamental characteristic of the biological realm is that organisms are complex patterns, and, for its creation, *life* requires extensive, and essentially maximal templates.

"Behe presents several examples of irreducibly complex systems to prove his point, but I'll just focus on one: the cilium. Cilia are hair-like structures, which are used by animals and plants to move fluid over various surfaces (for example, cilia in your respiratory tree sweep mucous towards the throat and thus promote elimination of contaminants) and by single-celled organisms to move through water.

"Cilia are like oars which contain their own mechanism for bending. That mechanism involves tiny rod-like structures called microtubules that are arranged in a ring. Adjacent microtubules are connected to each other by two types of *bridges* – a flexible linker bridge and an arm that can *walk* up the neighboring microtubule. The cilia bend by activating the *walker arms*, and the sliding motion that this tends to generate is converted to a bending motion by the *flexible linker bridges*.

"Thus, the cilium has several essential components: stiff microtubules, linker bridges, and the *motors* in the form of *walker arms*. While my description is greatly simplified (Behe notes that over 200 separate proteins have been identified in this particular *system*), these 3 components form the basic system, and show what is required for *functionality* (Think of being a cell mechanic and having to check all 200 proteins to find out what's wrong). For without one of these components, the system simply will not function (And we're supposed to believe that all these thousands, if not millions of decision-making steps, came about as a result of a singularity blast in outer space, that then put this *single life-bearing cell* on our planet? C'mon man! Really? If you believe that, I've got some property in Florida to sell you! Ha-ha-ha!).

"We can't evolve a cilium by starting with microtubules alone, because the microtubules will be fixed and rigid – not much good for moving around. Adding the flexible linker bridges to the system will not do any good either – there is still no motor and the cilia still will not bend. If we have microtubules and the walker arms (the motors) but no flexible linker arms, the microtubules will keep on sliding past each other till they float away from each other and are lost.

(This is only one of many *biochemical systems* that Behe discuses in his book, 'Darwin's Black Box'. Other examples of *irreducible complexity* include the light-sensing system in animal eyes, the transport system within the cell, the bacterial flagellum, and the blood clotting system, just to name a few. All consist of a very complex system of interacting parts which cannot be simplified while maintaining functionality by reducing the system back to its tiniest-of-tiny parts).

"Since the publication of "Darwin's Black Box" in 1986 [430], Behe has refined the definition of *Irreducible Complexity*. In 1996 he wrote that *"any precursor to an irreducibly complex system that is missing a part is by definition nonfunctional."* (Behe, M, 1996b. "Evidence for Intelligent Design from Biochemistry", a speech given at the Discovery Institute's God & Culture Conference, August 10, 1996, Seattle, WA.) [431]

By defining *irreducible complexity* in terms of non-functionality, Behe casts light on the fundamental problem with evolutionary theory: *"evolution cannot produce something where there would be a non-functional intermediate* (This is just one of many of the rules that Natural Selection must follow or it falls apart). *Natural selection only preserves or selects those structures which are functional."*

"If it is not functional, it cannot be naturally selected (Because it would prove dis-functional, and thus not fit for preserving one's survival, which is natural selections' chief principle and rule that supposedly gives rise to its existence). Thus, Behe's latest definition of irreducible complexity is as follows:

"An irreducibly complex evolutionary pathway is one that contains one or more unselected steps (That is, one or more necessary-but-unselected mutations). The degree of *irreducible complexity* is the number of unselected steps (Or mutations) in the pathway." (A Response to Critics of Darwin's Black Box, by Michael Behe, PCID, Volume 1.1, January, February, March 2002; iscid.org) [432]

Evolution simply cannot produce complex structures in a single generation as would be required for the formation of irreducibly complex systems (Another rule required by Natural Selection). To imagine that a chance set of mutations (Its cells being provided by one or both parents) would produce all 200 proteins required for cilia function in a single generation, stretches the imagination beyond the breaking point. And yet, producing one or a few of these proteins at a time, in standard Darwinian fashion, would convey no survival advantage because those few proteins would have no function indeed, they would constitute a waste of energy for the cell to even produce (Therefore, once again, this goes against natural selections' rules for survival so that they would be discarded).

Darwin recognized this as a potent threat to his theory of evolution – "The issue that could completely disprove his idea" – So, the question must be raised: "Has Darwin's theory of evolution absolutely broken down?" [433]

According to Michael Behe, Stephen Meyers, and other eminent scientists, the answer is a resounding "yes". Richard Dawkins states however, "Darwin devoted an entire chapter of the "Origin of Species" to 'difficulties' on the theory of descent with modifications, and it is fair to say that this brief chapter anticipated and *disposed* of *every single one of the alleged difficulties that have since been proposed*." [434]

C'mon man. Every single one Richard? Darwin's "Origin of Species" was written in 1859, so I respectfully disagree with Richard's claim that every single difficulty since 1859 has been resolved. Consider all that's been discovered since 1859 (*Review my discovery chart I included starting on page 199)". Richard continued, saying, "No one has found, nor has he himself found, a single case of *irreducible complexity* that disproves Darwin's statement that everything has been formed by numerous, successive, slight modifications (Coming by way of the *'smooth, gradient of Mount Improbable'* I suppose, which is an example from his book 'Climbing Mount Improbable")." [435]

In another one of Richard's books, titled "Climbing Mount Improbable", Richard wrote an entire chapter on the eye and the wing, in-order-to demonstrate how easy it was for them to evolve by slow (or, even, maybe, not so slow) gradual degrees (Iterations). Richard also mentions the flatworms' eye as being one such example of how "it went from simple to complex, it being far from the perfection of an eagle's eye, yet *functional for its purpose*." Richard uses it as an example of an eye being in the *"process of evolutionary improvement."* [436]

I could make a few arguments regarding these so-called examples offered up by Richard, but I'll let you, my readers, make the decision if you want to believe Richard's example of something living today that is, with its so-called *imperfect* eye, in a stage of evolution and that it will contribute to other offspring that will be part of the millions of gradations or iterations yet to take place, which iterations are required to take place over the next millions of years, before the flatworms' so-called *imperfect* eye reaches completion. So far, this seems to be the one and only example that Richard and other scientists have held up as proof of *natural selection* working today? Richard? You've got to be kidding.

Casey Luskin wrote the article titled, "Evolution and the Problem of Non-Functional Intermediates" in 1980.[437] Behe's articles regarding *Irreducible Complexity* were written 137 years after Darwin's time of 1859. Richard first published *The God Delusion* in 2006, and since then books like Stephen Meyer's "Signature in the Cell" [438] 2010, and "Darwin's Doubt" [439] 2013, and "Return of the God Hypothesis" [440] 2021, and many more books, have come on the scene, describing the many new discoveries that relate to this very interesting topic. Certainly, in my opinion, neither Richard nor anyone else can claim that Darwin *"anticipated and disposed of every single one of the alleged difficulties* that have since been brought to light, right up to the present day." [441]

Since Richard, to this very day, still supports his claim that Darwin's theory of evolution has disposed of *every single one of the alleged difficulties* that have been put forth opposing Darwin's theory, when in fact there have been hundreds come forth, including the ones I have listed here, it certainly is evidence, to me, that Richard, in my humble opinion, is indeed suffering from what I have been calling *an atheist's delusion*. I suggest you, my readers, read another article that I think lends additional support for Behe's conclusion regarding Irreducible Complexity and Functionality of Systems, which break down Darwin's theory of evolution and its tenet of natural selection ... piece-by-piece. Do a search for:

"Evolution and the Problem of Non-Functional Intermediates" by Casey Luskin (Evolutions Fundamental flaw at www.IdeaCenter.org) [442]

Richard's next Subtitle is – 'The Worship of Gaps

THE WORSHIP OF GAPS

Richard begins this subtitle by saying, "Creationists eagerly seek a gap in our present-day knowledge and understanding. If an apparent gap is found, it is assumed that God, by default, must fill it. What worries thoughtful theologians is that gaps shrink as science advances, and God is threatened with eventually having nothing to do and nowhere to hide. What worries scientists is something else. It is an essential part of the scientific enterprise *to admit ignorance*, even to exult in ignorance as a challenge to future conquests. *Admissions of ignorance and temporary mystification are vital to good science.* It is therefore unfortunate, to say the least, that the main strategy of creation propagandists is the negative one of seeking out gaps in scientific knowledge and then claiming to fill them with Intelligent Design by default." [443]

Richard gives what he thinks is an analogical example of how *irreducible complexity* could be accomplished by small, iterated steps. He uses an archway made of stones where scaffolding is used to set it all in place, and *then* the scaffolding is taken away. He then posits the question "Could not the *biological process* of some supposed irreducibly complex organism have had *scaffolding* (Of some kind) to get it to the completed stage after which the scaffolding is then removed"?" [444]

I suppose it is possible, but the fact is that there aren't any such biological scaffolding examples, that I'm aware of, in existing cells today. None. And if it was found I would ask, "What about the scaffolding's origin? Where would it have come from? Who or what created it? In other words, isn't Richard's proposition subject to infinite regression too? My perspective on this *gap* issue is that God not only fills the *unanswered gaps* that still exist today, God is also the answer to what's behind *all* of the *already answered gaps* from the past. God is the source and answer to all scientific advances and that's because He is the source of all scientific truth and knowledge about our reality, seen and unseen, even the Author and Finisher of all things physical and spiritual.

Next Richard attacks Behe, who I spoke of earlier, by referring to a book named "Finding Darwin's God" [445]. It was written by Kenneth Miller. Richard uses words like 'evidently', and 'an obvious way', and 'could climb', all of which shows Richard is simply exercising *faith* in his hope of getting irreducibly complex systems over on the side of his Mount Improbable. But, 'evidently' and 'could' are words he uses to express the fact that he's still just guessing how things *might* work with complexities. Richard's theory of the *Mount Improbable*, requires millions of years and millions of iterations to achieve the *simple-to-complex systems* process he describes, which systems Richard believes are the result of evolution.

I'm always amazed how atheist scientists constantly set aside their own Scientific Method and its rules to which they hold theists to, like myself, yet they interject words like 'possible', 'could', and 'evidently' into their arguments, without having performed the testing to back up all of their claims. Let me share what Dr. Hugh Ross, who I introduced to you early on in my book's Introduction, said about "The-God-of-the-Gaps" reasoning and its criticisms given by the likes of Richard and other atheist scientists who bark and yap loud and long about this 'God-of-the-Gap' theory, and I quote:

"The work of an apologist in some ways parallels the work of a scientist. Both seek to prove (as in 'establish by testing') the truth of their explanation for something, and thus, to defend their idea against challenges. Both look for solutions to problems, specifically inconsistencies and unanswered questions arising from their proposed explanations. A Christian apologist's job is to prove and defend the veracity of the Gospel, chiefly by establishing the reliability of Scripture and by solving apparent problems in biblical interpretation or theology. This brief background sheds light on the rise—and the fall—of an apologetics hypothesis popularly known as 'the gap theory'. When science is unable to explain how the universe came into being or how life originated on earth, most Christian apologists immediately point to God as the causal explanation. Upon suggesting this God-of-the-gaps solution, the skeptics immediately accuse the Christian apologist of oversimplifying the science by giving these gaps in science a name—God. "Having no adequate explanation themselves'", says the atheist, "they simply appeal to God as being the causal cause in the causal chain. The atheist naturalist (a person who believes that the physical cosmos is the ultimate reality) assumes that, given enough time, scientific exploration will one day discover *the naturalistic explanation to everything* (The 'Theory of Everything') that is now inexplicable (I guess one could call this ' naturalism-of-the-gaps').

"Regardless of the course taken by naturalists, most sophisticated Christian theists refrain from dependence on a god-of-the-gaps form of reasoning. Rather, Christian scholars tend to appeal to God as an *inference to the best explanation (The highest Percentage of probability inferring God's existence).*

"This form of logical reasoning resembles the way detectives, lawyers, historians, and scientists go about reasoning through difficult questions. For example, scientists sometimes postulate ideas that are unobservable, in order to try and explain the data that is observable" [446] (That's what I just said Richard did. Consider how they view dark matter and dark energy. I suggest you, my readers, watch the YouTube Video titled 'Genesis Impact'." [447] The full movie shows how far scientists will go in the way of promoting *unverified evidence* to try and prove their theory of evolution).

Hugh Ross continues:

"Informed Christian thinkers do not naively assume divine activity or divine intervention as the explanation for whatever humans have not yet found evidence for the unexplainable. They offer their best theories for life's unexplainable realities. For me, inference to the best explanation (It's called 'abduction') serves as the most powerful and cogent approach to explaining reality." [448]

End of Dr. Ross's excerpts

Once again, Richard reverts to sarcasm in describing such statements made by the likes of Dr. Ross, by saying: "A lot more work needs to be done, of course, and I'm sure it will be. Such work would never be done if scientists were satisfied with *a lazy default* such as Intelligent Design Theory would encourage. Here is the message that an imaginary *Intelligent Design* theorist might broadcast to scientists: 'If you don't understand how something works, never mind: just give up and say God did it … Please don't go to work on the problem, just give up, and appeal to God. Dear scientists, don't work on your mysteries. Bring us your mysteries, for we can use them … We need those glorious gaps as a last refuge for God." [449]

You can take what Richard wrote on this topic and the little summary I have commented about it and be done with it. But I would encourage that in addition to reading my book, you, my readers, should read Stephen Meyer's Book "Signature in the Cell" and review the research he's done regarding *Intelligent Design* that came out well after Darwin's and Richard's books were published. In addition, if you would like to know more about the court case that was held in 2010 regarding a group of Creationists desiring that a course on *'Intelligent Design'* be allowed to be taught in a Pennsylvania school as a science course, you can access it by doing a Search for:

Judge Rejects Teaching Intelligent Design by Laurie Goodstein. Here are some excerpts:

"HARRISBURG, Pa., Dec. 21 - A federal judge ruled on Tuesday that it was unconstitutional for a Pennsylvania school district to present 'Intelligent Design' as an *alternative* to 'evolution' in high school biology courses because it is a *religious viewpoint* that advances a particular version of Christianity (And therefore it is not a scientific view. Really? Didn't Richard want to make this God question a scientific research question?). In the nation's first case to test the legal merits of Intelligent Design, the judge, John E. Jones III, issued a broad, stinging rebuke to its advocates and provided strong support for scientists who have fought to bar Intelligent Design from the science curriculum." [450]

Do you, my readers, find it interesting like I do, that this particular subtitles' topic stirs such vitriol towards those who simply want to posit an *alternative* theory or viewpoint to the now questionable theory – Darwin's Theory of Evolution – and its tenet of Natural Selection? I would ask, "Who of these groups seems the more scared or anxious to you? The atheists or the theists?"

Hearing both sides to any scientific debate seems only fair and balanced to me, but apparently not to atheist scientists like Richard or to liberal judges like the one overseeing this case for that matter. To them, just one theory, one opinion, one point-of-view, and only one voice is fair, because they believe (or feel) it (Science curriculum) must only be sound science, and to these self-promoting intellectuals, *Intelligent Design* is *not* coming from a sound science place. Again, I ask you, my readers, "Just what are these so called eminently intelligent folks afraid of?"

The work being done on Intelligent Design, in my opinion, is incredibly scientific in terms of the scientific methods being performed to research it. Go and check this research out for yourself and don't take mine or their critics word for it. I think you'll come away with a new reference leg of evidence for your circular support stand that says this work is truly scientific.

The next subtitle is – 'The Anthropic Principle – Planetary Version'

THE ANTHROPIC PRINCIPLE – PLANETARY VERSION

Richard begins this subtitle by saying, "The next big God-of-the-Gaps submitted by theists is that of the 'Origin of Life'. Subsequent evolutionary steps are duplicated in more-or-less similar ways, throughout millions and millions of species (But none whatsoever in 'Kinds') independently, continually, and repeatedly throughout geological time."

"Therefore, to explain the evolution of complex life, we cannot resort to the same kind of statistical reasoning as we are able to apply to the origin of life. The events that constitute run-of-the-mill evolution, as distinct from its singular origins (and perhaps a few special cases), cannot have been very improvable. This distinction may seem puzzling, so I must explain it further, using the so-called *anthropic principle* (For those of you, my readers, who may not know what the anthropic principle is, it's the principle that says there is a restrictive lower bound on how statistically probable our observations of the universe are, given that we could only exist in the particular type of universe capable of developing and sustaining sentient life. In other words, a 'Goldilocks Zone')." [451]

"The anthropic argument is usually applied to the cosmos ... We exist here on earth, and therefore, earth must be the kind of planet that's capable of generating and supporting us, however unusual, even unique, that kind of planet might be. Around a typical star like our sun, there is a so-called 'Goldilocks Zone', not too hot and not too cold, but just right." [452]

Richard goes on to describe what I would say is the *fine-tuning* of the universe, and our solar system that makes it possible for *'life'* to have started and continued on in support of life and us: "Two main explanations have been offered for our planet's peculiar friendliness to life. The design theory says that God made the world, placed it in the Goldilocks Zone, and deliberately set up all the *details* (Fine-tuned it) for our benefit. The anthropic approach is very different, and it has a faintly Darwinian feel."

"The anthropic principle, like natural selection, is an alternative to the design hypothesis. It provides a rational (Implying that the God Hypothesis is irrational), design-free explanation of the fact that we find ourselves in a situation propitious (Extremely favorable) to our existence. Liquid water is a necessary condition for life as we know it, water, and the origin of life, may have been a highly improbable occurrence. Darwinian evolution proceeds merrily *'once life has originated'* (I thought Natural Selection is the director, the causal cause of all things. Who or what causes *'life'* itself to originate Richard?). But how does life get started?" [453] (How indeed? "Once life has originated?" is the 64,000-dollar question, isn't it? I bet this question irks Richard something fierce, since scientists have never been able to produce any answer to it what-so-ever).

"The origin of life was the chemical event, or *series of events*, whereby the vital *conditions* for natural selection first came about." [454] Chemical event Richard? Life in the parental-cells of animals and humans most certainly activates a new creation, a new animal, and a new human being, but where does the *'life'* or *'life giving power'* in these cells come from Richard? If it is just a chemical event, then why don't biologists just go ahead and dig up the minerals or purchase the chemicals from *The Lab Depot* and make the so-called *event or series of events* happen spontaneously? Richard goes on giving what he thinks *'probably'* happened, or *'perhaps'* happened. No facts. No evidence. No scientifically tested, proven events to point to. Just unreliable postulates and speaking as though it's settled science. Richard then says, "Once the vital ingredients – *some kind of genetic molecule* – is in place (Richard has absolutely no clue what those so-called vital ingredients that generate 'life' in cells are), true Darwinian natural selection can follow, and complex life emerges as the eventual consequence." [455]

Vital ingredients? Some kind of genetic molecule? Are you kidding me Richard? C'mon man. I say this *life power* that's already existing in these parental-cells, is what starts and gives 'life' to these parental-cells, and once these parental-cells come together, *that event* of life's beginning, this life activation of the DNA *system that directs all life-filled cells,* causes it to start directing the protein manufacturing process. The life in-dwelling in all cells cannot be created out of nothing, otherwise scientists would have already created it. The 'information' in the DNA code is what directs the 'life' and not the 'hijacked' term or concept that Richard calls natural selection. Richard does admit that "The *spontaneous* arising by chance of the *first* hereditary molecules (Parental-molecules making up our cells cells) strikes many as improbable. Maybe it is – very, very improbable, and I shall dwell on this, for it is central to this section of my book." [456]

Richard fully expects chemistry and biological scientists, in the next few years, will report that, "they have successfully *midwifed* a *'new origin of life'* in the laboratory. Nevertheless, it hasn't happened yet, and it is still possible to maintain that the probability of it happening is, and always was, exceedingly low – although it ('Spontaneous arising?') did happen once!" [457] No. It was not spontaneous Richard.

Richard says 'once' because we are all here, aren't we? And the 'Big' question is "Who or what was the causal cause of that so-called '*Spontaneous arising*'? I came across an online string on 'Quora's Q & A'. It was a string of comments by several people, one of whom was a man by the name of John Cousins. John's just an ordinary guy like myself, from what I could find out about him. You, my readers, will be the judge, but I found John's comments to be fair and balanced. He didn't list any scientific credentials, but I found him to be credible and authentic in his statements on this subject. John said, and I quote:

"Over the years, I have investigated the arguments for God by studying the Bible in depth, from the beginning to the end, and I read about 25% of the Quran in the same fashion. Eventually my interests moved me onto the notion of the Anthropic Principle and its offshoot the Fine-Tuning Principle through reading books by physicists from the likes of Paul Davis with his controversial titles of '*The Mind of God*' or the '*Fifth Miracle*', Martin Rees (Astronomer Royal) with his book '*Just Six Numbers*' (that indicates that there are just 6 numbers that are finely tuned for the universe we see) and more recently a dip into Sean Carroll's deterministic universe with '*The Big Picture*', where it touches on fine tuning.

"Having read these and many others, it seems to me we have had for years two protagonists to the universe's unfolding drama with each defending their patch of territory with vigor. On the one hand are the religiously minded who want to believe in a loving benevolent God who built the universe for the pleasure of free moral agents (us).

"On the other hand, at the opposite extreme, are the 'determinist' atheists, who wish to see the universe as an enormous snooker table full of atoms like snooker balls, all predictably behaving according to pre-defined rules (Laplacian demon). Thus like any other rule-based machine, they feel it has no free agency nor does any component of such a universe (Homo Sapiens), therefore no special relationship exists between a single component and the whole; the component is just an emerging quality of the whole (I ask, "Who or what set those rules in place to begin with?").

"Thus, the Anthropic Principle and Fine-Tuning Principle cannot be extracted from the polarizing debates from which the ideas have come which brings with it understandable biases. That is not to say, there aren't interesting facts about our universe worth knowing, there indeed are, but one must be aware of the continuous battle going on in the background and try to separate the data from the passion.

The Data and Anthropic Principle

Let's start with looking at the data first, before returning to the two principles?

- The Sun is just the right category of star, not too old and not too young, but just right, fortuitously at its most stable period in-order-to supply consistent steady light and heat.

- The proto-Earth was in just the exact position 4.5 billion years ago, relative to the other planets, to weather the stormy beginnings and become a substrate upon which life could form.

- The Earth is exactly at the right distance for the Sun's energy output to enable just the exact amount of heat and light necessary for molecular life to evolve.

- The Earth happens to have an almost circular orbit stopping the extremes of cold and heat that would have hampered the emergence of life had it had an excessively elliptical orbit.

- Our planet happens to have volcanism and thus a molten interior of iron and other heavy elements that creates the earth's unique magnetic field without which life could never have started due to cosmic ray bombardment from the Sun killing it off. Fortunately, that gets deflected by the earth's magnetism.

- Human life with eyes that allow a very small percentage of the visible electro-magnetic spectrum through, yet coincidentally the vast majority of what we have learned and understood about the universe has come from that very limited window of that spectrum.

- Using those eyes, humans have been able to fortuitously observe a unique moon whose orbit is just right compared to the sun's distance from us to produce a perfect eclipse without which certain deductions about light from the corona could not have been made. If the moon had been bigger the corona would not have been seen and thus analyzed. If smaller the peripheral light would have swamped the optics making measurements impossible.

- With humankind's intellect, we have now even found, through mathematics, at least 6- mathematical constants (there are others) that define natural processes. Changing their value by some insignificant amount would, it seems, be enough to render the universe devoid of life. So, for life to exist these six numbers are like positions on six dials with any one dial even slightly off position stopping the emergence of life.

Fine Tuned Universe

"Atheists unhappy with the hijacking of their own scientific findings (of the various intellectual fields from biology to astronomy) by the religionists, understandably cause them to start fighting back. But how can one counter such strong circumstantial evidence that there is at least *a designer* that purposed mankind's arrival, even if you don't want to accept the notion of a loving benevolent God? One physicist who could not help but see the contrived nature of the universe, Freeman Dyson (Physicist) in his book 'Disturbing the Universe', said this:

"The more I examine the Universe and study the details of its architecture, the more evidence I find that the universe in some sense must have known that we were coming."

"Atheists counter such arguments the way religionists do. Religious people who don't wish to face the idea there is no God, avoid talking about it, because it's too uncomfortable. In the case of atheists, they too avoid talking about the Anthropic Principle, not wishing to engage it, for the same uncomfortable reason. Another defense atheists use is what I call 'The rabbit out of the hat' theory. That rabbit is an equally astonishing untestable theory called 'The Many Worlds theory', or by its other names the 'Multiverse or Multiple Universe' theory. Unhappy that religionists were gaining the upper hand they concluded that if they could show that there were as many universes out there as there are stars in the universe, and perhaps a bit more, then *that* would show that our world was not so unique after all.

"Such a theory postulates that each universe could well have a random selection of mathematical constants of nature with most not able to sustain life as we know it, and perhaps all except our universe not congenial for intelligent life. The theory says that the one universe 'just right' for intelligent existence of conscious life, would likely conclude their world looks contrived and designed without the wider knowledge that they are just one of many universes. For someone like me who tries to be objective, this theory is no more testable than a belief in a benevolent God and has to be equally based on faith.

Virtual World Theory

"Another theory that sits far better but equally untestable, so still in the realms of hypothesis at this time, is the 'Virtual World Theory'. This theory while lurking in the background for several years is gaining ground. It has been held down by both religiously inclined and atheists who with equal measure dislike the uncomfortable ramifications of this theory to their respective world views, hence their keenness to starve it of oxygen. The virtual world theory, like the others, explains the contrivance we see in nature and explains it through its champion, Nik Bostrom, a Swedish Philosopher working at Oxford University (See "Simulation Hypothesis" - Wikipedia).

"He mentions that our advancing technology one day will (He suggested within 40 years) produce computers powerful enough to program into it every neuronal connection within a human brain. The result, we will be able to interact with the computerized virtual person to see how it responds to us, does it display emotion, can we attribute consciousness to it, etc. etc.? In fact, we will be able to use it as a research tool manipulating various connections to see what it does and whether it enhances or deteriorates the virtual person's functionality, all to learn how the brain really works."

"Eventually maybe within a hundred years the computers would allow for programming thousands of human brains into it, that way whole societies of humans can be analyzed and researched sociologically interacting with one another, again to find the optimum way of controlling human society. This is not science fiction. This is going to happen such is the progress of technology. The question though that Bostrom and a growing number of others makes is, "how do we know that *our* world is not *some kind of virtual computerized one* itself, rather than being the real one? Others have extended this theory stating that once such technology was available, we would want eventually to connect humans somehow to such computers, this in order to create a mental world manipulated by the computer with an individual's existing memories temporarily switched off.

"They say this would allow youths at 14, say, to live a fast-tracked computerized 70-year life (perhaps over a weekend), making life's mistakes in a virtual world rather than with real people. The effect after coming out of the experience with their original memories switched back on, would be to produce a wise head on young shoulders. Is this not what our present life achieves? Are we not changed and wiser on average after 70 years than when a teenager? Such a machine could also be used as an employment recruitment tool as part of the employment interview. ... One could be placed over a weekend into the computer via some pod where the person lies with their memories temporarily removed to live out their virtual life, profiled to test the potential candidate for characteristics needed for the job.

Conclusion

"From all the theories, how does one know if any are correct? Occam's Razor says, "out of all the competing theories that vie for supremacy in any field, choose the one with least assumptions because it is more testable, and test it if you can. Which theories, from the foregoing, seems to have the least assumptions? The only one that's potentially testable is Bostrom's, at least to a degree that either rules it out or makes it more plausible. I'm for objectivity. Let's keep a clear playing field for *all* the competing theories rather than the truth being restricted to just two with the loudest voices." [458]

End of Comments by John Cousins

Richard says, "Just as we did with the 'Goldilocks orbits', we can make the point that, however improbable *the origin of life* might be, we know it happened on earth because we are here." [459]

I would ask you, my readers, to ask yourselves this question, "Which is more improbable, the coming to existence of possibly trillions of universes all exploding from their own singularity the size of a pea (Or even smaller as Stephen Hawking described it), so that the math is there for one of those trillions of universes to pop out an earth like ours, so life can spontaneously originate? Or the probability of an incomprehensible, intelligent mind that is capable of producing the magnificence of information that makes up the DNA code and the power to activate the life-essence-bearing parent-molecule(s) that can begin life?" In other words, which causal cause (Or source) is more probable to have *the power to give and start life*?

Richard says, "There are two 'hypotheses' to explain what happened – the design hypothesis and the scientific or anthropic hypothesis (My understanding of the word science, is that it's a systematically organized body of 'knowledge', and therefore it makes me ask "Aren't both hypothesis scientifically knowledge-based in their very nature?").[460]

Richard goes on to say, "The design approach postulates a God who wrought a deliberate miracle, struck the *prebiotic soup* with divine fire, and launched DNA, or something equivalent, on its momentous career." [461] Ha-ha-ha, there's Richard doing his humorous wordsmithing again. I love it.

In response to what Richard just said, I would simply ask you, my readers, to watch a YouTube video titled "Scientists Speak Out About Evidence of Intelligent Design in Nature". It's incredible because it has world renown scientists speaking in support of Intelligent Design. One such scientist is Charles H. Townes, a Nobel Laureate in physics. Charles, as a practicing Christian, has always seen religious faith and scientific investigation as convergent paths to ultimate truth (Sound a lot like my illustration of Pure Science and Pure Religion or Faith converging at the Millennium, right?). Here is what Mr. Townes said:

"Intelligent Design, as one sees it from a scientific point of view, seems to be quite real." [462]

The video's only two-and-a-half minutes long, but I'm confident you will appreciate its contribution to the discussion we're having here. Now listen to this next statement made by Richard. If it isn't wishful thinking, then I don't know what is. Richard continues: "We live on a planet where we are surrounded by perhaps ten million species, each one of which independently displays a powerful *illusion* of apparent design (Intelligent Design). Each species is *well fitted* to its particular way of life." [463]

The question then becomes, "Who did the fitting Richard?"

I would have you consider the number of years it would take for these ten millions of species to evolve to the point where they're all so 'well fitted' for their particular, individual environments, including individualized fingerprints finding their way onto our fingers. Everything's perfectly fitted; perfectly finished; perfectly good, which is exactly what God said when He finished His creative work. He declared, "It is Good" after each creative period (Keep in mind this was a paradisical state, it being perfect, for it was before "The Fall"). If Richard's theory is correct, the time that would be required to do all of this *fitting* would be far beyond the 4.7 billion years of our earth's existence, wouldn't it? Do the math.

Richard continues: "Could we get away with the 'huge numbers of planets' argument to explain all these separate *illusions* of design? No, we could not. I repeat, we could not. Don't even think about it. This is important, for it goes to the heart of the most serious misunderstanding of Darwinism. We really need Darwin's powerful 'crane' to account for the diversity of life on earth (If we're going to eliminate God as the causal cause for all of it), and especially the persuasive *illusion* of design. The *origin of life*, by contrast, lies outside the reach of that crane, *because natural selection cannot proceed without it* (Did you read that? Now, prepare for it! See what Richard says next). We can deal with the unique *origin of life* by postulating (Guessing) 'a very large number of planetary opportunities."

"Once that initial *stroke of luck* (Chance) has been granted (By who or what?) – and the *anthropic principle* most decisively grants it to us (Oh. Really? C'mon man. Again, no proof, no testing, no observation, and yet Richard emphatically states this as though it is *settled science*). Natural selection takes over, and it emphatically is not a matter of luck!" [464]

Talk about speaking in circles. Luck? Chance? How about incredible, perfect, information-based creation from an incredibly brilliant, perfectly intelligent, and glorious Mind – the Mind of God?

Richard then says, "Natural selection works because it is a cumulative one-way street to improvement. It needs some 'luck' (A word atheists substitute in place of God) to *get started*, and the *billions of planets anthropic principle*, grants it that luck." [465]

A principle/idea granting luck? Really Richard? Now who's talking the impossible or improbable? The principle of trillions of universes coming into existence because of trillions more universes that came before them, back ad infinitum, ... granting this luck? Really? C'mon man. Doesn't this beg the question of "Infinite Regression" once again, as to "Who created the billions or trillions of Universes back into infinity"? Repeated Big Bangs? You can't have it both ways my atheist friends. Now who's delusional?

If *'trillions of universes'* isn't a statement of absolute blind faith, I again, don't know what blind faith is. There is absolutely no observable, tested proof to support the reality of these billions or trillions of universes existing or coming into existence through the process of trillions of *singularity Big Bangs taking place over billions of years by sheer luck,* which is how scientists say our own universe got started. Right? Talk about a low percentage of probability on Richard's probability spectrum. Good grief!

Let me interject a thought here. I ask you, my readers, to take a moment and imagine in your mind, that you're holding a gold wedding band, a gold ring between your thumb and index finger. As you do, consider the inside of that ring. Can you see a beginning and an end? No. This is a micro lesson of what *eternity* or *infinity* is. Infinity is the state or quality of being infinite, without a beginning or an end. Infinite is *"limitless or endless in space, extent, or size; impossible to measure or calculate"* (Meaning you cannot find the beginning from the end of the ring).

Both atheist scientists and theist scientists understand what *infinity* is and means, and I would even suggest that they believe in infinity or the infinite. So, if they believe in the concept of infinity, which has no beginning or end like the inside of the gold ring example I offered, why wouldn't this description be an accepted answer for the question of "Infinite Regression"?

If space and time are infinite, why can't the genealogy of our Father in Heaven be infinite? In the scriptures it is referred to as "Without a beginning or end of days". This concept is just as good an answer for this question of infinity or infinite regression as any other. My perspective is that our mind cannot comprehend these mysteries of godliness, nor can it comprehend what "Without a beginning or end of days" really is?

The eternality of God, our Creator, and the eternality of His creations, including you and I, is beyond man's limited, puny minds' understanding. Richard appears to be saying that there would be enough 'by-chance' power in his evolutionary 'cosmological crane' theory to bring into existence (Or crane-lift its scaffolding into existence) the billions or trillions of universes needed for them to pop out another one-of-a-kind planet earth like our own (The one-in-a-billion chance in other words). But then, for this to be probable there would have to be an *ancestral trillions of universes* that came into existence long before these trillions of universes, in order for each of them to have the numbers to pop into existence that one-of-a-kind--in-a-billion earth. Right? If this isn't totally improbable blind faith, then there's no such thing. Talk about a 'Flying Spaghetti Monster' Richard. C'mon man. It's more like *a trillion flying spaghetti monsters* popping out one improbable meat ball every billionth year, ad infinitum, until there's a full universe plate of celestial spaghetti and cosmological meat balls! That's what the Multi-Verse Theory sounds like to me. Once again, I say to you, this is one more reason why I called my book *An Atheist's Delusion!* Let's move on to the next subtitle – "The Anthropic Principle – Cosmological version" before my brain pops.

THE ANTHROPIC PRINCIPLE – COSMOLOGICAL VERSION

Richard begins this subtitles' topic by giving us a short summary of how the cosmos works, particularly how there are basically six constants (Six numbers or dials to align, just like John Cousins mentioned earlier) such as the magnitude of the so-called *strong force*, which is the force that binds the components of the atomic nucleus, versus the *weak force* which is the second of the four fundamental forces that govern all matter in the universe (The other two are gravity and electromagnetism).

Richard mentions Martin Rees, a British cosmologist and astrophysicist, and author of the book titled "Just Six Numbers". Rees, like many physicists, basically says, "Stars are a necessary prerequisite for the existence of most of the chemical elements and without chemistry there could be no life." [466]

This sounds like what Carl Sagan suggested. He said something similar in one of his original award-winning TV series episodes which was called 'Cosmos'. [467] The show recently got the reboot treatment, with the super space nerd Neil DeGrasse-Tyson as its new host. Richard continues:

"If the laws and constants of physics had been even slightly different, the universe would have *developed* in such a way that life would have been impossible. For example, a chemistry without hydrogen could not generate life as we know it. For one thing, there would be no water (I would ask my atheist scientist friends "The earth is 70% of the earth's surface, so where did it come from? I think I heard that some scientists say that it was on a super huge meteor that hit the earth or was used to help form the earth. Talk about an imagination!). Goldilocks value, .007, is just right for yielding the richness of elements that we need for an interesting and life-supporting chemistry." [468]

Richard goes on to explain the other 5 numbers representing the *constants of the universe*, and then says, "The bottom line for each of them is the same. The actual number sits in a Goldilocks band of values outside which life would not have been possible. How should we respond to this? Yet again, we have the other. The theist says that God, when setting up the universe, tuned the fundamental constants of the universe so that each one lay in its Goldilocks Zone for the production of life. It is as though God had 6 knobs that he could twiddle, and he carefully tuned each knob to its Goldilocks value. As ever, the theists' answer is deeply unsatisfying, because it leaves the existence of God unexplained (In other words, the "Who created God?" argument of infinite regression once again. But I partially answered this with the Ring Analogy micro lesson, didn't I? I certainly think so). [469]

"A God capable of calculating the Goldilocks value for the six numbers would have to be at least as improbable as the finely tuned combination of numbers itself, and that's very improbable indeed (I guess my God is "The Improbable God"). This is exactly the premise of the whole discussion we are having." [470]

Here's the bottom line with the argument Richard is giving here. Richard finds it impossible (Highly improbable) to imagine an eternal, glorified, perfected, infinitely intelligent being having such incredible intelligence, and unlimited knowledge that would give Him the power required to do this so-called *fine-tuning* referred to as Intelligent Design, and so, he dismisses it out of hand. There's a short verse of scripture that I think fits here, that I think will help you, my readers, understand and grasp how intelligent God truly is. That scripture, a revelation received from God by the Prophet Joseph Smith, says:

Doctrine & Covenants 93:36

36 The *glory (and power)* of God is *intelligence*, or, in other words, *light and truth.*

Intelligence; Light; Truth; Power; and Glory. These are incredibly sophisticated, divine attributes or character traits of God, and to understand the concepts of light and knowledge from which they spring, requires a great deal of study if we're ever going to acquire a scintilla of understanding of God's Mind, what He knows, and how He thinks. And so, it is understandable that Richard's limited scientific, naturalist-based mind is having a difficult time comprehending the idea that the Being we've decided to call God, could have such incomprehensible, unimaginable, highly improbable *intelligence*.

Here are a couple of verses of scripture that says as much. This is Jehovah (The Pre-Mortal Messiah Jesus Christ), once again, speaking to one of His prophet, Isaiah:

Isaiah 55:8-9

8 For my thoughts *are* not your thoughts, neither are your ways my ways, saith the Lord.

9 For *as* the heavens are higher than the earth, so are my ways higher than your ways, and my thoughts than your thoughts.

Richard finishes this line of thinking by saying, "I see no alternative but to dismiss it, while at the same time marveling at the number of people who can't see the problem and seem genuinely satisfied by the '*Divine Knob-Twiddler*' argument. Maybe the psychological reason for this amazing blindness (Who's blind here Richard?) has something to do with the fact that many people have not had their *consciousness raised* as (atheists) biologists have, by natural selection and its power to tame improbability" (On the other hand, we could say "… not had their consciousness, or mind, *deceived* like Richard's and his fellow atheist scientists' minds have been". I find it interesting that for a man who doesn't believe in 'mind', keeps uses the word 'consciousness' when scientists can't even tell us what consciousness is, or how it works. They only can describe it, and not tell us exactly what it is)." Richard continues:

"Biologists, with their raised consciousness of the power of natural selection to explain the rise of improbable things, are unlikely to be satisfied with any theory that evades *the problem of improbability* altogether. And the theistic response to the riddle of improbability is an evasion of stupendous proportions." [471]

Richard then moves to the "Anthropic answer", in its most general form, which is to say that "We could only be discussing the question in the kind of universe that was capable of producing us. Our existence therefore determines that *the fundamental constants* of physics had to be in their respective Goldilocks zones. Different physicists espouse different kinds of anthropic solutions to *the riddle of our existence*."

"When we finally reach the long-hoped-for *Theory of Everything* (*Bringing the four key forces in the universe into one theory, or one causal source*), we shall see that the six key numbers (Dials or knobs) depend upon each other, *or on something else as yet unknown (Maybe unseen, called God?)*, in ways that we today *cannot imagine* (Like I said, Richard can't imagine *the something else yet unknown. To him*, it couldn't be an eternal, immortal, glorified being with 'more intelligence than they all')." [472]

Richard continues: "The six numbers may turn out to be no freer to vary than is the ratio of a circle's circumference to its diameter. It will turn out that there is only one way for a universe to be. Far from God being '*needed*' to twiddle six knobs, there are no knobs to twiddle." [473]

Is it just my bias, or did Richard simply run on and on without giving any testable, provable, result-producing solutions to the fine-tuning, knob-twiddling of the universe question, and in particular, to these so-called six Goldilocks values that have to be perfectly precise for the universe to produce life? He even said, "The six key numbers depend upon each other, or on '*something else*' as yet unknown (Maybe unknown to him and other nonbelievers), *in ways that we today cannot imagine*." [474]

Again, let me repeat God's word that is found in the Book of Isaiah, chapter 55, verse 8: "My ways are not your ways". These so-called '*dials*' are unimaginable to our puny minds. For me it is "God 'speaking' them into existence" using the matter available in the universe. And the '*way*' God 'tunes them' is also unknown to us puny humans, except for what the prophets have said about it. The arrogance that Richard displays is so revealing to me. To me, that is a stark admittance that Richard and these atheist physicists have no clue as to how the fine-tuning in our, or any other universe for that matter, happens, or why things are the way they are. They just *know*, somehow, that *it absolutely cannot be the work of the 'Sky-God'* whom theists claim is the creator of everything, where He applied the four fundamental forces to intelligently design and organize our universe. For me, as I said, God *is* the 'Theory of Everything'!

Once again, Richard, with his *atheist delusion* being on full display, *chooses* to believe in (an exercise of faith) the anthropic solution of Multiverses, to answer this question of the 'six fine-tuning dials', or numbers. Here's what he says:

"There are many universes, co-existing like bubbles of foam, in a multiverse (Or mega-verse, as Leonard Susskin offers to call it). The laws and constants of any one universe, such as our observable universe, are by-laws. The multi-verse, as a whole, has a plethora of alternative sets of by-laws (Set by the '*Law-Giver*' of the Universe). The anthropic principle *kicks in* to explain that we have to be in one of those universes (or, *presumably*, a minority) whose by-laws happened to be propitious (Favorable for success) to our eventual *evolution* (That supposed all-knowing power and process that is called Evolutions' Natural Selection tenet), and hence contemplation of the problem". [475]

After explaining what he says has been '*the standard model*' of the universe, the model saying that time itself began with the singularity of the Big-Bang, along with space and time some 13.8 billion years ago, Richard then introduces the serial '*big crunch*' model saying:

"The serial big crunch model would amend the Standard Model and say, 'Our time and space did indeed begin in our Big-Bang, but this was just the latest in a long series of big-bangs, each one initiated by the '*big crunch*' that terminated the previous universe in the series'." [476]

Again, where has science produced trace evidence of these previous big-crunch terminations of universes? I certainly haven't seen any as yet. Have any of you, my readers? Here's the kicker. Richard says: "*Nobody understands* what goes on in singularities such as the Big Bang, so it is *conceivable* that the laws and constants are reset to new values, each time." [477] What does the resetting Richard?

Does this sound like Richard is simply guessing once again? Is that the scientific method he's describing? Shouldn't there be work done to prove out this predictive guessing that nobody understands how or what goes on in them? And that's the problem. Scientists, like Richard, can't prove them out because no one can observe the birth of these so-called multi-verses and their popping out an earth over a gestation period of 13.8 billions of years. It's all postulating and guess work, which by-the-way, is Richard's criticism of theists, isn't it? Do you want your reference legs of evidence, which are supposed to support your table of belief, to be based on untestable guesses? Richard continues:

"*If* '*bang-expansion-contraction-crunch-cycles*' have been going on forever like a cosmic accordion, we have a serial, rather than a parallel version of the multi-verse. Once again, the anthropic principle does its *explanatory duty*." Really Richard? You're saying that your stupendous guess is a '*principle*' doing something incredible such as its '*duty*'? C'mon man. You've got to be kidding. Does the word completely improbable mean anything to you? Hello! I am surprised that Richard is even going down this mental path and stupendous guessing game. Of all the universes in the series, only a minority have their 'dials' tuned to biogenic conditions (How do you know this Richard, so that you can state it so matter-of-factly'?). And, of course, the present universe (Meaning ours) has to be one of *that* minority, because we are in it." [478]

Good honk in the morning! Much like Richard's amazement for theist scientists who believe in an improbable God, with His resurrection, angels, and spirit bodies living in an unseen world, I'm amazed that this self-proclaimed *highly intelligent and eminent minded* evolutionary biologist (In order to avoid having to acknowledge the possibility of a super-intelligent *mind* being the *causal agent* of our universe), *chooses* to take this unbelievably extreme, cockamamie *multi-verse anthropic theoretical position* as his solution to the fine-tuning problem. The finely tuned universe is just as it seems. It is finely tuned, and that's because of an incredibly intelligent, gloriously powerful mind, even the great Causal-Cause Mind of God who designed everything we see and cannot see. Listen to the words of ancient prophets from the Book of Mormon where they spoke of Jehovah, and His creations:

I Nephi 17:36.

36 Behold, the Lord hath created the earth that it should be inhabited; and he hath created his children that they should possess it.

II Nephi 2:14

14 And now, my sons, I speak unto you these things for your profit and learning; for there is a God, and he hath *created all things*, both the heavens and the earth, and all things that in them are, both things to act and things to be acted upon.

Mosiah 4:9

9 Believe in God; believe that he is, and that he created all things, both in heaven and in earth; believe that he has all wisdom, and all power, both in heaven and in earth; believe that *man doth not comprehend all the things which the Lord can comprehend*.

Alma 18:28 (To the Lamanite King named Lamoni, Ammon said:)

28 And Ammon said: This is God. And Ammon said unto him again: Believest thou that this Great Spirit, who is God, created all things which are in heaven and in the earth?

Lamoni had been raised in the darkness of apostasy of the Lamanite tradition with its Great Spirit, and so he believed in a Great Spirit, but his life was about to be turned upside down on its head, and changed immensely on the day Ammon, who was one of the sons of Mosiah, crossed the borders into his land:

Alma 22:10

10 And Aaron said unto him: Yea, he is that Great Spirit, and he created all things both in heaven and in earth. Believest thou this?

Mormon 9:11

11 But behold, I will show unto you a God of miracles, even the God of Abraham, and the God of Isaac, and the God of Jacob; and it is that same God who created the heavens and the earth, and all things that in them are.

2 Ne. 8:13

13 And forgettest the Lord thy maker, that hath stretched forth the heavens, and laid the foundations of the earth, and hast feared continually every day, because of the fury of the oppressor, as if he were ready to destroy? And where is the fury of the oppressor?

Isaiah 51:13

13 And forgettest the LORD thy maker, that hath stretched forth the heavens, and laid the foundations of the earth; and hast feared continually every day because of the fury of the oppressor, as if he were ready to destroy? and where *is* the fury of the oppressor?

Once again, Richard's approach is simply a *grasping at straws* approach, and what I would call a '*non-proven-non-scientifically-based*' approach, in-order-to avoid accepting the more probable solution – the *God Hypothesis*. For me, it is another example of an atheist's delusion, the atheist being, of course, Richard Dawkins, who seems to be driven by a fear that theists are actually gaining what little ground is left on *the percentage of probability* spectrum, showing that God does in fact exist. Next is the subtitle – "An interlude at Cambridge."

AN INTERLUDE AT CAMBRIDGE

Richard begins this subtitle by telling his readers about a Cambridge conference on science and religion he once attended. He was one of the guest speakers, along with several speakers with varied backgrounds. The conference was sponsored by the Templeton Foundation. The John Templeton Foundation is a philanthropic organization that reflects the ideas of its founder, John Templeton, who became wealthy via a career as a contrarian investor and wanted to support progress in religious and spiritual knowledge, especially at the intersection of religion and science.

Upon learning that the foundation had paid several scientists and journalists $15,000 each to attend the conference (Boy! How can I participate in something like that? Just kidding), Richard's suspicion was aroused as to whether-or-not Templeton was using his money to suborn science journalists and subvert their scientific integrity.

While at the conference Richard challenged the theologians, with his go-to question. Richard asked them to consider his point that "a God capable of designing a universe, or anything else for that matter, would have to be complex and *statistically improbable*", which is Richard's main go-to-argument against there being a God, next to the *infinite regression* question.

The response Richard got from the journalists attending the conference was that Mr. Templeton was foisting a scientific epistemology upon an unwilling theology, and that scientific arguments, such as those Richard was accustomed to deploying in his own field, were inappropriate since theologians had always maintained that God lay *outside* of time-space and that He was a simple God, not a complex one.

Maybe other theists or theologians believe this, but I certainly do not. It is most definitely not my view regarding Richard's description of God's so-called *statistically improbable intelligence*. I think I've been clear in giving my Latter-Day Saint perspective of God's omniscience, and so I won't repeat myself here except to say that it appears that Richard is unable to comprehend how a divine being such as the Eternal, Divinely Intelligent God that I believe in, is capable of doing such incredible things. For example, answers to prayer, which is where God sends *messages* to us, His children, directly into our minds. This is just one example of His divine abilities that Richard just cannot get his head around. Richard also doesn't understand how "his messages can be intercepted by us with our human brains—and second, be capable of sending these intelligible signals to millions of people simultaneously, as well as Him receiving such messages from billions of us simultaneously." [479]

This says a lot about Richard's lack of spirituality, meaning his stunted understanding of spiritual things, but of course, you would expect this of an atheist. I've already given one analogy to answer Richard's criticism against the reality of God – an analogy about the spiritual principle called prayer.

The analogy was that of a 'Prayer Answering Search Engine' kind of Mind, much like the Google Search Engine tool of communication we all use every day of our lives. My question to Richard and other atheists was, "How were human brains capable of coming up with Googles' complex Search Engine with all of its power to receive and answer billions of queries coming in simultaneously?" If puny human beings' minds were able to produce such a complex, powerful communication tool, then most certainly the gloriously intelligent Mind of God, with its unfathomable degree of intelligence could at least match their puny brain power, don't you think? I sure do.

Certainly, one can imagine this kind of being that could surpass the human mind and therefore would be capable of having His own kind of Prayer-Answering-Search-Engine capacity for receiving and sending billions of prayers. Please note that I'm not saying that this is in fact how God does this. I'm just putting forth the idea that God certainly has a greater intellect than we humans have and so His Mind certainly surpasses us in how imaginative He is and in how He can communicate with His children.

This is just one example of how God's divine attributes, the main one being His Mind, which has the power and capacity to handle the spiritual principle we call prayer. God has many more divine attributes that we, as human beings, find next to impossible to imagine or comprehend. Everything God does with His divine attributes, shows "His ways are not our ways", that's for sure.

The following verses of scripture in the first book of Moses relates the account given by Moses where Jehovah appeared to Moses. After Moses was left to himself, he realized and declared that man, compared to God, is nothing, even as the dust of the earth. In other words, 'Oh puny man' with his 'arm of the flesh' being nothing, like dust is nothing when compared to God's mighty power and glory. Keep in mind that the person speaking in these verses, is Jehovah, who is speaking as though He is the Father. He does so, as I have suggested, by virtue of the principle called 'Divine Investiture of Authority'. Read them carefully, as they reveal a very complex understanding of who God the Father is and who His Only Begotten Son, Jehovah, who is Jesus Christ is:

Moses 1:1-10

1 The words of God, which he spake unto Moses at a time when Moses was caught up into an exceedingly high mountain,

2 And he saw God face to face, and he talked with him, *and the glory of God was upon Moses; therefore Moses could endure his presence.*

3 And God spake unto Moses, saying: Behold, I am the Lord God Almighty, and Endless is my name; for I am without beginning of days or end of years; and is not this endless?

4 And, behold, thou art my son; wherefore look, and I will show thee the workmanship of mine hands; but not all, *for my works are without end*, and also my words, for they never cease.

5 Wherefore, no man can behold all my works, except he behold all my glory; and no man can behold *all my glory*, and afterwards remain in the flesh on the earth.

6 And I have a work for thee, Moses, my son; and thou art in the similitude of mine Only Begotten; and mine Only Begotten is and shall be the Savior, for he is full of grace and truth; *but there is no God beside me*, and all things are present with me, for I know them all (Though Jehovah is God the Son, He is not above God the Father. Neither is God the Holy Ghost).

7 And now, behold, this one thing I show unto thee, Moses, my son, for thou art in the world, and now I show it unto thee.

8 And it came to pass that Moses looked, and beheld the world upon which he was created; and Moses beheld the world and the ends thereof, and all the children of men which are, and which were created; of the same he greatly marveled and wondered.

9 And the presence of God withdrew from Moses, that his glory was not upon Moses; and Moses was left unto himself. And as he was left unto himself, he fell unto the earth.

10 And it came to pass that it was for the space of many hours before Moses did again receive his natural strength like unto man; and he said unto himself: *Now, for this cause I know that man is nothing, which thing I never had supposed.*

These verses reveal a great deal about the God of the universe and about His Only Begotten Son Jehovah, who we know to be Jesus of Nazareth, who became clothed in flesh so He could fulfill His role and calling as the Savior of the world, even our advocate with the Father.

After this Cambridge experience, Richard reflected, "The theologians of my Cambridge encounter were defining themselves into an epistemological safe zone where rational argument could not reach them because they had declared by fiat that it could not. Who was I to say that rational argument was the only admissible kind of argument? There are these other ways of knowing that must be deployed to know God" (Meaning *spiritual experiences*, such as this account of Moses, which Richard knows little or nothing about it). Richard continues:

"The most important of these other ways of knowing turned out to be personal, subjective experiences of God (See? What'd I tell you?). Several discussants at Cambridge claimed that God spoke to them, inside their heads, just as vividly and as personally as another human might. I have dealt with illusion and hallucination in Chapter 3 (Titled "The argument against personal spiritual experience"), but at the Cambridge conference I added two points. First, that if God really did communicate with humans, that fact would emphatically not lie outside of science. Second, *a God who is capable of sending intelligible signals to millions of people simultaneously and of receiving messages from all of them simultaneously*, cannot be, whatever else he might be, simple. Such bandwidth!" [480]

Like I said Richard, it may be very much like a powerful *'Google Prayer Search Engine'* kind of mind, as well as it being a *super transmitter*, right? Or maybe He uses His angels to answer our prayers. Yes, that is some bandwidth. As I said, I am not saying that this power to receive and answer prayers is a Google type search engine. What I am saying, is that it's just one possible theorem for you, my readers, to consider and imagine in your mind, out of the many unimaginable possibilities that we might produce. One day God Himself will reveal to us the *'How'* He answers all our prayers, for He truly does in ways that give us hope and increased faith, and joy. Richard goes on to expose his deep lack of understanding of God's nature, or dare I say, his lack of having *his consciousness being raised by the mysteries of godliness*, as they relate to the nature of the original Prime Mover, God the Father. Here's Richard making my point perfectly:

"To suggest that the original prime mover was complicated enough to indulge in Intelligent Design, to say nothing of *mindreading millions of humans simultaneously*, is tantamount to dealing yourself *a perfect hand* at bridge. Look around at the world of life, at the Amazon rainforest with its rich interlacement of lianas, bromeliads, roots, and flying buttresses." Richard continues, "Its army ants and its jaguars, its tapirs, and peccaries, treefrogs and parrots. What you are looking at is *the statistical equivalent of a perfect hand of cards* ("And it was Good"; Complete; Finished; Perfect. You're right Richard), except that we *know* how it came about: by the gradualistic crane of natural selection." [481]

It's amazing to me that Richard can use words like *'we know'*, when in fact he *does not know*. Saying it is so, does not make it so. I don't think Richard is purposely lying (At least I hope not), and so that is why I say he suffers from an atheist's delusion. I don't think Richard realizes it, but he just said God's creations were *perfect* ('A perfect hand of cards'), which was the case when God said, "It is good" (Or perfect, complete, and finished, as they existed in the Garden of Eden, each being immortal, as all His creations were before the Fall of Man happened, which Fall changed everything).

Before the Fall of Man, God's creations were in fact perfect and immortal. But, after the Fall, everything fell to its fallen state – imperfect beings and imperfect creations – and things such as thorns and weeds were introduced into this fallen world, as was death, sin, and earthly evil such as tragedies like tsunamis, floods, and earthquakes, all of which come by way of so-called mother nature. This is just a few of the many kinds of what people call the 'evils' of this world. The fact is, the evidence of the *'perfection'* that all things once had at their beginning, is all around us, and it's nice to read that Richard admits it in his *'perfect hand of cards'* analogy, especially since he, and all his scientist friends for that matter, cannot offer one example of an animal in the *'process'* of iteration; being taken up the Mount Improbable by the *'process crane'* Richard calls natural selection. Not even one.

Although Richard admits that there must have been a first cause of everything, Richard says, "but it must have been simple (For that is where natural selection can only have its start) and therefore, whatever else we call it, God is not an appropriate name (unless we very explicitly divest it of all the baggage that the word *God* carries in the minds of most religious believers). To suggest that the first cause, the great unknown which is responsible for something existing rather than nothing, is a being capable of designing the universe and of *talking to billions of people simultaneously* (You mean like man-managed radio waves does to billions of TV's?), is a total abdication of the responsibility to find an explanation (In other words, Richard is saying that those who have this 'view' ... are being *intellectually lazy*, and so they have to come up with something better than an improbable God)."

Richard continues: "The very least that any honest quest for truth must have in setting out to explain such monstrosities of improbability as a rainforest, a coral reef, or a universe … is a *crane* and not a skyhook. The crane doesn't have to be natural selection. Admittedly, nobody has ever thought of a better one. But there could be others yet to be discovered". [482] A crane? Really? Now who's offering a monstrosity of a guess of improbable complexity? Of Richard's improbability argument, the atheist Dan Dennett describes it as "an unreputable refutation of the idea of God's existence." [483]

"This particular chapter", Richard says, "contains *the central argument* of my book, and at the risk of sounding repetitive, I shall summarize it as a series of six numbered points:

1. One of the greatest challenges to the human intellect, over the centuries, has been *to explain how* the complex, improbable appearance of design in the universe arises.

2. The natural temptation is to attribute the appearance of design to actual design itself. In the case of a man-made artefact such as a watch, the designer really was an intelligent engineer. It is tempting to apply the same *logic* to an eye or a wing, a spider, or a person (And yes, even to a universe?).

3. The temptation is a false one, because the designer hypothesis immediately raises the larger problem of "Who designed the designer?"

Again, this is the so-called infinite regression problem that Richard repeatedly brings up, "It is Richard's chief argument against the existence of God. The whole problem we started out with was obviously no solution to postulate something even more improbable. We need a crane, not a skyhook, for only a crane can do the business of '*working up gradually*' and plausibly from simplicity to otherwise improbable complexity." To believe that it's a gradual slope up Mount Improbable versus 'Speak it, and it is so' like God, our Heavenly Father spoke? Richard would say that that is far to improbable.

4. The most ingenious and powerful crane so far discovered is 'Darwinian evolution by natural selection'. Darwin and his successors have shown (Really? Have shown? Are there actual living iterations? Or just artist renditions and maybe a small number of tiny, broken pieces of old, worn-out bone? C'mon man!) how living creatures, with their spectacular statistical improbability and appearance of design, have evolved by slow, gradual degrees from simple beginnings (Using the crane to climb up 'Mount Improbable's' slope). We can now safely say that – an illusion of design in living creatures is just that – an illusion."

I think not Richard. The evidence does not affirm this proposition, but you continually state it is as though it's been successfully shown to be true, when in fact the evidence does not confirm this to be so. Saying it over and over again, doesn't make it true. The so-called evidence put forth for the theory of the evolution of man coming from a lower species like apes, is the illusion. Again, this is just Richard giving his opinion, though he won't admit to it. Here's what he listed:

5. We don't yet have an equivalent crane for physics. Some kind of multi-verse theory could in principle do for physics the same *explanatory work* as Darwinism does for biology. This kind of explanation is superficially less satisfying than the biological version of Darwinism because it makes heavier demands on *luck* (Correct! Evolution puts the entire weight of all creation on the back of *luck*). But the anthropic principle entitles us to postulate far more luck than our limited human intuition is comfortable with (Could we not use this same logic to explain God's improbability Richard?).

6. We should not give up hope of a better crane arising in physics, something as powerful as Darwinism is for biology. But even in the absence of a strongly satisfying crane to match the biological one (Evolution and natural Selection), the relatively weak cranes we have at present (Meaning his anthropic principle of multi-verses) are, when abetted by the anthropic principle, self-evidently better than the self-defeating skyhook hypothesis of an Intelligent Designer." [484]

After reviewing these six points, Richard goes on to say that the God Hypothesis and religion itself are *self-defeating* because of his infinite regression question of "Who created God?"

Richard says: "If the argument of this chapter is accepted, the factual premise of religion – The God Hypothesis – is untenable." [485] Richard then concludes this chapter by stating:

"God, most certainly, does not exist (Most certainly? Really? There you go again Richard, making a statement as though it is settled science, which it is not. "Most certainly does not" is a bit arrogant, don't you think? Especially when Richard has already admitted he cannot disprove God's existence?). Richard goes on to say, "This is the main conclusion of the book (His book *The God Delusion*)." [486]

If I've understood Richard's argument regarding *cranes*, I believe the reverse of Richard's argument of cranes would be: "<u>If</u> the argument of this chapter is NOT accepted – meaning the premise of Atheisms' claim that Darwinism is true – it is in fact, tenable". Right? You cannot have it both ways Richard. Richard keeps forgetting that his logic can be turned around and used against his own dogmatic claims, which he repeatedly has expressed as though they are settled science, when in fact they're not.

Like Richard's opinion he just expressed, my opinion of this chapter and its six points, is that it most certainly makes more logical sense to NOT accept the arguments laid out in this chapter. I'm particularly referring to Richard's argument that "*we're just waiting for scientists to come up with a crane for physics and the cosmos*", which has not happened in more than six thousand years (From the time of Adam and Eve 'til now), and the probability that it will come about in this way is extremely improbable. The *Darwinian Crane*, as Richard calls it, is, at best, a big guess stuffed by a series of misleading, and at times outright deceptions by scientists, in-order-to keep the big lie going. I would suggest, once again, that it is important for you, my readers, to watch the YouTube video titled "Genesis Impact (Full Move), [487] to see why I feel I can say that "It is the *Big Lie*".

Each of the six points become weaker and weaker as one moves from the first point on to the next point, and ending on the last point where Richard says:

"We should not give up hope of a better crane arising in physics, something as powerful as *Darwinism* is for biology. But even in the absence of a strongly satisfying crane to match the biological one, the relatively weak cranes we have at present are, when abetted by the *anthropic principle*, self-evidently better than the self-defeating skyhook hypothesis of an Intelligent Designer." [488]

With physics standing without a so-called crane, Richard offers the weak crane abetted by the anthropic principle, which is simply a theory of the multi-verse, which postulate is just a big, fat guess that scientists have named *The Multi-verse*.

Richard closes this subtitle and chapter by saying that "With the God Hypothesis being proven untenably (Incapable of being defended? Really Richard? C'mon Man! Good honk in the morning! You've got to be kidding me! Untenable?), we're ready to move on and answer the questions that religion itself poses."

Richard continues by asking, "Even if we accept that God doesn't exist, doesn't religion still have a lot going for it?" [489]

Having said this, Richard dedicates the next six (6) chapters to giving arguments on each of the subtitles found in "The Roots of Religion", beginning with the first subtitle "The Darwinian Imperative". In these subtitles Richard tries to destroy anything religion has going for it; meaning, anything that would or could possibly be used to prove God's existence.

CHAPTER 5

THE ROOTS OF RELIGION

Richard jumps right into the first subtitle with no introductory commentary on the chapters' title, and so I will jump right into it with him.

THE DARWINIAN IMPERATIVE

Wikipedia defines religion as *a social-cultural system of designated behaviors and practices, morals, beliefs, worldviews, texts, sanctified places, prophecies, ethics, or organizations, that generally relates humanity to supernatural, transcendental, and spiritual elements.* However, there is no scholarly consensus over what precisely constitutes a religion."

Richard says, "Everybody has their own pet theory of where religion comes from and why all human cultures have it." [490]

Richard too, has his own opinion where it comes from. He says, *"Knowing* (Once again Richard uses the term *knowing,* which more accurately should be *Believing, because saying knowing over and over again does not make it so*) that we are products of Darwinian evolution, we should ask *what pressure or pressures exerted by natural selection* originally favored the impulse to religion?" Richard is always looking through a pair of atheistic bifocal glasses. The first lens, as a scientist, and the second lens, or I should say simultaneously with the second lens, his evolution bias. Richard continues by saying: "Darwinian considerations of economy say, religion is so wasteful, so extravagant, and Darwinian selection habitually targets and eliminates waste."

"Nature is a miserly accountant, grudging the pennies, watching the clock, punishing the smallest extravagance. Unrelentingly and unceasingly, as Darwin explained, natural selection is daily and hourly scrutinizing, throughout the world, every variation, even the slightest; rejecting that which is bad, preserving and adding up all that is good."

(So, is Richard saying that natural selection has a moral compass; an *objective* standard that it follows? Really? Is he saying that 'it', a concept or principle, has a mind to determine from simply seeing these small extravagances, *it* makes decisions to keep or to discard certain traits that are *bad*?' I'll answer what I think Richard is really saying here a little later, and so, let's continue with his words):

"Silently and insensibly working, whenever and wherever opportunities offer, at the improvement of each organic being. If a wild animal habitually performs some useless activity, natural selection will favor rival individuals who devotes the time and energy, instead, to surviving and reproducing. Nature cannot afford frivolous jeux d' esprit (a lighthearted display of wit and cleverness). Ruthless utilitarianism trumps, even if it doesn't always seem that way." [491]

Next, Richard explains his theory of why religion is still practiced today. It's wild. Listen to this:

"To the evolutionist, religious rituals stand out like peacocks in a sunlit glade (Dan Dennett's phrase). Religious behaviors are the writ-large human equivalent of anting or bower-building. It is time-consuming, energy-consuming, often as extravagantly ornate as the plumage of a bird of paradise. Religion can endanger the life of the pious individual, as well as the lives of others."

I would suggest that this be changed just a little bit to say, "Man's interpretation and therefore man's actions regarding Religion, can endanger the life of the pious individual, as well as the lives of others." Richard continues:

"Thousands of people have been tortured for what is in many cases a scarcely distinguishable alternative faith. Religion devours resources, sometimes on a massive scale." Again, men and women choosing to act out what they believe their apostate religion is telling them. A medieval cathedral could consume a hundred man-centuries in its construction, yet was never used as a dwelling, or for any recognizably useful purpose. Was it some kind of architectural peacock's tail? If so, at whom was the advertisement aimed?

"Sacred music and devotional paintings largely monopolized medieval and Renaissance talent. Devout people have died for their gods and killed for them; whipped blood from their backs, sworn themselves to a lifetime of celibacy or to lonely silence, all in the service of religion. What is it all for?

"What is the benefit of religion? By benefit, the Darwinian normally means some enhancement to the survival of the individual's genes. What is missing from this is the important point that *Darwinian benefit* is *not* restricted to the genes of the individual organism.

"The fact that religion is ubiquitous *probably* means that it has worked to the benefit of *something*, but it may not be us or our genes. It may be to the benefit of only the religious ideas themselves, to the extent that they behave in a somewhat gene-like way, as replicators."

(Richard is obviously trying to manufacture a Darwinian natural selection answer to this question of how religion came about, and of what purpose are its cathedrals. Richard continues):

"Though the details differ across the world, no known culture lacks some version of the time-consuming, wealth-consuming, hostility-provoking rituals, the anti-factual, counter-productive fantasies of religion. Some educated individuals may have abandoned religion, but all were brought up in a religious culture from which they usually had to make a conscious decision to depart. ... *Universal features of a species demand a Darwinian explanation.*" [492]

Let me make one thing perfectly clear in regard to Richard's critique of religion and of its many cultures or societies that exist around the world today. My perspective as a Latter-Day Saint, is that religion is ubiquitous because God, our Heavenly Father, has taught his Plan of Happiness, His Redemptive Gospel, to the world repeatedly. First it was to His Son, who taught it to His angels, who, under the command of the Lord, taught it to His prophets here on earth, beginning with Adam and Eve, with the charge to take it to every nation, kindred, tongue, and people. Sounds pretty ubiquitous to me, doesn't it? It's pretty simple really. There's no need to conjure up some cockamamie evolution idea, but I'm okay with Richard taking that journey into the land of improbable guessing and delusion.

Before the time of the Great Flood when Noah's sons and their wives prepared to enter the ark, God's children had been taught the Plan of Redemption and Happiness from Adam, on throughout man's history up to the time Noah and his family entered the ark. The peoples of the world that sprang forth from these four couples (these eight people) had been taught the gospel before entering the ark so that their children would learn it firsthand. But over time, the generations that came from these four couples, apostatized from their ancestors' teachings, and that resulted in a multiplicity of false, apostate religions that sprang up and continued to exist up and until the time when Jesus Himself appeared on the scene to restore His gospel and set up His Church in its purity, and to complete His act of atonement.

The people of the world make their gods from their own imaginations, which is the substance of any idol – imaginations. It comes from apostate views of worship mixed with scripture, including what people want God to be. As a result, such apostasy brought forth idol gods made of stone, wood, animals, and even mythical godlike men and women such as Zeus and Dione, the goddess of love.

Due to the lack of understanding of the truth that God's prophets had taught their forebears, Noah's descendants fell into apostasy just like I mentioned when I discussed the *four consciousness-raisers* that Richard put forth. One need only do a Google search to learn about all the heathen religions that Moses and the House of Israel encountered while in Egypt, and upon entering the promised land of Canaan. The Old Testaments' history is a history of repeated apostasy by the House of Israel and its tribes, all the way down to the time of John the Baptist and his cousin Jesus, each focusing on teaching the House of Judah (The Jews of that Day) the pure gospel of God.

Over the centuries there has always been designing men in every age who are spurred on by Satan's spirit, the *spirit of anti-Christ*, to use their influence to take God's pure gospel and remold it and twist it to fit their own liking, often making it a means for controlling the people, and for usurping religion's power over them (It's called priestcraft). One only need look at the religionists of Jesus' Day to see the power that priestcraft gave to the religious leaders of that Day, and the power they had over the Jews.

These apostate priests of the Pharisees twisted the gospel and used their power-grabbing priestcraft to insight their followers into seeking the death of Jesus. Following the death of all the apostles, millions of people were murdered during the centuries that followed, all in the name God. The false gods that they worshipped were inspired by Satan. The so-called religion Richard speaks unfavorably of, is not God's pure gospel, nor is it his pure religion. They all are counterfeit religions that have brought forth all the evil and godless behavior that Richard speaks so vehemently about. It is the natural man's sinful nature that leads mortals to listen to Satan's voice and start these misguided belief systems, each born out of the spirit of unrighteous dominion. Most of these religious priests, or so-called spiritual leaders, exercise this unrighteous dominion by distorting the pure religion God Himself reveals to His prophets.

These designing men, with their apostate beliefs, use false interpretations of the scripture to deceive their unsuspecting followers into doing unspeakable evil acts in the name of their false gods. Saying they're doing it all in the name of their god is probably true however, because whether they know it or not, their god is Satan. He is behind all apostasy, for he is the father of lies and wants to be God. Under the influence of his *spirit of apostasy,* easily influenced men take the gospel hostage, making *it in the image of* their *religious designs and imaginations.* These apostate religious leaders, under the influence of the spirit of Satan, are the ones responsible for all these so-called religions that have produced all the evil, death, and corruption that Richard so vehemently criticizes as being the fault of religion itself. These religious leaders were and are not ordained by the authority and will of the True and Living God, or His prophets, nor do they teach the pure gospel that Christ Himself revealed to His living prophets.

As a side note, I know there are in fact examples in the Bible where God commanded his prophets to go in and *'cleanse'* a land being occupied by base and unbelievably wicked people. That's true. His command was to move in and inhabit the land that had been promised to their ancestors years before for an inheritance. I also understand why it's difficult to hear that *this kind of killing* is justified, especially when it's done by the command of the Israelites Lord God Almighty, even the Great I AM, Jehovah. But all is not as it seems. Due to the incompleteness of the information Richard has chosen to base his disdain for religion upon, his conclusions that he has shared with his readers, are faulty and ill-judged.

We weren't there and the Bible is not meant to be a complete and detailed account of the world's history, especially when there's so many incomplete mistranslations in these texts. Here's an example of men doing evil as though God commanded it – the Christian Crusades. They brought about a series of religious wars that were supported, and sometimes directed by the Latin Church in the medieval period. God did not sanction these wars, I assure you. The best known of these Crusades are those to the Holy Land in the period between 1095 and 1291 AD, which wars were intended to recover Jerusalem and its surrounding area from the heathenistic Islamic rule.

Atheists like Richard, see all such *bloodshed in the name of God,* as evidence that _all_ religions throughout all of mankind's history are false and reason enough to abandon religion altogether. Again, let me make my perspective perfectly clear. Religion is ubiquitous because God has given his Plan of Happiness, His Redemptive Gospel to every nation, kindred, tongue, and people, beginning with Adam and Eve and their posterity, and then it was preached to each of God's living prophets after Adam. Each prophet taught the gospel in its purity and fulness to their generation. Living prophets are still teaching the fulness of the Gospel in its purity to all the peoples of the world, even our generation.

Even though the Israelite leaders and parents of the generations that Joshua lead into the land of Canaan, taught the pure gospel to those members of their families, those members of the House of Israel ended up dwindling in unbelief and that unbelief rapidly turned into full blown apostasy so that their grandchildren *knew not the God of Jehovah.* Like these Israelites of old, the people of the world today are *'children of apostasy'.* The vast majority of the earth's population *'know not the True and Living God',* nor His pure gospel.

Today's living prophet, President Russell M. Nelsen, the president of the Church of Jesus Christ of Latter-Day Saints today, is continuing the clarion call to take the gospel to the four corners of the earth. He's doing so through the assistance of the Twelve Apostles who direct a legion of nearly 55,000 missionaries worldwide, consisting of young men and young women, as well as senior missionaries. It's been said this army of missionaries will grow to more than 100,000 as the Church grows. This doesn't count the seventeen plus million members who've been given the similar charge that says, *'every member be a missionary'* to their neighbors and friends in every corner of the globe. When God's restored gospel is taught in its purity, its fruit is goodness manifesting in the hearts of the people.

But, again, all of us know that God's children, including myself, and all of you, my readers, are imperfect, and so we sometimes stumble. This stumbling by Jesus' disciples often becomes a *stumbling block* for others in exercising their faith in God. However, man's weakness does not change the fact that pure religion comes from God Himself, in its perfection, to His prophets, and we, His children, are commanded to be vigilant in doing all we can to have a watchful eye in order to keep its doctrines pure and protected from Satan's influence, helping to protect them from his and his minions' efforts to distort and destroy the Church. They use such tactics as causing mistranslations, deliberate deceptions, and Satan putting forth his false prophets. As God's children we must do all we can to make sure that we not only teach His Plan of Happiness to those of His children who haven't heard about it, but we also must live His Plan as an example to those who haven't heard about it and do so in spirit and truth.

I'm speaking of the Gospel of Redemption, the gospel of Jesus Christ as He taught it in its purity, and we must do so in accordance with God's will and His will alone, and not ours. The next subtitle is – "Direct Advantage of Religion."

DIRECT ADVANTAGES OF RELIGION

I always get a chuckle out of Richard's sarcasm. Here's another example of it that I felt might be worth mentioning. It was right at the start of the subtitle 'Direct Advantages of Religion' where Richard quotes George Bernard Shaw, who's quite a character himself, like Richard is. Here's Richard quoting Mr. Shaw:

"The fact that a believer is happier than a skeptic is no more to the point than the fact that a drunken man is happier than a sober one." [493]

Richard later quotes an American comedian Cathy Ladman, who observed, "All religions are the same: religion is basically guilt, with different holidays." Ha-ha-ha. That's funny. Richard then says, "Religion is a large phenomenon, and it needs a large theory to explain it." [494]

This sums up Richard's reason for including this chapter where he tries to answer questions about religion. Richard tries to lay out what he hopes is a believable theory, or two, for why religion came into existence, and then gives a precedence as to why he believes Darwinian Natural Selection is the *large answer* that's needed for answering this 'need for religion' question. Richard asks:

"Why does a *mind* evolve (A mind Richard? Not a wet brain?) to find comfort in beliefs it can plainly see are false?" [495] 'Plainly see' Richard? A *mind* 'seeing'? Shouldn't it be "... find comfort in beliefs 'it' (The brain) can plainly imagine?" A person with eyes sees, and the mind of a person understands what they see, so that the person can then say, "I *see* that" "I understand that". Maybe it's in this context that Richard is referring when he says, "*it* can plainly see". Only Richard knows what he meant.

Richard's reasoning and *guess* as to why religion came about, truly seems to be a contradiction. Richard says, "What pressure or pressures exerted by natural selection originally favored the *impulse to religion*?" Good question Richard. Why indeed. ... "Religion is so wasteful, so extravagant; and Darwinian selection (With its rules) habitually targets and eliminates *waste*." [496]

So why didn't it reject this impulse Richard? In other words, if religion came from the process of an unguided, non-intended pressure that happens within the neurons exploding in the wet brains of some distant couple, all at the same time, who then produced (Or their egg and sperm coming together activated it) the start of a next generation, a supposed better generation of thinkers? Wouldn't this selective process have spit out this *wasteful impulse* to express some kind of faith before it finished its production of that offspring, since it and its so-called natural selecting *mind* (As Richard calls it) would be so destructive to the survival of a healthy, right-thinking person? Why did it not follow the rule? But it didn't, did it? Nope! This kind of reasoning, to me, is simply a *grasping at straws* that scientists like Richard often act out, when trying to produce a plausible theory for any implausible reality they can't explain or can't stand for that matter. In other words, they often back themselves into a corner, just as Richard has done to himself by putting forth this excuse of a theory about religions' beginnings.

Being aware of the criticism that will come to me for suggesting that religion is what I call '*the pure system supporting pure faith in God*', and that it is what follows any dispensing of pure truth by God Himself to His prophets, I ask my readers to hang in there with me as I try to give my perspective to questions about religion that Richard says are needing to be answered. Once I have, you can make your choice as to which perspective or argument makes more sense to you as a reference leg for your stand.

I know Richard would accuse me, once again, of trying to fill a gap in knowledge and calling it God. As long as atheists believe that religion, no matter whether it's pure or not, comes from mans' evolution and not from God's Mind, they will continue to say that this gap or lack of knowledge regarding the 'Big' questions, is just being filled with theists' God-of-the-Gaps ideas. Richard feels that one day this gap will be replaced by a theory postulated by a scientist who discovers the true reason for religion coming into existence. But I say that there is no gap here, and that Richard will be waiting for a very, very long time.

As you will see, Richard simply postulates a variety of *possible* theories about why religion is the way it is and how it came to be. But, in my opinion, Richard provides very little, if any well-in*formed evidence or reference legs* in this subtitle 'Direct Advantage of Religion' that support the claim that God does not exist. It's just Richard expressing his opinions in an annoyingly pompous and dogmatic way.

This chapter, as I read it, seemed to be a continual grasping at straws by Richard. I saw it as an atheist's delusion because Richard is incapable of imagining in his scientific mind that there might actually be something, some kind of elegant, eternal, magnificent being who is so incredibly brilliant and powerful that He could very well have created all that we see and don't see in this world, and in heaven (Including the unseen spirit world and its dimension) and including *pure* religion itself. That my friends, for those who have eyes to *see and ears to hear*, as I said before, is "The Theory of Everything".

What Richard postulated, for me, is as though he's taking the *skin of his theory* and stuffing it full of what I call *"delusional guessing"*, and this delusional guessing always seems to be constructed with or manufactured by the unseen crane of Darwinian natural selection, his go-to-answer for everything. Richard's next subtitle is another example of delusional guessing. It's called – "Group Selection."

GROUP SELECTION

Group Selection Theory is the idea that Darwinian selection *chooses* among species or other groups of individuals. Here's an example that Richard gives to describe what this kind of group selecting or group choosing is, as a theory that forms a particular religion. Here's Richard describing how it *might* look like:

"A tribe with a stirringly belligerent 'god of battles' wins wars against rival tribes whose gods urge peace and harmony, or tribes with no gods at all. Warriors who unshakably believe that a martyr's death will send them straight to paradise, fight bravely, and willingly give up their lives.

"'So, tribes with this kind of religion are more likely to survive in inter-tribal warfare, steal the conquered tribe's livestock and seize their women as concubines, etc. Such successful tribes prolifically spawn daughter tribes that go off and propagate more daughter tribes, all worshipping the same tribal god. The idea of a group spawning daughter groups, like a beehive throwing off swarms, is not implausible, by the way." [497]

Who says it's not implausible? Richard then states that he is not a supporter of group selection, because he feels it doesn't amount to a significant force in evolution. Again, it is always about evolutions' natural selection for Richard, just as it is always about God's intelligence for me. I have to ask this question, "Why is Richard even bringing in the theory of group selection then? I think it's to confuse or try and sound more credible to his peers, because other intellectuals agree that religion is manmade, and therefore they feel it necessary to produce what he calls 'plausible theories' as to why men have come up with different types of religion. Who knows. It just seems odd to me to even bring it up, because it doesn't move the belief cursor on the *percentage of probability spectrum* one fraction closer towards the 'God Does Not Exist' marker. It just seems to be a smoke screen put up by Richard, so he can avoid having to admit that natural selection can't possibly be the answer to *everything*.

In my way of thinking, there's certainly room for postulating a theory that a super-intelligent Designer is behind pure religion, and that the natural man, has a propensity for messing things up due to their state of carnality, which includes evil designs and a desire for power, etc., and that's so they can control other people in order to achieve their selfish purposes. Here's what I am talking about:

Doctrine & Covenants 121:39

39 We have learned by sad experience that it is the *nature and disposition* of almost all men, as soon as they get a little authority (power), as they suppose, they will immediately begin to exercise *unrighteous dominion*.

I suppose I could go into a long explanation of how religion today, with all its many stripes, originated from just one religion, God's pure religion itself, which religion was first revealed by God to His prophets, starting with Adam. But don't worry, I'm going to give just one example of this. It's the story of Nimrod from the Old Testament, who established his own slant on God's revealed pure religion which God revealed to Nimrod's great grandfather Noah, who in turn taught his children, on down to Nimrod.

Ham was Nimrod's grandfather as I said, and Cush was Nimrod's father. So, in just three generations time the pure gospel of God that was revealed to Noah, the patriarch of this family of eight, had degenerated into a state of apostasy, with Nimrod setting up his own false religion, with its own unauthorized power, authority, and organization, with Nimrod placing himself as its head, and not God.

After the Flood, the posterity of Noah began to multiply and establish cities and kingdoms upon the face of the earth. Many of the people turned from the Lord and became wicked and defiant.

In their rebellion they began to build a great tower in Babel. Because of the wickedness of the people, before they completed this tower the Lord confounded their language and scattered them across the globe. Hugh Nibley, author of *"Lehi in the Desert and The World of the Jaredites"*, and *"The Collected Works of Hugh Nibley"* [1980, pg. 156], wrote:

"Early Jewish and Christian traditions reported that Nimrod built the Tower of Babel, referred to as a pagan temple, in an attempt to contact heaven. Among the Jews, Nimrod's name has always been a *"symbol of rebellion against God and of usurped authority"*: he "established *a false priesthood and false kingship* in the earth to imitate God's rule and *'made all men to sin'*.

"The scriptural reference to Nimrod being a "mighty hunter" refers not only to his ability in killing animals, but also to his use of *'violence'* to gain power over and control over other people.

Genesis 10:8-10

8 And Cush begat Nimrod: he began to be a mighty one in the earth.

9 He was a mighty hunter before the LORD (THE JST IS "A MIGHTY MAN IN THE LAND"): wherefore it is said, Even as Nimrod the mighty hunter before the LORD.

10 And the beginning of his kingdom was Babel, and Erect, and Accad, and Calneh, in the land of Shinar.

"Though the words are not definite, it is very likely he was a very *bad man*. His name Nimrod comes from *marad, he rebelled;* and the Targum [ancient Jewish translations or paraphrases of the scriptures on 1 Chronicles 1:10], says: *Nimrod began to be a mighty man in sin, a murderer of innocent men, and a rebel before the Lord.* The meaning of Nimrod is "The Rebel". Thus "Nimrod" may not be the character's name at all. It is more likely a derisive term of a type, a representative of a system that is epitomized in rebellion against the Creator, the one true God. Rebellion began soon after the Flood as civilizations were restored. At that time, this person became very prominent and ultimately established his kingdom called Babylon."

"He was allegedly the first king to wear a crown. 'For this reason, people who knew nothing about it, said that a crown came down to him from heaven'. Later, the book describes how Nimrod established *fire worship and idolatry*, then received instruction in divination for three years from Bouniter, the fourth son of Noah (Bouniter being born after the flood)." [498]

This is just one example of a person of power, referred to in the Old Testament, living after the Global Flood of Noah's Day. Nimrod and his people turned from the pure gospel taught to them by prophets.

Nimrod decided to come up with his own *false god* and established a false religion that better served *his* personal desires. The Old Testament is full of such stories of apostasy and new religions springing up all across the earth. I don't want to take the time it would take to present all of them, but I decided to go ahead and tell you, my readers, about one more *people* who fell into apostasy.

As I mentioned before, the Book of Mormon is a history of such a falling away from God's revealed pure religion. It contains stories of many apostate leaders setting up their own religions and the effect this had on the people over the multiple centuries of apostasy that followed.

Today there are literally thousands of such strands of ancient religions, each having their own religious systems and views on the nature of the God they worship. As I've said before, such is the way of apostasy. My next example is about two groups of people coming from the prophet Lehi's parentage, both of which fell into apostasy. One group was the Lamanites who ultimately destroyed the other group, the Nephites, who started out as a delightsome and righteous people, but they became a tragic story of 'Paradise Lost" – the paradise being the life they had while following the True and Living God.

My comments on people and their apostasy, may not be the kind of sophisticated commentary Richard would put forth, but I think my analogy will be understood by everyone reading my book. The analogy is that of the *chain of whispers* game, or what's often called *Chinese Whispers*. This is a game where you have a number of people making up the chain. The first person is whispered an exact, pure statement by the one directing the game. The first person receiving the original, pure message, is then required to whisper that message to the person to their left, and this transference of the message is repeated until the entire chain has received and passed the message along. The last person to receive the message, then says out-loud what they heard. Almost without exception, the message declared by the last person to receive it, doesn't even come close to what the original message was.

These are people who have no ax to grind or evil designs to change the message. But, now think of the message being a typed message on paper or engraved on stone or papyrus being passed around the chain of people. Imagine that several of the people along the chain changing some of the writings before passing them to the next person. This is how apostasy happens. Now, imagine Nimrod, who decided to change the pure gospel message he was taught by his father. As I have said, this altering of the pure truth is the fruit or behavior of the natural man using their unrighteous dominion.

The next subtitle is another personal guess Richard offers up as another *'possible'* way religion was spawned ubiquitously. Its subtitle is — "Religion as a by-product of something else."

RELIGION AS A BY-PRODUCT OF SOMETHING ELSE

In this subtitle Richard turns to his own view of the Darwinian *'survival value'* of religion. Richard said, "I am one of an increasing number of biologists who see religion as a *by-product* of something else (The by-product of Biology, or the by-product of religion? In what way or ways are these two fields related? I'm sure Richard doesn't claim to be an expert on religion, does he? If so, he certainly doesn't understand it). I believe that we who *speculate* about Darwinian *survival value* need to think *by-product*."

"When we ask about the *survival value* of anything, we may be asking the wrong question. We need to rewrite the question in a more helpful way. Perhaps the *feature* we're interested in ('feature' of religion in this case) doesn't have a direct survival value of its own but is a by-product of something else that does." [499] This is going to get really interesting going forward, so pay close attention to what Richard says next.

Richard gives the analogy about moths flying into a candle flame and asks, "How could natural selection favor such an action by moths? (Good question Richard) My point is that we must rewrite the question before we can even attempt an intelligent answer. It isn't suicide. Apparent suicide emerges as an inadvertent side–effect of a by–product of something else. A by–product of what?" [500]

Richard then takes nearly a full page to describe how moths, who were designed to use the rays of light from the moon and stars to guide them while in flight, could be *mistaking* the light of a flame to be such a guide, and their biological nervous systems' *makeup* (Their makeup being their DNA programming) ends up driving them to fly right into the flame (This, to me, is a good description of how so many people are mistaking the loudest voice in the universe, and not the still small voice, for truth).

Richard continues: "When the question is rephrased, the mystery evaporates. It was never right to call it suicide." He says, "This flying into the flame of candles is *a misfiring by-product* of a normally useful compass within the makeup of the moth." [501] In other words, it was a mistake or accident, right?

Richard then asks his readers to apply this by-product lesson to religious behavior in humans. Richard says, "We observe large numbers of people–in many areas it amounts to 100 percent – who _hold_ beliefs that flatly contradict demonstrable scientific facts as well as rival religions followed by others." [502]

"Baffled, we ('We', being atheists) ask Why? But my point is that we may be asking the wrong question. The religious behavior may be *a misfiring*; an unfortunate by-product of an underlying psychological propensity (In other words a mental illness, malfunction, or delusion? But what is the human equivalent to this unique guidance–system which in other circumstances is, or once was, useful. On this view, the propensity that was 'naturally selected' in our ancestors, was not religion per se; it had some other benefit (What benefit Richard?), and it only incidentally manifests itself as religious behavior. We shall understand *religious behavior* ... only after we have *renamed* it." [503]

Wow! Talk about delusional, mental remapping. C' Mon man. If you're someone who believes this last statement by Richard, then you do not understand what Richard is trying to do here. Richard is saying, "We shall understand religious behavior *only after we have renamed it*?" [504] This is like someone renaming a cow pile of manure by calling it 'a chocolate pie', and then telling them 'Bona petit'. Richard's playing a verbal *word-shell-game* with his readers. He continues this ridiculous *shell-game* by saying:

"_If_ then, religion is a by-product of something else, what is that something else? What is the counterpart to the moth 'habit' of navigating by celestial light compasses? What is the primitively ' *advantageous trait*' (The result of the Darwinian rule) that sometimes *misfires* to generate religion?" Richard says, "I am much more wedded to the general principle that the question should be properly put, and if necessary rewritten, than I am to any particular answer." [505]

The main point of this particular subtitle was to denigrate the very idea of religion coming from God (by saying that religion "flatly contradicts demonstrable scientific facts"), and that believing in the eight (8) examples of miracles performed by Jesus (Healings etc.), is ridiculous. Richard then closes by saying:

"What would an objective anthropologist, coming fresh to this set of beliefs while on fieldwork in Cambridge, make of them?" [506] (Them being raising the dead, giving sight to the blind and resurrection)

Again, I see no argument value in the examples Richard postulated here, nor do they, in my opinion, in any way support the theory of God's non-existence. They just reflect Richard's distain for the idea of God, of His attributes, and for any-and-all religions that may spring forth from this false belief in God. I've replied to it only because I said I would give my perspective on Richard's atheist's delusion as I comment on all of his 'God does not exist' arguments, no matter how ridiculous or shallow some of them might be. Next is the subtitle – 'Psychologically Primed for Religion."

PSYCHOLOGICALLY PRIMED FOR RELIGION

In this subtitle Richard suggests the idea that a *psychological by-product* 'could' grow naturally out of the important and developing field of evolutionary psychology. Here's the heart of Richard's "*by-product, change the question by simply renaming the word*" theory:

"Just as the eye is an *evolved* organ for seeing, and the wing an *evolved* organ for flying, so the brain is a collection of organs (or modules) for dealing with a set of *specialist data-processing needs*." [507]

"Religion can be seen as a by-product of the *misfiring* of several of the modules involved in the brain (So, to me, what Richard is saying here is that religion is the result of a brain-flatulent? A misfiring of the brains' modules? C'mon man). For example, the modules for forming theories of other minds, for forming coalitions, and for discriminating in favor of in-group members and against strangers. Any of these could serve as the human equivalent of the moth's celestial navigation (Misfiring of its guidance system), vulnerable to *misfiring* in the same kind of way as was suggested for childhood gullibility." [508]

As you can see by Richard's comparatives here, "the eye is an evolved organ for seeing, and the wing an evolved organ for flying, so the brain is a collection of (evolved) organs (or modules) for dealing with a set of specialist data-processing needs (Or another way of stating it is, "the wet brains' hardware is all that is needed for thinking, and sometimes tis hardware *misfires, popping out religion*." Ha-ha-ha)." [509]

"This suggests that just as evolution does it in the biological world, it can produce new and improved ways of '*doing it*' in the world of religion. It is not far-fetched to imagine that in *the world of religious thought* or *mind*, evolution could easily produce or evolve this idea of religion being some sort of *survival value or purpose of something else*, and that's why it came into existence (In other words, it has a mind of its own?). And in this round-about way, religion meets the rules of natural selection, and it's why it continues to exist even today (This misfired by-product, in other words, *has survival purpose but it's being manifested somewhere else* (That, my friends, is truly an atheist's delusion, a grasping at straws, a 'changing the goal posts' move. The goal post being evolutions' rules for survival. I'll share why I say this, when I give my perspective on each argument Richard offers up on this topic)."

To me, this is a lot like the reasons professional basketball players choose to compete in a dunking contest, which is, of course, to entertain the public and elevate the players' market value. But I also believe these players participate in these kinds of contests because they want to impress their peers. And that is what I think Richard is trying to do with his book and its unusual arguments, and in particular this argument against religion. He's trying to entertain for sure, but he is also trying to elevate his own professionally perceived value in the minds of his peers – his atheist scientist peers.

Richard goes on to say, "Other by-product explanations of religion, besides the intention stance or the dualistic stance, have been proposed by Hinde, Shermer, Boyer, Altran, Bloom, Dennett, Kelemen, and others." [510]

Like I said, I think Richard has chosen to posit such grasping-at-straws kinds of theories in an effort to impress his atheist peers, and hopefully in the process, self-aggrandize himself. But, for me it does nothing to prop up or move the belief cursor in any way towards God's non-existence. You, my readers, will come to see that all the intellectualizing found in the remaining five chapters of Richard's book, doesn't add one scintilla of well-informed evidence to the argument of whether or not God exists.

After reading *The God Delusion* in its entirety, I came away with the feeling as though his arguments ran through my fingers like grains of sand, until I had nothing in my hand to substantiate God's non-existence. All that was left were my own Table of Belief's support stand of reference legs, each of which firmly supporting the belief that "God Exists"! Jesus, the very Son of God, came to restore His pure gospel on earth in the meridian of time because it had been corrupted. It was a time when the religionists of that Day (The Pharisees and Sanhedrin) were in full-blown apostasy. After Christ's and His apostles were all dead, many apostate doctrines began to sprang forth and flourish until Joseph Smiths' Day in 1820.

In a real sense, Richard actually confirms this about religion when he says, "Religions, like languages, evolve with sufficient randomness; from beginnings that are sufficiently arbitrary to generate the bewildering – and sometimes dangerous – richness of diversity that we observe today." [511]

That's exactly what I have been saying about apostasy and how it corrupts pure religion. It is replaced with man's so-called misfired belief systems. Richards' evolutionist mind has been conditioned to only see religion as a *feature* produced by the human species mind (Wet brain), and that's why he tries to convince his readers with his *grasping-at-straws theorizing*; his *atheistic guessing of where all these false religions come from*. The next subtitle is – "Tread softly because you tread on my memes."

TREAD SOFTLY BECAUSE YOU TREAD ON MY MEMES

Richard begins this subtitle by repeating his main point, which is, "Darwinian natural selection abhors waste, and so any ubiquitous *feature* of a species – such as religion – must have *conferred some advantage* or it wouldn't have survived (It being a rule of evolution and natural selection)."

Richard then says, "Such *advantages* can even be *replicators* such as viruses and memes – units of 'cultural inheritance' – these are the topic of this section" [512] How about a Divine Inheritance?

"To understand memes", Richard continues, "we have to first look a little more carefully at exactly how natural selection works. In its most general form, natural selection *must choose* between alternative *replicators*. A replicator is a piece of *coded information* that makes exact copies of itself along with inexact copies or mutations." [513] Is this making religious info biological coded info?

Get ready for Richard slight-of-words! Any ubiquitous *feature* of a species Richard? Really? The idea of an idea from a mind, meaning religion, being a coded *feature* of a species, or a *replicator* like a virus is? Really? That's unbelievable. I apologize if I sound like a broken record here, but isn't Richard actually referring to the *coded information found in DNA*? Richard seems to be saying that the *choosing* to keep, or the *choosing* to let go of any *feature* that confers advantages, is actually being done by natural selection (How does this concept have the info to do its thinking and deciding?), and NOT by the DNA coded information in each cell doing the directing within each cell. That seems so arrogant to me. To me, what Richard is saying about natural selection, sounds like *he's hijacking DNA's directive power by simply renaming it 'natural selection', and* then calling it a *'feature manager'*. He's saying that natural selection is keeping or discarding the so-called advantages or disadvantages of certain features etc. (It 'sees' the cells make-up? Really?), and it's NOT the DNA doing the directing. It's kind of like natural selection is doing what salespeople use to call 'riding the DNA bull'; getting the prospect to go where you want them to go.

Richard is saying that it's natural selection that sets in motion the *replication process*, and not DNA's coding itself. Richard is saying that *the power of natural selection* is some kind of *gene managing force* within the cells themselves, versus what science has been saying for years, which is that it's the DNA Code that's the *managing director force* within all cells (Who or what put this natural selection directive power and information in the cells?). DNA's coding is what's doing all the directing of the cells. It tells them to do what they're supposed to do within the bounds (laws) that were set in place (Or written in each cell) from the beginning by their creator – the Creator Designer called God.

I ask you, my readers, "Where does such *information*, coding, and *directions* come from? The species? The feature? The replicator? A watch did not come up with the mechanism for telling time, right? It is the DNA coding in the cell that is the directing force causing the cells to form the proteins, etc. It's the *coding information* that directs these features and replicators, and it was the Mind of God that placed the creative force in cells and is behind the incredible book-of-life story that's written within each and every one of our cells. God, and God's Mind alone, is the *coding programmer* so-to-speak, of all life, even *The Theory of Everything*, and not some unguided, mindless feature or replicator in the cell.

The fact is, we all know that strands of DNA are in fact information laden with DNA's alphabet like chemical representation letters A, T, C, and G (A single DNA molecule stores 215 million gigabytes of information), and we all know, or at least we should know, that all information flows from *a mind*. The DNA in the cells is where the *"how to"* information that directs the cell-related system or systems is found. This DNA directing information came from the "Mind of God". Richard, on the other hand, believes there's no such thing as *a mind*. There's just the wet brains' hardware that generates all the neurons bouncing around and firing off within it. Richard's arguments clearly reveal his delusion. He believes that man's wet brain alone (And not our mind), is what's generating all of the *mindless*, unguided, undirected neurons to fire off in such a way that they come up with the needed *information* for natural sections to direct of all our cells to do the work they do, *but only after life begins*.

Richard may be saying that natural selections' directing power lies dormant in the DNA alphabet code letters themselves (In the chemicals A, T, C, and G), and can only be activated when life begins. This incredible alphabet-laced strands of DNA code somehow knows when to activate its power so it can start directing the cells creation of molecules activities, but only when 'life' itself has started to form in the cell cluster. Richard said, "once *life* is there in the cell, *natural selection takes over.*" C'mon man. This is truly an atheist's delusion for sure, for he has absolutely no proof of it being so. Otherwise, show us how to give 'life' to these parent-cells Richard, so that you can say that God and His knowledge is unnecessary. Also, explain to me how the word *selection* is defined, so that an '*agent*' isn't necessary for making the preferred selections? Here is a definition I found on the internet for the word *selection*: "The '*action*' or fact of '*carefully choosing*' someone or something as being the best or most suitable. *This 'requires' evaluation*, a *principle of 'thought'*, and '*an agent*' to *choose* the '*best*' (An Intelligent Mind)." [514]

Now add this power to *carefully choose* or *to select*, in the biological sense of the word. Richard is saying that *natural selection* is a process in which 'biological', 'environmental' and 'genetic' influencers are what's determining which types of organisms thrive better than others and is therefore regarded as the main factor or *feature* in the evolution of religion. Good grief! Words like selecting, choosing, evaluating, determining, influencing, influences, or influencers, all seem to require the power of an agent's mind (To do something with the information) versus a concept itself doing the directing and the choosing, or the selecting. Where did the information contained in the cells come from Richard?

If you are going to produce the information needed to initiate an action or a process to be performed, like DNA forming proteins, coded information is needed, much like programs are needed for a computer to start computing. It is the source of the directions (The DNA's programming) that initiates the action to form the proteins. The *power or energy of life* and the *information* found in each and every cell of the body, are both put there by an *agent*, even the agent called God, who is the source of all life and information (Knowledge). Evolution didn't put it there. Evolution is just a *concept or a process*. Both the power of life and the information to direct it, are in each and every cell from their beginning, their organizing, their activation, and these powers are placed there by God, who is the source of all life.

This is likened to the hardware we call a computer. It requires *a word processor and operating system (Its 'mind')*, as well as the software programs (Intelligence, or DNA information for example) to do all its computing (Living and thinking). It also needs power of electricity pumped into it before it can do any computing (Its power of life). The same is true of our brains. They require a mind, or life and the intelligence or operating software program (It's directions), so-to-speak, so that the body can turn on and operate. The brains' mind is the mind of the spirit personage who resides within each of our bodies, giving it life (Our Spirit is our operating system living in our body). Our spirit (Our inner *self*) gives our brain (The hardware), its power to turn on and operate, function, think, dream, and do all that it does. Like I said earlier, I feel like Richard has tried to hi-jack the process and directing power that DNA performs, by simply *renaming* it natural selection. Does it have its own chemical coding alphabet letters forming the instructions it uses to direct the cells activity? How is it telling our DNA to do what it does?

Richard continues, "The point about this is the Darwinian one. Those varieties of replicators (A replicator being the Coded DNA information) that happen to be good at getting copied (Cells being directed to copy themselves), become more numerous at the expense of alternative replicators that are bad at getting copied. *That,* at its most rudimentary, is natural selection."

Listen to what Richard just said. The power behind the cells' ability to copy itself is natural selection (Natural Selections' process now has power to select and organize and copy? Really Richard? I think a whole lot of scientists would beg to differ). The archetypal replicator is a gene, a stretch of DNA" (There it is! Richard finally admits it. He just said it. *It* is the DNA, or a stretch of DNA) that is duplicated, nearly always with extreme accuracy, 'through' an indefinite number of generations (But by what means Richard?). "The central question, for *meme theory* is whether there are units of *cultural limitation* which behave as true replicators, like genes. And the purpose of this section is to ask whether *meme theory* (units of inheritance) might work for the special case of religion." [515] "It is not obviously silly to speak of a meme pool, in which particular memes might have a *frequency* which can change as a consequence of competitive interactions with alternate memes. The exact physical nature of a gene is now known (It is a sequence of DNA), whereas that of memes is not, and different memeticists confuse one another by switching from one physical medium to another." [516]

Good grief! I don't know about you, but to me the last few statements made by Richard, are saying that a *memes' nature* is not known, which is simply saying that "replicators in the memes that have the so-called *feature of religion* in them, either stay in one physical medium, or they switch to another one, but we don't know why".

Does that sound logical to you, my readers? It sure doesn't to me. It is, in my humble opinion, *science shhh-speak* and its hog wash. Here's even more *science shhh-speak*. Richard goes on to explain *meme pools* and *memeplexes*, in order to introduce his *memetic theory of religion*. Richard says:

"Some religious ideas, like some genes, might survive because of absolute merit. These *memes* would survive in any meme pool, regardless of the other memes that surround them. Some religious *ideas* survive because they are compatible with other memes that are already numerous in the meme pool – as part of a memeplex – which is called *survival value*." [517] C'mon Richard. Where's the scientific method behind all this? What testing have you done with it? Is this intellectual puffery and bloviating? Richard reveals his biased opinion, once again, regarding faith itself, which is that it is simply blind, meaning a belief without evidence (Scientific evidence specifically). He sarcastically says, "Faith (belief without evidence) is a virtue. The more your beliefs defy the evidence, the more virtuous you are." [518]

Of course, this is saying that people of faith are people who live by blind faith, for they have no evidence to back up their claims about the existence of God. This obviously comes down to how one defines evidence of course. At least that's what I believe. Here's what the apostle Paul wrote in the book of Hebrews, wherein he spoke on the principle of faith and evidence and their definition:

Hebrews 11:1
1 Now faith is the *substance* of things hoped for, the *evidence* of things not seen.

A good analogy of this '*kind*' of faith is a sailboat clipping along in a lake with its sails billowing. In this analogy the '*substance of the things hoped for*' is the hope that '*the boats sail will fill with air*', thus allowing the sailboat to move forward. The '*evidence of things not seen*' is the boats' sail actually filling up with the '*unseen power of wind or air*', making the sailboat clip along by its billowing sails' technology. The '*unseen thing*', of course, is '*the wind*'. This unseen '*power of the wind*' is making the sailboat '*move in the water*', which is '*evidence*', causing the water to split against its bow, which is also '*evidence*', but this evidence is the '*effect*' *evidence of things unseen*. In other words, there are *two* types of evidence in this example – the '*seen*' and the '*unseen*'. Both are very real evidence and do in fact exist for those who have eyes to see (Both literally and spiritually).

Like I said, it is obvious that Richard, though intelligent, is not schooled enough in his understanding of religious principles, or what's called the *mysteries of godliness*, and the '*eternal laws*' that they're predicated upon, and therefore he seems to be unable to see the forest for the trees. Faith, hope, charity, and pure religion. These are the '*things of the spirit*', even the '*mysteries of godliness*'. They all seem to be terms of which Richard has very little, if any experience with or understanding of, just like he accuses most theists of having very little understanding of evolutions' favorite tenant – natural selection. Anyway, even though I felt it important to bring your attention to the illustration of the sailboat, it being a good example of how the principle of faith works, I have gotten off script here, and so I won't repeat the entirety of the next paragraph Richard quotes, but I do want to share this part of it where it says: "Given this background, '*memeic natural selection*' of some kind seems to me to offer a *plausible* account of the detailed evolution of particular religions in the early stages of a religion's evolution, before it becomes organized, simple memes surviving by virtue of their universal appeal to human psychology." [519] This is just saying that people get or come up with ideas of their own and then get excited enough to go and recruit others to join them and creating an organized religion. Right?

Next Richard gives a couple examples to suggest the *plausibility* that religion can be and was intelligently designed. The examples Richard gives are Scientology and Mormonism. Let me share what is supposed to be an objective view of his '*memetic theory*'. However, it's a completely biased, derogatory opinion of Mormonism. I should know, don't you think? Here's what Richard said about it:

"Another candidate for a purely '*designed*' religion is Mormonism, Joseph Smith, its enterprisingly mendacious (Meaning 'lying') inventor, who went to the lengths of composing a complete new holy book, the Book of Mormon, inventing from scratch a whole new *bogus* American history, written in *bogus* seventeenth-century English. Mormonism, however, has '*evolved*' since it was *fabricated* in the nineteenth century and has now become one of the respectable mainstream religions of America – indeed." [520]

Another description of Mormonism was given by Jon Krakauer back in 2003. Mr. Krakauer is the author of "Under the Banner of Heaven". Jon said: "Joseph Smith lived out his days 'on stage' so-to-speak, for all to observe. As the Angel Moroni declared to Joseph, "Your name will be had for good and evil among all nations, kindreds, tongues, and people; some criticizing and some venerating. Joseph Smith was God's conduit for bringing back bold doctrines concerning the nature of God, the nature of man, the nature of the human experience, the purpose of life, and even the nature of the universe."

I guess there must be something wrong with me as a Latter-Day Saint because I should be offended by Richard's lambasting of my religious faith and its prophet founder Joseph Smith, but I'm not, and here's why. Richard, once again, reveals his true colors and to me it's laughable. Let me explain myself. In his criticism, Richard shows his *unscientific bias* towards Mormonism. Richard is constantly setting aside the *scientific method*, and simply expresses the alternative – subjective, philosophical, and often biased hatred towards the religious. In other words, Richard didn't do any kind of in-depth research that he should have done before he made such uninformed criticisms as though they were tested fact. Let me say that I don't mind his criticism. I just think Richard should have lived up to what he preaches – research; predictions; experiments; comparisons; all being the scientific method. He did none of these.

Using such words as mendacious, which means lying, or not telling the truth, inventor, bogus, and fabricated, doesn't sound like the fruit of the *scientific method* gained from a series of predictions while doing rigorous testing in order to find out if such-and-such claims are truthful or fabricated, founded, or made-up historically. Richard's criticisms are simply Richard's opinions stuffed with biased mockery.

Richard's views flow from his overall bias against religion as a whole, and so, I grant Richard the license to give his opinion about my faith, but I don't give him license to create his own facts about it. Since I don't want to make my perspective of Richard's book be about me, or about my faith alone, let me reply to Richard's criticism here by referring you, my readers, to a book titled, "A Marvelous Work and a Wonder", written by Elder LeGrand Richards, a past apostle (4-6-1952 – 1-11-1983) and a past member of the Quorum of Twelve Apostles of the Church of Jesus Christ of Latter-Day Saints. [521]

I'm suggesting this book as an alternative to you having to read the six-volume comprehensive history of the Church of Jesus Christ of Latter-Day Saints, which would be one of the better sources for learning the actual history of so-called Mormonism, as opposed to Richard's biased, prejudiced account. In my opinion, I think Elder Richard's work will do a wonderful job of informing you, my readers, about my Church. It's a fair and balanced history of the Restoration of the Gospel of Jesus Christ, and of Joseph Smith Jr. as the prophet, founder and first prophet of the Restored Church in this, the last dispensation of the fulness of times. I say that because it's a quick read versus a voluminous six-volume read.

If after reading "The Marvelous Work and a Wonder", you find yourself agreeing with Mr. Dawkins' assessment of the Church of Jesus Christ of Latter-Day Saints and its beginnings, then that's just fine with me. It just seems fair and balanced if both perspectives are represented here, and not just Richard's highly charged, highly biased, uninformed slam of my faith (By-the-way, Mormonism, as I said, is a slang word for my religious beliefs as practiced by Latter-Day Saints. I prefer you call me a disciple of Jesus Christ or a Latter-Day Saint). That way you can determine for yourself whether-or-not my faith is a deceitful, fabricated, invented, bogus, man-made religion set up by a fraudulent conman, or if it's what I say it is, the restored gospel of Jesus Christ with latter-day prophets and apostles being its foundation. Jesus Himself told Peter He would build His Church upon '*this rock*', the rock being Himself and His revelation to His prophets and apostles, and that His apostles and prophets (Like Peter, James, and John) were necessary "until we're unified in the faith and in the knowledge of the Son of God, that we *henceforth* be no more children, tossed to and fro, and carried about with *every wind of doctrine*":

Ephesians 4:11-15

11 And he gave some apostles; and some prophets; and some evangelists (Joseph Smith taught that an Evangelist is a Patriarch) in D & C 107:39-53); and some pastors and teachers;

12 For the perfecting of the saints, for the work of the ministry, for the edifying of the body of Christ:

13 Till we all come in the unity of the faith, and of the knowledge of the Son of God, unto a perfect man (A complete man), unto the measure of the stature of the fulness of Christ:

14 That we *henceforth* be no more children, tossed to and fro, and carried about *with every wind of doctrine,* by the sleight of men, *and* cunning craftiness, whereby they lie in wait to deceive;

Regarding Richard's *meme theory*, Richard says, "Whatever '*theory of religious evolution*' we adopt, it has to be capable of explaining the astonishing speed with which the process of '*religious evolution*', given the right conditions, can take off." [522]

Didn't Richard just say Mormonism evolved starting with its beginning in 1830? That's just 192 years ago, right? When I consider Richard's answer to religions' origin, I have to ask, "Why has the Church of Jesus Christ of Latter-Day Saints had such a meteoric rise since its beginning in 1830?" I ask this because it most certainly has. In fact, recently CBN.com reported that "Mormonism is the fastest growing faith in American history." The article reported that "If present trends continue there could be 265 million members of the Church of Jesus Christ of Latter-Day Saints worldwide by the year 2080." [523]

That's only a 250-year growth period compared to the thousands of years that the three other Abrahamic faiths have had, and the centuries that modern Christianity has had since it's coming forth during the reformation.

The Church of Jesus Christ of Latter-Day Saints certainly has taken off. This kind of meteoric growth for an evolution, memeic, mutated religion almost defies the theory itself, doesn't it? It's been less than 200 years, and not the millions of years that Richard's memetic theory of religions' "origin by evolution" theory Richard puts forth. I wonder why it has grown so fast in such a short period of time. Could it be because the LDS Church is true and is changing the mind and hearts of men and women worldwide?

For any kind of evolution to work, it takes millions of years, right? At least that's what evolutionists like Richard would have us believe. This restored Church sprang forth almost instantaneously, right after God spoke to His boy prophet, Joseph Smith. God's visitation to His prophet was foretold by ancient prophets, prophets who were allowed to *"peer around the corner"*, so-to-speak, into these latter-days, to see our Day as it was foretold. Anyway, I'll cover this more thoroughly a little later in a future chapter.

The next subtitle, "Cargo Cults", is a case study that Richard presents to illustrate how the process of *religious evolution works.*

CARGO CULTS

This subtitle's chief point is Richard's belief that "Christianity and all the ancient religions that have spread worldwide, *presumably* all began as local cults. Most of them died away, but the ones that have survived are the ones that we encounter today, which Richard says, "has been honed by further evolution (*memetic selection*) into the sophisticated system – or rather diverging sets of descendent systems – that dominate large parts of the world today." [524]

Again, we're back to seeing Richard defining the apostasy that we see throughout the world's history. This is apostasy in action today, or one could say, "Religion is still in the process of evolving" as Richard describes it. Richard goes on to describe the extreme rapidity with which a new religious cult could get started (Supposedly the Church of Jesus Christ of Latter-Day Saints is one such cult). Richard says:

"It (A cult) can spring up almost overnight and then become incorporated into a culture (Like a cancer), where it then play's a dominant role. For example, the *'cargo culture'* of Pacific Melanesia and New Guinea. The entire history of some of these cults, from initiation to expiry, is wrapped up within living memory. Unlike the *cult of Jesus*, the origins of which are not reliably attested, we can see the whole course of events laid out before our eyes" [525] (Is Richard saying that because the story of Jesus is more than 2,000 years old, you can't trust it? Really Richard? C'mon man).

Richard's definition of a cult is influenced by his belief that God does not exist, therefore any and all religions, as well as everything connected with them, are manmade, and as such all religions are simply cults, including what Richard calls *the cult of Jesus and Christianity.* The religion Jesus established during His earthly ministry some two thousand years ago, Richard says is simply a manifestation of manmade ideas, that man being Jesus, and not God.

"The pattern for the Cargo Cult and all other cults" Richard says, "is that in every case the islanders were bowled over by the wonderous possessions (Cargo) of the white immigrants that came to their islands. The islanders noticed that the white people who enjoyed these wonders never made them themselves. When these articles needed repair, they were sent away, and new ones kept arriving as *cargo* in great ships. Evidently then, the cargo must be of *supernatural origin.*" [526] What a reach!

Listen to Richard's creativity when he says, "The independent flowering of so many independent but *similar cults*, suggests some *'unifying features'* of human psychology in general (Duh Richard! I couldn't have said it any better than how you just described it. It is Apostasy! Richard. Apostasy *is* the *'unifying feature'* in mankind's psychology, thank you very much. The world's history is a constant repeating of mankind's dwindling in their faith in God. This dwindling is the *unifying feature of mind* called apostasy. It's the fruit of the *natural mans'* weakness for, and propensity towards *'rebellion against God and His commandments'*, leaving them to take their own path, and becoming a law unto themselves)."

Richard finishes this chapter with a short history of the legend of John Frum, the mythic god of the Islanders cultic religion that sprang from it, and then he says, "It has been honed by further evolution (*memetic selection*) into the sophisticated system that dominates large parts of the world today, and that is all I want to say about *the roots of religion* itself." [527] The next chapter is chapter 6" – "The Good Roots of Morality: Why Are We Good?"

CHAPTER 6

THE GOOD ROOTS OF MORALITY: WHY ARE WE GOOD?

Richard begins this chapter by saying: "Morality is often thought to have had its roots in religion, but I want to question this view. I shall argue that the origin of morality can itself be the subject of a Darwinian question (For Richard, like I have said over-and-over again, the answer to these 'Big questions is always evolution, evolution, and evolution!). Just as we asked, 'What is the Darwinian *survival value* of religion?', so we can ask the same question of morality. Morality, indeed, probably predates religion. Just as with religion we drew back from the question and replaced it, so with morality we shall find that it is best seen as a by-product of something else." [528]

Once again, this certainly sounds like a series of guesses to me. Richard says, "I *question* this view" and "Morality, indeed, *probably* ...". These descripts certainly don't sound like Richard has done his scientific homework in using the scientific methodology he usually touts in support of his theory of multi-verses, *memetic selection*, as two examples, and, like before, this new topic of morality and its beginnings, seems to be no different. It isn't another argument against God's existence. It's just Richard postulating an example of how a characteristic that most people think is an outflow of their belief in God, can be an outflow of religion which he feels consists of multiple manmade cults. Here's what Richard says about morality, and moral considerations:

"Many religious people find it hard to imagine how, without religion, one can be good, or would even want to be good. Moral considerations lie hidden behind religious attitudes to other topics that have no real link with morality." [529]

Here's an example of what Richard just described. He says, "A great deal of the opposition to the teaching of evolution has no connection with evolution itself, or with anything scientific, but is spurred on by moral outrage. This ranges from the naïve "If you teach children that they evolved from monkeys, then they will act like monkeys", to the more sophisticated underlying motivation for the whole *wedge* strategy of *Intelligent Design*, as it is mercilessly laid bare by Baron Forrest and Paul Gross in 'Creationism's Trojan Horse: The Wedge of Intelligent Design'." [530]

Next, Richard relates a few samples of the kind of hate mail he and other opponents receive from theists, and in particular from Christian organizations. I do not agree with most of Richard's or these other groups' theological opinions, but I also don't stand on the side of those folks who say they are followers of Christ, but then describe how they are ready to attack, kill, and go to war against the likes of Richard and his friends. It most definitely is not the behavior of what a true Christian, a follower of Jesus Christ should exemplify. It is most definitely not Christlike.

In my opinion, no true follower or disciple of the Savior Jesus Christ would use the kind of language presented in these letters or make the kind of threats that were made towards their intended recipients. Richard pretty much said the same thing as I just did. He said, "Nor does it (Sending hate letters) display to advantage the charity for which the founder of Christianity was notable." [531]

I stand apart from such vitriol, no matter towards whom it is directed. In other words, this kind of vitriol towards another child of God is certainly not Christlike, nor is it the kind of behavior of someone who truly exemplifies their Saviors' gospel. The bottom line of this chapter, for Richard, is that "It is about evil, and its opposite, good; it's about morality – where it comes from, why we should embrace it, and whether we need religion to do so." [532]

So, let's take a look at this chapters' first subtitle – "Does our moral sense have a Darwinian origin?"

Does our moral sense have a Darwinian origin?

The question Richard puts forth in this chapter's first subtitle is quite interesting. He asks, "What is *moral sense*?"

A definition given online says that moral sense is "A feeling of the rightness or wrongness of an action or the ability to have such feelings". As a member of the Church of Jesus Christ of Latter-Day Saints I would add the following to this secular definition of moral sense: It's "the attitude or mindset that comes from our conscience, our inner spiritual selves, and therefore, it is the fruit of or awareness of what is right and what is wrong, and this awareness, this reminding if-you-will, is from our conscience." Latter-Day Saints call this moral sense "The Light of Christ".

The Light of Christ is the divine energy, power, or spirit matters' light and influence that proceeds forth from the very beings of God and His Son, Jesus Christ (It being love's light and truth existing in all the world), and it is that which gives *life* and *light* to all things and is capable of residing in the heart and mind of every person who comes to reside on this earth, which, of course, includes all atheists hearts. We are all born with *a sense of right and wrong* – a conscience. This Light of Christ influences people for good and prepares them to receive the promptings of the Holy Ghost. The one manifestation of the Light of Christ that most of us are familiar with, as I said, is the fruit of our conscience – the *'sense of guilt'* that comes to our mind and heart when we are considering doing or in fact when we do something wrong, by reminding us who and what we really are – and that is ... a spirit son or spirit daughter of our Heavenly Father. The Light of Christ proceeds forth, as I said, from the presence of God to fill the immensity of space. It is "the light, which is in all things, which giveth life to all things, and is the law by which all things are governed." This power is an influence for good in the life of every person who ever lived or will ever live here on earth, including all unbelievers in God like Richard Dawkins:

John 1:9

9 *That* was the true Light, which lighteth every man that cometh into the world.

Doctrine & Covenants 93:2

2 And that I am the true light that lighteth every man that cometh into the world;

In the scriptures, the Light of Christ is sometimes called "the Spirit of the Lord", "the Spirit of God", "the Spirit of Christ", or "the Light of Life". As Joseph Smith described, *light* is made up of physical, yet unseen, refined, or more pure matter (Different kinds or types, different particles of matter). The Light of Christ should not be confused with the Holy Ghost. It is not a personage, as is the Holy Ghost. The Holy Ghost is a personage of spirit. His influence and power, His light, is manifested to lead people to Christ so they can find the true gospel, be baptized, and then have the Gift of the Holy Ghost conferred upon them when given the charge *to receive* the Holy Ghost as a testator and comforter. The following verses of scripture are the words Jesus spoke to His disciples on this subject, as well as the teachings of the prophet Alma, and then the teachings of the prophet Joseph Smith, and then Paul:

John 12:46

46 I am come a light into the world, that whosoever believeth on me should not abide in darkness.

Alma 26:14–15

14 Yea, we have reason to praise him forever, for he is the Most High God, and has loosed our brethren from the chains of hell.

15 Yea, they were encircled about with everlasting darkness and destruction; but behold, he has brought them into his everlasting light, yea, into everlasting salvation; and they are encircled about with the matchless bounty of his love; yea, and we have been instruments in his hands of doing this great and marvelous work.

Doctrine & Covenants 130:23

23 A man may receive the Holy Ghost, and it may descend upon him and not tarry with him.

Acts 10:1-48 (This story of Cornelius, a Gentile, shows how the Holy Ghost works in our lives to bring us to the truth of the gospel of Jesus Christ)

1 There was a certain man in Cæsarea called Cornelius, a centurion of the band called the Italian *band,*

2 *A* devout *man,* and one that feared God with all his house, which gave much alms to the people (I believe it was 'to the poor'), and prayed to God alway.

3 He saw in a vision evidently about the ninth hour of the day an angel of God coming in to him, and saying unto him, Cornelius.

4 And when he looked on him, *he was afraid*, and said, What is it, Lord? And he said unto him, Thy prayers and thine alms are come up for a memorial before God.

5 And now send men to Joppa, and call for *one* Simon, whose surname is Peter:

6 He lodgeth with one Simon a tanner, whose house is by the seaside: he shall tell thee thou oughtest to do.

7 And when the angel which spake unto Cornelius was departed, he called two of his household servants, and a devout soldier of them that waited on him continually;

8 And when he had declared all *these* things unto them, he sent them to Joppa.

9 On the morrow, as they went on their journey, and drew nigh unto the city, Peter went up upon the housetop to pray about the sixth hour:

10 And he became very hungry, and would have eaten: but while they made ready, he fell into a trance,

11 And saw heaven opened, and a certain vessel descending unto him, as it had been a great sheet knit at the four corners, and let down to the earth:

12 Wherein were all manner of four-footed beasts of the earth, and wild beasts, and creeping things, and fowls of the air.

13 And there came a voice to him, Rise, Peter; kill, and eat.

14 But Peter said, Not so, Lord; for I have never eaten anything that is common or unclean.

15 And the voice *spake* unto him again the second time, What God hath cleansed, *that* call not thou common.

16 This was done thrice: and the vessel was received up again into heaven.

17 Now while Peter doubted (Pondered with concern) in himself what this vision which he had seen should mean, behold, the men which were sent from Cornelius had made inquiry for Simon's house, and stood before the gate,

18 And called and asked whether Simon, which was surnamed Peter, were lodged there.

19 While Peter thought on the vision, the Spirit said unto him, Behold, three men seek thee.

20 Arise therefore, and get thee down, and go with them, doubting nothing: for I have sent them.

21 Then Peter went down to the men which were sent unto him from Cornelius; and said, Behold, I am he whom ye seek: what *is* the cause wherefore ye are come?

22 And they said, Cornelius the centurion, a just man, and one that feareth God, and of good report among all the nation of the Jews, was warned from God by an holy angel to send for thee into his house, and to hear words of thee.

23 Then called he them in and lodged *them*. And on the morrow Peter went away with them, and certain brethren from Joppa accompanied him.

24 And the morrow after they entered into Cæsarea. And Cornelius waited for them and had called together his kinsmen and near friends.

25 And as Peter was coming in, Cornelius met him, and fell down at his feet, and worshipped *him*.

26 But Peter took him up, saying, Stand up; I myself also am a man.

27 And as he talked with him, he went in, and found many that were come together.

28 And he said unto them, Ye know how that it is an unlawful thing for a man that is a Jew to keep company, or come unto one of another nation; but God hath shewed me that I should not call any man common or unclean.

29 Therefore came I *unto you* without gainsaying as soon as I was sent for: I ask therefore for what intent ye have sent for me?

30 And Cornelius said, Four days ago I was fasting until this hour; and at the ninth hour I prayed in my house, and, behold, a man stood before me *in bright clothing*,

31 And said, Cornelius, thy prayer is heard, and thine alms are had in remembrance in the sight of God.

32 Send therefore to Joppa, and call hither Simon, whose surname is Peter; he is lodged in the house of *one* Simon a tanner by the seaside: who, when he cometh, shall speak unto thee.

33 Immediately therefore I sent to thee; and thou hast well done that thou art come. Now therefore are we all here present before God, to hear all things that are commanded thee of God.

34 Then Peter opened *his* mouth, and said, Of a truth I perceive that God is no respecter of persons.

35 But in every nation he that feareth him, and worketh righteousness, is accepted with him.

36 The word which *God* sent unto the children of Israel, preaching peace by Jesus Christ: (He is Lord of all:)

37 That word, *I say,* ye know, which was published throughout all Judæa, and began from Galilee, after the baptism which John preached;

38 How God anointed Jesus of Nazareth with the Holy Ghost and with power: who went about doing good, and healing all that were oppressed of the devil; for God was with him.

39 And we are witnesses of all things which he did both in the land of the Jews, and in Jerusalem; whom they slew and hanged on a tree:

40 Him God raised up the third day, and shewed him openly;

41 Not to all the people, but unto witnesses chosen before of God, *even* to us, who did eat and drink with him after he rose from the dead.

42 And he commanded us to preach unto the people, and to testify that it is he which was ordained of God *to be* the Judge of quick and dead.

43 To him give all the prophets witness, that through his name whosoever believeth in him shall receive remission of sins.

44 While Peter yet spake these words, *the Holy Ghost fell on all them which heard the word.*

45 And they of the circumcision which believed were astonished, as many as came with Peter, because that on the Gentiles also was poured out the gift of the Holy Ghost.

46 For they heard them speak with tongues (In other words, spoke in their language), and magnify God. Then answered Peter,

47 Can any man forbid water, that these should not be baptized, which have received the Holy Ghost as well as we?

48 And he commanded them to be baptized in the name of the Lord. Then prayed they him to tarry certain days.

The Holy Ghost manifested His spirit within Cornelius's heart, confirming that what *the angel had told him was true.* This is the purpose of the Holy Ghost – to bring him and all of us to Christ – so that we have the kind of faith that leads us to repentant so we can then be baptized and *receive* the Gift of the Holy Ghost, which is different than just experiencing a manifestation of the Holy Ghost while we're searching for truth. Conscience, it being different than the Holy Ghost or a manifestation of the Holy Ghost, is the *fruit* of the Light of Christ, as I said, and it is what enables each of us to judge the good from the evil, and to feel the *moral sense* that invites us to do good. The prophet Mormon taught:

Moroni 7:16, 18

16 For behold, the Spirit of Christ is given to every man, that he may know good from evil; wherefore, I show unto you the way to judge; for everything which inviteth to do good, and to persuade to believe in Christ, is sent forth by the power and gift of Christ; wherefore ye may know with a *perfect knowledge* it is of God.

18 And now, my brethren, seeing that ye know the light by which ye may judge, which light is the light of Christ, see that ye do not judge wrongfully; for with that same judgment which ye judge ye shall also be judged.

Romans 2:15

15 Which shew *the 'work' of the law written in their hearts, their conscience also bearing witness,* and *their thoughts* the mean while accusing or else excusing one another;

Wikipedia says, "Moral Sense Theory" is a theory in moral epistemology and meta-ethics concerning the *discovery* of moral truths. Moral sense theory typically holds that distinctions between morality and immorality are *discovered* by emotional responses to experience."

These so-called distinctions are certainly an intellectual's scientific and secular attempt to try and define where morality comes from, in an effort to make sure that God is *not* considered to be its source. The fact is however, that naturalists and secularists (And atheists like Richard) haven't a clue of where our *moral sense* comes from, nor will they if they only look to a wet brain to try and figure it out. Their definition is that it comes from "Moral Discovery while experiencing emotions."

That may describe the experience, but it doesn't tell you what it is or where it actually comes from, and why and how we respond to it. For me, I'm going with the definition given by prophets of God, which certainly have a scientific basis when you consider that *light* has physical components that emanate from the very Being who has many titles, two of those titles being *'the light of lights'* and *'the light of the world'*, even Jesus Christ's 'Being' emitting His glorious light to the world.

I certainly understand how and why someone would have difficulty comprehending all of these principles regarding light and believing that this kind of power and influence actually exists in the universe, let alone emanating from a living Being with a human form of immortal flesh and bone, but lack of understanding or disbelief does not make such a Being non-existent or untrue.

Richard continues on, saying, "On the face of it, the Darwinian idea that evolution is driven by *natural selection* seems ill-suited to explain such goodness as we possess, or our *feelings of morality, decency, empathy, and pity*. Natural selection can easily explain hunger, fear, and sexual lust (Try sexual love), all of which straightforwardly *contribute to our survival for the preservation of our genes* (The core principle or tenet of Richard's quasi-religion once again is natural selection)."

Richard continues: "But what about the wrenching compassion we feel when we see an orphaned child weeping, an old widow in despair from loneliness, or an animal whimpering in pain? (Like the images and stories we're seeing on our T.V. screens about the war in Ukraine, as of today's writing in 2022-2023). *What* gives us the powerful urge to send an anonymous gift of money or clothes to the Ukrainians or the tsunami victims on the other side of the world whom we shall never meet, and who are highly unlikely to return the favor?" [533]

To Richard I say, "What indeed?" It is a question everyone should ask themselves with real intent and deep searching, because such 'urges' and *'feelings'* are ubiquitous in every human being (Unless, through whatever reason, a person has come to lose or reject this 'light of feelings' by rebelling against this spirit and light of Christ within themselves, so that they no longer feel such urges and feelings, the result being 'becoming amoral' in our beliefs and actions). Here's what the scriptures say about this spirit or moral sense within each of us if we reject or deny it long enough:

Genesis 6:3

3 For the Spirit of the Lord will *not* always *strive* with man.

These amoral individuals who have lost the Light of Christ within them, having no conscience anymore (Or a seriously diminished one), are an anomaly and not the norm, but the numbers of people becoming amoral is growing fast. Amorality is an absence of, indifference towards, disregard for, or incapacity to *be moral*, just like most serial killers, for example, are amoral. Some people simply refer to it as a case of not being moral or immoral. Amoral should not be confused with immoral, which refers to an agent doing or thinking something they know or believe to be wrong. Richard goes on to give his concept of what he calls the *'selfish gene'* in contrast with the *'selfish organism'*, or the *'selfish species'*.

He says: "The logic of Darwinism concludes that the *unit* in the hierarchy of life which survives and passes through the filter of natural selection will tend to be *selfish*. The *units* that survive natural selection will tend to be selfish. The *units* that survive in the world will be the ones that succeed in surviving at the expense of their rivals, at their own level in the hierarchy. That, precisely, is what *'selfish'* means in this context. The question is, what is the level of the action? The whole idea of the selfish gene, with the stress properly applied to the last word, is that the unit of natural selection (i.e., the unit of self-interest) is not the selfish organism, nor the selfish group or selfish species or selfish ecosystem, but the *'selfish gene'*. It is the *gene* that, in the form of *'information'*, either survives for many generations or it doesn't." [534]

Next, Richard relates several examples of his Darwinian evolution of the altruism idea, by explaining why they are possible reasons for individuals being altruistic. Altruism is when we act to promote someone else's welfare, even at a risk or cost to our own comfort. Evolutionary scientists like Richard, speculate that *altruism* has deep roots in human nature, and that's because the acts of helping and cooperation promote the survival of our species. In contrast, I believe that the feeling to be helpful and cooperative with others, comes from the Light of Christ residing within each of us, it being the source of all morality. It's what influences us to be good, to be kind, to be compassionate. It's the very source of the *'objective standard'* of morality. Atheists like Richard, on the other hand, believe altruism comes from "millions of years of Darwinian natural selection working in our genes so that we become *'helpful and cooperative'*, even though it's just moral misfiring's *promoting the survival of our species"*. That, my friends, is the spirit of anti-Christ at work on each of us. Its source is Satan and his angels wielding their influence upon each of us until we succumb, and the spirit or Light of Christ quits striving us.

Later on in this subtitle, Richard says, "It is important not to misstate the reach of natural selection. Selection does not favor the evolution of a *'cognitive awareness'* of what is good for your genes. Could it be that our *'Good Samaritan urges'* are misfiring's, analogous to the *misfiring* of a reed warbler's *parental instincts* when it works itself to the bones for a young cuckoo? An even closer analogy is the human 'urge' to adopt a child (A misfiring?). I must rush to add that *misfiring* is intended only in a strictly Darwinian sense. It carries no suggestion of the pejorative. The *mistake*, or *by-product idea*, (The misfiring consequence from an ancestral village life), which I am espousing, works like this: Natural selection (A name Richard is giving the programmer in the genes), in ancestral times when we lived in small and stable bands like baboons, *programmed* into our brain's *altruistic urges*, alongside sexual urges, hunger urges, xenophobic urges, and so on." [535] Natural selection is quite a busy bee pollinating or programming all these so-called urges in each of us, isn't it?

'A *process* programmed by a concept-programmer?' Really Richard? C'mon man. I have to stop here. I think I have been more than fair in repeating what Richard's stance is on morality and its origin. Nowhere does he give tested, proven data that supports his *altruistic theory* that says our *moral urges* come from a brain-flatulent misfiring or are simply *by-product* ideas. It's all hyperbole; his exaggerated postulating of what *might* have taken place in our human development that took hundreds of millions of years to, and I quote, "get it right". Richard's postulation is just an unproven guess with nothing to support it, and again, it doesn't add any evidence whatsoever to support the claim that God does not exist. On the other hand, anyone can *test* the principle of a *conscience* (Con = with, Science = knowledge, or 'With knowledge'), the true source of morality. That test being to simply perform the following steps:

Ray Comfort, a minister from the *Living Waters Ministry*, asks individuals to take this test by going through these questions. He takes people through a series of questions about God's Law (The Ten Commandments), in-order to find out whether-or-not their conscience is still alive and well. Our conscience is what convicts us when we break God's commandments. These questions determine if his interviewees still have their moral conscience, their moral sense, or not (Search YouTube for "Living Waters" and check out his interviews).

The first question Ray usually asks his interviewees is, "Have you ever lied?" and without blinking an eye almost everyone answers, "Oh, hundreds of times." Ray then asks, "What does that make you?" They say, "A liar". Ray then asks, "Have you ever stolen?" They answer, "Of course I have? Everybody does." Richard then asks, "And what does that make you?" And they say, "A thief". Richard corrects them and says, "Nope. You're a lying thief." Richard then asks them, "Have you ever taken the Lord's name in Vain?"; "Have you ever had sex before marriage?"; "Do you have any other God besides the Lord God?" The answers these folks give to Ray's questions are really quite revealing.

Ray reminds those who reply with, "I don't believe in the Ten Commandments or in that kind of God", is to tell them that "That's exactly what God meant when he said, 'Thou shalt have no other God besides Me'". In other words, we're commanded not to create our own God so we can free ourselves from feeling the responsibility of our actions in-order to avoid the consequences that come from breaking His commandments. The result of this *'Questionnaire Test'* is that nearly every single interviewee I have ever watched Ray interview, begin to show signs that they're *feeling* their conscience *convicting* them. They feel it within their heart and mind as it reminds them that they have broken God's law. Even when we begin to break God's commandments (*The Law*), our conscience convicts us on the spot. This convicting feeling is called *'guilt of conscience'* or *'our moral sense'*. Whereas *'shame'*, on the other hand, is a very different feeling than guilt. Shame is Satan's tool that he uses to get people to reject God.

Of course, there are some who try to deny their feelings of *'guilt of conscience'* by saying, "I don't believe in God or in the Bible. I believe God, if He's real, isn't that harsh or judgmental". These folks have reached the point in their lives where the *'spirit or voice of conscience'*, the 'Light of Christ', has ceased to strive within them, so that they no longer *feel* His voice. They now find themselves in open rebellion to God's commandments. They've become *'a law unto themselves'*. Some of these interviewees still have the spirit of truth, the spirit of conscience, the Light of Christs' flame of truth burning within them, much like a pilot light flickers continually. These folks acknowledge their sins and show a desire to know what they can do to resolve their *feelings of guilt,* which were manifested as their conscience convicted them while being asked the questions about the Law of God. For others, the *light* has ceased within them. The purpose of this *feeling of guilt* of course, is to bring us to Christ where we can exercise faith in Him and partake of the gift of repentance and enjoy the fruit from partaking of God's law of repentance. Guilt is meant to lead us to repentance and Shame is meant to destroy us. When we repent, we find forgiveness of our sins. At the heart of this law of repentance is Jesus' love for us. Sincere repentance allows the atonement of Jesus Christ to become activated and have efficacy in our lives.

Most of these interviewees say they don't believe in God, and that's because they love their sins such as: stealing, swearing, viewing pornography, lying to get what they want, having sex before marriage, or during marriage with someone other than their spouse, taking the Lord's name in Vain by saying 'Oh My God' as a cuss word time and time again. They love their sins more than they love God.

The truth is that all of us have sinned and come short of the glory of God, and so I'm not anyone's judge. However, God is. When a person commits a crime, they don't run to the police, do they? Why do you, my readers, suppose that is? The fact is that the offender doesn't want to be caught because *they know they've broken the law*, and they know that when they are caught, they will have to endure the punishment that is attached to that law that they've just broken, but only if they get caught, right? This ' nature within all men' to hide their sins is why the apostle John wrote:

John 3:19-20

19 And this is the condemnation (Convicting), that *light* is come into the world, and men *loved darkness* (Sins) rather than light, because their deeds were evil.

20 For every one that doeth evil hateth the light, *neither cometh to the light, lest his deeds should be reproved* (Made known and result in punishment).

As the apostle John just described, most people who break God's laws don't rush to Him to ask His forgiveness. Most people do everything they can do to keep from being caught or being found out. They want to keep their crimes or sins hidden in order to avoid being punished for having broken the law. They almost always go out of their way to try and hide, and cover up their sins and crimes, right? We see tons of examples of this *'hiding to cover up our sins'* being played out time-and-time again. We see 'extreme lengths being made to hide one's crimes. Consider TV shows like "Forensic Files" where they highlight a series of murderers. This is the nature and disposition of mankind when they have no relationship with God. When we have an awareness of the laws, but then choose to break them, it's man's nature to work hard to try and hide their crimes and lie about it continually.

The results of "this test" are incontrovertible. The *'conscience of man'* is made evident. It's in all of us, but it can cease to strive within us if we choose to rebel against God, and His laws, repeatedly by denying this spirit and light. This is what people do. We try to hide from or run away from these 'feelings of guilt' that convict us when we sin. When our conscience produces this *moral sense in us,* our nature is to try and hide from it in order to avoid being caught and *punished* for our bad behavior.

To me, this is 'well-informed evidence' that proves the existence of God. It's the *fruit* of His law working with in us, helping us to come unto His Son, Jesus Christ. It is this *sense of morality* that's triggered within us when we commit sin. It's this *'reminding power'* within us that tells us we did something wrong or are about to do something wrong. To me, this feeling or sense of guilt, this voice tells us what we are thinking of doing, or what we just did, is good and right or is wrong, is not the important thing here. The important principle behind this *feeling of guilt,* is the fact that it's a reminder to make a change, much like a GPS device tells us to get back on track. God wants us to become our better selves, so He uses His spiritual GPS, our conscience, this Light of Christ, to remind us of the fact that we are a child of God and that we can do better. This reminding voice is a gift from God. If we truly listen to this *sense of guilt* feeling in us, we will see that it's trying to ignite a desire in us to want to repent, and not to feel shame, for shame is from Satan. As I've said, our sense of guilt should lead us to repentance, which is a desire to change from who we've been and are right now, to become the better person we could be and were meant to be; the person who we truly are, ... God's child.

You only need to watch a crime series like "Forensic Files', which is a video series that you can find on YouTube, to see how the criminals go to incredible lengths to hide their crimes. Many of these criminals are actually pretty stupid, but they often think they're smarter than anyone. Now I know that Richard would say that the efforts to hide their crime is *a character feature, a survival meme* that has evolved over millions of years and this *'selective survival feature'* resides in all our genes, and therefore is in all of us and not just in the genes of these criminals. I bet Richard would also say that this drive to hide their crime is simply *the process of natural selection* working to help them survive.

I say that hiding one's crimes or sins, is a trait of fallen man, and not the fruit of evolution's natural selection working in us so that we can survive any law that might be put in place to protect society, and meet out its attended punishment, even a punishment called the death penalty. Which is the true system? I believe Richard's theory is a false system, and God's system of conscience is the true system, a system that helps us come unto repentance so we can one day return to Him. I say that this *drive to survive* or to keep from suffering the pain of exposure and punishment, is as old as dirt.

One only need look back at the story of Cain and Abel that's found in the Bible. Cain desired the flocks of his brother Abel, which was his chief motive for murdering his brother Abel. Cain came up with a plot for how and why he could kill his brother Abel. One of his motives, as I said, was to obtain his brothers' flocks because he believes owning them would make him 'free', meaning, wealthy enough so that he didn't have to labor as a dirt farmer anymore. And so, at the right moment, after days of fueling his hatred for his brother's righteousness, his rage against his brother took over, and he murdered Abel. Afterwards Cain declared, "I'm free"! Cain, like most murderers, denied having anything to do with his brother's death, saying to God, his inquisitor, who asked him "Where is your brother Abel?" Cain replied, "Am I my brother's keeper?" In other words, "I don't know anything about that!"

The fact is, all of us try to *rationalize* away our sins and transgressions, and one way we do it is to make up our own god so that we can feel comfortable in committing sins, instead of giving them up to the True and Living God as our gift of love to Him, who is our Eternal Judge, and be forgiven. People often tell themselves, "God loves everybody", and "He's made me this way", which is just another false god made in the image of their minds' imaginations, whose substance is a false ideology. Some say, "I'm human, so God isn't going to punish me for being human, is He? He made all of us this way. Was He wrong? And did He fail? Did He make a mistake?" Once again, these are the attributes of a manmade god, made in the image of the false idol one desires Him to be, so that they can continue in their sins without feeling any concern of punishment. It's simply an effort to free oneself of any feeling of guilt. This *sense of guilt* within all of us is the Light of Christ shining a light on our sins. This light will stop striving within us if we continue to rebel against God, and deny His existence, while refusing to repent.

Richard, like everyone else, though he doesn't call it God, has made up a substitute god for himself too, and it's called Evolution, with its chief tenet being natural selection. It is what's causing misfires in our genes. This is just one way he describes how his substitute god created morality, the moral sense that all of us have. He says: "Such feelings as sexual lust, and ambition (Like Greed?) etc., constitute a *misfiring*. This is true of the lust to be generous and compassionate. These are the *misfiring consequences* of ancestral village life. The best way for natural selection to build in both kinds of lust in ancestral times, was to install rules-of-thumb in the brain." [536]

This is quite something for a *process* to accomplish, isn't it? It builds; installs; considers multiple kinds of human behaviors and even comes up with its own rules-of-thumb. Really? C'mon man. What's sad is Richard is not kidding. He's just another man creating a god from the substance of his own minds' ideology, a false god that lets him do and think whatever the heck he wants to without any accountability or supposed consequences. Now if that isn't concocting a god in your own image and stuffing it full of the substance of humanistic secularism, mixed with the doctrine of Darwinian natural selection, then I don't know what creating or having your own false god means.

I could go on and on, giving a list of scriptures that lay out, in no uncertain terms, what the natural man (who is an enemy to God and always has been), does, but to save time I'll give just a couple for you, my readers, to consider. The natural man (meaning all of us), due to the Fall, is someone who fights the promptings of the Holy Spirit. The Holy Ghost uses the Light of Christ to help us bridle our passions, appetites, and desires of the flesh. Such a person can comprehend physical things but chooses not to comprehend or acknowledge spiritual things, with his or her real 'self' being one of the spiritual things.

All people, including myself, are carnal, sensual, and devilish *by nature*, which is being human, or what is called the Natural Man (This includes the Natural Woman too of course), and that's, as I said, because of the *effects of the Fall*, which resulted in all of us having the drives and passions that we experience with our mortal flesh. To overcome, or at least what's called 'bridle' our fleshes appetites and drives, is one of the reasons we were sent to earth. Another reason was to see if we would choose to obey God's commandments, which obedience would give us the strength to overcome our flesh.

Overcoming our flesh requires that we become born again through the power and gifts of the Atonement of Jesus Christ, and one of those gifts being the gift of repentance and forgiveness, which then opens to us the gift of the *enabling power* of Christ's Spirit. This enabling power gives us additional power to overcome the world's grasp that it has on each of us. When we accept our Savior's invitation to come unto Him and to abide in the light of His gospel, it is then that the gift of Christs' spiritual influence, His *enabling power*, begins to dwell within us. This is having Christ within us, or what Christians call indwelling. When we draw upon this divine strength and power to overcome the temptations of Satan and his unseen spirits, it is called overcoming the world. Satan, and the fallen angels who serve him, want to destroy each of us, literally and spiritual. Jesus' and Heavenly Father's desire is to love and strengthen and redeem every one of us so that we can overcome the world and return to Him once again and live in His presence as eternal families.

It is this indwelling of Christ's spirit within our heart and mind, w helps us *'put off'* and *'overcome'* the natural man, even the world. It's what gives us *the power and strength* to make the choice to bridle these drives and passions that each of us have as human beings. Our own power or will alone, is insufficient to fight the flesh. These passions and desires of the flesh are given to us by our creator for the wise and glorious purpose of creating a family to love and teach and provide for, but the procreative powers are only to be used within the bounds that God has set. Without this gift of the enabling power made available to us through the atonement of Jesus Christ, it's next to impossible for a human being to overcome the world and its influences on our own merits. It is only done through the merits of Christ.

In other words, we rely on ourselves and our weak arm of the flesh and our undisciplined 'will' alone, to overcome it, our lack of sufficient strength usually proves disastrous because people are easily succumbed by their thoughts and the resulting unbridled desires of their flesh, especially when they are fanned by the spirit of Satan. Our carnal thoughts lead to all kinds of sin against our individual temples, meaning our bodies, as well as against our fellow beings, and this is why Satan is called the 'god of pleasure'. He uses our flesh to tempt us with all kinds of pleasures. To prove this is true, one needs only to turn on their electronic devices. There's not a day that goes by where the news isn't broadcasting multiple stories about both men and women who were overcome by their flesh and the worlds' influence on them (The world again, is mankind being influenced by Satan and his unseen angels).

The key that unlocks the door to the power and efficacy of Christ's atonement in our lives, is faith in Jesus and the gift of repentance. It is the key principle to enjoying Christs' spirit and its enabling power, which power, as I've said, helps us make right choices for overcoming the world. The *Law of Repentance* is not a law of punishment. It provides *an opportunity for us to change our course* and avoid the guilt that comes from sin and ultimately the eternal punishment that follows if they're left unrepented. Forgiveness of sin is given on the *condition* of our repentance. When we sincerely repent, we're given access to Christ's atoning blood, and redemptive power which cleanses our mind and heart. This power's influence in our daily lives keeps us on the covenant path that leads us back to our Heavenly Father's presence, becoming perfect 'in' Christ and unspotted from the world. This *kind* of life is called Eternal Life. Here's just a few examples of this *process of changing our course and behavior* so that we can become clean and unburdened, receiving confidence to be in the presence of the Lord once again:

1 Corinthians 2:14

14 But the natural man receiveth not the things of the Spirit of God: for they are foolishness unto him: neither can he know *them,* because they are spiritually discerned.

Mosiah 3:19

19 For the natural man is an enemy to God, and has been from the fall of Adam, and will be, forever and ever, unless he yields to the enticing's of the Holy Spirit and putteth off the natural man and becometh a saint through the atonement of Christ the Lord, and becometh as a child, submissive, meek, humble, patient, full of love, willing to submit to all things which the Lord seeth fit to inflict upon him, even as a child doth submit to his father (This is the process of how we develop the 'Character of Christ', which is becoming Christlike. This is how we become like the child of God that we truly are. Our conscience within each of us, tries to remind us of this truth daily).

Mosiah 16:5

5 But remember that he that *persists in his own carnal nature*, and goes on in the ways of sin and rebellion against God, remaineth in his fallen state and the devil hath all power over him. Therefore he is as though there was no redemption made, being an enemy to God; and also is the devil an enemy to God.

Alma 42:7–24

7 And now, ye see by this that our first parents were cut off *both temporally and spiritually* from the presence of the Lord; and thus we see they became subjects to follow after their own will.

8 Now behold, it was not expedient that man should be reclaimed from this temporal death, for that would destroy the great plan of happiness.

9 Therefore, as the soul could never die, and the fall had brought upon all mankind a spiritual death as well as a temporal death, that is, they were cut off from the presence of the Lord, it was expedient that mankind should be reclaimed from this spiritual death.

10 Therefore, as they had become carnal, sensual, and devilish, *by nature,* this probationary state became a state for them to prepare; it became a preparatory state (For the immortal life to come).

11 And now remember, my son, if it were not for the plan of redemption, (laying it aside) as soon as they were dead their souls were miserable, being cut off from the presence of the Lord.

12 And now, there was no means to reclaim men from this *fallen state*, which man had brought upon himself because of his *own disobedience* (Adam's disobedience of choosing to transgress God's commandment to not eat of the fruit of the Tree of Knowledge of Good and Evil);

13 Therefore, according to *justice*, the plan of redemption could not be brought about, *only on conditions of repentance* of men in this probationary state, yea, this preparatory state; for except it were for these conditions, *mercy could not take effect* except it should destroy "the work of Justice". Now the 'work of justice' could not be destroyed; if so, God would cease to be God.

14 And thus we see that all mankind were fallen, and they were in the grasp of justice; *yea, 'the justice of God'*, which consigned them forever to be cut off from his presence.

15 And now, *the plan of mercy* could not be brought about *except an atonement should be made*; therefore God (The Lord God Jesus) himself atoneth for the sins of the world, to bring about the plan of mercy, *to appease the demands of justice*, that God (The eternal Father) might be a perfect, just God, and a merciful God also.

16 Now, repentance could not come unto men except there were a punishment, which also was eternal as the life of the soul should be, affixed opposite to the plan of happiness, which was as eternal also as the life of the soul.

17 Now, how could a man repent except he should sin? How could he sin if there was no law? How could there be a law save there was a punishment?

18 Now, there was a punishment affixed, and a just law given (By the Eternal Law Giver), which brought *remorse of conscience* unto man.

19 Now, if there was no law given—(Meaning) if a man murdered he should die—would he be afraid he would die if he should murder?

20 And also, if there was no law given against sin men would not be afraid to sin.

21 And if there was no law given, if men sinned what could justice do, or mercy either, for they would have *no claim* upon the creature?

22 But there is a law given, and a punishment affixed, and a repentance granted; which repentance, mercy claimeth; otherwise, justice claimeth the creature and executeth the law, and the law inflicteth the punishment; if not so, the works of justice would be destroyed, and God would cease to be God.

23 But God ceaseth not to be God, and mercy claimeth the penitent, and mercy cometh because of the atonement; and the atonement bringeth to pass the resurrection of the dead; and the resurrection of the dead bringeth back men into the presence of God; and thus they are restored into his presence, to be judged according to their works, according to the *law and justice*.

24 For behold, justice exerciseth all his demands, and also mercy claimeth all which is her own; and thus, *none but the truly penitent are saved.*

Doctrine & Covenants 20:20

20 But *by the transgression of these holy laws* man became sensual and devilish, and became fallen man.

Alma 26:19–22

19 Oh then, why did he not consign us to an awful destruction, yea, why did he not let the sword of his justice fall upon us, and doom us to eternal despair?

20 Oh, my soul, almost as it were, fleeth at the thought. Behold, he did not exercise his justice upon us, *but in his great mercy hath brought us over that everlasting gulf of death and misery, even to the salvation of our souls.*

21 And now behold, my brethren, what natural man is there that knoweth these things? I say unto you, there is none that knoweth these things, *save it be the penitent.*

22 Yea, he that repenteth and exerciseth faith, and bringeth forth good works, and prayeth continually without ceasing—unto such it is given to know *the mysteries of God*; yea, unto such it shall be given to reveal things which never have been revealed; yea, and it shall be given unto such to bring thousands of souls to repentance, even as it has been given unto us to bring these our brethren to repentance.

Here are a few more verses explaining God's Plan of Happiness and Redemption:

Alma 41:11

11 And now, my son, all men that are in a state of nature, or I would say, in a carnal state, are in the gall of bitterness and in the bonds of iniquity; They are without God in the world, and they have gone contrary to the nature of God; therefore, they are in a state contrary to the nature of happiness.

Doctrine & Covenants 29:41

41 Wherefore, I, the Lord God, caused that he should be cast out from the Garden of Eden, from my presence, *because of his transgression*, wherein he became spiritually dead, which is the first death, even that same death which is the last death, which is spiritual, which shall be pronounced upon the wicked when I shall say: Depart, ye cursed.

Doctrine & Covenants 67:12

12 Neither can any natural man abide the presence of God, neither after the carnal mind.

Moses 5:13

13 And Satan came among them, saying: I am also a son of God; and he commanded them, saying: Believe it not; and they believed it not, and they loved Satan more than God. And men began from that time forth to be carnal, sensual, and devilish.

Moses 6:49

49 Behold Satan hath come among the children of men, and tempteth them to worship him; and men have become carnal, sensual, and devilish, and are shut out from the presence of God.

With these scriptures fresh on our mind, I want to take a moment to share a few additional thoughts on the *Law and Gift of Repentance* and what it can bring to one's life. It became vividly clear to me that Richard really doesn't have a clue as to what the Atonement is, and more especially, what the principles involved in the Atonement of Jesus Christ are, and how they are supposed to operate in our lives.

So, at the risk of sounding like I am once again being preachy, which I most certainly am not, I want to share a few points regarding sin, which of course, Richard doesn't believe there is any such thing as a sin, and that's because he doesn't believe in the existence of God, and so, if there's no God, there's obviously no such thing as breaking His laws, which is what sin is, right? And therefore, there's nothing to feel guilty about, or to worry about anymore, right? To me, it appears that Richard has just a surface understanding of the principle of *repentance and what sin is*, as well as what *true guilt* is, and what real *shame* in fact is, as these terms relate to how they affect our spiritual and temporal lives.

I believe Richard, as a result of his lack of knowledge on these subjects, has developed a distorted, even a stunted or shallow view of the work performed by Jesus Christ on behalf of all mankind. God gave laws and commandments that defined for us what sin is, and He has revealed how we are to deal with the consequences of choosing sin over His desire that we keep His commandments. In my view, Richards' mindset about God and how his view of God was developed, was revealed early on in his book *The God Delusion*. At the beginning of Richard's book, he shared a few things about his childhood, which for me, revealed that he had been *shamed* during his early years, especially by the ministers or priests who had him in their supposed care. I can't say for sure, but I suspect that his parents may have shamed him as well, which most certainly would have shaped Richard's faith in God, and possibly destroyed it.

These so-called men of God should have been his spiritual teachers of the pure gospel of Jesus Christ. I believe that due to the continual use of the false spiritual tools of *shame and fear* by these adult authorities over Richards' spiritual life, in their effort to try and control him, scare him, and shame him into acting a certain way, it left Richard feeling self-loathing and feeling as though he had little to no personal worth as a person. I believe Richard rebelled against these painful feelings and emotions, leaving him to reject and stop believing there's a God. Richard was made to feel shame for mistakes that all children make in their early years of their life. Victimhood, and feelings of low self-worth, are what shame promotes in an individual's mind, if not immediately corrected. Rebelling against such feelings of shame and despair, is only natural, and that is why, I believe, Richard chose to reject these men and their false message about God and His Son, Jesus Christ, and as a result he turned to atheism.

There's an essay I found on www.churchofjesuschrist.org, written by McKell A. Jorgensen, a graduate student from Brigham Young University. McKell is also a Google scholar. Her essay is titled "Shame vs Guilt: Help for Discerning God's Voice from Satan's Lies". I really liked it, and so I hope you find it as interesting as I did. Here are a few excerpts from her essay, and I quote:

"The scriptures say that 'Shame' is a prompting from Satan's spirit and influence, whereas 'Guilt', the fruit of the spirit, is a prompting from God's spirit, and this influence regarding right and wrong leads to *a desire* to improve and change, even *a desire* to repent. ... The way you can tell the difference between these two promptings, these two voices – shame and guilt – is to consider what 'feelings' or 'thoughts' these promptings produce in you. Guilt is a feeling you get when you did something wrong, or perceived you did something wrong due to our sense of right and wrong, our *sense of morality within each of us.* Whereas *Shame is a feeling that tells you your 'whole self' is wrong, and that you now have no value or worth*, and it may not even be related to a specific behavior. This prompting or voice of Shame attacks your character, producing feelings that assert at your core you are worthless. Such lies from the 'father of lies', often lead to self-loathing like I said, and if not rejected, condemns you to a lifetime of misery because it causes you to forever believe you are unlovable and don't belong anywhere.

"The prompting of Guilt on the other hand, produces feelings of guilt that you have behaved different than your better self, the person you know you are and should be. These feelings do not attack your 'self-worth', and generally do not include 'self-loathing'. At least they shouldn't. So, parents, please stop shaming and making it tie to the sense of guilt. The prompting of guilt and the feelings it produces in your heart and mind, reminds you that your actions are not in line with your values and 'identity' as a child of God, and this realization, or remembering, often goes on to prompt you to change those actions or behaviors so you can become the person you know you should and want to be. Latter-Day-Saint doctrine is clear on how God wants us to 'feel' when it comes to our 'sins' and 'transgressions'. Our inherent worth as children of God means that we are never worthless, even when we have sinned. The Spirit's voice will never encourage us to hate 'ourselves' like the spirit of Satan does. Rather, it will remind us of our eternal worth as a child of God:

Moses 1:4, 12

4 And, behold, thou art my son; wherefore look, and I will show thee the workmanship of mine hands; but not all, for my works are without end, and also my words, for they never cease.

12 And it came to pass that when Moses had said these words, behold, Satan came tempting him, saying: Moses, son of man, worship me.

"Satan's prompting and influence of the spirit of shame, tries to convince you that you are not enough and shouldn't even be trying to do or be good anymore. Shame wants you to curl up in a corner and surrender as it whispers to you that you'll never get there. If shame's voice can convince you that those things are true, it has made the decision for you. It will keep you from trying again and becoming better by convincing you that you don't have agency (Or, Free Will), and don't have the ability to try again. It is such a heinous lie. Reject it immediately!

"On the other hand, the prompting and influential feelings of guilt tells you when something you did does not correspond with your values. Upon receiving that prompting, that knowledge, you are now 'free to choose' what to do with it. You can decide to change the behavior or ignore that still, small voice that's telling you, and even warning you, that what you are thinking of doing or are doing is wrong. Regardless of whether you are feeling guilt or shame, you are the agent who must decide what to do.

"The doctrine is clear: God has given you agency; He wants you to choose for yourself:

II Nephi 2:26–27

26 And the Messiah cometh in the fulness of time, that he may redeem the children of men from the fall. And because that they are redeemed from the fall they have become free forever, knowing good from evil; to act for themselves (as agents unto themselves) and not to be acted upon, save it be by the punishment of the law at the great and last day, according to the commandments which God hath given.

27 Wherefore, men are free according to the flesh; and all things are given them which are expedient unto man. And they are free to choose liberty and eternal life, through the great Mediator of all men, or to choose captivity and death, according to the captivity and power of the devil; for he seeketh that all men might be miserable like unto himself.

(Heavenly Father will not force anyone to love Him. We are free to choose His love, or Satan's lies)

Moses 4:3

3 Wherefore, because that Satan rebelled against me, and sought to destroy the agency of man, which I, the Lord God, had given him, and also, that I should give unto him mine own power; by the power of mine Only Begotten, I caused that he should be cast down; and ideally do it without you noticing ...,

II Nephi 28:21

21 And others will he pacify, and lull them away into carnal security, that they will say: All is well in Zion; yea, Zion prospereth, all is well—and thus the devil cheateth their souls, and leadeth them away carefully down to hell.

... and bind you to a life of misery and woe:

II Nephi 2:27

27 Wherefore, men are free according to the flesh; and all things are given them which are expedient unto man. *And they are free to choose liberty and eternal life, through the great Mediator of all men, or to choose captivity and death, according to the captivity and power of the devil*; for he (Satan) seeketh that all men might be miserable like unto himself.

"This prompting of Shame that one feels inside their head, is often dealt with by running away from our mistakes or failure; in other words, to hide from them and try to become invisible – "Don't see me!" Shame says that the worst thing that can happen is for someone to find out what you've done, because if people knew it, they would be disgusted by you. On the other hand, guilt, and its promptings, encourages one to keep moving forward. Guilt promotes change in one's behavior and allows you to reach out for help if you need it. Guilt is a tool of God that He's provided us, to bring us, His children, to repentance so that we can *improve* and *overcome* the natural man that's in us all, and ultimately enjoy true happiness. Thinking that we can hide our sins from God never elicits true repentance. It can't. Repentance is only possible through the Redeemer:

Alma 39:8

9 And now, my son, I have told you this that ye may learn wisdom, that ye may learn of me that there is no other way or means whereby man can be saved, only in and through Christ. Behold, he is the life and the light of the world. Behold, he is the word of truth and righteousness.

II Nephi 10:24

24 Wherefore, my beloved brethren, reconcile yourselves to the will of God, and not to the will of the devil and the flesh (By trying to hide your sins); and remember, after ye are reconciled unto God, *that it is only in and through the grace of God that ye are saved.*

Mosiah 16:13

13 And now, ought ye not to tremble and repent of your sins, and remember that only in and through Christ ye can be saved?

Alma 13:5

5 Or in fine, in the first place they were on the same standing with their brethren; thus this holy calling being prepared from the foundation of the world for such as would not harden their hearts, being in and through the atonement of the Only Begotten Son, who was prepared.

"We must all come unto Him to 'be made whole' and receive complete forgiveness. When Shame convinces us to *hide* our sins from God, repentance cannot occur, and that's exactly what Satan wants – for us to remain his captive. If we don't repent, if we don't call on the power of Jesus Christ and the blessings of His Atonement, Satan wins:

Alma 12:35

35 And whosoever will harden his heart and will do iniquity, behold, I swear in my wrath that he shall not enter into my rest.

Christ pleads for you to come unto Him and become better through His 'grace':

Matthew 11:28

28 Come unto me, all *ye* that labour and are heavy laden, and I will give you rest.

John 7:37

37 In the last day, that great *day* of the feast, Jesus stood and cried, saying, If any man thirst, let him come unto me, and drink.

"Messing up, learning from our mistakes, and moving forward through the 'repentance' process (the process of changing for the better), is an ongoing cycle on our journey to becoming more and more like the Savior and His example (In other words acquiring the Character of Christ). I argue that God will never attack our character, steal our agency, or prevent us from repenting. Rather, He reminds us of our worth, promotes our agency, and helps us repent through the instrumentality of guilt (and the gift of repentance) and His love for us. Guilt is a signal Heavenly Father has provided in our hearts (The Light of Christ), to let us know that something is not quite right and there *needs to be a change*.

"I consider 'guilt' to be the social-science synonym for 'godly sorrow'. I believe 'shame' is Satan's counterfeit of this signal. He wants us to believe that all hope is lost, that change cannot occur, and that we will never be able to live up to our potential as a child of God. Because shame is aimed at our *inherent worth rather than our actions and behaviors,* it isn't limited to sins or other behaviors that require change either. Satan, well-meaning people, and even one's own mind may shame us, our thoughts, actions, and even our decisions that don't require repentance." [537]

End of Excerpts by McKell A. Jorgensen

It is the power of shame, when used by others like Richard's spiritual leaders, or maybe even his own parents as they tried to control him, that steals one's hope. Possibly Richard's own thoughts may have been fueled by self-shaming and self-loathing at times too, and it's this power or 'spirit of shame', I believe, when we don't know how to correct it in our own mind and heart, that takes someone down the pathway to rebellion and disbelief in God, and ultimately embrace atheism, which is what I believe happened to Richard early on in his life.

Experiences with shame and self-loathing, I believe, was the chief reason why Richard made the choice to reject religion and his so-called spiritual leaders. It was his *conflating of shame with religion* that ultimately bore the fruit of Richard's disbelief in God. I also believe that a whole lot of other people have experienced this same spirit of shame in their lives, and it affected them in much the same way that it affected Richard, ultimately taking them down the same path to atheism. Now I may be wrong, but I don't think so. I do not fault Richard, or anyone else for that matter, who've chosen the paths they've taken with regards to belief in or lack of belief in God. That's why all of us we're sent here to earth – "to choose the path we want to take for our lives, for we are given the choice of being "agents unto ourselves". That way we only have ourselves to blame or to congratulate for our life's decisions.

I also want to say that I certainly do not hate Richard for the beliefs he has chosen as a result of his life's experiences, including his hatred for religion and anything else that speaks against religion, my faith included, and especially his feelings towards the incredible beings I love and worship, who are called 'The Godhead' – God the Father, God the Son, and God the Holy Ghost. I do, however, hate Satan. He certainly accomplished his goal for Richard, which is, in fact, the same goal he has for each and every one of us who have come to experience life here on earth. That goal being 'to destroy our faith in God'. Satan uses his most warn and effective tool – the power of shame – to accomplish his bidding.

What happened to Richard, and a great many others like him, truly saddens me. I love all of God's children and I'm pained by the success that 'shame' has had on the lives of so many people throughout the world's history. I so hope that you, my readers, will reject any shame you may be feeling at this time in your life, and turn to God, for you are worthy of His love. That's for sure! I promise you that Jesus Christ stands with outstretched arms, ready and willing to embrace you, heal, forgive, cleanse, strengthen, purify, and even sanctify you so that you can return to His and our Heavenly Fathers' presence.

The Church of Jesus Christ of Latter-Day Saints prophet, President Nelson, in a talk given back in the General Conference on April 2019, titled "We Can Do Better and Be better", taught the following about the law of repentance, and I quote:

"Nothing is more liberating, more ennobling, or more crucial to our individual progression than is a regular, daily focus on repentance. Repentance is not an event; it is a process. It is the key to happiness and peace of mind. When coupled with faith (In our Savior), repentance opens our access to the power of the Atonement of Jesus Christ."

End Quote

This is why we need the Atonement of Jesus Christ working in our lives. It blesses us with the gift of repentance, and that gift makes it possible for us to grow and change for the better. It is my hope that you, my readers, will at least consider if you're allowing the debilitating 'tool of shame' to take control and rule over your life. If it has led you to rebel against God so that it has destroyed your value, self-worth, and how you see yourself in your mind, please reject it now and use the blessing of repentance, coupled with the Light of Christ, to find forgiveness, peace, joy, and a feeling of eternal worth and happiness going forward. Let's go ahead and move on to the next subtitle – "A case study in the roots of morality".

A CASE STUDY IN THE 'ROOTS' OF MORALITY

Richard begins this subtitle on the *Roots of Morality* by saying, "If our 'moral sense', like our sexual desire, is indeed rooted deep in our Darwinian past, predating religion, we should expect that research on the human mind would reveal some moral 'universals' crossing geographical and cultural barriers, and also, crucially, religious barriers." [538] Richard has sure worked hard in coming up with his *possible solution* to all these religious questions, hasn't he? Man-oh-man. He's so creative, yet dead wrong.

Once again, Richard is making up his own God. To me, it doesn't sound convincing when he uses words like 'if our moral sense is rooted in' … and 'a fruitful line of thought experiments originally *suggested* by moral philosophers', etc. Richard is trying to come up with an answer as to 'why' religion and morality are ubiquitous, and why they cross all cultural barriers. In this subtitle he sets the table for what he *thinks* is the cause of 'moral universals', which is a scientists' way of describing 'the Light of Christ', or our conscience, which dwells in the hearts and minds of everyone (It being Ubiquitous), planted there by God Himself – universally – He being, no respecter of persons. But Richard doesn't know that this universal Light of Christ is the *'faculty'* he's been seeking in all his mental guessing.

A little later in this subtitle, Richard says, "Most people come to the same decisions when faced with the dilemma of what is right and wrong. This is what we should expect if we have a *moral sense* which is built into our brain (The supposed builder, he says, is natural selection using its unseen crane to select and remove unwanted *features* over a period of millions of years, one feature at a time, taking them up the Mountain Improbable) like our sexual instincts or our fear of heights or, like our capacity for language, but the underlying deep structure of grammar is universal." [539]

Next Richard says something very interesting. He says, "As we shall see, the way people respond to these moral tests, and their inability to articulate their reasons, seems largely independent of their religious beliefs or lack of them." Richard continues, "The message here is: Driving our moral judgements is a *universal moral programmer*, a *faculty* of the mind that evolved over millions of years to include a *set of principles* for building a range of possible *moral systems*." [540] Those principles or moral systems being built into the genes of everybody by natural selection? Really Richard? Built by natural selection? You've got to be kidding me. C'mon man. The universal moral programmer, *the faculty* of mind and its set of principles making up the moral system of right and wrong in our heart, is the Spirit of God, even the Light of Christ and God's Law, which is placed in all of us universally. Got it?

What I just described about everyone having a conscience, a sense of right and wrong, whether they believe in God or not, is Richard's so-called universal moral programmer. The difference is that it didn't come from millions of years of evolutionary processes of natural selection. It is God's own light; His own spirit of truth called The Light of Christ, it having been placed in all of us, whether we are good or evil, and that's why it's ubiquitous. It's in all things and was in us from our beginnings, and that is why I call it the Incomprehensible It. It's the conscience that's existed in our souls from our inception. It wasn't evolved over millions of years of trial and error that resulted in selected mutations. Adam and Eve, and all mankind, has had it since the dawn of time.

For me, Richard, though he doesn't realize it, is confirming what God has done in giving all men and women a conscience – the Light of Christ. God has also given each of us a *memory system* that records everything onto our spirits' hard-drive, so-to-speak. It records everything that we have done and everything we will do, say, or think. It's a lot like an airplanes' orange recorder box, but our recorder box stores a movie of our life's decisions and actions, not just an audio recording of it. Nothing will be held back at the time when we all stand at the judgement bar of God and watch our life's review with God, Himself. Can you picture your life being played before you and God, and maybe even in front of other people? Oh my! I certainly hope Jesus' promise to "Remember them no more" will be honored. I know that this judgment will be one hundred percent fair and true, because it will be based on our own words and our own deeds. There will be both praise, as well as condemnation in our life's review, and it will be in living color. It will also be about teaching us. Thank our God for the gift of repentance!

I'm just kidding about our life's review being played in front of everybody. Our life's review isn't to shame or browbeat us. It is not Jesus Christ's way. His purpose in having our spirits remember our choices is to help us see what we could have done to be our better selves; to be the child of God we truly are, and to help us realize the good as well as the bad that others experienced from our individual actions. Our life's review will show us the lessons we were meant to learn by coming here to earth and have this mortal experience, associating with God's other children. This life's experience will be its own disciplinary, or ministering council, but it will be a council of love … done in love, … and not a council of ridicule and shame.

I suggest that you, my readers, invest the time to watch a few YouTube videos of people who have had NDE's and afterwards talked about their life's review they had after they died, just so you can get to thinking about what it may mean for you going forward. I certainly have. As I watched many of these NDE stories, it made me consider my ways even more, and as a result I'm constantly working to change for the better, to become the very best me I can be, and to do my very best to have Christlike love and kindness for others at my core and to express loving intentions towards others every day of my life.

In other words. I am speaking of the work I call "taking on the character of Jesus Christ". This is a good time to mention a talk that was given by Elder David A. Bednar, an apostle of the Church of Jesus Christ of Latter-Day Saints, where Elder Bednar spoke on this very topic at the Missionary Training Center in Provo Utah. It was on Christmas Day, 2011. The title of his talk is, "The Character of Christ." You can watch it in its entirety by going to YouTube and doing a search for it there.

Elder Bednar began this talk by recalling an experience he had with another of God's modern-day apostles, Elder Neil Maxwell. The experience occurred back in 1995, while he was participating in a training meeting with Elder Maxwell. During the course of his instruction, Elder Maxwell made a statement that impressed Elder Bednar deeply. Elder Maxwell said: *"There would have been no Atonement except for the character of Christ."*

After returning home, this "penetrating statement" became a primary topic for Elder Bednar's studying, reflecting, and praying over the next several months. During a Mission Leadership Seminar at the Provo Missionary Training Center on June 25, 2019, Elder Bednar recounted:

"I read the New Testament and the Book of Mormon repeatedly focusing upon the question, 'What is the character of Christ?' I sought to learn more about the word 'character,' the relationship between Christ's character and the Atonement, and the implications of that relationship for each of us as disciples." Speaking to 164 couples attending that seminar, Elder Bednar said character refers to *"the moral qualities of an individual that are conscientiously and consistently lived."* The word character in the Topical Guide to the scriptures is cross-referenced to the topics of honesty, honor, and integrity, he noted (More on this definition can be found at www.churchofjesuschrist.org under 'Character').

In Elder Maxwell's talk, delivered to Church Educational System educators, "Elder Maxwell specifically linked Christ's character to the infinite and eternal atoning sacrifice", said Elder Bednar. "Jesus's character necessarily underwrote His remarkable atonement. Without Jesus's sublime character there could have been no sublime atonement! His character is such that He '[suffered] temptations of every kind' (Alma 7:11), yet He gave temptations 'no heed' (Doctrine and Covenants 20:22)," said Elder Bednar, quoting Elder Maxwell's address "O How Great the Plan of Our God."

One of the greatest indicators of righteous character "is the capacity to recognize and appropriately respond to other people who are experiencing the very challenge or adversity that is most immediately and forcefully pressing upon us," said Elder Bednar. "Character is revealed, for example, in the power to discern the suffering of other people when we ourselves are suffering; in the ability to detect the hunger of others when we are hungry; and in the power to reach out and extend compassion for the spiritual agony of others when we are in the midst of our own spiritual distress. Therefore, character is demonstrated by looking, turning, and reaching *outward* when the instinctive response of the natural man in each of us is to *turn inward* and to be selfish and self-absorbed."

"The Savior of the world is the source, the (Objective) standard, and the ultimate criterion of moral character and the perfect example of charity and consistency", said Elder Bednar. "The New Testament", he continued, "is replete with 'strikingly displayed' examples of the Savior's character. The character of Christ, the consistent capacity to turn outward and minister to others in the midst of affliction, is the very foundation of the infinite and eternal atoning sacrifice," he said. "Jesus, who suffered the most, has the most compassion for those who suffer so much less", said Elder Bednar. "As the awful agony of the Crucifixion commenced, the Savior pleaded with the Father to 'forgive them; for they know not what they do' (Luke 23:34)."

"While hanging on the cross, Jesus instructed the Apostle John about caring for His mother, Mary (see John 19:26-27). And in the midst of excruciating spiritual and physical pain, the Savior reassured one of the thieves on the cross, "To day shalt thou be with me in paradise" (Luke 23:43). Throughout His mortal ministry, and especially during the events leading up to and including the atoning sacrifice, the Savior of the world turned outward—when the natural man or woman in most of us would have focused inward. Latter-day Saints can in mortality seek to be blessed with and develop essential elements of a Christlike character", taught Elder Bednar. "Indeed, it is possible for us as mortals to strive in righteousness to receive the spiritual gifts associated with the capacity to reach outward and appropriately respond to other people who are experiencing the very challenge or adversity that is most immediately and forcefully pressing upon us. We cannot obtain such a capacity through sheer willpower or personal determination. Rather, we need and are dependent upon 'the merits, and mercy, and grace of the Holy Messiah' (2 Nephi 2:8)."

I think I will leave it there. If you want to check out what Elder Bednar said about Sesame Street's 'Cookie Monster' as being a type of each of us, and how we, through repentance, can stop turning inward and find the power to turn outward as we obtain the character of Christ, be sure to watch Elder Bednar's YouTube video in its entirety. He teaches some remarkable principles that can help each of us find the strength to put off any of the fruits of shame and victimhood that we may be suffering from in our lives and replace them with the power to turn outward and become a true disciple of Christ, even someone who reflects His character as we're serving others. I promise you will find it transformational.

Continuing with this subtitle, Richard finishes this subtitle by going through a variety of moral dilemmas and the results of studies done by Marc Hauser, Peter Singer, and Immanuel Kant. From such studies immerged the *Kant Principle* which states that, "a rational being should never be used as merely a non-consenting means to an end, even the end of benefitting others." [541] The main conclusion for Richard was that there is no statistically significant difference between atheists and religious believers in making these judgements. Richard says, "This seems compatible with the views, which I and many others hold, that *we do not need God in order to be good – or evil.*" [542]

At the risk of sounding as though my views are once again lining up with Richard's, let me say that I agree with Richard's thought that, "We don't need God to be good or evil", but that's because each of us do in fact have the *moral compass,* the moral GPS, so-to-speak, the *moral sense of the Light of Christ* in our hearts and minds *already, it being placed there by God.* It's part of the divine faculty within each of us, even our seeds of divinity. You could say it was placed there via our heavenly parent's spiritual genes. Because God is our Eternal parent of our spirit bodies, this moral compass is in us whether we believe in God or not. We can choose to follow its directives, or we can choose to follow our own wills' compulsions, which, more often than not, disregards the divine mapping or directives God has written on our hearts. Christ set the example and chose to follow His Fathers' will and directives, as should we all. Remember Him saying, "Not my will Father, but thine be done"?

I'm not speaking of the fleshy make-up of the neurological explosions going on in our so-called unguided, unintended brain matter either. I'm speaking of the light that's in our spirit bodies' mind, it being housed in our temporal bodies. This Light is called the Light of Christ, our conscience, which God placed in every person who has, or ever will live on this planet. So yes, we do not need God to be the Big Brother that Richard speaks of, where he says it's trying to force us to do and be good. Force is NOT part of God's character, nor is it part of His Plan. It was however in Satan's plan. Moral agency is the tool God gives us to choose which path we'll take. He'll never force us to love, obey, or come to Him.

Richard says the root or director of our moral agency and its sense of right and wrong, or good and evil, is the result of natural selection having worked in our cells for millions of years and somehow its *process* has apparently finished developing our moral sense, for we all seem to have it now. Right? Wrong! Not so. Whether we're a believer or nonbeliever in God, all of us originally had this moral sense in us from the get-go. It's always helping us know '*the good from the evil*'.

This fact leaves each of us to decide for ourselves if we are going to follow that light of truth within us, that sense of morality, or not. And as I said, if we choose not to follow it, the result is that over time this light of truth, even the spirit of truth, will cease to strive within us. In other words, it's a flickering 'pilot light' that can ultimately go out if we're not careful to keep it burning. Here's how the scriptures describes it:

Doctrine & Covenants 1:32-33

32 Nevertheless, he that repents and does the commandments of the Lord shall be forgiven;

33 And he that repents not, *from him shall be taken even the light which he has received; for my Spirit (The flickering pilot light) shall not always strive with man*, saith the Lord of Hosts.

This leads right into the next subtitle – "If there is no God, why be good?"

IF THERE IS NO GOD, WHY BE GOOD?

Richard starts this subtitle by expressing what he often feels tempted to do when asked, "If there is no God, then why be good?" Richard chooses to challenge his questioners by asking them, "Do you really mean to tell me ... the only reason you try to be good is to gain God's approval and rewards, or to avoid his disapproval and punishment?" That's not morality, it's just sucking up, apple-polishing, and looking over your shoulder at the great surveillance camera in the sky, or the small *wiretap* inside your head." [543]

Richard, "Do you mean by *wiretap*, life's recorder which is our spirits' memory written on our spirits' mind and heart?" If so, then yes. I'm being sarcastic here. But I will ask the question, "Why do we even have a memory? Why can't we just live without having to remember everything we do or everything we see and speak? Why is everything we ever do, from a tiny child until we die, recorded in our mind?" Are our memories only there to help us survive, and that's it? I would remind you, my readers, as well as Richard, that all memories are not about surviving and surviving alone, that's a fact.

Richard goes on to quote Dostoevsky and the words he put into the mouth of Ivan Karamazov. He also quotes Steven Pinkers' "Blank Slate" report of a police strike in Montreal, and H.L. Mencken's criticism of it. Here's what he said to all these public, cultural critics, "People say we need religion, when what they really mean is we need police." [544]

Richard makes the following statement, "It would be interesting to know whether there was any statistical tendency, however slight, for religious believers to loot and destroy less than unbelievers." [545] Richard is inclined to believe that "The prison populate of atheists is very low, and some atheists, being *more highly educated and having greater intelligence than others* (Like himself?)." [546]

Richards' mind is truly biased towards his fellow intellectuals, isn't it? Once again, he aggrandizes himself and other atheists because of their so-called *imminent intelligence*, saying it may be the reason they are *more restrained from committing crimes*. To support this idea, he says research evidence doesn't support the common view that religiosity is positively correlated with morality. Contrary to Richard's belief, I believe that if one were to do a survey of all prisoners in all the prisons throughout the world, by asking them, "Do you believe in God?", the majority of these prisoners would probably say, "No", but not all. But I guess we'll never know unless and until such a survey is taken, will we?

Next, Richard quotes fellow atheist Sam Harris who gives a list of statistics that implies more crime is committed in 'Red' states than in 'Blue' states, and then Richard concludes by saying that "systematic research, if anything, tends to support such correlation data." [547] And, quoting Gregory S. Paul from the "Journal of Religion and Society", who systematically compared seventeen economically developed nations, and reached the devastating conclusion that, "higher rates of belief in and worship of a Creator correlated with higher rates of homicide, juvenile and early mortality, STD infection rates, teen pregnancy and abortion in the prosperous democracies." [548]

After reading these statements by Sam Harris, as well as Richard's and Mr. Paul's statements, I decided to do a Google search, and the very first article that popped up, which was at the top of that first page list of articles, was an article titled, "Do red states report higher rates of violent crime than blue states?". It was written on Thursday, June 24, 2021, by a Mr. Stevie Rosignol-Cortez. Here's what it said (Be sure to read to the end of it so you can get the whole of his comments), and I quote:

"According to 2019 FBI data, seven out of ten states with the highest per-capita rates of violent crime voted Republican in the 2020 election. In contrast, seven out of ten states with the lowest rates voted Democrat. *However*, (And here's the chief point I want to bring to this discussion) the District of Columbia had the highest rate despite voting blue. The FBI cautions against using any one demographic marker to draw conclusions about the causes of crime, which they describe as manifold, complex, and often *not readily measurable*." Cited variables include:

- Population density and transience.
- Poverty
- Education levels

- Racial and ethnic makeup
- Family Cohesiveness
- Strength of law enforcement
- Youth concentration
- Climate

"Statistics are further complicated by the fact *that higher crime rates may reflect greater reporting rather than a higher incidence of crime* (Maybe Blue states hide such statistics? It's possible)." [549]

End of Article excerpts

It is obvious that one can go a bit overboard in trying to make their point. By overboard I mean 'blurring the line by conflating the facts' in-order-to try and convince someone of your point of view. It's called 'being unfair and imbalanced'. I don't want to judge Sam or Richard here, but it does appear that Sam was lopsided in his use of his statistical claims. I'll leave it there and let you, my readers, decide.

Richard's beef with God is found in his statement regarding morality wherein he says, "Even if it were true that we need God to be moral, it would, of course, not make God's existence more likely, merely more desirable. But that is not the issue here." [550]

My point exactly. All the answers Richard has put forth to try and answer why religion is here, do in fact lead me to feel an increased confidence in God's existence and a greater hope for those who love Him. And for those who have chosen darkness rather than light, I feel an increased hope that your consciousness will be raised once you've learned that your choices are being recorded by your own spirits' movie recorder in your own spirit's mind, which recorded content will be reviewed after you die, during what I've been calling your *life's review*.

Next, Richard goes on to give an analogy of an imaginary apologist. Richard shares with his readers what he thought his imaginary apologist would say regarding the question of "Where does *good* come from?", it being, once again, just his opinion put upon this imaginary apologist, like a ventriloquist speaking for their puppet. Here's what Richard said his imaginary apologist would answer:

"My imaginary religious apologist has no need to admit that sucking up to God is the religious motive to be good. Rather, his claim is that, wherever the motive to be good comes from, without God there would be no standard for deciding what is good (No objective standard in other words). My religious apologist would claim that only religion can provide a basis for deciding what is good. The springboard for this discussion of moral philosophy was a hypothetical religious claim that, without a God, morals are relative (Subjectively relative) and arbitrary. Men such as Kant and other sophisticated *moral philosophers* apart, and with due recognition given to patriotic fervor, the preferred source of *absolute morality* ... is usually a holy book of some kind." [551]

Again, Richard reveals his lack of understanding as to why believers, like myself, are motivated to try and do their best to keep God's commandments. *Good*, by-the-way, is *not* the objective here, as there are only two persons that I know of, that are and can be called *good,* or as Jesus said, *"Be ye therefore perfect as my Father in Heaven is perfect"*. After Jesus was resurrected, He included Himself by saying, "... even as I or your Father in Heaven is perfect", which is another way of saying "good", or "Complete".

The motive to *be good* is not to suck up to God. It is to *love God*, just as children are motivated to show that they love their parents, because their parents loved them first (Is loving one's parents just sucking up to them? I think not. Jesus counseled His disciples on this principle of love when He said:

John 14:15

15 If ye love me, keep my commandments.

Elder Jeffrey R. Holland taught, quote: "So we have neighbors to bless, children to protect, the poor to lift up, and the truth to defend. We have wrongs to make right, truths to share, and *good* to do. In short, we have a life of *devoted discipleship* to give in demonstrating our love of the Lord (This isn't sucking-up to God Richard. It is loving God). We can't quit and we can't go back. After an encounter with the living Son of the Living God, nothing is ever again to be as it was before." [552]

In response to Richard's comments on moral philosophy and where he feels our moral sense comes from, and in particular his belief that *absolute morality* comes from what is written in one's Holy books, and therefore it is manmade, I want to share an article I read recently, written by Ryan Leisure, an apologist with the Cross-Examined organization, titled, "Can We be Good Without God?"

I think you, my readers, will find it very enlightening. I took the liberty of inserting a few short comments of my own intermittently throughout Ryan's article. I put them in parenthesis, like I've done with other articles throughout my book, so that you would know who was saying what. My comments are those in parenthesis. Here's Ryan's article, and I quote:

"This past weekend, two mass-scaled shootings transpired on American soil. El Paso, Texas, and Dayton, Ohio, experienced unspeakable carnage. Two men, fueled by hatred for mankind, slaughtered dozens of innocent people in cold blood. In response, people of *all stripes* spoke out against these atrocities. Men and women, democrat and republican, Christian and Atheist, *all* condemned these crimes. In other words, the denunciation of these senseless and cowardly acts has been *universal*.

"But doesn't this universal agreement fly in the face of our relativistic cultural values? 'Don't force your morality on others' suddenly doesn't sound so appealing in situations like this. Don't we all want everyone else to adopt our same *moral position* on murder? This, of course, raises important questions. Does *objective* morality exist? That is, were those two men *objectively* wrong in what they did over the weekend? And if so, where does this *agreed-upon morality* come from?

'Relativists argue that there is no such thing as *objective morality*. Rather, morality is *subjective* — dependent on individual opinions. So, in situations like these mass shootings, the relativist cannot say that the shooters were wrong. If so, that would imply that an objective standard exists that these two individuals missed. Rather, the relativist can only say they didn't care for these events. They found them distasteful. "Murder is wrong," and "rape is evil" are just *opinions* on par with "pepperoni is better than sausage."

"But isn't it self-evident that mass murder is in a different category than pizza toppings? The very fact that society has *universally* condemned these acts ought to tip us off that something more than mere opinion is at work here. When we all cry *'foul'* in *unison*, we're implicitly affirming that *'fair'* exists. C. S. Lewis made this argument years ago when he wrote: "Just and unjust? A man does not call a line crooked unless he has some idea of a straight line. What was I comparing this universe to when I called it unjust?"

"What Lewis and so many others have argued is that *objective morality* exists, and this is most evident when people don't live up to that moral standard. If we learn, for example, that a man raped a little girl, brutally murdered her, and dismembered her body, would we say that he committed evil? If yes, then we recognize an *objective moral standard* exists that was not met. Our senses (Our conscience or the Light of Christ) tell us that acts such as abuse, rape, theft, deceit, murder, etc., all fail to measure up to a *standard* of some sort. This *moral standard* seems so patently obvious; it's odd when people try to deny it. A quick rule of thumb is that when a certain group can't condemn the Holocaust as evil, we conclude that their views are absurd. Of course, if those same relativists had been in those concentration camps, they'd drop their relativism and recognize evil for what it is.

"Even the most committed relativist will come around if you steal his wallet or spread false rumors about him. Phrases like "that's not right" or "that's not fair" will come spewing out faster than you can blink your eye.

"Where does *Objective Morality* come from then? The reality of objective morality raises a significant question. 'Where does it come from?' For the naturalists (those that believe the natural world is all that exists), these objective morals are mere illusory *by-products* of evolution and social conditioning (Just as Richard has said). For most naturalists, science is the only begetter of knowledge. But science itself is amoral. Science cannot tell us how things *ought* to be. It can only tell us how things *are*. That is, science can tell us how to make chemical weapons, but it cannot tell us whether we should use them.

"*Objective morals* simply cannot derive from something morally neutral like science. And they certainly don't arise from Darwinian evolution. According to Darwinists (Like Richard Dawkins), people only do good *because it aids in their survival*. But if that's the case, can we really call their actions morally good? Fundamentally, the motivation behind *good acts*, is self-serving, and thus not worthy of praise.

"Also, doesn't Darwinism, on the whole, make morality arbitrary (Based on random choice or personal whim, rather than any reason or system)? Couldn't the human race have found rape or killing each other for food acceptable if it would have evolved like other species from the animal kingdom? Sharks do this all the time, but are they immoral? Darwinists who find this notion uncomfortable typically adopt humanism — the belief that humans are the center of the universe and *morality is based on what helps them flourish*. But again, isn't humanism purely arbitrary in a Darwinian world?

"Darwin, after all, taught that every living species descended from the same common ancestor in the primordial soup. Thus, humans are simply one small branch on his tree of life (In other words, humans are nothing special). Other branches include crickets, lions, fungus, and every other living species. *Why should we think the human branch is the most valuable?* Why are we more important than crickets? Doesn't this make us guilty of speciesism?

"Ultimately, atheisms' understanding of morality is purely arbitrary. It simply cannot account for objective morality. In the end, God (And His gift of the Light of Christ or conscience, given to all of us) is the best explanation for *objective morality* (Which moral code is contained in His Laws).

"God's very nature grounds morality so that anything done that goes against his (Divine) character is wrong and/or evil. Furthermore, because God made humans in his image, each person possesses intrinsic value (Humans are His special creation because of this unique value – God creating us in His very image – which is proof that we are special, at least we are to Him).

'Without a doubt, the first objection raised to the claim that objective morality doesn't exist without God, is that atheists do good without believing in God. But this misses the point. Of course, people can still do good things without believing in God (All are given that freedom of choice, the moral agency to do good or not, or even to believe that there is no such thing as sin).

"The question is not: Do we have to believe in God to do good? Rather, the question is: If God doesn't exist, is anything objectively good at all? As I've argued, moral categories are arbitrary in an atheistic world. If we acknowledge, however, that the two mass-shooters committed evil, then objective moral categories exist. And if objective moral categories exist, then a transcendental lawgiver is the best (and the more probable) explanation we all feel that way about it.

"Which leads to the second objection — the '*Euthyphro Dilemma*'. The dilemma goes like this: Is something good because God wills it? Or does God will something because it is good? Skeptics raise this objection to put the theist between a rock and a hard place. For if we say something is good because God wills it, then good is ultimately arbitrary. But if we say God wills something because it's good, then the *objective standard* exists beyond God. But the skeptic presents us with a *false dilemma* here.

"A *third option* exists which states 'God wills something because He is good'. That is to say: *He is the standard* by which we get all moral categories (He is the *personification* of all that is good).

"Another frequent objection is that we don't need the Bible to know that we shouldn't murder or steal. After all, other religious books tell us the same as do most legal codes. But again, this is not the argument theists make.

"Nobody's arguing you need to read the Bible to know right from wrong (Our conscience does that job for us). Rather, we're arguing that objective right and wrong doesn't exist in a world without a *transcendent moral law*. But the very fact that every world religion and legal code agree on basic fundamental morals (Universally; Ubiquitously), which suggests that *a moral law exists that transcends the human race.* The Apostle Paul tells us:

Romans 2:14-15

14 For when the Gentiles, which have not the law, *do by nature* the things contained in the law, these, having not the law, are *a law unto themselves*:

15 Which shew the work of *the law written in their hearts*, their *conscience* also bearing witness, and *their* thoughts the mean while accusing (convicting) or else excusing one another;

"So, when Gentiles, who do not have the law, *by nature* do what the law requires, they are *a law unto themselves*, even though they do not have the law. They show that the work of the law is *written on their hearts*, while their *conscience* also bears witness, and their conflicting thoughts accuse or excuse them (Isn't it incredible that so-called peasants, as Richard calls these ancient apostles and prophets, living more than 2,000 years ago, were so well-informed about human psychology?)."

"That is to say; people don't need the Bible to know right from wrong. *God has instilled this moral code in the hearts of all people* (Via the Light of Christ/Our conscience as I've been saying all along. This, to me, is the greatest *proof* there is of God's existence, besides the universe he created). Which raises a final objection. If a moral law exists, why is there so much disagreement on morality?"

(*Disagreements certainly exists around issues like abortion and sexuality. But does that imply no right view exists? Of course not. Which is why we strive to make our views the accepted ones).

(*I encourage you to take a look at another YouTube video titled "This Turned Him from Friendly to Furious in a Second", where Ray Comfort asks multiple individuals questions about abortion. These are perfect strangers. Please note that I do not agree with everything Ray Comfort says or teaches in his evangelizing videos. I am just using his dialogue he has with these interviewees to point out the two very different points of view they seemed to fall into. First is the *objective standard* stance that says, 'abortion is killing a person' and 'thou shalt not kill'. Then there's the *subjective standard* that says, 'a woman has the right of control over her own body and its health, and that a fetus is not a human until it is born'. It's so interesting to me how people invariably contradict themselves when rationalizing their choice. You, my readers, will see this in living color as you watch this short video. It is quite interesting).

"In fact, if culture adopts our views, we'll say things like 'our culture is progressing'. Progressing toward what? The moral standard we believe to be right.

"Be that as it may, the human race generally agrees on several basic points. People have certain rights. We should treat others with respect. Love is better than hate. Honesty is better than deceit. Courage is better than cowardice. And so forth. As C. S. Lewis aptly states:

"Think of a country where people were admired for running away in battle, or where a man felt proud of double-crossing all the people who had been kindest to him. You might just as well try to imagine a country where two and two made five."

"The universal agreement on the most basic moral categories suggests a transcendent moral law. The Moral Argument for God.

(I believe that *objective morality* is one of the strongest arguments for God's existence. I have always said that the proof for God's existence lies behind our own belt buckle, meaning 'inside each of us')

Perhaps a more helpful way of looking at it would be this syllogism:

1. If God does not exist, objective morality does not exist.
2. Objective morality does exist.
3. Therefore, God exists.

"This argument is logically airtight. If premises 1 and 2 are true, then 3 necessarily follows. I've made a case for 1 and 2 in this article. It concludes then that God exists. So, can we be good without God? No, because if He doesn't exist, nothing objectively good exists either." [553]

End of article by Ryan Leisure

The key here is to understand that the world is coming from a secular, "'Man's Law' foundation, out of which from beliefs such as abortion, transgenderism, the Gay lifestyles, etc. immerge, and Theists, like myself, are coming from a 'God's Law' foundation, out of which immerge beliefs such as the sanctity of life, marriage between a man and a woman, the Law of Chastity, etc. These two ideologies, these two world views, are in opposition to each other. It truly is Satan plan against God, our Heavenly Father's plan. It is a war of ideologies continuing here on earth, just as it was in the ward in heaven.

The next chapter is titled – "The Good Book and The Moral Zeitgeist". This was a very interesting read for me. I really enjoyed it. I'm pretty sure you'll enjoy all the back and forth like I did.

CHAPTER 7

THE 'GOOD' BOOK AND THE CHANGING MORAL ZEITGEIST

Before I get too far into my perspective on this particular chapter's title, I want to say that because Richard takes full license to share his point of view and what he says are *facts* that prove his claims are incontrovertible, I too will take license here and freely share my point of view and perspective on what I feel are *facts* that support my claims regarding scripture, both ancient and modern.

Here is the point of view that Richard approached this chapters' title with, saying "Adherents of *scriptural authority* show distressingly little curiosity about the (normally highly dubious) historical origins of their holy books." Richard continues, "The next chapter will demonstrate that, in any case, people who claim to derive their morals from scripture do not really do so in practice." [554]

Again, in this entire chapter Richard tries to delegitimize scripture entirely. He says, "'holy books" as he calls them, or scripture, "may be considered by some to be a source of morals or rules for living, but that scripture is flawed and *weird documents that were composed, revised, translated, distorted, and improved by hundreds of anonymous authors, editors, and copyists, unknown to us and mostly unknown to each other, spanning centuries.*" [555] Once again, Richard gives a concise argument for apostasy and the mistranslation of scripture that often flows from it. In other words, both I and Richard do not believe the Bible to be *inerrant,* due to the apostasy that influenced its translators (But not all of course).

Richard is definitely put off by the claim most Christians make about the Bible, where they say, "the Bible is the *inerrant source* of our morals and rules for living", especially when "it came from such a checkered history of authorship." Richard continues, "Those who wish to base their morality literally on the Bible have either not read it or not understood it." [556]

Let me say that having *errors* intermittently dispersed throughout the Bible, is *not* a legitimate cause for throwing the baby (The entire Bible) out with the wash. As a Latter-Day Saint, let me share my perspective regarding the Bible itself. Like I said, I truly believe the Bible to be the word of God *as far as it is translated correctly. That disclaimer at the end of my statement, is in harmony with Richard's description of the Bible, it having many mistranslations made over the centuries since its first writings were written down by past prophets and apostles. The Bible's checkered history of translations prove that apostasy has taken its devastating course. However, I must also say that for the most part, in spite of these mistranslations, the Bible, overall, is true and therefore is a sacred record of God's dealings with His chosen people who lived in the eastern hemisphere, which were the Jews, and later with the gentiles when the apostle Paul served his missions.

Because of its errors I do not believe the Bible to be inerrant. In fact, the Prophet Joseph Smith, through revelation, spent a considerable amount of his time retranslating several mistranslated verses of the Bible, just as Richard described. This retranslation is called: "The Joseph Smith Translation" (JST) of the Bible. The prophet Joseph labored for months to clear up these mistranslations that the Lord, through revelation, was helping Joseph correct, at least up until Josephs' martyrdom, which left his work incomplete. I'm also not oblivious to what many critics of my faith have had to say, and still say today about Joseph Smith's translative work of the Bible (I call them recoveries or retranslations of what once was the original, pure writings of prophets). These critics often say that the prophet Joseph did it to try and make the Bible match the doctrines that Joseph was teaching. This is not a fair judgement of why Joseph did this work. But I allow any and everyone the privilege to say how they feel.

Please know, that I'm very much aware of the points of contention that other theists have about the Church of Jesus Christ of Latter-Day Saints, due to our view of scripture, and in particular our view of the Bible. I just want you, my readers, to be clear on the fact that although I'm making the point that I agree with *some* of what Richard says about the Bible's history, I do *not* agree with Richard's view that "scripture (or what I refer to as 'The word of God') cannot be a source and guide to morals and rules for living".

The scriptures, which includes what we as Latter-Day Saints call the Standard Works, absolutely can, and in fact do contain a *clearly defined pattern or model for living as God would have us live.* Following this divine pattern leads to a happy and joyous life, both as individuals and as families, communities, and nations. Here is a brief overview of what I believe about 'The Standard Works'. It can be found at www.churchofjesuschrist.org under the topic titled "Doctrinal Study: Scriptures":

"What is Scripture?"

"What is scripture? When holy men of God write or speak by the power of the Holy Ghost, their words 'shall be scripture, shall be the will of the Lord, shall be the mind of the Lord, shall be the word of the Lord, shall be the voice of the Lord, and the power of God unto salvation':

Doctrine & Covenants 68:3-4

3 And this is the ensample unto them, that they shall speak as they are moved upon by the Holy Ghost.

4 And whatsoever they shall speak when moved upon by the Holy Ghost shall be scripture, shall be the will of the Lord, shall be the mind of the Lord, shall be the word of the Lord, shall be the voice of the Lord, and the power of God unto salvation.

"The official, canonized scriptures of the Church of Jesus Christ of Latter-Day Saints, often called 'The Standard Works', are the Bible, the Book of Mormon, the Doctrine & Covenants, and the Pearl of Great Price. The principal purpose of the scriptures is to testify of Christ and to guide the children of God so we can come unto Him and receive eternal life (This is that pattern or pathway I just described):

John 5:39

39 Search the scriptures; for in them ye think ye have eternal life: and they are they which testify of me.

John 5:20-31

20 For the Father loveth the Son, and sheweth him all things that himself doeth: and he will shew him greater works than these, that ye may marvel.

21 For as the Father raiseth up the dead, and quickeneth them; even so the Son quickeneth whom he will.

22 For the Father judgeth no man, but he that committed all judgement unto the Son:

23 That all *men* should honour the Son, even as they honour the Father. He that honoureth not the Son honoureth not the Father which hath sent him.

24 Verily, verily, I say unto you, He that heareth my word, and believeth on him that sent me, hath everlasting life, and shall not come into condemnation; but is passed from death unto life.

25 Verily, verily, I say unto you, The hour is coming, and now is, when the dead shall hear the voice of the Son of God: and they that hear shall live.

26 For as the Father hath life in himself; so hath he given to the Son to have life in himself;

27 And hath given him authority to execute judgment also, because he is the Son of man.

28 Marvel not at this: for the hour is coming, in the which all that are in the graves shall hear his voice,

29 And shall come forth; they that have done good, unto the resurrection of life; and they that have done evil, unto the resurrection of damnation.

30 I can of mine own self do nothing: as I hear, I judge: and my judgment is just; because I seek not mine own will, but the will of the Father which hath sent me.

I Nephi 6:4

4 For the fulness of mine intent is that I may persuade men to come unto the God of Abraham, and the God of Isaac, and the God of Jacob and be saved.

Mosiah 13:33–35

33 For behold, did not Moses prophesy unto them concerning the coming of the Messiah, and that God should redeem his people? Yea, and even all the prophets who have prophesied ever since the world began—have they not spoken more or less concerning these things?

34 Have they not said that God himself should come down among the children of men, and take upon him the form of man, and go forth in mighty power upon the face of the earth?

35 Yea, and have they not said also that he should bring to pass the resurrection of the dead, and that he, himself, should be oppressed and afflicted?

The Book of Mormon prophet 'Mormon' taught:

Helaman 3:29-30

29 Yea, we see that whosoever will may lay hold upon the word of God, which is ^bquick and powerful, which shall divide asunder all the cunning and the snares and the wiles of the devil, and lead the man of Christ in a strait and narrow course across that everlasting gulf of misery which is prepared to engulf the wicked –

II Nephi 29:9

9 And I do this that I may prove unto many that I am the same … yesterday, today, and forever; and that I speak forth my words according to mine own pleasure. And because that I have spoken one word ye need not suppose that I cannot speak another; for my work is not yet finished; neither shall it be until the end of man, neither from that time henceforth and forever."

"God, who is the same 'yesterday, today, and forever', continues to reveal scripture in modern times as He did in ancient times. Latter-Day prophets counsel people everywhere to study the scriptures daily, including the Bible, the Book of Mormon, the Doctrine & Covenants, and the Pearl of Great Price. They encourage individual and family scripture study.

"They encourage us, as Nephi encouraged his brethren, to *liken the scriptures to ourselves*, finding ways that the sacred accounts of old apply in our lives today.

I Nephi 19:23–24

23 And I did read many things unto them which were written in the books of Moses; but that I might more fully persuade them to believe in the Lord their Redeemer I did read unto them that which was written by the prophet Isaiah; for I did liken all scriptures unto us, that it might be for our profit and learning.

24 Wherefore I spake unto them, saying: Hear ye the words of the prophet, ye who are a remnant of the house of Israel, a branch who have been broken off; hear ye the words of the prophet, which were written unto all the house of Israel, and liken them unto yourselves, that ye may have hope as well as your brethren from whom ye have been broken off; for after this manner has the prophet written.

"They exhort us to 'search the scriptures' and 'feast upon the words of Christ':

John 5:39

39 Search the scriptures; for in them ye think ye have eternal life: and they are they which testify of me.

II Nephi 32:3

3 Angels speak by the power of the Holy Ghost; wherefore, they speak the words of Christ. Wherefore, I said unto you, feast upon the words of Christ; for behold, the words of Christ will tell you all things what ye should do.

"Daily, meaningful scripture study *helps individuals be receptive* to the guidance of the Holy Ghost. It builds faith, fortifies against temptation, enlightens, and helps individuals draw near to their Heavenly Father and His Beloved Son.

The Bible

"The Bible is divided into two parts: the Old Testament and the New Testament. The Old Testament is a sacred record of God's dealings with His covenant people in the Holy Land. It includes the teachings of such prophets as Moses, Joshua, Isaiah, Jeremiah, and Daniel. The New Testament records the birth, mortal ministry, and Atonement of the Savior. It concludes with the ministry of the Savior's disciples. Because the Bible has been translated many times, it is printed in different versions. In English, the King James Version (KJV) of the Bible, is accepted as scripture by The Church of Jesus Christ of Latter-Day Saints, and in particular the more recent "New LDS Edition" of the KJV). In The Church of Jesus Christ of Latter-Day Saints, we revere the Bible and its sacred teachings. We can receive strength, comfort, and guidance from the biblical accounts of God's dealings with His people.

The Book of Mormon: Another Testament of Jesus Christ

"The Book of Mormon came forth in this dispensation by the will of the Lord. It is a record of God's dealings with the people who lived in the ancient Americas. Prophets of the Lord engraved the original records on gold plates. The Lord declared that the Book of Mormon contains "the fulness of the gospel of Jesus Christ".

Doctrine & Covenants 20:9

9 Which contains a record of a fallen people, and the fulness of the gospel of Jesus Christ to the Gentiles and to the Jews also;

Doctrine & Covenants 42:12

12 And again, the elders, priests and teachers of this church shall teach the principles of my gospel, which are in the Bible and the Book of Mormon, in the which is the fulness of the gospel.

"On September 22, 1827, an angel named Moroni—the last Book of Mormon prophet (Now resurrected)—delivered these records to the Prophet Joseph Smith. By the gift and power of God, the prophet Joseph translated the record into English. Since then, the Book of Mormon has been translated into many other languages. The primary purpose of the Book of Mormon is to convince all people "that Jesus is the Christ, the Eternal God, manifesting himself unto all nations" (See title page of the Book of Mormon). It teaches that all people 'must come unto him, or they cannot be saved':

I Nephi 13:40

40 And the angel spake unto me, saying: These last records, which thou hast seen among the Gentiles, shall establish the truth of the first, which are of the twelve apostles of the Lamb, and shall make known the plain and precious things which have been taken away from them; and shall make known to all kindreds, tongues, and people, that the Lamb of God is the Son of the Eternal Father, and the Savior of the world; and that all men must come unto him, or they cannot be saved.

"Joseph Smith said that the Book of Mormon is "the keystone of our religion, and a man [will] get nearer to God by abiding by its precepts, than by any other book" (See Introduction to the Book of Mormon). The Book of Mormon is another witness for the truths taught in the Bible (That's why it is called a second witness or Testament of Jesus Christ). It also restores "plain and precious" truths that have been lost from the Bible through errors in translation or "taken away" in attempts to "pervert the right ways of the Lord".

I Nephi 13:24–27, 38–41

24 And the angel of the Lord said unto me: Thou hast beheld that the book proceeded forth from the mouth of a Jew; and when it proceeded forth from the mouth of a Jew it contained the fulness of the gospel of the Lord, of whom the Twelve Apostles bear record; and they bear record according to the truth which is in the Lamb of God.

25 Wherefore, these things go forth from the Jews in purity unto the Gentiles, according to the truth which is in God.

26 And after they go forth by the hand of the Twelve Apostles of the Lamb, from the Jews unto the Gentiles, thou seest the formation of that great and abominable church, which is most abominable above all other churches;

" ... for behold, they have taken away from the gospel of the Lamb many parts which are plain and most precious; and also many covenants of the Lord have they taken away.

27 And all this have they done that they might pervert the right ways of the Lord, that they might blind the eyes and harden the hearts of the children of men.

1 Nephi 13:38–41

38 And it came to pass that I beheld the remnant of the seed of my brethren, and also the book of   the Lamb of God, which had proceeded forth from the mouth of the Jew, that it came forth from the Gentiles unto the remnant of the seed of my brethren.

39 And after it had come forth unto them I beheld other books, which came forth by the power of the Lamb, from the Gentiles unto them, unto the convincing of the Gentiles and the remnant of the seed of my brethren, and also the Jews who were scattered upon all the face of the earth, that the records of the prophets and of the Twelve Apostles of the Lamb are true.

40 And the angel spake unto me, saying: These last records, which thou hast seen among the Gentiles, shall establish the truth of the first, which are of the Twelve Apostles of the Lamb, and shall make known the plain and precious things *which have been taken away* from them; and shall make known to all kindreds, tongues, and people, that the Lamb of God is the Son of the Eternal Father, and the Savior of the world; and that all men must come unto him, or they cannot be saved.

41 And they must come according to the words which shall be established by the mouth of the Lamb; and the words of the Lamb shall be made known in the records of thy seed, as well as in the records of the Twelve Apostles of the Lamb; wherefore they both shall be established in ᵇone; for there is ᶜone God and one Shepherd over all the earth.

"The Bible and the Book of Mormon "shall grow together, unto the confounding of false doctrines and laying down of contentions and establishing peace".

II Nephi 3:12

12 Wherefore, the fruit of thy loins shall write; and the fruit of the loins of Judah shall write; and that which shall be written by the fruit of thy loins, and also that which shall be written by the fruit of the loins of Judah, shall grow together, unto the confounding of false doctrines and laying down of contentions, and establishing peace among the fruit of thy loins, and bringing them to the knowledge of their fathers in the latter days, and also to the knowledge of my covenants, saith the Lord.

"Near the end of the Book of Mormon, the prophet Moroni teaches us how we can know it is true:

Moroni 10:3-5

6　　Behold, I would exhort you that when ye shall read these things, if it be wisdom in God that ye should read them, that ye would remember how merciful the Lord hath been unto the children of men, from the creation of Adam even down until the time that ye shall receive these things, and ponder it in your hearts.

7　　And when ye shall receive these things, I would exhort you that ye would ask God, the Eternal Father, in the name of Christ, if these things are not true; and if ye shall ask with a sincere heart, with real intent, having faith in Christ, he will manifest the truth of it unto you, by the power of the Holy Ghost.

8　　And by the power of the Holy Ghost ye may know the truth of all things.

The Doctrine & Covenants

"The Doctrine & Covenants contains revelations given to the Prophet Joseph Smith. It also includes a few revelations given to other Latter-Day prophets following Joseph Smith. This book of scripture is unique because it is not a translation of ancient documents. It is a collection of revelations given by the Lord to His chosen prophets *in the latter days*.

"The Prophet Joseph Smith said that the Doctrine & Covenants is "the foundation of the Church in these last days, and a benefit to the world, showing that the keys of the mysteries of the kingdom of our Savior are again entrusted to man."

Section heading for Doctrine & Covenants 70:

'Revelation given through Joseph Smith the Prophet, at Hiram, Ohio, November 12, 1831. The Prophet's history states that four special conferences were held from the 1ˢᵗ to the 12ᵗʰ of November, inclusive. In the last of these assemblies, the great importance of the revelations that would later be published as the Book of Commandments and then the Doctrine & Covenants was considered. This revelation was given after the conference voted that the revelations were "worth to the Church the riches of the whole Earth."

Joseph Smith's history refers to the revelations as the foundation of the Church in these last days, and a benefit to the world, showing that the keys of the mysteries of the kingdom of our Savior are again entrusted to man."

The Pearl of Great Price

"The Pearl of Great Price contains the Books of Moses, the book of Abraham, the Prophet Joseph Smith's inspired translation of Matthew chapter 24, and some writings of the prophet Joseph. "The book of Moses is a small excerpt from Joseph Smith's inspired translation of the Bible. It is a more complete record of Moses's writings at the beginning of the book of Genesis in the Old Testament. It contains many doctrines and teachings that were lost from the Bible and gives additional information about the plan of salvation, the creation of the earth, and the Lord's dealings with Adam and Enoch.

"The book of Abraham is a translation of ancient records written on papyrus that came into the possession of the Church in 1835. The Prophet Joseph Smith translated the records by revelation. This book contains truths about the premortal Council in Heaven, the creation of the earth, the nature of God, and the priesthood.

"Joseph Smith—Matthew is an excerpt (Matthew 24) from Joseph Smith's inspired revision of the Bible and adds to our knowledge of the Savior's teachings about His 2nd Coming. The writings of Joseph Smith in the Pearl of Great Price include:

- Joseph Smith—History, which is an excerpt from the Prophet's history of the Church. It is a narrative of the events leading to the restoration of the Church, including the First Vision, the visits of Moroni to the Prophet Joseph, the obtaining of the gold plates, and the restoration of the Aaronic Priesthood.

- The Articles of Faith, which the Prophet Joseph Smith wrote as basic statements of belief and doctrine. [557]

End of the overview of Doctrinal Study – Scriptures

My view and perspective of 'scripture(s)' is that they are a divine source and guide for gaining an understanding of the morals and 'rules for living' that God wants us to take ownership of, by willingly choosing to live by them. The qualifiers on this view will become self-evident and even more clear as I give my thoughts and perspective on each of Richard's subtitle discussions that he puts forth in this chapter, starting with his first subtitle – "The Old Testament."

THE OLD TESTAMENT

Richard begins this subtitle by using the story of Noah, found in the Old Testament, claiming it came from the Babylonian *myth* of Uta-Napishti. Richard says, "the story of Noah is charming, but the moral of the story of Noah is appalling." Richard says this is due to the scriptures recording that God destroyed all flesh that moved upon the earth, both of fowl, and of cattle, and of beasts, and of every creeping thing, and every man, woman, and child by sending the great deluge, the global flood. Richard feels this shows that God had a dim view of His creations.

Richard says theists respond to his criticism of the Noah story by crying, "We don't take the book of Genesis literally!" [558] Richard then comes back at these theists saying, "It is a frighteningly large number who still take their scriptures, including the story of Noah, literally." [559]

Richard continues, "Theists and religionists pick-and-choose which bits of scripture to believe, which to write off as symbolic or allegories, just like atheists choose as a matter of personal decision, to follow this moral precept or that one. It is a personal decision, each without an absolute foundation. If one of these is morality 'flying by the seat of its pants', then so is the other." [560]

Let me say for the record, and I know I am going to be mocked for saying this, but I unequivocally believe in the story of Noah and the Ark, and the Great Global Flood. I do not pick and choose my bits of scripture when faced with what some would say is a lack of scientific evidence to support the stories revealed in scripture. It is my claim that there is in fact evidence that supports the Bible's record of the Global Flood, including Noah's Ark, it being the means of saving just eight (8) souls, Noah's family.

I listed several individuals in my Introduction who are experts in the fields of paleontology and the study of theology. These are experts who believe in the Global Flood, and in the story of Noah. These scientists say they have substantial evidence that supports it taking place. I won't go into what each of these specialists had to say about this, but here is the list of those folks whom I have looked into and studied their books and watched their videos. It is certainly worth checking into what they had to say in response to Richard's and other atheist's chidings on what they say is a fairytale.

After you, my readers, have read these folks books and watched their videos I've listed here, you too can decide for yourselves what you want to believe about the Global Flood and the story of Noah:

- o Dr. Marcus Ross – Paleontologist – The Study of Rock Formation and Fossils as they relate to The Global Flood & Intelligent Design
- o Dr. Kurt Wise – Paleontologist – Rock & Fossil Formation
- o Dr. Andrew Snelling – Geologist – Carbon-14 and Radiocarbon Dating
- o Dr. Art Chadwick – Taphonomy (The branch of Paleontology that deals with the processes of fossilization) – Study of Events and Systems as they relate to Fossils.
- o Ken Ham – Christian Apologist – Founded 'Answers in Genesis', a Video Series about Science and The Bible (Also see "Replacing Darwin: The New origin of Species)
- o Frank Turek – Christian Apologist – Founder of Cross Examined (A Masters' degree in 'Public Administration', and a Doctor of Ministry in Christian Apologetics.
- o Dr. Hugh Ross – Astrophysicist, Christian apologist, and old Earth creationist. Dr. Ross has a Ph.D. in Astronomy and a B.Sc. degree in physics. Some of his books are "Why the Universe is the Way it is", "Improbable Planet", and "The Creator of the Cosmos", and many, many more books.

If you, my readers, want to read what the Church of Jesus Christ of Latter-Day Saints has to say about Noah's Ark and the Great Global Flood, you can go to www.churchofjesuschrist.org and type into the search bar "Noah and the Ark". [561] An article will come up where this topic is covered briefly. And for a more in-depth, apologetics discussion of the Global Flood and Noah's Ark, you can go to the website www.fairlatterdaysaints.org [562] and type the following into the search bar:

"Mormonism and the reconciliation of the Flood of Noah with scripture and Church teachings"

Let me be clear, I am not saying that all of these are definitive, irrefutable studies, nor am I saying that the scientific studies that some of them have performed on the subject, and the claims they have made based on those studies, are immutable. Like most studies, they are just sharing their educated interpretation of the data they've found in the rocks and other layers of the earth's crust. I'm simply saying that you should study these works and make your own informed decisions as to their truthfulness, authenticity, and validity. I have, and I've concluded, or I should say, "I have *reaffirmed* my belief that the Great Global Flood happened, and the Biblical story of Noah and the Ark happened as a result of this cataclysm. Jesus Himself mentions it in the Book of Matthew, chapter 24, saying:

Matthew 24:37-38

37 But as the days of Noe *were,* so shall also the coming of the Son of man be.

38 For as in the days that were before the flood they were eating and drinking, marrying and giving in marriage, until the day that Noe entered into the ark,

39 And knew not until the flood came, and took them all away; so, shall also the coming of the Son of man be.

As I listed above, there are numerous sources on this subject, from PragerU to Frank Turek, to Dr. Marcus Ross, Ken Ham, and Dr. Kurt Wise, all of whom, along with many others, believe the Great Global Flood to be an actual event. Just type in the YouTube search bar 'Noah's Flood' and any one of these authors videos will pop up for your viewing. I think you, my readers, will be impressed. Richard, and his fellow atheist's so-called educated opinions and interpretations, certainly do not have the corner on what scientists have said about this event, and many other topics or stories discussed in the scriptures for that matter. Just to make a note, there are *published* scientists who believe the geological data that they've studied in researching the earth's crust, and as a result they've said that the *geological record,* such as the Grand Canyon, as well as other locations all across the globe, *affirm* the Great Flood.

Another interesting point made by Richard, after bringing up the fact that some religionists "blame the 2004 tsunami, for example, on human sins and not on a plate tectonic shift", is found in his question, "Why should a divine being, with creation on his mind, care a fig for petty human malefactions (Once again, Richard can't help himself for revealing his lack of understanding of God's Plan of Redemption nor the purpose and details of His Son's coming to the earth to perform His atoning sacrifice)? We humans give ourselves such airs, even aggrandizing our poky little *sins* to the level of cosmic significance." [563]

Richard then provides additional criticism of the Bible's account of Lot, and Sodom and Gomorrah, whose story is found in Genesis 19:8-10 in the (KJV) King James Version of the Bible. It is true that the Bible says *Lot was righteous*. So, one might ask, "Why would Lot offer to send out his two daughters, who were virgins, for the wicked Sodomites to rape, in exchange for them not taking the men (The Angels) visiting Lot in his home?" These wicked men wanted to sodomize the men (The Angels). The wicked men of Sodom, once they knew Lot had taken in these men (The Angels), surrounded Lot's house and were making mobocracy threats towards Lot if he didn't give the men (The Angels) up to them so that they could have wicked, non-consenting, sexual sodomy relations with them (I think I am fair in calling it non-consenting 'rape', but you, my readers, can make your own judgement).

In response to Richard's take on this story, I'm now going to share just one of many examples that I could give, where a living prophet has helped with such contradicting, even misleading scriptural mistranslations found in the Bible, like the one Richard used to criticize the Old Testament. First, I'll give the (KJV) King James Version account, and then I'll give the (JST) Joseph Smith Translation account:

Genesis 19:8-10 (KJV).

8 Behold now, I have two daughters which have not known man; let me, I pray you, bring them out unto you, *and do ye to them as is good in your eyes*: only unto these men do nothing; for therefore came they under the shadow of my roof.

9 And they said, Stand back. And they said *again,* This one *fellow* came in to sojourn, and he will needs be a judge: now will we deal worse with thee, than with them. And they pressed sore upon the man, *even* Lot, and came near to break the door.

10 But the men put forth their hand and pulled Lot into the house to them and shut the door.

The Prophet Joseph Smith's translation (JST) of Genesis 19:9-11 paints a far different picture than what the mistranslated Bible verses say in the KJV, starting with verse 9 of the JST version of Genesis 19. Here is the *JST* translation that the Lord revealed to Joseph Smith as its inspired version:

Genesis 19:9-11

9 And they said *unto him,* Stand back. *And they were angry with him.*

10 And they said *among themselves,* "This one *man* came into sojourn *among us,* and he will needs *now make himself to be* a judge; now we will deal worse with *him* than with them.

11 *Wherefore they said unto the man (Lot), "We will have the men (the Angels), and thy daughters also; and we will do with them as seemeth us good".*

12 *Now this was after the wickedness of Sodom.*

13 And Lot said, "Behold now, I have two daughters which have not known man; let me, I pray you, *plead with my brethren (The Angels) that I may not bring them (His daughters) out unto you; and ye shall not do unto them as seemeth good in your eyes;"*

14 *For God will not justify his servant in this thing; wherefore, let me plead with my brethren (The Angels), this once only, that unto these men (The Angels) ye do nothing, that they may have peace in my house;* for therefore came they under the shadow of my roof.

15 *And they were angry with Lot* and came near to break the door, but the *Angels of God* (The Joseph Smith Translation says there were actually *three* Angels*), which were holy men,* put forth their hand and pulled Lot into the house unto them, and shut the door.

The next few verses of the Bible, goes on to say that the angels smote the wicked Sodomite men *with blindness* so that they could not find their way to the door or anywhere else for that matter. We all know the rest of the story. My point in sharing the Joseph Smith Translation (JST) of this very unique story of Lot and his family, is to help you, my readers, understand that when there's only part of the facts, or in this case, when the facts have been *tampered with* in an effort to try and make the word of God contradictory and confusing, or when scribes had not the Spirit of the Holy Ghost helping them in the work of translation, we end up making judgements based on half-truths, just as Richard did with this story. When we're easily confused and deceived, we often find ourselves experiencing a *stumbling block*, just as I believe Richard and others have experienced with these scripturally mistranslated stories. I also believe Christendom has been deceived for the same reasons. They believe the Bible is completely *inerrant*. Since no righteous, God-fearing man, like Lot was, would ever commit such a heinous act of giving up his daughters as described in Genesis 19, one should give pause and search further for clarity.

It seems many, for whatever reason, do not do the work of clarification. That said, I do not feel I have to take each example that Richard uses to belittle and disprove the truths that the Bible puts forth as the Word of God, by giving the Joseph Smith translation (JST) for each and every one of his examples. I think I've made my point about the mistranslations of the Bible. Again, I believe the Bible to be the Word of God *as far as it is translated correctly.

Richard goes on to try and embolden his point about the Lot story, by following it up with a similar story found in Judges 19. It sounds eerily familiar because it basically has the same plot as the Lot story. This story, however, does not name names specifically, only that the man in the story was a *certain Levite*' whose concubine prostituted herself against him, so he dismembers her and presents her remains to the other tribes of Israel. Sounds pretty awful, does it not?

Let me just say, for those of my readers who may not have studied these chapters in the Old Testament, please note that in the closing chapters of Judges, the author has turned from stories of Israel's heroes and righteous prophets, *to writing about two incidents that illustrate the low state of religion at that time in history, which was a time of deep apostasy, and writes about the immorality that existed in the days when Israel had forsaken her covenant with the Lord*, and as a result of her apostasy, everyone '*did that which was right in his own eyes*' (In other words people had become *a law unto themselves*, just as this wicked Levite had. Nimrod is another example of being a law unto oneself):

Judges 17:6

6 In those days *there was* no king in Israel, *but every man did that which was right in his own eyes (They were a law unto themselves, and that law was to do whatever they chose to do).*

Judges 21:25

25 In those days *there was* no king in Israel: *every man did that which was right in his own eyes.*

Another way of saying this is that they were *ripened in apostasy* and so they did whatsoever thing that pleased them, having no desire to follow God's Plan for them or to make and keep any of the covenants He offered to them, and so, they rejected them. Once apostasy takes hold of the peoples' hearts, the first thing that happens is the breaking and discarding of the covenants they had previously made with God. The stories of Micah the Levite and the Danite migration, in chapters 17 and 18 of Judges, and the account just mentioned of the rape of the concubine at Gibeah, and the subsequent punishment of the Benjaminite's, in chapters 19–21, *are clear examples of Israel's worst days as an apostate people.* Nothing in these later stories show the Israelites doing what was right. Truly, apostasy had taken hold of the peoples' hearts completely, so that the spirit of the Lord had ceased to strive with them; so much so, that *they became a wicked and fallen, amoral people* ripe for destruction.

Next, Richard shares the story of an interview he did with a reverend named Michael Bray, where he asked Reverend Bray, "Why evangelical Christians were so obsessed with private sexual inclinations that don't interfere with anybody else's life?" [564] Reverend Bray's reply invoked something like self-defense. "Innocent citizens are at risk of becoming collateral damage when God chooses to strike a town with a natural disaster because it houses sinners." [565]

Let me say that Reverend Bray's reply here, in no way reflects what The Church of Jesus Christ of Latter-Day Saints leaders would ever give as their answer to such an entrapping question by the likes of Richard Dawkins. My perspective and answer would have been, "God has given *the Law of Chasity* for the preserving of the family unit and the moral cleanliness of His Children. By following it all societies may flourish and not decay into destruction." He who has ears to hear, let him hear.

Physical intimacy between a husband and wife is a beautiful and sacred part of God's Plan for His children. It's called His Plan of Happiness and Redemption. Sexual relations are an expression of love within the 'bonds of marriage' that allows a husband and wife to participate as partners with God in the creation of life. God has commanded that this *sacred power* is to be expressed ONLY between a man and a woman who are legally and lawfully married. This Law of Chastity applies to both men and women (Meaning the binary definitions of a man and a woman). It includes strict abstinence from sexual relations before marriage and complete fidelity and loyalty to one's spouse after marriage, and so, the Law of Chastity requires that sexual relations be reserved for marriage between a man and a woman, and only a man and a woman within the 'bonds of marriage'. Period.

"In addition to reserving sexual intimacy for marriage, we obey the Law of Chastity by controlling our thoughts, words, and actions." [566]

Psalms 24:3-4

3 Who shall ascend into the hill of the LORD? or who shall stand in his holy place?

4 He that hath clean hands, and a pure heart; who hath not lifted up his soul unto vanity, nor sworn deceitfully.

Jesus Christ taught:

Matthew 5:27–28

27 Ye have heard that it was said by them of old time, Thou shalt not commit adultery:

28 But I say unto you, That whosoever looketh on a woman to lust after her hath committed adultery with her already in his heart.

Ray Comfort, who I've mentioned before, is a New Zealand-born Christian minister who lives in the United States now. Comfort started 'Living Waters Publications', as well as the ministry 'The Way of the Master', in Bellflower, California. As I said, Ray does interviews with people all across America, as well as in other countries, during which all of his interviewees admitted that they have looked upon a woman or a man with lust, and therefore had broken the higher standard that Jesus commanded His disciples should keep. It was ubiquitous in other words. As I've mentioned, The Church of Jesus Christ of Latter-Day Saints calls this higher standard *The Law of Chastity*.

This is one of many reasons why I say that all of us have sinned and fallen short of the glory of God. If we're honest with ourselves and can admit that we have sinned, we then confirm the need we all have for a Savior. We all have need of rescue from the *consequences* of our sins (The consequences being Death & Hell). Jesus Christ is that *Rescuer*, that Savior from the consequences of our sins, which, as I said, are *physical death and spiritual death*, spiritual death being our *separation from our Heavenly Father*. God says that our sins can be forgiven, and that our debt or wages that we've earned by our breaking His Law, those wages being death, has been paid in full for us '*if*' and only if we accept God's *terms & conditions*. Those terms and conditions of Christ's Atonement are (1) belief in Jesus as our Savior and (2) sincere repentance. Through accessing Jesus' Atonement, we can go on to grow in our faith and become clean before Him, as we receive His gifts of repentance, mercy, and forgiveness.

As you can see, my answer is nowhere near what reverend Bray gave as his answer to Richards' question. All Christians do not believe all that I have just said, nor do they believe in the high standard of morality that's required when we choose to live by the Law of Chastity. Even though disbelievers disregard it entirely, the Law of Chastity is still Gods' Law. Richard goes on to mock some Christian televangelists like the Reverend Pat Robertson, who blamed specific tragedies like floods and hurricane's, on certain wicked people who lived and worked in those locations where the so-called *Acts of God* occurred. Richard says of such idea's: "You'd think an omnipotent God would adopt a slightly more targeted approach to zapping sinner's, such as a judicious heart attack, perhaps, rather than the wholesale destruction of an entire city ..." [567]

Zapping sinners? Ha-ha-ha. Richard, you make me laugh. That's funny. Ha-ha-ha. Anyway, Richard once again is showing his lack of biblical understanding when he puts forth another criticism of the Bible, the story of Abraham who lived in Egypt with his wife at the time of this incident. Richard says, "Lot's uncle, Abraham, was the founding father of all three *great monotheistic religions*. His patriarchal status renders him only somewhat less likely than God to be taken as a role model. But what modern moralist would wish to follow him?" [568]

In contrast to Richard's slanted view, consider this brief review of '*father*' Abraham and his supposed lies as viewed by the Church of Jesus Christ of Latter-Day Saints, and I quote:

"The idea that Abraham, the great man of righteousness, deceived Pharaoh in order to protect his own life, has troubled many students of the Old Testament. That his life was in danger because of Sarah's beauty seems quite clear. It seems peculiar, but whereas the Egyptian pharaohs had a strong aversion to committing adultery with another man's wife, they had no qualms or aversion about murdering a man to free his spouse for remarriage (Pretty crazy, huh?). To kill the husband, in order to possess himself of his wife, seems to have been a common royal custom in those days (This reminds me of the biblical story of King David, Uriah, and Uriah's wife Bathsheba). A papyrus tells of a Pharaoh who, acting on the advice of one of his princes, sent armed men to fetch a beautiful woman and make away with her husband. Another Pharaoh is promised by his priest on his tombstone, that even after death he will kill Palestinian sheiks and include their wives in his harem." [569]

The truth is that Abraham could *validly* state that Sarah was *his sister*, and here's why. In the Bible, the Hebrew words 'brother & *sister'* are often used for other *blood relatives*. In speaking of Lot, Abraham's nephew, the scriptures say:

Genesis 14:14

14 And when Abram heard that *his brother* was taken captive, he armed his trained *servants,* born in his own house, three hundred and eighteen, and pursued *them* unto Dan.

Lot, Abraham's *nephew*, is called his *'brother'* here. Because Abraham and Haran, Sarah's father, were brothers, Sarah was Abraham's niece, and thus could be called *'sister'* (I often think how our Black American friends often call each other 'brothers and sisters', just as members of The Church of Jesus Christ of Latter-Day Saints address each other brother and sister while at church). This is another ancient custom that might shed light on the relationship permitted a woman to be *adopted* as a man's sister upon their marriage to give her greater legal and social status.

Even though Abraham was correct in calling her his *sister*, he was disingenuous with the Egyptians. Because he was, one could fairly ask, "How can this action be justified?" The answer is very simple. His action was justified because God told him to do it:

Abraham 2:22–25

22 And it came to pass when I was come near to enter into Egypt, the Lord said unto me: Behold, Sarai, thy wife, is a very fair woman to look upon;

23 Therefore it shall come to pass, when the Egyptians shall see her, they will say—She is his wife; and they will kill you, but they will save her alive; therefore, see that ye do on this wise:

24 Let her say unto the Egyptians, she is thy *sister*, and thy soul shall live.

25 And it came to pass that I, Abraham, told Sarai, my wife, all that the Lord had said unto me— Therefore say unto them, I pray thee, thou art my sister, that it may be well with me for thy sake, and my soul shall live because of thee.

The Prophet Joseph Smith taught the following about this *hard* principle:

"That which is wrong under one circumstance, may be, and often is, right under another. God said, 'Thou shalt not kill;' at another time He said, 'Thou shalt utterly destroy.' This is the principle on which the government of heaven is conducted—by revelation adapted to the circumstances in which the children of the kingdom are placed. Whatever God requires is right, no matter what it is, *although we may not see the reason thereof till long after the events transpire* (*Teachings,* p. 256)." Since God is perfect and does not do anything that is not right …

Deuteronomy 32:4

4 *He is* the Rock, his work *is* perfect: for all his ways *are* judgment: a God of truth *and without iniquity, just and right is he.*

1 Samuel 15:29

29 And also the Strength of Israel will not lie nor repent: for he *is* not a man, that he should repent.

Alma 7:20

20 I perceive that it has been made known unto you, by the testimony of his word, that he cannot walk in crooked paths; neither doth he vary from that which he hath said; Neither hath he a shadow of turning from the right to the left, or from that which is right to that which is wrong; therefore, his course is one eternal round.

Doctrine & Covenants 3:2

2 For God doth not walk in crooked paths, neither doth he turn to the right hand nor to the left, neither doth he vary from that which he hath said, therefore his paths are straight, and his course is one eternal round.

… *Abraham's act was not wrong*. There are several examples of God directing His servants to take the life of an enemy. David killed Goliath; Nephi killed Laban; Moses killed the taskmaster, etc. To those who disagree with me on this principle of behind God directing prophets to take a life, or lives, in self-defense or when it's necessary to protect an entire nation, I would simply say that we can agree to disagree without being disagreeable and wait upon the Lord for more information to be revealed on the issue.

Richard mentions an additional puzzling story found in the Old Testament, in Judges 34:34-40, which is the story of Jephthah and his only daughter. Richard says this is another story of God requiring human sacrifice of one of His chosen deliverers of His people. You can go to the scriptures to reread it, but suffice it to say, I do not have the same view of this story as Richard does, and here's why:

Many have supposed that Jephthah offered his daughter as a human sacrifice, and a literal reading of the text may support that view. But if that is true, some difficult questions are raised. Jephthah was regarded as a great hero and deliverer of Israel, and even his sacrifice of his daughter is treated in a way that suggests the author of Judges viewed it as a commendable act.

In Hebrews 11:32–35 Jephthah is used as one of the examples of great faith by the apostle Paul.

Hebrews 11:32–35

32 And what shall I more say? for the time would fail me to tell of Gedeon, and *of* Barak, and *of* Samson, and *of* Jephthah; *of* David also, and Samuel, and *of* the prophets:

33 Who through faith subdued kingdoms, wrought righteousness, obtained promises, stopped the mouths of lions,

34 Quenched the violence of fire, escaped the edge of the sword, out of weakness were made strong, waxed valiant in fight, turned to flight the armies of the aliens.

35 Women received their dead raised to life again: and others were tortured, not accepting deliverance; *that they might obtain a better resurrection*:

"Would this case be true if he had engaged in human sacrifice, an act viewed as one of the greatest of abominations in ancient Israel? Why does Jephthah's daughter '*bewail her virginity*' rather than mourn the approaching loss of her life?

Judges 11:37

37 And she said unto her father, Let this thing be done for me: let me alone two months, that I may go up and down upon the mountains, and *bewail my virginity*, I and my fellows'.

39 And it came to pass at the end of two months, that she returned unto her father, who did with her *according* to his vow which he had vowed: *and she knew no man*. And it was a custom in Israel,

"After Jephthah had fulfilled his vow of '*sacrificing his daughter*', the text states that '*she knew no man*' (v. 39)".

"It is widely accepted by most Biblical scholars that Jephthah's vow was fulfilled by '*committing his daughter to a life without marriage and children*' (The sacrifice), hence the phrase "she knew no man." This would have been devastating indeed, for in that day marriage and children were critical parts of a woman's life. Likewise, it would have been devastating for Jephthah, as she was his only child, and he would have no more posterity because of his rash vow." [570]

End Quote

Now before I leave this topic, let me suggest to those of my readers who would like to get an even deeper understanding of what appears to be a *harsh history* of the God of the Old Testament, that you take the time to do a search for the topic titled "Understanding the Old Testament" on this website: www.churchofjesuschrist.org. It's the full article written by Edward J. Brandt, who's the director of the Evaluation Division of the Correlation of the Church of Jesus Christ of Latter-Day Saints and past President of the Columbus, Ohio Temple of The Church of Jesus Christ of Latter-Day Saints.

Here are just a few excerpts from Brother Brandt's article. I found them to be extremely helpful:

"Do you sometimes have difficulty understanding the Old Testament? Does the purpose of some of the book sometimes seems *veiled* to you? Do there seem to be *inconsistencies* in the record? If your response is 'yes', take heart; you're not alone. Yet the Old Testament doesn't really need to be as hard to understand as many think it is. Let's see if the following orientation is helpful.

Purpose of the Old Testament

"Many readers have not focused on the key fact that t*he Old Testament is primarily a witness of the Messiah—Jesus Christ*—who was known to the ancients as '*Jehovah*'. As President Spencer W. Kimball has said, "The Old Testament prophets from Adam to Malachi are testifying of the divinity of the Lord Jesus Christ and our Heavenly Father.

"Jesus Christ was the God of the Old Testament, and it was He who conversed with Abraham and Moses. It was He who inspired Isaiah and Jeremiah; it was He who foretold through those chosen men the happenings of the future, even to the latest day and hour" (*Ensign,* May 1977, p. 76).

"The Old Testament prophets witnessed of the reality of God and bore testimony that Jehovah was the Redeemer of the world throughout their record. This message from them about the future atonement of the Holy One of Israel is absolutely central to understanding the teachings in the Old Testament. Abinadi, an ancient American and pre-Christian prophet, also taught that all of the early prophets pointed to Jesus Christ:

Mosiah 13:33

33 For behold, did not Moses prophesy unto them concerning the coming of the Messiah, and that God should redeem his people? Yea, and even all the prophets who have prophesied ever since the world began—have they not spoken more or less concerning these things?

"Nephi's brother Jacob explained his own purpose—and, indeed, the purpose of all the ancient prophets—for writing what they did in their records:

Jacob 4:4

4 For this intent have we written these things, that they may know that we knew of Christ, and we had a hope of his glory many hundred years before his coming; and not only we ourselves had a hope of his glory, but also all the holy prophets which were before us.

"Even the Mosaic covenant—which, because of its many complex laws, often baffles and discourages Old Testament readers—is a specific, direct testimony of Jesus Christ. Jacob understood this:

II Nephi 11:4

4 My soul delighteth in proving unto my people the truth of the coming of Christ; for, for this end hath the law of Moses been given; and all things which have been given of God from the beginning of the world, unto man, are the typifying of him.

"If we keep this point in mind while reading the Old Testament, some of the more obscure parts of the record can become clearer to us. And just as importantly, events that have far-reaching, religious meaning in addition to their surface-level, literal meaning can become more significant.

"For example, when the 'Passover' feast was established, its immediate purpose was to remind ancient Israel of the time the destroying angel passed over the prepared, obedient Israelites in Moses's day. It also was a reminder of the redemption of Israel from the bondage of Egypt. Please keep in mind that the main purpose of the Old Testament is to testify of the Redeemer. As you do you will see *a Messianic theme* in this *ordinance*—the anticipated redemption of mankind by the Savior.

"The feast required a "lamb ... without blemish" which was to be completely consumed—a foreshadowing of "the Lamb of God, which taketh away the sin of the world" with "an infinite atonement".

Exodus 12:5

5 Your lamb shall be without blemish, a male of the first year: ye shall take *it* out from the sheep, or from the goats:

Exodus 12:4, 9–10

4 And if the household be too little for the lamb, let him and his neighbour next unto his house take *it* according to the number of the souls; every man according to his eating shall make your count for the lamb.

9 Eat not of it raw, nor sodden at all with water, but roast *with* fire; his head with his legs, and with the purtenance thereof.

10 And ye shall let nothing of it remain until the morning; and that which remaineth of it until the morning ye shall burn with fire.

John 1:29

29 The next day John seeth Jesus coming unto him, and saith, Behold the Lamb of God, which taketh away the sin of the world.

II Nephi 9:7

7 Wherefore, it must needs be an infinite atonement—save it should be an infinite atonement this corruption could not put on incorruption. Wherefore, the first judgment which came upon man must needs have remained to an endless duration. And if so, this flesh must have laid down to rot and to crumble to its mother earth, to rise no more.

"Further, the prescribed order required that the lamb's blood be placed as a sign on the lintel and doorposts of the places where true 'Passover' celebrants met.

Exodus 12:7

7 And they shall take of the blood and strike *it* on the two side posts and on the upper door post of the houses, wherein they shall eat it.

"This procedure takes on much greater meaning *when understood in the light of the Messianic mission*—it is a reminder that *personal redemption can be had only through the blood of the Anointed One, Christ*. Peter taught the Saints of former times that redemption comes only "with the precious blood of Christ, as of a lamb without blemish and without spot". And Paul testified that "Christ our 'Passover' is sacrificed for us".

1 Peter 1:19

19 But with the precious blood of Christ, as of a lamb without blemish and without spot:

1 Corinthians 5:7

7 Purge out therefore the old leaven, that ye may be a new lump, as ye are unleavened. For even Christ our passover is sacrificed for us:

"Readers are sometimes distracted from the Old Testament's important themes by what they consider inconsistencies in the *nature* of God or in *his manner of dealing with his children*. But I have found that these problems are usually caused by *incorrect interpretations* instead of caused by the record itself. And I've also found that most supposed inconsistencies can be resolved by *careful study*—sometimes aided by resources such as the Book of Mormon, trusted biblical commentaries and dictionaries, and the many *'study helps'* found in the new LDS edition of the King James Version of the Bible.

"The Book of Mormon can provide much helpful commentary on many Old Testament topics because the Nephites had an "Old Testament" record that was *more complete* than our current version is—the brass plates. Nephi tells us that our Bible is "a record like unto the engravings which are upon the plates of brass, save there are not so many", and he explains that the brass plates "did contain the five books of Moses, which gave an account of the creation of the world, and also of Adam and Eve, who were our first parents:

I Nephi 13:23

24 And the angel of the Lord said unto me: Thou hast beheld that the book proceeded forth from the mouth of a Jew; and when it proceeded forth from the mouth of a Jew it contained the fulness of the gospel of the Lord, of whom the Twelve Apostles bear record; and they bear record according to the truth which is in the Lamb of God.

I Nephi 5:11–13

11 And he beheld that they did contain the five books of Moses, which gave an account of the creation of the world, and also of Adam and Eve, who were our first parents;

12 And also a record of the Jews from the beginning, even down to the commencement of the reign of Zedekiah, king of Judah;

13 And also the prophecies of the holy prophets, from the beginning, even down to the commencement of the reign of Zedekiah; and also many prophecies which have been spoken by the mouth of Jeremiah.

"The Prophet Joseph Smith similarly indicated that "many important points touching the salvation of man, *had been taken from the Bible, or lost* before it was compiled" (*History of the Church,* 1:245).

"It is important to remember, too, that *the Old Testament doesn't even pretend to be a complete history*, an exhaustive chronicle of everything that transpired from the days of Adam to the birth of Jesus Christ. Often it includes only brief overviews to provide continuity to the overall general history of those centuries. Within this broad framework are found narratives of lesser and of greater detail. The four hundred years of the Israelites' sojourn in Egypt, for example, are passed over in just a few verses, with few details—*but the details surrounding their forty years in the wilderness cover over two hundred pages.*

"Old Testament *students* should remember, therefore, that what is contained in the writings is true, but often not complete in historical detail. Inherent in this type of history is the possibility that *parts of the record are treated with insufficient detail and could easily be misinterpreted.* Readers should keep this in mind, and not jump too hastily to conclusions (Some of the record of the Old Testament has also had some mistranslations that have to be considered as well).

Let's look at two areas in the Old Testament that commonly cause concern in readers, just as they have in Richard's mind.

"God's anger. Some readers complain that the supposed harsh, vengeful Old Testament God Jehovah, seems inconsistent with the loving, peaceful God Jesus, of the New Testament. The scales of justice and mercy seem to be out of balance.

"I feel that the reason people misconstrue the anger of the Lord is that they tend to assume that God's anger is identical to their own as fallen mortals—they don't *correctly understand the nature of 'divine anger'* (Nor do they understand what brings about the righteous indignation of God).

"Lehi gives us a more correct definition of *righteous anger.* When Laman and Lemuel complained of Nephi's anger toward them, Lehi explains:

II Ne. 1:26

26 And ye have murmured because he hath been plain unto you. Ye say that he hath used sharpness; ye say that he hath been angry with you; but behold, his sharpness was the sharpness of the power of the word of God, which was in him; and that which ye call anger was the truth, according to that which is in God, which he could not restrain, manifesting boldly concerning your iniquities.

"The *"anger"* of the Lord, then, is *"the truth of God's justice manifested against the disobedient".* When individuals are not in harmony with the eternal principles of justice and accountability, *they may perceive* the revelation of that truth (through God or his prophets) *as anger or harshness.*

I Nephi 16:2

2 And it came to pass that I said unto them that I knew that I had spoken hard things against the wicked, according to the truth; and the righteous have I justified, and testified that they should be lifted up at the last day; wherefore, the guilty taketh the truth to be hard, for it cutteth them to the very center.

"The guilty taketh the truth to be hard," Nephi said, *"for it cutteth them to the very center".* This was often the response of the rebellious Israelites to the consequences of their breach of eternal laws— laws which God is bound by and which he administers in long-suffering, mercy, and love.

(I want to interject a few a comments here regarding God's anger and Richard's comments on it where he said, "God is the most unpleasant character in all fiction. God is jealous and proud of it; petty, unjust, unforgiving; a control freak; *a vindictive, blood thirsty ethnic cleanser*; a misogynistic, homophobic racist; *an infanticidal, genocidal*, filicidal, pestilential, megalomaniacal, sadomasochist, capriciously malevolent bully", and, "You'd think an omnipotent God would adopt a slightly more targeted approach to zapping sinner's, such as a judicious heart attack, perhaps, *rather than the wholesale destruction of an entire city."*

Richard and his atheist friends, and I would even include some theists, who, like their atheist counterparts, do not understand what is called the "Righteous Indignation of God" and why He would wipe out an entire nation, or society from off the face of the earth, including women and children, and because of this lack of understanding, they view Jehovah as an angry God. In answer to this criticism, I call my readers attention to a YouTube video titled, "How Bad Does It Need to Get Before the Second Coming - Agency is the Key". Watch it for a full overview and one possible answer to this question.)

(I am going to share just a few thoughts from this video, in the hope that you, my readers, will be motivated to watch it in its entirety. The Lord's prophets, both past and present, have continually forewarned that God is going to destroy the wicked at the time of His Son's 2nd coming, and so the question becomes, "Why this wholesale sweeping out of existence of humanity? Why is God so angry with "mans' *poky little sins"*, as Richard called them? The following scriptures describe this forewarning and the reasons for God's *righteous indignation* towards the wicked. The prophet Nephi is speaking:)

II Nephi 28:16

16 Wo unto them that turn aside the just for a thing of naught and revile against that which is good, and say that it is of no worth! For the day shall come that the Lord God will speedily visit the inhabitants of the earth; and in that day that they are *'fully ripe'* in iniquity they shall perish.

The prophet Ether said something very similar:

Ether 2:15

15 And the brother of Jared repented of the evil which he had done and did call upon the name of the Lord for his brethren who were with him. And the Lord said unto him: I will forgive thee and thy brethren of their sins; but thou shalt not sin any more, for ye shall remember that my Spirit will not always strive with man; wherefore, if ye will sin *until ye are 'fully ripe'* ye shall be cut off from the presence of the Lord. And these are my thoughts upon the land which I shall give you for your inheritance; for it shall be a land choice above all other lands.

Alma 37:31

31 Yea, and cursed be the land forever and ever unto those *workers of darkness* and secret combinations, even unto destruction, *except* they repent before they are *'fully ripe'*.

(The 3rd President of the Church of Jesus Christ of Latter-Day Saints, Elder John Taylor, said: "After Noah had preached the gospel to the antediluvian world, and *after their 'cup of iniquity' was full;* and Zion and her cries had fled, *then* followed the judgement of God; *then* came desolation and destruction. *And why this wholesale sweeping out of the existence of humanity? To stop them from propagating a corrupt species.* Was that not right? Yes, it was. He said, "I will cut them off"; I will *prepare a prison for them,* in which they shall be confined for generations, (See I Peter 3:19-21) where they shall not have power to propagate their species; *for the pure spirits in the eternal world shall not be contaminated with their (The wicked) corruptions.* I will take them off the earth, and I will raise up another people. And He did do it" - JD 20:109 John Taylor).

(The justice of God requires that His children, sent from the eternal world to live here on earth, have the opportunity to exercise their *gift of moral agency* so that they can progress to live with Him again. When a society's wickedness has become so bad that it becomes *agency-destroying*, meaning that 'it's so bad that their little children, even before they reach the age of accountability, are so conditioned by evil surrounding them that they've already chosen their wicked parent's ideology, so that they do not have the opposite choice of righteousness before them', this is when the people's *cup of iniquity* is overflowing. This is when their society has become *fully ripe* and ready for destruction. I suggest you view the YouTube video titled "Drag Queens Reading to Kids in the Libraries" as just one example of how this state of wickedness is being pushed upon our children by wicked groomers of sin).

"God's favorites. Another complaint of some Old Testament readers is that God seems to have favorites—that he appears partial to some people. One common interpretation, for example, is that the young boy Joseph was unjustly favored over all the other sons of Israel—that his brothers had good reason to resent his dreams of superiority over them. However, the record reports that the brothers were involved with evil, and that Joseph, like Nephi in the Book of Mormon, earned the rights and blessings because of his faithfulness and his acquired birthright.

Genesis 37:2

2 These *are* the generations of Jacob. Joseph being *seventeen years old* was feeding the flock with his brethren; and the lad *was* with the sons of Bilhah, and with the sons of Zilpah, his father's wives: and Joseph brought unto his father *their evil report.*

"Jacob (Israel) could have said to his sons what Lehi said to Laman and Lemuel: "Ye have accused him [your brother] that he sought power and authority over you; … but I know that he hath not sought for power nor authority over you, but he hath sought the glory of God, and your own eternal welfare".

2 Ne. 1:25

25 And I exceedingly fear and tremble because of you, lest he shall suffer again; for behold, ye have accused him that he sought power and authority over you; but I know that he hath not sought for power nor authority over you, but he hath sought the glory of God, and your own eternal welfare.

"Joseph and Nephi were blessed because of their righteousness; their brothers were rejected because of their transgressions. Laman and Lemuel never did repent, but Joseph's brothers, long burdened with the guilt of their actions and feelings towards their brother, ... came to accept Joseph's foreordained presidency over them (In other words they repented).

"Another example of so-called favoritism is that Jacob appears to have stolen the birthright from his brother, Esau—that he received it unjustly through deceit and trickery. But what does the scriptural record say concerning this matter? The record indicates that Esau not only sold his birthright, but *"despised"* it, and that he further disqualified himself for these blessings by marrying nonbelievers which were a grief of mind unto Isaac and Rebekah.

Genesis 25:34

34 Then Jacob gave Esau bread and pottage of lentiles; and he did eat and drink, and rose up, and went his way: thus Esau despised *his* birthright.

"When the time came for Isaac to bless his two sons, Rebekah, who learned through a revelation she had received that Jacob was to rule over his brother, went against the 'cultural tradition' and helped Jacob, the younger son, receive the blessing.

Genesis 25:23

23 And the LORD said unto her, Two nations *are* in thy womb, and two manner of people shall be separated from thy bowels; and *the one* people shall be stronger than *the other* people; and the *elder shall serve the younger*.

"When Esau came to claim his blessing, Isaac realized that the important rights of priesthood presidency did, in fact, belong to faithful Jacob, *not to unworthy Esau*:

Genesis 27:33

33 And Isaac trembled very exceedingly, and said, Who? where *is* he that hath taken venison, and brought *it* me, and I have eaten of all before thou camest, and have blessed him? yea, *and* he shall be blessed.

"Yea," said Isaac, "and he shall be blessed". If the prophet-patriarch had acted improperly, he had the priesthood right to *revoke* Jacob's blessing. But he didn't do so, knowing that he had done the will of the Lord. *Perceiving that Esau's concern was for the loss of the temporal gain instead of spiritual blessings*, Isaac promised him prosperity, but he also reaffirmed the blessing of Jacob.

Genesis 27:37–40

37 And Isaac answered and said unto Esau, Behold, I have made him thy lord, and all his brethren have I given to him for servants; and with corn and wine have I sustained him: and what shall I do now unto thee, my son?

38 And Esau said unto his father, Hast thou but one blessing, my father? bless me, *even* me also, O my father. And Esau lifted up his voice, and wept.

39 And Isaac his father answered and said unto him, Behold, thy dwelling shall be the fatness of the earth, and of the dew of heaven from above;

40 And by thy sword shalt thou live, and shalt serve thy brother; and it shall come to pass when thou shalt have the dominion, that thou shalt break his yoke from off thy neck.

"Another problem: What is the justification for the destruction of the people in the land of Canaan by the children of Israel returning from Egypt? Although the land had been *promised to Abraham centuries earlier*, the people living there in Joshua's day had possessed it since Jacob and his family departed. What right did the Israelites have to drive out its inhabitants upon their return? Why did the Canaanites have to be destroyed as a people? Should such drastic consequences come upon people who seemingly were ignorant of the teachings or moral standards of Israel's God?

"Abraham and Isaac had negotiated peace with their neighbors and had purchased property in the land. The Lord told Abraham that the iniquity of the Amorites who possessed it was 'not yet full'. But how iniquitous were they *over four hundred years later* when the children of Israel returned? Did they deserve the treatment they received?

Genesis 15:16

16 But in the fourth generation they shall come hither again: for the iniquity of the Amorites is not yet *full*.

"The facts are that the people who possessed the land were obsessed with licentiousness, incest, adultery, same-gender attraction, bestiality, and even human sacrifice.

Leviticus 18:1–24

1 And the LORD spake unto Moses, saying,

2 Speak unto the children of Israel, and say unto them, I am the LORD your God.

3 After the doings of the land of Egypt, wherein ye dwelt, shall ye not do: and after the *doings* of the land of Canaan, whither I bring you, shall ye *not* do: neither shall ye walk in their ordinances.

4 Ye shall *do* my judgments, and keep mine ordinances, to walk therein: I am the Lord your God.

5 Ye shall therefore keep my statutes, and my judgments: which if a man do, he shall live in them: I *am* the LORD.

6 None of you shall approach to any that is near of kin to him, to uncover *their* nakedness: I *am* the LORD.

7 The nakedness of thy father, or the nakedness of thy mother, shalt thou not uncover: she *is* thy mother; thou shalt not uncover her nakedness.

8 The nakedness of thy father's wife shalt thou not uncover: it is thy father's nakedness.

9 The nakedness of thy sister, the daughter of thy father, or daughter of thy mother, whether she be born at home, or born abroad, even their nakedness thou shalt not uncover.

10 The nakedness of thy son's daughter, or of thy daughter's daughter, *even* their nakedness thou shalt not uncover: for theirs is thine own nakedness.

11 The nakedness of thy father's wife's daughter, begotten of thy father, she is thy sister, thou shalt not uncover her nakedness.

12 Thou shalt not uncover the nakedness of thy father's sister: she *is* thy father's near kinswoman.

13 Thou shalt not uncover the nakedness of thy mother's sister: for she is thy mother's near kinswoman.

14 Thou shalt not uncover the nakedness of thy father's brother, thou shalt not approach to his wife: she is thine aunt.

15 Thou shalt not uncover the nakedness of thy daughter in law: she is thy son's wife; thou shalt not uncover her nakedness.

16 Thou shalt not uncover the nakedness of thy brother's wife: it is thy brother's nakedness.

17 Thou shalt not uncover the nakedness of a woman and her daughter, neither shalt thou take her son's daughter, or her daughter's daughter, to uncover her nakedness; for they are her near kinswomen: it is wickedness.

18 Neither shalt thou take a wife to her sister, to vex her, to uncover her nakedness, beside the other in her lifetime.

19 Also thou shalt not approach unto a woman to uncover her nakedness, as long as she is put apart for her uncleanness.

20 Moreover thou shalt not *lie carnally* with thy neighbour's wife, to defile thyself with her.

21 And thou shalt not let any of thy seed *pass through the fire* to Molech, neither shalt thou *profane the name of thy God*: I *am* the LORD.

22 Thou shalt not *lie with mankind, as with womankind: it is abomination*.

23 Neither shalt thou *lie with any beast* to defile thyself there-with: neither shall any woman stand before a beast *to lie down thereto*: it *is* confusion.

24 Defile not ye yourselves in any of these things: *for in all these the nations are defiled which I cast out before you:*

Deuteronomy 12:31

31 Thou shalt not do so unto the LORD thy God: for every abomination to the LORD, which he hateth, *have they done unto their gods*; for even their sons and their daughters they have *burnt in the fire* to their gods.

"These unnatural practices brought the consequences required by *eternal law*. As the Lord declared, "The land is defiled: therefore, I do visit the iniquity thereof upon it, and the land itself vomiteth out her inhabitants".

Leviticus 18:25

25 And the land is defiled: therefore I do visit the iniquity thereof upon it, and the land itself vomiteth out her inhabitants.

"But how extensively must iniquity abound until a *'fulness of accountability'* is required by the Lord? Again, the Book of Mormon provides valuable information:

Helaman 13:14

14 But behold, it is for the righteous' sake that it is spared. But behold, the time cometh, saith the Lord, that *when ye shall cast out the righteous from among you, then shall ye be ripe for destruction*; yea, wo be unto this great city, because of the wickedness and abominations which are in her.

II Nephi 26:3

3 And after the Messiah shall come there shall be signs given unto my people of his birth, and also of his death and resurrection; and great and terrible shall that day be unto the wicked, for they shall perish; and they perish because they cast out the prophets, and the saints, and stone them, and slay them; wherefore the cry of the blood of the saints shall ascend up to God from the ground against them.

"The Book of Mormon also provides specific commentary about the driving out of the peoples of the land of Canaan:

I Nephi 17:32–35

32 And after they had crossed the river Jordan he did make them mighty unto the *driving out of the children of the land*, yea, unto the scattering them to destruction.

33 And now, do ye suppose that the children of this land, who were in the land of promise (the land of Canaan), who were driven out by our fathers, do ye suppose that they were righteous? Behold, I say unto you, Nay.

34 Do ye suppose that our fathers would have been more choice than they if they had been righteous? I say unto you, Nay.

35 Behold, *the Lord esteemeth all flesh in one*; he that is righteous is favored of God. But behold, this people had *rejected every word of God*, and *they were ripe in iniquity*; and the fulness of the wrath of God was upon them; and the Lord did curse the land against them, and bless it unto our fathers; yea, he did curse it against them unto their destruction, and he did bless it unto our fathers unto their obtaining power over it.

"They had *"rejected every word of God"* and were *"ripe in iniquity"*. They were a warned, a rebellious, and an accountable people—and they brought the rewards of unrighteousness upon their own heads. These three examples of God's "favoritism" illustrate the fact that God is, indeed, a *just* God and that his dealings with men *are based on their own righteousness and obedience*. The Apostle Paul said that:

2 Corinthians 3:14–16

14 But their minds were blinded: *for until this day remaineth the same veil untaken away in the reading of the old testament*; which *veil* is done away in Christ.

15 But even unto this day, when Moses is read, *the veil is upon their heart.*

16 Nevertheless when *it* shall turn to the Lord, the veil shall be taken away.

"Although there are difficulties in understanding the Old Testament, when we carefully study it in the spirit of its purpose, the record blesses our lives with testimony, teachings, insight, and examples of great worth." [571]

End of Article by Edward J. Brandt

For those readers who would like to get even further insight into who the God of the New Testament was, I suggest that you find a copy of Elder Bruce R. McConkie's book *"The Promised Messiah: The First Coming of Christ"*. This volume (One of five volumes in the series) presents a careful analysis of those prophecies concerning the first Coming of the Lord. As you read it, it becomes evident that *the fulness of God's everlasting gospel has been available to men in every age*, and that the Plan of Salvation and Happiness is eternal and unchanging from century to century. The Lord said that He is "the same yesterday, today, and Forever."

Richard's main point in sharing the Bible stories he deems horrific, is that "Morality, wherever else it comes from, does not come from the Bible." [572]

He continues later in this same chapter, "The Bible is held up to us as the source of our 'morality'." Richard exclaims, "What makes my jaw drop is that people today should base their lives on such an *appalling role model as Yahweh* (Jehovah, the God of the Old Testament, who later was known as Jesus of Nazareth in the New Testament) – and even worse, that they should bossily try to force the same *evil monster* (Whether fact or fiction) on the rest of us." [573]

After quoting Steven Weinberg, American physicist, and Blaine Pascal, a French mathematician, physicist, inventor, writer, philosopher, and Catholic theologian, both of which were quite critical of religion, Richard goes on to say:

"My main purpose here has been to show that we shouldn't get our morals from scripture. My purpose has been to demonstrate that we, as a matter of fact, *don't* get our morals from scripture" [574]

Again, this is just Richard's opinion. In response to Richard's opinion, I will repeat that I do not believe or say that we get our *moral sense* or our idea of morality from the scriptures *alone*. We get it directly from God, for it is His perfect morality that He operates by, and He is the *objective standard* for all morality. Our next topic is the subtitle – "Is the New Testament any better?"

IS THE NEW TESTAMENT ANY BETTER?

Richard begins this subtitle by holding up Jesus as an example of his belief that, "We do not and should not derive our morals from scripture." Here's the full quote:

"The moral superiority of Jesus precisely bears out my point. Jesus was not content to derive his ethics from the scriptures of his upbringing. He explicitly departed from them, for example when he deflated the dire warnings about breaking the sabbath. *'The sabbath was made for man, not man for the sabbath'*, has been generalized into a proverb. Since a principal thesis of this chapter is that we do not, and should not, derive our morals from scripture, Jesus has to be honored as a model for that thesis." [575]

I have to say that the example that Richard uses here about the Sabbath Day, proves my point about the religionists of Jesus' Day being in full blown apostasy. It proves that the writings of the prophets, the only scripture the Jews had available to them at the time of Jesus' ministry, had been misinterpreted by the religionists, the Pharisees and Sanhedrin's, due to apostasy (The only scripture the Jews had was known among the Jews as TaNaKh, an acronym derived from the names of its three divisions: Torah (Instruction, or Law, also called the Pentateuch), Nevi'im (Prophets), and Ketuvim (Writings)).

The Torah contained five books: Genesis, Exodus, Leviticus, Numbers, and Deuteronomy. In the Hebrew Bible, Psalms begins the third and last section of the biblical canon, known as Ketuvim (the Writings). The New Testament writers had not yet written down their letters yet, and so these were the only available scriptures for the Jews. Just like there are parts of the Bible that have been misinterpreted, Richard's story affirms that Jesus was correcting those misinterpretations. Jesus, the Jehovah of the Old Testament, was in fact the author and giver of The Law and thus these ancient scriptures. He was the Great I Am, whose law was contained in the ancient scriptures.

Jesus was simply correcting them by quoting the errors caused by apostasy. Now before you start thinking that Richard has changed his mind and is now a true fan of Jesus and His ministry, listen to what he says about Jesus next. Listen to this:

"Jesus encouraged his disciples to abandon their families to follow him. 'If any man come to me and hate not his father, and mother, and wife, and children, and brethren, and sisters, yea, and his own life also, he cannot be my disciple'." [576]

Richard adds a stinger to this last quote by quoting an American comedian Julia Sweeney who expressed her bewilderment in her one-woman stage show, 'Letting Go of God'. Here's what she said:

"Isn't that what cults do? They get you to reject your family in order to inculcate you?" [577]

Once again, Richard is revealing his lack of spiritual knowledge and understanding of spiritual principles expressed in the scriptures. In response to Richard's effort to take down Jesus as the moral authority, let me quote the 6th President of The Church of Jesus Christ of Latter-Day Saints, Joseph Fielding Smith (1970 - 1972). President Smith said the following, and I quote:

"To say that his disciples must *hate all that is dear to them* is surely a hard saying. But we discover, from other interpretations of the doctrine, the meaning is that anyone who *loves* his father, mother, wife, and all that is dear to him, even his own life, *more than he loves Christ*, is not worthy of him and cannot be his disciple. Here's Jesus own words as they're found in the New Testament:

Matthew 10:37-38

37 He that loveth father or mother *more than* me is not worthy of me: and he that loveth son or daughter *more than* me is not worthy of me.

38 And he that taketh not his cross, and followeth after me, is not worthy of me.

"The thought is very clear in this instruction that all who seek eternal life are required to come to Christ and *be willing to give up all that they possess, if necessary*. Should they be unwilling to do so, *even to the laying down of one's life in his cause*, then they are not worthy of his kingdom. This is reasonable; no unjust demand is made by our Savior, *for he came and laid down his life for us* that we might have life everlasting. He suffered for us; "*should we not love him more than we love our own lives?*" [578]

End of Quote by President Josepf Fielding Smith

Richard continues by saying, "There are other teachings in the New Testament that no good person should support." [579] Richard is referring to the central doctrine of Christianity, which is the atonement for original sin. Richard states, "This teaching, which lies at the heart of New Testament theology, is almost as obnoxious as the story of Abraham setting out to barbeque Isaac (Barbeque? That little comment made me chuckle out loud. Ha-ha-ha. Richard, you do some funny wordsmithing). Original sin itself comes straight from the Old Testament *myth* of Adam and Eve." [580]

Once again, Richard is showing his lack of understanding and spiritual maturity regarding spiritual things, especially what the Word of God says about the atonement in particular. The following is a brief overview of this topic as it's found on the website www.churchofjesuschrist.org. The topic is titled "The Fulness of the Gospel:

The Fall of Adam and Eve

Here are just a few excerpts to help us understand this doctrines of the 'Law of Consecration', and especially the principles undergirding the doctrine of 'Atonement' a little more fully and broadly:

"Most Christian churches teach that the Fall was a tragedy, that if Adam and Eve had not partaken of the forbidden fruit, they and all their posterity could now be living in immortal bliss in the Garden of Eden. But the fulness of truth revealed to Latter-Day prophets teaches that the Fall was not a tragedy— without it, Adam and Eve would have had no posterity. Thus, the Fall was *a necessary step* in Heavenly Father's Plan to bring about the eternal happiness of His children.

No Death, No Posterity, No Progress.

II Nephi 2:22–25

22 "If Adam had not transgressed", Lehi taught his son Jacob, "he would not have fallen, but he would have remained in the garden of Eden. ...

23 And they would have had no children; wherefore they would have remained in a state of innocence, having no joy, for they knew no misery; doing no good, for they knew no sin."

24 But behold, all things have been done in the wisdom of him who knoweth all things.

25 Adam fell that men might be; and men are, that they might have joy.

"After Adam and Eve partook of the fruit of the tree of the knowledge of good and evil, their eyes were opened, and Eve expressed gladness at the opportunity their transgression made possible for Adam and her and their posterity to come:

Moses 5:11

11 "Were it not for our transgression we never should have had seed, and never should have known good and evil, and the joy of our redemption, and the eternal life which God giveth unto all the obedient".

"Partaking of the fruit brought mortality, with its many opportunities to choose between good and evil, and enabled Adam and Eve to bear children. Thus, *the Fall opened the door for Heavenly Father's children to come into the world, obtain physical bodies, and participate in "the Great Plan of Happiness"*:

Alma 42:8

8 Now behold, it was not expedient that man should be reclaimed from this temporal death, for that would destroy the great plan of happiness.

Alma 12:24

24 And we see that death comes upon mankind, yea, the death which has been spoken of by Amulek, which is the temporal death; nevertheless there was a space granted unto man in which he might repent; therefore this life became a probationary state; a time to prepare to meet God; a time to prepare for that endless state which has been spoken of by us, which is after the resurrection of the dead.

Transgression, Not Sin

"President Joseph Fielding Smith (1970–1972) said: "I never speak of the part Eve took in this Fall as a sin, nor do I accuse Adam of a sin. This was a *transgression* of the law, but *not* a sin, for it was something that Adam and Eve *had to do*!"

Regarding this *distinction*, Elder Dallin H. Oaks, a current member of the First Presidency of the Church observed, quote:

"This suggested *contrast* between a *sin* and a *transgression* reminds us of the careful wording in the second article of faith: 'We believe that men will be punished for their own *sins,* and not Adam's *transgression*' (emphasis added). It also echoes a familiar distinction in the law. Some acts, like murder, are crimes because they are *inherently wrong*. Other acts, like operating without a license, *are crimes only because they are legally prohibited*. Under these distinctions, the act that produced the Fall was *not a sin—inherently wrong*—but a *transgression—wrong because it was formally prohibited*. These words are not always used to denote something different, but this distinction seems meaningful in the circumstances of the Fall." [581]

End Quote by Elder Dallin Oaks

"Even though Adam and Eve had not sinned, because of their transgression, having gone against what God had prohibited them from doing, they had to face certain *consequences*, two of which were *spiritual death and physical death*. Physical death came to Adam and Eve at the end of their earthly lives, but *their spiritual death occurred as they were cast out of the Garden of Eden*, having been cut off from God's presence.

Alma 42:9

19 Now, if there was no law given—if a man murdered he should die—would he be afraid he would die if he should murder?

"Original Sin – The *result* of our first parents' transgression, was banishment from the presence of God and bringing physical death into the world." The majority ... [of Christians] maintain that every child born into this world is tainted with 'original sin,' or partakers of 'Adam's transgression' with its birth (Most of them believing that Adam and Eve's transgression was inherently wrong).

"The Church of Jesus Christ of Latter-Day Saints second Article of Faith contradicts this foolish and erroneous doctrine. *It's true that all descendants of Adam and Eve inherit certain effects from the Fall of Adam and Eve*, but because of the Atonement of Jesus Christ *we are held accountable only for our own sins and NOT Adam's transgression.*

"The prophets teach that children who die before the age of accountability are *'alive in Christ'* and have no need of repentance or baptism (Little children certainly cannot perform the act of repentance, a requirement for salvation, as they have no concept of it).

Moroni 8:12

12 But little children are alive in Christ, even from the foundation of the world; if not so, God is a partial God, and also a changeable God, and a respecter to persons; for how many little children have died without baptism!

Moroni 8:8–11

8 Listen to the words of Christ, your Redeemer, your Lord and your God. Behold, I came into the world not to call the righteous but sinners to repentance; the whole need no physician, but they that are sick; wherefore, little children are whole, for they are not capable of committing sin; wherefore the curse of Adam is taken from them in me, that it hath no power over them; and the law of ᵍcircumcision is done away in me.

9 And after this manner did the Holy Ghost manifest the word of God unto me; wherefore, my beloved son, I know that it is solemn mockery before God, that ye should baptize little children.

10 Behold I say unto you that this thing shall ye teach—repentance and baptism unto those who are accountable and capable of committing sin; yea, teach parents that they must repent and be baptized, and humble themselves as their little children, and they shall all be saved with their little children.

11 And their little children need no repentance, neither baptism. Behold, baptism is unto repentance to the fulfilling the commandments unto the remission of sins.

Commandments in the Garden

"The Lord gave Adam and Eve commandments in the Garden of Eden, two of which were to multiply and replenish the earth:

Genesis 1:28

28 And God blessed them, and God said unto them, Be fruitful, and multiply, and replenish the earth, and subdue it: and have dominion over the fish of the sea, and over the fowl of the air, and over every living thing that moveth upon the earth.

"And to not partake of the fruit of the tree of knowledge of good and evil:

Gen. 2:17

17 But of the tree of the knowledge of good and evil, thou shalt not eat of it: for in the day that thou eatest thereof thou shalt surely die.

"These commandments were designed to place Adam and Eve in a position where they had to make a choice. President Smith taught:

"*The Lord said to Adam that if he wished to remain as he was in the garden, then he was not to eat the fruit, but if he desired to eat it and partake of death, he was at liberty to do so.* Faced with this dilemma, Adam and Eve chose death—both physical and spiritual—which opened the door for themselves and their posterity to gain knowledge and experience and to participate in the Father's plan of happiness leading to eternal life. [582]

End of Topic Overview of "The Fulness of the Gospel: The Fall of Adam and Eve"

Richard continues, "The Christian focus is overwhelmingly on sin … sin … sin … sin … sin … sin. What a nasty little preoccupation to have dominating your life." [583] Richard, once again, quotes his fellow atheist Sam Harris, who said, speaking to the Christian Nation:

"Your principal concern appears to be that the Creator of the universe will take offense at something people do while naked. This prudery (being a prude) of yours contributes daily to the surplus of human misery." [584]

Next, Richard takes aim at the Atonement of Jesus. He says, and I quote:

"But now, the sadomasochism. God incarnated and executed in atonement of the *'hereditary'* sin of Adam. Ever since Paul expounded this repellent doctrine, Jesus has been worshipped as the redeemer of all our sins." [585]

I am going to respond to Richard's and Sam's lack of understanding of the doctrine of the Atonement and the "Law of Chastity", by sharing with you, my readers, the first of four parts on the doctrine of the "Atonement of Jesus Christ", written by Hugh Nibley, an American scholar and apologist of The Church of Jesus Christ of Latter-Day Saints, whom I quoted earlier in my book (See page 271). Hugh, as I said, was also a professor at Brigham Young University for nearly 50 years. Professor Nibley was a prolific author, and wrote apologetic works supporting the archaeological, linguistic, and historical claims of Joseph Smith. Hugh was an absolutely brilliant man. He was 94 at the time of his death on February 24th, 2005, and has been greatly missed. If you want to read parts 2–4 of Dr. Nibley's work on the Atonement you can find them at www.churchofjesuschrist.org.

Here's part 1, quote:

"The Atonement of Christ is nothing less than the answer to the great and terrible question that life inevitably poses: "*Is this all there is?*" If you are a saint (A baptized member of The Church of Jesus Christ of Latter-Day Saints), you know that this is a wicked world; if you are the most cynical and worldly unbeliever (Sam and Richard, listen up. Just teasing!), you still know by experience that it is a vicious one. It seems that everything we want here is either destructive or trivial.

Peter was not philosophizing or theologizing but stating the unpleasant facts when he said:

1 Peter 1:17–18

17 And if ye call on the Father, who without respect of persons judgeth according to every man's *work*, pass the time of your sojourning *here* in fear:

18 Forasmuch as ye know that ye were not redeemed with corruptible things, *as* silver and gold, from your vain conversation *received* by tradition from your fathers;

"In other words, "Go about [*anastrophe,* conduct yourselves] in fear during your transient stay, knowing that perishables like silver and gold cannot free you from the futile way of life of your fathers." (Author's translation) Thus, he concludes his comment:

1 Peter 1:24–25

24 For all flesh *is* as grass, and all the glory of man as the flower of grass. The grass withereth, and the flower thereof falleth away:

25 But the word of the Lord endureth forever. And this is the word which by the gospel is preached unto you.

"Between these two statements of the problem, Peter gives us another choice; there is an order of things which goes back "*before the foundation of the world*" and is now emerging again to our advantage— "manifest in these last times for you."

1 Peter 1:20

20 Who verily was foreordained before the foundation of the world, but was manifest in these last times for you.

"It is the carrying out of the Atonement, for which the law of Moses was a preparation.

The Good News

"Jacob, in the Book of Mormon, goes right to the point. The problem is:

II Nephi 9:4, 6

4 For I know that ye have searched much, many of you, to know of things to come; wherefore I know that ye know that *our flesh must waste away and die; nevertheless, in our ᵇbodies we shall see God.*

6 For as death hath passed upon all men, to fulfil the merciful plan of the great Creator, *there must needs be a power of resurrection*, and the resurrection must needs come unto man by reason of the fall; and the fall came by reason of transgression; and because man became fallen they were cut off from the presence of the Lord.

"And without the resurrection, death becomes final:

II Nephi 9:7

7 Wherefore, it must needs be an *infinite atonement*—save it should be an infinite atonement this corruption could not put on incorruption. Wherefore, the *"first judgment"* which came upon man must needs have remained to an endless duration. And if so, this flesh must have laid down to rot and to crumble to its mother earth, to rise no more.

"And what is to stop it? Jacob grasps the situation: "There must needs be a *power*," he says, "a power of resurrection," and such a power has indeed been provided, "to fulfil the merciful plan of the great Creator":

II Nephi 9:6

6 For as death hath passed upon all men, to fulfil the merciful plan of the great Creator, there must needs be a power of resurrection, and the resurrection must needs come unto man by reason of the fall; and the fall came by reason of transgression; and because man became fallen they were cut off from the presence of the Lord.

"What a comfort to know that things are under control after all. *The Fall has put us into a state of corruption* in which it would be disastrous to remain if man should "put forth his hand and partake also of the tree of life and eat and live forever [in his sins]":

Moses 4:28

28 And I, the Lord God, said unto mine Only Begotten: Behold, the man is become as one of us *to know good and evil*; and now lest he put forth his hand and partake also of the tree of life, and eat and live forever,

"Nobody wants to live forever in a sewer, yet according to Shakespeare, even that is preferable to the alternative: 'The weariest and most loathed worldly life that age, ache, penury, and imprisonment can lay on nature, *is a paradise to what we fear of death*'. But it doesn't have to be that way. That is just the point. The Atonement makes available the only kind of lasting life worth having. The great Christian tract on the Atonement, *Paul's epistle to the Hebrews*, begins with an exhilarating prospect:

"God hath in these last days spoken unto us by his Son, whom he hath appointed heir of all things, by whom also he made the worlds; Who being the brightness of his glory, and the express image of his person, and upholding all things by the word of his power, when he had by himself purged our sins, sat down on the right hand of the Majesty on high":

Hebrews 1:1–3

1 God, who at sundry times and in divers manners spake in time past unto the fathers *by the prophets,*

2 Hath in these last days spoken unto us *by his Son*, whom he hath appointed heir of all things, by whom also he made the worlds;

3 Who being the brightness of *his* glory, and the express image of his person, and upholding all things by the word of his power, when he had by himself purged our sins, sat down on the right hand of the Majesty on high;

Atonement and Reconciliation

"People are usually surprised to learn that *atonement,* an accepted theological term, comes from neither a Greek nor a Latin word, but is good *old English* and really does mean, ... when we write it out, "at-*one*-ment," denoting both a state of *being "at one"* with another and the process by which that end is achieved. The word *atonement* appears only once in the New Testament in the King James Version, and in the Revised Standard Version it does not appear at all, the translators preferring the more familiar word *reconciliation* (See also footnote to Romans 5:11 in the LDS edition of the King James Version here):

Romans 5:11

11 And not only *so,* but we also joy in God through our Lord Jesus Christ, by whom we have now received the atonement.

"*Reconciliation* is a very good word for *atonement* there, since it means literally to be seated again with someone (*re-con-silio*)—so that atonement is to be reunited with God, just as Paul said:

"[The Lord] sat down on the right hand of the Majesty on High. The Greek word translated as "reconciliation" is *katallagein.* It is a business term, which the lexicon tells us means "*exchange, esp. of money; ... change from enmity to friendship, reconciliation; ... reconciliation of sinners with God.*"[2] It is the return to the status *ante quo,* whether as a making of peace or a settlement of debt. (The 'wages' of sin is death – Christ 'paid' the debt for all). The monetary metaphor is by far the most common, being the simplest and easiest to understand. Hence, frequently the word *redemption* literally means "to buy back"—that is, to reacquire something you owned previously. Thus, Moses said:

Deuteronomy 7:8

8 But because the LORD loved you, and because he would keep the oath which he had sworn unto your fathers, hath the LORD brought you out with a mighty hand, and redeemed you out of *the house of bondmen*, from the hand of Pharaoh king of Egypt.

"By redemption, someone has paid a price to get you off, restoring you to a former, happier condition. But the frequent use of the commercial analogy is not out of reverence for trade and commerce—just the opposite, in fact. *The redeemed are bought to clear them of all worldly obligation by paying off the world in its own currency, after which it has no further claim on the redeemed* (Justice has no more 'claim' on the redeemed). The Greek equivalent is *lutropins,* a ransoming. Paul tells the Saints to prepare for the salvation that has been made available by disengaging from this world:

Titus 2:12, 14

12 Teaching us that, denying ungodliness and worldly lusts, we should live soberly, righteously, and godly, in this present world;

14 Who gave himself for us, that he might redeem us from all iniquity, and purify unto himself a *peculiar people*, zealous of good works.—so that God "might redeem [*lutrosetai*] us from all iniquity and purify unto himself a peculiar people."

"Salvation likewise means "rescue" (*soteria,* also rendered "deliverance"). Another expression is "for a price," the word being *time,* "that which is paid in token or worth of value." He paid for us what he thought we were worth so he could join us with him. In the spirit of Article of Faith 8 ("We believe the Bible ... as far as it is translated correctly"), [A of F 1:8] a verse in Paul's letter to the Ephesians has always cried out for re-examination. The proposition actually reads like a business agreement, not binding but *releasing.* In whom we have bail [*apolutrosin*—our release pending the judgment] through his blood, the pardoning [*aphesin,* setting aside] of misdemeanors [*paraptomaton,* blunder, trespass] on consideration of the money [*ploutos*] of his generosity [*charitos*], which on our behalf has exceeded in all wisdom and understanding [*phronesei*]." (Author's translation from the Greek):

Ephesians 1:7–8

7 In whom we have redemption through his blood, the forgiveness of sins, according to the riches of his grace;

8 Wherein he hath abounded toward us in all wisdom and prudence;

Meanwhile, Paul counsels the Saints:

Ephesians 4:30, 32

30 And grieve not the holy Spirit of God, whereby ye are sealed unto the day of redemption [bought free, *apolutroseos*].

32 And be ye kind one to another, tenderhearted, forgiving one another, even as God for Christ's sake hath forgiven you.

"So, when the scriptures speak of atonement, it is always as re-conciliation, re-demption, resurrection, re-lease, salvation, and so on. *All refer to a return to a* former state."

Semitic Origins

"This theme is even more vividly and concretely expressed in the Hebrew terminology. In Semitic languages, where one root can have many meanings, the first rule is always to look for the basic or literal meaning of the word, which in Hebrew, Aramaic, and Arabic usually takes us back to early days and simple homely affairs of life in the desert or the countryside. One simple physical act often triggers a long line of derivatives—meanings which are perfectly reasonable if one takes the most obvious steps from one to the next, but which can end up miles from the starting-place.

"The basic word for atonement is *kafar,* which has the same basic meaning in Hebrew, Aramaic, and Arabic—that being *"to bend, arch over, cover; 2) [to pass over with one's palm &c., to wipe out, rub]* ... *to deny,* ... *to forgive,* ... *to be expiated,* ... *renounce."*

"The Arabic *kafara* puts the emphasis on a *tight squeeze,* such as tucking in the skirts, drawing a thing close to oneself. Closely related are Aramaic[4] and Arabic *kafata,*[5] meaning a close embrace, which are certainly related to the Egyptian *hpt,*[6] the common ritual embrace written with the ideogram of embracing arms. *Hpt* may be cognate with the Latin *capto*[7] and the Persian *kaftan,*[8] a monk's robe and hood completely embracing the body. Most interesting is the Arabic *kafata,*[9] as it is the key to a dramatic situation. It was the custom for one fleeing for his life in the desert to seek protection in the tent of a great sheik, crying out, "Ana dakhiluka," meaning "I am thy suppliant," whereupon the host would place the hem of his robe over the guest's shoulder and declare him under his protection. In one instance in the Book of Mormon we see Nephi fleeing from an evil enemy that is pursuing him. In great danger, he prays the Lord to give him an open road in the low way, to block his pursuers, and to make them stumble. He comes to the Lord as a suppliant:

II Nephi 4:33

33 O Lord, wilt thou encircle me around in *the robe of thy righteousness!* O Lord, wilt thou make a way for mine escape before mine enemies! (2 Ne. 4:33.)

"In reply, according to the ancient custom, the Master would then place the hem of his robe protectively over the kneeling man's shoulder (*kafata*). This puts him under the Lord's protection from all enemies. They embrace in a close hug, as Arab chiefs still do; the Lord makes a place for him and invites him to sit down beside him—they are at-one.

Alma 5:24

24 Behold, my brethren, do ye suppose that such an one can have a place to sit down in the kingdom of God, with Abraham, with Isaac, and with Jacob, and also all the holy prophets, whose garments are cleansed and are spotless, pure and white?

This is the imagery of the Atonement—the embrace:

II Nephi 1:15

15 But behold, the Lord hath redeemed my soul from hell; I have beheld his glory, and I am encircled about eternally *in the arms of his love.*

Alma 5:33

33 Behold, he sendeth an invitation unto all men, for the arms of mercy are extended towards them, and he saith: Repent, and I will receive you.

"This is the *hpt—the ritual embrace* that consummates the final escape from death in the Egyptian funerary texts and reliefs, where the son Horus is received into the arms of his father Osiris.

The Day of Atonement

"In Israel, when the sacrifices and sin offerings were completed on the Day of Atonement, the high priest went to the door of the *kapporet* to receive assurance from the Lord that He had accepted the offerings and repentance of the people and forgiven them their sins:

Exodus 29:42

42 "At the door of the tabernacle of the congregation before the Lord: where I will meet you, to speak there unto thee."

"The *kapporet* is usually assumed to be the lid of the ark of the covenant, yet it fits much better with the front, since one stands before it. The Septuagint, the old Greek text of the Bible, makes the verse clearer: "I will meet you *at the "door of the tent of the testimony in the presence of the Lord"*, on which occasion I shall make myself known to you that I might converse with you.

"The setting is clarified in the Gospel of Luke when Zacharias, a direct descendant of Aaron (as was also his wife), entered behind the veil into the Holy of Holies (*naon tou kuriou,* the *skene* or tent of the Old Testament) while people waited on the outside.

Luke 1:9–10

9 According to the custom of the priest's office, his lot was to burn incense when he went into the temple of the Lord.

10 And the whole multitude of the people were praying without at the time of incense.

"He did not meet the Lord, but rather his personal representative, a messenger of the Lord standing beside the altar, who identified himself as "Gabriel, that stand in the presence of God; and am sent to speak unto thee, and to shew thee these glad tidings."

Luke 1:11, 19

11 And there appeared unto him an angel of the Lord standing on the right side of the altar of incense.

19 And the angel answering said unto him, I am Gabriel, that stand in the presence of God; and am sent to speak unto thee, and to shew thee these glad tidings.

"The news was about *a great at-one-ment* that was to take place in which the children would "turn to the Lord their God" while the "hearts of the fathers" would be turned again [*epistrepsai*] "to the children, and the disobedient to the wisdom of the just; to make ready a people prepared for the Lord.

Luke 1:16–17

16 And many of the children of Israel shall he turn to the Lord their God.

17 And he shall go before him in the spirit and power of Elias, to turn the hearts of the fathers to the children, and the disobedient to the wisdom of the just; to make ready a people prepared for the Lord.

"It's all *a preparation for a great bringing together again* through the ordinance of baptism after they had been separated by the Fall:

Exodus 29:44–45

44 And I will sanctify the tabernacle of the congregation, and the altar: I will sanctify also both Aaron and his sons, to minister to me in the priest's office.

45 And I will dwell ᶜampong the children of Israel, and will be their God.

Jesus himself prayed on the eve of his crucifixion:

John 17:24

24 Father, I will that they also, whom thou hast given me, be with me where I am; that they may behold my glory, which thou hast given me: for thou lovest me before the foundation of the world.

They are going back to that premortal glory:

John 17:26

26 And I have declared unto them thy name, and will declare *it:* that the love where-with thou hast loved me may be in them, and I in them.

John 17:11

11 And now I am no more in the world, but these are in the world, and I come to thee. Holy Father, keep through thine own name those whom thou hast given me, that they may be ᵇone, as we *are.*

"Holy Father, keep [*tereo*] through thine own name those whom thou hast given me," in the King James Version; but in the Greek text, there is no direct object "whom," and the word *tereo* can mean to "*test by observation or trial.*" Instead, we have an instrumental dative, so in the spirit of Article of Faith 8, this verse could read, "*Holy Father, [test them on] thine own name [with which] thou hast given me, that they may be one, as we are one.*" [A of F 1:8]

This takes us back to the *kapporet,* for *only the high priest knew the name which he whispered for admission through the temple veil on the Day of Atonement.* It is understandable that the *kapporet* should be called the mercy seat, for *it was there*, in the most guarded and sacred part of the sanctuary, that Israel was reconciled *at-one* with God on the Day of Atonement. The apostle Paul said:

Hebrews 9:3, 5

3 And after the second veil, the tabernacle which is called the Holiest of all;

5 And over it the cherubims of glory shadowing the mercy seat; of which we cannot now speak particularly.

"Commenting on the ancient synagogue at Beth Alpha in Palestine, Erwin R. Goodenough notes, "The scene as designed shows the curtains drawn back at either side to disclose the objects behind them." The custom has persisted:

"In a synagogue the Torah shrine is still properly concealed by a curtain, but these curtains in the mosaic are not especially connected with the shrine: they serve when drawn to open up a whole stage, a whole world. ... So, the curtains have taken the place of the old carved screen which seemed to us to separate the world of man from heaven. ... Only the few were allowed to penetrate to the addition behind. ... The sense of distinction between the earthly and heavenly [was] still kept."

"Even more important than the idea that the veil introduces us into another realm is that "the curtains have also the value of suggesting the curtain in the Temple which separated the sanctuary from the world of ordinary life. And where does the Atonement motif come in? In a stock presentation found in early Jewish synagogues as well as on very early Christian murals, *"the hand of God is represented, but could not be called that explicitly, and instead of the heavenly utterance, the* bath kol *[echo, distant voice, whisper], is given."* From the hand "radiate beams of light." "To show the hand and light thus emerging from central darkness," writes Goodenough, "is as near as one could come in conservative Judaism to depicting God himself.

"In early Christian representations, *the hand of God reaching out of heaven is grasped by the human spirit who is being caught up into the presence of the Lord.*

To "Have Place" with God

"This yearly rite of atonement included the *teshuvah,* a *"return to God, repentance."* The prophets repeatedly *invite Israel to return to God*, who is waiting with open arms to receive them if only they will repent. They not only return and are welcomed in, but they also sit down. This is the yeshivah, "1) *sitting, rest,* 2) *settlement, dwelling, ...* 3) *... session, council, ...court."*

"The meanings all combine in the *Yeshivah shel ma^clah* or *Metivta de-Raki^ca* ("The Academy on High" or *"Academy of the Sky,"* respectively): Heaven (where the angels and the souls of the righteous are believed to dwell), a place of divine justice to which all will be summoned. The root *yashav* has the basic meaning of sitting or settling down to live in a place, *yashuv* "seated, [a] sitting." *You have a place because you have returned home.*

"All this we find in the Book of Mormon. Along with the embrace already mentioned, we find the formula "have place" used in exactly the same sense.

Alma 5:25 cf.

25 I say unto you, Nay; except ye make our Creator a liar from the beginning, or suppose that he is a liar from the beginning, *ye cannot suppose that such can have place in the kingdom of heaven*; but they shall be cast out for they are the children of the kingdom of the devil.

Mosiah 26:23–24 "a place at my right hand"

23 For it is I that taketh upon me the sins of the world; for it is I that hath created them; and it is I that granteth unto him that believeth unto the end a place at my right hand.

24 For behold, in my name are they called; and if they know me they shall come forth, and shall have a place eternally at my right hand.

Enos 1:27 ("there is a place prepared for you in the mansions of my Father.")

27 And I soon go to the place of my rest, which is with my Redeemer; for I know that in him I shall rest. And I rejoice in the day when my mortal shall put on immortality, and shall stand before him; then shall I see his face with pleasure, and he will say unto me: Come unto me, ye blessed, there is a place prepared for you in the mansions of my Father. Amen.

This is also the metaphor that Alma uses:

Alma 5:24, 27

24 Behold, my brethren, do ye suppose that such an one can have a place to sit down in the kingdom of God, with Abraham, with Isaac, and with Jacob, and also all the holy prophets, whose garments are cleansed and are spotless, pure and white?

27 Have ye walked, keeping yourselves blameless before God? Could ye say, if ye were called to die at this time, within yourselves, that ye have been sufficiently humble? That your garments have been cleansed and made white through the blood of Christ, who will come to redeem his people from their sins?

"Let us recall that it was on the Day of Atonement that the priest entered the tent and that the people's garments were all made white by the atoning sacrifice of the Lamb. The Book of Mormon is, of course, in the milieu of the old Hebrew rites before the destruction of Solomon's temple, for after that the ark and the covering (*kapporet*) no longer existed there, but the Holy of Holies was still called the *bait ha-kapporet.*

"*The loss of the old ceremonies* occurred shortly after Lehi left Jerusalem. "As long as the Temple stood," we read in the Talmud, "*the altar atoned for Israel, but now a man's table* [i.e., each man's temple] *atones for him.* Thus, the ordinances of atonement were, after Lehi's day, supplanted by allegory. Let us recall that Lehi and his people, who left Jerusalem in the very last days of Solomon's temple, were zealous in erecting altars of sacrifice and building temples of their own. It has often been claimed that the Book of Mormon cannot contain the "fulness of the gospel," since it does not mention *the temple ordinances.* As a matter of fact, *they are alluded to everywhere in the book if we know where to look for them,* and the dozen or so discourses on the Atonement in the Book of Mormon are replete with *temple imagery.* From all the Semitic variations of *kafar* (atonement), for example, we concluded that the literal meaning of the term is *a close and intimate embrace,* which took place at the *kapporet* or the front cover or flap of the tabernacle or tent. The Book of Mormon instances are quite clear:

Alma 5:33

33 "Behold, he sendeth an invitation unto all men, for the *arms of mercy are extended* towards them, and he saith: Repent, and *I will receive you.*"

II Nephi 1:15

15 "Behold, the Lord hath redeemed my soul from hell; I have beheld his glory, and *I am encircled about eternally in the arms of his love.*"

"To be redeemed is to be atoned. From this it should be clear *what kind of* oneness is meant by the Atonement—*it is being received by the Lord in a close embrace of the returning prodigal son, expressing not only forgiveness but 'oneness of heart and mind' that amounts to identity, like a literal family identity.* [586]

End of Part 1 on Atonement by Hugh Nibley

Richard finishes giving his critical rendition of the atonement by saying, "The story that Jesus had himself tortured and executed, in *vicarious punishment* for a symbolic sin committed by a non-existent individual (Adam), is barking mad." [587] I do appreciate Richard calling it a *vicarious act.* On more levels than I care to address however, Richard reveals his unschooled, spiritually stunted understanding of what he called the 'central doctrine' of Christianity – the Atonement. One statement, made by Richard, that I thought was particularly outrageous, due to the fact that he has no proven facts to say it, was, and I quote: "To cap it all, Adam, the supposed perpetrator of the original sin, never existed in the first place: an awkward *fact.*" [588]

Fact? Really Richard? Here again, is a stark example of why I called my book *An Atheist's Delusion.* Richard truly is delusional about these religious tenets. Like James R. Schlesinger said years ago, "Everyone is entitled to his own opinion, but not his own facts." [589]

I'm going to leave my perspectives' rebuttal to Richard's biased opinion on this most sacred of doctrines there, as I hope you've come to understand my point by now. In my mind, Richard is simply clueless, so it's easy to forgive his lack of understanding. Let's move on to the next subtitle – "Love thy neighbor".

LOVE THY NEIGHBOR

To begin this subtitle, Richard focuses, once again, on providing ammunition for shooting down the credibility of the Bible, and in particular the New Testament. Only in his delusional mind has he achieved delegitimizing the Old Testament. In trying to do delegitimize the New Testament, Richard reaches back, once again, into the Old Testament and brings forward the Canaanite question of "How do you reconcile certain scriptures in the Bible that appear to endorse genocide, pillage, and/or plunder?" I feel I have answered this already, but I'm going to go ahead and rebut Richards' efforts once again.

Richard begins his argument by mentioning a Black humorist named John Hartung, who tells of a study done by an Israeli psychologist George Tamarin, who also happens to be an atheist. Dr. Tamarin conducted a study of more than 1,000 Israeli schoolchildren between the ages of eight and fourteen, wherein he read to them the account of the battle of Jericho in the book of Joshua, and asked them:

"Do you think Joshua and the Israelites acted rightly or not?"

The verses said Joshua had 'utterly destroyed' all in the city, both men and women, young and old. To save time I won't go into all the breakdown of the answers given by each of the children who participated in the study, but suffice it to say that Richard felt that the results indicated that:

"The justification for the *genocidal massacre* by Joshua was religious in every case." And that, "It is a positive commandment to destroy the seven nations, as it is said: *Thou shalt utterly destroy them ... Thou shalt save alive nothing that breatheth."* [590]

Richard's point in bringing this bit of Israelite history up, was to point out that "It is religion that made the difference between children condemning genocide and condoning it." [591]

The most concerning point of Richard's conflating these points here, for me, is his blatant bias shown in the interpretations he uses to make his point. Richard uses '*his*' view of and '*his*' opinion of the "Canaanite question" as though it is "The truth, and nothing but the truth, so help me God", or should I say, "So help me, Darwin?" kind of argument. To save time I suggest you go to the YouTube video titled "Overview: Joshua" [592] and watch this short 8:46 minute animated video. It lays out the exact opposite view regarding the "Canaanite Question", and it's done in a fun, yet historical way. I think you'll enjoy it. I sure did.

I would also have you read a full article on this same question which gives an answer that I believe to be more in line with what really happened when the Israelites entered the promised land, using the related scriptures of the events. Just do a search in Google for "Question: How can one reconcile scriptures in the Bible that appear to endorse genocide, pillage, and/or plunder?" Here's a few excerpts from that article:

"War was a cultural reality for Israel and members of the ancient near east. It was a fight or die situation for many of them. Most of Israel's battles were fought on the defensive. It has been pointed out that Israel defended against the Amalekites who attacked them while traveling:

Exodus 17:8

8 Then came Amalek, and fought with Israel in Rephidim.

... and that the Canaanite king of Arad attacked and captured some of the Israelites:

Numbers 21:1

1 And *when* king Arad the Canaanite, which dwelt in the south, heard tell that Israel came by the way of the spies; then he fought against Israel, and *took some of them prisoners*.

"Israel countered the efforts of the Midianites who wanted to lead them away from Yahweh through sexual transgression and idolatry. Here are chapters 25 and 31 of Numbers:

Numbers 25

1 And Israel abode in Shittim, and the people began to commit whoredom with the daughters of Moab.

2 And they called the people unto the sacrifices of their gods: and the people did eat, and bowed down to their gods.

3 And Israel joined himself unto Baal-peor: and the anger of the LORD was kindled against Israel.

4 And the LORD said unto Moses, Take all the heads of the people, and hang them up before the LORD against the sun, that the fierce anger of the LORD may be turned away from Israel.

5 And Moses said unto the judges of Israel, Slay ye everyone his men that were joined unto Baal-peor.

6 And, behold, one of the children of Israel came and brought unto his brethren a Midianitish woman in the sight of Moses, and in the sight of all the congregation of the children of Israel, who *were* weeping *before* the door of the tabernacle of the congregation (He took this Midianite prostitute and began to have illicit sex with her).

7 And when Phinehas, the son of Eleazar, the son of Aaron the priest, saw *it,* he rose up from among the congregation, and took a javelin in his hand;

8 And he went after the man of Israel into the tent, and thrust both of them through, the man of Israel, and the woman through her belly. So, the plague was *stayed* from the children of Israel.

9 And those that died in the plague were twenty and four thousand.

10 And the LORD spake unto Moses, saying,

11 Phinehas, the son of Eleazar, the son of Aaron the priest, hath turned my wrath away from the children of Israel, while he was zealous for my sake among them, that I consumed not the children of Israel in my jealousy.

12 Wherefore say, Behold, I give unto him my covenant of peace:

13 And he shall have it, and his seed after him, *even the covenant of an everlasting priesthood*; because he was zealous for his God, and made an atonement for the children of Israel.

14 Now the name of the Israelite that was slain, *even* that was slain with the Midianitish woman, *was* Zimri, the son of Salu, a prince of a chief house among the Simeonites.

15 And the name of the Midianitish woman that was slain *was* Cozbi, the daughter of Zur; he *was* head over a people, *and* of a chief house in Midian.

16 And the LORD spake unto Moses, saying,

17 Vex the Midianites, and smite them:

18 For they vex you with their wiles, wherewith they have beguiled you *in the matter of Peor*, and in the matter of Cozbi, the daughter of a prince of Midian, their sister, which was slain in the day of the plague for Peor's sake.

Numbers 31

1 And the LORD spake unto Moses, saying,

2 Avenge the children of Israel of the Midianites: afterward shalt thou be gathered unto thy people.

3 And Moses spake unto the people, saying, arm some of yourselves unto the war, and let them go against the Midianites, and avenge the LORD of Midian.

4 Of every tribe a thousand, throughout all the tribes of Israel, shall ye send to the war. ... So there were delivered out of the thousands of Israel, a thousand of *every* tribe, twelve thousand armed for war.

6 And Moses sent them to the war, a thousand of *every* tribe, them, and Phinehas the son of Eleazar the priest, to the war, with the holy instruments, and the trumpets to blow in his hand.

7 And they warred against the Midianites, as the LORD commanded Moses; and they slew all the males.

8 And they slew the kings of Midian, beside the rest of them that were slain; *namely,* Evi, and Rekem, and Zur, and Hur, and Reba, five kings of Midian: Balaam also the son of Beor they slew with the sword.

9 And the children of Israel took *all* the women of Midian captives, and their little ones, and took the spoil of all their cattle, and all their flocks, and all their goods.

10 And they burnt all their cities wherein they dwelt, and all their goodly castles, with fire.

11 And they took all the spoil, and all the prey, *both* of men and of beasts.

12 And they brought the captives, and the prey, and the spoil, unto Moses, and Eleazar the priest, and unto the congregation of the children of Israel, unto the camp at the plains of Moab; which are by Jordan near Jericho.

And Moses, and Eleazar the priest, and all the princes of the congregation, went forth to meet them without the camp.

13 And Moses was wroth with the officers of the host, *with* the captains over thousands, and captains over hundreds, which came from the battle.

14 And Moses said unto them, "Have ye saved all the women alive?"

15 Behold, these caused the children of Israel, *through the counsel of Balaam (In the name of Balaam)*, to commit trespass against the LORD *in the matter of Peor (Sexual sin,* and there was a plague among the congregation of the LORD.

16 Now therefore kill every male among the little ones and kill every woman that hath known man by lying with him.

17 But all the women children, that have not known a man by lying with him, keep alive for yourselves.

18 And do ye abide without the camp seven days: whosoever hath killed any person, and whosoever hath touched any slain, purify *both* yourselves and your captives on the third day, and on the seventh day.

19 And purify all *your* raiment, and all that is made of skins, and all work of goats' *hair,* and all things made of wood.

20 And Eleazar the priest said unto the men of war which went to the battle, "This *is* the ordinance of the law which the LORD commanded Moses";

21 Only the gold, and the silver, the brass, the iron, the tin, and the lead,

22 Everything that may abide the fire, ye shall make *it* go through the fire, and it shall be clean: nevertheless it shall be purified with the water of separation: and all that abideth not the fire ye shall make go through the water.

23 And ye shall wash your clothes on the seventh day, and ye shall be clean, and afterward ye shall come into the camp.

24 And the LORD spake unto Moses, saying,

25 Take the sum of the prey that was taken, *both* of man and of beast, thou, and Eleazar the priest, and the chief fathers of the congregation:

26 And divide the prey into two parts; between them that took the war upon them, who went out to battle, and between all the congregation:

27 And levy a tribute unto the LORD of the men of war which went out to battle: one soul of five hundred, *both* of the persons, and of the beeves, and of the asses, and of the sheep:

28 Take *it* of their half, and give *it* unto Eleazar the priest, *for* an heave offering of the LORD.

29 And of the children of Israel's half, thou shalt take one portion of fifty, of the persons, of the beeves, of the asses, and of the flocks, of all manner of beasts, and give them unto the Levites, which keep the charge of the tabernacle of the LORD.

30 And Moses and Eleazar the priest did as the LORD commanded Moses.

31 And the booty, being the rest of the prey which the men of war had caught, was six hundred thousand and seventy thousand and five thousand sheep,

32 And threescore and twelve thousand beeves, (A beef creature)

33 And threescore and one thousand asses,

34 And thirty and two thousand persons in all, of women that had not known man by lying with him.

35 And the half, *which was* the portion of them that went out to war, was in number three hundred thousand and seven and thirty thousand and five hundred sheep:

36 And the LORD's tribute of the sheep was six hundred and threescore and fifteen.

37 And the beeves *were* thirty and six thousand; of which the LORD's tribute was three-core and twelve.

38 And the asses *were* thirty thousand and five hundred; of which the LORD's tribute was threescore and one.

39 And the persons *were* sixteen thousand; of which the LORD's tribute *was* thirty and two persons.

40 And Moses gave the tribute, *which was* the LORD's heave offering, unto Eleazar the priest, as the LORD commanded Moses.

41 And of the children of Israel's half, which Moses divided from the men that warred,

42 (Now the half *that pertained unto* the congregation was three hundred thousand and thirty thousand *and* seven thousand and five hundred sheep,

43 And thirty and six thousand beeves,

44 And thirty thousand asses and five hundred,

45 And sixteen thousand persons;)

46 Even of the children of Israel's half, Moses took one portion of fifty, *both* of man and of beast, and gave them unto the Levites, which kept the charge of the tabernacle of the LORD; as the LORD commanded Moses.

47 And the officers which *were* over thousands of the host, the captains of thousands, and captains of hundreds, came near unto Moses:

48 And they said unto Moses, Thy servants have taken the sum of the men of war which *are* under our charge, and there lacketh not one man of us.

49 We have therefore brought an *oblation for the LORD*, what every man hath gotten, of jewels of gold, chains, and bracelets, rings, earrings, and tablets, to make an atonement for our souls before the LORD.

50 And Moses and Eleazar the priest took the gold of them, *even* all wrought jewels.

51 And all the gold of the offering that they offered up to the LORD, of the captains of thousands, and of the captains of hundreds, was sixteen thousand seven hundred and fifty shekels.

52 *For* the men of war had taken spoil, every man for himself.

53 And Moses and Eleazar the priest took the gold of the captains of thousands and of hundreds, and brought it into the tabernacle of the congregation, *for* a memorial for the children of Israel before the LORD.

"Sihon refused peace offers from Israel and *attacked them* (Deuteronomy 2, Numbers 21), and so on. By this moment in Israel's history, they had become a *theocratic people-nation* that wanted to continue to show their counterparts *their faith in Yahweh and his sovereignty* as the only true God. The 'Canaanite command' came at this unique part of history w*here war was their reality.* God was giving a specific command for a specific purpose. The picture that we get from the whole of the biblical text tells a story of *gradual infiltration, strategizing, victory here and there.*

"As initial groundwork for understanding this picture, we need to understand what the Israelites thought of these texts as they wrote them. Did they intend the text to be *literal*? How would they have understood them? How did God "speak unto them according to their language that they might come to understanding?"

II Nephi 31:3

3 For my soul delighteth in plainness; for after this manner doth the Lord God work among the children of men. For the Lord God giveth light unto the understanding; ... for *he Spaeth unto men according to their language, unto their understanding.*

End of "Question: How can one reconcile scriptures?" [593]

"Paul Copan and Matthew Flanagan give an answer to this, which summarizes the view of "most scholars generally"—that the Canaanite account contains "*hagiographic hyperbole*". [594]

End of comments by Paul Copan & Matthew Flanagan

It is my hope that you, my readers, are more interested in seeking truth than you are in seeking those opinions that fit what you want to believe and feel more comfortable supporting. However, if not, then that is up to you. I do feel that this last article answers Richard's criticism of the harshness of the Day in which the Israelites lived. In my reading of Richard's criticism of Israel's' Day, with him being so steeped in hatred towards religion, and more particularly towards Christianity, Richard chose to give his readers a glossed-over, veneer kind of summary of his biased-interpretation of the Bible, in the hope of making the point that he already had in mind before he even began writing his book *The God Delusion*, which was that 'scripture is not the source of morality and neither is God', because there is no God. He simply went looking for examples from the Bible that supported his belief.

Richard's next comment says, "Religion is undoubtedly a divisive force ... Religion is a label of in-group/out-group enmity and vendetta, not necessarily worse than other labels such as skin color, language, or preferred football team, but often available when other labels are not" and "Without religion there would be no labels by which to decide whom to oppress and whom to avenge." [595]

And finally, to close off this subtitle Richard says, "Even if religion did no other harm in itself, its wanton and carefully nurtured divisiveness – its deliberate and cultivated pandering to humanity's natural tendency to favor in-groups and shun out-groups – would be enough to make it a significant force for evil in the world." [596]

I've chosen not to remark on every single example Richard put forth to make the point that "the New Testament, like the Old Testament, promotes hatred of out-groups that are not like them and their in-groups. So why would anyone follow such a belief system?" I just want to make the point that the Bible and its historicity, is not quite up to speed in terms of detail. Let me quote the Prophet Joseph Smith as a rebut to Richard's overall claim here. Joseph said, and I quote:

"Many important points touching the salvation of man, had been '*taken*' from the Bible, or lost before it was even compiled." [597]

End quote

So, I ask, is it possible that some of these peoples' history was lost, and that the biblical historians got some of their history wrong, and in doing so it opened the door for Richard, and other religious critics like him, to rail on the Bible and its sacred message? It's something to think about. If you, my readers, are honest truth seekers and not just part of the pack of barking dogs who are constantly yapping at the heels of the prophets and apostles who originally wrote the Bible, then I ask that you hold off making any judgement until I've finished giving my perspective on this topic in its entirety.

The truth is, that it wasn't God who went out in search for how He might wipe out a particular group or groups of people, but rather it was the wicked nations and their people who chose to go against God's message and commandments, which He gave to His prophets to declare to the nations – the good news. The prophets declared the words of the True and Living God, and because the people rejected them and their words, they reaped their punishment as they went to war against God's chosen people. They wanted to continue in their wicked living (In their sexual deviancy, as just one example), even after repeated years of warning (Just as God has warned against the wickedness that exists in the nations of the world today. He's proclaiming it just as He always has – through the voices of His living prophets).

In other words, the spirit ceased to strive with them to the point where they had become *ripe for destruction*, just as the people of Noah's Day were ready for their destruction, and just as the people of our Day are fast becoming *ripe for their destruction*. That Day of destruction will be the 2nd coming of our Lord and Savior Jesus Christ, so I would suggest you get an asbestos suit for the fire that's coming.

From my perspective, one need only be an honest fruit inspector, doing a thorough review of the wickedness that's taking place throughout the world today. Even as you're reading this book, I'm sure that you, my readers, have thought about the world and how it's fast approaching the point where it appears to be *ripening for destruction*. Evil is everywhere and it's getting worse with each passing year. The sad truth is, that the world will continue in its wicked ways until the Saviors' return, even the day where He promised He would come to cleanse the earth of all its evil, filth, and wickedness, even by fire (The earth has already had its 'baptism by water' by the Great Global Flood. This *cleansing by fire* will be the earth's 'baptism by fire', even to the sanctifying of the earth so it can receive its paradisical glory, the reception of the Holy Ghost being its type). The First Councilor in the First Presidency of the Church of Jesus Christ of Latter-Day Saints, Elder Dallin H. Oaks, gave a talk a few years back, titled, "Preparation for the Second Coming". There's also a video of it on YouTube titled, "Signs of the Second Coming Prophecy Fulfilled" wherein Elder Oaks said the following, and I quote:

"In modern revelation we have the promise that if we are 'prepared' we need not fear:

Doctrine & Covenants 38:30

30 I tell you these things because of your prayers; wherefore, treasure up wisdom in your bosoms, lest the wickedness of men reveal these things unto you by their wickedness, in a manner which shall speak in your ears with a voice louder than that which shall shake the earth; *but if ye are prepared ye shall not fear.*

"The scriptures are rich in references to the 2nd Coming, an event eagerly awaited by the righteous and dreaded or denied by the wicked. These references (or signs) include:

1 – The fulness of the gospel is restored and preached as a witness to all nations.

2 – False Christs and false prophets, deceiving many.

3 – Wars and rumors of wars, with nation rising against nation.

4 – Earthquakes in divers' places.

5 – Famine and pestilence

6 – An overflowing scourge, a desolating *sickness* covering the land (Could the COVID Pandemic be such a scourge? There is also the *spiritual scourge* of the evils we see today).

7 – Iniquity abounding.

8 – The whole earth in commotion.

9 – Men's hearts failing them.

In another revelation the Lord declares that some of these signs are His voice calling His people to repentance:

Doctrine & Covenants 43:23, 25

23 And again, the Lord shall utter his voice out of heaven, saying: Hearken, O ye nations of the earth, and hear the words of that God who made you.

25 How oft have I called upon you *by the mouth of my* [b]*servants*, and by the ministering of angels, and by mine own voice, and by the voice of thunderings, and by the voice of lightnings, and by the voice of tempests, and by the voice of earthquakes, and great hailstorms, and by the voice of famines and pestilences of every kind, and by the great sound of a trump, and by the voice of judgment, and by the voice of mercy all the day long, and by the voice of glory and honor and the riches of eternal life, and would have saved you with an everlasting salvation, but ye would not!

These signs of the Second Coming are happening all around us and seem to be increasing in frequency and intensity." [598]

End of quotes by Elder Dallin Oaks

I ask you, my readers, "Are the people of the world today obsessed with sex, violence, murder, hatred, fornication, adultery, licentiousness, incest, homosexuality, gender dysphoria, transgender ideology, greed, power, child trafficking, child sacrifice (Abortion), and in some cases even bestiality?" The answer is "Yes". These behaviors and actions by the people of the world are in fact taking place. The *'cycle of sin'* is speedily winding up to its climax. I ask you, my readers, "Is the aborting of millions of babies every year throughout the entire world (53 million plus annually) a form of human and child sacrifice?" It clearly is the taking of innocent, unprotected life, which act of abortion is breaking God's fifth commandment, "Thou Shalt Not Kill". Scientific studies show that the sperm and egg it fertilizes, contain all the DNA and information to form a human being. In its gestation period there is no additional DNA information added to the developing baby, and so it is a human being from its fertilization. This fact, and the fact that the woman's body has been designed to provide 'hCG' to protect this new, foreign being (The fertilized egg), in order for it to continue growing in the mother's womb. Otherwise, her body would protect itself from this foreign object and destroy it. God designed her body to provide this hormone protection so that it can grow to maturity and be born. That, my friends, is a scientific fact!

My fear is that the world is too busy with eating, drinking, and seeking the pleasures of the world, offered up by the god of pleasure, that they're basically being boiled like a frog is slowly boiled to death, unawares. Our next topic is the subtitle – "The Moral Zeitgeist". I really enjoyed reading about this concept and how I would respond to all of Richard's arguments about it. I hope you feel the same way.

THE MORAL ZEITGEIST

Richard began this subtitle by saying, "We do not – even the religious among us – ground our morality in holy books, no matter what we may fondly imagine. How, then, do we decide what is right and what is wrong?" [599]

Richard then says, "The majority of us don't cause needless suffering: we believe in free speech and protect it even if we disagree with what is being said; we pay our taxes; we don't cheat, don't kill, don't commit incest, don't do things to others that we would not wish done to us. Some of these *good principles* can be found in holy books, ... but the holy books do not supply any rules for distinguishing the good principles from the bad." [600]

Richard calls these good principles "*consensual ethics*" (Another name for subjective) and says of them:

"They produce rather similar results to each other, and what they produce is characteristic of the times in which they happen to live." Richard then relates a list of what he calls 'The New Ten Commandments' which he found on an atheist website which he describes as, "This little collection is not the work of a great sage or prophet or professional ethicist. It is just one ordinary web blogger's rather endearing attempt to summarize the principles of the good life today. The whole point is that it is the sort of list that any ordinary, decent person today would come up with." [601]

Richard then gives his own short list of *new* Commandments that he would add to the 'New' Ten Commandments other atheists have put forth. See if you think they sound like commandments of someone designing their own god and what they think He should be, even a god after their own imaginations, including His or Her laws that they want to live by; a life without guilt, or fear of punishment; a life where they can avoid having to live under the laws of the Living God and His restrictive Ten Commandments. Check out Richard's *New* Ten Commandments add-ons I've listed here:

- Enjoy your own sex life (so long as it damages nobody else) and leave others to enjoy theirs in private, whatever their inclinations, which are none of your (or God's) business.
- Do not discriminate or oppress on the basis of sex, race, or (as far as possible) species.
- Do not indoctrinate your children. Teach them how to think for themselves; how to evaluate evidence; and how to disagree with you.
- Value the future on a timescale longer than your own. [602]

I find this list offered by Richard, to be quite revealing. In my mind, what he and the other atheists have put forth, are simply lists of their own '*subjective standard*' of so-called moral values and what they think would be a foundation for living a good and happy life. For them, there is no '*objective standard*' to live by. But, if this is Richard's suggested way for everybody to approach the question of morality, it fails as an objective standard for living and socializing with each other. There's only a subjective standard here, and in my mind this subjective approach would open the door to all kinds of societal conflicts caused by the differences in opinions and priorities that everybody else would have, and that, like I said, would ultimately lead to absolute chaos. I would have you consider what the issue of "Transgenderism and LGBTQ+ Pronoun demands", as well as any kind of Wokism for that matter, is causing in almost every society throughout the world today. It's causing pure chaos in our social circles.

Next Richard mentions slavery, a woman's right to vote or lack of such rights, both issues due to a society regarding them as property. Richard offers the story of Abraham and his offering of his son Isaac as a human sacrifice (Though the angel stopped him), as an example of child abuse, and if he had not been stopped, he would have committed first-degree murder. Some scholars suggest that Abraham's son Jacob, was a young man in his early to mid-twenties, and not a little child, and as such could have overtaken his father, who was going to sacrifice him, but he chose to submit to his father's will, believing his prophet father could raise him back from the dead by exercising his priesthood power and authority. If you don't believe this part of the story, I would have you read this verse in the book of Hebrews:

Hebrews 11:19

19 *Accounting that God was able to raise him up, even from the dead*; from whence also he received him in a figure.

According to the *mores* of Abraham's time, Abraham's conduct was entirely admirable, as was Isaac's choice to obey God's commandment and submit to his father's will. Richard suggests, however religious we are, or not, we have all changed massively in our attitude to what is right and what is wrong.

So, the question then becomes, "What's the nature of this change, and what drives it?" [603]

To answer this question Richard puts forward the word "Zeitgeist", which means 'spirit of the times', and gives several examples of shifting Zeitgeists in our recent history, such as woman's suffrage and views of African Americans and racism being just two examples of many Zeitgeists' spirit of the times that have occurred over the centuries.

Richard concludes by saying, "There seems to be a steadily shifting standard of what is morally acceptable." ... "It has shifted in all of us, and the shift has no connection with religion. If anything, it happens in spite of religion, not because of it. Why does the moral Zeitgeist move in the broadly concerted way and direction that it does, and has done over the centuries? It is not driven by religion – and certainly not by scripture. It is probably not a single force like gravity, but a complex interplay of disparate exponential increase in computer power." [604]

Richard concludes this subtitle discussion by putting forth his dogmatic claim, "Whatever its cause, the manifest phenomenon of 'Zeitgeist progression' is more than enough to undermine the claim." [605] This has been Richard's goal here – To prove that we do not need God in order to be good, or to decide what is good, therefore there is no need for God, and that's why He claims that God not exist.

My-oh-my, where to begin? Let me start by sharing an article written by a blogger named James Michael Whitmore, titled "Zeitgeist in America: An Analysis of Societal Spirit in the United States". It provides a good foundation and understanding of where the concept of Zeitgeist came from. I want to let you, my readers, know that I have inserted my own thoughts here-and-there in parenthesis throughout Michael's article, as well as deleted some portions of the article in-order to save you time, but you can go to Google and look for the article there, if you want to read it in its entirety. I did and it was fantastic.

I've included what I thought would enhance our discussion and lend support to my response that I will give to Richard's points regarding the many Zeitgeist's that have taken place throughout history, as well as their relation to where morals come from. The following are excerpts from Mr. Whitmore's article, and I quote:

"This research focuses on the concept of zeitgeist— the particular 'spirit of an era' — and how it has changed and evolved in the modern American eras (As well as in all the societies of the nations of the world). Society is generally observed (and influenced) through five main categories (Five main influencers):

(1) politics, (2) economics (3) social trends (4) cultural trends, and (5) religion.

"Each of these categories play a significant role in shaping the Zeitgeist in each of the world's respective societies, some more than others, depending on its importance to the people of that time (Surely this gives us insight to what 'the cause or causes' of Zeitgeist are or is. But what or who drives the spirit of Zeitgeist in any society? I suggest Zeitgeist's are driven by two main influences, and all the 'influencers' that are natural outgrowths of these two voices/influences/spiritual influences).

(In the subtitle "Does our moral sense have a Darwinian origin?", in chapter 7 I discussed "The Spirit of God" and "The spirit of Satan" and shared how each and every person on the planet are given the opportunity to choose which of these two voices or spirit influences they want to follow, and this discussion about the spirit of an era, the Zeitgeist of the Day, is a reflection of one of these two voices or influencers swaying our societal norms)."

"Examples of categorial sources that influence these choices might include open sources from the Internet, novels from authors associated with specific time periods, artists and their creations, research reports from organizations focused on population trends, and even quotes from speeches or discussions of historical figures. The Zeitgeist of an era is best recognized when it has passed, rather than during its time, and the reason being that the people living in each of these eras are too caught-up in what surrounds them, to identify it for themselves. It is up to today's generation to analyze the Zeitgeists of previous time periods (Or eras, or societies) and be able to recognize 'trends' from those eras in today's society (If we fail to learn from our past history, we are doomed to repeat it). It is important for society to start learning to embrace the Zeitgeist of now, in order to determine if the trends are helpful or detrimental to one's future so we can create a greater future. Throughout the past two centuries, as an example, America has undergone vast developments in every aspect of society. Though many changes are identified, and the causes of those changes as well, it has not yet been well explained what (Or who) it is that drives such change.

"Many would reply that people drive that change, but what drove them? What compelled so great a transformation that it was encouraged by droves of people (I posit that it is the 'Light of Christ' that drives people to invent and create, and ultimately do good. However, when the spirit of Satan, the spirit of anti-Christ is the spirit that is followed by the majority of society, so that they choose darkness rather than light, the spirit and power of the Light of Christ soon ceases to strive with the masses, and soon it becomes a downward spiral, taking over their lives until that society crashes)?"

"It is indeed the energy (Spirit/Voice) itself of any reformation, the milieu surrounding the people, as-a-whole, that drives societal change. The word to describe this concept of change is Zeitgeist, meaning *the spirit of the time*' (I appreciate Richard having brought this concept up as one of his arguments. I don't necessarily agree with his belief that religion in no way drives the spirit of Zeitgeist, which then drives our morals, or that it may be a *'complex interplay'* of disparate exponential increase in computer power. I believe there's a *spiritual atmosphere* that exist in different societies, and it's due to the varied *influencers* that exist in these societies).

"Before delving into the spiritual makeup of an era, it is important to truly understand what Zeitgeist is. Zeitgeist is a word stemming from the root German words "Zeit" and "Geist," meaning time and spirit respectively (Zeitgeists). This word thus encapsulates the idea of *spiritual atmosphere*, and an incorporeal *feeling* that shifts and flows through society. Looking back on history, it is rather simple to identify the overall *psyche* of distinct time periods, the important figures with opinions of the Zeitgeist's ideals, and where *that* spirit led to shortcomings or successes (It's the spiritual influence that is accepted and even promoted during any given era). Authors, musicians, artists, and other such influential persons provide the most effective path towards understanding Zeitgeists of particular eras.

(These are people like the prophet of the 19th century, Joseph Smith Jr., who helped influence and shape religious America and the generations that followed. On the flip side there's Adolph Hitler. As a political despot, in just twenty-six short years he inspired an entire country to hate and kill every Jew they could get their hands on).

"Perhaps the most essential piece to understand about Zeitgeist is its effect on an individual. People are products of '*the continuum of Zeitgeists*' that ebb and flow across time and spirit. In the same way that parents instill values on their children (Richard would call this forcing religion down their throats, or child abuse), Zeitgeist promotes its ideals onto societies and individuals (Influencers also include sources like social media, movies, magazines, and the like. They are 'tools of influence' that often help drive the Zeitgeist ideals in society in any given era).

"This makes it far more difficult to comprehend the Zeitgeist of the present, rather than those of the past. Being 'in' the Zeitgeist inhibits the ability to clearly understand how its manifestations will affect the future. For example, the 1920's was a time known by many names: the Jazz Age, the Age of Intolerance, and perhaps the most famous name was the Roaring Twenties. People living in this time period (Era), later became known as the 'Lost Generation', a name popularized by American modernist writer Gertrude Stein ('Time Periods'). The name was accredited due to their disillusionment with the world, and their disinclination to move into a more settled way of life. The numerous labels given to this time period stand as a testament of the chaotic *spirit of the era*.

"The end of the Great War created a time where the only thing Americans wanted to do was experience anything and everything. This led to a rush into materialism and frivolousness. Spending skyrocketed, products were mass produced and sold cheap, and credit purchases were constant. The latter consumer practice would eventually lead into the economic collapse of the nation. But until then, Americans were too caught up in the 'Geist' to pay any attention to the consequences of their actions.

"In addition to economic changes, America was undergoing countless social and cultural developments. Women worked outside the home, were given the right to vote, dressed less conservatively, and were generally seen in a different light than before. In the Harlem Renaissance scene, music evolved into jazz, a form of music best identified by its use of improvisation, powerful rhythm, and the wide variety of dances that came with it. Art Deco was the overarching art form of the decade, with expressionism and surrealism close behind. It was best characterized by its use of vibrant color, dominant geometric shapes, and grand embellishment.

"From this time of vivacity emerged figures who are now regarded with significance, due to their contributions during the 1920s. One such man was Francis Scott Key Fitzgerald, an author best known now for his novel The Great Gatsby. Now a popular, required reading book in high school, the story provides numerous insights on a variety of societal themes that concerned Fitzgerald.

"Looking through the haze of the Zeitgeist surrounding him, Fitzgerald criticized the corruption and shallowness of America and its people. According to Fitzgerald, the American Dream — a prevalent theme criticized in The Great Gatsby — had long since died. The concept that any person could achieve success and prosperity by hard work and determination had been replaced by the acquisitiveness and short-term satisfactions of society.

"Gatsby, the tragic character of the story, is unable to grasp this concept as he holds on to a hope that had long since passed him by. Fitzgerald described this dying dream in his final words of the novel: "Gatsby believed in... the orgiastic future that year by year recedes before us. It eluded us then, but that's no matter — tomorrow we will run faster, stretch out our arms farther. And then one fine morning – we beat on, boats against the current, borne back ceaselessly into the past.

"(Fitzgerald 180–182) Fitzgerald's words perfectly encapsulate the melancholy that comes with endlessly reaching for dreams and never attaining them. And so, it was in the Zeitgeist (Or spirit of) the Roaring Twenties: a generation lost in their own endeavors, leading to a future uncertain and unstable.

"In the most abrupt Zeitgeist change in modern history, the Twenties spirit was driven headlong into a harsh reality. October 29, 1929, marked America's industrial descent into the Great Depression. The day of the American stock market crash — now referred to as "Black Tuesday" – initiated unemployment rates of twenty-five percent, leaving families broke and homeless. Those who found work or were lucky enough to keep their jobs had to ... start their savings from scratch.

"In this time of crisis, Americans looked towards the government to provide them with support. The president at that time, Herbert Hoover, made attempts to help in the nation's recovery. He believed the answer lied within the people instead of the government. However, his firm belief in 'self-determinism' was not the answer Americans were looking for.

"In 1932, Franklin D. Roosevelt was elected, and promised Americans a 'New Deal'. The government took on a whole new role in developing work programs for the unemployed and providing general relief to those in need. This marked the beginning of a political shift that would ripple into the future and change many Americans' ideas of government and its role in society. But as it is with Zeitgeist, those effects would not be recognized until decades later.

"By the arrival of the 1940s, the American Zeitgeist was on a much-desired upward trend. Though life wasn't as energetic as it was, a now humbled people lived life in a reasonable and more informed method. This pragmatic lifestyle, however, came with the side effects (For better or for worse) of a society that was far more aware of the world both near and far.

"The all too familiar shadow of war loomed over the American people once more, as conflicts in the Western hemisphere escalated. When war came to them in the form of Japan's attack on Pearl Harbor, the cry for war rang loudly. Production and the need to fight drove Americans towards a purpose that would carry the nation out of its rut. Industry boomed during this time, and by the end of the war, the distribution of wealth in America settled to a far more balanced state. Economics aside, the post war social changes created and would continue to form a much more diverse spirit in the United States. By the 1950's, paradoxical views of American society were being communicated across the media, especially with the phenomenon of mass culture. For instance, the beginning of civil rights movements and the fight against the spread of communism, showed the growing divisions in American society.

"With no set task ahead of it, America was waiting to find out what the next big steps were in store. This responsibility would not only affect the American people, but the world. This is best described in the words of Winston Churchill, and I quote:

"'... the United States stand at this moment at the summit of the world... Let them act up to the level of their power and their responsibility, not for themselves but for others, for all men in all lands, and then a brighter day may dawn upon human history...We must remold the relationships of all men...in such a way that these men do not wish or dare to fall upon each other for the sake of vulgar and outdated ambitions or for passionate differences in ideology, and that international bodies of supreme authority may give peace on earth and decree justice among men. Our pilgrimage has brought us to a sublime moment in the history of the world. From the least to the greatest, all must strive to be worthy of these supreme opportunities. There is not an hour to be wasted; there is not a day to be lost'."

End of quote by Winston Churchill

"With a Zeitgeist (The spirit of an era) beginning to form out of the ashes of an older era, the future of America took aim and rocketed into an *age of reform*. The next forty years of the United States would result in the largest and fastest growing conglomerate of change in any society. Generation X, the people born after the Baby Boomers, were the ones responsible for this change. Today's influencers are the 'Z' generation. For a general idea of the difficulties in analyzing this period's Zeitgeist, author Paul Taylor wrote in a research report, quote:

"Generation 'X' has a gripe with pulse takers, Zeitgeist keepers and population counters. We keep squeezing them out of the frame". This overlooked generation [is] often missing from stories about demographic, social and political change. They're smack in the middle innings of life, which tend to be short on drama and scant of theme. Gen Xers are bookended by two much larger generations — the Baby Boomers ahead and the Millennials behind — that are strikingly different from one another.

"And in most of the ways we take stock of generations — their racial and ethnic makeup; their political, social, and religious values; their economic and educational circumstances; their technology usage — Gen Xers are a low-slung, straight-line bridge between two noisy behemoths. Working in the working order prescribed by Taylor, bit by bit the Zeitgeist of Change can be pieced together.

"The issue of race had always been in American society, but the 1960s Civil Rights movement ultimately brought about the reformation being sought. Bringing full rights to African Americans set the precedent for all minority groups to be treated as equals and allowed the nation to move in a more racially open direction.

"In the world of politics, controversial issues poured into informants' laps and exploded into the public realm. The Korean and Vietnam War, the Cold War, Watergate, the Iran-Contra Affair, and the Monica Lewinsky affair are all prime examples of political scandals that left seeds of distrust planted in the American mind permanently (The so-called *seeds* becoming influencing drivers to the Zeitgeist. Where do these *seeds* come from? Are they *thoughts*, or ideals from the mind?).

"People would no longer view the government in as positive of a light as before. In the social and cultural elements of life, everything pushed as far left as hard as it could. People we're tired of living by the ideals of an older generation and fought for many reformations.

"This ranged from changes in the pop culture fads of music, dance, art, and fashion, all the way through the ideals of sexuality, drug use, law, and any other area of controversy. No decade was the same in this turbulent time, each differing vastly from the other as changes would come and go. Religion became decreasingly prevalent as each decade passed (This so-called *trend* of religious practice declining as we draw closer to the 2nd coming was foretold long ago by prophets, and the Zeitgeist ideals of this era were foretold as well. I'll address this a little later).

"The economy constantly grew, but the performance was inconsistent, leaving Americans unsure about their livelihoods. Technology, one of the strongest forces behind the Zeitgeist, drove onward and upward, but created issues for America and other countries.

"For a time, the Space Race between America and the U.S.S.R. led to a massive influx in technology production. This included progress in space travel, communication abilities, weapons development, and other major scientific breakthroughs. Though this proved to be beneficial as a whole to the consumer market and defense of the U.S., the delicate balance of brinkmanship with nations of differing political ideologies left a permanent scar of uneasiness on this Zeitgeist.

"The effects of this era's time are seen today in today's *spirit*, in the way politics are run, the technology used in daily life, and the common citizen's view on 'what it means to be human'. Quite simply, the people who invented the twenty-first century … saw things differently. The hierarchal systems… did not encourage this different type of thinking. [This] produced an anarchic mindset that is great for imagining a world not yet in existence.

(Consider the *trends* taking place at this very moment – Wokism, Black Lives Matter, Antifa, Extreme Rightwing Terrorism, Gender Ideology, the Trans movement with all of its gender dysphoria, and on and on it goes, each trend (Or what I would call issue coming forth from one of two foundations, the secular foundation of Man's Word, and the Theist foundation of God's word) helping to define *our* eras Zeitgeist).

"As seen through the observations of history, all people are framed by the Zeitgeist. The true question of the matter is whether-or-not society will be able to one day transcend it. Can it be seen, and can a nation steer itself on a path towards potential and construction? For now, the answer remains hidden, as it is with all Zeitgeists that have preceded.

"Just as it is hard to understand oneself entirely, it is near impossible to grasp *'the spirit of the time'* while being a part of it. When reflecting on the past, many wish to have known the consequences of actions not thought through. To have had *'the knowledge of now'* ... then.

"Can this practice of hindsight be applied to the future? Is foresight possible when using the trove of *'knowledge'* stored in the history of Zeitgeist? If society learns and listens to the wisdom found in its Zeitgeist, it can become possible to predict the Zeitgeist of the future. It is the responsibility of today's generation to shape that future as best as it can. While the plot of the future may change, let the theme echo true through the ages. Remember that while Zeitgeists of the past have indeed shaped this generation, they do not define what this generation is ... or what it will become." [606]

End of the Article by Michael Whitmore

Now then, with this as a foundation, I want to answer the articles and Richard's question of *"What or who drives the spirit of the time or the Zeitgeist?"* From my perspective, the two spiritual influencers we choose to follow or not, the two foundations – the word of man or the word of God – are the chief drivers and major 'influencer players' in all the Zeitgeist eras past, as well as the present. Our own Zeitgeist Era taking place today, in my opinion, is driven by both spiritual influencers. But, like James Whitmore said, "there's several *other* contributors."

Richard says, "as a matter of observed *fact*, it does move, and it is not driven by religion – and certainly not by scripture." [607] Like myself, Richard is so sure of himself when he says this is fact.

In contrast to Richard's opinion (And not a fact), I say, "It most certainly is the two influencers, the two spiritual voices making their daily case in the hearts and minds of all people throughout the entire world, each individual choosing daily which of these two voices they're going to follow. These two voices are *'the spirit of Satan'* and *'the Spirit of God'* (The foundations of the word of man or the word of God). Both voices influence everything we think about and what we end up doing with our spare time and money (Yes, this is my opinion). Today's Zeitgeist Ideals are identified in the following remarks given by Elder David A. Bednar, a living apostle of the Church of Jesus Christ of Latter-Day Saints, and I Quote:

"Doctrine & Covenants 45:26–27 describes the latter days as a time when there will be 'wars and rumors of wars', when the 'whole earth will be in commotion and men's hearts shall fail them' while 'the love of men shall wax cold, and iniquity abound' (This is a description of todays' Zeitgeist era, though in some ways its many characteristics isn't):

Doctrine & Covenants 45:26-27

26 And in that day shall be heard of wars and rumors of wars, and the whole earth shall be in *commotion*, and men's hearts shall fail them, and they shall say that Christ delayeth his coming until the end of the earth.

27 And the love of men shall wax cold, and iniquity shall abound.

Elder Bednar noted the word *'commotion'* from that verse, which denotes disturbance, uproar, turmoil, disorder, confusion, unrest, and disruption. Surely that word and the following verses are descriptive of our Day, 'Our Zeitgeist era', in which we now live.

"In the very first introductory section of the Doctrine & Covenants, verse 16, the Lord describes the Latter-Days with these words:

Doctrine & Covenants 1:16

16 They seek not the Lord to establish his righteousness, but every man *walketh in his own way*, and after the image of his own god, whose image is in the likeness of the world, and whose substance is that of an idol, which waxeth old and shall perish in Babylon, even Babylon the great, which shall fall (The Babylon of old being a type and shadow of the world today).

Elder Bednar continues: "Today, the world is witnessing the deconstruction of many principles, ideas, institutions, and established patterns and traditions, as people now *walk in their own way and after the image of their own gods*".

"May I suggest that many people presently are experiencing both a *'societal and an individual identity crisis'* (A Zeitgeist crisis?), a lack of understanding about who we are and 'Whose' we are."

Doctrine & Covenants 1:17 (the Lord says):

17 "He, knowing the calamity that would befall the inhabitants of the earth, called Joseph Smith Jr. and gave him commandments".

"Through the truths of the gospel of Jesus Christ that were restored to and through the Prophet Joseph Smith, we learn and know that we are 'sons and daughters' of our Heavenly Father, and we are covenant disciples of His beloved Son, the Lord Jesus Christ. In the commotion and confusion of the latter-days, we are blessed with a sure knowledge of who we are, who each of us is, and Whose we are," Elder Bednar explained.

"Moroni, the last Nephite prophet, and compiler of the record that would become the Book of Mormon, witnessed the atrocities leading up to the destruction of his people (Seeing around the corner). He was alone and being relentlessly hunted by his enemies. He saw the modern Day (Our Day, our Zeitgeist era) and chose to include in the record the things needed most for this time (Our time)."

Elder Bednar encouraged those listening to him, to read the final chapters of the Book of Mormon and consider Moroni's closing argument; this is Moroni's final invitation. Moroni is sharing the things of his soul that are most important, and in his loneliness, his heart is drawn to the topic of the priesthood, priesthood authority, properly performing ordinances, and the vital role of the Church in helping people come unto Christ.

Elder Bednar then directed his listeners to this verse:

Moroni 9:25

25 My son, be faithful in Christ; and may not the things which I have written grieve thee, to weigh thee down unto death; but may Christ lift thee up, and may his sufferings and death, and the showing his body unto our fathers, and his mercy and long-suffering, and the hope of his glory and of eternal life, rest in your mind forever.[608]

End of Elder Bednar's message

Richard says that "he doesn't know why moral Zeitgeist moves in a broadly concerned way, but he does observe it move." He then assures his readers, "It is not driven by religion, and certainly not by scripture" … and that "it is probably *not* a single force like gravity." [609] Richard admittedly says that *he doesn't really have a clear idea as to what drives moral Zeitgeist*, either an individual one or a societal one. To me, Richard doesn't have a clue as to what's behind our Zeitgeist Era; our Day.

As you and I consider the era in which we live, and its Zeitgeist ideals, I want you to know that you can identify what's causing all the commotion and confusion happing all around the world today. I ask you, "What do you think the spirit of our era is? What are the Zeitgeist Ideals, generally speaking, that are driving the *spirit of our time* … as far as you can identify them?"

Is it not commotion? Fear of the future? Ungoverned Iniquity? The age of pleasure and selfishness? Isn't this generation of Wokism, with social media as its main driver, driving this chaotic ideology? I suggest that you consider the thought that you and I, and every person on the planet, do in fact have the opportunity of choosing to follow the *influencers* that are driving our society, even the voices that we feel best satisfies our own desires, whether it's the Spirit of the Lord or the spirit of Satan and his influence to fulfill the passions of the flesh. Like I said, Satan is the god of pleasure, after-all. Our own personal Zeitgeist ideals are certainly manifesting themselves in the choices we've made as well as those we are making every moment of every day.

Next is the subtitle of – "What About Hitler and Stalin? Weren't They Atheists?

WHAT ABOUT HITLER AND STALIN? WEREN'T THEY ATHEISTS?

Richard begins this subtitle by saying "There have been some appalling '*reversals*' in our Zeitgeist's outstanding reversals, deep and terrible ones". These are provided by the dictators of the twentieth century. Hitler and Stalin were, by any standards, spectacularly evil men." [610]

Richard is often confronted with the question, "Hitler and Stalin were atheists, right? What have you got to say about that?" Richard relates two assumptions that his inquisitors confront him with, regarding this question: (1) Stalin and Hitler were atheists, and (2) they did their terrible deeds because they were atheists." [611]

Richard responds to the two assumptions with:

"Assumption (1) is true for Stalin and dubious for Hitler." He continues, "The interesting question is not whether evil (or good) individual human beings were religious or were atheists. What matters in not whether Hitler and Stalin were atheists, but whether atheism (ideologically) systematically influences people to do bad things. There is not the smallest evidence that it does." [612]

Specific to Stalin and his atheism, Richard says, "There is no evidence that his atheism motivated his brutality. His earlier religious training probably didn't either, unless it was through teaching him to revere absolutist faith, strong authority and a belief that ends justify means." [613]

Specific to Hitler and him being an atheist, Richard says, "The legend that Hitler was an atheist has been assiduously cultivated, so much so that a great many people believe it without question, and it is regularly and defiantly trotted out by religious apologists. The truth of the matter is far from clear. Hitler was born into a Catholic family and went to Catholic schools and churches as a child. Hitler never formally renounced his Catholicism, and there are indications throughout his life that he remained religious. If not Catholic, he seems to have retained a belief in some sort of divine providence. For example, he stated in Mein Kompf that, when he heard the news of the declaration of 'The First World War', "I sank down on my knees and thanked Heaven out of the fulness of my heart for the favor of having been permitted to live in such a time." [614]

Richard continues giving a brief history of Hitlers religious background, as well as a testimony by Hitler's close friend Rudolf Hess who said, "I know Herr Hitler very well personally and am quite close to him. He has an unusually honorable character (Really? An honorable character?), full of profound kindness, is religious, a good Catholic." [615] Richard then gives the true purpose of this review of Stalin, and in particular Hitler, saying, "Even if he (Hitler) didn't remain a sincerely believing Christian, Hitler would have to have been positively unusual not to have been *influenced by* the long Christian tradition of blaming Jews as Christ-killers." [616]

In support of this assumption, Richard introduces a quote by John Toland who wrote: "Adolf Hitler: The Definitive Biography". Mr. Toland wrote of Hitler's religious position at the time of the *'final solution'*, quote:

"Still a member in good standing of the Church of Rome despite detestation of its hierarchy, he carried within him its teaching that the Jew was the killer of God. The extermination, therefore, could be done *without a twinge of conscience* since he was merely acting as the avenging hand of God – so long as it was done impersonally without cruelty." [617]

As a follow up to Mr. Toland's comment, Richard returns to *Mein Kompf* to quote Hitler once again from that autobiographical manifesto where he said: "Hence today I believe that I am acting in accordance with the will of the Almighty Creator: *by defending myself against the Jew, I am fighting for the work of the Lord (1925).* [618]

In trying to be balanced in reporting Hitler's beliefs Richard said:

"Quotations like those have to be balanced by others from his *Table Talk*, in which Hitler expressed virulently anti-Christian views. Hitlers *Table Talk* contains quotations equating Christianity with Bolshevism. It could be argued that, despite his own words and those of his associates, Hitler was not really religious but just cynically exploiting the religiosity of his audience. Nobody could deny that Hitler was capable of such insincerity. If this was his real motive for pretending to be religious, it serves to remind us that Hitler didn't carry out his atrocities single-handed. The terrible deeds themselves were carried out by soldiers and their officers, most of who were surely Christian." [619]

It has become very apparent from Richard's weaving together of his arguments against Hitler's supposed atheism, that he wants his readers to believe that: "Either Hitler's professions of Christianity were sincere, or he faked his Christianity in order to win – successfully – cooperation from German Christians and the Catholic Church." [620] And here's Richard's clincher:

"In either case, the evils of Hitler's regime can hardly be held up as flowing from atheism." [621]

This is just one more example of an atheist's delusion. I find one comment that Richard included in his history about Hitler, to be quite revealing. He said, "Even when he was railing against Christianity, Hitler never ceased using the language of Providence: a mysterious agency which, he believed, had singled him out for a divine mission to lead Germany. He sometimes called it Providence, at other times God." [622]

One of the ways Hitler railed against God and Christianity, was how he berated God's Law. Adolf Hitler hated the Ten Commandments and wanted to free people from them. He called the commandments the "curse of Mt. Sanai". Hitler is quoted as saying:

"History will recognize our movement as the great battle of Humanity's liberation, a liberation from the "curse of Mt. Sanai" ... God is a tyrant who orders one to do the very things one doesn't like." [623]

End Quote

Clearly Adolf didn't like the thought of "Thou shalt not kill" because it didn't fit into his hate-filled worldview. As you've been reading these quotes provided by Richard, including the quote you just read, I suspect, much like myself, you've had come to your mind the argument that I made earlier, where I said, "there are two *'voices'*, two *'influencers'* competing for our attention, and that we have the opportunity to choose which of these two voices we want to listen to and follow". I hope you've also had the thought that I'm going to share with you now, which is.

Like Richard, who has been giving his personal opinion on Hitler and atheism, I too am going to give you my personal opinion about Hitler, Stalin, and other evil despots who've directed the genocidal murder of millions of people, supposedly in the name of God, albeit a false god. It is their manmade god, whom they've created wholly from the imaginations of their own sick minds. Both Stalin and Hitler, just like all of us, had average childhoods I'm sure, with all the normal influences one has while growing up in our families and the societies in which we live, such as Hitlers' alcoholic father, etc. All these influences helped shape his world view. It is my perspective that Hitler (Stalin too), listed to follow the *'voice of Satan'* and the 'spirit of evil' that Satan employs to not only get us to sin, but to go and recruit others to do his evil bidding – up to and including murder. This bidding cannot be accomplished unless and until his disciples, who choose to follow his evil voice, have been taught such mindsets and *principles* that form his evil ideology and tenets – 'power, corruption, deception, hate, and murder'.

I know that the following article, which I read recently, titled "Hitler Youth", is longer than I want it to be. However, it fully shows how the Nazi leaders did the very thing I'm talking about by brainwashing their country's youth over a period of many years, with the goal of preparing them to become the future of the Nazi party, and ultimately taking ownership of its misguided ideology of superiority and hatred for Jews. I hope you, my readers, see in these excerpts what I see – the influence of the *Spirit of Satan* hard at work creating the German's Zeitgeist of Hate, Murder & Destruction resulting in The Holocaust:

Hitler Youth:

"Kurt Gruber formed the first group of young members of the National Socialist German Workers Party (NSDAP) in 1926. Rudolf Hess suggested the name of the Hitler Youth (Hitler Jugend) and later that year transferred the leadership of the movement to Franz Pfeffer von Salomon of the Sturm Abteilung (SA), who was 38 at that time. Pfeffer's main intention was to train young men to *fight* against members of left-wing youth groups.

"The Hitler Youth organization was taken over by Ernst Röhm in 1930 and remained as an adjunct to the SA (Sturm Abteilung). After Röhm was murdered during the *Night of the Long Knives* the group came under the control of Baldur von Schirach, the Reich youth leader. In this post he had proved himself to be a master organizer. For example, he directed a massive youth demonstration in Potsdam, at which more than 100,000 youngsters marched past the Führer for seven hours. Schirach asked Adolf Hitler for permission to create an independent youth movement.

Hitler agreed and Schirach now made several important changes to the way the Hitler Youth was organized. His main objective was to re-educate German youth in the *'spirit of National Socialism'*. As Louis L. Snyder has pointed out: "Von Schirach would permit no opposition to his plans. As early as February 1933 he had led a surprise raid of fifty boys on the office of the rival Central Committee of Youth Organizations and confiscated its records. Cate Haste, the author of *Nazi Women* (2001) has argued: "The leadership immediately set about organizing youth into a coherent body of loyal supporters. Under Baldur von Schirach, himself only twenty-five at the time, *the organization was to net all young people from ages ten to eighteen to be schooled in Nazi ideology and trained to be the future valuable members of the Reich.* From the start, the Nazis pitched their appeal as the party of youth, building a New Germany. Hitler intended to inspire youth with a mission, appealing to their idealism and hope."

Hitler and the Hitler Youth

"In 1933 Hitler took power in Germany. At the time, the Hitler Youth only had 107,000 members. Non-Nazi youth organizations were far more popular. Hitler solved this problem by dissolving almost all the rival organizations (Only Catholic youth organizations survived this measure). All boys and girls in Nazi Germany came under great pressure to join the Hitler Youth. By the end of 1933 there were 2.3 million boys and girls between the ages of ten and eighteen in the Hitler Non-Nazi youth organization.

"At the 1934 Nuremberg Rally, described as the Rally of Youth, Hitler told Germany's young people: "Regardless of what we create and do, we shall pass away, but in Germany you will live on. And I know it cannot be otherwise for you are the flesh of our flesh, blood of our blood, and your young minds are filled with the same will that dominates us... And when the great columns of our movement march through Germany today, I know that you will join these columns. And we know that Germany is before us, within us and behind us."

"Herman Rauschning claimed Hitler told him: "In my great educative work I am *beginning with the young*. We older ones are used up. Yes, we are old already. We are rotten to the marrow. We have no unrestrained instincts left. We are cowardly and sentimental. We are bearing the burden of a humiliating past and have in our blood the dull recollection of serfdom and servility. But my magnificent youngsters! Are there finer ones anywhere in the world? Youth must be all those things.

"It must be indifferent to pain. There must be no weakness or tenderness in it. I want to see once more in its eyes the gleam of pride and independence of the beast of prey. Strong and handsome must my young men be. I will have them fully trained in all physical exercises. I intend to have an athletic youth - that is the first and the chief thing. In this way I shall eradicate the thousands of years of human domestication. Then I shall have in front of me the pure and noble natural material. With that I can create the 'new order'."

"Hitler proclaimed at the 1935 Nuremberg Rally: "In our eyes the German boy of the future must be slender and supple, swift as greyhounds, tough as leather and hard as Krupp steel. We must bring up a new type of human being, men and girls who are disciplined and healthy to the core. We have undertaken to give the German people an education that begins already in youth and will never come to an end ... Nobody will be able to say that he has a time in which he is left entirely alone to himself."

"It was through the youth organizations that Hitler sought to build the new Germans for the future. "Look at these young men and boys! What material! With them I can make a new world. My teaching is hard. Weakness has to be knocked out of them. In my Ordensburgen (New Order) a youth will grow up before which the world will shrink back. A violently active dominating, intrepid, brutal youth - that is what I am after."

"The authors of *What We Knew: Terror, Mass Murder and Everyday Life in Nazi Germany* (2005) carried out a detailed survey into life in Nazi Germany. They found that young people were much more likely to be supporters of Adolf Hitler than adult Germans: "This. probably reflects the Nazis' strong efforts to mold the new generation for the benefit of the regime after its seizure of power, through direct and indirect influence, such as through schools and the Hitler Youth.

Young people are characteristically less committed to previous conditioning than older people; they can be easily molded. (Doesn't this sound like the voice of the 'spirit of Satan' at work so that one day they too will do his bidding so he can enslave the entire world and destroy them?)

"Erwin Hammel pointed out; "As children, we didn't have the opportunity to travel, so we didn't get to know Germany from another point of view. We didn't have that at all. This made the propaganda that we were exposed to seem very plausible. We heard and saw nothing else. People today can't imagine this at all We didn't have the opportunity to hear about the world abroad. There were no foreign newspapers, and so on" (There was no *free speech* for they were told what they could and couldn't say, and they never heard or read any opposing view, as the government controlled all aspects of speech).

"In July 1936, the Hitler Youth had total control on the provision of sports facilities for all children below the age of fourteen. Soon afterwards, sports for 14-18-year-olds were subjected to the same monopoly. In effect, sports facilities were no longer available to non-members. On 1st December 1936, *the Hitler Youth was made a state agency*. Now, every young person was expected to belong to the Hitler Youth. The Hitler Youth now had *5 million members* and was by 1937 the largest youth organization in the world.

Life in the Hitler Youth

"Adam Grolsch has pointed out that before Hitler came to power in 1933, the Hitler Youth was not a popular organization. He believed that all his teachers disapproved of it. This all changed after he took over the country. "It is rather amazing from today's point of view that Hitler was so strongly supported by the teachers and the German middle class. This was not the case, however, when he was still struggling, not before 1933. They were all against him then. But after 1933, they discovered that he was actually just what the country needed. More than anybody, the teachers immediately did an about face and embraced *Nazism (Hitler's ideology)*.

Hitler Youth for Girls

"The Bund Deutscher Mädel (German Girls' League) was formed as the female branch of the Hitler Youth movement. The duties demanded of the (BDM) included the regular attendance at club premises and camps run by the Nazi Party. Christa Wolf joined the BDM in Landsberg. Her unit used to meet every Wednesday and Saturday. She remembers the importance of singing songs at meetings. This included the following: "Onward, onward, fanfares are joyfully blaring. Onward, onward, youth must be fearlessly daring. Germany, your light shines true, even if we die for you.""

"According to Richard Grunberger the ideal "German Girls' League type exemplified early nineteenth-century notions of what constituted the essence of maidenhood. Girls who infringed the code by perming their hair instead of wearing plaits or the 'Grechen' wreath of braids had it ceremoniously shaved off as punishment. As a negative counter-image Nazi propaganda projected the combative, man-hating suffragettes of other countries.""

"Melita Maschmann joined the League of German Girls on 1st March 1933 in secret because she knew her parents would disapprove. Like the other girls she was ordered to read *Mein Kemp* but she never finished the book. She argued that the BDM gave her a sense of purpose and belonging. Maschmann admitted that "she devoted herself to it night and day, to the neglect of her schooling and the distress of her parents"."

"In 1934, Trude Mohr, a former postal worker, was appointed as the leader of the BDM. In a speech soon after taking control of the organization she argued: "We need a generation of girls which is healthy in body and mind, sure and decisive, proudly and confidently going forward, one which assumes its place in everyday life with poise and discernment, one free of sentimental and rapturous emotions, and which, for precisely this reason, in sharply defined femininity, would be the comrade of a man, because she does not regard him as some sort of idol but rather as a companion! Such girls will then, by necessity, carry the values of National Socialism into the next generation as the mental bulwark of our people.""

Anti-Semitism & the Hitler Youth

"Armin Hertz was a Jewish schoolboy in Berlin. He remembers the children being allowed to sing Hitler Youth songs in the classroom. The anti-Semitism was very vivid in school ... They were trying to teach us Nazi songs. I vividly remember this song they were marching in the street with. The Hitler Youth, young boys actually of our age, were singing, *Das Judenblut vom Messer spitzt, geht's uns nochmal so gut.* (The Jews' blood spurting from the knife makes us feel especially good. They were also singing it in the school.")

'Some teachers attempted to provide a balanced *view,* but they were often reported by the children to the authorities. In a lesson that was devoted to those who had been killed in the First World War. The teacher said that some Jewish soldiers in the German Army had lost their lives in the conflict. Straight away one of the boys, who was a member of the Hitler Youth, shouted out, "They had died of fright. The Jews don't have a fatherland."

Herbert Lutz admitted: " We heard about a transport of people going out. There were rumors that people were killed, but there was never any mention of gas chambers. There were rumors that said people were squeezed together in these camps and most died of typhoid fever. I didn't really give it any thought. I was fifteen, sixteen years old. We heard this on the periphery. That was not, to kids of my age at the time, our primary interest. We didn't think about it. No, we didn't even think about it. They were out of sight. I'm talking about people who are fifteen years old. There weren't very many Jews, first of all. Even at the time when all the Jews were still in Cologne, you hardly ever saw any Jewish people where we lived in the Cologne suburbs of Sülz and Klettenberg."

The Hitler Youth in the Classroom

"According to one report the activities of the Hitler Youth and the Nazi government was slowly destroying the education system in Germany. "Everything that has been built up over a century of work by the teaching profession is no longer there in essence... They have been willfully destroyed from above. No thought any more of proper working methods in school, or of the freedom of teaching. In their place we have cramming and beating schools, prescribed methods of learning and... learning materials. Instead of freedom of learning, we have the most narrow-minded school supervision and spying on teachers and pupils. No free speech is permitted for teachers and pupils, no inner, personal empathy. The whole thing has been *taken over by the military spirit*.""

"Hildegard Koch was a member of the League of German Girls (BDM), the female branch of the Hitler Youth movement. She later recalled how the students controlled the curriculum: "As time went on more and more girls joined the BDM, which gave us a great advantage at school. The mistresses were mostly pretty old and stuffy. They wanted us to do scripture and, of course, we refused. Our leaders had told us that no one could be forced to listen to a lot of immoral stories about Jews, and so we made a row and behaved so badly during scripture classes that the teacher was glad in the end to let us out."

"Erich Dressler played an active role in getting rid of teachers he considered to be opponents of the Nazi Party: "In 1934, when I had reached the age of ten, I was sent to the Paulsen Realgymnasium. This was still a regular old-fashioned place with masters in long beards who were completely out of sympathy with the new era. Again, and again, we noticed that they had little understanding for the Führer's maxim - the training of character comes before the training of intellect.

"They still expected us to know as much as the pupils used to under the Jewish Weimar Republic, and they pestered us with all sorts of Latin and Greek nonsense instead of teaching us things that might be useful later on. This brought about an absurd state of affairs in which we, the boys, had to instruct our masters. Already we were set aflame by the idea of the New Germany and were resolved not to be influenced by their outdated ideas and theories, and flatly told our masters so. Of course, they said nothing, because I think they were a bit afraid of us, but they didn't do anything about changing their methods of teaching. Teachers encouraged members of the Hitler Youth *to inform on their parents*. For example, they set essays entitled "What does your family talk about at home?" According to one source:

"Parents... were alarmed by the gradual brutalization of manners, impoverishment of vocabulary, and rejection of traditional values... Their children became strangers, contemptuous of monarchy or religion, and perpetually barking and shouting like pint-sized Prussian sergeant-majors."

"Tomi Ungerer, who went to school in Colmar, claims that his teachers encouraged his students to inform on his parents. "*We were promised a reward of money if we denounced our parents or our neighbors* - what they said or did... We were told: Even if you denounce your parents, and if you should love them, your real father is the Führer, and being his children, you will be the chosen ones, the heroes of the future."

"By the end of 1938, the Hitler Youth numbered *7,728,259*. Although this number is very high, it meant that over 4 million youths had avoided joining. In March 1939 the government issued a law conscripting all young people into the Hitler Youth on the same basis as they were drafted into the German Army. "Recalcitrant parents were warned that their children would be taken away from them and put into orphanages other homes unless they enrolled."

"On the outbreak of the Second World War the Hitler Youth were given a role in air defense work. However, some former Hitler Youth members turned against Hitler. For example, former members, Hans Scholl, Sophie Scholl, Christoph Probst, Alexander Schmorell and Willi Graf formed the White Rose resistance group. In February 1943, these students were executed for distributing anti-Nazi leaflets. It has been pointed out that between "1940 and 1945, 1,807 inmates were executed in the Brandenburg prison alone for political reasons. Of these, 75 were under twenty years of age; 22 were high-school pupils or university students. In Hamburg between 1933 and 1945, of all those sentenced for political crimes, 11 per cent were youths."

"In the final months of the war members of the Hitler Youth, some aged only 14 and 15, fought on the front-line against the advancing Allies. Ilse Koehn, a schoolgirl in Berlin, remembers that on 3rd March 1945, her teacher, Dr. Graefe, made an announcement: "Today your Fatherland has called the class of 1929. Those born in 1929 are called up to bear arms. Those whose names I will read will report for duty as flak helpers in the assembly hall tomorrow morning at nine: Breller, Choenbach, Gerhard, Mertens, Mons, Mueller, Schubach and Tetzlaff." Koehn commented that "his voice is toneless" and as he leaves the room he mumbles "insanity". However, she points out that the boys whose names had been called out, "are clearly overjoyed they feel like men."

And to finish this article off "In the last few weeks of the war General Helmuth Weiding commanded underage Hitler Youth soldiers in the defense of Berlin. The lives of these young boys were sacrificed in order to prolong Hitler's life for just a few days. The last photograph ever taken of the Führer shows him decorating twenty Hitler Youth soldiers in the garden just outside his bunker. All the boys were war orphans." [624]

End of Article on Hitler Youth

I'm confident this insightful review of history has made my point. It's obvious that despots, like Hitler, had a multiplicity of opportunities to follow the voice of the Spirit, the Spirit of the Lord, but for whatever reason or reasons (and there were many I'm sure, much like the training Hitler perpetrated on the youth of Germany) like Hitler, they chose not to follow the voice or Spirit of the Lord. They chose to follow the spirit and voice of Satan, the spirit of anti-Christ, which was the Zeitgeist spirit of their Day and Era, and the tragic result, in Hitler's case, was the horrifying atrocities of the Holocaust.

It's my opinion and perspective that when someone is an atheist, someone who does not believe in God, they are someone who is not inclined, nor do they have the propensity to listen to, or more specifically, they do not *seek out* the Light of Life, and His spirit, the spirit of God. It doesn't mean it isn't there and trying to influence them. The Spirit of the Lord has its own so-called *'spirit station channel's transmissions'* that one can attune their heart and mind to. It's just that atheists usually ignore or even reject it due to their spirit of rebellion. As a result of this rejection of God, they're unschooled in how to attune to it, nor do they have any desire to attune to it or seek it out. Thus, they listen to the louder voices in society, meaning the six main influencers we discussed earlier, including religious voices.

From my observation, atheists usually listen to or follow the voice or channel I call S.A.T.A.N., which is the opposite voice or channel of God's L.O.V.E. The voice or channel S.A.T.A.N., is probably the loudest voice being transmitted out into the universe and it has many additional channels, whereas the Spirit of God's transmission is a still, small voice that requires its listeners to exercise a few disciplines like thought-management, scripture study, and prayer before they can really attune to it and hear it clearly. These are principles and steps of the law that, if followed, will attune one's heart to the Spirit of the Lord, even that still, small voice as it's described in the scriptures.

Consider the following experience of Elijah who lived in the ninth century BC. Elijah was a prophet of the Great I AM, even Jehovah (Who again, is the pre-mortal Messiah Jesus Christ). Each 'noise' can be likened to the loud voices of today's myriad of voices. Here's what the Lord told Elijah:

I Kings 19:11-13

11 And he said, "Go forth, and stand upon the mount before the LORD". And, behold, the LORD passed by, and *a great and strong wind* rent the mountains, and brake in pieces the rocks before the LORD; *but* the LORD *was* not in the wind: and after the wind *an earthquake*; but the LORD *was* not in the earthquake:

12 And after the earthquake *a fire*; *but* the LORD *was* not in the fire: and after the fire *a still small voice.*

13 And it was *so,* when Elijah heard *it,* that he wrapped his face in his mantle, and went out, and stood in the entering in of the cave. And, behold, *there came* a voice unto him, and said, *"What doest thou here, Elijah?"*

One need only become a fruit inspector to see the kind of behaviors that come from partaking of the fruit of '*the tree of the knowledge of good and evil*' so to speak, which more often than not, if not made with the spirit of Gods' influence, are choices of carnality, sensuality, and devilishness. It's pretty easy to see the *ideology of atheisms'* influence on the natural mans' mind and heart. This influence is best described as carnality, sensuality, and devilishness, which ultimately leads to, if not bridled and kept in check, a lifetime of breaking God's commandments. I have spent my entire adult life being a fruit inspector of such '*ideological trees*', even the trees of knowledge of both good and evil and their fruit.

The tree or ideology of atheism, more often than not, produces the fruit of carnality, sensuality, and devilishness. Some atheist's trees even end up producing abhorrent fruit like the fruit that Hitlers' ideological tree produced, which was outrageously evil – leading to the death of millions of people.

Do I believe all atheists behave in such a way that their fruit is always evil? Absolutely not. I am confident when I say, there were many voices, and many influences that were very influential in Hitler's '*epistemic philosophical journey*', each combining to influence Hitler to become the *Führer* of Germany. The voices he chose to listen to ultimately shaped his worldview, which he called 'Mein Kompf'. The main thesis of *Mein Kompf* was the thesis called "the Jewish peril", which Hitler used to posit his Jewish conspiracy upon his country's people. That way he could gain the power he hungered for, and believed he deserved in-order to achieve his goal of conquering the world. The bottom line is that Hitler suffered from paranoia, as well as anti-social, sadistic, and narcissistic personality disorders. Some may ask, "Are all atheists like Hitler and Stalin?" Again, absolutely not. But every atheist I have ever met or read about, are anti-theist and anti-Christ, knowingly and often unknowingly, which, from my perspective, is still promoting and doing the bidding of Satan as they espouse false ideologies that teach there is no God.

One clear characteristic of an atheist (And their ideology) is their need to try and convert other people to their same ideology of atheism, such as Evolution and Natural Selection. In other words, to convince people that God doesn't exist. I am not saying that all atheists do this. I think the majority just go about quietly living their lives. Having said that, you could say that one clear characteristic of a theist, or believer like myself, and our ideology, is our need or desire to try and convince or convert other people to our same ideology, which is a belief in God. The difference between the two, in my humble opinion, is what or who is behind this desire to influence? One is the spirit of God, and the other is the spirit of Satan. Of course, there is the middle ground where some of us simply remain quiet.

Hitler's life provided him a variety of opportunities from which he made his daily choices. Associations, reading and studying the books he chose to read, attending all the many meetings he attended, as well as having all the multiple experiences he had during his life; all of these influencers combined to influence and generate thoughts that laid down the *evil mapping onto his mind*. Some of these thoughts at times, in the beginning, I believe, led to Hitler feeling shame and guilt, and those feelings and emotions led to Adolph's choice to rebel against and reject the principle of sham and flee from it, and that rebellion gave birth to the behaviors and actions he ultimately exhibited. Those actions and behaviors, whether you see them as carnal, sensual, and devilish, or not, were the *fruit* of his thought-tree and the resulting feelings Hitler experienced, which feelings produced his "ideological mapping". That mapping then, in his case, produced the actions and behaviors that we know were unfathomably evil.

Hitler's life experiences provided many opportunities for him to choose which of the two voices he would follow and take ownership of. Adolf's thoughts and *what he made them mean*, led to the feelings which drove the actions he chose to take. These thoughts made Hitler who he was. They shaped his belief system, which ultimately led him to reject God. In fact, his thoughts led to his rebellion towards God and His commandments, especially during his later years as the Führer. I think this *fruit of rebellion* against God and his law, is described incredibly well in the *Hitler Youth* article you just read. The fruit of all those decisions, influenced by the influencer I am calling the spirit of Satan, as well as his spirit followers that are in the billions, led Adolf to become the evil despot and genocidal monster he became.

As I've already argued, the spirit of the Lord, the Light of Christ, will not always strive with man when we choose to ignore its voice for a long enough period of time. If it is rejected time and time again, the Spirit of the Lord will ultimately withdraw its influence from the heart and mind of man, who is then *left to himself* (or herself) and to his (or her) own devices and designs (Each becoming a law unto themselves). For some, they become dark and inhuman like we saw with Hitler. It can be a swift downward spiral. The Zeitgeist of Hitler and the society he built, truly was the fruit of the spirit of Satan working his plan to enslave mankind in their sins. He who has eyes to see, certainly can see this to be the Zeitgeist of Germany, Adolf Hitler's ideology of death and hate.

Although atheism itself is just a term given to someone who does not believe in God, it, as a belief system, is a *'quasi-religion'* which has its own prophets, Charles Darwin being its champion and chief cornerstone. Darwin offered up the 'doctrines of this faith', the main doctrine being Evolution with its chief tenant being Natural Selection. This *godless ideology* becomes the lens through which its adherents form their worldview. This perspectives' *ideological glasses* effects how its adherents see everything in the world, and this is exactly how Richard Dawkins' worldview has influenced him and all his atheist friends. In fact, this *atheistic system or ideology*, drove Richard to espouse his doctrine of "Godlessness" in his book, *The God Delusion*. He even said that it was his hope that putting *it* out into the world would raise the consciousness of even more people (With its goal of creating cognitive dissonance), so that his readers become disbelievers like himself. This is the goal of 'the spirit of Satan'.

The spirit and perspective of atheism is the spirit of anti-Christ, and it comes from the spirit of Satan. This spirit, this influential voice, has the power to influence new adherents' thoughts, and those thoughts lead its disciples to believe the way their quasi-prophets do. It's these thoughts that produce the feelings about the things that are and do happen in their lives. These feelings produce the actions that flow from them. The behaviors that atheisms' disciples exhibit, result in producing the fruit of godlessness that we see in every one of the worlds' societies. We only need to be a fruit inspector.

Now before you say it, I know that the same can be said of believers in God. It can also be said of the Later-day Saints, like myself, who look at life through our own unique *spiritual lenses*. Our lens of the 'Restored Gospel', with all of its doctrines and tenants, are the influencers that direct the choices we as members make every day of our lives. These influencers, depending on what we 'choose to think' about them and what we *make them mean to us*, drive us to feel a certain way, especially if we choose to follow *the still small voice* called the Spirit of God. These feelings and the emotions they generate in believers, produce their own unique behaviors and actions which hopefully is *godliness*.

As Latter-day Saints, our behaviors, and actions, for the most part, are positive, moral, and loving towards our fellow man. With that said, I ask you, my readers, to take a moment and become your own fruit inspector. I want you to *inspect* the fruit produced by the spiritual tree called the Gospel of Jesus Christ, as it's taught in The Church of Jesus Christ of Latter-Day Saints in its purity. Consider your own interactions with Latter-Day Saints like myself. I want you to ask yourself, "Do you see, *collectively*, good fruit as a whole?" Not on an individual basis, for there will always be a few bad apples amongst any large group. Check out our membership as a whole. "What kind of fruit do you see? Is it godliness?"

It is obvious to me that Hitler, having been influenced by the voices he chose to listen to his entire adult life, and the mental and spiritual thoughts they inspired in his mind, 'thoughts of anti-Christ', these 'spirt of anti-Christ' thoughts obviously gave birth to the 'spirit of atheism' in his heart and mind and that spirit of anti-Christ led him to stop believing in God. It is this disbelief in God's existence that ignited the *spirit of rebellion* against God and His laws within Hitler's heart, thus manifesting his godlessness.

Godlessness is a spiritual state of rebellion, a rebellion against God, and that rebellion opens the mental doorway to the twisted, antisemitic attitudes we saw from Hitler. This spiritual attitude of rebellion towards God and Hitlers hatred of His commandments, led Adolph to replace God's laws, once written on his heart and conscience, with his own law, resulting in Hitler becoming a law unto himself.

This spirit of rebellion permeated his thoughts over-and-over again, and that *mental mapping* finally led to the belief that '*Jews needed to be swept off the face of the earth*', and those godless thoughts finally drove Adolph to take the actions he did, and those actions included recruiting people of like mind (We attract who we are and not what we want) to help him bring about the atrocity called "The Holocaust". The visuals we have of it are horrifically stomach wrenching and reflect the epitome of 'evil'.

Richard believes, and said, that "the evils of Hitler's regime can hardly be held up as flowing from atheism." [625] I disagree. I believe that atheism is *a choice*, a worldview and ideology, and evil things do come from, and have flowed out of, this godless ideology. All atheists certainly do not end up perpetrating such heinous acts or atrocities as those perpetrated by Hitler, Stalin, Pol Pot, and other demonic despots. But, without the belief in the True and Living God influencing one's thoughts, one is void of having His spirit help them ward off the spirit of anti-Christ. By not having God's laws written on one's heart to protect you and provide you with the *objective standard* from which you can peacefully live your life, the resulting godless mentality (godlessness) soon opens the door more widely to the evil influence of the spirit of Satan. The spirit of anti-Christ leads men and women who no longer have natural affection guiding them, to do Satan's bidding and commit the kinds of evil we see today.

It also appears to me, from my 'fruit inspecting', that the choice to fashion a god after one's own desired imaginations, is driven by this spirit of rebellion and disbelief in the True and Living God and His Laws, and *that* lack of belief, *that* spirit of rebellion, is born of the spirit of anti-Christ, which I believe is what influenced Hitler during his early years as a teen and increased in his adulthood, Hitler having opened this horrific door. Adolf's 'ideology-tree' grew stronger and stronger as the years went by, until it bore the kind of bad fruit that history records – unchecked godlessness, chaos, and genocidal murders.

False Christ's, like Hitler's distorted view of the 'Divine Providence', are born out of the spirt of anti-Christ and apostasy. Hitler's Divine Providence was formed by the voice of the spirit of Satan. This voice, and its influence, continually pressed upon Hitler's mind in such a manner that it showed the tenacity and grim persistence that Satan relentlessly exerts towards everyone, especially towards despots like Hitler, and that's because he knows all of us. He knew the kind of person Adolf was and preyed on it.

Satan pressed upon Adolf until the spirit of the Lord withdrew itself from Adolf's heart all-together, leaving him to his own evil designs; designs that brought forth the fruit of the Holocaust. Being a law unto himself now, Adolf's thoughts spiraled downward until they became a deadly *spiritual cancer* in his mind; a cancer that mutated any principle of goodness he may have once had in his youth when he first believed in Gods' divine providence. Left unchecked, this deadly *mental cancer* mutated into the disgusting Mein Kompf's Nazi ideology, and that finally drove him, supposedly in the name of his false 'Divine Providence' god, to slaughter literally millions upon millions of innocent Jews whose ancestors supposedly killed Jesus. Hitler was also convinced by this same spirit of hatred into slaughtering others he considered to be the dross of the earth, such as Gypsies of the 'Forgotten Holocaust'.

Hitler is a personification example of what "*becoming a law unto themselves*" means. Adolf rejected the law that the True and Living God places in every man, woman, and child's heart. It's there until we rebel against it, by rejecting God and His laws altogether, like Richard and every other atheist does when they reject God's existence. As we've just read from *Hitler's Youth*, this spiritual cancer of evil and hate, brought forth the fruit of violence and the total destruction of all that is good and true in a society.

We've learned by sad experience and by inspecting the fruit of this and other similar societies, that this kind of evil fruit is the desired end that Satan has for every single one of God's children. Satan's one overarching objective is to supplant and usurp the role of Jesus Christ, and he's doing it by taking every godly society down as fast as he can, starting with individuals, and that's because Satan wants us to be miserable just like he and his fallen angels (The fallen pre-mortal spirit children of God) are most miserable, and they forever will be miserable as Nephi taught. His words are found in the Book of Mormon:

II Nephi 2:27

27 Wherefore, men are free according to the flesh; and all things are given them which are expedient unto man. And they are *free to choose liberty and eternal life*, through the great Mediator of all men, or to choose captivity and death, according to the captivity and power of the devil; for *he seeketh that all men might be miserable like unto himself.*

Richard finishes this chapter, as well as this subtitle by reaffirming his feeling that, "like all religions, Nazism was a cult that was turned into a religion in its own right." [626] Richard says, "Stalin was probably an atheist and Hitler probably wasn't, but even if they were both atheists, the bottom line of the Stalin/Hitler debating point is very simple – Individual atheists may do evil things, but they don't do evil things *in the name of atheism*." [627]

On this one single point – *that most atheists don't do evil things in the name of* atheism – I do agree with Richard. These despots did horrifically evil things in the name of their own imagined false god's, their actions and behaviors being influenced by the spirit of anti-Christ, which is at the heart of the spirit of Satan, and his voice, which voice is their god. All atheists seem to march to that same drummer however – the voice of Satan. Most atheists, like Richard, have not yet let their darkened minds mutate into darker thoughts and feelings that come from continual wicked thougths, such as the hateful and evil thoughts that Stalin and Hitler imagined. A mind that is in fact godless in its mapping, is certainly more susceptible to the spirit of Satan and his voice of anti-Christ, than it would be to the Spirit and voice of the Lord Jesus Christ. That's for sure.

Richard admits that "Stalin and Hitler did shatteringly horrible cruelties; extremely evil things, in the name of, respectively, dogmatic, and doctrinaire Marxism, and an insane and unscientific eugenics theory tinged with sub-Wagnerian ravings. Religious wars really are fought in the name of religion, and they have been horribly frequent in history. I cannot think of any war that has been fought in the name of atheism." In other words, "Why would anyone go to war for the sake of an *'absence of belief?'*" [628]

A 'lack of or absence of belief in God', or a belief in one of the many false gods being worshipped today, most definitely can be a source of, or a motivation for evil, if it's grown out of a mind *mapped with the* belief that war or violence is the answer for *forcing* people to do what you want them to do, and that 'now' is the time for doing any of the many atrocities we've been discussing. It is especially true of those minds that believe man is just another animal within the animal kingdom and as such has not divine value. This kind of mind sees an unwanted dog or cat or even a baby as disposable.

Even though Richard said that "I cannot think of any war that has been fought in the name of atheism", [629] I certainly can, and that war, as I explained in an earlier chapter, was the 'War in Heaven' (Faught in the name of anti-Christ, a disbelief or rejection of the calling of Jehovah to become the Savior of all mankind), which war and ideology continues to rage here on earth even to this very day. It is the same two ideologies, the same two conflicting foundations – Man's word versus God's word. It is the motivation one has, born out of a concrete cause or ideology called 'a motive', that often makes a person vulnerable to blindly perform tragically absurd or evil acts, such as going to war or perpetrating violence of any kind.

Motive and motivation are distinctly different from each other. Alexander Hamilton once said, "When you stand for nothing, you'll fall for everything" [630]. In other words, if you don't know what you stand for, *meaning what your foundational, concrete beliefs and motives are*, then you are vulnerable to falling for any kind of distorted, subjective idea. An example of this is the godless ideology that inspired and motivated Hitler's gutless followers to do his evil bidding of murdering and pillaging more than six million Jews. That idea was the superiority of a "Super race". I could go on and on, but I think I've said enough on this subject.

Let's go ahead and move on now, to the next chapter, chapter 8 – "What's Wrong with Religion? Why be so Hostile?

CHAPTER 8

WHAT'S WRONG WITH RELIGION? WHY BE SO HOSTILE?

Richard begins this chapter by quoting a sarcastic comment made by comic George Carlin, who is obviously an atheist like Richard. Besides, it being quite funny and a nice break from the serious topic we just left, I want to start by quoting it because it is a perfect example of what apostasy can do to undermine the culture of faith and pure religion, and the limited understanding of unbelievers regarding the complexities of pure religion. Here's Carlin's quote:

"Religion has actually convinced people that there's an invisible man – living in the sky – who watches everything you do, every minute of every day. And the invisible man has a special list of ten things he does not want you to do. And if you do any of these ten things, he has a special place, full of fire and smoke and burning and torture and anguish, where he will send you to live and suffer and burn and choke and scream and cry forever and ever 'til the end of time ... But he loves you!" [631]

End quote

Setting aside the fact that, at first glance, this made me laugh out loud, let me say what I really feel about Carlin's statement about religion. There are far too many doctrinal misstatements made by Mr. Carlin for me to take the amount of time it would take to break them down one-by-one in order to correct them for you, my readers. And so, suffice it to say that they are all evidence and a manifestation that there indeed has been an apostasy, and this has caused today's doctrines that are taught by its false teachers to be a stumbling block to most truth seekers.

Mr. Carlin and Sam Harris are fellow atheists that Richard quotes in his book, both of whom give the false impression that they have supposedly taken a sincere look at religion, and its objects of worship, God, and His Son, Jesus Christ, and have found religion to be wanting. The apostate teachings that we find being taught about Christ's gospel, has surely given them fodder to mock religion, as well as its believers. They especially mock the fulness of the Gospel of Jesus Christ as it's taught by members of the Church of Jesus Christ of Latter-Day Saints, and as a result, they choose to reject religion altogether.

Even though more than 70% of Americans believe in God or what's often called a supreme or supernatural being, more than 50% of those believers are in rebellion against God and His commandments. From their own imaginations they create their own god, a god whose laws justifies them breaking His commandments. As proof of this attitude, they say things like, "The god I believe in, saves me _in_ my sins, because He loves me. I'm a good person and I believe I'm going to heaven after I die."

Richard continues his attack on religion by saying, "Despite my dislike of gladiatorial contests (adversarial debate formats), I seem somehow to have acquired a reputation for pugnacity towards religion." [632] That, Richard, is an understatement. Richard goes on to summarize his book, saying quote:

"Colleagues who agree that there is no God, who agree that we do not need religion to be moral and agree that we can explain the roots of religion and of morality in non-religious terms, nevertheless, come back at me in gentle puzzlement, asking "Why are you so hostile? What is so wrong with religion? Does it really do so much harm that we should actively fight against it? Why not live and let live, as one does with Taurus and Scorpion, crystal energy and ley lines? Isn't it all just harmless nonsense?" [633]

Great Questions. Why indeed? Richard's answer to these questioners was, "My hostility is limited to words, but my interlocutor usually doesn't leave it at that. They go on to say something like this: "Doesn't your hostility mark you out as a *'fundamentalist atheist'*, just as fundamentalist in your own way as the wingnuts of the Bible Belt in theirs?" [634]

This is Richard's intro to the six (6) subtitles of chapter 8. Before I give my perspective on the first subtitle, "Fundamentalism and the Subversion of Science", let me say that Richard cannot tolerate anyone putting him in the same 'pool', the same 'group', or the same 'label' as the people he considers to be delusional. Richard sees himself *intellectually superior* to anyone who believes or espouses what he *knows* to be unscientific, or who he sees as someone that's unable to provide reasonable arguments for God's existence. Richard has invested his entire adult life to getting good at attacking theists, and I believe it's because it makes him feel superior, and therefore helps salve his wounds from his youth.

Richard likes to argue because it makes him feel as though he is in power and that his intelligence sets him apart and above everyone else. His so-called 'incisive logic' generates his interpretations, each feeding his ego, and this process of 'feeding his ego', to me, is the main reason Richard cannot and will probably never let go of it when presented with the True and Living God's pure gospel. I believe Richard continually resists the opportunity of having his heart changed because of having experienced the deep pain of shame and betrayal by those who should have been his protectors, and so now he cannot risk experiencing that kind of pain ever again. I don't want to beat a dead horse here, so I'll just leave it there, and go on to the first subtitle of chapter 8, titled – "Fundamentalism and the Subversion of Science."

Fundamentalism and the subversion of science

Richard begins this subtitle by criticizing fundamentalists view of holy books, and praises books on science. His argument centers on the word *'axiom'*, which, as you, my readers know means *'a statement or proposition which is regarded as being established, accepted, or self-evidently true'*.

Richard says, "Fundamentalists hold their holy books in reverence, believing them to be *true*, and not the end-product of a process of reasoning. The book is true (The word of God), and if the evidence seems to contradict it, it is the evidence that must be thrown out, not the book." Continuing he says, "By contrast, what I, as a scientist, believe (for example, evolution) I believe not because of reading a holy book but because I have studied the evidence. Books about evolution are believed not because they are holy. They are believed because they present overwhelming quantities of *mutually buttressed evidence*. In principle, any reader can go and check that evidence. When a science book is wrong, somebody eventually discovers the mistake, and it is corrected in subsequent books. That conspicuously doesn't happen with holy books." [635]

If I am honest with myself, I can certainly see Richard's point here. Having a scientists' mind like Richard's, has led him to think in a very different way than a fundamentalists' mind does. At least on most topics, I think. The scientific method is where you postulate theories, do tests, predict results, and have a skeptical mind so that you're driven to ask a ton of critical questions, and then you measure your results from all of your testing-after-testing, and on-and-on it goes. Richard has been *doing* the scientific method for the entirety of his adult life, and so, how could he *not* view things through the bifocal glasses with its lenses of atheism and science and not think as a skeptic? I feel the same could be said of the fundamentalist as well, which, I'm confident, Richard would describe me as being one.

I also have a lifetime of wearing colored glasses that have allowed me to see things in a very different way than Richard sees things, but for very different reasons than Richard sees them. Richard goes on to say, "All of us believes in the evidence in our own lives, whatever we may profess with our amateur philosophical hats on. Maybe scientists are fundamentalists when it comes to defining in some abstract way what is meant by 'truth'. But so is everybody else." [636]

But then Richard reveals his own so-called *axiom* when he says, "I am no more fundamentalist when I say evolution is true than when I say it is true that New Zealand is in the southern hemisphere. We believe in evolution because the evidence supports it, and we would abandon it overnight if *new* evidence arose to disprove it. No real fundamentalist would ever say anything like that" (I have a hard time believing that Richard would actually abandon evolution and its tenant of natural selection *if* incontrovertible proof was laid down right before his eyes)." [637]

Richard is just giving his interpretation here. He is making a judgement that, for me, weakens when he uses words like *'would ever'*. Like Richard, I believe most fundamentalist Christians have come to their so-called axiom about their faith and holy books, through their methods of prayer, study, and exercising reason, and these become their *mutually buttressed evidence*, just as Richard has come to his own axiom (Again, a proposition which is regarded by Richard as being established, accepted, or self-evidently *true* such as evolution). Richard studied scientific books on the subject and the evidence presented, and through exercising the principle of reason on that research and study he did on it, he came to his own personal conclusion that evolution was *incontrovertibly true*. But it's only in his mind. There's absolutely no *incontrovertible evidence* that *proves* Evolution is true with absolute certainty.

I admit that there are many fundamentalists who hold the axiom that holy books, such as the Bible, are inerrant (their axiom), which flies in the face of what multiple historians say about the evidence they've found concerning the methods that brought forth the Bible, and what these historians say regarding its history (This can be said of the Book of Mormon as well). I have dealt with this conflict earlier, and so I will only briefly comment on the subject a little more before moving on.

Because of apostasy's influence on some translators of the ancient manuscripts of more than 66 books that were compiled into what is now called the Bible (Bible meaning biblia, or many books), it does beg the question, "How can anyone come to the conclusion that it, meaning its current day interpretation, determined by multiple fundamentalists over the last two millennia, is inerrant?"

Their versions and interpretations of the Bible are *not* the *original* writings of the holy prophets. The fundamentalists' interpretations and versions of these ancient writings are what they're saying is the "Inerrant word of God". So, I ask, "Were 'they' interpreted correctly? How do you know that they were?" Just because men say that their interpretations of the copies of copies of copies of the Bible are inerrant, in my view, doesn't make them inerrant. It is simply their axiom.

It is sad that we do not have the actual handwritten accounts of Jesus' apostles when they were moved upon by the gift and power of the Holy Ghost to write down their testimonies. It would have been nice if their actual original manuscripts were protected in such a way that they were left untouched, pure, and undefiled. It is obvious that the Bible's history cannot make this claim. However, the Book of Mormon's history does make that claim, for it, the plates upon which the original prophet-authors wrote their words and testimonies, were hid up until the angel of God, Moroni, delivered them up to the prophet Joseph Smith who translated them into English, even the Old English of Joseph Smith's Day. The Book of Mormon contains the undefiled fulness of the gospel of Jesus Christ. But I understand those who don't see it the way I do and therefore cannot and do not accept Joseph Smith as God's prophet.

Like I said, I believe the Bible to be the Word of God as far as it is translated correctly, and I believe the Book of Mormon to be the word of God. I have come to this interpretation of the evidence, the book itself, and to my conclusion and testimony because of my own personal, intense study, and using my personal faculties of reason, prayer, inspiration, and personal experiences while researching and inspecting the *fruit of* the restored gospel and Joseph's work, particularly the delicious fruit called the Book of Mormon, the corner stone of the Church of Jesus Christ of Latter-Day Saints religion. Books of scripture like the Bible, the Book of Mormon, the Pearl of Great Price, and the Doctrines and Covenants, I believe, are only sacred because they contain the words of the Living God, who is perfectly holy so that everything that flows from His mouth is holy. That and that alone is why I reverence the scriptures.

Elder Dallin Oaks, current first councilor in the First Presidency of the Church of Jesus Christ of Latter-Day Saints (As of this writing), made the following comments regarding reason and personal revelation, and how they should be applied to the scriptures, and I quote:

"We seek learning by studying the accumulated wisdom of various disciplines and by using the *'powers of reasoning'* placed in us by our Creator. We should also seek learning by faith in God, the giver of revelation. Seekers who have paid the price in perspiration have been magnified by inspiration. The acquisition of knowledge by revelation is an extra bonus to seekers in the sciences and the arts, but it is the fundamental method for those *who seek to know God* and the doctrines of His gospel. In this area of knowledge, scholarship and reason are insufficient." [638]

End Quote

Members of the Quorum of the Seventy act as emissaries for the Quorum of the Twelve Apostles and First Presidency of the Church in organizing, training, proselytizing, and administering the gospel of Jesus Christ throughout the world. Elder Paul V. Johnson is a current member of the Seventy for the Church of Jesus Christ of Latter-Day Saints (At the time of this writing). While speaking at the Latter-Day Saint Seminaries and Institutes of Religion Satellite Broadcast on August 7, 2012, Elder Johnson taught, and I quote:

"In the scientific world *the scientific method* is used to learn truth and advance knowledge. It has been extremely helpful over the years and has yielded tremendous amounts of scientific knowledge and continues to push back the *'curtain of ignorance'* about our physical world. Learning spiritual things, however, requires a *different approach* than learning scientific things. The scientific method and intellect are very helpful, but *they alone* will never bring *'spiritual knowledge'*. Learning spiritual things involves the intellect (using the power of reasoning), but that is <u>not</u> enough. We only learn spiritual things *'by the Spirit'*.

1 Corinthians 2:14

14 But the natural man receiveth *not* the things of the Spirit of God: for they are foolishness unto him: neither can he *know them,* because they are *spiritually discerned.*

"Paul describes a trait of the Natural Man in the following verse. He said, "The natural man receiveth not the things *of the Spirit of God*: for they are foolishness unto him." Doesn't this sound familiar? Is not a *foolish* man a *delusional* man? "When Laman and Lemuel (from the Book of Mormon) wondered about the things Lehi (Their father) had taught them, they stated their concern to their younger brother Nephi, and Nephi explained how they could find the answers to their questions for themselves: (Laman, and Lemuel, inquired of their younger brother Nephi because they knew him to be spiritually minded):

I Nephi 15:7–10

7 And they said: Behold, we cannot understand the words which our father hath spoken the natural branches of the olive tree, and also concerning the Gentiles.

And I said unto them: Have ye *inquired of the Lord*?

9 And they said unto me: We have not; for the Lord maketh no such thing known unto us.

10 Behold, I said unto them: How is it that ye do not keep the commandments of the Lord? How is it that ye will perish, because of the *hardness of your hearts*?

"It's not surprising that Nephi asked them if they had inquired of the Lord. That seems like a reasonable requirement for learning spiritual truths, don't you think? But he also noted that they hadn't kept the commandments. You might ask, "What does that have to do with it?" Well, it happens to be a central part of *'the pattern in learning the things of the Spirit'*, the *Spiritual Method.* The Savior taught:

John 7:17

17 If any man will *a*do his will, he shall know of the doctrine, whether it be of God, or *whether I* speak of myself.

"Nephi continued with a brief summary of the process for learning spiritual things:

I Nephi 15:11

11 Do ye not remember the things which the Lord hath said?—If ye will not harden your hearts, and ask me in faith, believing that ye shall receive, with diligence in keeping my commandments, surely these things shall be made known unto you.

"This 'pattern for learning spiritual things' (This spiritual method) is crucial for our students to understand if they have questions about spiritual things. We can make the mistake of trying to resolve doubts about spiritual things by leaning *exclusively* on intellectual answers. Answers to *spiritual questions* are given to individuals who don't harden their hearts; who ask in faith, believing they will receive; and who diligently keep the commandments. Even when we follow this *pattern*, we don't control the timing of getting answers. Sometimes our answers come quickly, and sometimes we must *place questions on the shelf for a time* and rely on our faith that has developed from the answers we do know (Just as Elder McConkie taught that we should *withhold judgement* when we do not have enough facts.) [639]

Testing Spiritual Things

"Years ago, Hugh Nibley wrote a parable of a young man who ... found a diamond in a field. In his analogy the Book of Mormon was the diamond. This parable teaches us the necessity of applying *the proper method for testing something* (Here's the parable by Hugh Nibley):

"A young man once claimed he had found a large diamond in his field as he was ploughing. He put the stone on display to the public free of charge, and everyone took sides. A psychologist showed, by citing some famous case studies, that the young man was suffering from a well-known form of delusion (Sound familiar?). An historian showed that other men have also claimed to have found diamonds in fields and been deceived. A geologist proved that there were no diamonds in the area but only quartz: the young man had been fooled by a quartz. An English professor showed that the young man in describing his stone used the very same language that others had used in describing uncut diamonds: he was, therefore, simply speaking the common language of his time. A sociologist showed that only three out of 177 florists' assistants, in four major cities, believed the stone was genuine.

"Finally an indigent jeweler pointed out that since the stone was still available for examination the answer to the question of whether it was a diamond or not had absolutely nothing to do with who found it, or whether the finder was honest or sane, or who believed him, or whether he would know a diamond from a brick, or whether diamonds had ever been found in fields, or whether people had ever been fooled by quartz or glass, but was to be answered simply and solely by putting the stone to certain 'well-known tests' for diamonds." [640]

End of Mr. Nibley's Parable, and Elder Paul V. Johnson comments continue:

"Sometimes people, including some of our students, can get sidetracked trying to determine the veracity of spiritual things by subjecting them to '*tests*' that were *never* designed for spiritual things.

"*Debating spiritual things using only temporal evidence and methods doesn't settle the issues*, and yet this seems to be part of some externally imposed *set of rules* people use to explore questions about the gospel and the Church. This sounds familiar to what Korihor, the atheist asked:

Alma 30:15

15 How do ye know of their surety? Behold, *ye cannot know of things which ye do not see*; therefore ye cannot know that there shall be a Christ.

"If scientists tried to prove their hypotheses without following the scientific method, they would have no credibility. It is just as strange to think of people trying to prove or disprove spiritual things without following '*the pattern*' for learning spiritual things. "Changes of the Heart ... Open Spiritual Eyes" [641]

"Almost 20 years ago President Henry B. Eyring, then a member of the Quorum of the Twelve, spoke to the membership of the Church on this same subject where he said, and I quote:

"I would like to visit with you tonight about how we can best help in those moments of quiet crisis in the lives of our students. In your love for them you may decide to try to give them what they ask. You may be tempted to go with them through their doubts, with the hope that you can find 'proof' or 'reasoning' to dispel their doubts. Persons with doubts often want to talk about what they think are the facts or the arguments that have caused their doubts, and about how much it hurts. They may well want to explore some scientific theory, some historical study, some political position, or some reported failures in the leaders of the Church or in its members, which they see as the source of their doubts.

"But even at its best, the *resolution of doubts* by reason and appeal to evidence cannot take us far. It is *helpful* to meet a brilliant mind who defends gospel truths with fact and logic. There is comfort in finding that such a person has confronted the same questions with which you struggle and has retained his faith (Sounds a little like me I hope, except for the brilliant mind part. Ha-Ha. But I don't claim to have all the answers). But there is a hazard. Even the most brilliant and faithful person may defend the truth with argument *that later proves false* (This risk fits both myself as well as Richard. However, I have tried to rely solely on the words of prophets for in this regard).

"The best scholarship has, at least, incompleteness in it. But even flawless argument has a weakness if you come to depend on it: What happens to the next doubt, or the next? What if no physical evidence or persuasive logic can be produced to dispel it? You will find then what I have found—*that faithful scholar who reassured you with logic did not base his faith there*. It was the other way around. *His faith reassured him that someday, when God told him how it was all done, he would see all truth as perfectly logical, transparently reasonable* (I hope you, my readers, have seen that I have taken this exact approach as I have related my arguments and my perspective as a Latter-Day Saint thus far, especially as I have spoken of the intersection of Pure Science and Pure Religion, which I believe will take place at Christ's 2nd coming).

"You and I can do better if we do not stay long with what our students see as the source of their doubts. Their problem (Their cognitive dissonance that has caused their doubts) does not lie in what they think they see; *it lies in what they cannot yet see*. And so, we do best if we turn the conversation soon to the 'things of the heart', *those changes of the heart that 'open' spiritual eyes* (I have a suspicion that Richard would never be open to taking this approach, although he did say that "'If all the evidence in the universe turned in favor of creationism, I would be the first to admit it, and I would immediately change my mind." (I so hope that one day this statement by Richard will be proven true, for Richard's sake).

"The only sure way I know to soften a heart enough for that to happen, is to get the effects of the atonement of Jesus Christ into that person's life." [642]

"All of us know that we won't have every answer available to us in every branch of knowledge, including religion, except as it resides in the mind of God, which He has promised to reveal every bit of it to us in His own due time. President Ezra Taft Benson said, and I quote:

"We are not obligated to answer every objection, (Unlike what Richard says: "it's the theists responsibility to prove God's existence and not the Atheists"). *Every man eventually is backed up to the wall of faith, and there he must make his stand.*" [643]

End of President Benson's quote

Cautions while Helping Students with Questions

"There are some cautions we should remember as we try to help students with questions. We may feel such a desire to help students who are struggling that we 'grasp at straws' to give them any answer, even when there is no real answer available (Yet). Even the great prophet Alma explained this principle to his son Helaman (From the Book of Mormon:

Alma 37:11
11 Now these mysteries (of the spirit and of Godliness) are not yet fully made known unto me; therefore, I shall *forbear.*

"It may have been easy for Alma to speculate, but he didn't. I can't speak for you women faculty members, but "I don't know" is one of those three-word phrases men sometimes have a difficult time saying. It is right up there with "I love you," "I was wrong," and "Which direction to …?" But no matter how difficult, we all need to learn to acknowledge we don't know the answer to every question.

"It is not unhealthy for a student to see that the teacher doesn't know the answer to everything but does know the answer to the 'core questions' and has a strong testimony. When the angel asked Nephi if he knew the condescension of God, Nephi responded:

I Nephi 11:17
17 And I said unto him: I know that he loveth his children; nevertheless, *I do not know the meaning of all things.*

"Even if we don't know the answer to a specific question, we can remind our students of the things we do know. Another challenge we face, especially if we have taught for some time, is a tendency to hold on to old files and old explanations. We would be much better off keeping up with the current stance of the Church. One of the best ways to do this is to be familiar with material in the newsroom at www.newsroom.churchofjesuschrist.org.

"For example, there is currently an excellent interview with Elder Oaks and Elder Lance B. Wickman in the newsroom concerning same-gender issues that can help us understand the position of the Church on this matter (see "Official Statement: Same-Gender Attraction)." [644]

"I was hired in seminaries and institutes in the summer of 1978. In June of that summer, the revelation was announced that the priesthood was available to all worthy males. In August of that same year, Elder Bruce R. McConkie, a member of the Quorum of the Twelve, spoke to seminary and institute personnel in a gathering analogous to this one. He emphasized how the revelation had changed our understanding of the issue. He said, and I quote:

"Forget everything that I have said, or what President Brigham Young or President George Q. Cannon or whomsoever has said in days past that is *contrary* to the present revelation. We spoke with a limited understanding and without the light and knowledge that now has come into the world. We get our truth and our light *line upon line and precept upon precept*. We have now had added a new flood of intelligence and light on this particular subject, and it erases all the darkness and all the views and all the thoughts of the past. They don't matter anymore. It doesn't make a particle of difference what anybody ever said about the matter before the first day of June of this year (1978)". [645]

End of Elder McConkie's quote

"So, let's keep up to date with the light we have been given (I think that this statement, in some ways, is saying what Richard has said about scientific discovery. New things are discovered and so things change and that, more often than not, is the way with science, just as it is with faith). Many of us have a difficult time dealing with ambiguity, especially in issues concerning the Church. In fact, we may be drawn to use quotes in our teaching that are definitive because they seem to dispel the ambiguity. But some quotes are definitive on issues where there is no official answer. People who are more tentative on a subject that hasn't been revealed or resolved, don't get quoted as much, but may be more in line with where our current knowledge is. We plan to add helps to the curriculum for certain questions that are commonly raised.

"When I taught seminary many years ago, there was a lesson in the curriculum on the topic of 'The Mountain Meadows Massacre', and one on 'plural marriage'. Over the years these lessons have been dropped from the manuals because of limited page counts and the fact that many students were in countries where these types of things didn't seem like issues. However, with the spread of the Internet, attacks on the Church aren't limited by geography, so we must do more to help students understand the issues they likely will face.

Answers Come through Faithful Sources

"Great teachers are so crucial in the lives of students. One important pattern taught in scripture is:

Doctrine & Covenants 52:16

16 He that speaketh, whose spirit is contrite, whose language is meek and edifieth, the same is of God if he obey mine ordinances.

"When we fit this pattern, our students will sense it. They will also be able to tell the difference between their teacher, who fits this pattern, and other sources that don't. Our approach to students with doubts can be crucial in how they choose to respond. Earlier I read about President Hinckley having some doubts as a young person. Let me continue that story. Notice how his father handled the situation. Quoting again from the biography and speaking of President Hinckley, and I quote:

"Fortunately, he was able to discuss some of his concerns with his father, and together they explored the questions he raised: the fallibility of the 'Brethren' (The General Authorities of the Church), why difficult things happen to people who are living the gospel, why God allows some of His children to suffer, and so on. The environment of faith that permeated Gordon's home was vital during this period of searching, as he later explained: 'My father and mother were absolutely solid in their faith. They didn't try to push the gospel down my throat or compel me to participate, but they didn't back away from expressing their feelings either. My father was wise and judicious and was not dogmatic. He had taught university students and appreciated young people along with their points of view and difficulties. He had a tolerant, understanding attitude and was willing to talk about anything I had on my mind.'

"Underneath Gordon's questions and critical attitude lay a thread of faith that had been long in the weaving. Little by little, despite his questions and doubts, he realized that he had a testimony he could not deny. And though he began to understand that there wasn't always a clear-cut or easy answer for every difficult question, he also found that his faith in God transcended his doubts.

(Much like Richard Dawkins' faith in science and the theory of natural selection has transcended any doubts he may have had about it early on).

"The testimony which had come to me as a boy remained with me and became as a bulwark to which I could cling during those very difficult years. There was for me an underlying foundation of love that came from great parents and a good family, a wonderful bishop, devoted and faithful teachers, and the scriptures to read and ponder. Although in my youth I had trouble understanding many things there was in my heart something of a love for God and his great work that carried me above any doubts and fears." [646]

"Notice that President Hinckley sought help from someone who was faithful. We can help students seek faithful sources. We can also be like President Hinckley's parents—solid in our faith, wise, judicious, and not dogmatic—so we can help students who may be doubting but who have a destiny in this kingdom, as President Hinckley did. I am very thankful for you and your worthy lives. I know that your help and your love will bless many students as they become righteous disciples of Jesus Christ." [647]

End of Elder Johnson's Message

Richard says his passionate defense of evolution is not because of a rival fundamentalism of his own. It is because the evidence for evolution is overwhelmingly strong and he is passionately distressed that his opponents can't see it – or, more usually – refuses to look at it because it contradicts their holy book. Richard follows up by saying, "My belief in evolution is not fundamentalism, and it is not faith, because *I know what it would take to change my mind*, and I would gladly do so if the *necessary evidence* were forthcoming." [648]

Much like when Richard says:

"His passion for evolution is increased when I think about how much the poor fundamentalists, and those whom they influence, are missing." I feel much the same way about him, and individuals like him, who can't seem to see the forest for the trees. I have often said the following statement to those folks who can't seem to 'see' the gospel message of the restoration for what it is and in the way I see it. Here's what I say:

"I envy you and I pity you. I envy you because of what you are going to experience when you do come around and see it in the way I do for the first time, and I pity you because you haven't yet experienced the joy and happiness that comes from 'seeing it' right now."

Richard says the same thing but in different words when he says, "The truths of evolution, along with many other scientific truths, are so engrossingly fascinating and beautiful; how truly tragic to die having missed out on all that!" [649]

Richard describes Fundamentalist religion as "being actively engaged in debauching the scientific enterprise. It teaches us not to change our minds, and not to want to know exciting things that are available to be known. It subverts science and saps the intellect." [650]

After reading the excerpts of Elder Johnson's talk, it should be obvious that this criticism of fundamentalism, by Richard, certainly does not apply to me or to most members of The Church of Jesus Christ of Latter-Day Saints, and certainly not its leaders, and that's because we teach honest inquiry.

Richard gives an example of his critique of Fundamentalists, by mentioning Dr. Kurt Wise. You will remember that I listed Dr. Wise in my Introduction on page 17 (Dr. Kurt Wise – Paleontologist – Rock & Fossil Formation). Richard uses the words 'a proper university', implying Dr. Wise did not learn from nor does he work for a 'proper university'. Once again, Richard's self-aggrandizement of his own self pro-claimed intellectual pedigree, is raising its prideful head one again.

I won't take the time to repeat Dr. Wise's comments regarding the dilemma he faced while attending college as a young man, regarding science and his belief in young-earth creationism, which came from his studying and interpretation of what he felt the Bible prophets had said and what they meant, but what I will do is remind you, my readers once again, what I've said about *apostasy* and the scriptures being translated correctly, as well as what Elder Johnson said about '*how we should approach unanswered questions*' like the one Dr. Wise struggled with, especially when it comes to scripture.

Richard ends this first subtitle by saying, "I am hostile to religion because of what it did to Kurt Wise. And if it did that to a Harvard-educated geologist, just think what it can do to others less gifted and less well armed." [651]

Richard does make an honest gesture to not include '*all*' theists in his 'pool' of fundamentalists. He says, "Fundamentalist religion is hell-bent on ruining the scientific education of countless thousands of innocent, well-meaning, eager young minds. The Non fundamentalist, sensible religion may not be doing that. But it is making the world safe for fundamentalism by teaching children, from their earliest years, that unquestioning faith is a virtue." [652]

I am not exactly sure what Richard means by *sensible* religion. But I do know that Richard believes that people of faith are people of faith are operation from a position of blind faith. There are millions of believers, just like me, who operate from a position of research, reason, study, so that we have an affirmed, well-endorsed evidenced-based faith, and more especially a faith based on the principle of revelation in all its forms. I guess we would fit in Richard's group of non-fundamentalists and therefore are *sensible theists*. Right Richard? Ha-ha-ha.

I find it hypocritical when Richard says, "Fundamentalist religion is hell-bent on ruining the scientific education of countless thousands of innocent, well-meaning, eager young minds", when that's exactly what he's hell-bent on doing with his anti-Christ book *The God Delusion*. As he said, his goal for writing his book was to basically "ruin any religious training that young people have had and replace it with his ideology of atheism." I ask you, my readers, "Do you find this comment duplicitous like I do?"

The next subtitle is – "The dark side of absolutism."

THE DARK SIDE OF ABSOLUTISM

Richard begins this subtitle by saying:

"When trying to explain the shifting moral Zeitgeist, I invoked a widespread consensus of liberal, enlightened, decent people. I made the rosy-spectacled assumption that we 'all' broadly agree with this consensus, some more than others, and I had in mind most of the people likely to read this book (*The God Delusion*), whether they are religious or not. But of course, not everybody is of the consensus. It has to be admitted that absolutism (an absolute standard or principle) is far from dead. Indeed, it rules the minds of a great number of people in the world today, most dangerously so in the Muslim world and in the incipient American theocracy."

"Such absolutism nearly always *results* from strong religious faith, and it constitutes a major reason for suggesting that religion can be a force for evil in the world" [653]

Well Richard, so can atheisms' absolutism for that matter. Remember our discussion on Hitler? Next Richard introduces a powerful example of one such *'absolutist fruit'* ... that being the sin of Blasphemy. After running through a laundry list of examples where Blasphemy is punished by laws on the books of most countries throughout the world, even in America, Richard states, "All the ingredients are there: slavish adherence to a misunderstood old text; hatred of women, modernity, rival religions, science, and pleasure; love of punishment, bullying, narrow-minded, bossy interference in every aspect of life. The Afghan Taliban and the American Taliban are good examples of what happens when people take their (Misinterpreted) scriptures literally and seriously. They provide a horrifying modern enactment of what life might have been like under the theocracy of the Old Testament." [654]

My response to this brief attack on past and present examples of blasphemy, is to simply remind you, my readers, of a couple verses of scripture found in the book of Moses:

Moses 4:20-21

20 And I, the Lord God, said unto the serpent: Because thou hast done this thou shalt be cursed above all cattle, and above every beast of the field; upon thy belly shalt thou go, and dust shalt thou eat all the days of thy life;

21 And I will put *enmity* between thee and the woman, between thy seed (His seed are the followers of Satan) and her seed (Her seed is Jesus and therefore all of mankind); and he (Jesus Christ) shall bruise thy (Satan's) head, and thou (Satan) shalt bruise his heel (Get Jesus crucified).

Satan, with his spirit of hatred, evil, and anti-Christ, as he promised, uses this *enmity* (The state or feeling of being actively opposed or hostile to, or in rebellion of someone or something) to exploit fallen man, the natural man, in order to get God's children to do his bidding, which bidding is to destroy Jesus' authority and influence by destroying god's word. We see this *enmity* in all that Richard's laid out here.

Satan uses whatever means at his disposal to rule with blood and horror on this earth, in order to achieve his desired ends, which are most diabolical. Human history is strewn with examples of Satan's war on humanity. His first war was the war with God and His children long before we came to dwell on this earth. It took place in the pre-mortal world. That war continues today. It started when Lucifer tempted Adam and Eve, and continued when they left the Garden of Eden, after their fall. It is my view that Satan uses the enmity God placed between man and Satan to reign with the kind of blood and horror that's been recorded throughout our history, and the horror we see taking place in the world today.

Recorded in the *Journal of Discourses 21: by Orson Pratt, we find this commentary, Quote:*

"How different was the second or temporal work that existed in the beginning of the great work of creation (The first great work was that of the Spiritual Creation, like a blueprint creation), from the present order of things! Now we see, and according to history we learn, that all creation is at *enmity* one with another in their natural state. Hence, we find the lions with teeth, probably constructed since the fall, and adapted to devour their prey. I do not believe they had such teeth in the beginning. They had teeth with which they ate "straw like the ox". There weren't any thorns or thistles before the fall either. Let's see what the Bible says about this:

Genesis 3:17-19

17 And unto Adam he said, Because thou hast hearkened unto the voice of thy wife, and hast eaten of the tree, of which I commanded thee, saying, Thou shalt not eat of it: cursed *is* the ground for thy sake; in sorrow shalt thou *eat of it* all the days of thy life;

18 *Thorns* also and *thistles* shall it bring forth to thee; and thou shalt eat the herb of the field;

19 In the sweat of thy face shalt thou eat bread, till thou return unto the ground; for out of it wast thou taken: for *dust* thou *art,* and unto *dust* shalt thou return.

"But everything was changed in a great measure, in this beautiful temporal creation; and the beasts began to fight, and quarrel, and devour each other; and man began to be ferocious, like the beasts, desirous to kill his fellow man. We see him at this early stage in our race, seeking the blood of his fellows, and entering into secret combinations to kill, and destroy, and rob one another of their position and property, and to be at *enmity* one against another." [655]

Richard's blasphemy example is just one of thousands of examples I could bring forth to show that it is *not* just religious people taking their misinterpreted scriptures literally, that brings forth this enmity of which I speak. It is *fallen man's nature* manifesting this enmity, as do all of earth's animal kingdom.

Man in his fallen state lists to obey the voice of Satan. The spirit of Satan uses this enmity of which God spoke to Adam and Eve about, to bring about his designs, and many of the atrocities of which Richard speaks are in fact done in the name of apostate religions' false gods. The natural man is an enemy to God and ever has been, unless and until he (Or she) yields to the enticing of the spirit of God and puts off the natural man through accepting and then accessing the gift of the atonement provided by the Savior of the world, even Jesus Christ:

Mosiah 3:19

19 For the natural man is an enemy to God, and has been from the fall of Adam, and will be, forever and ever, unless he yields to the enticings of the Holy Spirit, and putteth off the natural man and becometh a saint through the atonement of Christ the Lord, and becometh as a child, submissive, meek, humble, patient, full of love, willing to submit to all things which the Lord seeth fit to inflict upon him, even as a child doth submit to his father.

Anyway, let's move on to the next subtitle – "Faith and homosexuality".

Faith and Homosexuality

Richard continues his discussion regarding '*religious absolutism*', by bringing up the tragic story of British mathematician Alan Turing. You, my readers, may remember a movie about this genius where he, with his '*ultra-team*' of brilliant minds from Berkley Park, provided the pivotal *intellect* that broke the German Enigma codes. The movie was called 'The Imitation Game'. When Turing's homosexuality was discovered, Britain's law and its courts convicted him of what Richard called the criminal offense of *homosexual behavior in private*.

Let me repeat exactly what Richard said of Turing, as I feel it captures Richard's personal disdain for religionists, and what he calls *faith-based moralizers*. Here is his Quote:

"After the war, when Turing's role was no longer top secret, he should have been knighted and feted as a savior of his nation. Instead, this gentle, stammering, eccentric genius was destroyed for a '*crime*' committed in private, which harmed nobody. Once again, the unmistakable trademark of the '*faith-based moralizer*' is to care passionately about what other people do (or even think) in private." [656]

End Quote

I don't want to put words into Richard's mouth, nor do I want to say I know what Richard thinks, but I do believe that when Richard uses the moniker '*American Taliban*' to describe those theists, religionists, or Christians who he feels are participants in one 'pool' of believers, I do believe he has shown himself as having become what he so vehemently hates in others – an *absolutist*. I'm referring to his attitude towards religion, just as he refers to their attitude towards nonbelievers. It's the attitude of labeling groups, motivated by vitriolic emotions like hate, where it often leads a person to become the victim of those very emotions that got them upset in the first place. I believe Richard has indeed become the victim of his own emotional hate towards religion, so-much-so that he's expressing exactly what he hates about these so-called religionists – It's called *bigotry* (prejudice against a person or people on the basis of their membership in or of a particular *group*) and sheer nastiness.

Now as far as Mr. Turing and him being a homosexual for which he was sent to jail, my position first-of-all, as with any sin – mine, yours, Richard's, and Mr. Turing's – is that I love the person and *not* the sin. So, I have a love for Mr. Turing, but I do not love the sin of homosexuality. Mine is not to judge the person's heart. I love myself; I love you, my readers; I love Richard; and I love Mr. Turing, for we are all children of a Heavenly Father, and because I love all of His children (a commandment he has asked us to follow as disciples of His Son, Jesus Christ), I try to do everything in my power to follow that commandment, which includes praying for the '*Gift of Love*', which I have done and in doing so I received this Christlike love as one of His gifts. I also want to agree that Turning's punishment did not fit his so-called crime. Here's what the Savior had to say about the Gift of love of which I am speaking (which kind of love, as an example, Jesus Himself extended to the woman caught in adultery). His love showed the kind of divine character Jesus has):

John 13:34
34 A new commandment I give unto you, That ye love one another; as I have loved you, that ye also love one another.

To keep from being seen as though I'm trying to dodge the question Richard is implying with his statements, let me say that I personally see the sin, or the behavior of homosexuality itself (and not the persons engaged in its same-sex behavior) as going against the law that God has commanded us to live by, which is "The Law of Chastity". In the book of Alma, in the Book of Mormon, the prophet Alma said:

Alma 45:15-16

15 And now it came to pass that after Alma had said these things to Helaman, he blessed him, and also his other sons; and he also blessed the earth for the righteous sake.

16 And he said: Thus saith the Lord God—Cursed shall be the land, yea, this land, unto every nation, kindred, tongue, and people, unto destruction, which do wickedly, *when they are fully ripe*; and as I have said so shall it be; for this is the cursing and the blessing of God upon the land, for *the Lord cannot look upon sin* (any sin) *with the least degree of allowance.*

The Lord says, "Cannot look upon *sin*"; he doesn't say "cannot look upon *the person* who sinned". To commit sin willfully (any sin) is to rebel against God's commandments or to fail to act righteously, despite having a knowledge of the truth (The Light of Christ within our hearts speaking this truth to our minds):

James 4:17

17 Therefore to him that *'knoweth' to do good*, and doeth *it* not, to him it is sin.

Doctrine & Covenants 1:31-32

31 For I the Lord cannot look upon sin with the least degree of allowance;

32 Nevertheless, he that repents and does the commandments of the Lord shall be forgiven;

Sin, if not repented of, results in the withdrawal of the Holy Ghosts' spiritual influence so that we are left to ourselves to become a law unto ourselves. It makes the one who sins unable to dwell in the presence of Heavenly Father (which is spiritual death), for "no unclean thing can dwell with God", unless and until we repent which requires that we change our behavior, and become perfect *in* Christ:

I Nephi 10:21

21 Wherefore, if ye have sought to do wickedly in the days of your probation, then ye are found unclean before the judgment-seat of God; and *no unclean thing can dwell with God*; wherefore, ye must be cast off forever.

It says "Cast off forever *unless* we repent", which repentance allows the grace and blood of the Savior to cover our sins, which is the gift of Mercy. Other than Jesus Christ, each person who has ever lived on this earth has broken commandments or failed to act according to a knowledge of the truth (Which is a knowledge of what's right and wrong and thus we're convicted by our conscience). But through the Atonement of Jesus Christ, every one of us can access forgiveness of our sins, thus obtaining mercy, but we must come unto Christ with a broken heart and a contrite spirit, which contrition comes by recognizing and then repenting of our sins. John, the Apostle taught his listeners the following:

I John 1:8–9

8 If we say that we have no sin, we deceive ourselves, and the truth is not in us.

9 If we confess our sins he is faithful and just to forgive us of sins, and to cleanse us from all unrighteousness.

10 If we say that we have not sinned, we make him a liar, and his word *is not in us*."

Let me first say, that it is my belief that the LGBTQIA+ community that promotes homosexuality and Transgenderism in all its forms and sexual lifestyle, are certainly entitled to their civil rights and civility towards them as children of God. I also affirm that those who avail themselves of the laws and court rulings that authorize this lifestyle, such as same-sex marriage, Trans persons participating in women's sports, etc., should not be treated disrespectfully at any time. Again, all are children of a loving Heavenly Father who has commanded that we love one another. However, I also believe what the Church of Jesus Christ of Latter-Day Saints leaders have said about 'Same-Sex Marriage' activists, which is:

"Just as those who promote same-sex marriage are entitled to civility, the same is true for those who oppose it (The 'It' being the lifestyle and not the persons themselves). The Church insists on its leaders and members right *to express and advocate religious convictions* on marriage, family, and morality free from retaliation or retribution (Such as being 'cancelled' for simply expressing opposing beliefs, which is just one example of retaliation and retribution). The Church is also entitled to maintain its standards of moral conduct and good standing for members." [657]

So, for me it boils down to how one chooses to *oppose* same-sex marriage, homosexuality behavior, and immorality itself. I know that Richard is right when he says that there are some *'faith-based moralizers'* who choose to really get in one's face, hold aggressive rallies, and even physically attack individuals they think are *evil* because of their behavior, which happens with both sides of this sensitive topic. This kind of contentious physicality isn't the Lord's way.

Shaming others is not the way I would ever choose to express and advocate my religious convictions regarding these sensitive issues. Period! Unlike Richard, who seems to love grouping everyone into a group, a pool, or to give them a label, just so he can say things like this:

"Attitudes towards homosexuality reveals much about the sort of morality that is inspired by (and here's the grouping or labeling) 'religious faith'," [658]

I choose not to take that path. I know there are individuals who conduct themselves in the way Richard describes, but I also know, that as far as I can tell, those folks are the exception and not the rule. At least it is my hope that it's not the norm. It certainly isn't how true disciples of Jesus Christ should act or be towards our brothers and sisters from our Heavenly Parents.

Richard's next pet-peeve is the subtitle – "Faith and the Sanctity of Human Life".

FAITH AND THE SANCTITY OF HUMAN LIFE

Richard summarized this subtitle by saying, "Suffering is hard to measure, and the details might be disputed. But that doesn't affect my main point, which concerns the difference between secular consequential and religiously absolute moral philosophies. One school of thought cares about whether embryos can suffer. The other cares about whether they are human. Religious moralists (There goes Richard labeling or branding folks into a single group again) can be heard debating questions like:

"When does the developing embryo become a person – a human being?" Secular moralists are more likely to ask questions like, "Never mind whether it is human (what does that even mean for a little cluster of cells?); at what age does any developing embryo, of any species, become capable of suffering?" [659]

President Russell M. Nelson, who, as I said, is the current President of the Church of Jesus Christ of Latter-Day Saints, and the chief apostle and prophet, gave a talk in October 2008 when he was a member of the Quorum of the Twelve Apostles, titled, *"Abortion: An Assault on the Defenseless"*. Let me mention that President Nelson was a highly regarded heart surgeon, and so, he most certainly understood science, biology, and the physical body. I'm going to share just a small portion of President Nelson's remarks where he outlines my personal stance and perspective on this sensitive topic, and I Quote:

"As sons and daughters of God, we cherish life as a gift from Him. His eternal plan provides opportunities for His children to obtain physical bodies; to gain experiences, and to realize their divine destinies as heirs of eternal life. With that understanding and reverence for life, we deplore the loss of life associated with warfare. These data are appalling. In World War I, more than 8 million military fatalities occurred. In World War II, more than 22 million servicemen and women died. Together, these two wars, covering portions of 14 years, cost the lives of at least 30 million soldiers worldwide. That figure does not include the millions of civilian casualties.

"These data, however, are dwarfed by the toll of another war that claims more casualties annually than did World War I and World War II combined. Worldwide reports indicate that more than 40 million abortions are performed per year (Worldwide). This war called abortion is a war on the defenseless and the voiceless. It is a war on the unborn. This war is being waged globally. Ironically, civilized societies that have generally placed safeguards on human life have now passed laws that sanction this practice. This matters greatly to us because the Lord has repeatedly declared this divine imperative:

'Thou shalt not kill.' Then He added, 'Nor do anything like unto it.' Even before the fulness of the gospel was restored, enlightened individuals understood the sanctity of human life. John Calvin, a sixteenth-century reformer, wrote, 'If it seems more horrible to kill a man in his own house than in a field, it ought surely to be deemed more atrocious to destroy a fetus in the womb before it has come to light.'

"Man-made rules have now legalized that which has been forbidden by God from the dawn of time! Human reasoning has twisted and transformed absolute truth into sound-bite slogans that promote a practice that is consummately wrong." [660]

End of quote by President Nelson

If I have understood the arguments Richard gave in this subtitle, he would place President Nelson, and myself, in his grouping of *'consequentialist's'* and *'absolutists'*, calling President Nelson's remarks 'slippery slope' arguments, and would call President Nelson a *'religious foe'* of abortion. Richard would describe President Nelsons' stance, as well as my stance on this issue, as being an absolutist stance because we believe 'An embryo is a baby, and killing it is murder, and that's that: end of discussion'.

Richard goes on to bring in the argument of IVF (In vitro Fertilization) and the inconsistency that Richard says is apparent when you reflect on the fact that society already accepts IVF, in which "doctors routinely stimulate women to produce surplus eggs, to be fertilized outside the body. Therefore, IVF kills conceptuses at two stages of the procedure and society has no problem with this." I would ask, "Are eggs in and of themselves at this stage of the life generating process, a 'life', a 'person'? Has the conception of life been consummated before the egg and sperm are fertilized upon their coming together?" The answer to both questions is 'No'. This is not murder any more than sperm dying before it reaches the woman's unfertilized egg is any kind of murder." [661]

In Richard's effort to condemn his grouping of 'Religious Absolutists', he continued by sharing what he sees as another inconsistency, "A certain kind of religious mind cannot see the moral difference between killing a *'microscopic cluster of cells'* on the one hand and killing a 'full-grown doctor' on the other (Richard is referring to extremist killing an abortion doctor, which I consider to be abhorrent)."

Richard points out those people who are in the camp of "right-wing anti-abortion extremists", such as the likes of Randall Terry and 'Operation Rescue', and 'The Army of God' (AOG), and any other extremist organization." [662] Richard then labels these far-right extremists, using Paul Hill as an example, as "Dangerous, yes, but not a psychopath. Dangerously religious. What was wrong with Paul Hill was his religious faith itself." [663]

Again, Richard doesn't seem to be able to separate religious faith, and the sick mind of a religious nut job. Since Richard has a hatred for all religion, he can't seem to help himself from being so biased or avoid his bigotry on this topic of religion and the religious. I do agree with Richard when he stays, "Strong opponents of abortion are almost all deeply religious. The sincere supporters of abortion, whether personally religious or not, are likely to follow a non-religious, consequential moral philosophy." [664] However, I am not sure what Richard means by 'strong' opponent. I oppose abortion and am therefore *pro-life*, but I do not have any hate in my heart for those who are *pro-choice* and want to protect their so-called pro-choice rights, even though their act of abortion appalls me.

Richard's last point is that early embryos have no nervous system and so most certainly 'they' (The 'embryos' at certain stages) do not *suffer* when aborted. Of course, this depends on how far along the embryo is at the time of the abortion. Is the embryo a fetus? In my mind, it is not a question of suffering either way. It is a question about 'life itself' and the 'value' God has placed on 'life' and its potential. "When does 'life' begin?", for me, is the most important question in this debate or what some call 'battle'. It is my belief that 'life' (Human life and not just life) begins at fertilized conception (I would have you, my readers, watch the YouTube video called, "The #1 Mistake Christians Make When Discussing Abortion", with Ken Ham, founder of Answers in Genesis, and the 'Ark Encounter' park).

My chief point is, 'killing is killing', whether you call it a so-called 'microscopic cluster of cells' being sucked out of the mother's womb by an abortion doctor, or it's a full-term baby who is killed by the doctor moments after its birth (which is called 'infanticide'), 'killing is killing'. Killing? Destruction? Removal? Dismembering? Causing death, no matter the stage the baby's development is in, all of it is killing a human being. If you were to stab a pregnant woman to death by plunging a long knife into her belly, the law of the land says there were two murders committed – the mother and the (not yet born) baby. What is the difference then if you plunge a sopher clamp up into the woman's womb and you grab, rip, and tear the baby into pieces? I'll comment about this ritual of abortion a little later on, so let's move off this topic for now. The next subtitle Richard brings up is – "The Great Beethoven Fallacy".

The Great Beethoven Fallacy

Richard introduces what he calls "the potential argument made by anti-abortionists". He says that they argue that "Abortion has deprived it [the fetus] of the opportunity for a full human life in the future." [665] Then Richard reveals his own feeling about abortion by saying, "The notion is epitomized by a rhetorical argument whose extreme stupidity is its only defense against a charge of serious dishonesty." [666]

Next Richard uses a hypothetical dialogue between doctors in-order-to introduce what is called the 'Beethoven Fallacy'. Richard says, "About the terminating of pregnancy, I want your opinion."

"The father was syphilitic, the mother tuberculous. Of the four children born, the first was blind, the second died, the third was deaf and dumb, the fourth was also tuberculous. What would you have done? I would have terminated the pregnancy. Then you would have murdered Beethoven." [667]

Richard explains that apparently a certain professor (L.R. Agnew at UCLA Medical School), was said to have been the source of this hypothetical, and I quote Richard as saying, "It is a 'ridiculous story'. Professor Agnew apparently put this dilemma to his students and told them 'Congratulations, you have just murdered Beethoven.'" [668]

Richard goes on to say that "Invented it certainly was. It is completely false. It is, in fact, a full-fledged urban legend, a fabrication, deliberately disseminated by people with a vested interest in spreading it." Then Richard concludes by saying:

"But the fact that it is a lie is, in any case, completely beside the point. Even if it were not a lie, the argument derived from it is a very bad argument indeed." [669]

Without going any further, let me remind you, my readers, of the argument made by Richard regarding "The Great Beethoven Fallacy" wherein he said it was a typical example of "the kind of logical mess we get into when our minds are befuddled by religiously inspired absolutism." [670]

Richard's statement here, is an example of how a society, having only a subjective standard they follow, will lead to a 'logical, befuddled mess', whereas, if you have an objective standard you follow, it removes all doubt and confusion on the matter.

Richard's arguments are often ridiculous as they are meant to raise eyebrows. An example of such a ridiculous argument is the argument Richard made against the loss of the 'human potential' (which resides within every human being). Richard is saying that pro-lifers are saying that "no matter the method of depriving said human beings from coming into existence, it is tantamount to murder".

Richard then tries to make the case that the Beethoven Story is a fallacy, by using a twisted attack on the sacred pro-creative power our Creator has given to all of us – the power to bring about human life. Richard's so-called logic seems to be saying that the fallacy of the pro-life proponents valuing 'human potential' is invalid, 'if' it doesn't include the idea that just the 'potential power a person has for creating life' (the opportunity to have sex in other words), *if not seized upon immediately* (if we fail to have sex at every given opportunity that presents itself), this too would be 'tantamount to murder'.

This kind of laughable, sick logic, especially coming from someone who holds himself up as having an *eminent intellect* and the highest powers of logic in the world, in my mind, is evidence that Richard is suffering from an atheist's delusion. No one that I have ever discussed this difficult subject with, has ever posited the argument that "like abortion, even the very opportunity to have sex, no matter when it presents itself, if not acted on right then and there, is a case for murder, because a life *could be made*, and that *life's potential could bless the world*, and if you don't seize upon that opportunity, then you're a murderer too". Surely Richard is kidding. I feel he could have imagined a far better argument than using this outrageous, and dare I say 'dull-witted' argument to make his point. My goodness Richard. C'mon man. Don't you have any dignity or refinement in you?

Using Richard's so-called logic is like a man saying to any woman he comes across, "Hey, I have an uncontrollable urge to have sex, and if you don't help me satisfy my urge, you will be an accomplice to murder. The death of the potential baby that could be born from having sex with me, and the death of its potential as a person, will be on your head!" Wow! Now that's what I call a pick-up line. To this I can only say, quoting the famous philosopher Charlie Brown, "Good grief!" Richard goes on to make a statement that I find quite arrogant. He says, "The granting of uniquely special rights to cells of the species Homo Sapiens is hard to reconcile with the *fact* of evolution. Admittedly, this will not worry those many anti-abortionists who don't understand *that evolution is a fact!*" [671]

There it is. Richard saying evolution is a *fact*, over, and over again ad infinitum, is so credulous to me. It doesn't make evolution a fact Richard. As I've said countless times, the jury on the 'Case for evolution' is still out and will stay out until it is 'incontrovertibly falsified' as a theory, or 'incontrovertibly proven' as a theory, and that day, when it is proven to be false, I believe, is fast approaching.

The last argument Richard makes against anti-abortionists, is evolution itself. Richard says, "The evolution point is very simple. The humanness of an embryo's cells cannot confer upon it any '*absolutely discontinuous*' moral status" [672] (Except when you consider that God made us in His divine image).

Richard continues, "The gradual continuity that is an inescapable feature of biological evolution, tells us that there must be some *intermediate* who would lie sufficiently close to the *borderline* to blur the moral principle and destroy its absoluteness."

"A better way to say this, is that there are no natural borderlines in evolution. The illusion of *a borderline is created by the fact that the evolutionary intermediates happen to be extinct.*" [673]

How convenient is that? Why is it that Richard seems to always cry "It's an illusion" whenever evidence is discovered that brings us closer to disproving evolution? Could it possibly be because of the fact that evolution isn't all that it's cracked up to be? In order for evolution to be a *fact* like Richard just claimed it was, there must be Intermediates existing in our world today. But Richard just admitted that "there aren't any, because they're *extinct*". An interesting choice of words, don't you think? Extinct? Really? Try "There never were any intermediates to begin with Richard, and that's because everything was created as 'finished' creations at their activation (at their fertilization), God being their creator."

Richard truly has bought into this anti-Christ dogma, hook, line, and sinker, and his 'full and complete conversion' to it is why I feel comfortable saying that Richard has an atheist's delusion when it comes to its godless tenet natural selection. It has colored, or should I say, it has distorted everything else he believes in, including his belief about God's non-existence.

This can also be said about me and other theists. I too have had a '*full and complete conversion*' to the gospel of Jesus Christ, including God's Plan of Redemption and Happiness, it having been restored by the instrumentality of the prophet Joseph Smith, who God raised up in the early 19th century. And so, by Richard's interpretation of the definition of delusion and delusional, one can say that it's a good description of me too.

The fact is, either I am delusional, or Richard is delusional. There is no middle ground where we both can be right. Is there? It's one or the other. You, my readers, must decide for yourselves which of us is delusional, and which of us is of a sound mind. Either God exists, or He doesn't. Let me ask you, "At this juncture of my book, how far has your belief cursor moved along *the Percentage of Probability spectrum regarding the existence of God?* Has it moved towards or away from 'God Exists', or towards or away from "God does not exist?" Hopefully, you've been keeping track of each '*reference leg of evidence*' I've provided so far, in an effort to help you decide whether-or-not your personal 'table of belief' stand is becoming more anchored and immoveable, or more unsteady and unanchored.

The last subtitle in this chapter is – "How moderation in faith foster's fanaticism".

HOW 'MODERATION' IN FAITH FOSTERS FANATICISM

In this last subtitle of this chapter, Richard posits what he calls, 'The Dark Side of Religious Absolutism' (Often called *religious extremism* or *the American Taliban*). Richard's main point or argument is that "Even mild and moderate religion helps to provide the climate of faith in which extremism *naturally* flourishes." [674] Doesn't atheism provide the climate for despots to flourish?

To lay the foundation for Richard's argument, he relates the story of four young British Muslims, who in 2005, living in London, perpetrated a concerted suicide bomb attack. Richard describes them as "British citizens, cricket-loving, and well-mannered; just the sort of men whose company one might have enjoyed." Richard then says this of these young men, "*Only* religious faith is a strong enough force to motivate such utter madness in otherwise sane and decent people." [675]

The question is: "Why did these cricket-loving young men do it?"

To answer this question Richard quotes Sam Harris who said:

"The answer to this question is obvious – if only because it has been patiently articulated ad nauseum by bin Laden himself. The answer is that '*men like bin Laden actually believe what they say they believe*'. They believe in the literal truth of the Koran. Why did nineteen well-educated middle-class men trade their lives in this world for the privilege of killing thousands of our neighbors? Because they believed that they would go straight to paradise for doing so. It is rare to find the behavior of humans so fully and satisfactorily explained. Why have we been so reluctant to accept this explanation?" [676]

Let me say this about what Sam Harris just said. Yes, what these men did, and every other extremist have done in the name of their god, is horrific and utter madness. However, to say that it is simply because they believed "they would go straight to paradise" is an oversimplification. The culture these men grew up in was desperate circumstances; the stoking of hatred towards government and anyone who they believed were their enemies; and the lack of feeling any hope of getting out of such circumstances; and yes, the extreme influence of the religion they were taught from their youth and throughout their entire adulthood (Might I say the influence of their *apostate* religion they grew up believing was absolutely true), all of these were *influencers* that inspired them to cause mass murder.

The mind, as well as the wet brain it's connected to, when engaged in creating thoughts that are evil, carnal, sensual, and devilish, which these men's minds in fact constructed, it can't help but produce images that are as realistic a movie as the digital movies produced by the best movie production companies in the world. Thought mapping is powerful, and like faith, it is often the source of all action. This *power of imagination and fantasizing*, magnifies one's appetites and desires, and when they are enhanced by chemicals such as dopamine, oxytocin, serotonin, and endorphins, the brain's chemistry fans this fantasizing flame to where the chemical reaction or reactions stimulated by these enhancing chemicals, do in fact become impactful in their influence upon a person to act out their mental fantasies.

Most serial killers are examples of these mental gymnastics. They are products of base and licentious repeated thoughts that they have entertained day-in-and-day-out for years. And probably many times a day. The extremists that Richard uses to condemn religious absolutism, had in fact constructed their specific fantasies over time as I said. I call it *'embedded mental mapping'* which gets laid down onto the wet brain's neuropaths, often over a period of many years, including the memory of every behavior and every evil 'fantasy-thought' that these psychopaths dreamed up. The fruit of their *fantasies of the mind mixed with the chemical soup they generated in their brains*, was the suicidal blowing up of hundreds of innocent victims, including themselves, on 9/1/11.

I am not a specialist about these sorts of things by any means, but here are a few thoughts that were written by one. She's the author of the book titled, "Inside the Minds of Serial Killers: Why They Kill". Her name is Katherine Ramsland. Of course, most, if not all serial killers, are psychopaths (A person suffering from chronic mental disorder with abnormal or violent social behavior) and have other mental behavior disorders going on in their heads as well. Here are a few excerpts from Katherine's book, where she states what's going on in the minds of these psychopathic deviants:

"There are many cultural myths about serial killers, often propagated even by mental health professionals. Many assume there is a profile of a serial killer, that serial killers always go for the same victim type or always use the same MO that they are more clever than ordinary people, and that they are inevitably charming and attractive. The truth is not as simple as that (Nor is labeling extremists like Richard and Sam are doing by saying the young men were simply *religious absolutists)*. There are different types of serial killers and while there are many books that discuss the serial killer phenomenon, especially in relationship to victim types or context, researchers have not yet been able to come up with a definition, or type (Or group) that covers the broad spectrum of serial killers and their complex psychological dynamics. [677]

Katherine's publisher, *Praeger Publishers*, goes on to say, "Katherine looks at serial killer types, illustrating that it is difficult to accurately depict these elusive, intriguing, and dangerous killers. Her book examines a variety of serial killers, from sexual predators to psychotic killers, from murder teams to odd eccentric stalkers, in-order to present the *distinct psychological dynamics* that set serial killers apart from other violent murderers."

"Among the motives addressed are lust, control, glory, profit, thrill, delusions, rage, the desire for company, the need to please a partner, and even murder as an intellectual (and yes, even religious) exercise. Serial killers live double lives, hiding their violence even from those who live with them, so along with a study of motives are chapters devoted to how close associates have described killers, including parents, siblings, co-workers, lovers, and survivors. There is no profile of a serial killer, and this book establishes that in vivid and frightening detail." [678]

End of quote by Katherine Ramslands' publisher

I believe this is true of the extremists Richard and Sam are talking about as well. There is no simple profile of an extremist like Richard and Sam Harris want to label as just being religious absolutists. Am I condoning what these nut-job extremists did? Absolutely not. I'm just not ready to condemn a small handful of so-called cricket-loving Brits, as being totally and completely driven to commit these horrific acts of murder, simply because of the fruit of their religious beliefs *alone*, or as Richard described it, 'Only religious faith'. It was certainly a major factor, for sure, but it was *not* 'the only' factor as Richard and Sam would have us believe. Consider what Sam said of the question 'Why'? Here again is Sam's comments, and I quote:

"The answer to this question of 'why' is obvious – men like Bin Laden and these four young suicide bombers – actually believe what they say they believe religiously." [679]

End of Sam's quote

The fact is, Sam and Richard have an atheists' axe to grind. They hate religion and possibly even religious people themselves at times. Richard mentions a respected journalist Muriel Gray, who in writing for the (Glasgow) Harold on the 24th of July, 2005, made a similar point referencing the London bombings. Richard included her comments to help bolster his argument. Here's her quote:

"Everyone is being blamed. From the obvious villainous duo of George W. Bush and Tony Blair to the inaction of Muslim communities. But it has never been clearer that there is only (There's that absolute word 'only' again) one place to lay the blame and it has ever been thus. The cause of all this misery, mayhem, violence, terror, and ignorance is of course *'religion'* itself, and if it seems ludicrous to have to state such as obvious reality, the fact is that the government and the media are doing a pretty good job of pretending that it isn't so." [680]

End Quote

Again, is some form of *religious motivation* a factor in how these evil men's minds work? No question. It is. But it is not 'the only' factor, nor is 'pure religion' at play here at all. It is apostate religion that is at play here. Wrongly interpreted beliefs born from the mistranslated words in their so-called holy books, are what's at play, which Richard tried to delegitimize in his earlier subtitles. I must give a nod of respect to Richard and Sam for their approach however, even though it's one-sided. Just as no prosecuting attorney worth his or her salt would introduce the other side's point of view in support of their case. So, it is with Richard's and Sam's case. They don't feel they have to be fair and balanced in other words.

This being true, I'm giving you, my readers, my perspective as an alternative view to their one-sided view. That way you, my readers, can consider both perspectives and decide for yourselves whether-or-not the bombings were caused simply by religious fervor alone, or that there was more to it.

Richard goes on to make an interesting claim. He says: "Our Western politicians avoid mentioning the 'R' word (religion), and instead characterize their battle as a war against *terror*, as though terror were a kind of spirit or force with a will and mind of its own (Did we just read Richard questioning the idea that something like *terror*, which is an emotion, is a kind of force with a mind and will of its own? How then can Richard suggest that natural selection is a kind of force that directs, makes to stack up, and sets up a series, etc.? He can't have it both ways). He's characterizing terrorism as motivated by pure 'evil', but then says they're not motivated by evil. However, misguided we may think they are (These terrorists); they are motivated – like the Christian murderers of abortion doctors – by what they perceive to be righteousness; faithfully pursuing what their religion tells them." [681]

Their religion "tells them what to do, such as 'go and murder the innocent'?" Really Richard? Just as Richard has said that 'science *says* this and science *says* that', he is now repeating that same 'error of reasoning' when he tells us that "religion says to do this, and religion tells us to do that."

Religion, like science, DOES NOT SAY or DOES NOT TELL US ANYTHING. It's the men and women of science who say things about the data of science, and it's the men and women within the various religions who do all the thinking, and then do the saying, and the doing.

Is it possible that people of science and people of religion can be misguided, misdirected, and mistaken, or maybe even be under the influence of evil thoughts coming from the spirit of Satan's whisperings in their minds and hearts? Or maybe, could they even be influenced by their own repeating thoughts that they've conjured up from their own *'vain imaginations'*, thus driving their actions over many years of sick mental mapping? Could they have possibly imagined outrageous ideas as coming from their so-called faith or religion, and then they chose to act out on those evil imaginations? Religion, meaning religious experience, certainly does influence, but they *don't* make anybody do evil by holding a gun to their congregants' heads. People *choose* to do evil, or they choose to do good. No religion that I am aware of forces its believers to do evil or forces them to do good. Just ask yourself, "Is your faith or lack of faith, *forcing* you to do something bad? Does it force you to do something good?" Again, I would ask that you, my readers, to become an honest fruit inspector and listen to what comes into your heart and mind when you ask yourself these questions.

The fact is that such evil ideas and imagined beliefs are far from what pure religion teaches. Again, religion does *not* say anything in-and-of itself. The same is true of pure religion. It is people themselves that go about saying what 'their' religion teaches them to think, do, and speak. So, to Richard and Sam I say … C'mon man. Lighten up. Let's not do the *'one size fits all'* condemning of an entire group of people here, okay? Individuals are the ones doing the evil things. That said, I will agree that false religion does provide the climate for such anti-social religious behaviors to flourish, but I submit that pure religion absolutely does not.

Richard continues with his diatribe against religionists, saying: "They are not psychotic; they are religious idealists who, by their own lights, are rational. They perceive their acts to be good, not because they have *been possessed by Satan*, but because they have been brought up, from the cradle, to have total and unquestioning faith." [682]

If that isn't a biased, bigoted opinion, (which means obstinately or unreasonably attached to a belief, opinion, or faction, in particular prejudiced against or antagonistic toward a person or people on the basis of their membership of a particular group) then I don't know what is.

Having lived in the '*Land of the Free and the Home of the Brave*', as an American, I have and continue to enjoy religious freedom, at least so far. Our nations' founding fathers had the wisdom to establish laws that protect this freedom so that as an American citizen, I'm able to enjoy the privilege of worshiping Almighty God according to the dictates of my own conscience, and I allow all men that same privilege. Let them worship how, where, or what they may, ... but ... that privilege cannot be expressed outside of the law. If it is, then the full weight of the law must be applied to any such lawbreaker.

I do not believe in allowing extremists, or anyone else for that matter, to cross the line of religious freedom, over to the side of lawlessness in the name of one's God, where they commit heinous acts of violence in the name of their religion and God. For example, having been motivated by the lure of their heightened visions of grandeur and the promised pleasures of paradise (Apparently 70 wives each), the cricket-players stepped out of the bounds of the law and murdered people. That's not expressing religious freedom. That's breaking the law. As long as anyone stays on the side of the law and allows everyone's religious freedom to be expressed freely within the law, so that everyone can enjoy the privilege of worshiping whom or what they choose to worship, or, to not worship anything or anyone at all; if that's their choice, then we can live in peace and harmony. This religious freedom was granted to every American by our constitution – both the freedom *of* and the freedom *from* religion – under the law.

Let me share what Richard said Sam Harris said about the lure of paradise that these terrorists imagined in their warped minds. I won't quote the entire statement, but I will give the last paragraph to make my point. Here it is, and I quote:

"The young men and the planner then knelt and placed their right hands on the Koran. The planner said: "Are you ready? Tomorrow you will be in Paradise." [683]

End Quote

This promise that "tomorrow you will be in paradise" is, of course, a statement of false doctrine born of apostasy (because if you are a murderer, you certainly will not go to paradise). It's a belief born of and steeped in the falling away from pure truth and the pure religion that existed from the beginning. Would I prefer they come to the belief in the pure gospel of Jesus Christ? Yes. But as I said, I believe in allowing all men the privilege of worshiping as they choose, as long as their acts of worship don't cross the line to where they break the law, such as committing mass murder as these extremists did. When someone crosses that line, they forfeit their privileges and must be made subject to the consequences and full extent of the law, and hopefully the fear of suffering the punishment that is commensurate with their crime will keep them, and others, from stepping over that line.

Richard and Sam are correct when they say – "These people actually believe what they say they believe". And what *they* believe can lead to their acting out on the fantasies that have finally reached their emotional peak, and that peak, for them, was to blow themselves and others up. But you cannot hang their behavior, and the evil it produced, on the shoulders of '*pure, undefiled religion*'. If you do, then you're just being prejudiced towards religion in general, which Richard, Sam, and the other atheists that Richard has quoted throughout his book, all seem to be. Richard manifests his prejudiced, biased, and bigoted opinion when he says such things like the following statement, and I quote:

"The take-home message is that we should blame religion itself, not religious extremism – as though that were some kind of terrible perversion of *real, decent religion* (Richard is trying to remove the possibility that there is any such thing as pure religion, or real, decent religion). Voltaire got it right long ago when he said: 'Those who can *make* you believe absurdities can make you commit atrocities." [684]

End quote

Using the word *make* in this quote implies that someone is holding something like a gun to someone's head or is threatening someone in such a way that it *makes* that person believe something that's absurd when they don't want to believe it, or do it. Nobody makes anybody think a certain way. I would say that Voltaire used a poor choice of words here. He may have been better served if he would have said:

"Those who can *convince you* to believe absurdities can probably *convince you* to commit atrocities".

I hope by now you understand the point I've been trying to make here. Next Richard once again shares his scientific, atheist, logic when he says:

"As long as we accept the principle that religious faith must be respected simply because it is religious faith, it is hard to withhold respect from the faith of Osama Bin Laden and the suicide bombers. The alternative, one so transparent that it should need no urging, is to abandon the principle of *automatic respect* for religious faith (I'm not convinced that it is automatic). This is one reason why I do everything in my power to warn people against *faith* itself, not just against so-called *extremist* faith. The teachings of moderate religion, though not extremist in themselves, are an open invitation to extremism." [685]

As I've said many times, this is just Richard's opinion. In my Latter-Day Saint mind, Richard has failed to come to an understanding of the difference between true or pure religion (Which Richard called *real, decent religion*) versus apostate or moderately defiled religion. I give Richard, once again, a little slack here because what he sees in the many false religions of our Day, is apostasy's fruits fully ripened on its many trees. It is these fruits of apostasy, I believe, that have led Richard to state legitimate claims about these apostate religions, but they are not legitimate claims about pure, prefect religion. Here is an excerpt from a talk given by Kent P. Jackson, an assistant professor of ancient scripture at Brigham Young University, that I want to share with you, my readers, because it relates perfectly to this topic of apostasy, and I quote:

"The Church of Jesus Christ of Latter-Day Saints has proclaimed to the world consistently since its beginning that there was an apostasy of the church founded by Jesus during his Palestinian ministry and led by his apostles following his ascension. This is a fundamental belief of the Latter-Day Saints. If there had not been an apostasy, there would have been *no need* for a restoration. Latter-Day Saint theology asserts that the Church established by the Savior and led by his apostles in the Old World, *came to an end within a century after its formation*. The doctrines which its inspired leaders taught were *corrupted* and *changed* by others not of similar inspiration, the authority to act in God's name was taken from the earth, and none of the Christian systems that existed after those developments, though they did some good things, enjoyed *divine endorsement* as the Lord's own Church.

JS—H 1:19

19 I was answered that I must join none of them, for they were all wrong; and the Personage who addressed me said that all their creeds were an abomination in his sight; that those professors were all corrupt; that: "they draw near to me with their lips, but their hearts are far from me, they teach for doctrines the commandments of men, having a form of godliness, but they deny the power thereof."

Doctrine & Covenants 1:30

30 And also those to whom these commandments were given, might have power to lay the foundation of this church, and to bring it forth out of obscurity and out of darkness, the only true and living church upon the face of the whole earth, with which I, the Lord, am well pleased, speaking unto the church collectively and not individually —

"Possibly, the best single witness of the apostasy of New Testament Christianity is the New Testament itself. The *New Testament writers prophesied that apostasy would take place in the Church and that the Church in fact would be overcome by it.* Just as significantly, the New Testament actually records that apostasy was happening even as their records were being written. As time progressed, the heresies against which the apostles contended, became increasingly virulent and successful, as the record attests. Near the end of the first century, the apostolic record came to a sudden close." [686]

End of excerpt

The full talk can be found by searching "Early Signs of the Apostasy" at www.churchofjesuschrist.org. My point in sharing it is simple. It is disingenuous for Richard to place Christ's pure religion, and its pure doctrine, into the group that Richard has placed all religions in, saying, "religious extremism is NOT some kind of terrible perversion of real, decent (Or what I'm calling PURE) religion." [687]

This statement shows Richard's ignorance of apostasy and how it has ravaged the pure religion God gives His children through His apostles and prophets. Once the apostles and prophets were killed off, God's children were left to fend for themselves until ultimately, they fell away, leaving the generations that followed believing in a *'form of godliness'*, but *'denying the power thereof'*. The pure gospel of Jesus Christ, when replaced with the precepts of men, mingled with scripture, becomes an apostate religion.

Richard repeats his firm belief that, and I quote:

"More generally (and this applies to Christianity no less than to Islam), what is really pernicious is the practice of teaching children that faith is a virtue. Faith (To Richard this means any kind of religious faith) is evil precisely because it requires no justification and brooks no argument.

"Teaching children that unquestioned faith is a virtue primes them – given certain other ingredients that are not hard to come by – to grow up into potentially lethal weapons for future jihads, or crusades. Immunized against fear by the promise of a martyr's paradise, the authentic faith-head deserves a high place in history.

"Faith (I think Richard is still referring to Unquestioned Faith here, at least I hope so) can be very, very dangerous, and to deliberately implant it into the vulnerable mind of an innocent child is a grievous wrong. It is to childhood itself, and the violation of childhood by religion, that we turn in the next chapter." [688]

End Quote

Unlike what Richard says of theists, I do not have, nor do I believe in 'unquestioned faith', or 'blind faith' as Richard suggests all theist believe. I'm confident that as you, my readers, have been reading my perspective on Richard's arguments so far, you have come to understand why I say that one only needs to become a fruit inspector and review the actions and behaviors of any of these various devotees of various religions, to conclude that the 'pure gospel' as it was once observed, even the pure gospel of the True and Living God, has in fact been corrupted. Anyone of a sound and open mind would know that God would never require His devotees to commit the kind of unprovoked acts of senseless murder that the cricket-loving Islamists Richard spoke about.

It's not my intent here to ridicule Richard, or any of the religions of the world, including Islam, but I do see Richard as being spiritually blinded by spiritual cataracts of hatred and bias towards God and religion of any kind. Richard developed these spiritual cataracts early on by reading books that contain only half-truths, as well as associating with other atheists with his same worldview disease, and as a result these spiritual cataracts have confined Richard to a view of life that is full of spiritual darkness; a life where religious bigotry and the spirit of Satan reigns freely in his and other atheists' minds.

Richard's bigotry manifests itself in his obstinate and what I feel is an unreasonable attachment to atheism and evolution, which often produces prejudice against any person who claims membership in any form of religion or declares their faith and belief in God as our creator and not accepting evolutions' natural selection as our creator and director. These spiritual cataracts have kept and continue to keep Richard, and more than half the world's population, blinded spiritually and unable to recognize the pure gospel of Jesus Christ for what it truly is – God's Plan of Happiness and Redemption for His children. This spiritual blindness is one more reason I feel I have license to say that "Richard suffers from an atheist's delusion".

Okay, on to the next chapter, chapter 9, which is – "Childhood Abuse and the Escape from Religion".

CHAPTER 9

CHILDHOOD, ABUSE AND THE ESCAPE FROM RELIGION

Richard begins chapter 9 by sharing an anecdote that describes the *attitude of mind* that children of our Day have, due to their growing up in religious homes. This anecdotal story is from a book written by David I. Kertzer, titled, "The Kidnapping of Edgardo Mortara", and as Richard says, "This nineteenth-century human tragedy sheds a pitiless light on present-day *religious attitudes* towards children." [689]

Edgardo's story is one of priestly abduction with the purpose of converting (I use that word loosely) non-Catholic children such as Jews, to the Roman Catholic faith. It occurred in 1858. You can read the book if you want to read the full story. It's about a child, Edgardo, who was secretly baptized at some earlier date, and the Inquisition came to hear about it at some later date. This practice was a central part of the Roman Catholic belief system at that time. My point in bringing up this story, is to highlight the point Richard made about this story, which was "In their mental world, to allow a Christian child to stay with his Jewish parents was not an option, and they (The Catholic Priesthood holders) maintained this bizarre and cruel stance steadfastly, and with the utmost sincerity, in the face of worldwide outrage." [690]

Richard continues, "Being brought up in a stupor of belief that a child who dies unbaptized, would suffer forever in hell, Edgardo's baby-sitter (The illiterate Catholic girl who looked after Edgardo) sought advice from a Catholic neighbor who told her how to do a baptism." [691] Richard goes on to describe a perfect example of *apostasy in full display*, and I quote:

"Amazingly for a rite (A rite is called an ordinance in my faith) that could have such monumental significance for a whole extended family, the Catholic Church allowed (and still allows) *anybody* (Baptized member or otherwise) to baptize anybody else. The baptizer doesn't have to be a priest. Neither the child, nor the parents, nor anybody else has to consent to the baptism. Nothing need be signed. Nothing need be officially witnessed. All that is necessary is a splash of water, a few words, a helpless child, and a superstitious and catechistically brainwashed babysitter." [692]

Next Richard summarizes this story by saying, "In my book, I have deliberately refrained from detailing the horrors of the Crusades, the conquistadores, or the Spanish Inquisition. Cruel and evil people can be found in every century and of every persuasion. But this story of the Italian Inquisition and its attitude towards children is particularly revealing of the *religious mind (of just Catholics?)*, and 'the evils that arise' specifically because it is religious" (I wonder why Richard keeps using the term religious 'mind' instead of 'brain' since he doesn't believe there is a mind. For him there's just the brain at work here). [693]

My perspective is that it is apostasy that is at work here, and more specifically it's the spirit of anti-Christ, the spirit of Satan, and not simply because it is religious. Richard continues: "Has there ever been a more flagrant misdirection of words like 'forced', 'compulsorily', 'ferocious', and 'bigotry'? Yet all the indications are that Catholic apologists, from the Pope down, sincerely believed that what they were doing was right; absolutely right morally, and right for the welfare of the child. Such is the power of (mainstream 'moderate') religion to warp judgement and pervert ordinary human decency." [694]

End Quotes

I don't think I could have said it any better than how Richard describes apostasy once again, though not knowing that it is apostasy that he is describing. This warped perversion of what Richard calls 'moderate religion' is indeed a perfect example of how Satan, the father of lies, goes about distorting Jesus' pure gospel. Satan wants to destroy each-and-every form of religion that exists throughout the world, and in particular He wants to destroy those principles that teach the purpose of God's eternal plan that He prepared for His children so that they can become like Him and return to His presence. This destruction of the pure gospel of Jesus Christ, which is pure religion, has ever been the way of apostasy, for it is the way of Satan, even the way of 'anti-Christ'.

Richard concludes his introduction to this chapter by saying:

"What mattered to Edgardo was not his religion (he was too young to possess thought-out religious opinions) but the love and care of his parents and family, and he was deprived of those by celibate priests whose grotesque cruelty was mitigated only by their crass insensitivity to normal human feelings – an insensitivity that comes all too easily to a mind hijacked by (Apostate) religious faith." [695]

One can't help but see what happens to men and women when they choose to disregard the Light of Christ and its influence for doing good. Without the Light of Christ's spirit *'striving'* with man, man ends up with perversions like the one Richard described here in Edgardo's sad story. Let me now share what I believe is the reason for Richard's belief that *'teaching religion to a child is child abuse'*. Richard gives the reason himself as he concludes his intro to chapter 9. Here's what he said about his claim:

"Even without physical abduction, *isn't it always a form of child abuse to label children as possessors of beliefs that they are too young to have thought about*? Yet the practice persists to this day, almost entirely unquestioned. *To question it is my main purpose in this chapter.*" [696]

Before we get too far into chapter 9, let me share a few of my thoughts regarding when it's appropriate to teach little children spiritual principles, and when it is not. Because little children don't have the mental or spiritual maturity to understand the commitments that must be made at baptism, the Lord instructed His prophet, Joseph Smith, that children must be at least eight years old, and older, before they can be baptized. Age eight is the *'age of accountability'* (Being accountable for one's choices) one must reach before they can make the baptismal covenant with God. The Church of Jesus Christ of Latter-Day Saints, therefore, does not baptize or confirm little babies, toddlers, or even three-to-seven-year-old children.

As the Church of Jesus Christ, we do however, perform an *ordinance* for our little ones where we take an infant in our arms and pronounce upon them a name and a blessing. This ordinance is simply called a 'Baby Blessing', which can only be performed by the father, grandfather, brother, uncle, or a male friend who holds the Melchizedek priesthood and is in good standing, meaning, they hold a current temple recommend. That way the entire Church can know and bear witness that this ordinance, like all other ordinances in Christ's Church, was performed *"by one having authority"* to do so. But that is not the rite or ordinance we are talking about here. We're talking about the false practice of *Infant Baptism*.

At the time Jesus came on the scene, John the Baptist had the authority to perform the ordinance called Baptism. Because John held the office of Priest in the Aaronic Priesthood, which office included bearing the priesthood keys necessary to baptize people with that authority, Jesus Himself submitted to John's authority and waded down into the river Jordan to be baptized by John, who was his cousin. John the Baptist laid Jesus back into the river and immersed Him fully under the water, which symbolized a new birth, fulfilling Heavenly Father's commandment to willingly obey Him in all things.

As members of the Church of Jesus Christ of Latter-Day Saints, we follow Jesus' example by being baptized by one having this same Priesthood authority and its keys. That said, we do not baptize infants. Infant Baptism is a fruit of the false tree of apostasy. Babies cannot know nor can they understand the gospel sufficiently to make the baptismal covenant with God. Toddlers cannot possibly understand the principle of repentance, yet the Catholic church, as I understand their doctrine, still baptize little infants by their priests sprinkling or pouring water over the infants' forehead, which rite shows a lack of understanding of Christ's atonement and its purpose in our spiritual lives.

A story regarding Mormon, a prophet from the Book of Mormon, provides wonderful insight on what God has revealed on this subject of 'Infant Baptism', sin, and the process of repentance. Not long after Mormons' son Moroni was called to be a prophet leader for a community of people living in what is now called North America, certain disagreements arose within the Church membership that Moroni presided over. Their disagreement was whether or not little children should be baptized. In other words, Infant Baptism. Moroni decided to write a letter to his father, Mormon, who was the senior prophet and presiding authority over the entire land but lived in a different part of the land than Moroni lived in. In the letter Moroni asked for counsel on this point of doctrine. Mormon prayed to Heavenly Father and received the following answer to his inquiry, which he then sent back to his son Moroni:

Moroni 8:8

8 Listen to the words of Christ, your Redeemer, your Lord, and your God. Behold, I came into the world not to call the righteous but sinners to repentance; the whole need no physician, but they that are sick; wherefore, *little children are whole*, for *they are not capable of committing sin*; wherefore the curse of Adam is taken from them in me, (The Lord Jehovah, who later came to earth and was known as Jesus of Nazareth, even the Son of God, is speaking here) that it hath no power over them; and the law of circumcision is done away in me.

Moroni 8:9–12

9 And after this manner did the Holy Ghost manifest the word of God unto me; wherefore, my beloved son, I know that it is *solemn mockery* before God, that ye should baptize *little children*.

10 Behold I say unto you that this thing shall ye teach—repentance and baptism *unto those who are accountable and capable of committing sin*; yea, teach parents that they must repent and be baptized, and humble themselves as their little children, and they shall all be saved with their little children.

11 And their little children need no repentance, neither baptism. Behold, baptism is *unto* repentance (Leads to repentance) to the fulfilling the commandments unto the remission of sins (which leads to the remission of sins).

12 But little children are alive in Christ, even from the foundation of the world; if not so, God is a partial God, and also a changeable God, and a respecter to persons; for how many little children have died without baptism!

As I said earlier, in our own dispensation the Lord revealed to the prophet Joseph Smith that children should be baptized at the age of eight (The age of accountability) and older:

Doctrine & Covenants 68:25, 27

25 And again, inasmuch as parents have children in Zion, or in any of her stakes which are organized, that teach them not to understand the doctrine of repentance, faith in Christ the Son of the Living God, and of baptism and the gift of the Holy Ghost by the laying on of the hands, when eight years old, the sin be upon the heads of the parents.

26 For this shall be a law unto the inhabitants of Zion, or in any of her stakes which are organized.

27 And their children shall be baptized for the remission of their sins when *eight years old*, and receive the laying on of the hands (For the receipt of Gift of the Holy Ghost).

As Later-Day Saints we do not believe that it is necessary for people, (eight and older), to have an apologetic understanding of all the doctrines of God before baptism can be performed, and that's because increased knowledge will come line upon line as newly baptized persons study and continue to pray after their baptism. But we do believe, however, as God has directed, that baptismal candidates have a basic understanding of right and wrong; who Jesus is; what repentance means; the truthfulness of the Restoration; and a few additional teachings of the gospel of Jesus Christ, at least by the time they reach the age of accountability, which, as the Lord said, 'when eight years old'.

Let's go on to the subtitles of this chapter now. The first subtitle is – "Physical and mental abuse" (See Footnote 698 at the end of this book – "Preventing and Responding to Abuse", to read what the Church of Jesus Christ of Latter-Day Saints current policies & guidelines are regarding abuse) [697]

Physical and Mental Abuse

I do not want to say I know or understand exactly what Richard describes next, as he writes about the hysteria people express about the heinous crime of pedophilia. The example of hysteria and vigilantism Richard gives, occurred around the year 2,000 when zealot vigilantes were attacking pedophiles in England (I didn't avail myself to any news stories that spoke of these events in England).

After reviewing his view on the subject, Richard said something that really caught my attention. He said, "All three of the boarding schools I attended employed teachers whose *affection* for small boys overstepped the bounds of propriety. That was indeed reprehensible. Nevertheless if, fifty years on, they had been hounded by vigilantes or lawyers as no better than child murderers, I should have felt obliged to come to their defense, (And here is the comment that caught my attention) *'even as the victim of them'* (an embarrassing but otherwise harmless experience)." [698]

Knowing but little of Richard's upbringing, including his Anglican background and the boarding schools he attended as a youth, I do know that he had some religious experiences as a youth for he mentioned he attended public schools that had a Church of England ethos. I was saddened to learn that while attending a boarding school in Salisbury during his early years, he had the unfortunate experience of being quote, "mildly molested by overstepping teachers". Notice Richard said teachers in the plural.

Richard in an interview for Times Magazine said, "while he was under the care and stewardship of an unnamed School Master in Salisbury, he was *mildly molested*". This being true, I believe that it became an additional factor that helped take Richard down the path to atheism from around the age of fifteen. Today Richard considers this reprehensible experience as simply *"an embarrassing but otherwise harmless experience"*. "Wow! I'm flabbergasted at that statement: "otherwise a harmless experience?"

Let's continue. Listen carefully as Richard expresses his dislike of the Roman Catholic Church. He says, "The Roman Catholic Church has borne a heavy share of such retrospective opprobrium (the public disgrace arising from their shameful conduct). For all sorts of reasons, I dislike the Roman Catholic Church. But I dislike unfairness even more, and I can't help wondering whether this one institution has been unfairly demonized over the issue (of child molestation), especially in Ireland and America. I suppose some additional public resentment flows from the hypocrisy of priests whose professional life is largely devoted to arousing guilt about 'sin' (I would switch the word *guilt* out with the words "arousing shame about sin" in its place)." [699]

A little later Richard continues, "Horrible as sexual abuse no doubt was, the damage was arguably less than the long-term psychological damage inflicted by bringing the child up Catholic in the first place." [700]

This truly shows Richard's hatred towards any and all religions. Richard goes on to relate the story of a woman from America who wrote him. The woman said that she had been brought up as Roman Catholic, and at the age of seven she was sexually abused by her parish priest in his car. She also said that around this same time, a little schoolfriend of hers, who had tragically died, went to hell because she was a Protestant, or so this woman had been led to believe by the then official doctrine of her friends' church, which she learned from her parents.

This woman's view as a mature adult now, was that, of these two examples of Roman Catholic child abuse, the one physical and the other mental, the second example of mental abuse was by far the worst. Richard goes on to say, "Sticks and stones may break my bones, but words can never hurt me". This adage is true as long as you don't really believe the words. But if your whole upbringing, and everything you have even been told by parents, teachers, and priests, has led you to believe, really believe, utterly and completely, that sinners burn in hell (or some other obnoxious article of doctrine such as that a woman is the property of her husband), it is entirely plausible that words could have a more long-lasting and damaging effect than deeds." [701]

Richard finishes his point by saying, "I am persuaded that the phrase *child abuse* is no exaggeration when used to describe what teachers and priests are doing to children whom they encourage to believe in something like the punishment of unshriven (not confessed or absolved) mortal sins in an eternal hell." [702]

I've chosen not to go into the examples of pastors Roberts and Haggard, that Richard gives from his interviews during his documentary on religion. Suffice it to say that I agree with Richard's criticism of the false doctrine regarding what 'hell' is. Many religious leaders and teachers preach that it is a place where '*actual brimstone and eternal flames of hellfire continually burning you*'. I ask my Christian friends, "If it is just a person's spirit that goes to Hell at one's death until they are resurrected and receive their body once again, how do these spirit persons 'feel' the pain of 'burning flames' upon their spirits? I thought only bodies of flesh and bones 'feel' physical pain.

Or are you saying that people after death immediately receive their resurrected bodies of flesh and bone and that they're sent to hell at the time of their death, so that they can 'feel' the flames heat, but not be consumed? This doctrine is a false, apostate doctrine, and it is used as a *spiritual club* to terrify and shame people into coming to Christ, yet it seems to me, to be an abject failure at doing so, as this woman's experience shows.

Richard continues, "If I think back to my childhood, it's one dominated by *fear*. And it was the fear of disapproval (The fruit of shame) while in the present, but also of eternal damnation (To me it sounds like Richard was shamed over and over. Does it appear that way to you too?). And for a child, images of hellfire and gnashing of teeth, are actually very real. They are not metaphorical at all." [703]

Richard then asked the woman we've been discussing here, to spell out what she had actually been told about hell, as a child, and her eventual reply, after a long hesitation, was: "It's strange, isn't it? After all this time it still has the power to … affect me … when you … when you ask me that question. Hell is a fearful place. It's complete rejection by God (Again, the power of shame, which is rejection or condemnation of the person and not just the sin or behavior. That's the message and fruit of shame). It's complete judgement, there is *real fire*, there is *real torment*, *real torture*, and it goes on forever so there is no respite from it." [704]

You may be asking yourself, "Okay Marty, what does your Church teach about hell, if hell is not an actual place of continually burning flames that burn its' residents without consuming them?" Well, the answer to this question is found in the Doctrine & Covenants, section 76. Elder Bruce R. McConkie, a past member of the Quorum of the Twelve Apostles, said the following about *hell, and I quote:*

"That part of the spirit world inhabited by wicked *spirits,* who are awaiting the eventual day of their resurrection, is called *hell.* Between their death and resurrection, these souls of the wicked are cast out into *outer darkness,* into the gloomy depression of Sheol, into the hades of waiting wicked spirits; into hell" (This part of the spirit world is often called "Spirit Prison"). There they suffer the 'torments of the damned' (*Not* actual flames of fire though); there they welter in the vengeance of *'eternal fire'* (What does Elder McConkie mean by 'Eternal Fire' here? Read on); there is found 'weeping and wailing and gnashing of teeth'; ... there the *fiery indignation* of the wrath of God is poured out upon the wicked (Please continue reading for a much clearer picture of what 'eternal fire' and 'fiery indignation' are before you jump to any conclusion):

Alma 40:11–14

11 Now, concerning the state of the soul between death and the resurrection—Behold, it has been made known unto me by an angel, that the spirits of all men, as soon as they are departed from this mortal body, yea, the spirits of all men, whether they be good or evil, are taken home to that God who gave them life.

12 And then shall it come to pass, that the spirits of those who are righteous are received into a state of happiness, which is called *paradise,* a state of rest, a state of peace, where they shall rest from all their troubles and from all care, and sorrow.

13 And then shall it come to pass, that the spirits of the wicked, yea, who are evil—for behold, they have no part nor portion of the Spirit of the Lord; for behold, they chose evil works rather than good; therefore the spirit of the devil did enter into them, and take possession of their house—and these shall be cast out into *outer darkness*; there shall be weeping, and wailing, and gnashing of teeth, and this because of their own iniquity, being led captive by the will of the devil.

14 Now this is the state of the souls of the wicked, yea, in darkness, and a state of awful, fearful looking for the *fiery indignation* of the wrath of God upon them; thus they remain in this ᵉstate, as well as the righteous in paradise, *until the time of their resurrection.*

Doctrine & Covenants 76:103–106

103 These are they who are liars, and sorcerers, and adulterers, and whoremongers, (someone who participates with whores), and whosoever loves and makes a lie.

104 These are they who suffer the wrath of God on earth.

105 These are they who suffer the vengeance of eternal fire.

106 These are they who are cast down to hell and suffer the wrath of Almighty God, *until the fulness of times,* when Christ shall have subdued all enemies under his feet, and shall have perfected his work;

Doctrine & Covenants 76:44

44 Wherefore, he saves all except them—they shall go away into everlasting punishment, which is endless punishment, which is eternal punishment, to reign with the devil and his angels in eternity, where their worm dieth not, and the *'fire'* is not quenched, which is their torment (Read on to learn what kind of *fire* this is).

"Thus, for those who are heirs of some salvation, which includes all except the sons of perdition, *hell has an end.*" [705]

End of quote by Elder McConkie

The Latter-Day Saint Bible Dictionary says:

"As Later-Day Saints we believe the scriptures use the term 'hell' in at least *two* ways:

First, hell is the part of the *spirit world* inhabited by the wicked *until* they repent and at some time during the millennium are resurrected. This hell is a *literal* but *temporary* condition or state of *spiritual torment and suffering (And not in the physical sense as Christians believe it is).*

Second, the scriptures sometimes use the word *hell* to refer to a *permanent* condition of torment and suffering for those who are *sons of perdition.*" [706]

If one stops here, they may think that Latter-Day Saints believe hell to be exactly what the examples Richard said his interviewees believed hell to be. But remember, Elder McConkie used the words ' spiritual torment' and not physical, flesh torment that would come by way of real fire on real flesh.

Let me share a message given by Elder Dallin H. Oaks, who is currently the First Counselor in the First Presidency of the Church of Jesus Christ of Latter-Day Saints (at the time of this writing). His talk is titled "Sin and Suffering". It will give you, my readers, a much clearer understanding, and sense of what my view, as a Latter-Day Saint, is on 'spiritual torment'. Here are a few excerpts from his talk, and I quote:

"I begin by describing an event that happened here on campus. About fifteen years ago, a group of newspaper editors from various western states came to Salt Lake City to learn more about the Church. They visited with Church authorities, went to Temple Square, saw the welfare program in action, and then came to BYU. At dinner in the Wilkinson Center, I sat with an editor from California. He was immensely impressed with what he had seen. "You Mormons really know how to do it," he said. Then he praised the various things he had seen. I enjoyed his positive reactions to everything. Later, he asked the location of the nearest rest room and excused himself. When he returned, he had a triumphant smile on his face. "Well, I found out that you Mormons are just like everyone else," he said. In response to my question, he explained.

"When I go into a rest room in another public place, I find there are things written on the wall. When I went to the rest room here in the Wilkinson Center, I found it was just like other rest rooms. There was something written on the wall. Sorry that the man's gleaming impressions had been tarnished, I began to apologize about how difficult it was to keep current on the maintenance in a public place. He smiled and raised his hand to stop me. "Oh, I'm just kidding," he said. "It's true there was something written in there, but I've never seen anything like that written on the wall in a public place. It was just one word: *repent.*"

"Whoever wrote that word on a rest room wall in the Wilkinson Center many years ago at least knew the word *repent,* which is more than can be said for many people in the world today. But I wonder how many of us understand the principle and purpose of repentance, including its relationship to sin and suffering.

The Subject of Sin

"We are concerned that some young people who are anticipating serving a mission or being married in the temple have *a very lax attitude toward sin.* I'll just have a few free ones," they say, "and then I'll repent quickly, and go on my mission (or get married in the temple), and everything will be all right."

"Young people are not the only ones with a lax attitude toward sin. We know of mature members of the Church who commit serious transgressions *knowingly and deliberately*, relying on their supposed ability later to repent speedily and be "as good as new." Such persons want *the present convenience or enjoyment of sin and the future effects of righteousness*, in that order. They want to experience the sin but avoid its effects. The Book of Mormon describes such persons:

II Nephi 28:8

28 And there shall also be many which shall say: Eat, drink, and be merry; nevertheless, fear God— he will justify in committing a little sin; yea, lie a little, take the advantage of one because of his words, dig a pit for thy neighbor; there is no harm in this; and do all these things, for tomorrow we die; and if it so be that we are guilty, God will beat us with a few stripes, and at last we shall be saved in the kingdom of God.

"The attitude and position of such persons is exactly the opposite of the Savior, who never experienced sin (And that's because He never did sin Himself), but whose atoning sacrifice subjected Him to all of its 'anguish'. When I was a young man, I accompanied a Protestant friend to his church service. There I heard a minister take on the subject of sin. It was an uneven contest. *That minister really beat up on sin.* "He condemned it. He denounced it. He castigated it. He left no doubt in the mind of anyone that he was against sin. But he didn't give the congregation one word of definition or explanation about what it was.

"To minimize misunderstanding, I will give some illustrations of the kinds of things I mean when I refer to sin or transgression. In its widest application, *sin* includes every irregularity of behavior, every source of uncleanliness. But many things that are sins under this widest definition are just grains of sand or specks of dirt that come out in the weekly wash and do not block our progress on the path toward eternal life. When I speak of *sin* in this message, I refer to *serious transgressions*, the 'boulder-size' obstacles that block the path and cannot be removed without *prolonged repentance*. During one-week last month a knowledgeable observer listed some of the crimes reported in a Utah newspaper and then struck off those where the accused was not a member of this Church. The following list illustrates the kinds of sins in which Latter-Day Saints were involved:

Fraud
Sale of illegal drugs
Aggravated assault
Aggravated kidnapping
Sexual abuse by a woman upon a child
Sexual abuse by a man upon a child
A professional having sexual relations with a client

"Church disciplinary records make us aware of other serious transgressions rarely reported in the press: adultery, fornication, polygamy, and apostasy. When the Savior appeared to the people of this continent, He spoke of the final judgment. Here's what He said:

III Nephi 24:5

5 And I will come near to you to judgment; and I will be a swift witness against the sorcerers, and against the adulterers, and against false swearers, and against those that oppress the hireling in his wages, the widow and the fatherless, and that turn aside the stranger, and fear not me, saith the Lord of Hosts.

"Those are some illustrations of serious transgressions. Others could be given. As background, let us review some familiar principles. One of the principal purposes of this life is to test the children of God, to see whether we will keep his commandments:

Abraham 3:25

25 And we will prove them herewith, to see if they will do all things whatsoever the Lord their God shall command them;

Therefore, this life is "a probationary time," as Alma called it, "a time to repent and serve God":

Alma 42:4

4 And thus we see, that there was a time granted unto man to repent, yea, a probationary time, a time to repent and serve God.

Breaking of a commandment of God is sin. For every sin there is "a punishment affixed":

Alma 42:18

18 Now, there was a punishment affixed, and a just law given, which brought remorse of conscience unto man.

Amos 3:1–2

1 Hear this word that the LORD hath spoken against you, O children of Israel, against the whole family which I brought up from the land of Egypt, saying,

2 You only have I known of all the families of the earth: therefore I will punish you for all your iniquities.

In the final judgment, we will stand before God to be judged according to our works:

Alma 11:41

41 Therefore the wicked remain as though there had been no redemption made, except it be the loosing of the bands of death; for behold, the day cometh that [b]all shall rise from the dead and stand before God, and be judged according to their works.

III Nephi 26:4

4 And even unto the great and last day, when all people, and all kindreds, and all nations and tongues shall stand before God, to be judged of their works, whether they be good or whether they be evil—

Doctrine & Covenants 19:3

3 Retaining all power, even to the destroying of Satan and his works at the end of the world, and the last great day of judgment, which I shall pass upon the inhabitants thereof, judging every man according to his works and the deeds which he hath done.

"Those who have broken the commandments of God and have not repented of their sins in this life, will 'stand with awful guilt before the bard of God'":

Jacob 6:9

9 Know ye not that if ye will do these things, that the power of the redemption and the resurrection, which is in Christ, will bring you to stand with shame and awful guilt before the bar of God?

They will have "an awful view of their own guilt and abominations":

Mosiah 3:25

25 And if they be evil they are consigned to an awful view of their own guilt and abominations, which doth cause them to shrink from the presence of the Lord into a state of misery and endless torment, from whence they can no more return; therefore they have drunk damnation to their own souls.

The scriptures describe this as:

Mosiah 2:38

38 Therefore if that man repenteth not, and remaineth and dieth an enemy to God, the demands of divine justice do awaken his immortal soul to a lively sense of his own guilt, which doth cause him to shrink from the presence of the Lord, and doth *fill his breast with guilt, and pain, and anguish, which is like an unquenchable fire*, whose flame ascendeth up forever and ever.

"There it is. The definition of what the *suffering* actually is; what the *unquenchable fire* actually is; *a lively sense of one's own guilt, and pain, and anguish,* which is *"like"* an *unquenchable fire.* The awful *demands of justice* upon those who have violated the laws of God, the "*state of misery and endless torment*" described in these scriptures, can be mediated, and eliminated by the Atonement of Jesus Christ. This is the very essence of the gospel of Jesus Christ."

Elder Oaks continues:

"What do these basic principles mean in the case of a Latter-Day Saint who deliberately commits a serious transgression in the expectation that he or she will enjoy the effects or benefits of the sin now, and then make a speedy and relatively '*painless repentance*' and soon be as good as new (This applies to all of God's children and not just to members of the Church)?

The Book of Mormon teaches that the Savior does not redeem men "*in* their sins":

Alma 11:34, 36, 37

34 And Zeezrom said again: Shall he save his people *in* their sins? And Amulek answered and said unto him: I say unto you he shall *not,* for it is impossible for him to deny his word.

Now Amulek saith again unto him: Behold thou hast lied, for thou sayest that I spake as though I had authority to command God because I said he shall not save his people in their sins.

37 And I say unto you again that he cannot save them in their sins; for I cannot deny his word, and he hath said that no unclean thing can inherit the kingdom of heaven; therefore, how can ye be saved, except ye inherit the kingdom of heaven? Therefore, ye cannot be saved *in* your sins?

Helaman 5:10

10 And remember also the words which Amulek spake unto Zeezrom, in the city of Ammonihah; for he said unto him that the Lord surely should come to redeem his people, but that he should not come to redeem them *in* their sins, but to redeem them *from* their sins.

"The wicked remain as though there had been no redemption made, except it be the loosing of the bands of death (Resurrection, which comes to all)"

Alma 11:41

41 Therefore the wicked remain as though there had been no redemption made, except it be the loosing of the bands of death; for behold, the day cometh that *b*all shall rise from the dead and stand before God, and be judged according to their works.

"The Savior came to redeem men *from* their sins because of repentance" and upon the "conditions of repentance".

Helaman 5:11

11 And he hath power given unto him from the Father to redeem them from their sins because of repentance; therefore he hath sent his angels to declare the tidings of the conditions of, which bringeth unto the power of the Redeemer, unto the salvation of their souls.

"One of those *conditions of repentance* is faith in the Lord Jesus Christ, including faith in and reliance upon his atoning sacrifice. As Amulek taught:

Alma 34:16

16 And thus mercy can satisfy the demands of justice, and encircles them in the arms of safety, while he that exercises no faith unto repentance is exposed to the whole law of the demands of justice; therefore only unto him that has faith unto repentance is brought about the great and eternal plan of redemption.

Personal Suffering for Sin

"Another *condition of repentance* is suffering or punishment for the sin. In the words of Alma:

Alma 42:16

16 Now, repentance could not come unto men except there were a punishment, which also was *b*eternal as the life of the soul should be, affixed opposite to the plan of happiness, which was as eternal also as the life of the soul.

"Where there has been sin, there must be *suffering* (Or punishment)."

"Perhaps the greatest statement of this principle in all the scriptures is the revelation the Lord gave to the Prophet Joseph Smith in March 1830, the month the Book of Mormon was published and the month before the Church was organized. Here the Lord reminds us of "the great day of judgment" when all will be judged according to their works.

"He explains that the "endless" or "eternal torment" or "punishment" that comes from sin is <u>not</u> '*punishment without end*', but it is "*the punishment 'of' God*", who is endless and eternal (In other words, '*eternal*' is another *name* of God, thus eternal punishment is '*God's punishment*').

"In this setting, the Savior of the world commands us to repent and keep his commandments:

Doctrine & Covenants 19:15–20

15 Therefore I command you to repent—repent, lest I smite you by the rod of my mouth, and by my wrath, and by my anger, and your sufferings be sore—how sore you know not, how exquisite you know not, yea, how hard to bear you know not.

16 For behold, I, God, have suffered these things for all, that they might not suffer if they would repent;

17 But if they would not repent they must suffer even as I;

18 Which suffering caused myself, even God, the greatest of all, to tremble because of pain, and to bleed at every pore, and to suffer both body and spirit—and would that I might not drink the bitter cup, and shrink—

19 Nevertheless, glory be to the Father, and I partook and finished my preparations unto the children of men.

20 Wherefore, I command you again to repent, lest I humble you with my almighty power; and that you confess your sins, lest you suffer these punishments of which I have spoken, of which in the smallest, yea, even in the least degree you have tasted at the time I withdrew my Spirit.

"As we consider these sobering words of the Savior, we realize that there is something very peculiar about the state of mind or "heart" of the person who deliberately commits sin in the expectation that he or she *will speedily and comfortably repent* and continue as a servant of God preaching repentance and asking others to come unto Christ. I will illustrate *the peculiarity of this attitude* with two analogies. Picture a father who labors tirelessly to support a large family. He denies himself many things in order to provide their urgent needs: food, clothing, housing, health care, and education. This father works every waking hour, scraping, saving, and praying that there will be enough to go around. The children see his tireless work and his sacrifices for them.

"Finally, a day comes when the family gathers for a celebration. They go to a restaurant where the father, with carefully saved resources, plans to treat everyone to a nice meal. Mindful of their financial circumstances and the sacrifices the father has made to bring them to this place, most of the children are very considerate about what they order. But some are heard to say, "We don't have to pay, so we're going to order everything we want, no matter how expensive. We'll enjoy it, and he'll pay for it."

"*Second example.* The mother of a large family is burdened almost past the point of endurance. Every waking hour is spent serving the needs of her large family: meals, mending, transporting, counseling, caring for those who are sick, comforting those who mourn, and administering to every other need a mother can understand. She has committed herself to do everything within her power to serve the needs of her children.

"She is giving her life for them. The children know she will attempt to carry whatever load is placed upon her. Most of them are considerate and do all that they can to minimize her burden. But some, knowing of her willingness to serve, heedlessly pile more and more tasks on the weary mother. "Don't worry about it," is their attitude, "she'll carry it. She said she would. Drop it on Mom, and we'll just have a good time."

"In these two analogies, I am obviously likening the heedless children to those who sin in the expectation that someone else will bear the burden of suffering. The one who bears the burden is our Savior. Am I suggesting that the benefits of the Atonement are not available for the person who heedlessly sins? Of course not. But *I am suggesting that there is a relationship between sin and suffering that is not understood by people who knowingly sin in the expectation that all the burden of suffering will be borne by another*, that the sin is all theirs, but the suffering is all his (This is what self-righteous means. They sin but still say they are a good person).

"This is not the way. Repentance, which is an assured passage to an eternal destination, is nevertheless *not a free ride*. Let us recall two scriptures quoted earlier: (1) "Repentance could not come unto men except there were a punishment":

Alma 42:16

16 Now, repentance could not come unto men except there were a punishment, which also was *b*eternal as the life of the soul should be, affixed opposite to the plan of happiness, which was as eternal also as the life of the soul. And (2) the Savior said that he had suffered these things for all, "that they might not suffer if they would repent; But if they would not repent, they must suffer even as I":

D&C 19:16–17

16 For behold, I, God, have suffered these things for all, that they might not suffer if they would repent;

17 But if they would not repent, they must suffer even as I;

"*Does this mean that a person who repents does not need to suffer at all because the entire punishment or suffering is borne by the Savior?* That cannot be the meaning because it would be inconsistent with the Savior's other teachings. What is meant is that the person who repents does not need to suffer "*even as*" the Savior suffered. Sinners who are repenting will experience '*some*' suffering (A recollection of their sins), but because of their repentance and the Atonement, they will not experience the '*full exquisite extent*' of the *eternal torment* that the Savior suffered.

"President Spencer W. Kimball, who gave such comprehensive teachings on repentance and forgiveness, said that "*personal suffering* is a very important part of repentance. *One has not begun to repent until he has suffered intensely for his sins.*" [TSWK, p. 88]

"*If a person hasn't suffered, he hasn't repented ... He has got to go through a change in his system whereby he suffers and then forgiveness is a possibility.* [p. 99] *(*I am well aware of the Christian belief that all one needs to do to be forgiven of all their sins is to confess the name of Jesus, to ask His forgiveness, and vocalize their repentance, and he will take on their sins *as well as any suffering*. They seem to be saying repentance is to *give a lip-service declaration* that they are sorry for committing their sins, and forgiveness is 'assured' so that they can declare 'I'm Saved!').

"The Savior taught this principle when he said that his atoning sacrifice was for "all those who have *a broken heart and a contrite spirit* (*Some suffering* is what brings about a broken heart and a contrite spirit); and unto 'none' else can the ends of the law be answered":

II Nephi 2:7

7 Behold, he offereth himself a sacrifice for sin, to answer the ends of the law, unto all those who have a broken heart and a contrite spirit; and unto [b]none else can the ends of the law be answered.

Alma 5:48

48 I say unto you, that I know of myself that whatsoever I shall say unto you, concerning that which is to come, is true; and I say unto you, that I know that Jesus Christ shall come, yea, the Son, the Only Begotten of the Father, full of grace, and mercy, and truth. And behold, it is he that cometh to take away the sins of the world, yea, the sins of every man who steadfastly believeth on his name.

Alma 11:40

40 And he shall come into the world to redeem his people; and he shall take upon him the transgressions of those who believe on his name; and these are they that shall have eternal life, and salvation cometh to none else.

"The repentant sinner who comes to Christ with a broken heart and a contrite spirit has been through a process of personal pain and suffering for sin. He understands the meaning of Alma's statement that *"none but the truly penitent are saved"*:

Alma 42:24

24 For behold, justice exerciseth all his demands, and also mercy claimeth all which is her own; and thus, none but the truly penitent are saved.

"Bruce C. Hafen, author of "The Broken Heart" and "Faith is Not Blind", has described how some people think that repentance is too easy. They look "for short cuts and easy answers, thinking that quick confessions or breezy apologies alone are enough" *(The Broken Heart,* 1989, p. 150). President Kimball, past President of The Church of Jesus Christ of Latter-Day Saints said: "Very frequently people think they have repented and are worthy of forgiveness when all they have done is to express sorrow or regret at the unfortunate happening" *(TSWK,* p. 87). There is a big difference between the *"godly sorrow [that] worketh repentance"*:

2 Corinthians 7:10

10 For godly sorrow worketh repentance to salvation not to be repented of: but the sorrow of the world worketh death.

"This involves personal suffering, and the easy and relatively painless sorrow for being caught or the misplaced sorrow Mormon described as "the sorrowing of the damned, because the Lord would not always suffer them to *'take happiness in sin'*":

Mormon 2:13

13 But behold this my joy was vain, for their sorrowing was not unto repentance, because of the goodness of God; but it was rather the sorrowing of the damned, because the Lord would not always suffer them to *take happiness in sin.*

"Alma the Younger certainly understood that easy and painless sorrow was not a sufficient basis for repentance. His experience, related in detail in the Book of Mormon, is our best scriptural illustration of the fact that *the process of repentance is filled with personal suffering for sin.* Alma said after he was stopped in his wicked course, he was "in the darkest abyss", *racked with eternal torment, for my soul was harrowed up to the greatest degree and racked with all my sins (This is the 'spiritual fire' or 'spiritual suffering' we will feel due to unrepented sins):*

Alma 27:29

29 My soul hath been redeemed from the gall of bitterness and bonds of iniquity. I was in the darkest abyss; but now I behold the marvelous light of God. My soul was [c]racked with eternal torment; but I am snatched, and my soul is pained no more.

"Yea, I did remember all my sins and iniquities, for which I was tormented with the pains of hell":

Alma 36:12–14, 17

12 But I was racked with eternal torment, for my soul was harrowed up to the greatest degree and racked with all my sins.

13 Yea, I did remember all my sins and iniquities, for which I was tormented with the pains of hell; yea, I saw that I had rebelled against my God, and that I had not kept his holy commandments.

14 Yea, and I had murdered many of his children, or rather led them away unto destruction; yea, and in fine so great had been my iniquities, that the very thought of coming into the presence of my God did rack my soul with inexpressible horror.

17 And it came to pass that as I was thus racked with torment, while I was harrowed up by the memory of my many sins, behold, I remembered also to have heard my father prophesy unto the people concerning the coming of one Jesus Christ, a Son of God, to atone for the sins of the world.

"He tells how "the very thought of coming into the presence of my God did rack my soul with inexpressible horror": (verse 14). He speaks of being "harrowed up by the memory of my many sins" (verse 17). After three days and three nights of what he called "the most bitter pain and anguish of soul," he cried out to the Lord Jesus Christ for mercy and received "a remission of [his] sins":

Alma 38:8

8 And it came to pass that I was three days and three nights in the most bitter pain and anguish of soul; and never, until I did cry out unto the Lord Jesus Christ for mercy, did I receive a remission of my sins. But behold, I did cry unto him, and I did find peace to my soul.

"All of our personal experience confirms the fact that we must endure personal suffering in the process of repentance—and for serious transgressions that suffering can be severe and prolonged. I believe that every one of us who is truly honest with ourselves, recognizes the truth of this principle. We have felt it in our own lives, and we have seen it in the lives of others.

"The *Ensign* (August 1990) contains an anonymous article describing such an experience. Under the title "Yearning to Return," a repenting transgressor who was excommunicated describes his personal feelings: "tearful hours," "misery," "wishing to be covered by a million mountains," "crushed by the shame," "dark blackness," "unbearable pain," and "anguish. . . as wide as eternity" (pp. 22–24).

"Why is it necessary for us to suffer on the way to repentance for serious transgressions?"

"We often think of the results of repentance as simply cleansing us from sin. But that is an incomplete view of the matter. A person who sins is like a tree that bends easily in the wind. On a windy and rainy day, the tree bends so deeply against the ground that the leaves become soiled with mud, like sin. If we only focus on cleaning the leaves, *the weakness in the tree* that allowed it to bend and soil its leaves may remain. Merely cleaning the leaves does not strengthen the tree. Similarly, a person who is merely sorry to be soiled by sin will sin again in the next high wind. *The susceptibility to repetition continues until the tree has been strengthened.*

"When a person has gone through the process that results in what the scriptures call '*a broken heart and a contrite spirit*', that person is not only eligible to be cleansed from sin, but he is also strengthened, and that strengthening is essential for us to realize *the purpose of the cleansing*, which is *to return to our Heavenly Father*. To be admitted to his presence we must be more than clean. We must also be '*changed*' from a weak person who once transgressed into a strong person with the spiritual stature that qualifies one to dwell in the presence of God. We must, as the scripture says, become "*a saint through the atonement of Christ the Lord*":

Mosiah 3:19 (also see Hafen, *The Broken Heart,* p. 149).

19 For the natural man is an enemy to God, and has been from the fall of Adam, and will be, forever and ever, unless he yields to the enticings of the Holy Spirit, and putteth off the natural man and becometh a saint through the atonement of Christ the Lord, and becometh as a child, submissive, meek, humble, patient, full of love, willing to submit to all things which the Lord seeth fit to inflict upon him, even as a child doth submit to his father.

"This is what is meant by the scriptural explanation that a person who has repented of his sins will "confess them and forsake them":

Doctrine & Covenants 58:43

43 By this ye may know if a man repenteth of his sins—behold, he will confess them and forsake them.

"Forsaking sins is more than resolving not to repeat them. It involves *a fundamental change* in the individual. King Benjamin and Alma both speak of *"a mighty change of heart"*. King Benjamin's congregation described that mighty change by saying that they had *"no more disposition to do evil, but to do good continually"*:

Mosiah 5:2

2 And they all cried with one voice, saying: Yea, we believe all the words which thou hast spoken unto us; and also, we know of their surety and truth, because of the Spirit of the Lord Omnipotent, which has wrought a mighty change in us, or in our hearts, that we have no more disposition to do evil, but to do good continually.

"Alma illustrated that change of heart when he described a people who "awoke unto God," "put their trust in" him, and were "faithful until the end":

Alma 5:7, 13

7 Behold, he changed their hearts; yea, he awakened them out of a deep sleep, and they awoke unto God. Behold, they were in the midst of darkness; nevertheless, their souls were illuminated by the light of the everlasting word; yea, they were encircled about by the bands of death, and the chains of hell, and an everlasting destruction did await them.

13 And behold, he preached the word unto your fathers, and a mighty change was also wrought in their hearts, and they humbled themselves and put their trust in the True and Living God. And behold, they were faithful until the end; therefore they were saved.

"He challenged others to "look forward with an eye of faith" to the time when we will "stand before God to be judged" according to our deeds:

Alma 5:15

15 Do ye exercise faith in the redemption of him who created you? Do you look forward with an eye of faith, and view this mortal body raised in immortality, and this corruption *b*raised in incorruption, to stand before God to be judged according to the deeds which have been done in the mortal body?

"Persons who have had that kind of change in their hearts have been cleansed from their sins and *have attained the strength and stature* to dwell with God. *That* is what we, as Latter-Day Saints, call *'being saved'*.

Heed the Warnings

"Some Latter-Day Saints who think repentance is easy, maintain that a person is better off after he has sinned and repented. "Get a little experience with sin," one argument goes, "and then you will be better able to counsel others and sympathize with others. Anyway, it won't hurt to sin a little. I plead with you, my brothers and sisters, my young friends, and my older friends, avoid transgression! The idea that one is better off after one has sinned and repented is a devilish lie of the adversary.

"Does anyone here think that it is better to learn firsthand that a certain blow will break a bone, or a certain mixture of chemicals will explode and sear off our skin? Are we better off after we have sustained and then healed such injuries? I believe we all can see that it is better to heed the warnings of wise persons who know the effects on our bodies of certain traumas (It is far better to learn from someone else's broken nose, than your own broken nose).

"Just as we can benefit from someone else's experience in matters such as these, we can also benefit from the warnings contained in the commandments of God. We don't have to have personal experience with the effects of serious transgressions to know that they are destructive of our eternal welfare.

"Some years ago, one of our sons asked me why it wasn't a good idea to try alcohol or tobacco to see what it was like. He knew about the Word of Wisdom, and he also knew the health effects of these substances, but he was questioning why he shouldn't just try them out for himself. I replied that if he wanted to try something he ought to go out in the barnyard and eat a little manure. He recoiled in horror. "Ooh, that's gross," he reacted. I'm glad you think so," I said, "but why don't you just try it out so you will know for yourself? While you're proposing to try one thing that you know is not good for you, why don't you apply that principle to some others?" That illustration of the silliness of 'trying it out for yourself' proved persuasive for one sixteen-year-old.

"He Who Has Repented"

"Most of what I have said here has been addressed to persons who think that repentance is too easy. At the opposite extreme are those who think that repentance is too hard. That group of souls are so tenderhearted and conscientious that they see sin everywhere in their own lives, and they despair of ever being able to be clean. The shot of doctrine that is necessary to penetrate the hard shell of the easygoing group is a massive overdose for the conscientious. What is necessary to encourage reformation for the lax can produce paralyzing discouragement for the conscientious. This is a common problem. We address a diverse audience each time we speak, and we are never free from the reality that a doctrinal underdose for some is an overdose for others.

"I will conclude with a message of hope that is true for all, but especially needed for those who think that repentance is too hard. Repentance is a continuing process, needed by all because "all have sinned, and come short of the glory of God":

Romans 3:23

23 For all have sinned, and come short of the glory of God;

Elder Spencer W. Kimball said:

"Repentance is possible, and then forgiveness is certain. *Sometimes, when a repentant one looks back and sees the ugliness, the loathsomeness of the transgression, he is almost overwhelmed and wonders, "Can the Lord ever forgive me? Cam I ever forgive myself?" But when one reaches the depths of despondency and feels the hopelessness of his position, and when he cries out to god for mercy in helplessness but in faith, there comes a still, small, but penetrating voice whispering to his soul, "The sins are forgiven thee." (Miracle of Forgiveness", 1969, p. 344)* [707]

End Quote

"When this happens, how precious the promise that God will take "away the guilt from our hearts, through the merits of his Son":

Alma 24:10

10 And I also thank my God, yea, my great God, that he hath granted unto us that we might repent of these things, and also that he hath forgiven us of those our many sins and murders which we have committed, and taken away the guilt from our hearts, through the merits of his Son.

"How comforting the promise that "though your sins be as scarlet, they shall be as white as snow":

Isaiah 1:18

18 Come now, and let us reason together, saith the LORD: though your sins be as scarlet, they shall be as white as snow; though they be red like crimson, they shall be as wool.

"How glorious God's own promise that "he who has repented of his sins, the same is forgiven, and I, the Lord, remember them no more":

Doctrine & Covenants 58:42

42 Behold, he who has repented of his sins, the same is forgiven, and I, the Lord, remember them no more.

Jeremiah 31:34

34 And they shall teach no more every man his neighbour, and every man his brother, saying, Know the LORD: for they shall all know me, from the least of them unto the greatest of them, saith the LORD: for I will forgive their iniquity, and I will remember their sin no more.

Hebrews 8:12

12 For I will be merciful to their unrighteousness, and their sins and their iniquities will I remember no more.

This is the end of Elder Oaks message. [708]

With his words still fresh in your mind, I would have you consider these words in the Doctrine & Covenants 76, verses 84–85 and 104–106 that describe *the suffering* the wicked will experience after they die:

Doctrine & Covenants 76:84-85, 104-105

84 These are they who are thrust down to hell.

85 These are they who shall not be redeemed from the devil until the *b*last resurrection, until the Lord, even Christ the Lamb, shall have finished his work.

104 These are they who suffer the wrath of God on earth.

105 These are they who suffer the vengeance of eternal fire.

In verse 105, the phrase "eternal fire" is a figurative expression referring to the *type or kind* of suffering the wicked will experience. These individuals will inherit the telestial kingdom. As we've just learned, It does not mean that their suffering will never end:

Doctrine & Covenants 19:4–12

4 And surely every man must repent or suffer, for I, God, am endless.

5 Wherefore, I revoke not the judgments which I shall pass, but woes shall go forth, weeping, wailing and gnashing of teeth, yea, to those who are found on my *c*left hand.

6 Nevertheless, it is not written that there shall be no end to this torment, but it is written *endless torment*.

7 Again, it is written *eternal damnation;* wherefore it is more express than other scriptures, that it might work upon the hearts of the children of men, altogether for my name's glory.

8 Wherefore, I will explain unto you this mystery, for it is meet unto you to know even as mine apostles.

9 I speak unto you that are chosen in this thing, even as one, that you may enter into my rest.

10 For, behold, the mystery of godliness, how great is it! For, behold, I am endless, and the punishment which is given from my hand is endless punishment, for Endless is my name. Wherefore—

11 Eternal punishment is God's punishment.

12 Endless punishment is God's punishment.

"The conditions in 'hell' experienced by those who will inherit the telestial kingdom will be temporary. Because these individuals would not repent and apply the blessings of the Atonement in their lives, they will remain in hell throughout the Millennium, paying the penalty for their sins by *the things which they suffer* while in spirit prison. The following statement by President Joseph Fielding Smith, past president of The Church of Jesus Christ of Latter-Day Saints (July 19, 1876 – July 2, 1972), speaks of the results of the suffering that the wicked will experience in hell, or spirit prison, and I quote:

"This suffering will be a means of cleansing, or purifying, and through it the wicked shall be brought to a condition whereby they may, through the redemption of Jesus Christ, obtain immortality. Their spirits and bodies shall be again united (through their resurrection), and they shall dwell in the telestial kingdom. But this resurrection will not come until the end of the world." [709]

End quote

Doctrine & Covenants 76:106–108 explains that the wicked will suffer for their sins until Jesus Christ completes His work and delivers up the kingdom of God on earth to His Father. Christ will then be crowned with glory:

Doctrine & Covenants 76:106–108

106 These are they who are cast down to hell and suffer the wrath of Almighty God, until the fulness of times, when Christ shall have subdued all enemies under his feet, and shall have perfected his work;

107 When he shall deliver up the kingdom, and present it unto the Father, spotless, saying: I have overcome and have trodden the wine-press alone, even the wine-press of the fierceness of the wrath of Almighty God.

108 Then shall he be crowned with the crown of his glory, to sit on the throne of his power to reign forever and ever.

Doctrine & Covenants 76:109–111 and Doctrine & Covenants 137:9 teaches what will happen when those who are to inherit the telestial kingdom come before the throne of God to be judged. These verses teach that they will kneel and acknowledge Jesus Christ as their Savior. According to verse 111, the kingdom of glory we inherit will be determined by our actions in this life ... and the *desires* of our hearts.

Doctrine & Covenants 76:109–111

109 But behold, and lo, we saw the glory and the inhabitants of the telestial world, that they were as innumerable as the stars in the firmament of heaven, or as the sand upon the seashore;

110 And heard the voice of the Lord saying: These all shall bow the knee, and every tongue shall confess to him who sits upon the throne forever and ever;

111 For they shall be judged according to their works, and every man shall receive according to his own works, his own dominion, in the mansions which are prepared;

Doctrine & Covenants 137:9

9 For I, the Lord, will judge all men according to their works, according to the desire of their hearts.

Doctrine & Covenants 76:86–89, 98, 112 describes what immortality will be like for those who inherit the telestial kingdom:

Doctrine & Covenants 76:86–89, 98, 112

86 These are they who receive not of his fulness in the eternal world, but of the Holy Spirit through the ministration of the terrestrial;

87 And the terrestrial through the ministration of the celestial.

88 And also the telestial receive it of the administering of angels who are appointed to minister for them, or who are appointed to be ministering spirits for them; for they shall be heirs of salvation.

89 And thus we saw, in the heavenly vision, the glory of the telestial, which surpasses all understanding;

Doctrine & Covenants 76:98

98 And the glory of the telestial is one, even as the glory of the stars is one; for as one star differs from another star in glory, even so differs one from another in glory in the telestial world;

Doctrine & Covenants 76:112

112 And they shall be servants of the Most High; but where God and Christ dwell they cannot come, worlds without end.

Doctrine & Covenants 76:91–98 describes how the glory of the celestial kingdom differs from the glory of the terrestrial and telestial kingdoms.

Doctrine & Covenants 76:91–98

91 And thus we saw the glory of the terrestrial which excels in all things the glory of the telestial, even in glory, and in power, and in might, and in dominion.

92 And thus we saw the glory of the celestial, which excels in all things—where God, even the Father, reigns upon his throne forever and ever;

93 Before whose throne all things bow in humble reverence, and give him glory forever and ever.

94 They who dwell in his presence are the church of the Firstborn; and they see as they are seen, and know as they are known, having received of his fulness and of his grace;

95 And he makes them equal in power, and in might, and in dominion.

96 And the glory of the celestial is one, even as the glory of the sun is one.

97 And the glory of the terrestrial is one, even as the glory of the moon is one.

98 And the glory of the telestial is one, even as the glory of the stars is one; for as one star differs from another star in glory, even so differs one from another in glory in the telestial world;

Joseph Smith and Sidney Rigdon explain how others can receive the knowledge they received. In Doctrine & Covenants 76:113–119 it says that after describing this vision, Joseph Smith and Sidney Rigdon stated that the Lord had commanded them not to write all that they had been shown. They also explained what we must do to be able to see and understand the mysteries of the kingdom of God:

Doctrine & Covenants 76:113–119

113 This is the end of the vision which we saw, which we were commanded to write while we were yet in the Spirit.

114 But great and marvelous are the works of the Lord, and the mysteries of his kingdom which he showed unto us, which surpass all understanding in glory, and in might, and in dominion;

115 Which he commanded us we should not write while we were yet in the Spirit, and are not lawful for man to utter;

116 Neither is man capable to make them known, for they are only to be seen and understood by the power of the Holy Spirit, which God bestows on those who love him, and purify themselves before him;

117 To whom he grants this privilege of seeing and knowing for themselves;

118 That through the power and manifestation of the Spirit, while in the flesh, they may be able to bear his presence in the world of glory.

119 And to God and the Lamb be glory, and honor, and dominion forever and ever. Amen.

Doctrine & Covenants 76:85, 106 teaches about the redemption of the wicked:

Doctrine & Covenants 76:85

85 These are they who shall not be redeemed from the devil until the *b*last resurrection, until the Lord, even Christ the Lamb, shall have finished his work.

Doctrine & Covenants 76:106

106 These are they who are cast down to hell and suffer the wrath of Almighty God, until the fulness of times, when Christ shall have subdued all enemies under his feet, and shall have perfected his work;

President Brigham Young explained how some people in his day responded to the truth that most of the wicked would eventually be redeemed and not suffer in 'hell' forever. Here what he said:

"When God revealed to Joseph Smith and Sidney Rigdon that there was a place prepared for all, according to the light they had received and their rejection of evil and practice of good, it was a great trial to many, and some apostatized because God was not going to send to everlasting punishment heathens and infants, but *had a place of salvation, in due time, for all*, and would bless the honest and virtuous and truthful, whether they ever belonged to any church or not. It was a new doctrine to this generation, and many stumbled at it." [710]

The scriptures describe how the celestial kingdom excels in all things and is glorious:

Doctrine & Covenants 76:92–95

92 And thus we saw the glory of the celestial, which excels in all things—where God, even the Father, reigns upon his throne forever and ever;

93 Before whose throne all things bow in humble reverence, and give him glory forever and ever.

94 They who dwell in his presence are the church of the Firstborn; and they see as they are seen, and know as they are known, having received of his fulness and of his grace;

95 And he makes them equal in power, and in might, and in dominion.

Elder Orson Pratt of the Quorum of the Twelve Apostles taught of the difference between 'being saved' in the celestial kingdom and inheriting other kingdoms of glory. Here's his quote:

"There is quite a difference between being saved in some kingdom, where there is some glory, some happiness, and being saved in the kingdom where our Father resides. ...

"Our Father who dwells in yonder heavens, and his Son Jesus Christ, inhabit the highest degree of glory in eternity.

"They are possessed of all the fulness of glory. They have a fulness of happiness, a fulness of power, a fulness of intelligence, light, and truth, and they bear rule over all other kingdoms of inferior glory, of inferior happiness, and of inferior power. ... The gospel is intended to exalt the children of men to that same degree of glory, where our Father and His Son resides." [711]

End Quote

Doctrine & Covenants 76:99–101 teaches:

99 For these are they who are of Paul, and of Apollos, and of Cephas.**100** These are they who say they are some of one and some of another—some of Christ and some of John, and some of Moses, and some of Elias, and some of Esaias, and some of Isaiah, and some of Enoch;

"They who are of Paul, and of Apollos, and of Cephas". To condemn disunity, Paul wrote to the Corinthians:

1 Corinthians 1:11–13

11 For it hath been declared unto me of you, my brethren, by them *which are of the house* of Chloe, that there are contentions among you.

12 Now this I say, that every one of you saith, I am of Paul; and I of Apollos; and I of Cephas; and I of Christ.

13 Is Christ divided? was Paul crucified for you? or were ye baptized in the name of Paul?

"Similar wording in Doctrine & Covenants 76:99–101 refers to those who are not in harmony with Jesus Christ or His prophets. Some will say that they follow Jesus Christ or particular prophets, yet these people willfully reject the Savior and refuse to accept His gospel or follow His prophets.

"Doctrine & Covenants 76:113–116 teaches that Joseph Smith saw more in this vision than what is written. Referring to the vision recorded in Doctrine & Covenants 76, the Prophet Joseph Smith said, quote:

"I could explain a hundred-fold more than I ever have of the glories of the kingdoms manifested to me in the vision, were I permitted, and were the people prepared to receive them." [712]

End Quote

The prophet Joseph Smith also taught, quote, "It is our duty to concentrate all our influence to make popular that which is sound and good, and unpopular that which is unsound." [713]

End Quote

Please believe me when I say that my response to Richard's perspective on religion and the worlds' doctrine of sin, repentance, hellfire, and eternal suffering, is not an effort to be preachy in any way. It is simply my effort to make clear what my perspective is, as a Latter-Day Saint, on what the sound, pure doctrines of 'sin and suffering' truly are, and what it means to access the atonement of Jesus Christ, which blessing allows us to find peace in this world, and joy and eternal life in the world to come.

In concluding this first subtitle, Richard relates the brief story of a handful of individuals who came to a *crossroad* in their lives, and experienced cognitive dissonance and a faith-crisis, many of them having similar experiences with hellfire preachers, but who ultimately made their *escape* to go on to live happily ever after as atheists. One woman's description of how difficult it was to leave her faith, I think her name was Jill, was particularly poignant to me, so I want to share her comments with you, my readers. If you haven't read Richard's *The God Delusion* recently, here it is:

"The process of leaving is extraordinarily difficult. Ah, you are leaving behind a whole social network, a whole system that you've practically been brought up in, you are leaving behind a belief-system that you have held for years. Very often you leave families, and friends ... You don't really exist anymore for them." [714]

"Jill also described this kind of religious upbringing as a form of mental abuse, and Richard asked her, "You use the words religious abuse. If you were to compare the abuse of bringing up a child really to believe in hell (the kind that Richard describes), how do you think that would compare in trauma terms with sexual abuse?" [715]

Jill replied, quote:

"That's a very difficult question. I think there are a lot of similarities actually, because it is about *abuse of trust*; it is about denying the child the right to feel free and open and able to relate to the world in the normal way; it's a form of denigration; it's a form of denial of the true self in both cases." [716]

End quote

I cannot and I will not argue against the abominable actions of these so-called spiritual teachers. The resulting pain and suffering experienced by their victims, is the fruit of false, apostate teachings by these degenerate spiritual leaders' priestcraft. But what I will do, is ask that you, my readers, avoid attributing their apostate doctrines and their wicked actions to the *pure religion* offered by the Savior Jesus Christ, which He's revealed to His past prophets as well as to the prophets that have been called to this holy calling since the restoration of Christ's true Church, beginning with the prophet Joseph Smith Jr.

Let us agree on the fact that evil men, and in some cases evil women, are lurking in nearly every organization there is, including the Church of Jesus Christ of Latter-Day Saints, but such deviants are not the norm. In my mind, for Richard to lump all religious organizations in their entirety into one grouping, and calling it *Religion*, and then vilifying *it* as being a cesspool of child molesters, holding up the Catholic Church as evidence of such evil (in particular because of its high percentage of pedophile priests who are peppered throughout the body of the church's priesthood serving its parishioners), is totally unfair and unjustified. Any spiritual leader who breaches their calling is an abuser of the trust they were extended, and are deserving of condemnation, but this does not include the entirety of religion.

I think everyone would agree that the Catholic Church has a serious problem with pedophilia in its priesthood ranks, and this should move its parishioners to give serious thought regarding the organization they've aligned their hearts, minds, faith and souls to. To me, this level of breach within the leadership of their church, is a major red flag that cries out *apostasy*, and this cancer is still growing within its priesthood body, the very heart of that organization. Anyway, that's just my opinion.

But, for Richard to lump all religions into a single grouping or *pool of believers* and then say that 'it' – religion itself – is evil because there are a few individual spiritual leaders who should have been representing the Savior Jesus Christ, but due to their own wicked, perverted thoughts and behaviors, they spiraled down to where they ultimately became abusers of the trust given them by their file leaders by committing these horrendous acts against children, in my mind, is an outrageous characterization by Richard, and a distortion of the truth about pure religion and faith in God. These bad apples, though having tainted the basket they're in, does not define Religion as a whole, and I think any fair-minded person would agree with me. Or, so I would hope. The next subtitle is – "In defense of children."

IN DEFENSE OF CHILDREN

For this subtitle, Richard summarizes his case for defending children from their adult overseers – parents, religious leaders, political leaders, and more – by saying the following:

"There is something breathtakingly condescending, as well as inhumane, about the sacrificing of anyone, especially children, on the '*alter of diversity*' and the virtue of preserving a variety of religious traditions." [717]

First, let me say, that a condemnation of adults who Richard says, "are sacrificing children on the '*alter of diversity*' in order to preserve a variety of religious traditions", is so hypocritical to me, especially when you consider the fact that Richard is *pro-sacrifice of the unborn,* meaning he's *pro-abortion.* Roughly 121 million unintended pregnancies occur each year, worldwide. Of these unintended pregnancies, approximately 61% of them end in abortion. This translates to the slaughter of 73 million unborn babies annually, the majority being aborted just to satisfy the '*god of convenience*'. So, I would say to Richard, that "Teaching *little children* about Jesus Christ and His gospel of love, versus promoting the ideology that says 'babies' are just a part of the animal kingdom that is over populating, and so the slaughter of millions of unborn babies is somehow virtuous and justified, is outside of the bounds of acceptable behavior. One teaches the virtue of the love for life, and the other ideology promotes the tragic taking of life from tiny, unborn babies. By now you, my readers, have come to realize that I am pro-life, but I grant others their own opinion and belief regarding this most serious, polarizing issue.

Prior to making the statement where Richard criticizes parents teaching children their religious beliefs early on in their childhood, Richard shared several religious traditions, beginning with that of the Inca Nation. He gives the example of a young Inca girl whose 500-year-old remains were found in the mountains of Peru in 1995. The anthropologist who discovered her, Johan Reinhard, wrote that she had been the victim of a '*ritual sacrifice*'. Richard expressed:

"The decent liberal reader may feel a twinge of unease. Immoral by our standards, certainly, and stupid, but what about Inca standards? Surely to the Incas, the sacrifice was a moral act and far from stupid, sanctioned by all that they held sacred. Who are we to use a word like *murder*, judging Inca priests by our own standards rather than theirs (I hope Richard is being a bit cynical here)? Perhaps this girl (from her birth was taught the Inca ways and so) she was rapturously happy with her fate? Or perhaps – as seems far more likely – she screamed in terror." [718]

Nicholas Humphrey, an anthropologist colleague of Richard's, did a documentary on this young 'ice maiden'. His point, which is Richard's point for this subtitle, is that "Regardless of whether she was a willing victim or not, there is strong reason to suppose that she would *not* have been willing if she had been in full possession of the facts." [719]

In other words, when informed, this young woman, it is assumed, would have probably made a different choice, or, if being forced to submit to this atrocity, maybe she would have tried her very best to escape from her captures. Viewers of Humphrey's documentary on this young girl were invited to marvel at *the spiritual commitment* of the Inca priests and to share with the girl on her last journey, her pride and excitement of having been selected for the signal *honor* of being sacrificed.

Richard goes on to say that "the message of Humphrey's television program was in effect that the practice of human sacrifice was in its own way *a glorious cultural invention* – another jewel in the crown of multiculturalism, if you like (With its religious bent). It promoted the idea that the Inca priests cannot be blamed for their ignorance, and it could perhaps be thought harsh to judge them stupid and puffed up." [720]

Humphrey then gets to the point of his documentary which was, "But they can be blamed for foisting their own beliefs on a child too young to decide whether to worship the sun or not." [721]

Richard then gives a few more examples of ethnic religious habits and how they justify cruelties in their name. He says, "It crops up again, and again. It is the source", Richard says, "of squirming internal conflict in the minds of nice liberal people who, on the one hand, cannot bear suffering and cruelty, but on the other have been trained by postmodernists and relativists to respect other cultures no less than their own." [722]

In addition to human sacrifice, Richard briefly reviews Female Genital Mutilation, Hasidim, Gypsies, and the Amish's right to bring up their own children in *'their own way'*, as examples of how society has an excitement for maintaining *'cultural diversity'* and their cultural traditions. As I read what Richard described here as liberals' excitement for *maintaining cultural diversity*, I couldn't help but think about their full-throated support of the LGBTQIA+ community, as well as the "Gender Neutral" community who are pushing a total rewrite of the definition of male and female, an example being the definition of 'what is a *woman?*", etc. It is my opinion that maintaining this so-called *cultural diversity* will ultimately be the ruin of our American society as we know it, due to subjective moral standards replacing the objective moral standard given to mankind by God Himself, through His prophets and apostles.

Richard continues: "It's a shame, maybe, when individuals have to be sacrificed to maintain such diversity. But there it is, *it's the price we pay as a society*. Except, I would feel bound to remind you, we do not pay it, they do." [723]

Once again, this is an example of the old adage, "Remember, remember, if you pick up one end of the stick you automatically pick up the other end of the stick, so you'd better know what that other end is, for it may be the opposite of what you wanted when you picked up the stick". [724]

Richard finishes this subtitle by saying to the adults that do the sacrificing of the children (Once again I think Richard is being sarcastic here), "Of course you must be allowed to trap your children with you in your seventeenth-century time warp, otherwise something irretrievable would be lost to us: a part of the wonderful diversity of human culture. A small part of me can see something in this. But the larger part is made to feel very queasy indeed." [725]

My response to Richard's point he just gave, is to simply remind you, my readers, what Jesus Himself said on this subject. The Savior spoke seriously of *abuse when He said:

Matthew 18:2-7

2 And Jesus called a little child unto him, and set him in the midst of them,

3 And said, Verily I say unto you, Except ye be converted, and become as little children, ye shall not enter into the kingdom of heaven.

4 Whosoever therefore shall humble himself as this little child, the same is greatest in the kingdom of heaven.

5 And whoso shall receive one such little child in my name receiveth me.

6 But whoso shall *offend* (*Abuse or cause to stumble) one of these little ones *which believe in me*, it were better for him that a millstone were hanged about his neck, and *that* he were drowned in the depth of the sea.

7 Woe unto the world because of offences (Abuse)! for it must needs be that offences come; but woe to that man by whom the offence (Or abuse) cometh!

Mark 9:42

42 And whosoever shall one of *these* little ones that believe in me, it is better for him that a millstone were hanged about his neck, and he were cast into the sea.

Luke 17:2

2 It were better for him that a millstone were hanged about his neck, and he cast into the sea, than that he should *offend* one of these little ones.

(*Abuse is the mistreatment or neglect of others (such as a child or spouse, the elderly, or the disabled) in a way that causes physical, emotional, or sexual harm (Verbal abuse being just one more form of abuse). The Church of Jesus Christ of Latter-Day Saints position is that abuse cannot be tolerated in *any of its forms).*

While some types of abuse may cause physical harm, all forms of abuse affect the mind and spirit. This kind of abuse often destroys faith and can cause confusion, doubt, mistrust, guilt, and fear in the victim, all of which can cause the child or adult to stumble and lose their faith in their Lord and Savior Jesus Christ (Isn't this exactly how the women in Richard's examples described their stories of abuse?). Let me also address the infant baptism issue that Richard brought up earlier, and that I expressed my perspective on, as it relates to this topic of abuse.

To Latter-Day Saints, age eight, as I said, is when we become *'accountable for our behavior'*, knowing right from wrong, and are able to comprehend the principle of repentance in its simplicity. It is interesting to note that research indicates that from early history the approximate age of seven was commonly accepted as *the age of responsibility and accountability.* Under Roman law, a child under the age of seven (7) was not considered to have developed sufficient discretion or judgment to be responsible for his or her actions.

"That Roman law and most of Rome's paternal customs were undoubtedly influenced by Greek and Spartan paternal customs. Under Roman law, "minors" were divided into three classes:

1. Infants;
2. *Impubes,* those prior to puberty; and
3. *Upberes,* those after puberty.

"Infants were those under the age of seven, and *impubes* were those from age seven to puberty. Under the law all those who had not reached puberty were subject to guardianship laws. Infants and insane persons were considered "without intelligence" and could not act for themselves. Their 'tutor' or 'guardian' acted for them. After age seven, each child was granted full legal rights. He was then considered to have 'intelligence', even though it was not *mature judgment*. He could perform legal acts on his own, unless his guardian demonstrated that an action was not in his best interest. The laws, as recorded by both Justinian and Gaius, demonstrate the evolution of Roman law into the great civilizing force that it became, and one constant was the attitude toward children and the age of accountability.

"Roman and Greek laws regarding infants affected the laws of most, if not all countries, that eventually came under Roman influence; this involved most of the countries of Europe. More than 2,000 years after the early Greeks and Romans, the Lord revealed that *age eight*, and not seven or nine, was *the proper age of accountability.*" [726]

I bring this little tidbit of information from the age of the Roman Empire up, to make the point that, like Richard and Humphrey, I too recognize that young children do in fact need *protection* from the outrageous and dangerous societal traditions that push its own beliefs on their children who are far too young to decide for themselves what they want and don't want to believe, like these examples that Richard described. An example from our Day is Trans Adults going into our grade schools and dancing provocatively. It is my belief that they are grooming little children who are innocent and vulnerable.

I mention that these supposed adults are, in my opinion, grooming little children in order move them towards the idea of gender transitioning. Transsexual dancing at grade schools by these individuals as well as the parents themselves normalizing this grooming, has led to an explosion of children as young as ten to twelve years old experiencing gender dysphoria, which of course has led to an explosion of children seeking puberty blockers and transition surgery. I've included this in my book in order to make the point that someone has to protect our youth from such 'debauchery motivated' behaviors.

That said, I do not feel it is fair to lump every religion into Richard's *pot of religious extremism*, and their extreme practices.

As you have seen, my perspective and arguments regarding these religious questions, have been to simply provide you, my readers, with the doctrines of the Church of Jesus Christ of Latter-Day Saints regarding these topics, and that's because it is the only religion that can unabashedly claim that it has never, nor does it now teach such extreme apostate doctrines as *infant baptism, human sacrifice*, hedonism, or anything *like unto it*. Nor does it sacrifice its little one's on the *'alter of diversity'* or *'convenience'* in-order to preserve its *religious traditions* like Richard has accused all religions of doing. The Lord revealed to the prophet Joseph Smith that children, when eight years old, have developed sufficient discretion or judgment to be responsible and accountable for their own actions. That said, all of us still need to protect them from any extremist view, including, but not limited to abuse of *any* kind.

Now I am very much aware, as a member of the Church of Jesus Christ of Latter-Day Saints, that Latter-day Saints are accused, by some folks like Richard and the pack of barking dogs he runs with, to be abusers of our little ones because we teach them the basic doctrines of faith in Heavenly Father; in His Son Jesus Christ; Commandments; the principle of repentance and other basic doctrines from the time they're just 3 years olde and up (We teach them during what's called 'Primary', so that by the time they're 8 years old they're ready to make and keep the covenants they'll be making at baptism with their Heavenly Father.

There are other unrelated accusations that our critics use to justify calling the Church of Jesus Christ of Latte-Day Saints an extremist, immoral Church, but I will only address two of the more notable ones. Because some of its leaders (But not all), as well as some of the members of the Church of Jesus Christ of Latter-Day Saints (But not all), once practiced the principle of Plural Marriage over 130 years ago, which practice has long since been set aside by the Church leaders in compliance with the laws of the land, and because there are LDS *Fundamentalists (*who are *not* members of the Church of Jesus Christ of Latter-Day Saints), that still practice what many call the perverse practice of polygamy (One such group is Warren Jeffs followers), we, as members of the Church of Jesus Christ of Latter-Day Saints are still considered extremist, immoral cultists.

In addition to our limited past practice of polygamy, the Latter-Day Saints are also accused of being racist as well, because the Church of Jesus Christ of Latter-Day Saints once had restrictions on its African American *members, keeping them from being* ordained to the priesthood and receiving their temple ordinances, including their marriage sealings. This restriction ended in 1978 when the prophet and President of the Church, President Spencer W. Kimball (December 30th, 1973 – November 5, 1985), received a revelation every worthy male member of the Church could now be ordained to the priesthood, no matter their skin color, and therefore, having had this restriction in the first place, for some outside and looking in on our religious practices, makes every Latter-Day Saint a racist.

You, my readers, can go into a deeper dive regarding these two practices and their history, as well as other controversial topics, by doing a search for 'Gospel Topics Essays' at www.churchofjesuschrist.org, where you'll find a more comprehensive review of both of these practices history, as well as review the Church leaders *official position* on both practices as it stands today.

That said, going back to what Richard said about children being taught religion when they're just little children, I do agree with Richard when he says that little children should have been protected from their extremist authority figures, and they weren't. The resulting travesties stirs an intense sense of *righteous indignation* in me, as I'm sure it does in you, my readers. I know that it absolutely stirs righteous indignation in the Father of all mankind. I testify, God will not be mocked! His eternal judgement will be the 'abusers *wages'* for their heinous sins, even death:

Romans 6:23

23 For the *wages* of sin *is* death; but the gift of God *is* eternal life through Jesus Christ our Lord.

Next is the subtitle – "An educational scandal".

AN EDUCATIONAL SCANDAL

This subtitle begins by Richard relating his disdain for the people who started, run, and teach at one of England's academies that was part of an initiative of the Tony Blair administration, the *Emmanuel College in Gateshead*. Richard says of its benefactor Sir Peter Vardy, who is a wealthy car salesman, "Peter had a credible desire to give today's children the education he wishes he had had, and a less credible desire to imprint his *personal religious convictions* upon them." [727]

In describing the sometime headmaster of the Emanuel School, Nigel McQuoid, former director of a whole consortium of various schools, Richard's *standard for measuring any academic's credibility and qualification as a teacher* is their 'scientific understanding', and in particular *whether or not they believe in evolution and natural selection*. Richard said of McQuoid:

"The level of McQuoid's scientific understanding can be judged from his belief that the world is less than ten thousand years old, and also from the following quotation:

"But to think that we just evolved from a bang, that we used to be monkeys, seems unbelievable when you look at the complexity of the human body ... If you tell children, there is no purpose to their life – that they are just a chemical mutation – that doesn't build self-esteem'." [728]

Richard goes on to refute McQuoid's statement saying, "No scientist has ever suggested that a child is a *'chemical mutation'*." [729] That may be true, but Richard himself has called them a *'microscopic cluster of cells'*, and I quote: "A certain kind of religious mind cannot see the moral difference between killing a *'microscopic cluster of cells'* on the one hand and killing a full-grown doctor on the other." [730]

Richard goes on to reference the Bishop of the Christian Life City Church in Hackney, Bishop Wayne Malcolm, who disputes the scientific evidence for evolution. Malcolm said, and I quote: "There is clearly *an absence in the fossil record for intermediate levels of development*. If a frog turned into a monkey, shouldn't you have lots of fronkies?" [731] That quote made me laugh out loud! Fronkies! Ha, ha, ha!

After saying that both Nigel McQuoid and Bishop Malcolm are not experts on science, Richard says, "In fairness, I turn to the head of science (At Emmanuel College), Stephen Layfield. Mr. Layfield gave a lecture at Emmanuel College on 'The Teaching of Science: A Biblical Perspective'." [732]

To save time I won't go into the story Richard gives of the school taking down this lecture from its website or give Richard's many points to try and show the school's efforts to hide what the lecture said, but I do want to repeat the following comment made by Richard:

"You have to keep pinching yourself. You are not dreaming. This is not some preacher in a tent in Alabama but the head of science at a school into which the British government is pouring money, and which is Tony Blair's pride and joy." [733]

Then Richard's hatred for religion, and anything related to it, once again rears its bigoted head so that he starts barking about Layfield's comment when Stephen said, "It would seem particularly prudent for all who deliver this aspect of the course to familiarize themselves with the Flood geology papers of Whitcomb and Morris."

Reading this Richard decries: "Flood geology? We're talking Noah's Ark here. Noah's Ark! – When the children could be learning the spine-tingling fact that Africa and South America were once joined and have drawn apart at the speed with which fingernails grow." [734] I am not sure, but I suspect Richard doesn't know that the scriptures speak of the great *dividing* of the earth's crusts in the book of Genesis, which is exactly what Richard is talking about. Here's what the scriptures says about it:

Genesis 10:25

25 And unto Eber were born two sons: the name of one *was* Peleg; for in his days *was the earth divided*; and his brother's name *was* Joktan (That's a biblical statement postulated by science. Isn't that interesting?).

Richard concludes his disquisition of Latfields' lecture by saying:

"It is nothing less than a propaganda manual, a resource for religious teachers of biology, chemistry, and physics who wish, while remaining just inside the 'guidelines' of the national curriculum, to subvert evidence-based science education and replace it with biblical scripture (Young earth creationism in other words)." [735]

Richard's basic argument is that truth comes from evidence (Richard means 'evidence-based science' alone), rather than a variety of additional evidence, including evidence put forth from the scriptures. I've already covered where I believe pure truth comes from and what 'truth' is ('Truth' is the knowledge of things as they were, as they are, and as they are to come), so I won't be overly repetitive here, but I will make just one observation on this educational scandal which Richard has used to buoy up his argument that '*only the voice of science*' should be taught in our schools and colleges, as it, ("evidence-based science education alone") is the *only* source of truth, or so he says.

Here are excerpts from a talk given by Joy D. Jones, past Primary General President of the Church of Jesus Christ of Latter-Day Saints (As I mentioned earlier, Primary is the Church's organization for teaching the gospel to our young children who are three years old, on up to twelve years old). Joy has an 'associate of science' degree from Brigham Young University (BYU). Joy's talk is titled "Conversation, Conviction, and Civility: Sharing Religious Values in Schools and the Public Square". I feel it is a good comparative view on the subject of what should and shouldn't be taught in our public schools as well as in the public square, versus the view expressed by Richard where he believes science should be at the foundation of all education. Here's Joy's message, and I quote:

"Do you think of yourself as standing outside the noise of society? As hovering above the confusion of the world? As immune to the messiness of democracy? Well, that noise is all around us. But I believe that we are better off when we don't think of it as noise; it's real life. We are inescapably part of society. We benefit from its goodness at the same time as we work to improve its flaws.

"Even as we don't think of circumstances as noise, we will find that there will always be challenges to face. Consider the following scenarios and even think of your own:

"A teacher tells her students they cannot talk about God in class."

"A high school coach suspends a Jewish student from the basketball team for refusing to play the few Friday night games on the schedule due to his Sabbath observance."

"Your sophomore brings you a notice to attend a required health class that includes issues of sexual behavior that go against your beliefs."

"A Muslim student prays in a corner of the playground during recess, and your child sees a teacher order him to stop. The teacher then tells your child's class that absolutely no prayers are allowed *in* school."

"A rally on your college campus condemns the lobbying efforts of The Church of Jesus Christ of Latter-Day Saints in the passage of a legislative bill that promotes the rights of religious institutions. Signs with the phrase "We demand the separation of church and state" rise with the shouts."

"Colleagues at work take down from your cubicle wall your framed copy of the "Family Proclamation." (*See full printing of "The Family: A Proclamation to the World" at the end of this book on page 435).

"Your boss says she'll reprimand the culprits but then warns you that anti-LGBTQ bigotry is not allowed in the workplace."

"A young woman speaks out in class about why she doesn't believe in God or organized religion and gets booed by the rest of the students."

"These examples represent situations that actually have happened or could happen. The list goes on and on. The questions I want to pose include these: How do we, as parents, students, citizens, neighbors, and human beings react to such conflicts? What is our first impulse? Evade or engage? The answer determines what kind of a society we will live in—whether we splinter apart into our own warring groups or flourish together as citizens seeking the common good. It is sometimes necessary to turn to the administration or the law for recourse, but often situations can end up being handled by the parties involved—regular people who have a stake in the outcome. However, if you think nice words or kind gestures alone will solve these conflicts, then you may be in for an education. While niceness and kindness are important, engaging in open and honest dialogue in the public square is *hard work*. The short-term outcome is always in question. Good will is a work in progress. We ultimately find that societal harmony is more of a negotiation than it is a total victory for any one side or any other.

"As we are figuring out that truth, we don't have the luxury of cloistering ourselves in a safe, hermetically sealed environment, closed off from any and all disagreement. In the beautiful rough-and-tumble of a republic, there is no option for religious people to retreat, only a call to engage. When we engage, we often feel threatened by differences. And we don't have to go far to find them. The peculiarities of our lives can estrange us from each other. We often see things from different perspectives, and sometimes the fear of differences threatens us more than the actual differences.

"Our differences, therefore, have more meaning when they enter into conversation with other differences. Otherwise, we get stuck in our own social echo chambers.

Connection vs. Protection

"When we live among people who have immeasurably different opinions, experiences, upbringings, beliefs, personalities, and politics, we can approach our interactions in two ways. We either connect ourselves *with* people or protect ourselves *from* people.

"Someone who makes connection through their creed will make people their focus, listen more than talk, shake hands with someone even if they are shy or don't know what to say, become vulnerable to ridicule, and so on. Someone who sinks into a protective mode worries how they are perceived, frets about pleasing their tribe, competes instead of cooperates, and wins points instead of hearts. Protection is so much easier. In fact, it's human nature. We all do it. But a connective mind-set is what keeps civilization going. Connection comes with risk, but it also comes with greater rewards. Protection from the messiness of other people has a veneer of safety but ends up shrinking our ability to influence society.

"This paradigm applies to almost every area of life, especially how we share our faith in public life. Connecting always creates more space for growth and creativity, while protection and guarding oneself from others always contracts and reduces and limits the space of possibilities for human understanding and social progress. What are the stakes here in connecting or protecting? A few are that it can prove the difference between making friends or enemies. Between resolving an issue and allowing it to harden. Between trust and suspicion. Between progress and stalemate. Between open arms and clenched teeth.

"Think of this contrast, these two ways to approach life, as we return to our examples. "Speaking 'about' religion in public schools, for both teachers and students, is constitutional and legal. But, as in all things, it should be done in a reasonable, sincere, thoughtful way. Just because something is legal does not mean that we don't have to be considerate. Remember, we are working with both hearts and minds here.

"According to this wonderful resource titled '*A Parent's Guide to Religion in the Public Schools*': 'Generally, individual students are free to pray, read their scriptures, discuss their faith, and invite others to join their particular religious group'. Only if a student's behavior is disruptive or coercive should it be prohibited. No student should be allowed to harass or pressure others in a public-school setting. If doing so is relevant to the subject under consideration and meets the requirements of the assignment, students also have the right to express their religious views during a class discussion or as part of a written assignment or art activity.

"And regarding prayer, according to that same parent's guide, "Students are free to pray alone or in groups, as long as the activity is not disruptive and does not infringe upon the rights of others. These activities must be truly voluntary and 'student-initiated'. The classroom is a place of education, not of proselyting or religious competition, so differing perspectives about God and religion certainly have a place in public schools. The companion resource for 'teachers' states:

"As the Supreme Court has made clear, study about religion in public schools is constitutional. Inclusion of study about religion is important in-order for students to be properly educated about history and cultures. Religion must be taught objectively and neutrally. Some circumstances don't have a definitive answer or solution but must be worked out in the specific context of the situation. Instead, we must consider the circumstances, personalities, policies, and environments involved; read the situation; and then engage in conversation.

What Can We Say?

"Most of the examples I spoke of earlier can be resolved without resorting to legal action. What is usually needed is good old honest dialogue.

"If we look deeply and closely enough, all sides of a disagreement usually have a legitimate, defensible viewpoint and stake in a good outcome. It is often the case that the interests of the involved parties are not, objectively speaking, better or worse, but just different. And it takes time, care, and honesty to disentangle those interests and present them plainly to the other side. Safety comes in engaging, not avoiding.

"One other thing to remember is that not all school administrators, teachers, or staff have been trained on these matters. And, of course, many parents haven't either. For that reason, we all need to be patient with each other and *find civil solutions based on law*. Workplace politics can be even more challenging because of the diversity of the sector. But the same principles apply. The Church has a resource page that spells out the specifics. It says:

"You have a right to express your faith, as long as you don't harass others or lead people to mistake your private expressions of faith for your employer's views. You can talk to coworkers about your beliefs, hang a religious picture or keep personal items at your work station, wear religious clothing or jewelry, have personal devotionals (like reading your scriptures in the break room), or even start a voluntary prayer group, unless the company has job-related policies that apply the same to everyone (such as keeping desks clear of any personal items when customers can see them) and can't give you an accommodation.

"What kinds of situations have you faced? What will you do? Hunker down, or lend a voice of reason and shape society as much as we can, knowing that the final outcome is decided, but we have a way to go before we get there? Whenever we express our values in the public square, we need to be mindful, prayerful, and sensitive to the Spirit in order to determine how we interact in each situation and to know what the particular moment calls for. Not all moments are the same, and some require different styles and tones.

"Years ago, our oldest son was beginning junior high in California. My husband and I were invited to attend a health education class preview led by the teacher. During the presentation, we viewed videos that would be included in the course. As we watched, we both felt impressed that one of the videos was very inappropriate for that age group. At the end of the class, the teacher asked if there were any questions. After a brief pause, my husband raised his hand and said, "With all due respect, we don't feel that the last video is appropriate and would like our son excused from class the day it is shown. With some hesitancy, the teacher agreed and asked us to talk to her after the meeting. As she returned to the group, another parent made the same request. Then additional hands went up, each parent seeking the same exemption. Finally, the teacher said, "I'm getting the feeling you don't want this video shown. Is that correct?" The entire group agreed, and the teacher assured the group that it wouldn't be used.

"Here's the point—it took only one voice speaking up to make a difference for the entire group. We can each provide that tactful, respectful voice that can make a difference. In the public discourse of our day, we often see both sides of the extreme—either full-throttle condemnation and shaming of opponents on the one hand, or a passive agreeability without conviction on the other. Real life may take us across the range of this spectrum, but it takes faith to speak with both conviction and civility. The two are not mutually exclusive. Let's find the right degree of firmness and cooperation to fit what the moment calls for. [736]

Our Current Social Environment

"The law is obviously important and foundational, but the culture and values of a society are also crucial in maintaining freedom and justice. As Elder Patrick Kearon, a member of the Presidents of the Seventy recently said, Quote:

"Healthy societies run on trust, confidence, and a sense of safety. With freedom of religion and belief, people feel safe in their deepest convictions and can express and exercise them publicly. The great enemy of religious freedom is estrangement and alienation. When a society or government divides people based on what they believe, how they think, the words they say, whom they worship, or the manner in which they worship, common ground is lost, and life together becomes a battle. The test of a pluralistic society is to achieve unity without diminishing the diversity within it." [737]

End of Quote

President Joy D. Jones continues:

"We live in a peculiar time. The public life of our country seems to be getting more and more secular. Mentions of religion and truth claims must be brief, almost veiled, for fear of offending others. And yet, we've never lived in a time when so many fascinating and unique religious practices live side by side with each other. This pluralism of religious experience is simply a fact of our changing society, and we have the pleasure of learning how to navigate it.

"We can no longer assume that the Christian beliefs and values that were once so common will now be shared by everyone. But we can hope that everyone feels empowered to live out their religion." [738]

Elder Kearon also said, Quote:

"In terms of numbers and inherited culture, the United States has a Christian majority, but unless it honors the lawful practices of Hindus, Sikhs, Muslims, Jews, Buddhists, Native American religions, and everyone else, including individuals and groups who profess no faith at all, it will fail to live up to its own ideals." [739]

End Quote

President Joy D. Jones continues:

"Our modern world is teeming with choices and possibilities. Endless philosophies, ideologies, and truth claims clamor for attention, magnified by instantaneous media. Globalization pushes peoples and cultures together. Different religions and worldviews interact and collide. In many instances, personal preferences alone shape efforts to deal with moral dilemmas. In this state of flux, individuals can feel isolated and become disconnected from their communities, so let's take up this challenge with confidence.

"Let's follow the counsel of Latter-Day prophets, learn of "the perplexities of the nations," and gain a knowledge of "countries and of kingdoms." A major part of any nation or country is its religious history, beliefs, and practices. To really understand a people, a nation, or a neighbor, you have to understand their religion. We call this religious literacy. This greater understanding and appreciation will broaden our perspective and equip us to handle societal dialogue much more deeply. It will also inspire people to have more respect for us.

"Be sensitive and cognizant of the shifting dynamics between religious majorities and minorities. This dynamic can change depending on location and social context. You may be in the religious majority in Utah, but you will find yourself to be a minority most anywhere else. Majorities have the moral responsibility to treat their outnumbered brothers and sisters with respect as well as kindness.

We, as Latter-Day Saints, often view ourselves as being on the receiving end of mistreatment, but we can be on the offending end, too. Don't let the power of being in a majority make you complacent, and don't let the imbalance of being in a minority make you resentful. In either situation, we can act as disciples of Jesus Christ. We can connect with those who disagree, be firm in our rights, empathize with those around us, and develop a broader perspective.

Conclusion

'When you do venture out to connect and create goodwill, you will find kindred spirits—both those who disagree and those who agree with you. They may be hiding, but they will emerge. And those who don't agree with you will find respect for you and perhaps soften their disagreement because of your civility. In this process, both sides gain faith in humanity and feel a greater sense of belonging to each other. Follow your conscience and convictions. Ordinary people such as you and I can influence our communities in simple, yet profound ways. Let me suggest seven simple guidelines for speaking up and speaking out:

- Be informed.
- Be civil.
- Be sincere.
- Be clear.
- Be natural.
- Be meek.
- Be patient.

"The Prophet Joseph Smith said, "It is a love of liberty which inspires my soul—civil and religious liberty to the whole of the human race". In the end, brothers, and sisters, we are the guardians of our religious liberty. And as the Apostle Paul said:

II Cor. 3:17

17 Where the Spirit of the Lord is, there is liberty.

End of Joy D. Jones' Message [740]

The last point I want to make regarding the topic discussed in this subtitle, is to say that Richard's desire to make his atheists' delusion the only legitimate view that should be taught exclusively in every schools' science curriculum, is a deliberate, self-serving effort to undermine the possibility of teaching any views different than his own, especially the science-based evidence that supports the views of theist scientists who happen to interpret the same scientific data differently than Richard and his fellow atheist scientists interpret it.

Next is the Subtitle – "Consciousness-raising again."

CONSCIOUSNESS-RAISING AGAIN

In this subtitle Richard's goal is to raise the consciousness of his readers so that their reaction is to wince whenever they hear a small child being labelled as or belonging to some particular religion or another. His desire is driven by his belief that, … "Small children are too young to decide their views on the origins of the cosmos, of life and of morals. The very sound of 'Christian child', or 'Muslim child' (Dare I add or 'Latter-Day Saint child'?) should grate like fingernails on a blackboard." [741]

Richard can be so melodramatic, can't he? I've actually come to like this about Richard. He makes me chuckle, and even laugh out loud at his sense of humor at times, although I am sure he would be offended at me chuckling at his view on child abuse. For him, it is serious business. He is trying to get us to wince at the very idea of labelling children Catholic, Muslim, Christian, Latter-Day Saint, or any number of religious labels. That is the consciousness-raising Richard wants to take place in our societies all around the globe.

Here's what he says in closing out this particular subtitle:

"Let children learn about different faiths, let them notice their incompatibility, and let them draw their own conclusions about the consequences of that incompatibility. As for whether any are valid, let them make up their own minds *when they are old enough to do so*." [742]

As you can see, Richard is repeating what he said as his introduction to this chapter – "Childhood Abuse, and the Escape from Religion", and in particular his comments regarding the subtitle "In Defense of Children". So, I need not repeat myself, except to mention a quote made by the prophet Joseph Smith, and another one from the book of Proverbs:

The Prophet Joseph Smith Jr. said:

"*It is our duty to concentrate all our influence to make popular that which is sound and good, and unpopular that which is unsound.*" [743]

Proverbs 22:6

6 Train up a child in the way he should go and when he is old he will not depart from it.

End Quote

Coming from Richard's point of view, acquired from his own life experiences, I cannot fault him for expressing what he feels is his duty, which is to make popular that which he feels is sound and good, and unpopular that which he feels is unpopular and unsound. But this is true for me as well. Richard should not fault me for what I feel is my duty, and that is *to concentrate all my influence to make popular that which I feel is sound and good, and unpopular that which I feel is unsound.*

We should all agree that '*we can choose to disagree without being disagreeable*' and allow others to draw their own conclusion as to which view their heart and mind more easily attunes to, deciding for themselves which perspective has the greater percentage of probability of being true.

Next is the subtitle – "Religious education as a part of literacy culture."

RELIGIOUS EDUCATION AS A PART OF LITTERACY CULTURE

In chapter 9's last subtitle, Richard shares a very interesting point. He says:

"*An atheistic worldview provides no justification for cutting the Bible, and other sacred books (Like the Book of Mormon and the Koran, etc.) out of our education*. And of course, we can retain a sentimental loyalty to the cultural and literary traditions of, say, Judaism, Anglicanism, or Islam, and even participate in religious rituals such as marriages and funerals, without buying into the *supernatural beliefs* that historically went along with those traditions. *We can give up belief in God while not losing touch with a treasured heritage.*" [744]

Richard expresses the need for making religious education a part of 'literary culture', and admits he is taken aback by the biblical ignorance commonly displayed by supposedly religious people (I find that statement quite ironic). Richard goes on to say, "The King James Bible of 1611 – the authorized version – includes passages of outstanding literary merit in its own right. For example ..." [745]

Richard lists more than two pages of Bible-inspired phrases and sentences that occur commonly in literary or conversational English, from 'great poetry to backyard cliché, from proverb to gossip', and then says, "Every one of these idioms, phrases or clichés comes directly from the King James Authorized Version of the Bible. Surely ignorance of the Bible is bound to impoverish one's appreciation of English literature. And not just solemn and serious literature." [746]

And then Richard brings me back to who Richard really is, an atheist. He closed this subtitle by saying: "We can give up belief in God while not losing touch with a treasured heritage." [747]

The complier of the book titled "Joseph Smith's Commentary on the Bible", Kent P. Jackson, states that "The prophet Joseph Smith loved the Bible, and that in his sermons and writings he often expounded on biblical themes, reflecting his careful study of and appreciation for the word of God. In this commentary on the Bible, the statements in which Joseph Smith discussed, analyzed, and drew significant application from biblical verses, are gathered into one place to enhance one's personal study of the Bible through Joseph Smith's eyes". Kent said, quote: "A wealth of excerpts from the Prophet's letters, articles, and discourses that shed light on verses in the Old and New Testaments are found throughout its pages".

"The fact that there are Christians, or Muslims who do not enjoy even a scintilla of knowledge about the Bible or the Koran which they hold as inerrant, is not evidence that their faith is false, it is just evidence that those individuals lack true conversion to the faith they claim to believe in. Their lax in reading and studying the pages of their most cherished religious books (Their holy books), is also not evidence that those books are not the word of God. It's simply evidence that they're just poor examples of the teachings contained in those books." [748]

End Quote

I mention Mr. Jackson's book and a description by his publisher, because it reflects Joseph Smith's love of the Bible. It shows how we, as believers in this book of scripture, should approach the Bible. As disciples of Jesus Christ, Joseph Smith felt that we should have at least a modicum of familiarity of the Bible and its contents. Richard seems to think however, that most of us theists haven't come close to following that council, and he may be right.

Next is chapter 10, the last chapter of The God Delusion. Its title is – "A Much-Needed Gap?'

CHAPTER 10

A MUCH-NEEDED GAP?

Richard introduces his last chapter by asking the question: "Does religion fill a much-needed gap?" He continues later, "*Historically, religion aspired to explain our own existence and the nature of the universe in which we find ourselves. In this role it is now completely superseded by science.*" [749]

I would say this quite differently. I would say that "Scientists have '*tried*' to interpret the data that relates to our origin and have tried to explain how we and our universe came to be. They're also still *trying* to answer all the other 'Big' questions as well, such as "Is there life after death?", as well as determine "What our life's purpose is as sentient beings living here on this globe called earth; one tiny planet in a vast, never-ending universe", and "Why there is a universe as opposed to nothing at all?"

For Richard to say that "Science has *completely* superseded religions' explanation or interpretation of the data that gives birth to the 'Big' Questions about our universe and our place in it", is going far beyond the mark. At least I think so. Yes, scientists have discovered answers to many of the questions that mankind has sought to answer over its multi-millennia of existence, but they have yet to answer the really "Big" ones. The biggest question, of course, being, "Does God exist"? It is my belief that God, in His infinite wisdom has provided science its discoveries on a timeline He has set. Richard continues:

"At one time religion has been thought to *fill four main roles* in human life: explanation, exhortation, consolation, and inspiration. By exhortation I mean moral instruction on how we ought to behave." [750]

Richard says these four *roles* – explanation, exhortation, consolation, and inspiration – are arguments that need to be filled in order to prove God's existence, and so Richard feels that any such evidence as far as these four roles go, roles which theists say support God's existence, must be disproved. Richard says, "he has dealt with '*explanation*' in chapter 4, and '*exhortation*' in chapters 6 and 7, and so in this chapter, chapter 10, he is going to take upon himself the dealing with the remaining two – 'consolation' and 'inspiration'." [751]

Richard describes this gap as a 'much-needed gap', or a 'psychological need for God', that believing theists choose to fill with the *imaginary friend theory – the Sky-God*. In response he basically says, disregard your Sky-God and "Just fill it with my quasi-religion atheism with its 'doctrine of evolution' and all will be well". Of course, that's me putting words into Richard's mouth, which really isn't fair.

As Richard sees it, the age-old gap question "Does God exist or not?" is filled by believers with what he calls the 'imaginary friend theory'. Until 2006, when Richard wrote *The God Delusion*, Richard felt that the questions he presents in chapter 10, hadn't really been objectively answered yet, and so, in his mind, writing his book finally answered this 'much needed gap' question; the *gap* being the 'human need to find purpose in their lives, as well as what the answers were to the 'Big' questions like, "Where did I come from? Why am I here? and, 'Where am I going when I die, if there is life after death?" All of mankind has felt the need to answer these much-needed gap questions, each of them forming in the hearts and minds of all mankind. Richard claims to have answered them with his scientific guesses.

To me, it's as though Richard is saying that '*he, and he alone*' has once-and-for-all disproved the 'God Hypothesis'. He, and he alone has done what all of science has never been able to do for millennia. I can hear him saying to himself, "I did it! I did it! I've answered all the gap questions, and it's not God! It's evolution! It's Darwin's' crane of 'natural selection'! Atheism is right! Yippee! Hip-Hip-Hurray!"

Of course, Richard's never said this, but it sure seems that is what he is saying throughout his book The God Delusion. I do appreciate Richard's mental strength and the confidence he's shown in sharing his reasoning behind his arguments regarding the 'Big' questions of life. In fact, I don't fault him for being so adamant about them either. I too have mental strength and confidence in my perspective on what I believe with all my heart and soul, which is that 'God does exists'. I too am adamant about my table of belief stand that supports and has stabilized my table of belief! I'm just set aback at times, by Richard's logic. A lot of it is sound and makes good sense, of course, but then there's the times when Richard seems to become void of any common sense whatsoever when positing some of his outlandish theories, especially his 'Big' questions arguments. To me, many of Richard's arguments seem to have come from way out in left field. In other words, from la-la land, and this is why I believe I can say that Richard suffers from an atheist's delusion. With that said, let's address Richard's first subtitle of this last chapter of The God Delusion, it being the subtitle called 'Binker'. This subtitle is a perfect example of why Richard cracks me up. You're going to love this chapter, and hopefully my [perspective of it too.

BINKER

As a preliminary to the first role of religion– 'consolation'–Richard begins his subtitle of 'Binker' by talking about Christopher Robin and his imaginary friends Winnie the Pooh and Binker (Richard believes Christopher's *imaginary friends* Winnie the Pooh and Binker have affinities with religious belief).

After quoting from A. A. Milne's 'Now We Are Six', Christopher Robins' description of his *secret friend* Binker, Richard says, "I suspect that the 'Binker' phenomenon of childhood may be a good model for understanding theistic belief in adults (Richard's scientific, evolution believing, atheistic mind cannot allow itself to wrap around how grown adults can believe in an unseen God) a companion and confidant, a 'Binker' for life, is surely one role that God plays – one gap that might be left if God were to go." [752]

Richard then relates a story of a little girl and her imaginary 'purple man', and then gives this commentary on it: "The story makes me almost tearful, and it brings me as close as I shall probably come to understanding the *consoling and counseling role* of imaginary gods in people's lives. Perhaps even better (than giving real comfort and good advice), imaginary friends – and imaginary gods – have the time and patience to devote *all* their attention to the sufferer. And they are much cheaper than psychiatrists or professional counsellors." [753]

Richard then, as always, reverts back to his answer for all the 'Big' questions, that answer being evolution, and asks, "Did gods, in their role as consolers and counsellors, *evolve* from *Binkers*, by a sort of psychological *pedomorphosis*? Pedomorphosis is the retention into adulthood of childhood characteristics. It is a well-known pattern in evolution, widely accepted as important for the development of such human characteristics as our bulbous foreheads and short jaws."

"Could religions have evolved originally by *gradual postponement*, over generations, of the moment in life when children gave up their 'binkers' – just as we slowed down, during evolution, the flattening of our foreheads and the protrusion of our jaws?" [754]

Wow! Ha-ha-ha. That's a good one Richard! Amazing! You've convinced me that evolution is true! Not! I'm just kidding of course! In trying to give validation and credibility to his *Binker* theory and its evolutionary pathology, Richard introduces psychologist Julian Jaynes, and refers to Jayne's book, which is titled, "The Origin of Consciousness in the Breakdown of the Bicameral Mind." In it, Mr. Jaynes says:

"Many people perceive their own thought processes as a kind of dialogue between the 'self' and another internal protagonist inside the head"

In other words, Jaynes is suggesting that there are two main *imaginary* characters or voices going on in one's head. Jayne's suggestion that "some time before 1,000 BC people in general were unaware that the second voice – the *Gilbert Pinfold voice* – came from within themselves. They thought the Pinfold voice was a god: Apollo, say, or Astarte or Yaweh, offering them advice or orders. The breakdown of the *bicameral mind* was, for Jaynes, a historical transition". [755]

Both Jaynes and Dawkins are saying that evolution was at play here. Jaynes even goes so far as to define this time of *'transition to the two voices at battles with each other'*, as the 'dawning of human consciousness'. I'm not kidding. It's unreal. As an evolutionary biologist, Richard knows, as do most neuroscientists, that the nature of consciousness is problematic, in particular because of man's mental ability to 'introspect'; to have 'awareness' of oneself. Jaynes, like many neuroscientists, believes our 'ability to introspect' must be distinguished by sensory awareness and other processes of cognition, and so he posits a solution to this *'problem'* by saying that *consciousness is a learned behavior* (Really? A learned behavior? C'mon man!), based more on language and culture than on biology (This is just Jaynes' interpretation of things without offering any tested, irrefutable evidence).

This solution that came into Jaynes' mind (He'd say into his wet brain), points to the *origin of consciousness* as having started in ancient human history, rather than to metaphysical processes. Furthermore, Jaynes believes "archaeological and historical evidence indicates that prior to the (so-called) *'learning'* of consciousness, *human mentality* (Or intelligence) was called the 'bicameral mind' – a mentality based on verbal hallucination." [756]

What? Are you kidding me Jaynes? Our consciousness is a hallucination? C' Mon man! There's absolutely no scientific evidence or data from any scientific study that you can hold up in support of this theory. Again, this is just one scientist postulating a wild guess. I added this additional detail on Jaynes' writings since Richard chose not to. I wanted to make it clear that this theory of the *bicameral mind* being the launching point of man's conscientiousness, is most definitely *not* settled science, as Jaynes, and other scientists would have us believe. It is, in fact, a big guess by Jaynes.

This goes for Richard's theorizing or guessing that the 'Binker' phenomenon of childhood is supposedly a good model for understanding theistic belief in adults, as well. Both of these postulates are just big, fat, guesses. They are wild examples of what I've been calling an atheist's delusion. As you can see, supposedly highly intelligent individuals, like Dawkins and Jaynes, have an incredible ability to imagine a plethora of improbable theorems. Most of them being outlandish and an affront to common sense. It's so interesting to me how the mind of scientists, like Dawkins and Jaynes's minds work. To them, this is called 'doing science'. They often get off track and forget to follow the scientific method for many of their theories, making it impossible for other scientists to duplicate their supposedly tested theory's results.

With that said, I would like you, my readers, to consider what Daniel C. Peterson, a former professor of Islamic Studies and Arabic in the Department of Asian and Near Eastern Languages at Brigham Young University, had to say about *conscientiousness*. The following excerpts are from a talk given by Dr. Peterson where he discusses secular arguments in support of the Gospel of Jesus Christ, and in particular in support of the '*restored*' gospel as it is taught in the Church of Jesus Christ of Latter-Day Saints. Here are those excerpts, and I quote:

"One other issue that I want to talk about is the whole issue of consciousness. We (Meaning everybody) don't know what consciousness is. Now that's odd because consciousness is the '*thing*' we are most closely acquainted with. We know about our own consciousness. That's precisely the point. I can cut into somebody else's head. I can see how the brain functions. We can measure what parts of the brain fire up at certain points. But we cannot have the sense of what's going on in *that* head. My personal subjective experiences are mine; they're not yours. And I can never have yours; you can never have mine. And we don't know what that means.

"Where did consciousness come from? Even if you create a really elaborate computer, is it conscious? And how would we know? What's his name, the mathematician who's big, the movie was just done about him? Yeah, the Turing machine, you know, the Turing machine problem. You could have something that behaves as if it's conscious, but how would you know, unless you can gain access to it? We don't know how to gain access to it. The whole question of intentionality.

"I had a dialogue with someone just yesterday – I have these dialogues all the time on the internet, but they're useful to me. I learn what's going on out there, what's agitating the hive, if you will – and this fellow was saying, "Look, thought is nothing more than" ... he's quoting someone; he probably doesn't know he is, but ... "thought is something secreted by the brain in the same way the liver secretes bile," right? And "it's just a chemical thing." I said, "Well, then, why should I listen to you, any more than I should listen to your toaster?

He says, "What does that mean? My toaster doesn't have thoughts", and I said, "Well, by your standards, neither do you. If thought is just a neurochemical event, then what is it? And how can a neurochemical or an electrochemical event be about anything else? I mean, he may be thinking that he's thinking about the nature of the brain, but toasters aren't doing anything. I mean, physical events and physical objects aren't about anything else. If your brain ... your liver, when it's secreting bile, that secretion is not about the planet Mars. The astronomer may be thinking he's thinking about the planet Mars, but if his brain is no different than his liver or his kidney, it's hard to know what that would even mean.

"But the fact is, we know that we do think, OK? I mean, it's funny to me to see some philosophers of consciousness now saying consciousness is an '*illusion*'. Well then, who's having the illusion? What in the world are you talking about?" Then Mr. Peterson wrote: "Albert Einstein said that 'the eternal mystery of the world is its comprehensibility'. Why in the world does it make sense?"

"Or there's a Hungarian-born American theoretical physicist and also a Nobel laureate by the name of Eugene Wigner, who wrote a very famous paper entitled "*The Unreasonable Effectiveness of Mathematics*". And what struck him was how weird it was that mathematicians could sit in their studies inventing mathematical theorems and so on, imaginary numbers and so on, and then they would apply them to the universe. Why? Why is a creature who just evolved sort of randomly in the savannas of Africa or something like that? Why do we even have to have 'minds', brains that can do this sort of thing? (Why indeed?) And why does the mathematics that we think of fit the universe? It's odd. It's very strange that it applies to the real outside world (When, like Julian Jaynes' postulates, 'The breakdown of the bicameral mind was just a historical transition that was the dawning of human consciousness')."

"In other words, the result of trillions of neurons firing off until they generated (Or oozed out) a 'thought' that says, "One and one equals two", and from there it just transitioned into the physics and mathematics we have today (over millions of years), allowing mathematicians to sit in their studies, inventing mathematical theorems and so on, imaginary numbers that they could apply to the universe, and everything in it (All of this imagining math being an illusion too? C'mon man)." [757]

End of Excerpt from Dr. Daniel Peterson's talk

This talk by Dr. Peterson is basically a summary of what professor Peterson says will become a six volume, maybe even seven volume series on the arguments he wanted to offer a friend who was going through a faith crisis and leaning towards atheism. Obviously, Dr. Peterson's first desire to help, has grown to become an enormous project.

Dr. Petersons' full talk goes into greater details on the arguments he gives on several topics that I've been covering as I've given my perspective on Richard's book *The God Delusion*. At the end of his talk, Dr. Peterson included a lengthy list of footnotes and resources he used in writing his full talk. You can check all of them out at www.fairlatterdaysaints.org under the title of, "The Reasonable Leap into Light: A Barebones Secular Argument for the Gospel". I'm hoping that what I've just covered, shows you, my readers, that there are most certainly *two sides* to every argument (probably more) regarding the God Hypothesis Theory, and any other topic for that matter.

There is Richard's so-called *scientific* arguments against God's existence, and then there's my perspective and informed arguments, coupled with thousands of believing theist scientists' arguments for God's existence. Each argument becomes another informed reference leg of evidence that you, my readers, can add to your *table of beliefs'* support stand, which support stand has hopefully widened considerably as we've plowed through each chapter of Richard's book, and hopefully it has made your table of belief even more stable than it was before you began reading my book.

The resources and references I listed in my Introduction, are just a drop in the bucket of the kind of support material I could have listed. There are hundreds of published, accredited theist scientists, as well as expert intellectuals who've produced their own materials on this "much-needed gap" question. Richard supports one side of this debate and has his own list of accredited, published atheist scientists whose research he has used to support his arguments against the 'much needed gap' question.

After you, my readers, have considered the arguments, interpretations, and perspectives from both sides of this 'Does God Exist?' debate, I'm confident you'll be able to make an informed, well-supported decision about which of the arguments, interpretations, and perspectives makes more sense to you, and which of them aligns with your mind and heart. In other words, "Which one feels right and actually moved your belief cursor the most as you've read my book? As you decide, hopefully you'll agree that the arguments that Richard has put forth, implying that 'they are settled science and because they have falsified the God Hypothesis', has in fact not been settled, nor has the 'God Hypothesis' been falsified. The fact is … the jury is still out. Until the verdict comes back, we must continue deliberating on the data.

It is my belief that "By the time we're finish with this last chapters' review, I'm absolutely confident that you, my readers, will know my perspective on the 'God Hypothesis' and will have gained a clear understanding of all my informed reference legs that I've shared with you, and will yet share with you, and from that understanding I hope your belief cursor will have moved closer and closer to the *'God Exists'* marker on the *Percentage of Probability Spectrum,* and for some of you, I am hoping that it has moved even farther away from the *God Doesn't* Exist' marker. At least that's my hope. I can't help it, and that's because I love you and want the very best for all of my readers. Okay, let's get on with the first of the three remaining subtitles of this last chapter, it being – "Consolation".

CONSOLATION

Richard, as he himself said, thinks that "It is *infantilism* that lies behind the 'need' for a god. The true *adult view*, he contrasts, is that our life is as meaningful and as full and wonderful as we choose to make it. And we can make it very wonderful indeed." [758]

What Richard is really saying here, is that "anyone can fill this need for finding meaning for their life, without having to believe in some kind of, or any kind of childish fantasy, which Richard calls the Sky-God. In other words, "Just decide to make it so, and it is".

Richard continues, "It is time to face up to the important role that God plays in consoling us; and the humanitarian challenge, if he does not exist, to put something in his place." [759]

Here is the 'consolation' issue reasoning Richard hopes his readers will buy into. He says, "If you take religion away, people truculently ask (meaning aggressively self-assertively ask), 'What are you going to put in its place? What have you to offer the dying patients, the weeping bereaved, the lonely Eleanor Rigby's for whom God is their only friend?" [760]

Richard immediately responds to his own question saying, "Religions' power to console doesn't make it true. Even if it were conclusively demonstrated that belief in God's existence is completely essential to human psychological and emotional well-being; even if all atheists were despairing neurotics driven to suicide by relentless cosmic angst – none of this would contribute the tiniest jot or tittle of evidence that 'religious belief' is true." [761]

I appreciate Richard's relentless doggedness to take down any argument for God's existence, no matter how insignificant it may be. That seems to be what new atheists do. This *'argument from Consolation'*, in my mind, is one such insignificant argument. But I do want to interject one personal thought here. It is something that Daniel Petersen referenced to in his talk we just covered. It's an analogy given by William James, who was, some have argued, one of the greatest philosophers ever produced in the United States. He was the brother of the novelist Henry James. His *'Principles of Psychology'* was a foundational text in the discipline of psychology, but he, more importantly, has become famous as a founder of pragmatism.

William's analogy was about a carriage ride. William is talking about 'decision making' under *conditions of uncertainty* where you don't know with absolute certainly whether *'x'* is true or *'y'* is true, but you must decide, nonetheless (This sounds very much like the 'Big' questions to me, don't you think?). William begins by saying, and I quote:

"Imagine yourself in a carriage. The driver has gone in to get a drink. Suddenly the carriage begins to roll down the hill and it's going faster and faster. You must decide. How are you going to react to this? You're not sure whether it would be safer to stay in the carriage. You know, that might be safe, but on the other hand, it might smash into something at the base of the hill, and you die. Would it be wiser to jump out? On the other hand, if you jump out you might be killed. You just don't know'." William says, "Under conditions like that, either decision is rational". That's a statement of rationality that says: "If you can't really decide, you have to just kind of go with one and it's, you know, as long as it's roughly 50-50 or 60-40, or something like that, not an irrational decision. You might turn out to be wrong, but you were *'reasonable'* in making that decision." [762]

End of analogy

I mention this analogy, and Dr. Peterson's comments about it, because I think this is what Richard is getting at when he says, "There's a difference between belief in God and *belief in belief* itself: the belief that it is 'desirable' to believe (Which is one choice), even if the belief is false (Which is the other choice). It might be evidence in favor of the desirability of convincing yourself that God exists (Which is one choice), even if he doesn't (Which is the other choice)." [763]

Richard says, "Doesn't this appear to be a 50-50 choice?", and then uses a Bible verse to make his point. It is found in the Book of Mark:

Mark 9:24

24 Lord, I believe (One choice); help thou mine unbelief (the other choice).

Next, Richard makes a sarcastic comment:

"The faithful are encouraged to profess belief, whether they are convinced by it or not." [764]

Richard certainly did not get this verses' meaning at all. To me Richard's understanding of it sounds like what William's carriage ride analogy was describing. It's a basic statement on rationality. It says that "if you can't really decide, you have to just kind of go with one of the choices, and it's, you know, as long as it's roughly 50-50 or 60-40, or something like that; you're not making an irrational decision" (either way). You might turn out to be wrong (Which Richard says belief in God is), but at least you were reasonable in making that decision (Because it gives you some kind of *consolation* from making it)."

Richard believes that when people feel *consolation* from believing in God, it's really just them *believing in belief,* and not because God's real. This sounds a lot like that feeling a young woman gets when she's 'being in love with love', and not so much from actually being in love. It's enjoying the *'idea of love'* and not actually having a real love relationship with someone. Richard gives an example of this to prove his point. He says:

"I think we all know people who enjoy the idea of religious faith, and resent attacks on it, while reluctantly admitting that they don't have it themselves." Richard then gives an example of this by introducing a hero of his, Peter Medawar, who said in his book "The Limits of Science", the following:

"I regret my disbelief in God and religious answers generally, for I believed it would give *'satisfaction and comfort'* to many in need of it if it were possible to discover good scientific and philosophical reasons to believe in God." [765]

Richard's atheistic mind sees belief in God, in any way, shape, or form, as being an "irrational belief", and argues "One can live a happy and fulfilled life without *supernatural* religion." [766]

To me, what Richard is saying, is that all this talk about mans' need for consolation being one of many proofs that God is real, is just hogwash. It is irrational just like belief in a supernatural God is irrational. So, where do we derive *'consolation'* from then? What are its sources? Is one's belief in God simply the result of our mind trying to come up with a way to fill this human need to find consolation when life, with all its suffering, happens? I ask, "If we're just another animal in the animal kingdom, then why the need for consolation? Why would natural selection keep this need for consolation in us, and not in other animals? Richard continues:

"False beliefs can be every bit as consoling as true ones, right up until the moment of disillusionment. This applies to both non-believers and believers." [767]

Again, here's an example to describe what Richard is saying:

"A man with terminal cancer may be consoled by a doctor who lies to him that he is cured, just as effectively as another man who is told truthfully that he is cured. Sincere and wholehearted belief in life after death is even more immune to disillusionment than belief is from a lying doctor. The doctor's lie remains effective only until the symptoms become unmistakable, yet a believer in life after death can never become disillusioned." [768]

Richard then says, "This being true, wouldn't you expect that religious people would be the least likely to cling unbecomingly to earthly life? Why deem mercy killing, abortion, or euthanasia to be a sin if you sincerely believe you are (simply) accelerating a journey to heaven?" [769]

Well, here's my answer to Richard's sarcastic queries in order to make his point that all of this consolation business is wasted energy. For me, mercy killing, abortion, and euthanasia, is killing someone, and the act of killing is a serious sin. A person's life is shortened unnecessarily when you kill them. Our life here on earth is a time *to prepare to meet God before this life's test is over*. Ending our probationary time prematurely, shortens our ability to repent in order to be prepared to meet God.

Through his questions Richard reveals his atheist mindset and how little he understands the sanctity and purpose of life. Richard further shows it when he asked, "Isn't there an important difference between having your appendix removed (Under anesthesia) and having your life removed (by drugs that kill you quietly and quickly)? [770]

Richard answers his own question saying, "Not if you are going to die anyway, and not if you have a sincere religious belief in life after death, so that life is just a transition from one life to another." [771]

In other words, "What's the big deal of euthanasia? You're just getting to the next ride faster, and it's a happier ride than this one." If Richard truly believes what he is suggesting here, (And I am confident he does not), then using his logic, the entire population of the world should be terminated, because 'life's a pain and then we all die'. If what Richard says is true, then why not just kill everyone which would make it possible for all of us to leave this life of pain and disappointment and simply go on to the next state of 'happiness' that's found in heaven?" Right?

Of course, that's ridiculous and Richard knows this argument he's given here is ridiculous. Richard is simply mocking believers who believe in the afterlife. Richard continues, "It is those of us who view death as 'terminal' rather than 'transitional' who might naively be expected to resist euthanasia or assisted suicide. Yet, we (The atheists of the world) are the ones who support it." [772]

"When I am dying" Richard says, "I should like my life to be taken out under general anesthetic" [773]

Richard, and all atheists I suppose, say this because an atheist reasons that this act would simply stop the *unnecessary pain*, and induce death, and death, in Richard's way of thinking, is becoming just like he was before he showed up here on earth – he was nothing, nothing at all – just as death will make him become nothing, nothing at all once again (Do you, my readers, truly believe that you are nothing at all?). Let me insert a quick quote from The Church of Jesus Christ of Latter-Day Saints' website, stating its leader's position on the *sanctity of life* and their opposition to euthanasia, and I quote:

"The Church of Jesus Christ of Latter-Day Saints believes in the sanctity of human life and is therefore opposed to euthanasia. Euthanasia is defined as deliberately putting to death a person who is suffering from an incurable condition or disease. Such a deliberate act ends life immediately through, for example, *'frequently termed assisted suicide'*. Ending a life in such a manner is a violation of the commandments of God (The commandment being the 6th commandment, "Thou shalt not kill or do anything like unto it").

"The Church of Jesus Christ of Latter-Day Saints does not believe that allowing a person to die from natural causes by removing a patient from artificial means of life support, as in the case of a long-term illness, falls within the definition of euthanasia. When dying from such an illness or an accident becomes inevitable, it should be seen as a blessing and a purposeful part of eternal existence. Members should not feel obligated to extend mortal life by means that are *unreasonable*. These judgments are best made by family members after receiving wise and competent medical advice and seeking divine guidance through fasting and prayer." [774]

End Quote

Richard quips, "Religious people who fear death, doesn't speak strongly of religions' power to comfort the dying. Is it fear of punishment?" [775] No Richard. It is fear of *the unknown*. It is fear *of purgatory*. It is fear *of another kind*. There certainly are more than one reason why people *fear* death. Richard asks, "Why don't all Christians and Muslims say something like this when they hear that a friend is dying - "Do give my love to Uncle Robert when you see him" (Especially those who are soon to die), if they know there is life after death? Why do they fear it so?" [776]

I would ask Richard, "Just how, in your way of thinking, should the theological mind work in terms of how they should speak and act when a loved one is soon to pass on? Should they set aside their feelings of losing their loved one's companionship? Or their close association with a friend, which friendship will no longer be available to them? Or the loss of ever enjoying any and all future special events with them, such as marriages, the birth of their loved one's baby, etc. etc. "Talk to you soon?" ... Are you kidding me Richard? Talk to you soon? C' Mon Man!

Richard then goes into a long rant on the doctrine of Purgatory, an example he gives of how Catholic parishioners pay monies to minimize the time they think they will have to spend in purgatory, or to even avoid it. Of this bounty Richard quips, "I'm sure the proportion of medieval treasures of art and architecture started out as down payments on eternity." [777]

This of course, is Richard's unique way of slamming Catholics, and their unique Catholic belief in what they call purgatory. Richard sees this belief as a form of 'consolation' and as deserving scorn. I choose not to scorn it. There are some theists who think that mankind's constant search for a source of consolation to help fill the holes in their lives, is proof of God's existence, otherwise, life would be empty, pointless, futile, a desert of meaninglessness and insignificance, and full of all kinds of pain for which there is no consolation. "That argument" Richard says, "is infantile," and putting it forward as one's 'Need for God' to be filled, is going back to 'Binker-ville'!" Once again, that quip actually made me laugh out loud. Ha-ha-ha. Binker-ville!

The next subtitle topic is 'inspiration', the last of the four roles religion plays in human life. Richard of course, begs to differ.

INSPIRATION

First of all, since the title of this subtitle is 'Inspiration" you would think Richard would use that word while making his points about it, but I have thoroughly reviewed his comments and arguments on this topic several times, and I could not find where he even refers to the word 'Inspiration' in this subtitle. So, I'm just going to respond to what he did say about this forth role religion plays in a theists' life.

Richard begins this subtitle by saying this is a matter of private judgements, and so, the method of argument he had to employ against what religious people say the role that inspiration plays (though he didn't use the word inspiration like I just did) in the lives of human beings, is going to be *'rhetoric'* rather than *'logic'*, and that's because "the process of being mentally stimulated to do or feel something, especially to do something creative, (Which is the fruit of the 'inspiration' he's discussing in this subtitle) is simply a matter of private judgement and personal taste." [778]

Richard's rhetoric begins with his atheistic view that life is the 'luck' of being alive. I have not read it, but Richard mentions his books' title "Unweaving the Rainbow", within which he quotes:

"I tried to convey how lucky we are to be alive, given that the vast majority of people who could potentially be thrown up by the combinatorial lottery of DNA will in fact never be born." [779]

As an atheist Richard's mindset doesn't seem to permit his mind to imagine the idea of an existence or a life *before* this life, nor imagine the idea of existence *after* this mortal one. Richard doesn't believe, as I do, that there is a God in heaven who has billions of spirit children, all of whom are meant to come to this earth to experience what all of us are experiencing (Our pilgrim's progress, so-to-speak), where all of us come here to experience mortality. For Richard, this life of mortality, and only this life … is all there is, and then at death it's over. In other words, "Lights out!". Period! We were nothing before coming into existence, and then at death we, our individual *'selves'*, will obliterate into the nothingness that was before, even nothing at all, or I should say "into dust". No spirit person, just dirt!

Richard says his "atheist view is correspondingly life-affirming and life-enhancing, while at the same time never being tainted with self-delusion, wishful thinking, or the whingering self-pity of those who feel that life owes them something." [780] I had to look up whingering, which means 'to complain or protest, especially in an annoying or persistent manner'. In other words, "Do you serve *'whine'* with your cheese?" Many atheists have said that "The knowledge that 'we have only one life' should make this life all the more precious." I particularly enjoyed Richard's analogy of how it's lucky to be alive at all. Here's what he said:

"For those of us lucky enough to be here, I pictured the relative brevity of life by imagining a laser-thin spotlight creeping along a gigantic ruler of time. Everything before or after the spotlight, is shrouded in the darkness of the dead past, or the darkness of the unknown future. We are staggeringly lucky to find ourselves in the spotlight at all. However brief our time in the sun (spotlight), if we waste a second of it, or complain that it is dull or barren or (like a teen might say) boring, couldn't this be seen as a *callous insult* to those *unborn* trillions (Of what?) who will never even be offered life in the first place?" [781]

Trillions, who will never be born? Really Richard? Man-oh-man. The way an atheists' mind works is so fascinating to me. Implied in what Richard calls rhetoric, where he says he imagines trillions of unborn, non-existent *people*, would be 'insulted', if you or I wasted our lives while here on earth, is the imaginative thought that these so-called unborn, *'non-existent'* people would actually feel something at all, let alone insults. Wow!

In other words, 'they (these non-existent potential beings) have non-existent 'minds' that have non-existent 'feelings' about <u>not</u> being able to have a possible life experience of 'their' own'? How would 'a nothing' even have a thought, let alone a thought like this one? Didn't Richard just say that he believes that there was *nothing* before his life here on earth, and that there is *nothing* after he dies? Richard believes that 'he', his 'individual self', didn't come from any other place; that there was no 'he' before this life here on earth, and so, when his 'individual self' dies (His body of flesh and bones), 'he' doesn't go anywhere after death except into the ground where his body will just rot away into dust. 'He', whatever 'he' is right now, simply goes back to being the dust his cells came from, meaning he'll become 'nothing', just like 'he' was before 'his' life here on earth. Good honk in the morning Richard! What a poverty-stricken belief and view of one's life! It's so sad to me. No wonder atheist dictators place little to no value on human life except for the 'work-unit' they represent for their utopian goals.

If that view of life is true, then why does it matter at all whether we make the most of it, or not? Don't atheists believe this life is all there is? In other words, our minutes, our hours, our days, or whatever length of (time) life we have on this earth, and the contribution we may or may not have made to the world around us, it's all there is. Period! Nothing more. Nothing less. And once it's over (your personal time on earth), its' over. This view or belief reminds me of a song by the indomitable American singer, Peggy Lee, who sang "Is That All There Is?"

> I know what you must be saying to yourselves,
> If that's the way she feels about it, why doesn't she just end it all?
> Oh, no, not me, I'm not ready for that final disappointment,
> Because I know just as well as I'm standing here talking to you,
> That when that final moment comes and I'm
> Breathing my last breath, I'll be saying to myself
> Is that all there is, is that all there is?
> If that's all there is my friends, then let's keep dancing.
> Let's break out the booze and have a ball,
> If that's all there is …

This mindset also reminds me of the verses of scripture in the Book of Mormon that says:

II Nephi 28:7-9

7 Yea, and there shall be many which shall say: Eat, drink, and be merry, for tomorrow we die; and it shall be well with us.

8 And there shall also be many which shall say: Eat, drink, and be merry; nevertheless, fear God— he will justify in committing a little sin; yea, lie a little, take the advantage of one because of his words, dig a pit for thy neighbor; there is no harm in this; and do all these things, for tomorrow we die; and if it so be that we are guilty, God will beat us with a few stripes, and at last we shall be saved in the kingdom of God.

9 Yea, and there shall be many which shall teach after this manner, false and vain and foolish doctrines, and shall be puffed up in their hearts, and shall seek deep to hide their counsels from the Lord; and their works shall be in the dark.

"Eat, drink, and be merry, for tomorrow we die!" To atheists like Richard, life is like a memory we have from looking at a photo in a photo album of a loved one. How do we know that that picture of that young woman with her baby in her arms, glued in a photo album, isn't just a made-up, imaginary photo-shopped digital fake photo, *unless* we were there, experiencing this event shown in the picture of her and her baby, in person? Who cares anyway? Once she's dead, she's dead, and nothing matters about that dead person and her baby anymore, right?

There's no reason to feel happy or sad, or feel nostalgic or despairing, while we're here. Life is just a falls' breeze that stirs up a pile of fallen leaves and then passes on, and the leaves soon settle down as though there was never a blast of wind in the first place. Tell me, "Who remembers it? Or why would it even be remembered if tomorrow we die and that's all there is to it?"

I know what Richard would say. He'd say that the feelings that our *mind* (wet brain I mean) produces – the love we feel for others, our passions, our accomplishments, our mistakes, and any and every thought we've ever had – can stir us to greatness or spiral us down to the very depths of baseness, because that's just being human. But the question remains, "If there isn't anything before this life and there's nothing after it, then why do we have any of these emotions or feelings in the first place?

What purpose did evolutions' natural selection 'see' in us having our brief moment in the '*spotlight*' where we experience memories and emotions and passions, just for them to fade away and be forgotten? Did natural selection malfunction? Were our memories just to remind us of dangers? Are they a driving force of evolution and not the force behind our need to keep our memories of others so we don't forget them? Why do we have memories of ourselves when they're just going to disappear once we die? The only ones with our memories of 'making the best of our lives', once we're dead, are those who continue to live after we die. What's the point of memories Richard? Are they just to protect and keep us safe from past dangers, and that's it? C'mon Man. That doesn't ring true to me at all.

Yes, we can choose what we want to make our lives mean. Coming from Richard's atheistic view, this choosing is not the question to be asked, however. The question we should be asking ourselves, if Richard and all the atheists are right about all of this, is, "Why? Why should we even have the thought that we 'make the best of our lives' while we're alive, because at death it dissolves away and becomes meaningless vapors of nothingness, right?

If what Richard, and every other atheist believes about life is true, then where in heaven's name do all the feelings of nostalgia for family come from, and why do they come to us in the first place? How do they lend to our '*survival*'? Where does the feeling or desire to make this 'one' life, the best life it can be, come from? And if our lives aren't or weren't the best they could be and could have been, what does it matter? Tell me, why is there this feeling in all of mankind that says, "Life is precious"? And "Why is this feeling ubiquitous? Why do I want to know who I am, and who my parents were, and where they were from, if I don't know? Why do we have such feelings and longings to know such things?

Todays' atheist Chinese leader Xi Jinping, as well as every past and present despot who has ever lived, doesn't and didn't see life as being precious. Or do they? No, they don't. So, 'what' or 'who' is telling each of us that it is? William Wadsworth, an American poet wrote:

"Our birth is but a sleep and a forgetting; the soul that rises with us, our life's star, hath had elsewhere its setting, and cometh from afar; not in entire forgetfulness, and not in utter nakedness, but trailing clouds of glory do we come from God, who is our home ..."

If evolution is all about survival and tossing out that which doesn't provide a means for us to survive, then I ask you, "Survive what? Survive death? Survive sickness? Is it to protect us from dying, when dying is simply the end of a meaningless 'self-life' where we end up becoming a dirt pile, and nothing forevermore? If we're honest with ourselves, I would say that this built-in drive to survive is another divine trait we got from our divine heavenly parents. All parents know that life is precious.

The fact is, we can't stop death from ravaging all of us. That said, our lives have a purpose and it's not just to survive until we die. Our purpose is three-fold. *First*, it is to gain the physical bodies we each have. *Second*, is to experience the good with the bad that life on earth brings. Each experience providing the opportunity for us to choose whether or not we believe in God and His principles of truth, and whether-or-not we want to keep His commandments, so we can live a happy life here, and after we die.

And the *third* purpose, is to experience the process of how to become a disciple of Jesus Christ by exercising faith in Him, and in His atoning sacrifice, which offers each of us two special gifts. The first gift is without any conditions. It is the gift of immortality. Every last one of us are going to be resurrected and live forever, whether we live good or evil lives. The *second gift* is conditional. It is the gift of eternal life in the presence and heavenly society of Jesus Christ and our Heavenly Father, but it's based on the conditions of repentance and exhibiting a willingness to be obedient to God's commandments. This greatest of all gifts of God, provides us the possibility of living forever with our families. This gift requires that we do our best to obey the laws and ordinances of the gospel of Jesus Christ, and then endure to the end of our lives here on earth. This earth life is a preparatory state where we prepare to meet God.

Richard's analogy is like me saying, "You didn't have any knowledge that you need to have a happy, successful life *before* college, because there is no *before* college experience, or life *before* college, and so, you need to make your college life as meaningful as you possibly can, because at the end of your four, eight, or ten years of intense study, your knowledge and experience gained from your college life here on earth's campus, will be over, and useful for nothing, because that'll be the end of it all."

To me, this atheist belief is like saying, "There is no future life to apply your incredible college learning and experience to, because there is no 'after-college' existence, just like there was no 'before-college' existence. When you graduate from your 'college-life'; after you've received your diploma and then shouted and tossed your cap up high into the air, you simply walk into a future of 'educated nothingness'. Ooops! That's wrong. You don't even walk into it; you simply evaporate into dust."

"And don't forget to think about all the millions of non-existent people who would have loved to have had your 'college-life experience', but weren't lucky enough to have it (Oh, and by-the-way, they are the non-existent people who now feel insulted about your college experience). Remember, you, and those lucky enough to have attended college, or who are now attending college, if you and they don't make the very best of it, you'll be callously insulting those non-existent potential college students who don't exist and didn't get to attend college." This, to me, is an atheist's delusion, that's for sure.

Recently I was impressed even more on this subject of "There's nothing before life and nothing after life" belief that atheists hold to, when I read an essay written by a woman whose name is May Wang. She is a Harvard Graduate as well as a reporting fellow at Harvard Art Museum, Dumbarton Oaks, in Washington D.C. May titled her essay "If We All End Up Dying, What's the Purpose of Living?" The following excerpts are from that essay. They pretty much sum up, not only her view as an atheist, but the view of almost every atheist I know, including Richard, on the question of "What's the purpose of life (If there's nothing after death)?", and I quote:

"I may be accused of not answering the question in the title "If we all end up dying, then what is the purpose of living?" head on, and that's fine. So, you are a part of the 'everything' of life, which will continue on infinitely after the *self* "dies". But how does that translate to finding meaning in 'individual' life? To that, I say, "If you truly understand and believe in the idea of 'oneness', then the question answers itself." There is 'no purpose of living'. Living, itself, is the purpose. You (Your 'self') contributes to 'life'. And call me crazy, but I find happiness and satisfaction in that." [782]

End of first excerpt

May leads up to her conclusion that 'life' or '*living itself*' is, for her, the only purpose of existence, and *not* continual living. She says, and I quote: "This is such a great question because it is the most intensely personal question you could ever ask someone. A persons answer to this question will immediately reveal a number of things: his/her religion, his/her thoughts about the present world and the future, and this strange little thing we call *spirituality*, or as I like to define it, 'a personal belief and approach to living … that reconciles the tricky concepts of life, death, and subjective experience.'

"I used to associate the word *spirituality* exclusively with new age hippies who did tons of yoga and believed in healing crystals and astrology, but I also used to be a staunch anti-theist and Richard Dawkins worshipper, who handed out postcards about not believing in God during college. Over the past year or two, my views on life, death, religion, and whatnot, have evolved significantly, and I've finally discovered my own personal *spirituality*, for lack of a better word, which continues to help me live my life in a way that makes me happy.

"Around November of last year, I began having trouble sleeping because I couldn't stop myself from thinking about death. Even if I did fall asleep, I'd often wake up in the middle of the night in a cold sweat because my mind would inevitably wander to the certainty of death and trying to imagine the subjective experience of death, which of course was a futile exercise. The unknown (unexperienced) scared the crap out of me and the fact that it was going to happen whether I liked it or not, filled me with despair. Each night this incredible fear would engulf me as I imagined that never ending darkness edging closer and closer, until it eventually swallowed me whole, alone, helpless and flailing. And then the next night it would happen again, no matter how hard I tried to push the thought out of my mind. Rinse and repeat. This period lasted for about three months. I have no idea what triggered it. It may have had something to do with the fact that I was turning twenty-five soon.

"As a 25-year-old, I was officially a not-so-young adult who needed to start thinking about the rest of her life, and it could have had something to do with the fact that I had newly moved to Hong Kong, didn't love it, didn't know what my next step was, and was consumed by a constant uncertainty that unsettled me in general. Either way, it was terrifying and awful, but also necessary to trigger the intensely rewarding journey of personal discovery that followed. This is starting to sound really cheesy, I know, but stay with me. On a trip to Seattle in early 2014 I purchased "The Little Book of Atheist Spirituality" by Andre Comte-Sponville at the Left Bank Bookstore next to Pike Place Market.

"The title intrigued me because I had been used to reading very strongly opinionated atheist texts like *The God Delusion* by Dawkins and 'God is Not Great' by Hitchens, and this seemed like an interesting, albeit slightly unconventional take, on the subject of atheism.

"However, before moving to Hong Kong I'd only been able to get through the first two chapters, "Can We Do Without Religion' and 'Does God Exist,' which were pretty much similar (though arguably more eloquent) rehashes of subject matter I had encountered before. During my period of existential crises, however, I decided to crack the book open again and take a shot at the third chapter, "Can There Be an Atheist Spirituality?"

"Trust me, I am not exaggerating when I tell you that this chapter of this book changed my life. Before reading the book, I had already begun juggling some ideas in my head about the *meaning of life* and what happens to *subjective experience* (Individual, subjective self-experience of the *self*?) after death. I knew I did not believe in God, in the sense that I did not believe in the very specific idea of an anthropomorphic, all-knowing being who resides in the sky (The Sky-God Richard speaks of) and has control over every movement and action of life on earth.

"However, I was beginning to open myself up to the idea of many different *kinds of truths*, and to really think about these as possibilities, rather than focus all my energies on the denial of God's existence because I believed it improbable. My focus shifted from the one-track denial of a certain belief to the exploration of many beliefs of which, maybe, I could find a home (May is just one example of the millions of people who are in search for the truth regarding the 'Big' questions of life ... and know not where to find it)."

May continues: "I was searching for something to sustain me and help me find *meaning* in life despite knowing that human death was certain (Why is this searching or longing showing up again? "(Why the feeling of a hole, or gap that May felt she *needed* to fill? It even seems to be ubiquitous for all of humanity, does it not?). The idea of reincarnation has always fascinated me. Not necessarily the idea of a person dying and then becoming a frog or other animal in the next life per se, but the idea of '*cyclical of life*' contained within itself. This has been explored by many philosophers, poets, village prophets alike, and something in it has always rung true to me. Ashes to ashes, dust to dust.

"There are so many observable cycles here on earth, and it didn't seem entirely impossible that the '*end of life*' itself could coincide entirely with the 'beginning'. Perhaps, I thought, 'life' is contained entirely in itself (Self?). we live the same 'life' over and over again infinitely, and perhaps there is no time, since linear time is a human construct, so though we feel we are living life linearly from beginning to end that is only our subjective experience and in reality, we are just going from point A to point B, which is also point A, and going round and round and being at all points of our life at once. Is that confusing yet?

"But that idea is also highly unsatisfying. It makes life seem like a trap that we can't get out of. It also places such a huge emphasis on *'individual life'*, making each person 'one unit of life', only mattering to oneself (Just to oneself? Really?). Why, as humans then, do we seek camaraderie, identify with people, feel love, wander the world, breathe the air, and reap so much satisfaction from being with others and among the world. It didn't make sense (In other words, "Why the strong bonds to family?" as an example) And then, I read Comte-Sponville.

"Comte-Sponville speaks of a feeling of 'oneness of (Or with?) the universe' as the pinnacle (or core) of atheist *'spirituality'*. This spirituality does not need God or some other deity in the middle of it. The *'universe and the present'*, he says, is enough, in *fact* (Fact? Really?), it's all there is. (Let me insert here my definition of spirituality and personality. Spirituality is our ability to relate to God, and our personality is our ability to relate to other people).

May continues:

"The universe is all we know, it contains us, we operate in it, and we interact with it every day. It is real to us, so far as our subjective experience dictates. And he (Comte-Sponville) gives an example of this *'feeling of oneness'* (Connectedness) which he terms 'the oceanic feeling':

"Walking in the woods with friends on a cool summer evening, stopping to gaze up at the stars and feeling overwhelmed by the beauty of the night sky — Suddenly feeling like more than yourself, that the wind in your hair, the chirping of night birds, your friends' cool arm in yours, is sublime and *'true'* and all that matters.

"His descriptions rang so *true* to me because I've definitely felt like that before, many times. And I think many of you have as well. Remember that super cheesy scene in "The Parks of Being a Wallflower," when Charlie and his friends race through the night in a convertible and declare that in that moment, they felt 'infinite?' Moments like those? Lucid moments of *recognition* that you are alive and part of this infinite world (Infinite? Really? Don't scientists say that this world is coming to an end quicker than we think, and that our bodies are all going to have a worm-fest? Where will this feeling of 'infinite' come from then?).

"It's as simple and as obvious as that. And according to Comte-Sponville, it is exactly this 'oneness of (With?) the universe' that makes life worth living, because it is complete, incredible, everything. We _must_ accept it because we are a part of it. And that very fact is marvelous and incredible. This is probably the trickiest part to wrap your head around, so here's a wonderfully eloquent except from Comte-Sponville that perfectly expresses this idea in a much better way than I can, quote:

"*Love of fate, loving what is — not because it is good, but because it is the set of all things that occur (the universe, reality), and because nothing else exists... This is a tragic wisdom: 'The Dionysiac affirmation of the universe as it is, with no possibility of subtraction, exception, or choice.' It means participating in the 'innocence of becoming,' the 'eternal yes of being,' which is the self-affirmation of all... 'Not what should be, but what is,'- neither hope nor regret.*

"*It is the only path: 'There is no way out except acceptance.'* We must say yes to all that is and to all that occurs, but it is the *'yes of acceptance'* (all is true, all is real), not the *'yes of approval'* (all is well). It is the *'yes of wisdom'*, not of religion- or, more accurately, it is not a word, and neither wisdom nor religion exists. All that exists is the eternal necessity of becoming, which is true being. In other words, life is everything. And I (My subjective self?) am irresistibly a part of that 'everything of life' (So, what 'part of you' after you have died and your body has become a worm-banquet of dust, is still part of the universe you're calling 'life'? Is it just the dust? Or is it all the memories that others will continue having of you, held in *their* minds while they're still living? If not that, then what is it?)."

"Gandhi once said, 'all life is one.' He might have been using the phrase to encourage people of all castes and colors to come together and end discrimination, but I subscribe to this phrase as a belief, and I subscribe to it 'literally'. As humans our primary instinct and goal is to *'stay alive'* ourselves and help each other *stay alive* too (It may be for atheists, but for theists it's to live in such a way so that we can return to our Creator and become one with Him. Christ said He is one with the Father. Of course, we want to live as long as we possibly can, but that's not our primary goal in life).

"We are naturally inclined to sustain life. So, what if all life is one? We are only 'identified' as individuals because we have different bodies which 'carry' different subjective experiences of life (What about our individual thoughts and desires? Are these *'subjective experiences'*, our individuality, our individual-selves?). But each individual is living 'life' itself. Perhaps as individuals, we are all just vehicles, really.

"Vehicles living out 'life' because life (Life itself?) demands to be 'lived'. A vehicle can grow old physically and wither and die, but after death of an individual 'vehicle', 'life itself' continues, anew, and in others who are still living (So it is 'life' itself continuing on forever in those still alive, and not the man?).

"So, _if_ (I'm sure glad May put this 'if' in all her guessing) all life is one (One what? One big pile of 'memories', thoughts, ideas, guesses, forever getting bigger and bigger like Google's search engine?), and you (Or my experiences) are (and will become) a part of that 'one' (Or oneness of experience and knowledge?); you ARE that one (Or oneness?), then why would you (My living 'self') care about the death of the individual 'self', which is merely a _vehicle_ (Are you talking about the physical shell that carries around the 'mind', the mind or spirit being the true self, the conscious self with its 'consciousness' and all that makes it a person, an individual 'self')?

"You are a part of the universe, of _life_ (I certainly am). And 'life' will continue, and so will you (When you say 'you', do you mean all my contributed memories that are in the minds of those still living life even though I am no longer alive? Or do you mean my conscious self? My spirit self?). What a beautiful thought. Spirituality happens when the 'self' is transcended, and the 'all' of the universe, (This big pile of memories and memory making that exists in the minds of all those still living, or just the physical parts of the universe?) is _accepted._ As articulated by Comte-Sponville:

"We are separated from 'the-all' only by thought, only by ourselves. When the ego is relinquished (Or transcended, given up and accepted), when thought ceases, the-all remains (What? I thought that the 'all' was our thoughts, our memory making while living and the accumulation of memories in the big pile of memories called 'life' out there in the universe? Now you're saying thought itself is to cease for 'the-all' to remain? C' Mon May)."

"I may have lost you already. And you may be thinking – what a load of bollock (A British vulgar slang word), 'what a cop-out, what desperate grasping at straws to avoid confronting the certainty of death and that your loved ones will all die. You're no better than those religious fanatics' (You're reading my mind May). I've had all of these thoughts, trust me. I've turned this subject around in my head so many times, yet somehow the concept rings so true to me. The eternal 'yes' of 'being', because being is all we have and is all there is (Or so you believe. It is only your opinion May). It (This eternal 'yes of being' we call 'life') is not God, it's not Buddha, it's not heaven and prancing around on fluffy white clouds and 72 virgins after death, it's just as simple as 'letting go of' that rigid idea of the 'self' and taking joy in 'being a part of _life_' and the universe and now (At death there'll be no more 'taking joy in being part of life').

"I have never agreed with the idea that atheism is the lack of belief. I prefer to think that as an atheist, I am a healthy skeptic. I gather information, I question everything, and I evaluate all options before I '_choose to believe_' in something (Now that is possibly the first thing that I have agreed with May on so far. We do in fact 'choose' to believe). My atheism is the lack of belief in the conventional tenets of organized religion, most of which worship a single deity and contain elaborate, comprehensive theorems about the origin of life. Yet it does not mean that I will not and do not believe in anything, and that I cannot develop my own spirituality and understanding of life (May's a great candidate for placing her atheism on Richard's probability scale. I don't think it would land at 7, or even 6. May asks:)

"What is spirituality? (Like I said earlier, spirituality is 'our relatability to God', and personality is 'our relatability to people', but for May and other atheists like her, spirituality is something quite different. She quotes Andre's definition:)

"Quoting Andre Comte-Sponville once again – "_Our finite relationship to infinity or immensity, our temporal experience of eternity, our relative access to the absolute."_

(Sounds like a wordy way of saying what I said spirituality was. Ha, ha. May continues):

"Of course, that doesn't answer the question- 'What happens to "subjective experience" (All our thoughts and memories stored in the mind, etc.) after we die, if it's not going to heaven or reincarnation? Because there is still no getting around the idea that at least the particular 'subjective experience' you are living now, is tied to the 'self' and the 'individual' (You got that right May. All that we are and have been and all that we have done and are going to do, is certainly tied to the 'Self'; ...our spirit Self indeed, and that 'Self' will live on forever, and then be resurrected with its body). But even that is a tricky subject that can be written and postulated endlessly about. I highly recommend a "Wait but Why" article on 'What makes you 'you'?", that sheds more light (or adds more confusion to, depending on which way you see it) the subject, and I have to admit, I still do not know and don't know if I ever will know 'the answer'. Yet _that_ very question ("What makes you, you?") does not seem to matter so much when the importance of the 'self' and 'subjective experiences' ceases to be everything."

"But even that is a tricky subject that can be written and postulated endlessly about. I highly recommend a "Wait but Why" article on 'What makes you 'you'?', that sheds more light (or adds more confusion to, depending on which way you see it) the subject, and I have to admit, I still do not know and don't know if I ever will know 'the answer'. Yet *that* very question ("What makes you, you?") does not seem to matter so much when the importance of the 'self' (The importance of the 'you'?) and 'subjective experiences' ceases to be everything." [783]

End of May's Essay

This is one side – the atheistic side – of the two-sided debate on the 'value of life', or the 'sanctity of life', and the 'purpose of life', and ultimately what one believes 'life' really is. The other side of the debate is a religious-based one, the theistic side of the debate. Like Richard taking the liberty to quote his hero's, I'm now going to quote one of my hero's, who gave some beautiful comments on the 'sanctity of life'. His name is James E. Faust. Elder Faust was one of several past apostles of the Church of Jesus Christ of Latter-Day Saints, who have since passed away. I'm taking an excerpt from a talk Elder Faust gave titled, "The Sanctity of Life".

Because we are talking about 'life', it's value, and what role it plays in our lives, now and after death (And I submit even before this earth life), I want to give my belief and perspective as to what the sanctity of life means to me. Although Elder Faust is talking about the unborn here, I want you, my readers, to focus on the specifics of what he says about 'life' itself. Here's some excerpts from his talk, and I quote:

"I have chosen to speak on the sanctity of life. I desire also to speak with reverence about the *'hallowed hallmark of life'*, which is *'the ability to reproduce itself'*. I wish also to be an advocate for the unborn. For this reason, I direct my remarks primarily to women, because only they can *honor the holy calling of motherhood* (because they're the ones who cross over to the shadow of death to bring a little one into this world), which is the most exalted good that can be rendered to mankind. In the Talmud we read that *'he who saves one life is as if he had saved an entire world'*. Since the beginning of man, God has taught of an absolute respect for *human life*. From the very first moment of his (man's) being, until the last breath of his *life* (the life within him and the life he lived), there is a veneration for life which includes those in 'being', but not yet born. One wise teacher tells us, "One human life is as precious as a million lives, for each is infinite in value."

James E. Faust excerpts continued

"The exercise of a man or woman's *sacred procreative powers* makes each a partner with God in creation and brings to them in parenthood their greatest happiness. This *divine partnership* also brings their greatest privileges and most weighty responsibilities. Since becoming a parent is such a transcending blessing, and since each child is so precious and brings so much happiness, a cardinal purpose of marriage and of 'life' (The life we live) itself is to bring forth *'new' life* within this partnership with God. Obligations inherent in the creation of precious human life are a *sacred trust*, which if faithfully kept, will keep us from degenerating into moral bankrupts and from becoming mere *addicts of lust*. The responsibilities involved in the divine life-giving process, and the functions of our body, are so *sacrosanct* that they are to be exercised only within the marriage relationship. Those who do not accept and meet those responsibilities, for any reason, as well as those who do, should never depart from '*the law of chastity*' if they wish to be truly happy.

"All members of this Church (The Church of Jesus Christ of Latter-Day Saints) seeking eternal joy and peace, are expected to and will wish to come to the marriage altar free from sexual transgressions—chaste and pure. Any who fail to do so may find that they have cheated themselves of their own self-respect, dignity, and much of the great '*joy*' they seek in marriage. Because of the special inner peace, strength, and happiness it brings, Chastity, as the law of God, is and always has been really "in", and unchastity is and always has been really "out".

"In times past we have looked upon a person who saves another human life as a great hero; yet now we have come to a time when the taking of an *unborn human life* for nonmedical reasons has become tolerated, made legal, and accepted in many countries of the world. But making it legal to destroy 'newly conceived life' will never make it right. It is consummately wrong. [784]

"President Spencer W. Kimball (A past prophet and President of the Church) said, "This is one of the most despicable of all sins—to destroy an unborn child to save one from embarrassment or to save one's face or comfort." [785]

"Some say, as did the Supreme Court of the United States, that *it is only a theory that human life is present from conception*. This is contrary to insurmountable medical evidence (Even more true considering today's scientific updated discoveries as of 2022). Dr. Bernard N. Nathanson recently revealed that he was among those who were militantly outspoken in favor of legalized abortion and joined in using every device available in political action to *promote* it. He helped set up and became director of the first and largest abortion clinic in the western world. After the center had performed some *sixty thousand abortions*, Dr. Nathanson resigned as director.

Dr. Nathanson said, quote:

"I am deeply troubled by my own increasing certainty that I had in fact presided over 60,000 deaths. There is no longer serious doubt in my mind that *human life* exists within the womb *from the very 'onset of pregnancy'*." [786]

End Quote

"Way back in the sixteenth century, Arantius showed that maternal and fetal circulations were separate, thus clearly demonstrating that there are two separate *'lives'* involved. The unborn 'babe' is certainly alive because it possesses the *'token'* of life which is *'the ability to reproduce dying cells.* [787]

"For the unborn, only two possibilities are open: It can become a live human being or a dead unborn child.

"Dietrich Bonhoeffer, a German Lutheran pastor, theologian, anti-Nazi dissident, and key founding member of the Confessing Church, referring to the unborn 'babe' in the mother's womb, said: "The simple fact is that God certainly intended to create a human being." [788]

"Because she feels it, every mother knows there is *'sacred life'* in the body of her unborn babe. There is also 'life' in the spirit, and *some time before birth the 'body' and the 'spirit' are united*. When they do come together, we have a human soul. For the Lord has said:

D&C 88:15

15 And the spirit and the body are the soul of man.

"Experts tell us that the necessity of terminating unborn life, is rarely justified for purely medical or psychiatric reasons. (Dr. James H. Ford, M.D., *California Medical Journal,* Nov. 1972, pp. 80–84. [789]) Some justify abortions because the unborn may have been exposed to drugs or disease and may have birth defects. Where in all the world is the physically or mentally perfect man or woman? Is life not worth living unless it is free of handicaps? Experience in working with handicapped children would suggest that human nature frequently rises above its impediments and that in Shakespeare's words, 'They say best men are molded out of faults, and, for the most, become much more the better for being a little bad" in the physical sense' [790] (*Measure for Measure,* 5, I, 445).

"At 8:53 AM, August 20th, 2024 – on Tweetbot for iOS, Richard Dawkins tweeted "Abort it and try again. It would be immoral to bring it into the world if you have the choice." [791] Quite an opposite view by Richard, isn't it?

Continuing with Elder Faust Comments:

"Many parents who have known the heartache and concern of caring for a handicapped child would agree with Pearl Buck, Nobel prize-winning author who said, "A retarded child, a handicapped person, brings its own *gift* to 'life', even to the life of normal human beings." [792]

"What a great gift to mankind the 'life' of Helen Keller brought. It is the belief of those who are members of this Church that *'human life'* is so hallowed and precious that there is an accountability to God on the part of those who *'invoke the sacred fountains of life'*. The destruction of such a treasure is so abhorrent that the First Presidency of the Church has clearly and repeatedly counseled the world—against the taking of unborn life. I quote, *"Abortion must be considered one of the most revolting and sinful practices in this day. … Members of the Church guilty of being parties to the sin of abortion must be subjected to the disciplinary action of the councils of the Church as circumstances warrant."* [793]

"Members are counseled neither "to submit to or perform an abortion except in the rare cases where it is medically necessary", and, as the First Presidency has further counseled, "even then it should be done only after counseling with the local presiding priesthood authority and after receiving divine confirmation through prayer." [794]

"The First Presidency has advised that it will be amenable to the laws of repentance and forgiveness. It is my feeling that we grossly underestimate the sacred nature of motherhood. Psychiatric experts remind us that there are certain fundamental, biological facts which *influence the psyche* of those who bring new life into the world. Dr. S. Bolter says, "The ability of mothers to accept infants after they are born is underrated and underestimated." [795] Childbearing is a basic biological and psychological, privileged function of womankind.

"One of the most-evil myths of our day is that a woman who has joined hands with God in creation can destroy that creation because *she claims the right to control her own body*. Since the life within her *is not her own*, how can she justify its termination and deflect that life from an earth which it may never inherit?

"The great medical profession, for which I have such great respect, that for centuries has been committed to the preservation of 'life' (Compare May's definition of life here to the definition being laid out here by Elder Faust) under the cardinal principles of treatment— "do no harm" and "protect life"—now finds itself destroying almost a million unborn children a year in the United States alone (There are over 53 million abortions per year worldwide). Each of these, because of tiny 'chromosomal differences', would have been different from any other person born in the world. How many with special gifts like unto Moses, Leonardo da Vinci, Rembrandt, and Abraham Lincoln might have been among them?

"These and all others are '*entitled*' to a defense in their unborn, natural state of existence. One great physician, Dr. Henry G. Armitage Jr. says, "We do that much for seagulls, flamingos, and whooping cranes (Meaning their eggs)." [796] This same physician states, "Not without comment shall it come to pass that a state (so fretful for the preservation of the praying mantis but holding an unborn baby to be of no account) can send *a spark of immortality* swinging out into limbo and conspire with citizen and physician to turn a fragile, living object of simple innocence and *complex wonder* into a pathetic pulp and consign it by rude and peremptory passage to the furnace or sewer—unknown, unwanted [and] undefended." [797]

Continuing: "He further questions how a woman as "the fertile adornment of our race can be deluded into the notion that she is a mere portress of *unwanted luggage* (An unwanted microscopic mass of gelatinous cells) or be by blandishment seduced into believing that she has dominion over life *not her own*." He says, "An abortion is never commonplace, for the world holds no heartbreak like the death of innocence. Whenever and wherever it occurs, we all suffer another loss from that little which sustains us and holds us together. It is the degradation of humanity. It is fulness emptied, innocence defiled, song unfinished, beauty discarded, hope un-sprung. In our absence, housebreakers are robbing us of everything that we own: of virtue, honor, integrity, trust, innocence, truth, beauty, justice, and liberty." [798]

"I urge all who may have 'dipped into the *fountains of life*' to respect the divinity inherent in that 'life' and to protect this sacred treasure and its transcending blessings. For the Savior said:

Matt. 25:40

40 Inasmuch as ye have done it unto one of the least of these ... ye have done it unto me.

End of excerpts by Elder Faust [799]

I would ask that you compare this description of 'life', and its value, expressed by Elder Faust, to May's and Richard's description of it. When you do you will see a stark difference in the two sides of this debate concerning 'life' and what it truly is, and what its *unique value* is for each of us, and for society as a whole. Another piece to this complex, two-sided debate-puzzle of whether or not there is 'life before life here on earth, and life after death', and whether life itself is valuable or not, and if there's any reason to make of it the best we can, the 'it' being the 'life's *value*' we each attach to it.

My perspective on this whole debate was recently widened when I read a speech given by an associate professor of English and coordinator of the American Studies Program at BYU. Her name is Kristin L. Matthews. Here's a few excerpts from a talk she gave to BYU's student body, and I quote:

"Good morning, friends. A few months ago, I had the opportunity to travel to Italy for the first time. While there I saw art created by the great masters: Michelangelo, Botticelli, Fra Angelico, and many others. In Milan I was able to see the famed '*The Last Supper*' of Leonardo da Vinci. This mural is in the refectory of the 'Convent of Santa Maria delle Grazie', and to see it one must purchase tickets ahead of time and wait for one's fifteen minutes with the painting. When my time drew near, I was corralled with twenty-four others into a waiting area, guided through two air-locked chambers, and finally allowed in front of the painting for fifteen minutes of communion.

"As I sat there, I contemplated the painting and why it is considered *'priceless'*—the value of which is beyond measure. Is it because the painting is old, created in the fifteenth century? Is it because of where it is located—in Milan? Is it because access is limited—few people can see it, so it is more valuable than paintings just anyone can, see? Is it because it has been threatened in the past—like when Napoleon used the convent as an armory, a prison, and a stable or when it was partially destroyed by bombs during World War II? Is it because it was painted in an unconventional style—on a dry wall versus in the wet plaster—making it more fragile, and rare? Is it because of who painted it—the great master da Vinci? Is it because of its subject?

"These questions and others I chewed on while sitting and looking at this painting. I'd like to say that I came up with profound answers that shook me to my core, but instead, I came up with more questions. How do we measure value? What makes 'something'—and, more important, 'someone'—of worth? As a professor of literature and culture, it is my job to look at systems of meaning and value, language being the first and foremost. If we go to the *Oxford English Dictionary*—the fifth standard work for all English majors—excerpts from the entry for the word *value* (n) read:

- *worth or quality as measured by a standard of equivalence*
- *a standard of estimation or exchange*
- [something] *worth having*
- *material or monetary worth of something*
- *an appraisement*
- *relative rank or importance*
- *worth based on esteem*
- *estimation* [based on] *real or supposed desirability or utility* [later extended] *to an individual or group*
- *opinion of or liking for a person or thing*
- *worth or worthiness . . . in respect of rank*

"According to these definitions, a thing's value is contingent on ideas of estimation, desirability, likeability, and worthiness. It is at the center of the word *evaluate*—to analyze—yet often we do not ask the questions, "Who determines the system of value by which we are considering, classifying, and ranking people or things? Who determines the mechanism of evaluation and the indices of what is evaluated? Who sets the *"standard of equivalence"* that says some things have greater worth than others?

"As human beings, one of the things that we do to understand our world is to create systems of meaning that help us organize the sensations, experiences, and objects we encounter. I remember a time when I was reading with my oldest nephew, Connor, as he was learning different categories of animals—how a dog is not a cow, and a cow is not a zebra. What the animal looked like, how it sounded, and what it ate all factored in as he learned how to identify these different species. Similarly, we have created categories such as nationality, race, ethnicity, sex, religious affiliation, political party, marital status, and so on to organize and make sense of *humankind's diversity*. However, too often we use these seemingly descriptive systems to determine the worth of others. *These human-made hierarchies of value can cause division, contention, and skewed understandings of self-worth.*

"Conversely, God's system of valuing us promotes connection, compassion, and love. We are His children. He loves us unconditionally, eternally, and unchangingly. Our worth is infinite because we are His daughters and sons. No one spirit is more valuable than the other. So why, then, do we fall short of loving and "measuring right" God's children?

We read in Doctrine & Covenants:

Doctrine & Covenants 18:10

10 Remember the worth of souls is great in the sight of God;

… but do we really believe that, or do we bookmark that scripture in our minds as only for missionary purposes? Today I'd like to reflect upon how we might better align how we 'value' others with how the Lord values His children so that we might be true disciples of Christ.

What Are You Worth?

"So, what are you worth?" This is a question I overheard as I may or may not have been eavesdropping on a recent flight. (In my defense, it is hard not to hear everything going on around you on a plane.) In response to the question, the petitioned gentleman cited portfolio figures, property holdings, and his net financial wealth. My first thought was, "Holy cow! I hope nobody measures my worth by what's in my savings account; otherwise, I'm in trouble. Then I sat and thought more about how externalities like wealth are used to ascribe value to individuals. I was reminded of Edith Wharton's novel 'The Age of Innocence'. In this text Wharton satirizes the intricate set of codes that the very wealthy used to dictate behavior and measure worth in Gilded Age New York. People who abided by these strict codes were accepted into high society as a valued member. Those who did not or could not abide by these codes were dismissed as vulgar, low class, and—the worst of all designations— "unpleasant."

"When I teach this novel, my students have no trouble laughing at these characters and their shallowness. But we as early twenty-first-century folk too have codes that separate the "hots" from the "nots" (to quote a Facebook page that has been in the local news recently). As a class we started to identify various *markers or codes* that could be used to rank others and came up with a list: what people wear, what cell phone they have, what laptop they use, what car they drive, what bands they listen to, what size their jeans are, what status their relationship is in, what apartment complex they live in, what films they watch, what facial hair they grow, and so on. My students found that these things that seemingly describe, actually *prescribe* certain behaviors and beliefs deemed important to acceptance and worth.

"Oftentimes we are unaware that we are ascribing worth to people in ways that contradict or challenge our professed beliefs as Christians. Wealth, physical appearance, education, race, ethnicity, gender, sexuality, religious affiliation, and political party are just some *categories* that can be used to lift some folks up and bring others down. Whether we like to admit it or not, it is human to *rank and ascribe value to others*, and more often than not we ascribe higher value to people who are like us than to those who are different. It is now cliché to say this, but we fear what we don't know, so difference is made suspect or "bad," whereas familiarity breeds comfort, so sameness becomes more valuable. In addition, fear of coming up short or fear of not being enough often propels these negative behaviors. Because we fear we are somehow less, we seek to elevate ourselves above others to convince ourselves that we are valuable.

False Systems of Value

"Where do these systems that evaluate worth come from? (From fallen, natural man) These systems are neither eternal nor transcendent but are *'human creations'* based on place and time that, more often than not, benefit those in positions of power who have created these systems.

"For example, pseudoscientific ideas of racial superiority elevating Anglo-Saxons above all others were perpetuated for centuries in order to justify devaluing and dehumanizing persons of color so that their land might be seized, and their bodies be used as slaves or subjects. Until recently, social narratives said that humans in possession of two X chromosomes were intellectually inferior, predisposed to emotional irrationality, and incapable of governing others—let alone governing themselves. This valuation barred women from holding property, gaining an education, voting in elections, and participating in the public sphere.

"These human systems by which human beings have been evaluated, categorized, and ranked have changed with time and place. Obviously, these systems that elevate some and denigrate others are destructive and have led to wars, enslavement, and discrimination—violence of a social and global scale (This is true especially today as we see 'Woke-ism' rise its ugly head). These false *systems of value* also have a negative impact on a smaller scale—on the individual and his or her sense of self-worth and place in the community. Being told that you are less, that you'll never fit in or add up, or that you'll be accepted only when you change who you are is destructive emotionally, spiritually, and, at times, physically.

"One system of valuation that has negative consequences for feelings of individual worth is *beauty*. Human beings go to great lengths to achieve some ideal beauty—extreme workouts, plastic surgery, eating disorders, elaborate makeup rituals, extensive hair and nail treatments, and compulsive shopping. All of these behaviors stem from the desire to be beautiful because *we are taught to believe that beautiful people are more valuable than others.*

"Here in Utah, we are not immune to this trend. In November 2007 *Forbes* magazine named Salt Lake City the vainest city in America because it had more plastic surgeons and used more beauty products per capita than any other large city in the United States.[2] Drive down I-15 and you'll see sign after sign offering to fix how you look to make a better you. Scroll through a Facebook feed or watch one commercial break during prime-time television viewing hours and you'll see several examples in which bodies are objectified, shamed, and tied to one's individual worth. If we are prisoners in the wasteland that is reality TV, we are subjected to scores of plastic surgery shows, makeover shows, "dating" shows, and dangerous weight-loss competitions inundating us with the message that one can never be beautiful enough and that happiness is predicated upon one's skin, teeth, hair, weight, shape, and wardrobe. We read in 1 Samuel 16:7:

1 Samuel 16:7

7 But the LORD said unto Samuel, Look not on his countenance, or on the height of his stature; because I have refused him: for *the LORD seeth* not as man seeth; for man looketh on the outward appearance, but the LORD looketh on the heart.

"Our modern culture's obsession with beauty indeed confirms that. This obsession is not without its costs. In a general conference talk Elder Jeffrey R. Holland remarked on this *false system of value* and its destructive nature, pleading with women young and old, quote:

"Please be more accepting of yourselves, including your body shape and style, with a little less longing to look like someone else. We are all different . . . If you are obsessing over being a size 2, you won't be very surprised when your daughter or the Mia Maid in your class does the same and makes herself physically ill trying to accomplish it. It is spiritually destructive, and it accounts for much of the unhappiness women, including young women, face in the modern world. And if adults are preoccupied with appearance—tucking and nipping and implanting and remodeling everything that can be remodeled—those pressures and anxieties will certainly seep through to children. At some point the problem becomes what the Book of Mormon called "*vain imaginations.*"

End quote

"As Elder Holland said, this preoccupation with appearance and this *socially constructed* idea of beauty as that by which we find worth, or value is physically and spiritually destructive—and it isn't just limited to women. Men too have to negotiate pressures of appearance, and eating disorders, exercise bulimia, and psychological troubles associated with achieving beauty are on the rise among men. Are beautiful people better people? Does God love them more? I am sure we would all respond with a resounding no; however, do you say no when you look in the mirror and criticize yourself or when you criticize others for their appearance? Do we believe what we say?

"Remember: *ideal beauty is a construction of this world*. We can point to the usual suspects for this false system of value—the fashion industry, advertising, television, and so on. And yes, we are bombarded with images that say, "This is beautiful. If you are this, you will be popular, you will be important, you will be datable, you will be marriageable, you will be worth loving." While we know this to be false, the rates of "tucking and nipping and implanting and remodeling," as Elder Holland said, and the rates of eating disorders and depression among college students on this campus and others, tell us that this is very real.

Loving Thy Neighbor

"One of my favorite works of literature is Lorraine Hansberry's play '*A Raisin in the Sun*'. This play examines the ways in which *socially constructed categories of worth* can grind down individuals and offers a corrective. The Younger family is poor and black, living in Southside Chicago after World War II. The degradations of racist housing and hiring practices have worn them out, eating away at familial relationships and draining each individual of hope. At the beginning of the third act the 'Younger' family is reeling from the news that Walter Lee Younger's actions have lost the small inheritance that could have helped them better their situation. His sister, Beneatha, turns against him, saying he is no longer a man but "a toothless rat."

"Her mother corrects her, reminding her that she taught her to love him, to which Beneatha replies, "Love him? There is nothing left to love." Indeed, the oppressive weight of racism has told the Youngers that they are worth nothing so many times that they are starting to believe it.

Yet Mama rightly says in this memorable speech:

"There is always *something left to love . . . Child, when do you think is the time to love somebody the most? When they done good and made things easy for everybody? Well then, you ain't through learning—because that ain't the time at all. It's when he's at his lowest and can't believe in hisself 'cause the world done whipped him so! When you starts measuring somebody, measure him right, child, measure him right. Make sure you done taken into account what hills and valleys he come through before he got to wherever he is.*

"Mama reminds Beneatha that all individuals are of worth, that there is always something to love, and that we must rethink how we measure each other. Ultimately, she argues that *correct measurement is not contingent on external factors but instead is based upon one's immutable worth as a human being.* And for Mama, a practicing Christian, there's more: worth cannot be diminished and there is always something to love because all are children of God. Heavenly Father knew that we would have trouble with this. Indeed, the scriptures are full of commands to resist the human impulse to 'rank people' and instead to see them as God does. For example, Leviticus contains several injunctions to the Israelites to accept and love all those among them. We read:

Leviticus 19:33–34

33 And if a stranger sojourn with thee in your land, ye shall not vex him.

34 But the stranger that dwelleth with you shall be unto you as one born among you, and thou shalt love him as thyself; for ye were strangers in the land of Egypt: I *am* the LORD your God.

"God commanded the Israelites to look past human-made constructions of nationality or religious practice and to see and love a "stranger" as "one born among you." He commanded that we not 'vex' others we perceive as different. He asked that we recognize that us/them divisions are artificial because *all* are God's children. He also reminded the Israelites that they too were strangers and that we *all* are strangers at one point or another in our lives. If God did and could show mercy to them—His children—then so should they to others.

In addition to that, God commanded the Israelites:

Leviticus 19:18

18 Thou shalt not avenge, nor bear any grudge against the children of thy people, but thou shalt love thy neighbour as thyself: I *am* the LORD.

"There are no caveats here—no "love thy neighbor unless he is X, Y, or Z"—but *a command for total inclusion.* The final statement "I am the Lord" underscores who is speaking and distinguishes the divine commandment to love inclusively from the human tendency to distinguish, evaluate, discriminate, and tolerate. So, what are you worth? I hope you know that you are above and beyond those false measures of worth that we humans have created. You have an infinite value that has nothing to do with what your portfolio contains, what size you wear, what party you vote, what color your skin is, what your gender is, and so on. Why?

First, because you are a human being, and all human beings have value. Second, because you are a child of God who loves you and sees you for the valuable person you are." [800]

End of Kristen's excerpts

I almost want to apologize for adding these lengthy quotes and essays to make my point about 'inspiration', but I felt that Kristin's talk in particular, would add some unique twists to the conversation we're having about the 'Big questions of 'life', 'value', and 'inspiration', and the real reason *why* we should make it the best life it can be, and whether or not our mortal life is all that there is, and why it's important to ask ourselves, "How do we go about making our life the best it can be?"

For me, I can understand Richard's point, that as an atheist, he is having a wonderful life because he has determined to make it a great one, especially because he believes it is the *only one* he's got; the only 'life' he'll ever have, which life will soon come to an end in the next few years if not sooner (Be it 1 year from now, 60 years from now, or 100 years from now. When Richard dies, he dies and turns to dust!).

As far as Richard's concerned, there wasn't a life before he was born into this world, and there isn't going to be a life after he dies, and his world of mortality ends. It is not a progressive, continuation into an eternal life experience for him. It is just a 1 to a 100-year life journey, max, before his eternal dirt nap! And because he believes this and has lived his life according to this belief, Richard's *'philosophy of life'* closely resembles the following quote by one of the ancient prophets of the Book of Mormon, the prophet Nephi, who said:

II Nephi 28:7

7 Yea, and there shall be many which shall say: Eat, drink, and be merry, for tomorrow we die; and it shall be well with us.

Or as Richard puts it:

"That it will never come again, is what makes life so sweet." [801]

I get it Richard. I really do. But I find Richard's next comment as one more example of what I've been calling *an atheist's delusion*. Richard says, "If the demise of God will leave a gap, different people will fill it in different ways. *My way includes a good dose of science, and the honest and systematic endeavor to find out the truth about the real world.* I see the human effort to 'understand the universe' as a model-building enterprise. Each of us builds, inside our head, *a model* of the world in which we find ourselves." [802]

Why do humans seek to understand themselves and the universe they find themselves in? Why do they want to build a model of the world in which they live? Could it be because we have a spark of divinity in us, it being the desire to create, just like our Heavenly Father does? Did this desire to create come from our mortal parents? Or could this desire in each of us be divine, innate 'desire' genes? Or is it just evolution driving us so we can survive? Period. You, my readers, can decide for yourselves. I choose my heavenly parents as the source of my divine 'desire' genes.

Richard continues: "The minimal model of the world is the model our ancestors needed in-order to survive in it. Its *'simulation software'* was *constructed and debugged* by natural selection (Really? Constructed and debugged Richard? C'mon man), and it is most adept in the world familiar to our ancestors on the African savannah: a three-dimensional world of medium-sized material objects, moving at medium speeds relative to one another." [803]

And here's the kicker. Richard goes on to say, "As an unexpected bonus, our brains turn out to be powerful enough to accommodate a much richer world model than the mediocre utilitarian one that our ancestors needed in order to survive (Ancestors like amoeba's and frogs? Ha-ha, ha)." [804]

Let me tell you what I was thinking when I read this. If I were one of those ancestors Richard is describing here, and I was told I had a 'mediocre utilitarian brain', even though I am not easily offended, I do think I would have probably taken it as an insult. Wouldn't you have? Look, as far as Richard's belief that there is no God, and that there is no life before our life here on earth, and that there is no life after our death except maybe the memories of the dead living on in the minds of those still living after our passing, and that there is no purpose to any of it, and that this is just life, and this life alone is all that matters, it certainly begs the question, at least in my mind it does, "How is that view life-affirming and life-enhancing? Affirming of what and life-enhancing to whom?"

The side I have and am presenting as my perspective, in contrast to Richard's, and all atheists view for that matter, is a perspective that gives meaning and purpose to life, and it is the view that fills the gaps of needing to understand our universe and our place in it. We all want the answers to the 'Big' questions, much like the tens-of-thousands of people who've been adopted and grew up wanting to know who their biological parents are. One need only watch a handful of a T.V. series like "Who Do You Think You Are" to see the intense desire people have to know their ancestry. It's, like I said, an innate, ubiquitous driving force within one's psyche to 'know who we are and where we came from'. 'Family' is the most important experience there is to be had from our existence and our life we experience here on this globe we call earth. One should ask themselves "Why is that?" Do ameba's have this same need to know, since they're our ten-millionth great grandparents? I believe this desire to know if God exists comes from the same source as the desire to know one's biological origins.

Without such a view, these longings don't make any sense, especially in a so-called evolutionary and natural selective way. Coming to know and understand the *'meaning of life'*, or how large our universe is, and what our relationship to all of this really means, both short and long-term, as well as coming to understand all the other 'Big' questions that all of us have, in the view of atheism, it just doesn't matter. We're all just 'dust' (Star dust apparently) or 'a pile of dirt' anyway. Right? But if one is a believer in God, all of this absolutely matters. In fact, it matters a great deal. To theists, it is everything. These feelings of 'luck' for being alive, the feeling or sense that life is precious and that we each have intrinsic value, and the feeling that what we do and how we live our lives matters, if these feelings don't, in fact, really matter at all, … then why try to figure out why we have such feelings and desires in the first place? Think about it. It's like they are internally programmed right into our minds' operating system. It's like there's a homing device driving and directing us to 'come home' (E.T. Come home).

For example, why do we create art and music? Is it to enjoy personal expression and provide enjoyment to others, and that's it? If so, then why? Why didn't evolution reject this desire since they don't really help us survive? What does painting a Mona Lisa have to do with our survival? What does the idea that we matter to each other even mean, and more particularly why do we matter to ourselves, if we're just going to become a dirt pile anyway? To me, the answer to these questions is obvious. It's because we're children of a living, loving Heavenly Father who loves us and wants us to grow and learn all that we can and need to learn, so that we can return and live with Him 'once again' forever.

Why are we creatures that have the capacity for enjoyment? For love? Why do we have a passion for something, with that passion being different than everybody else's passion? Why the difference? Why do we have a need to be accepted and appreciated by others? Why do we seek out to get a sense of personal worth and to feel personal value? Worth to who? And why do we need to feel valued as a person? And if there's an answer to the 'worth to who?' question, then why that 'who' instead of nobody at all. Why do we need to feel this sense of worth and value in ourselves?

The philosopher, Schopenhauer, was writing just as the first translations of Buddhist texts into Western languages were being made. These texts mentioned the Buddhist idea that "life is suffering," that is, "that suffering is the substance of life". Think on that one for a while. I have often said, "Life's a pain and then we die." Of course, I was being a bit facetious when I said that.

There's a theory called The James-Lange Theory of Emotion [805]. What is it you ask? William James, an American philosopher, and psychologist, and the first educator to offer a psychology course in the United States, postulated it back in the 1880's. His theory was that bodily changes come first and form the basis of an emotional experience. Thus, emotions are caused by bodily sensations (For example, you become happier when you smile). This connection between mind and body led him to develop what came to be known as the James-Lange Theory of Emotion.

Simply put, the human experience of emotion arises from physiological changes in response to external events. Sound familiar? I'm including Mr. James-Lange's theory in my response for Richard's benefit, 'cuz I know he would agree with Mr. James-Lange. However, the opposite side of this two-sided view can be summed up by a quote made by a hero of mine who I've quoted before. I'm speaking of course, of the prophet Nephi from the Book of Mormon. Nephi wrote:

I Nephi 2:25

25 Adam fell, that men might be; and men are, that they might have *joy*.

There you go. The atheist side basically says that man's memories and human experience, all become part of life, meaning they remain in the memories of the living *only*. But on the other hand, God, our Creator says that man 'is' that he might have joy, especially as we become more and more like He and His Son Jesus Christ. Jesus Himself said, we are to become perfect, or complete, just as our Father in Heaven is perfect and complete. Matthew quoted Jesus as saying:

Matthew 5:48

48 Be ye therefore perfect, even as your Father which is in heaven is perfect.

This is the view of life's purpose that I believe in. It, to me, is what a purposeful life is all about. Of course, Jesus was not saying that you and I have to '*be*' perfect as human beings. We all know we've made and will continue to make mistakes throughout our lives, and that's why we say, "I'm human, aren't I?" Like I explained before, *being* perfect is *becoming complete in Christ*, becoming 'one' with God and His Son; becoming perfect and complete '*in*' Christ, our Savior and Redeemer.

You've got both sides now for your consideration. My Latter-Day Saint perspective on the purpose of life, which is to 'have Joy'; Joy coming from having an eternal family in God's divine and exalted society, versus Richard's Atheistic perspective on the purpose of life, which is 'to make it be the best life you can', while living in 'the here and now', knowing that it doesn't really matter in the end, and that's because we're all going die and become dirt piles anyway, or what I call taking a '*forever dirt nap*'.

Again, it is, "Eat, drink, and be merry, for tomorrow we die". In other words, "we can kiss our hind-ends goodbye, because we're just going to be a dirt pile very soon. Or, it is to have "JOY"."

Okay, are you ready for the last subtitle? I certainly am. It's called – "The Mother of All Burkas". This was quite a ride of sorts when I first read it. I had to read it a couple, three times. It was amazingly fun for me as I read through it over and over again. It opened my mind to a wider view of life itself.

THE MOTHER OF ALL BURKAS

Richard's main objective of his last subtitle – "The mother of all burkas" – is to convince us that *science* and *evolution* are the two vision-slits that make up the glasses or lenses through which we must look at the world. For Richard, science and evolution are the only lenses by which truth is discovered. Richard gives several illustrations to try and convince us, his readers, of his world view reality, starting with the symbolic metaphor of a black a burka and its 'vision-slit'. Richard begins this subtitle by saying that, "He wants to use the narrow vision-slit in the egregious male cruelty and tragically cowed female submission of the Burka, as a symbol of the worldview we each have." [806]

Richard wants us, his readers, to imagine the imagery of a symbolic, gigantic burka, with its gigantically wide *vision-slit*, as a representation of how we *should view our world*. He asks us to imagine the *view* we'd have as we look out through this gigantic *vision-slit*, and how wide our view might and could be when we do. Richard then compares this metaphoric analogy to science, saying, "What science does for us is *widen the window*, the vision-slit's view. Science opens this vision-slit so wide that the imprisoning black garment drops away almost completely, exposing our senses to airy and exhilarating freedom." [807]

I submit that there is an additional '*view-master*', an additional tool, or vision-slit for 'widening our view of the world'. It's a principle all of us have available to us if we but exercise the faith needed to make it work in our lives. It is called *Revelation*. Now I know atheists, and even some theists don't believe in this gift of the spirit. I'm speaking of course of my Christian friends. My Christian friends say that *after* Jesus died and rose from the dead and ascended into heaven, and *after* His apostles were all killed off or died off, the revelation these followers of Christ enjoyed ceased, for there was no need for it anymore. Right? However, that is not what the Lord and Savior of the world said to his apostles just before He ascended to heaven. Let me set the table for what Jesus told them.

A definition of revelation can be found at www.churchofjesuschrist.org, under "Revelation: A Doctrinal Study". Here are a few excerpts from this essay that lays the foundation for what Jesus taught, and I quote:

"Revelation, simply put, is communication from God to His children. This guidance comes through various *channels* according to the needs and circumstances of individuals, families, and the Church as a whole (This guidance is available not only to the members of The Church of Jesus Christ of Latter-Day Saints, it's also available to anyone who desires to know what God would have them 'know and do')."

"When the Lord reveals His will to the Church collectively, He speaks through His living prophets. Today's prophets are those men who receive revelation for the Church as a whole, but they are not the only people who can and do receive revelation. According to our faithfulness, everyone, men, and women alike, can receive revelation and inspiration to help guide them in their specific and personal needs and responsibilities, especially with their families and church callings, as well as provide answers to their sincere, personal questions.

"The scriptures tell of different *types* of revelation, such as visions, dreams, and visitations by angels. Through such *channels*, the Lord has restored His gospel in the latter-days and revealed many truths (Much of which I have touched on in my book). Revelation comes to both leaders as well as individual members of the Church through the whisperings of the voice of the Holy Ghost to our hearts and minds. It's called "the still small voice" (We've talked about this voice already). Quiet spiritual promptings (Whisperings) may not seem as spectacular as visions or angelic visitations, but they are just as powerful and lasting and life changing as any other form of revelation. The witness of the Holy Ghost makes an impression on the soul that is more significant than anything we can see or hear. Through such revelations, we receive lasting strength to help us stay true to the gospel and help others do the same.

Preparing to Receive Revelation

"The following counsel regarding revelation will help us prepare to receive promptings from the Holy Ghost. The Lord Jesus Christ himself said:

Matthew 7:7–8

7 Ask, and it shall be given you; seek, and ye shall find; knock, and it shall be opened unto you:

8 For every one that asketh receiveth; and he that seeketh findeth; and to him that knocketh it shall be opened.

"This is just one of many scriptures that describe the very essence of personal revelation and inspiration. In order to find and receive it, we must make the effort to seek and ask.

"We must also *be reverent*. Reverence is profound respect and love. When we are reverent and peaceful, we invite revelation (We're told to 'be still' and know that I am God'). Even when everything around us is in commotion, we can have a reverent attitude and be prepared to receive guidance from the Lord.

"*Be humble*. Humility is closely related to reverence. When we are humble, we recognize our dependence on the Lord.

"*Keep the commandments*. When we keep the commandments, we are prepared to receive, recognize, and follow the promptings of the Holy Ghost.

"*Partake of the sacrament worthily*. The sacramental prayers teach how to receive the constant companionship of the Holy Spirit:

D&C 20:79

76 And the elder or priest shall administer it; and after this manner shall he administer it—he shall kneel with the church and call upon the Father in solemn prayer, saying:

77 O God, the Eternal Father, we ask thee in the name of thy Son, Jesus Christ, to bless and sanctify this bread to the souls of all those who partake of it, that they may eat in remembrance of the body of thy Son, and witness unto thee, O God, the Eternal Father, that they are willing to take upon them the name of thy Son, and always remember him and keep his commandments which he has given them; that they may always have his Spirit to be with them. Amen.

78 The manner of administering the wine—he shall take the cup also, and say:

79 O God, the Eternal Father, we ask thee in the name of thy Son, Jesus Christ, to bless and sanctify this wine to the souls of all those who drink of it, that they may do it in remembrance of the blood of thy Son, which was shed for them; that they may witness unto thee, O God, the Eternal Father, that they do always remember him, that they may ... always have his Spirit to be with them. Amen.

"When we partake of the sacrament, we witness to God that we are willing to take upon ourselves the name of His Son and that we will always remember Him and keep His commandments. In return our Heavenly Father promises that He will send us His Spirit so that we can always have His Spirit to be with us, to help and guide us as we journey on the covenant path back to His presence.

"*Study the scriptures every day*. As we diligently study the scriptures, we learn from the examples of men and women whose lives have been blessed as they have followed the Lord's revealed will (We can also learn from men and women who didn't follow the Lord's revealed will. Their stories reveal what results of not following the commandments. These stories are recorded in the scriptures for us and are a witness of how we can be blessed when we follow His will). We also become more receptive to the Holy Ghost in our own lives. As we read and ponder, we may receive revelation about how a certain scripture passage applies to us or about anything else the Lord desires to communicate to us. *Take time to ponder*. When we take time to ponder the truths of the gospel, we open our mind and heart to the guiding influence of the Holy Ghost:

I Nephi 11:1

1 For it came to pass after I had desired to know the things that my father had seen, and believing that the Lord was able to make them known unto me, as I sat pondering in mine heart I was caught away in the Spirit of the Lord, yea, into an exceedingly high mountain, *which I never had before seen*, and upon which I never had before set my foot.

Doctrine & Covenants 76:19

19 And while we *meditated* upon these things, the Lord touched the eyes of our understandings and they were opened, and the glory of the Lord shone round about.

Doctrine & Covenants 138:1–11

1 On the third of October, in the year nineteen hundred and eighteen, I sat in my room *pondering* over the scriptures;

2 And *reflecting* upon the great atoning sacrifice that was made by the Son of God, for the redemption of the world;

3 And the great and wonderful love made manifest by the Father and the Son in the coming of the Redeemer into the world;

4 That through his atonement, and by obedience to the principles of the gospel, mankind might be saved.

5 While I was thus engaged, my mind reverted to the writings of the apostle Peter, to the primitive saints scattered abroad throughout Pontus, Galatia, Cappadocia, and other parts of Asia, where the gospel had been preached after the crucifixion of the Lord.

6 I opened the Bible and read the third and fourth chapters of the first epistle of Peter, and as I read I was greatly impressed, more than I had ever been before, with the following passages:

7 For Christ also hath once suffered for sins, the just for the unjust, that he might bring us to God, being put to death in the flesh, but quickened by the Spirit:

8 By which also he went and preached unto the spirits in prison;

9 Which sometime were disobedient, when once the longsuffering of God waited in the days of Noah, while the ark was a preparing, wherein few, that is, eight souls were saved by water.

10 For, for this cause was the gospel preached also to them that are dead, that they might be judged according to men in the flesh but live according to God in the spirit.

11 As I *pondered* over these things which are written, the eyes of my understanding were opened, and the Spirit of the Lord rested upon me, and I saw the hosts of the dead, both small and great.

"Pondering takes our thoughts from the trivial things of the world, helping us gain a more eternal perspective and bringing us (Our heart, mind, and spirit) closer to the Spirit.

"When seeking specific guidance, we should study the matter out in our minds. At times, the Lord's communication will come only after we have studied a matter out in our minds. Patiently seek God's will. God reveals Himself "in his own time, and in his own way, and according to his own will":

Doctrine & Covenants 88:63–68

63 Draw near unto me and I will draw near unto you; seek me diligently and ye shall find me; ask, and ye shall receive; knock, and it shall be opened unto you.

64 Whatsoever ye ask the Father in my name it shall be given unto you, that is expedient for you;

65 And if ye ask anything that is not expedient for you, it shall turn unto your condemnation.

66 Behold, that which you hear is as the voice of one crying in the wilderness—in the wilderness, because you cannot see him—my voice, because *my voice is Spirit*; my Spirit is truth; truth abideth and hath no end; and if it be in you it shall abound.

67 And if your eye be single to my glory, *your whole bodies shall be filled with light*, and there shall be no darkness in you; and that body which is filled with light comprehendeth all things.

68 Therefore, sanctify yourselves *that your mind become single to God*, and the days will come that you shall see him; for he will unveil his face unto you, and it shall be in his own time, and in his own way, and according to his own will.

"Revelation will often come *line upon line, precept upon precept, here a little and there a little*. We should be patient and trust in the Lord's timing.

Recognizing the Promptings of the Holy Ghost. Amid the many noises and messengers (voices) in the world today, *we must learn to recognize the whisperings of the Holy Ghost.* The following scriptures describe some of the principal ways in which the Holy Ghost (The mediator of revelation; the Testator) communicates with us:

Doctrine & Covenants 8:2–3

2 Yea, behold, I will tell you In your mind and in your heart, by the Holy Ghost, which shall come upon you and which shall dwell in your heart.

3 Now, behold, this is *the spirit of revelation*; behold, this is the spirit by which Moses brought the children of Israel through the Red Sea on dry ground.

"Although such revelation can have a powerful effect on us, it almost always comes quietly, as a still small voice":

1 Kings 19:9–12

9 And he came thither unto a cave, and lodged there; and behold, the word of the LORD *came* to him, and he said unto him, What doest thou here, Elijah?

10 And he said, I have been very jealous for the LORD God of hosts: for the children of Israel have forsaken thy covenant, thrown down thine altars, and slain thy prophets with the sword; and I, *even* I only, am left; and they seek my life, to take it away.

11 And he said, Go forth, and stand upon the mount before the LORD. And, behold, the LORD passed by, and a great and strong wind rent the mountains, and brake in pieces the rocks before the LORD; *but* the LORD *was* not in the wind: and after the wind an earthquake; but the LORD *was* not in the earthquake:

12 And after the earthquake a fire; *but* the LORD *was* not in the fire: and after the fire *a still small voice.*

Helaman 5:30

30 And it came to pass when they heard this voice, and beheld that it was not a voice of thunder, neither was it a voice of a great tumultuous noise, but behold, it was *a still voice of perfect mildness,* as if it had been a whisper, and it did pierce even to the very soul –

Doctrine & Covenants 85:6

6 Yea, thus saith the *still small voice,* which whispereth through and pierceth all things, and often times it maketh my bones to quake while it maketh manifest, saying:

"He prompts us through our feelings. Although we often describe communication from the Spirit as a voice, that voice is one that we *'feel'* more than we *'hear'* (Let me interject here: It is much like a transmitter sending out waves of light and knowledge, and our receiver, meaning our spirits' heart and mind, when attuned to the spirits' transmissions from the Lord, we receive those waves of light and knowledge).

(It is our choice to choose to attune our hearts and minds to this transmitting stations' message waves (so-to-speak), the waves that are coming directly from God. There are two transmitting channels from which we can choose to listen to. One channel or station is called 'S.A.T.A.N.', and the other is called 'The Light of Christ'. I'm calling this spiritual channel 'J.E.S.U.S.').

"The Holy Ghost uses the Light of Christ to bring peace. He is often called the Comforter":

John 14:26

26 But the *Comforter, which Is the Holy Ghost, whom,* the Father will send in my name, he shall teach you all things, and bring all things to your remembrance, whatsoever I have said unto you.

Doctrine & Covenants 39:6

6 And this is my gospel—repentance and baptism by water, and then cometh the baptism of fire and *the Holy Ghost,* even the Comforter, *which showeth all things, and teacheth the peaceable things of the kingdom.*

"As He reveals the will of the Lord to us, He will 'speak peace' to our minds":

Doctrine & Covenants 6:23

23 Did I not speak peace to your mind concerning the matter? What greater witness can you have than from God?

End of excerpts from the essay on Revelation [808]

To continue with this principle of revelation, here are a few more excerpts from a talk given by Elder Terence M. Vinson of the Presidency of the Seventy of the Church of Jesus Christ of Latter-Day Saints, where he spoke on this principle of revelation, and particularly about *'personal revelation'*, and how each of us can *grow in the principle of revelation* and enjoy its power in our daily lives.

"The Lord's admonition to us with respect to learning is clear. He tells us":

Doctrine & Covenants 88:118

118 And *as all have not faith,* seek ye diligently and teach one another words of wisdom; yea, seek ye out of the best books words of wisdom; seek learning, even by study and also by faith.

"In this verse in the Doctrine & Covenants, the Lord is saying that *both* knowledge and wisdom are necessary. As stated simply in the words of this proverb from Guinea, West Africa: *'Knowledge without wisdom is like water in the sand'."*

"A more complete explanation of the importance of both knowledge and wisdom is given in the words of Jacob, the son of Lehi, another prophet quoted in the Book of Mormon":

II Nephi 9:28–29

28 O that cunning plan of the evil one! O the vainness, and the frailties, and the foolishness of men! *When they are learned they think they are wise, and they hearken not unto the counsel of God, for they set it aside, supposing they know of themselves,* wherefore, their wisdom is foolishness and it profiteth them not. And they shall perish (I couldn't have described Richard and many of his learned friends better, even if I tried).

29 But to be learned is good if they hearken unto the counsels of God.

"Here, we have a hint at how to find wisdom: *we must hearken to the counsels of God.* As the Lord has said concerning those who put their trust in Him":

Doctrine & Covenants 76:9–10

9 And their wisdom shall be great, and their understanding reach to heaven; and before them the wisdom of the wise shall perish, and the understanding of the prudent shall come to naught.

10 For *by my Spirit will I enlighten them,* and by my power will I make known unto them the secrets of my will—yea, even those things which eye has not seen, nor ear heard, nor yet entered into the heart of man.

"But most people do not understand this or do not live it; for them education is purely an intellectual pursuit. We are easily indoctrinated in modern society to believe that we can really only know something through our intellects and our physical senses (Supposedly, doing science is achieved by the wet brain and not with the 'mind'. The wet brain apparently uses *reason* and the physical senses *alone*).

There is no tolerance in the modern world for things that can't be proven scientifically."

"Nobel Prize–winning Russian novelist Alexander Solzhenitsyn expressed the idea that the problems of the Western world began in the Renaissance. He indicated that the thought processes enshrined during the Renaissance "did not [see in] the existence of … man … any higher task than the attainment of happiness on earth. … Modern Western civilization [has developed] on the dangerous trend to worship man and his material needs." …

"… We have placed too much hope in political and social reforms, only to find that we were being deprived of our most precious possession: our spiritual life."

Two Ways to Know

"Latter-Day Saints understand that there are, instead, two different ways of knowing things: scientifically (through the use of reasoning and the physical senses) and *spiritually* (through revelation and the spiritual senses). Like others, I have not always clearly understood what it means to 'know' spiritually. As a young man, I met a beautiful young lady who was a member of The Church of Jesus Christ of Latter-Day Saints. I had never before heard of this Church. Having grown up in a different Christian church, I felt that to accept the teachings of the restored Church, I needed to be totally convinced intellectually that my previous beliefs were mistaken and that these new teachings were truly teachings of the gospel that Jesus Christ had previously established.

"Several consecutive sets of missionaries taught me, but I always had questions for them. When they could not answer my questions, they would go away and then return the following week with the answers. By then I had more questions. This continued for several weeks as I tried to receive an *'intellectual conversion'*. Then, one day as I sat in a church meeting, I clearly felt this message from the Holy Ghost: *"Terry, all of your questions have answers. It is not important for you to know them all now. As the questions come to you, they will be answered. But I need you to act and to be baptized now."*

"Do you see what had happened? *My study and pondering gave rise to 'revelation'.* I immediately acted and was baptized. Over the subsequent 44 years, the prophecy contained in that (personal) *revelation* has been fulfilled. All of my questions have been answered, including those I had not even considered 44 years ago.

"President Dallin H. Oaks, First Counselor in the First Presidency, has spoken about the different ways of knowing. Here's what he said:

"What do we mean when we testify and say that we (1) *'know'* the gospel is true? Contrast that kind of knowledge with (2) 'I know it is cold outside' or (3) 'I know I love my wife.' These are *three* different kinds of knowledge, *each learned in a different way.* Knowledge of outside temperature can be verified by scientific proof. Knowledge that we love our spouse is personal and subjective. While not capable of scientific proof, it is still important. The idea that all important knowledge is based on scientific evidence is simply untrue.

"While there is some evidence for gospel truths, scientific methods will *not* yield spiritual knowledge:

Psalm 19:1

1 The heavens declare the glory of God; and the firmament sheweth his handywork.

Helaman 8:24

24 And now, seeing ye know these things and cannot deny them except ye shall lie, therefore in this ye have sinned, for ye have rejected all these things, notwithstanding so many evidences which ye have received; yea, even ye have received all things, both things in heaven, and all things which are in the earth, as a witness that they are true.

"This is what Jesus taught in response to Simon Peter's testimony that He was the Christ:

Matthew 16:17

17 And Jesus answered and said unto him, Blessed art thou, Simon Bar-jona: for flesh and blood hath not revealed it unto thee, but my Father which is in heaven.

"The Apostle Paul explained this. In a letter to the Corinthian Saints, he said:

1 Corinthians 2:11

11 For what man knoweth the things of a man, save the spirit of man *which is in him*? even so the things of God knoweth no man, but the Spirit of God.

John 14:17

17 *Even* the Spirit of truth; whom the world cannot receive, because it seeth him not, neither knoweth him: but ye know him; for he dwelleth with you and shall be in you.

"In contrast, we know the things of man by the ways of man:

1 Corinthians 2:14

14 But the natural man receiveth not the things of the Spirit of God: for they are foolishness unto him: neither can he know *them,* because they are spiritually discerned.

"The Book of Mormon teaches:

Moroni 10:4–5

4 And when ye shall receive these things, I would exhort you that ye would ask God, the Eternal Father, in the name of Christ, if these things are not true; and if ye shall ask with a sincere heart, with real intent, having faith in Christ, he will manifest the truth of it unto you, by the power of the Holy Ghost.

5 And by the power of the Holy Ghost ye my know the truth of all things.

"In modern revelation God promises us:

Doctrine & Covenants 8:1–2

1 Oliver Cowdery, verily, verily, I say unto you, that assuredly as the Lord liveth, who is your God and your Redeemer, even so surely shall you receive a knowledge of whatsoever things you shall ᶜask in faith, with an honest heart, believing that you shall receive a knowledge concerning the engravings of old records, which are ancient, which contain those parts of my scripture of which has been spoken by the manifestation of my Spirit.

2 Yea, behold, I will tell you in your mind and in your heart, by the Holy Ghost, which shall come upon you and which shall dwell in your heart.

Elder Vinson continues quoting President Oaks:

"One of the greatest things about our Heavenly Father's plan for His children is that *each of us can know the truth of that plan for ourselves*. That *revealed knowledge* does not come from books, from scientific proof, or from intellectual pondering. As with the Apostle Peter, we can receive that knowledge directly from our Heavenly Father through *the witness of the Holy Ghost* (It's a personal, spiritual revelation that is a spirit-to-spirit connection and communication)."

"When we know spiritual truths by spiritual means, we can be just as sure of that knowledge as scholars and scientists are of the different kinds of knowledge they have acquired by [scientific] methods."

"Although *spiritual knowledge and intellectual knowledge* are different, both are important. To comprehend the things of the world, we must be *intellectually enlightened*; to know and understand the things of God, we must be *spiritually enlightened*.

"You have all been in high school or college classes with people of greater or lesser intellect than yourself. A good portion of our intelligence is due to genetics. How fair would it be if God favored people of greater intellect over those with lesser ability *by making the acceptance of gospel truths a function of our intellects alone*? Why would He give some an advantage based on inherited intellect? He would not, and He does not! Rather, *we learn spiritual truths as a function of our spiritual receptivity*. Such is a spiritual gift, nurtured by individual faith, prayer, humility, and goodness, as well as a desire to respond and to act.

"Despite the apparent conflict between reason and revelation, *the rational view and the religious view of the world are not opposites of one another*. The religious view (At least the view of a religion that is untarnished by apostasy) includes reason as well as revelation, and it embraces the truths determined by both. In contrast, the rational view excludes what is spiritually revealed.

"Our focus should not just be on acquiring *knowledge* but also on acquiring *wisdom—the practical application of knowledge for purposes of good.*

"Finally, these things are acquired through both study and faith, with *faith* being a word that encompasses our *acting on* what we believe in-order-to gain knowledge and wisdom." [809]

End of Excerpts from "Personal Revelation" by Elder Terence M. Vinson

I'm sure you, my readers, noticed that there are big differences between the principles of the *Scientific Method* for getting knowledge (a specific kind of knowledge), and the principles of the *Revelatory Method* or the *Spiritual Method* for gaining knowledge and wisdom (a specific kind of knowledge and wisdom). *The method we use to seek knowledge depends on* the kind of knowledge we are seeking. Let's continue now with Richard's discussion on widening our view through the lens of science, and science alone.

Richard says: "This metaphor of the 'narrow window of light', broadening out into a spectacular wide spectrum (supposedly where our consciousness is raised), serves us in other areas of science too. We are at home with objects ranging in size from a few kilometers (the view from a mountain top), to about a tenth of a millimeter (the view down to as small as the point of a pin). Outside this range even our imagination is handicapped." [810]

Richard continues, "The range of sizes, distances, or speeds with which our imaginations are comfortable, is a tiny band (vision-slit), set in the midst of a gigantic range of the possible, from the scale of quantum strangeness at the smaller end to the scale of Einsteinian cosmology at the larger (Those things that our natural eyes cannot see or comprehend without the use of telescopes and microscopes)." [811]

"Our imaginations are not yet tooled-up (Or not yet conditioned through the glasses of evolution and natural selection) to penetrate the neighborhood of the quantum. Nothing at that scale behaves in the way matter – as we are 'evolved' to think – ought to behave. Nor can we cope with the behavior of objects that move at some appreciable fraction of the speed of light." [812]

As I was reading this, I wondered why, as an example, our tooled-up, evolving wet brains didn't think of the need to evolve or *tool-up* our eyes capacities or capabilities to see like a bat sees things using radar; or to hear like the Bushbuck hears while in the desert of Africa? These physical attributes most definitely would have given us a much greater advantage for survival than not having them does, wouldn't they? I would certainly think so, 'if' in fact the rules of natural selection that are supposed to help us survive are truly locked in place, right? Yet, natural selection short-changed us on at least two of these life protecting physical traits. It didn't do it for the flatworms eyes either. I wonder why?

Richard answered my question when he describes how animals *model* their brains (That's quite a medical feat or surgery for these animals, isn't it? Just kidding. I know Richard is saying here that it is the director called 'Natural Selection' doing all of this) and bodily features to meet the challenges in their own unique kind of world and experience, and so, we as humans, *don't need to develop that kind of brain model to survive* in our human or unique kind of experiential Middle World (This is a descript Richard uses to describe our present world. I of course would give a very different answer here).

Richard's evolutionary and biologically educated and trained mind, along with the atheistic influence he's had on his thinking over his many years, have all combined to tool-up his brain (Meaning *mapped* his brains' neuropathways) to the point where Richard emphatically and automatically believes that our brains, in fact, have evolved to where they project illusions onto our imagining, illusion-making software system, fueled simply by the data our senses collect in our wet brains.

Richard believes our senses send the data collected, into the wet machine he calls the brain – what we see, feel, taste, smell, and hear – as we go about living in what he calls our Middle World. Our brains, using this data, *construct* a brain model, supposedly a little bit at a time in its evolutionary way, due to millions of years where the director called natural selection, has directed our genes to constantly mutate its cells, thus *adjusting themselves* so that we ultimately have the brain model we each have and enjoy today. That's quite a feat, don't you think? It's natural selections' construction crane is at work, continuously moving our brains development up Mt. Improvable, one iteration-step at a time. Wow!

Here's an example of what I am talking about. Richard says:

"As we observe the movement of the world's rotation, objects that seem large because they are near, such as – mountains, trees and buildings, even the ground itself that is far away from our view – all moving in exact synchrony with each other and with the stars, our brains take in this data and projects an *illusion* onto these large objects, rather than on the smaller objects such as the mountains, trees, and buildings right before us." [815]

Do you get it? It took me awhile before I got it. In other words, Richard is saying, as an example, that we see the horizon of a paved highway as *water* (An illusion). We see the earth as *standing still* (an illusion), and therefore we think the sun is moving around it (Another illusion), etc. Richard's purpose in going through this metaphoric exercise regarding our mind's ability to create illusions, is to prop up his final point, which is, and I quote:

"The way we see the world, and the reason why we find some things intuitively easy to grasp and others hard, is that our brains are themselves evolved organs: on-board computers, evolved to help us survive in a world where the objects that matters to our survival were neither very large nor very small; a world where things either stood still or moved slowly compared with the speed of light; and where the very improbable could safely be treated as impossible. Our mental burka window (Vision-Slit) is narrow because it didn't need to be any wider in order to assist our ancestors to survive (So, if I understand Richard, he's saying that our peasant ancestors didn't need their consciousness raised in order to survive in their world, but today we do need our consciousness raised to survive? C'mon Richard)."

"Science has taught us, against *all evolved intuitions*, that *apparently* solid things like crystals and rocks are really composed almost entirely of empty space. The familiar illustration represents the nucleus of an atom as a fly in the middle of a sports stadium. The next atom is right outside the stadium. The hardest, solidest, densest rock, then, is really almost entirely empty space, broken only by tiny particles so far apart that they shouldn't count." [814]

Richard then asks: "So why do rocks look and feel solid and hard and impenetrable (Or large, walnut, coffee tables for that matter)? As an evolutionary biologist I would answer it like this: Our brains have evolved to help our bodies find their way around the world on the scale at which those bodies operate. *We never evolved to navigate the world of atoms* ... We are evolved denizens of *Middle World*, and that *limits* what we are capable of imagining. The narrow window of our burka permits us, unless we are especially gifted *or peculiarly well educated* (Richard, once again, is saying, *gifted and well educated like he is*), to see only Middle World." [815]

Evolved, evolved, evolved. To Richard everything evolved and or is evolving. For Richard, nothing is created and placed in its bounds by the laws of God called physics and genetics, so that they never go outside of the boundaries that God has set. If these things were created in the way I believe they were, with laws that set them in their individual bounds, then obviously evolution by natural selection didn't happen. I want to remind you, my readers, of the alternative view to what Richard says caused everything – evolution.

To me, that's a very narrow vision-slit indeed. The brain uses perceptions, or what Richard calls "*internal labels* such as colors to construct its model of external reality, to make distinctions that are especially salient to the animal concerned." [816]

In other words, the evolutionary labeling process of the flying bat or of the Weenie dog, constructs their specific brains' world models so that they can *live* in *that* or *their unique* world and survive. I'd be interested in seeing the world through the mind of a Weenie dog and see what its world actually looks like to it. In their minds' world do they try to imagine themselves with long legs? Ha-ha, ha. Just kidding.

Richard continues his argument:

"On one planet, and possibly only one world of a bat or a rhino, a pond skater or a mole, a bacterium or a bark beetle, is one of the privileges science grants us when it tugs at the black cloth of our burka and shows us the wider range of what is out there for our delight." [817]

I truly do get a kick out of how Richards' mind works. This was quite a creative guess, don't you think? I agree that science does in fact widen the range of our understanding and knowledge of the physical world, the world on which each of us lives and breathes, and the physical universe in which we exist as well, not to mention all of the things that will yet be discovered by scientists like Richard.

All of this is certainly exciting and can provoke within us feelings of delight and awe. But there are other vision-slits to which we can and should direct our eyes, in order to gain new and undiscovered knowledge, understanding, and wisdom. The wider the expanding range of the vision-slit called Revelation, the more *spiritual knowledge and wisdom* regarding this world in which we live can be revealed, and regarding the universe in which our world exists, as well as the unseen world that exists all around and through us, all of it will be revealed to us in due time.

Revelation offers us a continuum of greater knowledge – even the knowledge called *the mysteries of godliness* – which godliness I've spent my entire adult life seeking and studying in order to increase my understanding of its principles.

As was mentioned earlier, these additional vision-slits are the spiritual lenses called Scripture Study, Personal Prayer, Quiet Spiritual Promptings, Reverence, Humility, Worship, Obedience to God's Commandments, Pondering, and Exercising Faith and Patience, all of which the Lords' Spirit uses to expand our vision, knowledge, and understanding, even the greater light called the "light of truth".

I like the quote Richard mentioned early on in this subtitle. It was by J. B. Haldane. Haldane, a biologist, said in his essay titled, "Possible World's", and I quote: "Now, my own suspicion is that the universe is not only queerer *than* we suppose, but queerer than we *can* suppose." [818]

Such can be the search for truth and our understanding of God's doings, for His ways are not our ways. They can seem more queerer than we can suppose. Anyway, after a few scientific ramblings, and a brief 'cat-thought-experiment' to help illustrate Richard's final point, Richard closes this last chapter by giving the pet answer he's given to every one of the 'Big' questions covered so far, especially those covered in this final chapter, that pet answer being – Evolution, evolution, evolution. It seems evolution, for Richard, is the "Theory behind everything, even The Theory of Everything".

Richard says, and I quote: "On one planet, and possibly only one planet in the entire universe, *molecules,* that would normally make nothing more complicated than a chunk of rock, *gathered themselves together into chunks of rock-sized matter* of such staggering complexity that they are capable of running, jumping, swimming, flying, seeing, hearing, capturing and eating other such animated chunks of complexity; capable in some cases of 'thinking and feeling', and *falling in love,* with yet other chunks of complex matter." [819]

Molecules gathered together into 'Chunks of complexity', or 'Chunks of complex matter'? Really Richard? That is an interesting way of describing you and me, isn't it? Chunks of rock '*gathering themselves together*'? Really? That my friends, is why I called my book "An Atheists' Delusion".

Richard continues:

"We now understand essentially how *the trick* is done, but only since 1859. Before 1859 it would have seemed very odd indeed (Queerer than we suppose, right?). Now, thanks to Darwin, it is merely very odd. Darwin seized the window of the burka and wrenched it open, letting in a flood of understanding whose dazzling novelty, and power to uplift the human spirit, perhaps had no *precedent* – unless it was 'the Copernican realization' that the Earth was not the center of the universe." [820]

This last statement is basically the last of Richard's arguments in his book *The God Delusion*. After I finished reading this last chapter, I came away thinking and feeling that Richards' purpose in writing his book, from my perspective, was to engage in an *intellectual exercise* that would strengthen his own atheist's mental muscles (Much like a comedian tries out his newest set of jokes on a fresh, new audience) so that Richard could enhance his debating prowess on the subjects of science, evolution, natural selection, and of course, the God Hypothesis, so he can better prove God's non-existence.

In addition to that, he, as a preacher of atheism, of course wanted to help strengthen his fellow atheist's mental muscles regarding these same topics, as well as win a few more converts to his quasi-religion of atheism. I'm confident when I say that he, in fact, has accomplished these goals to some degree. I'm sure the consciousness for some of his readers, has been raised and new converts have been added, at their own peril.

But, let me say that even though I do believe that Richard tightened up his theorems regarding God's non-existence, I do not believe he provided any *new*, incontrovertible evidence that proves his claim that God is a delusion. In other words, there were absolutely no new earth-shattering arguments for his obsequious converts to reverentially applaud him evermore. Nor did he, in my humble opinion, push everyone's belief cursor along the *percentage of probability spectrum* towards the 'God does not Exist' marker, or even beyond the 50%/50% point on this spectrum, which is where we started.

I actually believe that most of you, my readers, having read my book now, have had your belief cursor moved towards the God Exists marker. At least I hope so. Like I said in my Introduction, I found myself feeling a duty to jump into the middle of this debate so I could share my perspective as a Latter-Day Saint on Richard's arguments against God's existence. On the subject of putting forth one's best arguments or influence, let me again remind you, my readers, of the quote by the prophet Joseph Smith:

"It is our duty to concentrate all our influence to make popular that which is sound and good, and unpopular that which is unsound". [821]

That quote, in a nutshell, is why I wrote my book *An Atheist's Delusion*, and why I included as many quotes and excerpts as I did, from the ancient day apostles and prophets of the Church of Jesus Christ of Meridian-Day Saints to the Later-Day prophets and apostles. I wanted these men and women's inspired comments to influence and make popular my perspective on God and His existence, as well as make Richards' atheistic claims about God's non-existence unpopular.

I felt that the prophetic comments made by God's prophets, past and present, would add insightful commentary to the arguments and perspective I would be presenting for your consideration. Their confirming and prophetic influence, for me, is the *glue* that holds together all the reference legs of evidence in my support stand, upon which my table of belief rests, and it's my hope that my perspective on Richard's book *The God Delusion,* and on God's existence, has in some way added multiple reference leg evidence to your personal support stand upon which your table of belief rests. I sincerely hope and pray that as a result of reading my book, your 'belief cursor' has moved along the 'Percentage of Probability Spectrum' well beyond 51% that God exists, and I am confident that many of your belief cursors may have even reached close to the 100% 'God Exists' marker, and maybe even steadfastly on "God Exists" where mine rests.

When I started this journey of writing *An Atheist's Delusion,* I hardly knew any of the specifics about Richard Dawkins' views on religion, other than what he expressed in the title of his book. I soon learned that he hated any kind of religion. The specifics of his hatred for religion were quickly discovered as I traveled the onerous journey of reading each chapter of *The God Delusion*.

When I started reading Richard's book I knew even less about Richard's life or upbringing. And so, I wouldn't describe my feelings about Richard as feelings of distain or disgust for him personally, or for him as an atheist, and that's because I didn't know him. I just knew of him. Before reading his book, I admit that I maybe have had some degree of enmity towards his atheist views about the God I worship and love. I'm a disciple of Jesus Christ, my Lord and King, and I love Him as my Savior, and so, when I read Richard's vitriolic description of God, and of His Son, Jesus Christ, it stung my heart a little.

However, as I read Richard's thoughts and learned more about his mindset, especially the little bits of information about his life growing up in Kenya and later moving to England, my enmity and opinion of him softened. I now see Richard in a whole new light. Of course, I still have a little angst about his criticism of religion and especially his disgust towards our Father in heaven, and towards His Son, Jesus Christ, the Savior of the world, but that too has softened as I've come to understand the paradigm out of which Richard's distain for God and religion has sprung.

With all that said, I would have Richard know, that I love him, just like I love all of God's children. I would want Richard to know that my attitude at this moment says, "I have no ill will towards you Richard, as a person. I've actually grown to enjoy your humor and brilliance, and so, I truly do wish you no harm." I would also say to him, "Going forward, let's simply agree to disagree on the question of God's existence, and I promise to not be disagreeable about it." I would also want to say to Richard, "Who knows, maybe one day we will meet and find some common ground on which we could build an amicable connection, and maybe even a friendship. Until then, I wish you well."

Okay, I'm almost done, but before I close this off, I want to quote once again, what Elder Bruce R. McConkie said about questions that still seem to be unanswerable at the present moment, and I quote:

"There are some questions which seem to invite intellectual forays into unknown areas, or which seem to ensnare in endless contention those who are somewhat less than spiritually literate. If you cannot believe all of the doctrines of the gospel, *withhold judgment* in the areas in question, do not commit yourself to a position which is contrary to that espoused by the prophets and apostles who preside over the kingdom. Study, pray, work in the Church, and *await further light and knowledge.*

"If you are troubled about so-called evolution (As the main argument in Richards' book) and have not learned that Adam was both the first man and the first mortal flesh, and that there was no death of any form of life until *after* the fall—*withhold judgment* and do not take a stand against the scriptures. If you suppose God is progressing and gaining more knowledge and truth, and that he is not really omnipotent, omniscient, and omnipresent as Joseph Smith taught—*withhold judgment.* Remain silent. Do not lock yourself into a position contrary to the revealed word.

"If you think there will be progression from one kingdom of glory to another after the resurrection; or that people who reject the gospel in this life will have a second chance to gain salvation in the world to come; or that couples who are married in the temple can commit all manner of sin and still gain salvation; or any of a host of the common heresies of the hour—*withhold judgment.*

"Do not commit yourself to the defense of a false cause. Study something else and await the day when you will be prepared for more light on the matter that troubles you. Conversion is not born of contention. He that hath the spirit of contention is not of God. Our divine commission is to declare glad tidings to the world, not to quarrel with others about the meaning of texts. There are, of course, answers to all of the false claims of those who array themselves against us—*I do not believe the devil has had a new idea for a hundred years*—but conversion is not found in the *'dens of debate'*. It comes rather to those who read the Book of Mormon in the way Moroni counseled.

"Most members of the Church would be better off if they simply *ignored the specious claims of the professional anti-Christs*. Often those who ask questions are more interested in sustaining a pre-chosen position than in learning *what* the facts are.

"Our concern should be to find and cleave to the truth. It should not matter to us what the doctrine is, only that we come to a knowledge of it. Our espousal and defense of a false doctrine will not make it true. Our concern is to come to a knowledge of the truth, not to prove a point to which we may unwisely have committed ourselves." [822]

End quote by Elder McConkie

It is my hope that you, my readers, did not find that my book promoted contention. If so, it was not my intention, and please forgive me. I hope you saw it as just a Latter-Day Saint sharing his perspective and interpretation of each of the many subtitle topics Richard put forth in his book, *The God Delusion*. Nothing more, and nothing less.

In conclusion, like I said in my Introduction, this debate boils down to the self-evident truth that every individual I've ever talked with about this 'Big' question, "Does God Exist?", has *chosen* to believe what they *want* to believe regarding His existence. Both sides are still in search for any-and-all arguments or pieces of evidence (the smoking gun so-to-speak) that might certify *their own beliefs* and *falsify* the other sides point of view. Both sides are also in a constant search for as many *allies as they can find; allies who will support their worldview and refute the opposing sides' view. These are people who* believe as they do and think the same way as they do.

The reality is, both sides have well-informed evidence that supports their worldview. However, the evidence that Richard has put forth is, as I said, *not incontrovertible*, nor is it *settled science* as he has claimed it is throughout his book. On the other hand, my evidence is also not incontrovertible.

So, this leaves us asking ourselves – "Which claim do we *want* to believe?" Or "Which claim do we *feel* the most comfortable with?", and then, "What do we want to make the evidence we do have, mean to us?" As I said in my Introduction, most of us believe what we *want* and what supports our worldview.

Almost the entirety of Richard's book was filled with *opinions* regarding the 'Big' questions about God's existence, and because they're just *opinions*, I say, "they didn't move the 'belief cursor' on the "percentage of probability spectrum" that God Exists, beyond the 50/50 draw we started with. But it is my hope that you, my readers, have come away with the same conclusion that I did. I hope you've come to the realization that Richard's arguments *not only didn't move* the probability spectrums' Belief Cursor one scintilla of an inch towards "God Does Not Exist", but that you found my Latter-Day Saint perspective actually helped move your individual belief cursor along the "percentage of *probability spectrum*" closer to the "God Exists" marker, even well beyond the 50/50 split. For some of you, I hope it's even moved your Belief Cursor on the Percentage of Probability Spectrum, all the way to the 100% God Exists marker, which as I have said, is where my Belief Cursor currently rests.

I *choose* to believe *the stack of well-informed reference legs I've shared with you.* I believe my stack of evidence shows my Latter-Day Saint perspective and worldview of theism to be the *"more probable"* of the two stacks of evidence. My reference legs stand includes, as I've shared, my personal experiential *evidence* I've collected over more than 68 years of living here on earth, especially those experiences with the very Beings we've been discussing throughout my book. I'm talking about the True and Living God, even God the Eternal Father, and His only Begotten Son, in the Flesh, His Living Son Jesus Christ, who was Jehovah of the Old Testament and became known as Jesus Christ of the New Testament, even the very 'Savior and Redeemer of the world'.

For me, the entirety of both the *well-informed and experiential evidence* I've presented for your consideration, allows me to say unequivocally that the *evidentiary stand* supporting my *table of belief* has most certainly moved my 'belief cursor' along the *Percentage of Probability Spectrum* all the way to 100% God Exists! That said, the reality is, the ultimate reason I came to *know* God exists, when my *belief* changed to *knowledge*, was when the power of the Holy Ghost affirmed this truth to my heart and mind, spirit-to-spirit, as a gift of testimony affirming that these things were true. This gift of testimony came from my Heavenly Father, and it continues to live in me to this very day.

This same power will confirm these truths to your heart and mind too if you haven't already experienced it. I believe anyone who reads my book with an open mind will experience their individual belief cursor moving along the percentage of probability spectrum towards the God's Exists marker, until it's well beyond the 50/50 split and on to the "God Exists" end of the spectrum. It is my hope that your belief cursor has reached 100% probability, so that you too can now say with reverential confidence, "I know my God and my Redeemer lives, and I know that They love me dearly!"

If, after reading my perspective as a Latter-Day Saint on God's existence, you still do *not believe* He exists, ask yourself, "What is your *percentage of probability* that God exists after reading my book?" You can answer this by measuring what my Latter-Day Saint perspectives' impact and influence has had on your mind and heart. Meaning, "In what direction has your 'feelings and common-sense thoughts' moved your belief cursor?" Has your belief cursor moved closer to the 'God Exists' marker on the *percentage of probability spectrum*, or has your belief cursor moved closer to the 'God Does Not Exist' marker on the *percentage of probability spectrum*? I hope, you find that your belief cursor has moved ever so closer to the "God Exists" marker on the spectrum. Your happiness depends on it.

Just like Richard's worldview, my worldview boils down to the fact that there's no absolute, irrefutable, incontrovertible evidence that proves God's existence *or* His non-existence. Neither the atheist camp of scientists nor the theist camp of scientists, have been able to produce incontrovertible evidence that *proves* without question their case for or against God's existence. And so, the Caravan of Truth I spoke of early on, with its pack of barking dogs continually yapping at its heels, will continue to press on through the *desert of doubt* until the answers to the 'Big' questions about God's existence are either discovered, or, as I believe, they will be fully revealed to the entire world at Jesus' 2nd coming.

Jesus Christs' 2nd coming will usher in the millennium. The heavens will be rolled back like a scroll and Jesus Himself will show His face for all the world to see, proving that His Father exists and lives in His sidereal heavenly abode with all His holy angels, those angels being His spirit children. On that great and dreadful Day, I will either be here on earth at Christ's coming, or I will come with him as a resurrected being with all the righteous sons and daughters of God. God's Son's coming will prove that Jesus was and is His Only Begotten Son in the flesh, even the crucified Christ, the foretold Messiah.

On that great and dreadful Day, the Jews will confess that Jesus is in fact the Christ, the very Son of God who came to earth to fulfill His role as our Savior and Redeemer, whom their fathers crucified. I testify that we'll all come to know God exists, and that He alone is the "Theory of Everything", even the answer to all the 'Big' questions, both the seen and unseen. I testify that God is as real as you and I are, and these truths will be confirmed on that Great and Dreadful Day, the glorious Day of His 2nd coming, and I can't wait for that Day to come. I hope you do not fear or dread that Day of Christ's coming. It will be glorious!

Because you, my readers, have made it this far, I want you to know that what I have shared is true. I want you to know that I love you as a brother or sister, because you are part of God our Father's eternal family, and that you are of great worth to Him and to me. I want you to know that I have prayed that you'll have all of your sincere questions answered. In closing, let me quote John Lennox once again, by sharing his closing remarks for his book "God and Stephen Hawking". I feel John said exactly what my heart is feeling at this very moment, and I quote him now:

"Many of the topics that have been mentioned deserve much more consideration. I do hope, however, that I have at least managed to communicate to you that the widespread belief that atheism is the default intellectual position is untenable, and, I hope that for many of you this investigation of Richard's atheistic belief system will serve to confirm your faith in God, as it has mine, and that it will encourage you not to be ashamed of bringing God unto the public square by joining in the debate yourself.

"I even dare to hope that, for some of you, this little book may be the start of a journey that will eventually lead to your coming to believe in the God who not only made the universe but also conferred on you the immeasurable dignity of creating you *in his image*, with the capacity for thought and the intellectual curiosity that got you reading this book in the first place. In turn that could even be, as it was for me, the first step in embarking on what is, by definition, life's highest adventure–*getting to know the Creator through the Son that has revealed Him.*" [823]

End of John Lenox's Quote

Conclusion

In the Introduction to my book An Atheist's DelusioOn, I shared Richard's list of four consciousness-raisers that he predicted would be answered by the arguments he would present in his book, *The God Delusion*, and in doing so it would *knock out* Intelligent Design and the God Hypothesis as well as disprove each and every belief or argument made by believers in God, like myself. Let me remind you what the four consciousness-raisers were that Richard said he'd answer:

- Why belief is so ubiquitous, but not because God exists.
- Why religion isn't needed to have objective morals.
- Why religion comes from childhood indoctrination and not from God.
- And 'Why atheism is something to be proud of and not to be embarrassed about'.

Richard's belief system, his quasi-religion *Atheism*, along with Richard's quasi-prophet Charles Darwin, and Darwin's false doctrine of *Evolution,* with its chief anti-Christ tenant *Natural Selection*, were offered to us, his readers, time and time again throughout the entirety of his book *The God Delusion,* with Evolution being the supposed knock-out blow to *Intelligent Design*, the *God Hypothesis*, and *all religious claims* made by believers like myself. Richard's claim that he, and he alone, finally knocked out *all of these theistic claims*, in my humble opinion, is "An Atheist's Delusion".

Hebrews 12:1-2

1 Wherefore seeing we also are compassed about with so great a *cloud of witnesses*, let us lay aside every weight, and the sin which doth so easlly beset *us,* and let us run with patience the race that is set before us.

2 Looking unto Jesus *the author and finisher of our faith*; who for the joy that was set before him endured the cross, despising the shame, and is set down at the right hand of the throne of God.

As I close my book An Atheists Delusion, it is my hope that you, my readers, have come to a greater understanding of the reality of God the Fathers' existence, and that of His Son, Jesus Christs' as well. I wish to add my testimony to the many testimonies that I have quoted throughout my book, even the many testimonies of the living prophets and apostles of the Church of Jesus Christ of Latter-Day Saints.

I testify that the third member of the Heavenly First Presidency of the Universe, the third member of the Godhead who is the Holy Ghost and Testator of all truth, will confirm these truths to your heart and mind *if* you're a sincere truth seeker, just as God has promised He would to all those who seek after Him. All you need to do is to ask Him in faith, with a sincere heart, nothing wavering, for He is no respecter of persons. I so testify to this truth in the name of Jesus Christ, my Lord and King, even the Redeemer and Savior of the world, ... Amen.

*The proclamation I've listed below was referred to on pgs. 164 and 396 of this book. It is called – *"The Family: A Proclamation to the World"*. During a Women's General Conference address given in 1995, the First Presidency and the Quorum of the Twelve Apostles issued "The Family: A Proclamation to the World". In introducing it to the women in attendance at that meeting, President Gordon B. Hinkley said the following just before reading the proclamation in its entirety, and I quote:

"With so much of sophistry that is passed off as truth, with so much of deception concerning standards and values, with so much of allurement and enticement to take on *the slow stain of the world*, we have felt to warn and forewarn.

"In furtherance of this we of the First Presidency and the Council of the Twelve Apostles now issue a proclamation to the Church *and to the world* as a declaration and reaffirmation of standards, doctrines, and practices relative to the family which the prophets, seers, and revelators of this Church have repeatedly stated throughout its history. I now take the opportunity of reading to you this proclamation."

End of President Hinkley's brief introduction of the proclamation. [824]

The sum and total of this proclamation *summarizes my personal perspective of God and the purpose of my life as a Latter-Day Saint, and in particular it clarifies my beliefs* about God, His Son Jesus Christ, the Holy Ghost, and the pure and restored gospel that Jesus revealed to the prophet Joseph Smith Jr. early in the nineteenth century, when He came to restore His Church and earthly kingdom to the earth.

The Family: A Proclamation to the World
First Presidency and Quorum of the Twelve Apostles

Ensign, *Nov. 1995,*

WE, THE FIRST PRESIDENCY and the Council of the Twelve Apostles, of The Church of Jesus Christ of Latter-Day Saints, solemnly proclaim that marriage between a man and a woman is ordained of God and that the family is central to the Creator's plan for the eternal destiny of His children.

ALL HUMAN BEINGS—male and female—are created in the image of God. Each is a beloved spirit son or daughter of heavenly parents, and, as such, each has a divine nature and destiny. Gender is an essential characteristic of individual premortal, mortal, and eternal *identity* and purpose.

IN THE PREMORTAL REALM, spirit sons and daughters knew and worshiped God as their Eternal Father and accepted His plan by which His children could obtain a physical body and gain earthly experience to progress toward perfection and ultimately realize his or her divine destiny as an heir of eternal life. The divine plan of happiness enables family relationships to be perpetuated beyond the grave. Sacred ordinances and covenants available in holy temples make it possible for individuals to return to the presence of God and for families to be united eternally.

THE FIRST COMMANDMENT that God gave to Adam and Eve pertained to their potential for parenthood as husband and wife. We declare that God's commandment for His children to multiply and replenish the earth remains in force. We further declare that God has commanded that the sacred powers of procreation are to be employed *only* between man and woman, lawfully wedded as husband and wife.

WE DECLARE the means by which mortal life is created to be divinely appointed. We affirm the sanctity of life and of its importance in God's eternal plan.

HUSBAND AND WIFE have a solemn responsibility to love and care for each other and for their children. "Children are an heritage of the Lord" (Psalms 127:3). Parents have a sacred duty to rear their children in love and righteousness, to provide for their physical and spiritual needs, to teach them to love and serve one another, to observe the commandments of God and to be law-abiding citizens wherever they live. Husbands and wives—mothers and fathers—will be held accountable before God for the discharge of these obligations.

THE FAMILY is ordained of God. Marriage between man and woman is essential to His eternal plan. Children are entitled to birth within the bonds of matrimony, and to be reared by a father and a mother who honor marital vows with complete fidelity. Happiness in family life is most likely to be achieved when founded upon the teachings of the Lord Jesus Christ.

Successful marriages and families are established and maintained on principles of faith, prayer, repentance, forgiveness, respect, love, compassion, work, and wholesome recreational activities. By divine design, fathers are to preside over their families in love and righteousness and are responsible to provide the necessities of life and protection for their families. Mothers are primarily responsible for the nurture of their children. In these sacred responsibilities, fathers and mothers are obligated to help one another as equal partners. Disability, death, or other circumstances may necessitate individual adaptation. Extended families should lend support when needed.

WE WARN that individuals who violate covenants of chastity, who abuse spouse or offspring, or who fail to fulfill family responsibilities will one day stand accountable before God. Further, we warn that the disintegration of the family will bring upon individuals, communities, and nations the calamities foretold by ancient and modern prophets.

WE CALL upon responsible citizens and officers of government everywhere to promote those measures designed to maintain and strengthen the family as the fundamental unit of society.

About The Author

Martin L. Braden was born in Boise, Idaho, and lived there until the age of nineteen when, as a member of the Church of Jesus Christ of Latter-Day Saints, he was called to serve a mission in the Gulf States, which consisted of the southern states of Mississippi, Arkansas, Louisiana, and the western half of Tennessee. Upon returning home from his two years of missionary service, Martin attended college at Boise State University where his focus of studies was on the Fine Arts and Business Management, which Martin has used repeatedly throughout his forty-five-year career consulting small businesses.

Seven months after returning home from his mission, Martin met and fell in love with a young woman, Kathleen Smart, and six months later they were married and sealed in the Salt Lake Temple for time and all eternity. Martin has said that God made Kathleen beautiful so that Martin would ask Kathleen to marry him, and then made Kathleen dumb so that she would say yes. Kathleen has been the love of Martin's life for forty-six years and counting, and they are the proud parents of eight children and fifteen grandchildren.

During Martin's early years as a husband and father, Martin provided for his family by taking on several sales jobs with local businesses throughout Boise. After eight years of living in Boise, Martin and Kathleen moved their small family to West Covina California. After just two years in West Covina, Martin and Kathleen decided to make their long-term home in Bountiful Utah. For the rest of Martin's career, he worked with hundreds of small business owners along the Wasatch Front, providing a permission-based email marketing service that helped his owner-clients expand their customer base.

For the last five years of his career, Martin worked as a Sr. account manager for an Internet Marketing company called TopTenReviews.com, which is a website that provides reviews of products and services manufactured by large companies like Intuit, Microsoft, Adobe, and Norton Anti-virus to name just a few. During his time with TopTenReviews.com Martin earned more than one-and-a-half million dollars before the company closed out his department, but that financial boon allowed Martin to become 100% debt free, including his home and vehicles. Martin's success as a Sr. account manager not only allowed him to become debt free, but it also allowed him the luxury to invest his full time to research and then write his book *An Atheist's Delusion*, which was inspired by the need Martin saw for helping individuals who had experienced or were still experiencing cognitive dissonance about their faith and God's existence.

Another reason Martin wrote *An Atheist's Delusion*, was due to a request that was made of him to read Richard Dawkins' anti-Theist/anti-Christ book *The God Delusion*. After reading Richard's book, Martin felt driven to take on the formidable task of rebutting Mr. Dawkins' arguments against the existence of God, as well as his hatred for religion itself, by giving his Latter-Day Saint perspective on each of Richard's arguments. It's important to note that Martin's perspective comes from a lifetime of study, daily prayer, and personal experience with God and His Son Jesus Christ, both of whom he loves with all his heart, might, mind and strength.

Martin's consumption of literally hundreds of well-informed, highly endorsed resources, and in particular the revealed words of both past, as well as modern-day living apostles and prophets, have provided Martin with a plethora of evidence that supports both the reality of God's existence, as well as Martin's claim that it is not he who suffers from a God delusion, but that it is in fact Mr. Dawkins who is suffering from *An Atheist's Delusion*.

FOOTNOTES: - (From the 2008 edition of The God Delusion - First Mariner Books)

1. The God Delusion, pp. 70, 73 (see #6); and p. 77

2. Ibid p. 73 Available evidence and reasoning may yield an estimate of probability of more than 50 per cent.

3. Ibid, p. 78 (The God Hypothesis is very close to being ruled out by the laws of probability').

4. New Atheism and its critics - Kaufman – Nov 7, 2018 — Andrew Johnson, for example, claims that the New Atheists have successfully made the case that atheism is "presumptively true".

5. *"God and Stephen Hawking*: Whose Design is it Anyway?" by John C. Lennox - Paperback. $6.99. Can Science Explain Everything?

6. Ibid, p. 11

7. Mind Matters News - "James Webb Space Telescope Shows Big Bang Didn't Happen? Wait ... by Physicist Eric J. Learner, founder, president, and chief scientist of Lawrenceville Plasma Physics, Inc. [Aug. 13, 2022]

8. *God and Stephen Hawking*: Whose Design is it Anyway?" by John C. Lennox - Paperback. $6.99. Can Science Explain Everything?

9. "Stanford researchers uncover patterns in how scientists lie about their data". Nov 16, 2015 — 'When scientists falsify data, they try to cover it up by writing differently in their published works.' Also, see 'The 7 biggest problems facing science, according to 270 scientists.

10. See Enlightenment | Definition, Summary, Ideas, Meaning, History

11. YouTube - Dr. Hugh Ross Conference Weekend // Session 3 //Cosmic Reasons to Believe in Christ

12. Hugh Ross – Reasons to Believe – "Like it or Not, Dark energy is Real". Lisa Dyson, Matthew Kleban, and Leonard Susskind, "Disturbing Implications of a Cosmological Constant," *Journal of High Energy Physics* 2002 (November 12, 2002): id. 011, doi:10.1088/1126-6708/2002/10/011.

13. Philip Ball, "Is Physics Watching Over Us?" *Nature*, August 13, 2002, doi:10.1038/news020812-2.

14. Ibid.

15. Ibid.

16. "The Irrational Atheist: Dissecting the Unholy Trinity of Dawkins, Harris, and Hitchens"" – A book by American writer and technology entrepreneur Vox Day, a weekly columnist on WorldNetDaily and member of the SFWA, MENSA and IGDA.

17. Wikipedia – New Atheism - https://en.wikipedia.org/wiki/New_Atheism - Also see the 'about the four Horsemen" commentary on book titled "The Four Horsemen", written by Christopher Hitchens and published by 'Penguin Random House publishers – 'At the dawn of the new atheist movement, the thinkers who became known as "the four horsemen," the heralds of religion's unraveling—Christopher Hitchens, Richard Dawkins, Sam Harris, and Daniel Dennett –

18. The God Delusion – See Preface, second paragraph – "This book is intended to raise consciousness – raise aspiration, and a brave and splendid one."

19. Ibid, See Preface, second paragraph – "This book is intended to raise consciousness – raise aspiration, and a brave and splendid one."

20. Search "Einstein showed Newton was wrong about gravity. Now scientists are coming for Einstein" by Jeremy Deaton – Aug 3, 2019 — "New research confirms Einstein's theory of gravity but brings scientists a step closer to the day when it might be supplanted by ...

21. "The Grand Design: Has the Grand Master of Physics checkmated the Grand Designer of the Universe?" by Stephen Hawking, London, Bantam Press 2010Ibid, by Stephen Hawking, London, Bantam Press 2010

22. Ibid, by Stephen Hawking, London, Bantam Press 2010

23. *God and Stephen Hawking*: Whose Design is it Anyway? by John C. Lennox – Page 18-22

24. The God Delusion, Chapter 9 – 'Childhood, Abuse and the Escape from Religion'

25. Hymns of The Church of Jesus Christ of Latter-Day Saints – "Come, Thou King of Kings", Hymn #59 - Text: Parley P. Pratt, 1807-1857

26. Lectures on Faith' by Joseph Smith Jr. – Desert Book publishing

27. See "School of the Prophets" on www.churchofjesuschrist.org

28. See "What Is a Quorum?" on www.churchofjesuschrist.org

29. See Bible Dictionary for definition of Death and Hell: www.churchofjesuschrist.org

30. See John 17:3 – "And this is ªlife eternal, that they might know thee the only true God, and Jesus Christ, whom thou hast ᵉsent."

31. "The God Makers" - a book and film co-authored by Ed Decker and Dave Hunt

32. Sandra Tanner (& her late husband Jerald) founders of The Lighthouse Ministry whose purpose is to document problems with the claims of Mormonism and compare LDS doctrines with Christianity.

33. The Promised Messiah: The First Coming of Christ by Bruce R. McConkie – Desert Book - The Promised Messiah: The First Coming of Christ presents a careful analysis of those prophecies concerning the First Coming of the Lord. "What is here considered," says the author, Elder Bruce R. McConkie of the Council of the Twelve, "was the heart and core of the teachings of all the preachers of righteousness who lived before he dwelt among men.

34. 'The Mortal Messiah: From Bethlehem to Calvary' – Deseret Book – A four volume series by Bruce R. McConkie – Through Elder McConkie's fluent writing style, you'll discover how every word the Savior spoke, every action He took, and even the timing of His experiences are wonderful parts of the Master's divine plan. Written by a man of God who was called as a special witness of Jesus Christ, *The Mortal Messiah* examines the mission, ministry, and accomplishments of our Savior.

35. 'The Millennial Messiah: The Second Coming of the Son of Man' – by Bruce R. McConkie – Deseret Book – The crowning work of his trilogy on the life of Christ-preceded by The Promised Messiah and The Mortal Messiah (in four volumes)-The Millennial Messiah lays out before the reader every pertinent bit of information to be gleaned from the four standard works and inspired prophets.

36. 'Answers to Gospel Questions' by Joseph Fielding Smith – Deseret Book – Journal of Discourses - Complete 26 Volume Set Plus Index by Brigham Young, George Q. Cannon, et al. | Jan 1, 1974

37. 'The Journal of Discourses' by Brigham Young, George Q. Cannon, et al. | Jan 1, 1974 – Deseret Book – A complete 26 Volume Set plus an Index

38. History of the Church, 4:185; from a letter from Joseph Smith and his counselors in the First Presidency to the Saints, Sept. 1840, Nauvoo, Illinois, published in Times & Seasons, Oct. 1840, P. 178

39. William Smith, interview by E. C. Briggs and J. W. Peterson, Oct., or Nov. 1893, originally published in Zion's Ensign (periodical published by the *Reorganized Church of Jesus Christ of Latter-Day Saints*, now called *Community of Christ*); reprinted in Deseret *Evening News*, Jan. 20, 1994, p. 2; punctuation modernized.

40. 'The Journal of Discourses' by Brigham Young, George Q. Cannon, et al. | Jan 1, 1974 – Deseret Book – A complete 26 Volume Set plus an Index

41. Joseph Smith, History 1832, pp. 2-3; Letter Book 1, 1829-35, Joseph Smith, Collection, Church Archives.

42. History of the Church, 6:305; from a discourse given by Joseph Smith on Apr. 7, 1844, in Nauvoo, Illinois; reported by Wilford Woodruff, Willard Richards, Thomas Bullock, and William Clayton.

43. *History of the Church*, 4:595; from "Baptism for the Dead," an editorial published in *Times and Seasons*, Apr. 15, 1842, p. 759; Joseph Smith was the editor of the periodical.

44. *History of the Church*, 2:12, 14; paragraph divisions altered; from "The elders of the Church in Kirtland, to Their Brethren Abroad," Jan. 22, 1834, published in *Evening and Morning Star*, Feb. 1834, p. 136; Mar. 1834

45. *History of the Church*, 1:317; from a letter from Joseph Smith to w2illiam W. Phelps, Jan. 11, 1833, Kirtland, Ohio; this letter is incorrectly dated Jan. 14, 1833, in *History of the Church*.

46. *History of the Church*, 4:185; from a letter from Joseph Smith and his counselors in the First Presidency to the Saints, Sept. 1840, Nauvoo, Illinois, published in *Times and Seasons*, Oct. 1840, p. 178.

47. *History of the Church*, 6:303-5, 308; capitalization modernized; paragraph divisions altered; from a discourse given by Joseph Smith on Apr. 7, 1844, in Nauvoo, Illinois; reported by Wilford Woodruff, Willard Richards, Thomas Bullock, and William Clayton; see also the appendix in in Teachings of the Presidents of the Church: Joseph Smith, p. 562, item 3.

48. Articles of faith 1:1

49. Doctrine & Covenants 130:22; instructions given by Joseph Smith on April 2, 1843, in Ramus, Illinois.

50. *History of the Church*, 6:474; from a discourse given by Joseph Smith on June 16, 1844, in Nauvoo, Illinois; reported by Thomas Bullock.

51. Quoted by William Clayton, reporting an undated discourse given by Joseph Smith in Nauvoo, Illinois; in L. John Nuttall, "Extracts from William Clayton's Private Book," p. 7, Journals of L. John Nuttall, 1857- 1904, L. Tom Perry Special Collections, Brigham Young University, Provo, Utah; copy in Church Archives.

52. *History of the Church*, 5:426; from a discourse given by Joseph Smith on June 11, 1843, in Nauvoo, Illinois, reported by Wilford woodruff and Willard Richards.

53. Quoted by William Clayton, reporting a discourse given by Joseph Smith in Nauvoo, Illinois; in L. John Nuttall, "Extracts from William Clayton's Private Book," pp. 10-11, Journals of L. John Nuttall, 1857- 1904, L. Tom Perry Special Collections, Brigham Young University, Provo, Utah; copy in Church Archives.

54. Quoted by William O. McIntire, reporting a discourse given by Joseph Smith in early 1841 in Nauvoo, Illinois; William Patterson McIntire, Notebook 1840-45, Church Archives. William McIntire made brief reports of several discourses given by Joseph Smith in Nauvoo in early 1841. This book quotes from four of these reports, none of which is dated.

55. Quoted by George Laub, in compilation of excerpts from Joseph Smith's discourses, ca. 1845; George Laub, Reminiscences and Journals Jan. 1845-Apr. 1857, pp. 29-30, church Archives.

56. Mark 12:29-30; see also Matt. 22:37-38; Deut. 6:5

57. *Lectures on Faith* (1985), 38, 42.

58. *History of the Church* 6:305

59. Article of Faith 1:1

60. John 17:3 New Testament

61. John 8:38; John 6:38;

62. "The Grandeur of God" – A talk given by Elder Jeffrey Holland, October 2003 General Conference, Saturday Morning Session

63. Ibid, "The Grandeur of God" – A talk given by Elder Jeffrey Holland, October 2003 General Conference, Saturday Morning Session

64. Ibid, The Grandeur of God" – A talk given by Elder Jeffrey Holland, October 2003 General Conference, Saturday Morning Session

65. Ibid, "The Grandeur of God" – A talk given by Elder Jeffrey Holland, October 2003 General Conference, Saturday Morning Session

66. Ibid, "The Grandeur of God" – A talk given by Elder Jeffrey Holland, October 2003 General Conference, Saturday Morning Session

67. Ibid, The Grandeur of God" – A talk given by Elder Jeffrey Holland, October 2003 General Conference, Saturday Morning Session

68. Ibid, The Grandeur of God" – A talk given by Elder Jeffrey Holland, October 2003 General Conference, Saturday Morning Session

69. Ibid, The Grandeur of God" – A talk given by Elder Jeffrey Holland, October 2003 General Conference, Saturday Morning Session

70. Ibid, The Grandeur of God" – A talk given by Elder Jeffrey Holland, October 2003 General Conference, Saturday Morning Session

71. Ibid, The Grandeur of God" – A talk given by Elder Jeffrey Holland, October 2003 General Conference, Saturday Morning Session – William Barclay, The Mind of Jesus (1961), especially the chapter "Looking at the Cross" for a discussion of this modern tendency.

72. Ibid, The Grandeur of God" – A talk given by Elder Jeffrey Holland, October 2003 General Conference, Saturday Morning Session

73. The God Delusion, p. 296

74. Ibid, p. 23

75. Ibid, p. 17

76. Ibid, p. 18

77. Ibid, p. 49

78. Ibid, p. 19-21

79. Ibid, p. 23

80. Ibid, p. 23

81. Ibid, p. 23
82. Ibid, p. 23
83. Ibid, p. 23
84. Ibid, p. 85
85. Mormon Doctrine by Bruce R. McConkie, "Apostacy" p. 42
86. The God Delusion, p. 23
87. The True Church by Elder LeGrand Richard's of the Quorum of the Twelve Apostles (See Sunday Afternoon Session of General Conference on April 9, 1972)
88. The God Delusion, p. 351
89. *Choose to Believe* by Elder L. Whitney Clayton *of the Presidency of the Seventy*
90. The Bible Dictionary – The Light of Christ – Got to Mormon Doctrine or to the Church website www.thechurchofjesuschrist.org and do a search for The Light of Christ.
91. The God Delusion, p. 56
92. Oxford Languages - Definition of Religion
93. *Man, His Origin and Destiny*, by Joseph Fielding Smith, p. 186
94. *Ibid*, p. 186-187
95. *Ibid*, p. 187
96. JS History 1:19
97. The President of the Board of Education, Whitehall, London, S. W. I. October 6th, 1941
98. *Man, His Origin and Destiny*, by Joseph Fielding Smith, p. 189-190; *Decent of Man* by Charles Darwin-Chapter 2: *p. 78*
99. The God Delusion, p. 241
100. *Joseph Smith's 21st Century View of the World: Truths He Knew Before the World Accepted Them* – Joseph Smith, Nauvoo, Illinois, October 9, 1843, *History of the Church*, 6, p. 50.
101. Ibid, p. vi
102. Ibid, p. vii
103. Ibid, p. vii – Journal of Discourses, Albert Carrington Pub., Liverpool, 1875, 17, p. 52; Brigham Young discourses, 3 May 1874.
104. Ibid, p. vii
105. Ibid, p. viii
106. Ibid, p. 4
107. Ibid, p. 4-5
108. Joseph Smith, Nauvoo, Illinois, October 9, 1843, *History of the Church*, 6, p. 50. *Teachings of the Presidents of the Church: Joseph Smith*
109. Joseph Smith's 21st Century View of the World: Truths He Knew Before the World Accepted Them – p. 3-5
110. Ibid, p. 5
111. Ibid, p. 15
112. Ibid, p. 16
113. Ibid, p. 19 – Carl Sagan, Cosmos, Digitally Remastered Disc Collector's Edition, Cosmos Studios Inc., 2000.
114. Ibid, p. 20-21
115. Ibid, p. 22
116. Ibid, p. 23
117. Ibid, p. 24 – I highly recommend C. S. Lewis's book Mere Christianity, first published in 1952 and still in print from Harper One Publishers.
118. World's Most Powerful Microscope by Lynn Charles Rathbun - Posted on Nanooze on November 5, 2013
119. Doctrine & Covenants 131:7 – 7 There is no such thing as immaterial matter. All spirit is matter, but it is mores fine or pure, and can only be discerned by purer eyes.

120. Pratt, Parley P. "Eternal Duration of Matter." HC 4:55; Selections from *Times and Seasons,* 1 Apr. 1842, in *JSP*, D9:329.

121. Joseph Smith's 21st Century View of the World: Truths He Knew Before the World Accepted Them – p. 31-32

122. Ibid, p. 32

123. Ibid, p. 32

124. Ibid, p. 35

125. Ibid, p. 36

126. "What is Consciousness?" – Episode 1302 I Closer to Truth – Robert Kuhn and Dr. Sam Parnia

127. *"Teachings of Presidents of the Church: Brigham Young"* [1997], 279; www.churchofjesuschrist.org – Search for 'Spirit World'."

128. Joseph Smith's 21st Century View of the World: Truths He Knew Before the World Accepted Them – p. 36

129. Georges Lemaître, father of the Big Bang Theory – This startling idea first appeared in scientific form in 1931, in a paper by Georges Lemaître, a Belgian cosmologist and Catholic priest. The theory, accepted by nearly all astronomers today, was a radical departure from scientific orthodoxy in the 1930s.

130. Dark energy was discovered in 1998 with this method by two international teams that included American astronomers Adam Riess (the author of this article) and Saul Perlmutter and Australian astronomer Brian Schmidt.

131. *Key to the Science of Theology* by Parley P. Pratt, - Deseret Book Company, Salt Lake City, Utah, published in 1966 tenth edition, pp. 45-48; and – *Joseph Smith's 21st Century View of the World: Truths He Knew Before the World Accepted Them* – p. 44-45

132. Joseph Smith's 21st Century View of the World: Truths He Knew Before the World Accepted Them – by Dr. Lamb

133. *Decent of Man* by Charles Darwin - Chapters 3-4

134. *Man, His Origin and Destiny*, by Joseph Fielding Smith

135. *Decent of Man* by Charles Darwin - Chapters 3-4

136. *Man, His Origin and Destiny*, by Joseph Fielding Smith

137. The Church & BYU: An evolution — of evolution by Rachel Keeler - July 30, 2019 (The Daily Universe)

138. *Evolution: Bacteria to Beethoven* – You Tube video by Stephen Meyer, an American author, a former geophysicist, and college professor, and now the director of Discovery Institute's Center for Science and Culture in Seattle.

139. The God Delusion, p. 29

140. Ibid, p. 35-36

141. Ibid, p. 40

142. Ibid, p. 30-31

143. Ibid, p. 39-40

144. Ibid, p. 39-40

145. Ibid, p. 36, 40

146. Ibid, p. 40

147. Ibid, p. 41

148. Ibid, p. 37

149. Ibid, pp. 41-42

150. Ibid, p. 39-40

151. Ibid, pp. 41

152. Ibid, pp. 47

153. Ibid, p. 39

154. Ibid, p. 48

155. Ibid, p. 49

156. Ibid, p. 49
157. Ibid, p. 49
158. Ibid, p. 49
159. Ibid, p. 49
160. Ibid, p. 49
161. Ibid, p. 51
162. Ibid, p. 49
163. Ibid, p. 50
164. Ibid, p. 50
165. Ibid, pp. 17, 51
166. Ibid, p. 51
167. Ibid, p. 51
168. Ibid, p. 52
169. Ibid, p. 52
170. Ibid, p. 52
171. Ibid, p. 52
172. Ibid, p. 53
173. Ibid, p. 54
174. Ibid, p. 54
175. Ibid, p. 56
176. Ibid, p. 56
177. Ibid, p. 56
178. Ibid, p. 56
179. Ibid, p. 56
180. Ibid, p. 56
181. Ibid, p. 56
182. See www.churchofjsesuschrist.org and search for "Priestcraft".
183. See John 21:21-23; Also do a search for "Are John the Beloved and the Three Nephites actually still on the earth? If so, what are they doing?" at www.churchofjesuschrist.org
184. The Pearl of Great Price - Joseph Smith's History – 1:17-20
185. See Ephesians 6:11–18 and D&C 27:15–18
186. "The True Nature of God", by Jeffrey Holland – Doctrine & Covenants 130:22
187. The God Delusion – p. 58-59
188. Ibid, p. 61
189. Ibid, p. 59
190. "Earthly Governments and Laws" – Section 134, Earthly Governments and Laws," *Doctrine & Covenants Student Manual* (2002), 344–47. For the entire article go to: www.churchofjesuschrist.org and search for 'Earthly Governments and Laws".
191. The God Delusion – p. 58
192. *"We Will Witness What Nephi Saw in Vision"* (Parts 1 & 2) – YouTube
193. A talk titled 'Hear Him', by President Russell M. Nelson, April 2020s General Conference: https://www.churchofjesuschrist.org/study/general-conference/2020/04/45nelson?lang=eng
194. "We Will Prove Them Herewith" – A talk by Elder David A. Bednar, October General Conference, Saturday morning session: https://www.churchofjesuschrist.org/study/general-conference/2020/10/12bednar?lang=eng
195. A talk title "I testify" by President Ezra Taft Benson in October 1988 Saturday morning sessionhttps://www.churchofjesuschrist.org/study/general-conference/1988/10/i-testify? lang=eng

196. "What is Secularism" by National Secular Society –https://www.secularism.org.uk/what-is-secularism.html

197. The God Delusion, p. 68

198. Ibid, p. 68

199. Ibid, p. 68

200. Ibid, p. 69

201. Ibid, p. 69

202. Ibid, p. 69

203. Ibid, p. 69

204. Ibid, p. 70

205. Ibid, p. 69

206. Ibid, p. 70

207. Ibid, p. 72

208. Ibid, p. 72-73

209. Ibid, p. 73

210. Ibid, p. 72

211. Ibid, p. 73

212. Ibid, p. 73

213. "Becoming Converted" by Elder D. Todd Christofferson of the Quorum of the Twelve Apostles: www.churchofjesuschrist.org"

214. Bob Saget Talks About Life, Death, and Jesus www.YouTube.com

215. "Becoming Converted" by Elder D. Todd Christofferson of the Quorum of the Twelve Apostles – www.churchofjesuschrist.org

216. The God Delusion – p. 74

217. Ibid, p. 73-74

218. Ibid, p. 73-74

219. Ibid, p. 77

220. Ibid, p. 77

221. Teachings of Presidents of the Church: Joseph Smith (2007), 210

222. Joseph Smith's 21st Century View of the World: Truths He Knew Before the World Accepted Them–p. 36

223. "Knowing God" by Elder Bernard P. Brockbank, Assistant to the Council of the Twelve Apostles, at the April 1972 General Conference, Thursday morning session: https://www.churchofjesuschrist.org/study/general-conference/1972/04/knowing-god?lang=eng

224. President Harold B. Lee, Teachings of Presidents of the Church: Harold B. Less (2000), 134

225. President David O. McKay, Teachings of Presidents of the Church: David O. McKay (2000), 131

226. Austin Farrer – Published statement from 1966, quoted by Elder Neil Maxwell: https://fornspollfira.blogspot.com/2013/01/history-of-quote.html

227. The God Delusion, pp. 77-78; also in Dawkins' God: Genes, Memes, and the Origin of Life, by Alister McGrath

228. Ibid, p. 79

229. Ibid, p. 79

230. Ibid, p. 79

231. Ibid, p. 80

232. Ibid, p. 81-82

233. Ibid, p. 83

234. Ibid, p. 87

235. Ibid, p. 87

236. "The Millennium" – Joseph Smith Jr. – Essay at www.chirchofjesuschrist.org

237. See *Teachings of the Prophet Joseph Smith,* sel. Joseph Fielding Smith [1976], 268.

238. *Teachings of Presidents of the Church: Joseph Smith* [2007], 258); See Joseph Fielding Smith, *Doctrines of Salvation,* comp. Bruce R. McConkie, 3 vols. [1954–56], 2:167, 251–52.

239. *Teachings of Presidents of the Church: John Taylor* [2001], 225).

240. The God Delusion – p. 79

241. Ibid, p. 86

242. Ibid, p. 86

243. Question: "Nephi states that God gives liberally to those who 'ask not amiss' (2 Ne. 4:35)." See "What guidelines can help us pray in accordance with God's will?" search on www.church of jesuschrost.org. Response given by Alan L. Wilkins, *academic vice president of Brigham Young University.*

244. The God Delusion – p. 89

245. Ibid, p. 93

246. Ibid, p. 90

247. "All Things Shall Work Together for Your Good" by Susan W. Tanner Young Women General President (see www.churchofjesuschrist.org)

248. "Melchizedek Priesthood" –www.churchofjesuschrist.org/study/manual/gospeltopics

249. *"Healing the Sick"* by Dallin H. Oaks of the Quorum of the Twelve Apostles – (see www.churchofjesuschrist.org)

250. You Tube video titled, "Does Science Prove God's Glory? Dr. Hugh Ross, Regent University"

251. You Tube video titled, "Does Science Prove God's Glory? Dr. Hugh Ross, Regent University"

252. YouTube videos on Near Death Experiences (NDE's)

253. YouTube video "LDS Perspective on Near Death Experiences" by Vincenzo Covino

254. Joseph Smith *HC* 6:50

255. Bioethics Research Library – "Death Rate is 120 per Minute" - 65 million people die each year

256. See YouTube - "Lawrence M. Krauss || A Universe from Nothing || Radcliffe Institute"

257. See www.churchofjesuschrist.org – "Resurrection" – A doctrinal study overview.

258. See JST John 1:19 [Appendix or John 1:18 note c]; JST 1 Jn. 4:12 [1 Jn. 4:12 note a].

259. See JS—H 1:11–20.

260. See 'Mysteries of Godliness' – www.churchofjesuschrist.org - For other references to God, see Heb. 1:1–3; Jacob 4:5; D&C 20:17, and also *Holy Ghost; Jehovah* in the Bible Dictionary.

261. The God Delusion – p. 93

262. Ibid, p. 94-97

263. Ibid, p. 94-97

264. Ibid, p. 96-97

265. Ibid, p. 97

266. Ibid, p. 97

267. "Remember Carl Sagan by Joel Achenbach in the Washington Post Interview by Joel Achenbach December 21, 2016.

268. "Carl Sagan denied being an atheist. So, what did he believe?" [Part 1] by Joel Achenbach of the Washington Post, July 10, 2014, To Robert Pope, of Windsor, Ontario, Oct. 2, 1996.

269. The God Delusion – p. 98

270. Ibid, p. 100

271. Ibid, p. 100

272. Ibid, p. 102

273. Ibid, p. 102

274. Ibid, p. 102

275. Ibid, p. 102

276. Ibid, p. 102

277. A discourse given by Joseph Smith on April 8, 2843, in Nauvoo. Illinois; reported by Willard Richards

and William Clayton: History of the Church 5:340

278. The God Delusion – p. 101

279. Church Resources - "First Vision Accounts," Gospel Topics, topics.lds.org; First Vision Accounts videos, josephsmithpapers.org; Primary Accounts of Joseph Smith's First Vision of Deity, josephsmithpapers.org; "Ask of God: Joseph Smith's First Vision," history.lds.org.

280. "If You Could Hie to Kolob" to be interesting and informative. It was written by William W. Phelps (1792–1872)

281. The God Delusion – p. 102

282. See www.churchofjesuschrist.org and do a search for "Why can't we remember our premortal life as spirits, and when will those memories return?"

283. The God Delusion, p. 103

284. Wikipedia – "Intelligent Design"; and "Center for Science and Culture"

285. YouTube – "5-Part Series: Science and God"

286. YouTube - "What's Wrong with Atheism?"

287. "Roger's Version" by John Updike; Requoted in Los Angeles Times by David Briggs in article titled "Science, Religion Are Discovering Commonality in Big Bang Theory: Creationism: New findings are seen by some as supporting belief that Earth was formed out of chaos by divine intervention". https://www.latimes.com/archives/la-xpm-1992-05-02-me-1350-story.html

288. The God Delusion – p. 102

289. Ibid, p. 102

290. Ibid, p. 102

291. HC 6:308-309, The King Follett Sermon; and "Spirit Children of our Heavenly Parents" https://www.churchofjesuschrist.org/study/manual/gospel-topics/spirit-children-of-heavenly-parents?lang=eng

292. "Intelligence, Intelligences" (A Guide to the Scriptures) – www.churchofjesuschrist.org

293. History of the Church, 5:340.

294. "Mormonism and the Concept of infinite Regress of God" – www.fairlatterdaysaints.org https://www.fairlatterdaysaints.org/answers/Mormonism_and_the_nature_of_God/Infinite_regress of Gods

295. Blake T. Ostler, "Review of The Mormon Concept of God: A Philosophical Analysis by Francis J. Beckwith and Stephen E. Parrish," FARMS Review of Books 8/2 (1996): 99–146.

296. "Becoming Like God" – www.churchofjesuschrist.org

297. "The Cost of Discipleship", by Dietrich Bonhoeffer, 1963, p. 45).

298. "Law and Gospel Re-examine" by Paul L. Homer, "Sage journals" – "Theology Today", 1953-54: 474 https://journals.sagepub.com/doi/abs/10.1177/004057365401000405?journalCode=ttja

299. "Articles of faith" by James Talmage, p. 480

300. Hafen, Bruce C.. "Grace" – In Encyclopedia of Mormonism, Edited by Daniel H. Ludlow. Vol. 2. New York: Macmillan, 1992. – Quoting John Dillenberger author of "Grace and Works in Martin Luther and Joseph Smith".

301. "The Enabling Power of Jesus Christ and His Atonement" – www.churchofjesuschrist.org https://www.churchofjesuschrist.org/study/liahona/2017/03/the-enabling-power-of-jesus-christ-and- his-atonement?lang=eng

302. The God Delusion – p. 102

303. Ibid, p. 103-104

304. Stephen E. Robinson – "Yet another way in which anti-Mormon critics often misrepresent LDS doctrine is in the presentation of anomalies as though they were the doctrine of the Church" by Stephen E. Robinson@www.fairlatterdaysaints.org

305. The God Delusion, p. 103

306. Ibid, p. 103

307. Ibid, p. 103

308. Joseph Smith, Teachings of the Prophet Joseph Smith, 56.

309. John A. Widtsoe, Evidences and Reconciliations, 19–21.

310. "The Father and the Son: A Doctrinal Exposition by the First Presidency and the Twelve," in James E. Talmage, *The Articles of Faith,* 466.

311. Brigham Young, *Discourses of Brigham Young,* 50

312. John Taylor, in *Journal of Discourses,* 21:14.

313. The Apostle Boyd K. Packer, in Conference Report, Oct. 1984, 82; or *Ensign,* Nov. 1984, 66–67.

314. Joseph Smith, *Teachings,* 345–46).

315. Spencer W. Kimball, *The Teachings of Spencer W. Kimball,* 25.

316. Joseph Smith, *Teachings,* 347–48.

317. Bruce R. McConkie, *Mormon Doctrine,* 317.

318. Joseph Smith, comp., *Lectures on Faith,* 10.

319. Bruce R. McConkie, "Our Relationship with the Lord," in *Brigham Young University 1981–82 Fireside and Devotional Speeches,* 101.

320. "Mormon Doctrine", p. 319 - by Elder Bruce R. McConkie

321. Joseph Smith, *Teachings,* 190.

322. Joseph F. Smith, "Answers to Questions," *Improvement Era,* Jan. 1901, 228

323. The God Delusion, p. 105

324. Ibid, p. 105

325. "Objective Morality: Much Ado About Nothing", by Terry Lewis, an American apologist for Cross Examined, headed up by Frank Terek, American apologist, author, public speaker, and radio host.

326. The God Delusion, p. 106

327. Ibid, p. 106

328. Ibid, p. 107

329. Ibid, p. 107

330. William Lane Craig's website www.reasonableFaith.com

331. The God Delusion, p. 114

332. Ibid, p. 114

333. Ibid, p. 115

334. Ibid, p. 115

335. "Infidelity Statistics (2022): How much Cheating is going On?" by Paul Brian 3/31, 2022 – Hack Spirit: https://hackspirit.com/infidelity-statistics/

336. "Bestiality is much, much more common than you think" by News24: https://www.news24.com/health24/sex/sexual-diversity/Bestiality-is-much-much-more-common-than-you-think-20150218

337. "The True History of Moloch" by Marco Margaritoff, October 2, 2021 https://allthatsinteresting.com/moloch

338. Ibid, https://allthatsinteresting.com/moloch

339. The God Delusion p. 117

340. Ibid, p. 117

341. Ibid, p. 118

342. Ibid, p. 119

343. "Do Animals Dream?" – Earthsky 2-7-2019 - https://earthsky.org/earth/animal-dreams

344. "Quiet Slumber: Revelation through Dreams" by Ryan C. Jenkins

345. Charles W. Penrose, JD 26:21 (Page 221)

346. "Light, Visions, and Dreams" by Merrill J. Bateman, *President of Brigham Young University September 19, 2000*

347. The God Delusion, p. 121

348. The PEW Forum on Religion & Public Safety – PEW Research Center - "U.S. Religious Landscape Survey" – Religious Affiliation: Diverse and Dynamic – February 200

349. The God Delusion, p. 122

350. Ibid, p. 122

351. Ibid, p. 122

352. Ibid, p. 125

353. "God Will Yet Reveal", by Elder Neil Maxwell – Do a search for this talk by Elder Maxwell at www.churchofjesuschrist.org

354. "The Scriptures" – Go to www.churchofjesuschrist.org and do a search for 'The Scriptures' and scroll down until you see 'Bible'.

355. The God Delusion, p. 129

356. Ibid, p. p. 129

357. Ibid, p. 129

358. Ibid, p. 130

359. Ibid, p. 130

360. Ibid, p. 131

361. Ibid, p. 131

362. Ibid, p. 132

363. Ibid, p. 135

364. Ibid, p. 136

365. Ibid, p. 137

366. Ibid, p. 137

367. Ibid, p. 138

368. Ibid, p. 139

369. "Doctrines of Salvation", comp. Bruce R. McConkie, 3 vols. [1954–56], 2:311).

370. "Teachings of the Presidents of the Church – Joseph Fielding Smith p. 99:https://www.churchofjesuschrist.org/bc/content/shared/content/english/pdf/languagematerials/369 07_eng.pdf

371. General Conference Report, Oct. 2002, 89; or Ensign, Nov. 2002, 83; Elder Joseph B. Wirthlin (1917–2008), who served as an apostle in the Quorum of the Twelve Apostles from 1986 – 2008.

372. "Christ and the New Covenant" [1997], 169). Elder Jeffrey R. Holland of the Quorum of the Twelve Apostles emphasized the importance of studying Alma 32–34 as a coherent whole.374 Conference Report, Oct. 2003, 104; or Ensign, Nov. 2003, 98).

373. Bishop Richard C. Edgley of the Presiding Bishopric taught that humility and submissiveness are virtues allowing one to access gospel blessings:

374. Family Pecan Trees: Planting a Legacy of Faith at Home [1992], 193–94). For more information and a diagram depicting the pride cycle, refer to "The Cycle of Righteousness and Wickedness" in the appendix (page 414).

375. Conference Report, Apr. 1989, 6; or Ensign, May 1989, 6–7). III Nephi 11:11; 13:33; Moroni 10:32)

376. President Ezra Taft Benson – The Faces of Pride - Excerpted from an April 1989 General Conference

377. The Lord's Way [1991], 85–86), Elder Dallin Oaks, Alma 32:21 – Faith and Hope

378. "Lectures on faith" – Lesson 1 - #12 - Joseph Smith

379. "What Is Faith?" in Faith [1983], 42–43). Boyd K. Packer,

380. Elder Neil Maxwell – Ether 12:4; see also Romans 8:24; Hebrews 11:1; Alma 32:21)" (In Conference Report, Oct. 1994, 45; or Fnsign, Nov. 1994, 35).

381. Elder Neal A. Maxwell; III Nephi 26:14)" – Conference Report, Apr. 1996, 95–96; or Ensign, May 1996, 69–70).

382. Conference Report, Oct. 2000, 97; or Ensign, Nov. 2000, 75; M. Russell Ballard of the Quorum of the Twelve Apostles

383. "Of Seeds and Soil" by President James E. Faust, Second Councilor in the First Presidency until his death in 2007 - Conference Report, Oct. 1999, 61; or Ensign, Nov. 1999, 48). Commentary for Alma 30:15–16 on page 214; see also "The Candle of the Lord," Ensign, Jan. 1983, 51–52). https://www.churchofjesuschrist.org/study/general-conference/1999/10/of-seeds-and-soils?lang=

384. Elder Boyd K. Packard – Mosiah 4:27)" (in Conference Report, Apr. 2005, 7; or Ensign, May 2005, 8).

385. The Prophet Joseph Smith (1805–44); *History of the Church,* 6:312; italics added).

386. Conference Report, Oct. 1997, 104; or *Ensign,* Nov. 1997, 75); Sister Janette Hales Beckham, former General Young Women President.

387. Commentary on Alma 32-35 contains a quote by Elder Neal A. Maxwell who has since passed away.

388. Elder Bruce C. Hafen of the Seventy – Conference Report, Apr. 2004, 100–101; or *Ensign,* May 2004, 97).

389. President Dieter F. Uchtdorf of the First Presidency – ("The Way of the Disciple, *Ensign,* May 2009, 76–77)."

390. President Henry B. Eyring of the First Presidency – (In the Conference Report, Oct. 2001, 17; or *Ensign,* Nov. 2001, 16)

391. Elder Dallin H. Oaks – (in Conference Report, Oct. 1992, 51; or *Ensign,* Nov. 1992, 37).

392. Elder Bruce R. McConkie – (In *Mormon Doctrine,* 2nd ed. [1966], 64; see also Moses 7:30).

393. Elder Russell M. Nelson, when he was a member of the Quorum of the Twelve Apostles – (in Conference Report, Oct. 1996, 46; or *Ensign,* Nov. 1996, 35).

394. Elder Robert E. Wells, past president of the Seventies – ("The Liahona Triad," in Bruce A. Van Orden and Brent L. Top, eds., *Doctrines of the Book of Mormon: The 1991 Sperry Symposium* [1992], 6–7).

395. President Joseph Fielding Smith; *The Way to Perfection* [1970], 202)

396. President Harold B. Lee of the First Presidency – (*The Teachings of Harold B. Lee,* ed. Clyde J. Williams [1996], 59).

397. Melvin J. Ballard – *The Three Degrees of Glory: A Discourse* [Sept. 22, 1922], 11–12).

398. The God Delusion, p. 139

399. Ibid, p. 140

400. Ibid, pp. 141

401. Ibid, p. 142-143

402. "We Believe in being Perfect – In Christ" – an Essay from www.churchofjesuschrist.org

403. "Perfect" from the Bible Dictionary at www.churchofjesuschrist.org

404. "Becoming Perfect in Christ" by Elder Gerrit W. Gong of the Quorum of the Twelve Apostles: https://www.churchofjesuschrist.org/study/ensign/2014/07/young-adults/becoming-perfect-inchrist?lang=eng

405. The God Delusion, p. 143

406. Ibid, p. 144

407. Ibid, p. 145

408. Ibid, p. 145

409. Ibid, p. 146

410. Ibid, p. 146

411. Ibid, p. 147

412. Wikipedia; PragerU is short for Prager University   https://en.wikipedia.org/wiki/PragerU - www.prageru.com

413. YouTube.com – "Evolution: Bacteria to Beethoven" by PragerU – Presenter - Stephen Meyer.

414. The God Delusion, p. 148

415. Ibid, p. 150

416. "Douglas Adams and God – Portrait of a radical atheist" - https://douglasadams.eu/douglas-adams-and-god-portrait-of-a-radical-atheist/

417. The God Delusion, p. 154

418. Ibid, p. 154

419. Ibid, p. 154

420. Ibid, p. 154

421. Ibid, p. 155

422. Ibid, p. 154

423. Ibid, p. 156-157

424. "A Mousetrap for Darwin: Michael J. Behe Answers His Critics Paperback" – November 17"; and "Irreducible Complexity.

425. The God Delusion, p. 161

426. "The Origin of Species", p. 226, by Charles Darwin

427. "A Mousetrap for Darwin: Michael J. Behe Answers His Critics Paperback" – November 17"; and "Irreducible Complexity".

428. "Evolution: A Theory in Crisis" by Michael Denton; ISBN 979-8-218-12163-1; Released 4 of 1986; Publisher – Adler & Adler Publishers Inc.

429. *"Templets and the explanation of complex patterns"* (Cambridge: Cambridge University Press, 1986) by Michael J. Katz

430. "Darwin's Black Box: The Biochemical Challenge to Evolution" by Michael J. Behe, Paperback. The Challenge to the Darwinian Evolutionary Explanations of many Biochemical Structures". A Response to Critics of Darwin's Black Box, by Michael Behe, PCID, Volume 1.1, January, February, March 2002; iscid.org.

431. "Evidence for Intelligent Design from Biochemistry" by Michael Behe, 1996b., a speech given at the Discovery Institute's God & Culture Conference, August 10, 1996, Seattle, WA. - http://www.arn.org/docs/behe/mb_idfrombiochemistry.htm.

432. "A Response to Critics of Darwin's Black Box", by Michael Behe, PCID, Volume 1.1, January, February, March 2002; iscid.org 383 The God Delusion, p. 158

433. A Response to Critics of Darwin's Black Box, by Michael Behe, PCID, Volume 1.1, January, February, March 2002; iscid.org 383 The God Delusion, p. 158

434. The God Delusion, p. 159

435. Ibid, p. 161

436. Ibid, p. 160-161

437. "Evolution and the Problem of Non-Functional Intermediates" – "Evolution's Fundamental Flaw" by Casey Luskin; Non-functionality and Irreducible Complexity: In the *Origin of the Species*, by Charles Darwin.

438. *"Signature in the Cell: DNA and the Evidence for Intelligent Design"*, by Stephen C. Meyer"

439. "Darwin's Doubt: The Explosive Origin of Animal Life and the Case for Intelligent Design" by Stephen Meyer –

440. "Return of the God Hypothesis" by Stephen C. Meyer

441. The God Delusion, p. 158 -159

442. "Evolution and the Problem of Non-Functional Intermediates" – "Evolution's Fundamental Flaw" by Casey Luskin; Non-functionality and Irreducible Complexity: In the *Origin of the Species*, by Charles Darwin.

443. The God Delusion, p. 162

444. Ibid, p. 167

445. "Finding Darwin's God"', written by Kenneth Miller. 'Finding Darwin's God: A Scientist's Search for Common Ground Between God and Evolution', is a 2000 book by the American cell biologist and Roman Catholic Kenneth R. Miller wherein he argues that evolution does not contradict religious faith.

446. "Closing the Gap: A Scientist's Response to the Gap Theory" by Dr. Hugh Ross – www.reasons.org

447. "The Genesis Impact" – A You Tube Video that is an animated presentation explaining the Ruin Reconstruction interpretation of the Bible's Genesis creation account.

448. "Closing the Gap: A Scientist's Response to the Gap Theory" by Dr. Hugh Ross – www.reasons.org

449. The God Delusion, p. 171

450. "Judge Rejects Teaching of Intelligent Design" by Laurie Goodstein, Dec. 21, 2005, The New York Times.

451. The God Delusion, p. 174

452. Ibid, p. 174

453. Ibid, p. 174

454. Ibid, p. 177

455. Ibid, p. 177

456. Ibid, p. 177

457. Ibid, p. 177

458. Quora.com – What is the difference between the anthropic principle and fine-tuning argument? – Contributor John Cousins, June 25, 202

459. The God Delusion, p. 177

460. Ibid, p. 177

461. Ibid, p. 177

462. Discovery Science – "Scientists Speak Out About Evidence of Intelligent Design in Nature" – Scientists from around the world speak out about the convincing evidence of purpose and Intelligent Design they see in nature. Explore at: https://www.intelligentdesign.org

463. The God Delusion, p. 180

464. Ibid, p. 181

465. Ibid, p. 182

466. Ibid, p. 183

467. "We Are Stardust", by Neil DeGrasse Tyson – You Tube Video May 11, 2015.

468. The God Delusion, p. 183

469. Ibid, p. 185

470. Ibid, p. 185

471. Ibid, p. 186

472. Ibid, pp. 186-187

473. Ibid, p. 186-187

474. Ibid, p. 186

475. Ibid, p. 187

476. Ibid, p. 188

477. Ibid, p. 188

478. Ibid, p. 188

479. Ibid, p. 200

480. Ibid, p. 200

481. Ibid, p. 200

482. Ibid, p. 201

483. Ibid, p. 204

484. Ibid, p. 205

485. Ibid, p. 205

486. Ibid, p. 205

487. "Genesis Impact (2020) Full Movie I Hannah Bradley I Reggie McGuire I Becky Emerick – You Tube"

488. The God Delusion, p. 205

489. Ibid, p. 205

490. Ibid, p. 206

491. Ibid, p. 207

492. Ibid, p. 211

493. Ibid, p. 212

494. Ibid, p. 213

495. Ibid, p. 213

496. Ibid, p. 207

497. Ibid, p. 216

498. *"Lehi in the Desert and The World of the Jaredites" by Hugh Nibley,* and *"The Collected Works of Hugh Nibley"* [1980], pg. 156; Adam Clarke, *The Holy Bible … with a Commentary and Critical Notes,* 6 vols., 1:86; see also *Old Testament Student Manual: Genesis–2 Samuel,* 3rd ed. [Church

Educational System manual, 2003], 57–58. See also "The Kitab al-Megall". Sacred-texts.com, retrieved 5 April 2012.

499. The God Delusion, p. 218

500. Ibid, p. 219

501. Ibid, p. 220

502. Ibid, p. 220

503. Ibid, p. 221

504. Ibid, p. 221

505. Ibid, p. 221

506. Ibid, p. 228

507. Ibid, p. 228

508. Ibid, p. 228

509. Ibid, p. 228

510. Ibid, p. 235

511. Ibid, p. 242

512. Ibid, p. 243

513. Ibid, p. 244

514. Oxford Dictionary – #1 Definition of "Selection"

515. The God Delusion, p. 244

516. Ibid, p. 245

517. Ibid, p. 245Ibid, p. 254

518. Ibid, p. 254

519. Ibid, p. 255

520. Ibid, p. 257

521. Ibid, p. 257"A Marvelous Work and a Wonder" written by Elder LeGrand Richards, who served as an apostle of the Church of Jesus Christ of Latter-Day Saints, in the Quorum of the Twelve Apostles beginning in 1952.

522. The God Delusion, p. 257-258

523. U.S. News & World Report article – "Study shows Mormonism is fastest-growing faith in half of U.S. states" by Kevin Eckstrom| Religion News Service, May 1, 2012.

524. The God Delusion, p. 263

525. Ibid, p. 258

526. Ibid, p. 259

527. Ibid, p. 263

528. Ibid, p. 264

529. Ibid, p. 265

530. Ibid, p. 266

531. Ibid, p. 268

532. Ibid, p. 270

533. Ibid, p. 270

534. Ibid, p. 271

535. Ibid, p. 277

536. Ibid, p. 279

537. "Shame vs Guilt: Help for Discerning God's Voice from Satan's Lies" by McKell A. Jorgensen, a graduate student from Brigham Young University and a Google scholar.

538. The God Delusion, p. 280

539. Ibid, p. 281

540. Ibid, p. 281

541. Ibid, p. 283

542. Ibid, p. 285

543. Ibid, p. 286

544. Ibid, p. 289

545. Ibid, p. 289

546. Ibid, p. 289

547. Ibid, p. 290

548. Ibid, p. 290

549. "Do red states report higher rates of violent crime than blue states?". It was written on Thursday, Jun 24, 2021, by Stevie Rosignol-Cortez.

550. The God Delusion, p. 291

551. Ibid, p. 291

552. "The First Great Commandment" by Jeffrey R. Holland, at www.churchofjesuschrist.org

553. "Can We be Good Without God?" by Ryan Leisure, Tuesday, Aug. 27, 2019 – on www.crossedexamined.org

554. The God Delusion, p. 295

555. Ibid, p. 297

556. Ibid, p. 297

557. "Gospel Topics" – 'Doctrinal Study Scriptures' at: www.churchofjesuschrist.org The God Delusion, p. 297

558. The God Delusion, p. 297

559. Ibid, p. 298

560. Ibid, p. 298

561. "Noah and the Ark" – Search at www.churchofjesuschrist.org

562. "Mormonism and the reconciliation of the Flood of Noah with scripture and Church teachings" – Search at www.fairlatterdaysaints.org

563. The God Delusion, p. 299

564. Ibid, p. 299

565. Ibid, p. 299

566. "What is the Law of Chastity" – Do a search for this articles title at www.churchofjesuschrist.org

567. The God Delusion, p. 299

568. Ibid, p. 302

569. Kasher, *Encyclopedia of Biblical Interpretation,* 2:128. Type "Genesis 12–17 -Abraham—Father of the Faithful" into the search bar: www.churchofjesuschrist.org– (see *Encyclopedia Judaica,* s.v. "Sarah," 14:866).

570. Old Testament Student Manual: Genesis–2 Samuel, 3rd ed. [Church Educational System manual, 2003], 256 www.churchofjesuschrist.org

571. "Understanding the Old Testament" - www.churchofjesuschrist.org, for the full article, written by Edward J. Brandt, the director of the Evaluation Division of the Correlation Department of The Church of Jesus Christ of Latter-Day Saints and past President of the Columbus, Ohio Temple of the Church of Jesus Christ of Latter-Day Saints.

572. The God Delusion, p. 309-310

573. Ibid, p. 310

574. Ibid, p. 313

575. Ibid, p. 314

576. Ibid, p. 315

577. Ibid, p. 315

578. *"The Way to Perfection"* [Salt Lake City: Genealogical Society of Utah, 1949], 272 - 273.

579. The God Delusion, p. 315

580. Ibid, p. 315

581. "The Great Plan of Happiness" by Elder Dallin H. Oaks of the First Presidency of the

Church — https://www.churchofjesuschrist.org/study/general-conference/1993/10/the-great-plan-of- happiness?lang=eng

582. "The Fulness of the Gospel: The Fall of Adam and Eve"– wwww.churchofjesuschrist.org

583. The God Delusion, p. 316

584. Ibid, p. 317

585. Ibid, p. 317

586. www.churchofjesuschrist.org - The Atonement of Jesus Christ, Part 1 by Hugh W. Nibley

587. The God Delusion, p. 318

588. Ibid, p. 318

589. Column on January 18, 1983, The Washington Post. Based on an earlier quote by James R. Schlesinger."

590. The God Delusion, p. 322

591. Ibid, p. 323

592. YouTube video "Overview: Joshua" – Animated video regarding the Canaanite Question.

593. www.fairlatterdaysaints – Do a search for "Question: How can one reconcile scripture in the Bible that appear to endorse genocide, pillage, and/or plunder?

594. Paul Copan and Matthew Flanagan give an answer to this question, which summarizes the view of 'most scholars generally'—that the Canaanite account contains "hagiographic hyperbole"

595. The God Delusion, p. 326

596. Ibid, p. 330

597. Joseph Smith - History of the Church, 1:245

598. See "Preparation for the Second Coming" by Elder Dallin H. Oaks of the Quorum of the Twelve Apostles by doing a search for this talk at the website: www.churchofjesuschrist.org.

599. The God Delusion, p. 330

600. Ibid, p. 331

601. Ibid, p. 332

602. Ibid, p. 332

603. Ibid, p. 333

604. Ibid, p. 338

605. Ibid, p. 342-343

606. "Zeitgeist in America: An Analysis of Societal Spirit in the United States" by James Michael Whitmore, Aug. 22, 2018

607. The God Delusion, p. 342

608. Elder David A. Bednar, an apostle of the Church of Jesus Christ of Latter-Day Saints and a member of the Quorum of the Twelve Apostles, given at a devotional in the Cannon Activities Center in Laie, Hawaii, on Sunday, November 14, 2021.

609. The God Delusion, p. 342

610. Ibid, p. 343

611. Ibid, p. 343

612. Ibid, p. 343

613. Ibid, p. 344

614. Ibid, p. 344

615. Ibid, p. 344

616. Ibid, p. 346

617. Ibid, p. 346

618. Ibid, p. 347

619. Ibid, p. 348

620. Ibid, p. 349

621. Ibid, p. 349

622. Ibid, p. 349

623. "Hitler Speaks" by Herman Rauschning

624. "Hitler Youth" by John Simkin, September 1997 (updated June 2020) https://spartacus-educational.com/GERyouth.htm

625. The God Delusion, p. 349

626. Ibid, p. 350

627. Ibid, p. 351

628. Ibid, p. 351

629. Ibid, p. 351

630. Alexander Hamilton

631. Ibid, p. 352

632. Ibid, p. 353

633. Ibid, p. 353

634. Ibid, pp. 353-35

635. Ibid, p. 355

636. Ibid, p. 355

637. Ibid, p. 355

638. "Alternate Voices", *Ensign,* May 1989, 29, by Elder Dallin H. Oaks of the Church of Jesus Christ of Latter-Day Saints.

639. Elder Paul V. Johnson is a member of the Seventy in the Church of Jesus Christ of Latter-Day Saints, and was speaking at the 'Seminaries and Institutes of Religion Satellite Broadcast' on August 7, 2012, and referred to *"Lehi in the Desert; The World of the Jaredites; There Were Jaredites"* [1988], 121–22)

640. *"Lehi in the Desert; The World of the Jaredites; There Were Jaredites"* [1988], 121–22)

641. Elder Paul V. Johnson is a member of the Seventy in the Church of Jesus Christ of Latter-Day Saints, and was speaking at the 'Seminaries and Institutes of Religion Satellite Broadcast' on August 7, 2012, and referred to *"Lehi in the Desert; The World of the Jaredites; There Were Jaredites"* [1988], 121–22)

642. "And Thus We See: Helping a Student in a Moment of Doubt" [an evening with Elder Henry B. Eyring, Feb. 5, 1993], 2–4, 6–7; a member of the Quorum of the Twelve Apostles at the time of this talk.

643. *The Teachings of Ezra Taft Benson* [1988], 206.

644. "Official Statement: Same-Gender Attraction" by Elder Dallin Oaks and Elder Lance B. Wickman https://newsroom.churchofjesuschrist.org/article/interview-oaks-wickman-same-gender-attraction

645. Elder Bruce R. McConkie - "All Are Alike unto God" [CES symposium on the Book of Mormon, Aug. 18, 1978], 2; http://si.lds.org

646. President Gordon B. Hinkley, *"Go Forward with Faith"* by Sheri Dew, April 2, 2001, p. 47.

647. Elder Paul V. Johnson, a member of the Seventy in the Church of Jesus Christ of Latter-Day Saints, and The Quorum of the *Seventy, speaking at* 'Seminaries and Institutes of Religion Satellite Broadcast on August 7, 2012'.

648. The God Delusion, p. 356

649. Ibid, p. 356

650. Ibid, p. 356

651. Ibid, p. 359

652. Ibid, p. 359

653. Ibid, p. 359

654. Ibid, p. 363

655. *Journal of Discourses 21: by Orson Pratt.*

656. The God Delusion, pp. 363-364

657. www.churchofjesuschrist.org – "Same-Sex Marriage'

658. The God Delusion, p. 366

659. Ibid, p. 375

660. *"Abortion: An Assault on the Defenseless"* & *"Reverence for Life"* – Both by Elder Russell M. Nelson of the Quorum of the Twelve Apostles (See full talk at www.churchofjesuschrist.org).

661. The God Delusion, p. 370

662. Ibid, p. 370-371

663. Ibid, p. 373

664. Ibid, p. 373-374

665. Ibid, p. 375

666. Ibid, p. 375

667. Ibid, p. 376

668. Ibid, p. 377

669. Ibid, p. 377

670. Ibid, p. 378

671. Ibid, p. 378

672. Ibid, p. 378

673. Ibid, p. 378

674. Ibid, p. 379

675. Ibid, p. 382

676. Ibid, p. 382

677. "Inside the Minds of Serial Killers: Why They Kill" by Katherine Ramsland.

678. Praeger Publishers – An imprint of Greenwood Publishing Group, Inc.

679. The God Delusion, p. 383

680. Muriel Gray, writing for the (Glasgow) Harold on 24 July 2005: https://www.goodreads.com/author/quotes/237540.Muriel_Gray

681. The God Delusion, p. 383

682. Ibid, p. 384

683. Ibid, p. 384

684. Ibid, p. 385

685. Ibid, p. 385

686. "Early Signs of the Apostacy" by Kent P. Jackson, an assistant professor of ancient scripture at Brigham Young University (Do a search at www.churchofjesuschrist.org for the title of this talk).

687. The God Delusion, p. 385

688. Ibid, p. 388

689. Ibid, p. 389

690. Ibid, p. 390

691. Ibid, p. 390

692. Ibid, p. 391-391

693. Ibid, p. 392

694. Ibid, p. 393

695. Ibid, p. 395

696. Ibid, p. 395

697. "Preventing and responding to Abuse" – Current Church policies and guidelines on abuse. https://newsroom.churchofjesuschrist.org/multimedia/file/Preventing-and-Responding-to-Abuse-attachment-final.pdf

698. The God Delusion, p. 396

699. Ibid, p. 397

700. Ibid, p. 398

701. Ibid, p. 399

702. Ibid, p. 399

703. Ibid, p. 403

704. Ibid, p. 404

705. *Mormon Doctrine,* 2nd ed. By Elder Bruce R. McConkie [1966], 349, 350, 351; see also *Doctrine &Covenants Student Manual,* 2nd ed. [Church Educational System manual, 2001], 165–166.)

706. "Bible Dictionary, "Hell"; 'Guide to the Scriptures', 'Hell' www.churchofjesuschrist.org – Scriptures.

707. The Miracle of Forgiveness by President Spencer W. Kimball, 1969, p. 344.

708. "Sin and Suffering" – Elder Dallin H. Oaks, who is currently the First Counselor in the First Presidency of the Church of Jesus Christ of Latter-Day Saints

709. "*Doctrines of Salvation,* comp. by Bruce R. McConkie, 3 vols. [1954–56], 2:298), quoting President Joseph Fielding Smith.

710. *Teachings of Presidents of the Church: Brigham Young* [1997], 292

711. *Elder Orson Pratt of the Quorum of the Twelve Apostles – Teachings of presidents of the Church: Brigham Young [1997], 292. Deseret News, Nov. 10, 1880, 64*

712. Joseph Smith Jr. the Prophet of the Restoration – *History of the Church,* 5:402)

713. Joseph Smith Jr. the Prophet of the Restoration – *History of the Church,* 5:286).

714. The God Delusion, p. 404

715. Ibid, p. 407

716. Ibid, p. 408

717. Ibid, p. 415

718. Ibid, p. 411

719. Ibid, p. 412

720. Ibid, p. 412

721. Ibid, p. 412

722. Ibid, p. 412

723. Ibid, p. 413

724. Ethiopian Proverb – "Remember, Remember, when you pick-up one end of a stick, you automatically pick-up the other end" – Article by Moshood Adenekan. https://www.linkedin.com/pulse/when-you-pick-up-one-end-stick-automatically-pick-up-other-

725. The God Delusion, p. 415

726. Ibid, p. 416

727. Ibid, p. 416

728. Ibid, p. 416

729. Ibid, p. 370-371

730. Ibid, p. 417

731. Ibid, p. 417

732. Ibid, p. 419

733. Ibid, p. 419

734. Ibid, p. 421

735. Ibid, p. 421

736. "Conversation, Conviction, and Civility: Sharing Religious Values in Schools and the Public Square" by Sister Joy D. jones, past Primary General President of the Church of Jesus Christ of Latter-Day Saints.

737. "Of Rights and Responsibilities: The Social Ecosystem of Religious Freedom", a keynote address by Elder Patrick Kearon, a member of the Presidents of the Seventy. At the Religious freedom Annual review at Brigham Young University on June 19, 2019

738. "Conversation, Conviction, and Civility: Sharing Religious Values in Schools and the Public Square" by Sister Joy D. jones, past Primary General President of the Church of Jesus Christ of Latter-Day Saints.

739. "Of Rights and Responsibilities: The Social Ecosystem of Religious Freedom", a keynote address by Elder Patrick Kearon, a member of the Presidents of the Seventy. At the Religious freedom Annual review at Brigham Young University on June 19, 2019

740. "Conversation, Conviction, and Civility: Sharing Religious Values in Schools and the Public Square" by Sister Joy D. jones, past Primary General President of the Church of Jesus Christ of Latter-Day Saints.

741. The God Delusion, p. 425

742. Ibid, p. 427

743. Joseph Smith Jr. the Prophet of the Restoration – *History of the Church,* 5:286].

744. The God Delusion, p. 432

745. Ibid, p. 428

746. Ibid, p. 430

747. Ibid, p. 432

748. "Joseph Smith's Commentary on the Bible" by Kent P. Jackson, Inside jacket of Book Cover.

749. The God Delusion, p. 434

750. Ibid, p. 434Ibid, p. 434

751. Ibid, p. 436

752. Ibid, p. 437

753. Ibid, p. 438

754. Ibid, p. 438

755. Ibid, p. 439

756. Ibid, p. 439

757. "The Reasonable Leap into Light: A Barebones Secular Argument for the Gospel" by Daniel C. Peterson, a former professor of Islamic Studies and Arabic in the Department of Asian and Near Eastern Languages at Brigham Young University (www.fairlatterdaysaints.org).

758. The God Delusion, p. 452

759. Ibid, p. 440

760. Ibid, p. 440

761. Ibid, p. 440

762. "The Reasonable Leap into Light: A Barebones Secular Argument for the Gospel" by Daniel C. Peterson, a former professor of Islamic Studies and Arabic in the Department of Asian and Near Eastern Languages at Brigham Young University (www.fairlatterdaysaints.org)

763. The God Delusion, pp. 440-441

764. Ibid, P. 441

765. Ibid, p. 441

766. Ibid, p. 442

767. Ibid, p. 445

768. Ibid, p. 445

769. Ibid, p. 446

770. Ibid, p. 447

771. Ibid, p. 447

772. Ibid, p. 447-448

773. Ibid, p. 447

774. "Euthanasia and Prolonging Life" – www.churchofjesuschrist.org.

775. The God Delusion, p. 448

776. Ibid, p. 446

777. Ibid, p. 451

778. Ibid, p. 452

779. Ibid, p. 452

780. Ibid, p. 453

781. Ibid, p. 452

782. "If We All End Up Dying, What's the Purpose of Living?" by May Wang, postgraduate, writing and

reporting fellow at Dumbarton Oaks.

783. "If We All End Up Dying, What's the Purpose of Living?" by May Wang, postgraduate, writing and reporting fellow at Dumbarton Oaks

784. "The Sanctity of Life" by Elder James E. Faust (*Ensign,* Nov. 1974, p. 7.) "Jewish Views on Abortion" by Rabi

Immanuel Jakobovits, Jewish Views on Abortion, p. 4

785. Spencer W. Kimball – Ensign, Nov. 1974, p. 7

786. Dr. Nathanson – New England Journal of Medicine, vol. 291, no. 22, p. 118

787. Arantis – Dr. Eugene F. Diamond, Illinois Medical Journal, Nov. 1972, pp. 80-84

788. Dietrich Bonhoeffer, a German Lutheran pastor, theologian, anti-Nazi dissident, and key founding member of the Confessing Church.

789. Dr. James H. Ford, M.d., California Medical Journal, Nov. 1972, pp. 80-84

790. "Measure for Measure", 6; I, 445 – Shakespeare

791. August 20th, 2004 – on Tweetbot for IOS, Richard Dawkins tweeted this quote

792. *"Death Before Birth"*, the Constitutional Right to Life Committee, Providence, Rhode Island.

793. *"The Death of Innocence"*, First Presidency - *Ensign,* March 1973, p. 64.

794. *"The Death of Innocence"*, First Presidency *Ensign,* March 1973, p. 64.

795. Dr. S. Bolter, *American Journal of Psychiatry,* Oct. 1962, pp. 312–16.

796. Dr. Henry G. Armitage, Jr., *The Death of Innocence.*

797. Dr. Henry G. Armitage, Jr., *The Death of Innocence.*

798. Dr. Henry G. Armitage, Jr., *The Death of Innocence.*

799. "The Sanctity of Life" by James E. Faust, past Apostles of the Church of Jesus Christ of Latter-Day Saints.

800. "The Worth of Souls is Great" by Kristin L. Matthews, associate professor of English and coordinator of the American Studies Program.

801. The God Delusion, p. 453

802. Ibid, p. 453

803. Ibid, p. 453

804. Ibid, p. 453

805. SimplyPsychology.org – "The James-Lange Theory of Emotion": https://www.simplypsychology.org/what-is-the-james-lange-theory-of-emotion.html#:~:text=James%2DLange%20theory%20of%20emotion%20(1880s)%20proposed%20tha t%20bodily,are%20afraid%20because%20you%20run).

806. The God Delusion, p. 454

807. Ibid, p. 454-455

808. "Revelation" Go to: www.churchofjesuschrist.org and search for "Revelation" a Doctrinal Study.808 "Personal Revelation" by Elder Terence M. Vinson *of the Presidency of the Seventy of the Church of Jesus Christ of Latter-Day Saints. Go to: www.churchofjesuschrist.org and search for "Personal Revelation".*

809. "The Essential Role of Revelation" by Elder Terence M. Vinson of the Presidency of the Seventy of the Church of Jesus Christ of Latter-Day Saints, quoting Elder Dallin H. Oaks

810. The God Delusion, p. 455

811. Ibid, p. 455

812. Ibid, p. 456

813. Ibid, p. 461

814. Ibid, p. 461

815. Ibid, p. 461-462

816. Ibid, p. 468

817. Ibid, p. 469

818. Ibid, p. 456 - "Possible World's" by J. B. Haldane, a biologist; p. 655 of my book.

819. Ibid, p. 460

820. Ibid, p. 460

821. Joseph Smith in HC 5:286

822. "Finding Answers to Gospel Questions" by Elder Bruce R. McConkie, a past Apostle in the Quorum of the Twelve Apostles, in an open letter, about 1980, Historical Department Archives, The Church of Jesus Christ of Latter-Day Saints.

823. "God and Stephen Hawking" by John Lennox, p. 96.

824. "Stand Strong Against the Wiles of the World" by President Gordon B. Hinkley of the Church of Jesus Christ of Latter-Day Saints at the Women's Conference in 1998.